# CRITICAL SURVEY
# OF
# POETRY

# CRITICAL SURVEY
## OF
## POETRY

# English Language Series

## Authors
### Chau–Dur

# 2

*Edited by*
# FRANK N. MAGILL

*Academic Director*
### WALTON BEACHAM

**SALEM PRESS**
Englewood Cliffs, N. J.

LIBRARY OF CONGRESS CATALOG CARD NUMBER: 82-62168
Complete Set:          ISBN 0-89356-340-4
Volume 2:              ISBN 0-89356-342-0

PRINTED IN THE UNITED STATES OF AMERICA

# LIST OF AUTHORS IN VOLUME 2

# CRITICAL SURVEY
## OF
## POETRY

# GEOFFREY CHAUCER

**Born:** London(?), England; c. 1343
**Died:** London, England; October 25(?), 1400

## Principal poems

*The Book of the Duchess*, c. 1370; *The Romance of the Rose*, c. 1370 (translation, possibly not by Chaucer); *The House of Fame*, 1372-1380; *The Legend of St. Cecilia*, 1372-1380 (later used as "The Second Nun's Tale"), *Tragedies of Fortune*, 1372-1380 (later used as "The Monk's Tale"), *Anelida and Arcite*, c. 1380; *The Parliament of Fowls*, 1380; *Palamon and Arcite*, 1380-1386 (later used as "The Knight's Tale"); *The Legend of Good Women*, 1380-1386; *Troilus and Criseyde*, 1382; *The Canterbury Tales*, 1387-1400.

## Other literary forms

In addition to the early allegorical dream visions, the "tragedy" of *Troilus and Criseyde*, and the "comedy," *The Canterbury Tales*, Geoffrey Chaucer composed various lyrical poems, wrote a scientific treatise in prose, and translated two immensely influential works from Latin and Old French into Middle English. The shorter works have received little attention from critics. *ABC to the Virgin*, Chaucer's earliest poem adapted from the French of Guillaume Deguilleville, and the various ballades, roundels, and envoys are in the French courtly tradition. They also reflect the influence of the Roman philosopher Boethius and often include moral advice and standard *sententiae*. Somewhat longer are the *Anelida and Arcite* and the complaints to Pity and of Venus and Mars, which develop the conventions of the languishing lover of romance.

The prose works include the interesting astrological study, the *Treatise on the Astrolabe* (1387-1392), written for "little Lewis my son," and the *Boece* (c. 1380) a translation of Boethius' *The Consolation of Philosophy* (523) which particularly influenced Chaucer's *Troilus and Criseyde* and "The Knight's Tale." The prologue to *The Legend of Good Women* notes that Chaucer also translated *The Romance of the Rose* (c. 1370). Certainly the great Old French dream vision, particularly the first part by Guillaume de Lorris, influenced Chaucer's early dream allegories as well as his portrayal of certain characters and scenes in *The Canterbury Tales*—the Wife of Bath, for example, and the enclosed garden of "The Merchant's Tale." Scholars, however, are uncertain whether the extant Middle English version of *The Romance of the Rose* included in standard editions of Chaucer is by the poet.

## Achievements

Seldom has a poet been as consistently popular and admired by fellow poets, critics, and the public as has Chaucer. From the comments of his French contemporary, Eustache Deschamps (c. 1340-1410) and the praise by imitation

of the fifteenth century Chaucerians to the remarks of notable critics from
John Dryden and Alexander Pope to Matthew Arnold and C. S. Lewis, Chaucer has been warmly applauded if not always understood. His poetic talent,
"genial nature," wit, charm, and sympathetic yet critical understanding of
human diversity are particularly attractive. To D. S. Brewer, Chaucer "is our
Goethe, a great artist who put his whole mind into his art."

Yet sometimes this praise has been misinformed, portraying Chaucer rather
grandly as "the father of English literature" and the prime shaper of the
English language. In fact, English literature had a long and illustrious tradition
before Chaucer, and the development of Modern English from the London
East Midland dialect of Chaucer has little to do with the poet. Chaucer has
also been credited with a series of firsts. G. L. Kittredge identified *Troilus
and Criseyde* as "the first novel, in the modern sense, that ever was written
in the world." Its characters, to John Speirs, are also poetic firsts: Pandarus
"the first rounded comic creation of substantial magnitude in English literature," and Criseyde "the first complete character of a woman in English
literature." Others see Chaucer's poetry as "Renaissance" in outlook, a har-
binger of the humanism of the modern world. Such views reveal an element
of surprise on the critics' part that from the midst of Middle English such a
poetic genius should emerge. In fact, typical discussions of Chaucer's career,
dividing it into three stages as it develops from French influence (seen in the
dream allegories) to Italian tendencies (in *Troilus and Criseyde*, for example)
and finally to English realism (in *The Canterbury Tales*), imply an evolutionary
view not only of Chaucer's poetry, but also of English literary history. These
stages supposedly reflect the gradual rejection of medieval conventionalism
and the movement toward modern realism.

Whatever Chaucer's varied achievements are, the rejection of conventions,
rhetoric, types, symbols, and authorities is not among them. Charles Muscatine has shown, moreover, that Chaucer's "realism" is as French and conventional as are his early allegories. Chaucer's poetry should be judged within
the conventions of his time. He did experiment with verse forms, establishing
a decasyllabic line which, to become the iambic pentameter of the sonnet,
blank verse, and heroic couplet, is English poetry's most enduring line. His
talent, however, lies in manipulating the authorities, the rhetoric, and conventional "topics," and in his mastery of the "art poetical." As A. C. Spearing
notes, "Once we become aware of Chaucer's 'art poetical,' we gain a deeper
insight into his work by seeing how what appears natural in it is in fact
achieved not carelessly but by the play of genius upon convention and con-
trivance."

Such an approach to Chaucer will recognize his achievement as the greatest
poet of medieval England, not as a forerunner of modernism. It will note his
remaking of French, Latin, and Italian sources and treatment of secular and
religious allegory as being, in their own way, as original as his creation of

such characters as the Wife of Bath and the Pardoner. Chaucer's achievement is in his ability to juxtapose various medieval outlooks to portray complex ideas in human terms, with wit and humor, to include both "heigh sentence" and "solaas and myrthe," and to merge the naturalistic detail with the symbolic pattern. In this attempt to synthesize the everyday with the supernatural and the homely with the philosophical, and in his insistence on inclusiveness—on presenting both the angels and the gargoyles—Chaucer is the supreme example of the Gothic artist.

## Biography

For a medieval poet, much is known about Geoffrey Chaucer's life, his association with the English court, his diplomatic activity on the Continent, and his public appointments. He was born in the early 1340's, the son of John Chaucer, a London wine merchant. He spent time in the military, serving with the English forces in France in 1359 where he was captured; he was ransomed in 1360. Around 1366 he married Philippa Roet and probably fathered two sons. He served the crown most of his life. Originally (c. 1357) he was connected to the household of Princess Elizabeth, who was married to Prince Lionel, the son of King Edward III. He also served another son of the king, John of Gaunt, the Duke of Lancaster, who later married Chaucer's sister-in-law, Katherine Swynford. Chaucer's public service survived the death of Edward III and the tumultuous reign and deposition of Richard II. It included numerous diplomatic missions to the Continent, his appointment as Controller of Customs and Subsidy for the port of London (1374-1386), his service as a justice of the peace and member of parliament for Kent (1386), his demanding duties as Clerk of the King's Works (1389-1391), and, finally, his appointment as deputy forester of North Petherton royal forest in Somerset (after 1391). Chaucer lived in London, Greenwich, and Calais, the French port then controlled by the English. In 1399, he leased a house in the garden of Westminster Abbey. He probably died on October 25, 1400, and was buried in the nearby abbey, the first of a long line of English authors to rest in the Poets' Corner.

These biographical details provide little evidence of Chaucer's position as a poet, although in a general way they do cast light on his poetry. Chaucer's association with courtly circles must have provided both the inspiration for and the occasion of his early poetry. It is certain that he wrote *The Book of the Duchess* to commemorate the death of Blanche, the wife of John of Gaunt. He probably also composed *The Legend of Good Women* for a courtly patron (the queen, according to John Lydgate), and read *Troilus and Criseyde* to a courtly audience, as he is portrayed doing in a manuscript illustration. In more general terms, his early poetry reflects the French literary taste of the English court.

Chaucer's public career, furthermore, reveals that he was far from being the withdrawn versifier of artificial courtly tastes. His duties at the port of London and as chief supervisor of royal building projects suggest that he was a practical man of the world. Certainly these responsibilities brought him into contact with a wide variety of individuals whose manners and outlooks must have contrasted sharply with those of members of the court. In the past, such scholars as J. M. Manly searched historical records to identify specific individuals with whom Chaucer dealt in an attempt to locate models for the portraits of the pilgrims in *The Canterbury Tales*. Like any artist, Chaucer was no doubt influenced by those with whom he worked, but such research gives a false impression of Chaucer's characters. Even his most "realistic" creations are often composites of traditional portraits. Nevertheless, the recent studies of J. A. W. Bennett (*Chaucer at Oxford and at Cambridge*, 1974) show that careful attention to the records of fourteenth century England can enlighten modern understanding of the social, intellectual, and cultural trends of Chaucer's time and thus provide a setting for his life and work.

One aspect of Chaucer's public career must certainly have influenced his poetry. Repeatedly from 1360 to 1387 Chaucer undertook royal missions on the Continent. During these journeys he visited Flanders, Paris, perhaps even Spain. More important, in 1373 and again in 1378 he visited Italy. These trips to what in the fourteenth century was the center of European art brought him into contact with a sophisticated culture. They may have also introduced him to the work of the great Florentine poets, for Chaucer's poetry after these visits to Italy reflects the influence of Dante, Petrarch, and particularly Boccaccio. Finally, the diplomatic missions suggest certain features of Chaucer's personality that lie behind his poetry, although these features seem deliberately masked by his self-portraits in the poetry. Of middle class origin, expert in languages and trusted at court, Chaucer as a diplomat sent on at least seven missions to the Continent must have been not only convivial and personable—the usual view of the poet—but also self-assured, intelligent, and a keen judge of character.

**Analysis**

When reading Geoffrey Chaucer's works one is struck by a sense of great variety. His poetry reflects numerous sources, Latin, French, and Italian, ranging from ancient authorities to contemporary poets and including folk tales, sermons, rhetorical textbooks, philosophical meditations, and ribald jokes. Equally varied are Chaucer's poetic forms and genres: short conventional lyrics, long romances, exempla, fabliaux, allegorical dream visions, confessions, saints legends, and beast fables. The characters he creates, from personified abstractions, regal birds, and ancient goddesses to the odd collection of the Canterbury pilgrims and the naïve persona who narrates the poems are similarly varied. Finally, the poems present a wide variety of outlooks on an unusual number of topics. Like the Gothic cathedrals, Chaucer's poetry seems all-inclusive. Not surprisingly, also like the Gothic cathedrals, his poems were often left unfinished.

"Experience, though no authority," the Wife of Bath states in the prologue to her tale, "is good enough for me." Unlike her fifth husband, Jankin the clerk, the Wife is not interested in what "olde Romayn gestes" teach, what Saint Jerome, Tertullian, Solomon, and Ovid say about women and marriage. She knows "of the woe that is in marriage" by her own experience. This implied contrast between, on the one hand, authority—the established positions concerning just about any topic set forth in the past by scripture, ancient authors, and the Church fathers and passed on to the present by books—and, on the other hand, the individual's experience of everyday life is central to medieval intellectual thought. It is a major theme of Chaucer's poetry. Often Chaucer appears to establish an authority and then to contrast it with the experience of real life, testing the expected by the actual. This contrast may be tragic or comic; it may cast doubt on the authority or further support it. Often it is expressed by paired characters, Troilus and Pandarus, for example, or by paired tales, the Knight's and the Miller's. The characters' long recital of authorities may be ludicrous and pompous, Chaucer's parody of the pedant; but the pedant may be right. After Chanticleer's concern with what all the past has said about the significance of dreams, readers probably sympathize with Pertelote's comment that he should take a laxative. Nevertheless, once the rooster is in the fox's mouth, the authorities are proven correct. Similarly, the sum total of the Wife of Bath's personal experience is merely the proving, in an exaggerated form, of the antifeminist authorities. As Chaucer states in the prologue to *The Parliament of Fowls*, out of old fields comes new corn, and out of old books new knowledge.

Related to the contrast between authority and experience are a series of other contrasts investigated by Chaucer: theological faith versus human reason, the ideal versus the pragmatic, the ritual of courtly love versus the business of making love, the dream world versus everyday life, the expectations of the rule versus the actions of the individual, the Christian teaching of free will versus man's sense of being fated. Again, these contrasts may be treated seriously or comically, may be represented by particular characters and may be brought into temporary balance. Seldom, however, does Chaucer provide solutions. The oppositions are implicit in human nature, in the wish for the absolute and the recognition of the relative. As Arthur Koestler comments on a modern political version of this dilemma (as represented by the extremes of the Yogi and the Commissar), "Apparently the two elements do not mix, and this may be one of the reasons why we have made such a mess of our History." Chaucer's poetic and highly varied treatment of these nonmixers may help to explain why his poetry continues to speak to the twentieth century.

Chaucer's concern with these topics—a fascination not unusual in the dualistic Gothic world—imbues his poetry with a sense of irony. Since the 1930's, readers have certainly emphasized Chaucer's ironic treatment of characters and topics, a critical vogue that may be due as much to the fashions of the New Criticism as to the poetry itself. Yet Chaucer's characteristic means of telling his stories clearly encourages such readings. One can never be sure of his attitude because the poet stands behind a narrator whose often naïve attitudes simply cannot be identified with his creator's. Perhaps the creation of such a middleman between the poet and his audience was necessary for a middle-class poet reading to an aristocratic audience, or perhaps it is the natural practice of a diplomatic mind, which does not speak for itself but for another. Whatever the reasons, Chaucer's narrators are poetically effective. They provide a unifying strand throughout his varied work. Spearing notes that "the idiot-dreamer of *The Book of the Duchess* develops into the idiot-historian of *Troilus and Criseyde* and the idiot-pilgrim of *The Canterbury Tales*." Later, he comments that when Chaucer assigns the doggerel poem, "Sir Thopas," to Chaucer the pilgrim as a joke, he "takes the role of idiot-poet to its culmination."

One result of the use of such narrators is that, in contrast with the contemporary dream vision, *The Vision of William Concerning Piers the Plowman* (c. 1395)—with its acid attacks on English society, the failures of government, and the hypocrisy of the church—Chaucer's poetry seems aware of human foibles yet accepting of human nature. He implies rather than shouts the need for change, recognizing that in this world at least major reform is unlikely. His essentially Christian position, hidden behind the naïve narrator and his concern with surface details, naturalistic dialogue, and sharp description, is implied by the poem's larger structures. They often provide symbolic patterning. The contrast in *The Parliament of Fowls* between the steamy atmosphere of the temple of Venus and the clear air of Nature's dominion, or in *Troilus and Criseyde* between the narrator's introductory devotion to the god of love and his concluding epilogue based on Troilus' new heavenly point of view imply Chaucer's position concerning his favorite topic, human love. Similarly, the traditional Christian metaphor identifying life as a pilgrimage and the Parson's identification of Canterbury with the New Jerusalem suggest that the pilgrimage from a pub in Southwark to a shrine in Canterbury is a secular version of an important traditional religious theme. The reader of Chaucer, while paying careful attention to his realism which has been found so attractive should also be aware of the larger implications of his poetry.

Behind the medieval interest in dreams and the genre of dream visions lies a long tradition, both religious and secular, originating in biblical and classical stories and passed on to the Middle Ages in the works of Macrobiuss and Boethius. As a literary type, the dream vision, given impetus by *The Romance of the Rose*, was particularly popular in fourteenth century England. The obtuse dreamers led by authoritative guides found in such works as *Piers*

*Plowman* and *The Pearl* (c. 1375-1400) are typical of dream visions and may have suggested to Chaucer the creation of his characteristic naïve narrator. Certainly Chaucer's four dream visions, as different as they are from one another, already develop this narrative voice as well as other typical Chaucerian characteristics.

The earliest of Chaucer's very long poems, *The Book of the Duchess* (1,334 lines), is a dream elegy in memory of the duchess of Lancaster. The poem begins with the narrator reading in bed about dreams, specifically the Ovidian story of the tragic love of Ceyx and Alcyone. After her husband's death, Alcyone is visited in a dream by Ceyx, leading to Alcyone's eventual brokenhearted death. This introductory section, which as usual refers to numerous authorities on dreams, combines Chaucer's concern with both dreams and love. These authorities provide background for the narrator's experience in a dream. After praying to Morpheus, the narrator falls asleep to dream of another couple divided by death, a man in black (John of Gaunt) and his lost lover, "faire White" (Blanche). The dreamer's foolish and tactless questions allow the grieving knight to express his love and sense of loss, sometimes by direct statement, on other occasions by such elaborate devices as describing a game of chess in which fortune takes his queen. The traditionally obtuse dreamer is here used in a remarkably original way. The poet is able to place the praise of the dead and the feelings of anguish in the mouth of the bereaved. Thus this highly conventional poem, with its conscious borrowing from Ovid, *The Romance of the Rose*, Jean Froissart, and Guillaume de Machaut, is an effective elegy in the restrained courtly tradition.

*The House of Fame*, Chaucer's second dream vision, breaks off suddenly after 2,158 lines. It creates a series of allegorical structures and figures in an analysis of the relationship between love, fame, rumor, fortune, and poetry. The dreamer is here provided with a guide, Jupiter's eagle, that probably derives from Dante's *Purgatorio IX*. In Book I he relates the romance of Aeneas and Dido, two lovers of some poetic fame whose story is portrayed in panels on a temple of glass dedicated to Venus. This temple is contrasted with the house of Fame which the dreamer sees in Book III when the eagle rather unceremoniously whisks him into the heavens. In this second allegorical structure, the dreamer views the goddess Fame surrounded by the great poets of antiquity on pedestals. They represent the authorities who, like Vergil, record the stories of such lovers as Aeneas and Dido. The dreamer realizes, however, that Fame (and thus presumably the poets of Fame) deals out good and bad at random, suggesting that there is little relationship between actuality and reputation. He next sees the house of Rumor. Full of noise and whispering people, it is perhaps an allegorical representation of the character of everyday life. In any case, this chaotic structure is no more attractive than the house of Fame. Still searching for "tydinges of Loves folk," the dreamer sees "a man of greet auctoritee," but the poem breaks off before the man can speak.

The reader, like the dreamer, is left in the air; the poem is left without an ending. As Muscatine comments, "It is hard to conceive of any ending at all that could consistently follow from what we have." In fact, the poem lacks a sense of unity. Its multiple topics and elaborate descriptions are best studied as set pieces. Of particular interest is the often comic dialogue between the dreamer and the eagle in Book II.

*The Parliament of Fowls* (699 lines) is a more satisfactory poem, although it shares much in common with *The House of Fame*, including a series of allegorical portraits and locales, a guide who tends to shove the dreamer around, and birds as characters. A poem describing the mating of birds on Saint Valentine's day, *The Parliament of Fowls* begins, like *The Book of the Duchess*, with the narrator reading a book about a dream. The book is Cicero's *Dream of Scipio*, the standard textbook on dreams, found in the last part of *De republica* (52-51 B.C.). Its guide, Scipio Africanus the elder, becomes the dreamer's guide in *The Parliament of Fowls*. He dreams of the typical enclosed garden of romance, guarded by a gate. The gate's contrasting inscriptions alluding to the gates of Dante's *Inferno*, suggest the dual nature of love: bliss, fertility, and "good aventure" on the one hand, and sorrow, barrenness, and danger on the other. Within the garden the dreamer again sees two versions of love, although, as naïve as ever, he seems bewildered and unsure of what he witnesses.

Like the Renaissance masterpiece, Titian's painting of "Sacred and Profane Love," the poem contrasts two traditional ideals of love. One is symbolized by Venus, whose entourage includes Flattery, Desire, and Lust as well as Cupid, Courtesy, and Gentleness. Her religion of love is the subject of the poets and ancient authorities whom the narrator so often reads. Her palace is dark and mannered, painted with the tragic stories of doomed lovers. In contrast, the dreamer next sees in the bright sunlight "this noble goddesse Nature," who presides over the beauty of natural love and mating of the birds. These ceremonies include description of all levels of the hierarchy of the birds, from the pragmatic arrangements of the goose and the love devotion of the turtledove to the courtly wooing of the former by the eagles. The language of the birds, often comic, similarly ranges from the sudden "kek, kek!" and "kukkow" to elaborate Latinate diction. Although lighthearted and sometimes chaotic, the openness and social awareness of Nature's realm is clearly to be preferred to the artificiality and self-absorption of the temple of Venus. The poem ends under Nature's skillful guidance as the birds sing a song of spring, which awakens the dreamer. In the prologue, the narrator states that he wishes to learn of love. This dream has provided much to learn, yet he seems in the end unchanged by his experience and once again returns to his authorities.

Of great interest as a forerunner of *The Canterbury Tales*, *The Legend of Good Women* is Chaucer's first experiment with decasyllabic couplets and with the idea of a framed collection of stories. Like the much grander later collection, it begins with a prologue and then relates an unfinished series of stories. Although the prologue plans nineteen stories, the poem breaks off near the conclusion of the ninth, after 2,723 lines. Unlike "The General Prologue" to *The Canterbury Tales*, with its detailed portraits of the pilgrims set in the Tabard Inn, the prologue to *The Legend of Good Women* is set as yet another dream. It presents the god of love and his daisy queen in conversation with the Chaucerian narrator. Once again, the narrator is a reader of books anxious to learn from life about love. More interesting, he is here also a writer of books, and is harassed by the god of love for not presenting lovers in a good light in his poetry. Specific reference is made to his translation of *The Romance of the Rose* and to *Troilus and Criseyde*. As penance for his grievous sins against the religion of love, the narrator promises to write about the faithful lovers of ancient legend.

Comparisons with *The Canterbury Tales* are perhaps unfair, but the poem, lacking the dynamic characters and varied tales of the later collection, seems grievously repetitious. Its recital of love tragedies is borrowed from Ovid and other authorities. Nevertheless, the legends do encompass a wider range of classical stories than might at first be expected, including the stories of Cleopatra and Medea, who to the modern reader, at least, hardly qualify as "good women." The luscious yet natural scenery of the prologue is superb. Furthermore, the work is fulfillment of Chaucer's poetic development in the courtly tradition. Whatever the poem's weaknesses, it is unlikely that Chaucer would have agreed with Robert Burlin's judgment that the poem was "a colossal blunder."

In his elaborate panegyric, the French poet Émile Deschamps refers to Chaucer as a "Socrates, full of philosophy, Seneca for morality . . . a great Ovid in your poetry. . . ." The poem that most fully deserves such praise is *Troilus and Criseyde*, Chaucer's longest complete poem (8,259 lines) and, to many readers, his most moving work. Here for the first time in a long poem, Chaucer turns from the dream vision form and the participating narrator, but not from his concern with authorities and the nature of love. He now adds, however, a Boethian philosophical touch. Although it is a poem about love, Fortuna rather than Venus is the controlling goddess of Chaucer's "little tragedy." Although the career of Troilus is based on Boccaccio's *Filostrato* (c. 1335-1340), it would seem that *The Consolation of Philosophy* exerted the greatest influence on the poem.

The five books of *Troilus and Criseyde* rather than being, as modern critics like to assert, the first novel or a drama in five acts, represent the various stages of Troilus' tragic love affair. Describing the "double sorrow" of Troilus, the son of King Priam of Troy, the poem begins with his initial love-longing, then traces his increasingly successful courtship of Criseyde culminating in their fulfilled love, the intervention of the Trojan War in the midst of their happiness, their forced separation, Criseyde's eventual acceptance of the Greek Diomede, and finally Troilus' gallant death at the hand of Achilles. While telling this story, Chaucer paints a series of scenes, both comic and serious, sometimes absurd, often movingly romantic, examining various outlooks on human love. Troilus' excessive idealism seems to parody the courtly lovers of French romances, whereas the pragmatic, often cynical attitudes of Pandarus, the uncle of Criseyde and confidant of Troilus, remind one of the waterfowl in *The Parliament of Fowls* and the later fabliaux of *The Canterbury Tales*. Criseyde's views of love shift between these two extremes, varying according to her feelings and the exigencies of circumstance.

Calling *Troilus and Criseyde* Chaucer's "great failure," Ian Robinson (*Chaucer and the English Tradition*, 1972) believes that the poem includes "many great parts but they don't cohere into a great whole." Yet the poem does have a unifying structure, based on the rising and falling stages of the Wheel of Fortune. The notion of Fortune turning a wheel which sometimes takes man to the height of success and sometimes drags him down to failure is standard in medieval thought and very popular in both literature and art. The stages of the wheel, along with the poem's narrative units, are set forth in the invocations which introduce the books of *Troilus and Criseyde*. In the first, when Troilus is at the bottom of the wheel, the narrator invokes Tesiphone, "thou cruel fury." As Morton Bloomfield comments ("Distance and Predestination in *Troilus and Criseyde*"), Tesiphone was characterized as the "sorrowful fury" who laments her torments and pities those whom she torments. The choice is thus appropriate for the description in Book I of the hero's initial love torments and for the events of the entire poem. The Chaucerian narrator presents himself as "the sorrowful instrument" of love, required to tell the "sorrowful tale."

The invocation in Book II, to Clio the muse of history, suggests that the second stage represents a rather neutral and objectively historical description of the rise of Troilus on the wheel, whereas the invocation to Venus in Book III is appropriate for the stage when the lovers are at the top of the wheel and consummate their love. As all readers of Boethius know, however, if one chooses to ride to the top of the wheel, one in all fairness cannot be surprised when the wheel continues to turn downward. Thus, Book IV begins with an invocation to Fortune and her wheel, which throws down the hero and sets Diomede in his place. There is also an appropriate reference to Mars, suggesting the growing influence of the war on the romance. Book V follows without an invocation, probably because it is a continuation of the fourth book and implying that the downward movement of the wheel is one continuous stage. Certainly the poem's last book does not introduce any new elements. Its major concerns are Troilus' fatalism and the details of the Trojan War.

This pattern clearly interweaves two problems which dominate the poem:

the perplexities of human love and man's sense of being fated. Troilus is the character overwhelmed by both problems. Although many critics are fascinated by the inscrutable Criseyde and attracted by the worldly-wise Pandarus, Troilus is the poem's central figure. Readers may become frustrated by his passive love-longing and swooning and his long-winded and confused discussion of predestination and free will; however, he is treated sympathetically and his situation must be taken seriously. One can argue, using Boethius as support, that the solution to the human predicament is simply never to accept the favors of Fortune—to stay away from her wheel—but what man would not do as Troilus did for the love of Criseyde? Similarly, one can agree with the moralizing narrator at the poem's conclusion that the solution is to avoid worldly vanity and the love associated with Venus and to look instead to heavenly love.

Certainly Troilus recognizes this view as his soul ascends to the seventh sphere. Yet the poem as a whole hardly condemns the love of the two Trojans. On the contrary, it describes their long-awaited rendezvous in bed with great sensitivity and poetic beauty, with warmth and sensuous natural imagery. As Spearing states, "There is probably no finer poetry of fulfilled love in English than this scene." In this great tragic romance, Chaucer seems to juxtapose human and divine love and to intermingle the sense of predestination and the Christian teaching of free will; not until the end does he speak as the moralist and condemn worldly vanity. Perhaps the tragedy of Troilus and of the human situation in general is that the distinctions are not sufficiently clear until it is too late to choose.

Near the end of *Troilus and Criseyde*, Chaucer associates his "little tragedy" with a long line of classical poets and then asks for help to write "some comedie." Donald Howard and others have seen this as a reference to the poet's plans for *The Canterbury Tales*. Whether Chaucer had this collection planned by the time he had completed *Troilus and Criseyde*, *The Canterbury Tales* can certainly be understood as his comedy. If, as the Monk notes at the beginning of his long summary of tragic tales, a tragedy deals with those who once "stood in high degree, and fell so that there was no remedy," in the medieval view comedy deals with less significant characters and with events that move toward happy endings. *The Canterbury Tales* is thus a comedy, not because of its comic characters and humorous stories—several tales are actually tragic in tone and structure—but because its overall structure is comic.

Like Dante's *The Divine Comedy* (c. 1320) which traces the poet's eschatological journey from hell through purgatory to heaven, shifting from a pagan guide to the representatives of divine love and inspiration, and concluding with the beatific vision, Chaucer's comedy symbolically moves from the infernal to the heavenly. From the worldly concerns of the Tabard Inn in Southwark and the guidance of the worldly-wise Host, through a variety of points of view set forth by differing characters on the pilgrimage road, the poem moves to the religious goal of the saint's shrine in Canterbury Cathedral and the Parson's direction of the pilgrims to "Jerusalem celestial."

Although with differing effects, since the Christian perspective of *Troilus and Criseyde* lies beyond the narrative itself, Chaucer's tragedy and comedy thus share a similar moral structure. Like the tragedy, *The Canterbury Tales* moves from an ancient story of pagan heroes to a Christian perspective. In *Troilus and Criseyde* the narrator develops from being the servant of the god of love to being a moralist who condemns pagan "cursed old rites" and advises the young to love Him who "for love upon a cross our souls did buy." The collection of tales similarly moves from the Knight's "old stories" set in ancient Thebes and Athens and relating the fates of pagan lovers to the Parson's sermon beginning "Our swete lord god of hevene." In contrast with the earlier poem, *The Canterbury Tales* is a comedy because its divine perspective is achieved within the overall narrative. Yet as in the earlier poem, this divine perspective at the end does not necessarily cancel out the earlier outlooks proposed. The entire poem with its multiplicity of characters and viewpoints remains.

Such an approach to *The Canterbury Tales* assumes that, although unfinished, the poem is complete as it stands and should be judged as a whole. Like the Corpus Christi cycles of the later Middle Ages, which include numerous individual plays yet can (and should) be read as one large play tracing salvation history from creation to doomsday, *The Canterbury Tales* is more than the sum of its parts. "The General Prologue," that masterpiece of human description with its fascinating portraits of the pilgrims, establishes not only the supposed circumstances for the pilgrimage and the competition to tell the best story, but also the strands that link the tales to the characters and to one another. Although only twenty-four tales were finished, their relationship to one another within fragments and their sense of unity within variety suggest that Chaucer had an overall plan for *The Canterbury Tales*.

The famous opening lines of "The General Prologue," with the beautiful evocation of spring fever, set forth both the religious and the secular motivations of the pilgrims. These motivations are further developed in their description by the pilgrim Chaucer. He again is the naïve narrator whose wide-eyed simplicity seems to accept all, leaving the discriminating reader to see beyond the surface details. Finally, in his faithful retelling of the stories he hears on the way to Canterbury—for once his experience has become an authority to which, he explains, he must not be false—the narrator again unwittingly implies much about these various human types. Several of the prologues and tales that follow then continue to explore the motivations of the individual pilgrims. The confessional prologue of "The Pardoner's Tale" and its sermon filled with moral exempla, for instance, ironically reflects the earlier description of the confidence man, Pardoner, as one "with feigned flattery and tricks, made the parson and the people his apes."

It would be a mistake, however, to interpret the various tales simply as dramatic embodiments of the pilgrims. Certainly Chaucer often fits story to storyteller. The sentimental, self-absorbed, and prissy Prioress tells, for example, a simplistic, anti-Semitic tale of a devout little Christian boy murdered by Jews. The implications of her tale make one question the nature of her spirituality. The tales given the Knight, Miller, and Reeve also reflect their characters. The Knight tells at great length a chivalric romance, a celebration of his world view, whereas the Miller and Reeve tell bawdy stories concerning tradesmen, clerks, and wayward wives.

Yet these tales also develop the larger concerns of *The Canterbury Tales* implied by Chaucer's arrangement of the tales into thematic groups. "The Knight's Tale," with its ritualized action and idealized characters, draws from Boethian philosophy in its symmetrically patterned examination of courtly love, fate, and cosmic justice. The Miller then interrupts to "quite" or answer the Knight with a bawdy fabliau. Developing naturalistic dialogue and earthy characters, it rejects the artificial and the philosophical for the mundane and the practical. In place of the Knight's code of honor and courtly love, elaborate description of the tournament, and Stoic speech on the Great Chain of Being, the drunken Miller sets the stage for sexual conquest, a complex practical joke, and a "cherles tales" involving bodily functions and fleshly punishment. In "The Miller's Tale," justice is created not by planetary gods but by human action, each character getting what he deserves. The Reeve, offended by both the Miller and his tale, then follows with another fabliau. His motivations are much more personal than those of the Miller: the Reeve feels that the Miller has deliberately insulted him and he insists on returning the favor. Yet even in this tale Chaucer provides another dimension to the issues originally set forth by the Knight.

The clearest example of Chaucer's thematic grouping of tales is the so-called "Marriage Cycle." First noted by G. L. Kittredge and discussed since by various critics, the idea of the cycle is that Chaucer carefully arranged particular tales, told by suitable pilgrims, so that they referred to one another and developed a common theme, as in a scholarly debate. The "Marriage Cycle" examines various viewpoints on love and marriage, particularly tackling the issue of who should have sovereignty in marriage, the husband or the wife. The cycle is introduced by the Wife of Bath's rambling commentary on the woes of marriage and her wishful tale of a young bachelor who rightly puts himself in his wife's "wyse governance." After the Friar and Summoner "quite" each other in their own personal feud, the cycle continues with an extreme example of wifely obedience, "The Clerk's Tale" of patient Griselda. Such an otherworldly portrait of womanly perfection spurs the Merchant, a man who is obviously unhappy in marriage, to propound his cynical view of the unfaithful wife. The saint's legend of the scholarly Clerk is thus followed by the fabliau of the satirical Merchant and the debate is no nearer conclusion.

Finally, the Franklin appears to "knit up the whole matter" by suggesting that in marriage the man should be both dominant as husband and subservient as lover. Yet the Franklin's view is hardly followed by the characters of his tale. Interestingly, the two solutions to the issue of sovereignty proposed—those of the Wife of Bath and of the Franklin—are developed in Breton lays, short and highly unrealistic romances relying heavily on magical elements. Is it the case that only magic can solve this typically human problem? Chaucer, at least, does not press for a definitive answer.

The great sense of variety, the comic treatment of serious issues, the concern with oppositions and unsuccessful solutions, and the lively and imaginative verse that so typifies *The Canterbury Tales* are best exemplified by "The Nun's Priest's Tale." A beast fable mocking courtly language and rhetorical over-abundance, the tale at once includes Chaucer's fascination with authorities, dreams, fate, and love and marriage, and suggests his ambivalent attitudes toward the major philosophical and social concerns of his day. The elevated speeches of Chanticleer are punctuated by barnyard cries, and the pompous world of the rooster and hen are set within the humble yard of a poor widow.

Here the reader is provided with a comic version of the detached perspective that concludes *Troilus and Criseyde*. After deciding that dreams are to be taken seriously and refusing to take a laxative, Chanticleer disregards his dream and its warning and makes love to his favorite wife in a scene that absurdly portrays chickens as courtly lovers. Interestingly, Chanticleer now cites a standard sentiment of medieval antifeminism: *In principio/ Mulier est hominis confusio* ("In the beginning woman is man's ruin"), which alludes to the apostle John's famous description of the creation (John 1:1). The learned rooster, moreover, immediately mistranslates the Latin as "Womman is mannes ioye and al his blys," perhaps the Priest's subtle comment on the Nun he serves or the rooster's joke on Pertelote. Yet the joke ultimately is on Chanticleer when "a colfox ful of sley iniquitee" sneaks into this romance "garden." Noting that the counsel of woman brought woe to the world "And made Adam fro paradys to go," the Nun's Priest then relates the temptation and fall of Chanticleer and the subsequent chasing of the fox and rooster out of the barnyard. The adventure is full of great fun, a hilarious scene, yet strangely reminiscent of the biblical story of the fall of man. It is not clear what one is to make of such a story.

Although Chaucer was not the first author to create a framed collection of stories, *The Canterbury Tales* is assuredly the most imaginative collection. Earlier the poet had experimented with a framed collection in *The Legend of Good Women*. His Italian contemporary, Boccaccio, also created a collection of stories in *The Decameron* (1348-1353), although scholars cannot agree whether Chaucer knew this work. Earlier collections of exempla and legends were probably known by the poet, and he certainly knew the great collection of Ovid, *The Metamorphoses* (c. 8 A.D.). Like Ovid's collection,

*The Canterbury Tales* is organized by thematic and structural elements which provide a sense of unity within diversity. Chaucer's choice of the pilgrimage as the setting for the tales is particularly effective, since it allows the juxtaposition of characters, literary types, and themes gathered from a wide range of sources and reflecting a wide range of human attitudes.

Here, perhaps, is the key to Chaucer's greatness. Like the medieval view of the macrocosm, in which constant change and movement take place within a relatively unchanging framework, Chaucer's view of the microcosm balances the dynamic and the static, the wide range of individual feeling and belief within unchanging human nature. *The Canterbury Tales* is his greatest achievement in this area, although earlier poems, such as *The Parliament of Fowls*, with its portrayal of the hierarchy of birds within Nature's order, already show Chaucer's basic view. Ranging over human nature, selecting from ancient story and supposed personal experience, with a place for both the comic and the tragic, Chaucer's poetry mixes mirth and morality, accomplishing very successfuly the two great purposes of literature, what the Host calls "sentence and solas," teaching and entertainment.

## Major publications other than poetry

NONFICTION: *Boece*, 1380 (translation of Boethius' *The Consolation of Philosophy*); *Treatise on the Astrolabe*, (1387-1392).

MISCELLANEOUS: *The Complete Works of Chaucer*, 1957 (second edition, F. N. Robinson, editor).

## Bibliography

Brewer, Derek, ed. *Chaucer: The Critical Heritage*, 1978.

Burlin, Robert B. *Chaucerian Fiction*, 1977.

Donaldson, E. Talbot. *Speaking of Chaucer*, 1972.

Howard, Donald R. *The Idea of the Canterbury Tales*, 1976.

Hussey, Maurice, A. C. Spearing, and James Winny. *An Introduction to Chaucer*, 1965.

Kittredge, G. L. *Chaucer and His Poetry*, 1970.

Muscatine, Charles. *Chaucer and the French Tradition*, 1957.

*Richard Kenneth Emmerson*

# G. K. CHESTERTON

**Born:** London, England; May 29, 1874
**Died:** Beaconsfield, England; June 14, 1936

## Principal collections

*The Wild Knight and Other Poems*, 1900; *Greybeards at Play*, 1900; *The Ballad of the White Horse*, 1911; *The Flying Inn*, 1914; *Poems*, 1915; *The Ballad of St. Barbara and Other Verses*, 1922; *The Queen of Seven Swords*, 1926; *Collected Poems*, 1926; *Gloria in Profundis*, 1927; *Ubi Ecclesia*, 1929; *The Grave of Arthur*, 1930; *Collected Poems*, 1933.

## Other literary forms

G. K. Chesterton's literary output was almost equally distributed among poetry, fiction, and nonfiction prose. Chesterton's literary criticism is dismissed by many contemporary scholars because of his tendency to thrust forward his own views on particular periods of literary history—views not always clearly supported. Nevertheless, his works in that vein deserve some consideration for their method, if not for their content.

In certain circles, Chesterton is best known for his stories of Father Brown, the diminutive detective-priest whom Chesterton fashioned after Father John O'Connor, a lifelong friend of his who received him into the Catholic faith. Chesterton's output of novels and essays was also extensive, although he remains recognized for his literary criticisms and stories of Father Brown.

## Achievements

Chesterton's prose as well as his personality have tended to obscure his poetry, which has received little serious critical attention. Among those who have studied the poetry, critical reaction is not always based entirely upon literary criteria. For example, George Orwell, in his lengthy essay entitled "Notes on Nationalism" (1945), claimed that everything Chesterton wrote seemed to demonstrate the superiority of Roman Catholicism over everything and everyone else. Such superiority, observed the author of *Nineteen Eighty-Four* (1949), Chesterton translated into matters of national prestige and military power, as well as into intellectual and spiritual terms. In discussing such poems as "Lepanto" or "The Ballad of St. Barbara," Orwell focused upon what he viewed as silly and vulgar glorifications of the process of war, concluding that both pieces served as examples of pure "romantic rubbish."

Less politically motivated readers, however, see Chesterton's verse in a quite different context. What Orwell interpreted as exercises in political Catholicism tended to be the poet's attempts to discover relationships between the present and the old ways of life, which, in terms of the traditions governing the latter, happened to include Anglo-Catholicism. What Orwell described as silly and vulgar glorifications were actually sincere attempts at poetic experiment; in such pieces as "The Holy of Holies" and "The Earth's Shame," Chesterton manipulated ambiguity and paradox in an attempt to express the presence of God amidst the intellectual, political, and theological activities of humankind. The whole issue of the presence of God among men provides an important clue to Chesterton's poetic achievement.

Chesterton worked quite comfortably with older literary forms and conventions, particularly the long ballad. Such poems as "The Ballad of the White Horse" allowed him to reveal the best of two artistic worlds—fiction and poetry. Within the ballad form, he could rely easily upon recitation and narration. If one looks hard enough, spiritual and intellectual conflicts similar to those developed in the religious poems may be uncovered; however, Chesterton subordinated those struggles to the sheer force of the major ballad conventions: movement, excitement, and elaborate themes. In addition, the old times and the old ways received free reign; indeed, a strain of medieval romanticism lingered with considerable fire in Chesterton's large frame, and the ballad form gave him sufficient room to develop extravagant re-creations from the pages of England's history.

## Biography

The elder son of Edward Chesterton, the head of a firm of auctioneers and estate agents situated in Kensington, and Marie Louise Grosjean (of French and Scottish ancestry), young Gilbert Keith Chesterton studied at St. Paul's School from 1887 to 1892. His literary career began, officially, at the age of sixteen, when at school he founded a junior debating club and a magazine entitled *The Debator*. Such pursuits revealed, at a relatively early age, the young schoolboy's ability to create something that aroused his interest; at the same time, however, he gave ample evidence of an absolute inability to cope with the practicalities of life. For example, his friend Lucian Oldershaw had to assume full responsibility for producing and distributing *The Debator*, labors that Chesterton's absentmindedness and thoroughly good nature would not enable him to endure or to complete. Young Chesterton was more inclined toward sketching and daydreaming than applying himself to his books, and because of his artistic talent, Chesterton's father entered him in the Slade School of Art. At about the same time (1892), Chesterton began to study English literature at London University. After leaving the Slade School in 1895, he worked for several publishing houses (Fisher Unwin being foremost among them) and then gradually drifted into journalism (principally with the *Daily News*), a profession that he maintained as his principal interest and occupation.

Chesterton's liberal politics took shape around 1899-1900, during which time he developed a relationship with the versatile essayist and critic Hilaire Belloc (1870-1953), and with a number of young liberals employed by *The*

*Speaker*. He also became engaged to Frances Blogg (whom he married in 1901), an Anglo-Catholic who influenced his religious feeling and thinking. In 1900, his first published volumes appeared: *The Wild Knight* and *Greybeards at Play*, the latter complemented by his own illustrations. The success and enthusiasm resulting from those volumes was dampened, however, by political differences occasioned by the Boer War, specifically Chesterton's sympathies for the Dutch Afrikaners who challenged British rule. During the next decade, he plunged into a number of religious, critical, and political controversies with certain of his contemporaries—most significantly with Bernard Shaw, H. G. Wells, and Rudyard Kipling. He also devoted his energies to literary analysis, literary and art criticism, and various other forms of scholarship; his studies of Robert Browning (1903) and Charles Dickens (1906) emerged as the most prominent results of that period. During those first ten years of the twentieth century, Chesterton sported a number of different hats: journalist, novelist, artist, poet, political essayist, philosopher, social critic, biographer, and theologian; beneath them all, however, he projected the image of one determined to avoid the serious and to laugh at his critics as well as at himself. Those who failed to understand the image also failed to understand the man and his work.

Shortly after the Chestertons moved, in 1908, from Battersea to Beaconsfield, the writer launched a series of short fictional pieces that were to secure his fame as a man of letters. The first of the Father Brown detective stories was published in 1911, after which the Chestertons embarked upon a motor trip throughout the west of England (known as "the King Alfred country") that would lead to Chesterton's most significant poem, "The Ballad of the White Horse," published in 1911. Three years later, England rushed into the Great War, but Chesterton had other problems. Overeating, excessive work, and heavy drinking nearly ruined his health, although his devoted wife managed to nurse him back to full life and even fuller energy. He then turned his attention to history, which served as a prologue to his conversion to and eventual acceptance by the Anglo-Catholic Church in July, 1922. This event produced two popular and extremely important books, *St. Francis of Assisi* (1923) and *The Everlasting Man* (1925). The latter work focused upon the meaning of Chesterton's own discovery of Christianity and the necessity for committing both the individual and all mankind to the Christian concept. Following that 1925 publication, Chesterton lectured in the United States and Canada (1930-1931), pausing at Notre Dame University to offer undergraduate seminars. Still, he continued to produce essays, fiction, poetry, and even some dramatic pieces (lacking in distinction). After his return to England, he found time for several series of radio discussions for the British Broadcasting System. Although his youthful attitudes and almost juvenile high spirits continued to the end of his days, his literary contemporaries recognized his seriousness (even a certain degree of genius) as a philosopher, poet, and biographer. Chesterton died at Beaconsfield on June 14, 1936, after having returned from a visit to Lourdes and Lisieux, in France.

## Analysis

The year 1915 proved to be a mixture of good and bad circumstances for the forty-one-year-old Gilbert Keith Chesterton. He had spent almost four months, from November, 1914, until the following March, in critical physical condition; the convalescence lasted until June, 1915. Nevertheless, that year witnessed the publication of the first collected edition of his poems—a collection noted for its extreme variety, with subjects and themes ranging from the deeply devotional to the highly satiric. On first reading, the satirical pieces capture the attention, and justifiably so. Although Chesterton maintained, throughout his life, that he functioned principally as a journalist, his strength as a man of letters resides in his wit, in a tradition of English verse developed and fostered during the Restoration and Augustan periods by John Dryden, Alexander Pope, and Jonathan Swift and, in the next century, by Lord Byron and William S. Gilbert. Despite its Augustan echoes, however, the 1915 collection contains a number of pieces that required much of Chesterton's original intellectual and spiritual effort, particularly the romantic ballads, the religious songs, and the political satires.

Of the romantic verse, the often-quoted "The Ballad of the White Horse," is highly representative of Chesterton's historical themes. The poet relates the story of the defense of England by the Christian Alfred the Great against the invading heathen Danes. Chesterton was enthralled by the events of the late ninth century, during which Alfred fought the Danes in six great battles. Beaten back from the valley of the Thames during the first six years of his reign, Alfred gathered the last remnants of his force in the marshes of the Parret in Somerset, and at last, by superior strategy, managed to overwhelm Guthrum, the Danish leader and self-styled king, somewhere on the borders of Somerset and Wilts (in 878). That battle proved to have turned the tide. Guthrum agreed to receive baptism and to retire behind the line which the Treaty of Wedmore (or Chippenham) drew from London to Chester. The Danes would have no claim in Wessex or in western Mercia.

Chesterton's poem surveys the battle of Ethandune (or Edington), Alfred's final victory, and lingers upon the final acceptance of Christian baptism by Guthrum. As long as King Alfred follows the cause of Christianity for its own sake, and not for any worldly advantage that he might derive for himself or for his nation, he knows that he will emerge victorious. In opposition to that view, the pagan Danes, especially the young among them, boast of a life built upon the thrill and the violence of victory, a life and a world of pagan joy and beauty. The eight books of this long ballad are held together by Chesterton's own love for the ancient traditions of Britain and his even stronger Christian faith. Thus, the white horses carved in the chalked hillsides symbolize, for him, not only the art of early man, but also the history and culture of the island kingdom that are protected by a Christian God, rather than by a pagan system.

A similar theme may be seen in "Lepanto," also from the 1915 collected edition (although written in 1912), a piece embraced and popularized by British troops during the early battles of World War I. Again, Chesterton reached back into history for his version of the conflict between Christian Europe, led by John of Austria (1547-1578), and the pagan forces of the Turkish sultan. On this poetic occasion, Chesterton returns to 1571, when—at the head of the fleets of Spain, the Pope, and Venice—John defeated the Turks in the great sea battle of Lepanto, near Greece. The Allies virtually destroyed the Turkish fleet, commanded by Ochiali Pasha, captured or killed almost fifteen thousand Turks, and liberated approximately ten thousand Christian galley slaves. Interestingly, among the wounded Spanish soldiers was one Miguel Cervantes, who lost his left arm.

In glorifying the engagement at Lepanto, Chesterton allows his readers to sense the echoes of Alfred's triumph over the pagan Danes at Edington. "Lepanto," however, differs from "The Ballad of the White Horse" in the sheer force of its strong rhythm. Certainly, the lines of the poem read well and recite even better, but somehow Chesterton failed to capture the force of a truly serious anti-Christian menace. From another point of view, Chesterton's John of Austria comes off in much the same manner—as a rhetorician rather than as a militant Christian agent. The Austrian sovereign emits clear images of sound and color; his pounding "from the slaughter-painted poop,/ Purpling all the ocean like a bloody pirate's sloop" speaks well for Chesterton's proficiency in alliteration. In the end, however, the poem does not promote Christian sentiment; rather, it glories in the sheer color of a romanticized victory.

One of the more noteworthy of Chesterton's satiric poems, written in 1912 and appearing, again, in the 1915 collected *Poems*, bears the title "Anti-Christ: Or, The Reunion of Christendom" and concerns Frederick Edwin Smith, afterward first Earl of Birkenhead (1872-1930). Chesterton reacted to the parliamentarian's insincerity in a speech denouncing the Welsh Disestablishment Bill. Smith had labeled the proposed statute a shock upon "the conscience of every Christian community in Europe." Chesterton's satiric artillery tended to take the form of rhythmic banter associated with the London music halls rather than the neoclassical subtleties of his Augustan and Hanoverian predecessors. Thus, he relied upon direct language, almost to the point of name-calling: "Sooth me, Smith"; leave this theme alone, "Holy Smith"; "Chuck it, Smith"; "Really, Smith." Chesterton had no patience with the rhetoric of overly impassioned parliamentarians, and he found the softness of his Edwardian contemporaries totally inadequate in dealing with pure political wind. "What happens," he asks the future Lord Birkenhead,

In the mountain hamlets clothing
Peaks beyond Caucasian pales
Where Establishment means nothing
And they never heard of Wales?

Chesterton also went after a parliamentary colleague of Smith, Walter Long, who once claimed that he would never stand idle in the midst of revolution. In "The Revolutionist," the poet satirically cautions, "Walter, beware! scorn not the gathering throng"; the reader almost knows what will come next: the mob "suffers, yet it cannot suffer Long." When a group of self-styled worshipers of Shakespeare organized themselves into the Shakespeare Memorial League, Chesterton pounced upon them, labeling them as souls having been "fed with Shakespeare's flame" who could do nothing more than sit about and remember the bard's name. Then, in a moment of seeming irreverence, he turned his satiric attention to a Reverend Isaiah Bunter, an overseas missionary apparently done in by a cannibalistic tribe that he had attempted to convert. By entering the heavenly kingdom in that manner, Bunter, according to Chesterton, further "spread" religion in a manner "he did not intend."

The 1922 collection, *The Ballad of St. Barbara and Other Verses*, carries a scathing but still lighthearted attack upon the British education system, especially the tendency to promote half-truths and outright lies to advance the glorification of the nation. For example, one of the "Songs of Education" identifies the meaning behind Empire Day, a time when Lancashire merchants "can water the beer of a man in Klondike,/ Or poison the meat of a man in Bombay. . . ." Chesterton could even strike out at the over-seriousness among his fellow poets, admonishing them for their erudition and wishing that they got more fun out of it."

Chesterton's early poems on religious themes—an obvious choice being "Adveniat Regnum Tuum"—emphasize the negative aspects of modern religious institutions and organizations. He struggled very hard to bridge the gap between human weakness and failings and the greatness that lies beyond human powers. A shift from a negative to a positive tone occurred when Chesterton began to realize that the core of religion lies in the idea of God's existence and His direct inspiration of man. Thus, in "The Song of Labour," the poet tried to depict man's attempts to manifest inspiration: modern religious and political institutions can only produce words, while the actual voices of laborers communicate directly upward. Even art, Chesterton maintained, may be an inadequate instrument through which to provide an expression of nature; the laborer, capable of pure and uncontaminated action, may actually hear "The roar of the endless purpose."

In his later work, Chesterton seems to have been guided by an especially strong belief in the beneficent presence of God. Even in his early poems, such as "By the Babe Unborn," he captured the shifts and changes in man's religious ideas that make their actual expression so difficult and, at best, so ambiguous. Chesterton demands, in the same poem, that for the experience of inspiration to be personally relevant, it must permeate and then transcend current dogma. In other words, man must get out from under the idea of prescribed notions of God; he must refresh his perspective and recognize the wonder of a world infused with the power and glory of God. In later poems such as "The Holy of Holies" and "The Earth's Shame," Chesterton continued to explore the paradox and the ambiguity needed for poetic descriptions and analyses of the presence of God.

The real essence, for Chesterton, of poetry and religion—and thus the real essence of his poetry—may be found in two sentences in *Orthodoxy* (1908), a collection of essays which provides the background to his religious and philosophical beliefs. "God was a creator," wrote Chesterton, "as an artist is a creator. A poet is so separate from his poem that he himself speaks of it as a little thing he has 'thrown off.'" Man needs God, according to Chesterton, to reveal his (man's) identity, while the artist gives meaning to that identity. Finally, as all human beings must remain aware of human limitations, art must acknowledge its own limitations, particularly as existing in a subordinate creative role to that of God. Chesterton sought to express, in as many poetic forms as possible, the ultimate truth of nature. That truth, he believed, lay in an almost unending string of paradoxes: in "an older place than Eden,/ And a taller tower than Rome"; at "The end of the way of the wandering star,/ To the things that cannot be and that are." For Chesterton, the purpose for writing poetry in any form and at any level was to bring mankind to a place in life and in time "where God was homeless/ And all men are at home."

**Major publications other than poetry**

NOVELS: *The Napoleon of Notting Hill*, 1904; *The Man Who Was Thursday*, 1908; *The Ball and the Cross*, 1909; *Manalive*, 1912; *The Return of Don Quixote*, 1927.

SHORT FICTION: *The Innocence of Father Brown*, 1911; *The Wisdom of Father Brown*, 1914; *The Incredulity of Father Brown*, 1926; *The Secret of Father Brown*, 1927; *The Scandal of Father Brown*, 1935.

NONFICTION: *The Defendant*, 1901; *Twelve Types*, 1902; *Robert Browning*, 1903; *Heretics*, 1905; *Five Types*, 1905; *Charles Dickens*, 1906; *Orthodoxy*, 1908; *All Things Considered*, 1908; *George Bernard Shaw*, 1909; *Tremendous Trifles*, 1909; *Defiance of Nonsense*, 1909; *What's Wrong with the World and Alarms and Discussions*; 1910; *William Blake*, 1910; *A Miscellany of Men*, 1912; *The Victorian Age in Literature*, 1913; *The Barbarism of Berlin*, 1914; *The Crimes of England*, 1915; *A Shilling for My Thoughts*, 1916; *Utopia of Usurers*, 1917; *The Uses of Diversity*, 1920; *Fancies vs. Fads*, 1923; *St. Francis of Assisi*, 1923; *The End of the Roman Road*, 1924; *The Everlasting Man*,

1925; *The Superstitions of the Skeptics*, 1925; *Culture and the Coming Peril*, 1927; *Social Reforms and Birth Control*, 1927; *Robert Louis Stevenson*, 1927; *Generally Speaking*, 1928; *Come To Think of It*, 1930; *Sidelights on New London and Newer York*, 1932; *Chaucer*, 1932; *Christendom in Dublin*, 1932; *St. Thomas Aquinas*, 1933; *Avowals and Denials*, 1934; *As I Was Saying*, 1936.

## Bibliography
Barker, Dudley. *G. K. Chesterton: A Biography*, 1973.
Carol, Sister M. *G. K. Chesterton: The Dynamic Classicist*, 1972.
Clipper, Lawrence J. *G. K. Chesterton*, 1974.
Evans, Maurice. *G. K. Chesterton*, 1972.
Hollis, Christopher. *G. K. Chesterton*, 1950.
_____ . *The Mind of Chesterton*, 1970.
Hunter, Lynette. *G. K. Chesterton: Explorations in Allegory*, 1979.
Kenner, Hugh. *Paradox in Chesterton*, 1947.
Lea, F. A. *The Wild Knight of Battersea: G. K. Chesterton*, 1945.
Marie Virginia, Sister. *G. K. Chesterton's Evangel*, 1937.
Sullivan, John. *G. K. Chesterton: A Bibliography*, 1958.
_____ . *G. K. Chesterton Continued: A Biographical Supplement*, 1969.
_____ . *G. K. Chesterton: A Century Appraisal*, 1974.

*Samuel J. Rogal*

# JOHN CIARDI

**Born:** Boston, Massachusetts; June 24, 1916

**Principal collections**

*Homeward to America*, 1940; *Other Skies*, 1947; *Live Another Day*, 1949; *From Time to Time*, 1951; *The Inferno of Dante*, 1954 (translation); *As If: Poems New and Selected*, 1955; *I Marry You: A Sheaf of Love Poems*, 1958; *39 Poems*, 1959; *Dante's Purgatorio*, 1961 (translation); *In the Stoneworks*, 1961; *In Fact*, 1962; *Person to Person*, 1964; *This Strangest Everything*, 1966; *Dante's Paradiso*, 1970 (translation); *Lives of X*, 1971; *The Little That Is All*, 1974.

**Other literary forms**

John Ciardi's career as a poet has both generated and nourished his other remarkably varied and prolific literary activities, particularly his influential work as a teacher and critic, and author of two popular textbooks, *How Does a Poem Mean?* (1959) and *Poetry: A Closer Look* (1963). Ciardi served as an often controversial poetry editor of the *Saturday Review* (originally the *Saturday Review of Literature*) from 1956 to 1977. There he was responsible for selecting the verse that would be published in the magazine, as well as writing highly subjective columns covering a broad range of aesthetic subjects. Two volumes of his selected essays have been published: *Dialogue with an Audience* (1963) and *Manner of Speaking* (1972). These titles suggest two basic aspects of Ciardi's ideological stance—his awareness of the vital role of the reader (or "audience") with whom the artist must communicate and interact, and his single-minded delight in the power and versatility of words.

Ciardi's work as a translator of Dante's *The Divine Comedy* (c. 1320) is closely related to his recognition as a poet, for he chose to present all three sections of the classic work in his characteristically forceful, idiomatic American verse, professing not to offer yet another scholarly translation, but one that based its appeal on its ability to be understood by the average reader. Ciardi worked more than twenty years on Dante's poem. The first section, *The Inferno*, appeared in 1954, *The Purgatorio* in 1961, and *The Paradiso* in 1970. A one-volume edition, with a new introduction by Ciardi, was published in 1977. Although critical opinion of his translation has varied, Ciardi himself has evaluated his effort as one that "has not been a scholar's but a poet's work."

On innumerable other occasions, Ciardi has chosen to comment on his own poetry (he is an especially good self-analyst), and on the art in general. Essays of this sort have appeared not only in his *Saturday Review* columns, but also in various periodicals and prefaces to his poetry collections.

Other facets of Ciardi's talent and personality are revealed in his numerous volumes of poetry for children, mostly nonsense verse in the grand tradition of Edward Lear and Lewis Carroll. The first of these collections, *The Reason for the Pelican*, appeared in 1959 and the most recent volume, *Fast and Slow Poems for Advanced Children and Beginning Parents*, was published in 1975. Ciardi also published *Limericks Too Gross* (1978) with Isaac Asimov and *A Browser's Dictionary* (1980).

Not content with the printed word, Ciardi has recorded many of his poems for children, as well as his more serious work (including the Dante translations), and several discussions of poetry in general and how it can be understood. Currently he presents a series of programs on National Public Radio entitled *A Word in Your Ear*, in which he both instructs and entertains his listeners with nontechnical etymological lore.

## Achievements

Ideally, Ciardi's poems should be read as a whole, not as individual works, for their total effect is much greater than the sum of their various parts. Ciardi's engaging "personality" constitutes an integral informing intelligence, a presence that becomes more complex and developed as the experience of his poetry grows. His work is comparatively accessible—indeed his "first law" for all poetry is that it be easily understood by the general reader.

Whether Ciardi ranks among the finest of contemporary poets remains to be seen; he himself defined a "modern poet" as one who has yet to stand the test of continued critical acclaim. Because he has never been identified with a so-called "movement," or been the spokesman for a conspicuous cause, his popular reputation has been solely based on his poetry, essays, and personal efforts to effect a mutually meaningful dialogue with a middlebrow audience.

## Biography

Born in 1916 in the Italian neighborhood of South Boston, John Ciardi was the fourth child and only son of Neopolitan immigrants Concetta DeBenedictis and Carminantonio Ciardi. When he was only three years old, his father died in an automobile accident. In 1921 his mother moved the family to the Boston suburb of Medford, where Ciardi attended public school. After finishing high school in 1933, he worked a year to earn money before entering the pre-law program at Bates College in Maine, where his academic career was not very successful. In 1935 he transferred to Tufts College in Boston, where he abandoned his pre-law studies for literature and took his A.B. degree *magna cum laude* in 1938. In that same year he entered University of Michigan graduate school on a tuition scholarship.

Ciardi's main interest in the Michigan program was its Avery Hopwood Awards in poetry, and he was determined to compete for both the money and the prestige. He won first prize, a stipend of $1,200, and saw his first book of poetry, *Homeward to America*, published the following year; his career as a poet was launched. His Master of Arts degree was granted in 1939, and in 1940 he began his teaching career, a vocation he pursued, with only the interruption of service in World War II, until 1961. His first position was in Missouri as instructor in English at the University of Kansas City.

In 1942 Ciardi enlisted in the United States Army Air Force, and was discharged in 1945 as a technical sergeant after duty as an aerial gunner on a B-29 bomber in the air offensive against Japan. In both 1943 and 1944, while still in the service, he received prestigious prizes for his verse from *Poetry* magazine. After discharge from the Air Force, he returned briefly to his teaching post in Kansas City in 1946, that year marrying Myra Judith Hostetter, an instructor in journalism. He also received another prize from *Poetry* and in the fall joined the faculty of Harvard University as an instructor.

In 1947, Ciardi's second volume of poetry was published and he joined the staff of the Bread Loaf Writers Conference, an affiliation he continued until 1972. In 1948 he became an assistant professor at Harvard, a position he held with distinction until 1953, once being voted "the most popular professor at Harvard." The depth and strength of his vocational commitment is evident in his 1949 statement that "I make my living by writing and by teaching others to write." During this period he was an editor at Twayne Publishers, and another collection of his poetry appeared, *Live Another Day*. In 1950 he edited his anthology *Mid-Century American Poets*, and in 1951 lectured in Salzburg, Austria. In 1952 he was elected a Fellow of the American Academy of Arts and Sciences.

That same year the first of his three children, a daughter, was born; in 1953 and 1954 two sons were born. In 1953, Ciardi left Harvard for Rutgers University, where he remained until his resignation as a tenured professor in 1961, no longer determined to pursue the academic life of "planned poverty." In 1956 he spent much of the year in Rome on a Fellowship in Literature at the American Academy of Arts and Letters, also beginning in that year his long association (lasting until 1977) as poetry editor of the *Saturday Review*. In 1958 he served as president of the College English Association, and the following year published his initial juvenile poetry book. In 1960, Ciardi received the first of many honorary degrees, and in 1961 he began performing on educational television.

Working on his Dante translations, on his almost annual publication of verse collections, and at the *Saturday Review* (he reported reading approximately a thousand poems a week in his position as poetry editor), Ciardi produced an enormous literary output. From 1973 to 1974 he was a visiting professor at the University of Florida, and for a number of years was a literary "circuit rider," filling year-round lecture engagements throughout America. Still active in various literary activities, he lives in Metuchen, New Jersey.

**Analysis**

In an important prefatory essay to the 1949 volume *Live Another Day*, John Ciardi set down thirteen prescriptive principles of his poetic creed. These fundamental rules have served him as a guideline for his own poetry and also as a standard for the evaluation and judgment of the works of others. An understanding of these critical precepts is important to the analysis of Ciardi's poetry.

Ciardi's first and most important rule is that the reader should be able to understand a given poem. Ciardi has little use for certain poets (T. S. Eliot and Ezra Pound among them) whom he calls "baroque," inbred mannerists writing to other writers rather than generating their work from the raw material of nature "outward to the lives of men." Moreover, Ciardi believes that a poem should be affirmative and specific "about the lives of people." He recalls the origins of the genre by reminding readers that poetry should be read aloud, that its effect is to the ear, not the eye. Ciardi asserts that poetry can be about any subject, and may utilize any diction (no word is "not fit"), thus echoing William Wordsworth's democratic principles set forth in his Preface to *Lyrical Ballads* (1800). Ciardi also believes that "personality" must emerge from the work, otherwise it "is dead." Pursuing more technical prosodic elements, his premises include the opinion that to succeed a poem "must create its own form," and that ambiguities must be recognized and understood in each of their separate possibilities.

One can recognize that much of Ciardi's poetic credo is derivative, especially from the modern New Critical approach. In reference to his translations of Dante, Ciardi confessed unabashedly that he was "a thief of other men's scholarship," but argues logically and persuasively that such work has "no better purpose" than to serve other men's needs. In his own poetic principles, however, he goes beyond any limited doctrinaire critical tenets, and stresses the totality of a specific work, each line being "a conceived unit" of the whole. His final points are technical: he sees rhyme in the poem as "part of the total voice-punctuation," and metrics as being more successful when the conventional iambic pentameter line is less strictly observed.

Critics have declared that no two of Ciardi's poems are alike. While that observation may be something of an overstatement, certainly both his subjects and his forms, his diction and his tone, all demonstrate both poetic inventiveness and a remarkably broad range of personal interests. Indeed, in their subjectivity lies the primary theme of this most autobiographical poet: himself and his search for orientation and stability in a protean and often hostile and uncertain world. Readers, however, soon notice certain recurring themes: the pervasive influence of his first-generation Italian background, the shattering personal loss of his father, and the anxieties and contradictions, as well as the joys, of everyday contemporary urban life. The universal problem of discovering "a self" amid its distractions lies at the heart of Ciardi's work.

In his preference for the short, usually lyric poem, Ciardi consistently uses closed forms and tightly structured traditional stanzas, whether or not he employs rhyme; more often than not the reader is aware of a beginning, middle, and end. Following his own dictum advocating "common speech," Ciardi's lively vernacular diction is honestly direct, sometimes irreverent, and even crude, often employing colloquialisms.

In Ciardi's first book, *Homeward to America*, the volume that launched his career by winning the Hopwood Prize at the University of Michigan, he exhibited many of the characteristics that mark all his work—the search for and development of a self presented with wit and irony. Drawing obvious analogies between his parents' migration to America—their search for a "home"—and his own experience, he concludes (in "Letter to Mother") that despite their courageous and dramatic precedent, he must find his way alone. While the weaker poems in the collection are little more than externalizations of emotions dimly felt by the young poet, in his maturity this same protesting voice rings true.

A tone of protest is a distinctive characteristic of Ciardi's verse, especially in his early work, yet the iconoclast is no nihilist. Affirmation of life underlies even his most violent social criticism. Beginning in 1947, Ciardi began publishing strongly worded, often cynical poems. The volume *Other Skies* reflects Ciardi's war years; the forty-two poems reveal the intellectual growth forged by his military experience. Indicative of his new personal confidence and his mastery of the ironic tone is the tightly rhymed "Elegy Just in Case" that begins "Here lie Ciardi's pearly bones," in which he speculates about what would become of his decaying corpse rotting in the jungle. The bantering observations belie the grisly truth of war and its victims, yet the poem is no less effective for its flippant tone. More somberly intense is his "Poem for My Twenty-Ninth Birthday," in which he identifies himself with "the soaring madness of our time," a crewman of a bomber whose mission is "to save or kill us all" by destroying the lives of unseen and unknown enemy victims. Also in this important collection is "On a Photo of Sgt. Ciardi a Year Later," one of his most widely read poems. Here he considers himself in an earlier snapshot. He appears as an illusory costumed figure, and he concludes that the reality of a subject invariably eludes the camera's eye: "The shadow under the shadow is never caught."

In succeeding collections the flippancy diminishes; perhaps the newly married poet underwent a humanizing transformation, an affirmation of his growing responsibilities. In *Live Another Day*, *From Time to Time*, and *As If: Poems New and Selected*, he continues to recall and chronicle earlier experiences, the raw material of his emerging consciousness of self. In *Live Another Day* he includes both his prefatory credo as a poet and a profile of his hypothetical reader. In these transitional volumes the poet begins his attempt to reconcile his own introspective incursions with the interests of the public with whom he feels increasingly compelled to create a "dialogue."

In *As If: Poems New and Selected*, Ciardi includes several poems inspired by his wife Judith, later reprinted in *I Marry You*. At the time of this collection, Ciardi was deeply involved in his translations of Dante, an involvement which forced him to reexamine his Italian roots. Much of this personal exploration is evident in powerful poems about his father. In a sharply drawn poem typical of another less elegiac strain ("Thoughts on Looking into a Thicket") the poet offers one of his most succinct statements of his thematic stance: "I believe the world to praise it."

*I Marry You*, despite its popularity, is a private collection, a tribute by the poet to his happy and inspirational marriage and family life. Some critics see it as self-conscious sentimentality, but perhaps this opinion is a judgment on modern attitudes toward such intimate revelations rather than on the emotions themselves or the quality of their presentation. Not all of the poems in this collection, however, are conjugal, for what some consider to be Ciardi's finest poem, "Snowy Heron," is included. Here the poet follows his earlier admonition to praise, and extends the idea of espousal to include the world of nature; "I praise without a name," he proclaims, the power of the heron's flight. He feels that by whatever name one calls this spirit, the crucial act is to express glorification, adding emphasis by both beginning and ending the second six-line stanza with the imperative "But praise."

With the publication of *I Marry You*, Ciardi approached the height of his poetic powers. In his next collection, *39 Poems*, which appeared in 1959, he strives to illustrate his belief that intensely personal truths about one man might well illumine the life of another. "Bridal Photo, 1906" was inspired by a picture of his parents in a frozen moment; it ends with a prayer and a benediction by their son. In his explanatory notes for this poem, Ciardi says that from this communion of a man with a piece of paper, he found himself "knowing more and more truly about myself, and about all of us."

Four collections by Ciardi appeared during the 1960's: *In the Stoneworks*, *In Fact*, *Person to Person*, and *This Strangest Everything*. The first two works are generally seen as competent, but merely covering Ciardi's familiar and recognized poetic territory. His third volume of the decade is more successful. The title poem of *Person to Person* reaffirms his ceaseless efforts to make connections with his readers despite the difficulty of any genuine personal communication ("I can reach no one.") Another commendable poem in this group is "Autobiography of a Comedian," in which "Lucky John" Ciardi honestly profiles himself; being a comic, he confesses, is the only alternative to death. Materialistic rewards, however, do not satisfy the humanist instincts and yearnings of the soul: the comedian admits, "I'm still winning what I have no real use for." Protesting the absurdity that "even scholars take me seriously," he asks plaintively and in desperation (apparently extending himself to be a spokesman for Everyman), "How do we make sense of ourselves?"

A well-known poem in this important collection is "Tenzone," an ironic debate between the poet's soul and his body. In the guise of "soul," the effaced poet (again obviously Ciardi) describes himself complacently and realistically as "the well-known poet, critic, editor, and middle-high aesthete of the circuit" for whom "some weep" because he wastes his talents, while others find the very thought of his abilities laughable. "Soul" denounces him as a "greedy pig," dead to art, a confidence man concerned only with money and whiskey. In response, "body" accuses "soul" of having a father-fixation, of being a failed poet who knows it after discovering that a "poem is belly and bone." In "Nothing Is Really Hard But to Be Real" the poet taunts his readers by declaring that the aphoristic title is "fraudulent," only hollow "gnomic garbage." What is important is to find the truth of "our own sound" that reveals "what a man is." This argument, as well as his rhetorical gambit, is familiar Ciardi material, the theme and style not only of much of his poetry but also of his essays and lectures.

Less successful than *Person to Person*, his best and most significant volume of this decade, is *This Strangest Everything*. Here there are no excellent poems, nor, for that matter, any embarrassments; Ciardi seems content to cover old ground, to write not for critical acclaim but to fulfill the expectations of his growing audience of devoted readers.

In *Lives of X*, the first of Ciardi's two collections of the 1970's, the poet offers fifteen longer narratives in blank verse, one critic seeing it as "the closest thing to a formal autobiography [Ciardi] has yet attempted." Here he traces his rich and varied life from birth onward, recalling and expanding on events described in earlier poems and offering new details from memory, especially on his desperate search for a name and an identity, as well as his struggle with the Catholic Church. The other collection of this decade, *The Little That Is All*, has been called "vintage Ciardi," and is a random yet ultimately affirmative collection that expresses his concerns with objects and events in the life of a typical twentieth century man. Ranging from power mowers and blue movies to hiring a lawyer to fix his son's fourth "pot bust," the volume reflects both Ciardi's wit and his hard-won wisdom, and above all his ultimately triumphant coming to terms with life. His terse yet perceptive self-assessment of the chaos of suburban existence (in "Memo: Preliminary Draft of a Prayer to God the Father") is: "I do not complain: I describe." To date, this collection is the last volume of serious verse he has published.

Often faulted for being repetitious and belaboring the obvious as well as for lacking a direct emotional charge in his choice of diction, Ciardi has nevertheless refused to assume a philosophical stance alien to his nature, nor has he departed from his own particular "sense of the form." Perhaps his anecdotal subjects are often not equal to his masterful technical skills, but when one considers the number of poets of whom the reverse is true, Ciardi's remarkable poetic achievement comes into focus.

**Major publications other than poetry**

NONFICTION: *How Does a Poem Mean?*, 1959; *Poetry: A Closer Look*, 1963; *Dialogue with an Audience*, 1963; *Manner of Speaking*, 1972.

CHILDREN'S LITERATURE: *The Reason for the Pelican*, 1959; *Scrappy the Pup*, 1960; *I Met a Man*, 1961; *The Man Who Sang the Sillies*, 1961; *You Read to Me, I'll Read to You*, 1962; *The Wish-Tree*, 1962; *J. J. Plenty and Fidler Den*, 1963; *You Know Who*, 1964; *The King Who Saved Himself from Being Saved*, 1965; *An Alphabestiary*, 1966; *Someone Could Win a Polar Bear*, 1970; *Fast and Slow Poems for Advanced Children and Beginning Parents*, 1975.

ANTHOLOGY: *Mid-Century American Poets*, 1950.

MISCELLANEOUS: *Dante's Divine Comedy*, 1977 (translation); *Limericks Too Gross*, 1978 (with Isaac Asimov); *For Instance*, 1979; *A Browser's Dictionary*, 1980.

**Bibliography**

Cifelli, Edward. "The Size of John Ciardi's Song," in *CEA Critic*. November, 1973, pp. 21-23, 26-27.

Hughes, John W. "Humanism and the Orphic Voice," in *Saturday Review*. May 22, 1971, pp. 31-33.

Krickel, Edward. *John Ciardi*, 1980.

Southworth, James C. "The Poetry of John Ciardi," in *English Journal*. December, 1961, pp. 583-589.

White, William. *John Ciardi: A Bibliography*, 1959.

Williams, Miller, ed. *The Achievement of John Ciardi*, 1969.

*Maryhelen C. Harmon*

# JOHN CLARE

**Born:** Helpston, England; July 13, 1793
**Died:** Northampton, England; May 20, 1864

## Principal collections

*Poems Descriptive of Rural Life and Scenery*, 1820, 1821; *The Village Minstrel and Other Poems*, 1821; *The Shepherd's Calendar*, 1827; *The Rural Muse*, 1835; *The Later Poems of John Clare*, 1964 (Eric Robinson and Geoffrey Summerfield, editors); *The Shepherd's Calendar*, 1964 (Eric Robinson and Geoffrey Summerfield, editors); *Selected Poems and Prose of John Clare*, 1967 (Eric Robinson and Geoffrey Summerfield, editors); *The Midsummer Cushion*, 1979.

## Other literary forms

John Clare attempted little systematically except poetry. He left manuscript drafts of several unfinished essays, and part of what was intended as a natural history of Helpston. He wrote two lengthy autobiographical essays, one of which was published in 1931: *Sketches in the Life of John Clare, Written by Himself*. The other appeared in a collection of his prose in 1951. He also left one year of a journal in which he recorded his reading and his speculations on religion, politics, and literature. His best-known essay is probably his "Journey out of Essex," an account of his escape from an asylum and his harrowing journey home on foot with no food or shelter; it has been published several times.

## Achievements

Clare overcame obstacles that would have defeated most other people and became an important poet of the Romantic period in England. His family was illiterate and desperately poor, though ambitious for their son to rise in the world. His formal schooling was minimal, and he lived all his life isolated from the literary currents of his day. His editors censored his work heavily, misled him about royalties, and were generally insensitive to what he was trying to do in his verse. He suffered for years from malnutrition and then from incurable mental illness. Despite everything, he was not only enormously prolific as a poet—more than three thousand poems in a fifty-five-year career that began at the age of sixteen—but also wrote a number of poems that may deservedly be called masterpieces. In particular, his descriptive poems have come in recent years to be recognized for their originality and anticipation of certain trends in twentieth century nature poetry. His dedication to poetry was intense, surviving, in addition to all other trials, the almost complete financial failure of three of the four books he published during his lifetime. His "The Shepherd's Calendar" is one of the truest and most delightful evocations of English rural life ever written. The "animal" poems of his middle years (the most famous of which is probably "Badger") are stark and powerful expressions of his increasing alienation and despair. He carried his dedication to poetry undiminished into confinement in an asylum, where he wrote poems which show his "sane" grasp of his own insanity. These later poems rise to a universality which has made them widely admired ever since some of them were published in 1873.

Clare was almost completely ignored by the critics until the commentary of Arthur Symons in 1908, and the first textually reliable selection of his poems did not appear until 1920. Even at that, the student of Clare must still exercise extreme caution when using certain editions. In particular, the largest existing selection of his poems, the most complete editions of his prose, and the only one of his letters (all edited by J. W. and Anne Tibble), as well as one of the two existing selections of his asylum poems (edited by Geoffrey Grigson), contain serious misprintings of the manuscripts on almost every page. Much better selections have appeared more recently, but even today there is no complete edition of Clare's poetry or prose, although one is well under way. His reputation began to rise after the work of Symons, and especially after the edition by Edmund Blunden in 1920. Much criticism and analysis has appeared since the centennial of Clare's death in 1864, and his reputation has risen rapidly since then.

**Biography**

John Clare's childhood was spent laboring in the fields near his native village, and in the "dame schools" which provided a rudimentary education for those of the rural poor who understood their value. Clare's father was a ballad singer of some local note, and this early exposure to village folk-culture, together with his bent for reading, provided a solid base for his later accomplishments. His interest in writing seems to have awakened at the age of sixteen when he acquired a copy of James Thomson's narrative-descriptive poem, *The Seasons* (1746). Finding time and opportunity to write at all, however, proved difficult. Unable to afford much paper, he recorded his earliest efforts on scraps kept in his hat; thus they were easily lost or damaged. The extremely long hours of an agricultural laborer and the distrust of learning among his fellow villagers restricted him further. Nevertheless, by his early twenties he had assembled a fairly substantial body of work which he showed to a nearby storekeeper with literary connections in London. His first book, *Poems Descriptive of Rural Life and Scenery*, was brought out in 1820 by John Taylor, publisher of Charles Lamb and John Keats. It was an immediate success, going through four editions within a year. Taylor then published a second volume, *The Village Minstrel and Other Poems*, in 1821, but its sale was disappointing. Clare's first book had caught the very end of a craze for "peasant poets." Over the next several years he made a few trips to London, meeting and socializing with Lamb, William Hazlitt, Thomas De Quincey, and others. Nevertheless, problems quickly developed. He began to have disagreements with his publishers over the editing of his poems, the size of his family increased rapidly (he had married a local woman in 1820), and so did his debts. He could not seem to get an accurate or satisfactory explanation of how much of his royalties were needed to pay publishing expenses.

From then until 1837, Clare lived in Helpston almost without interruption, writing increasingly good poetry with almost no public recognition at all. A third volume, *The Shepherd's Calendar*, was finished in 1823 but not published until four years later when it, too, sold poorly. He suffered from malnutrition and his mental health began to deteriorate. Little regular employment was available in his region, and a move to a neighboring village in 1832 (to a cottage given him by a patron) did not substantially alter his prospects. His sense of place was so strong that he found it difficult to adjust to the move, and he grew increasingly deluded. In 1835 he managed to have a fourth volume published, *The Rural Muse*. It was well received by the critics but did not sell well.

Finally, in late 1837, he was taken to Matthew Allen's experimental asylum at High Beech, in the Epping Forest near London. There he was well-treated and recovered some of his physical health; but he wrote little for several years. In the spring of 1841, he began writing poetry again, and in July he escaped. He made his way home by walking for several days, surviving by eating grass along the roadside. Although he was not violent, he was clearly not sane, and in late 1841, he was again committed, this time nearer home at the asylum in Northampton. There he remained until his death in 1864 at the age of seventy-one. His asylum poetry was written almost entirely in the last few months at High Beech, and during the brief stay at home and the first several years at Northampton. When a sympathetic asylum supervisor who had preserved his work departed in 1850, his deteriorating condition and lack of encouragement from the staff seemingly closed off his inspiration.

**Analysis**

The poetry of John Clare shows throughout its development the influence of three forces: the culture of his village and social class; nature; and the topographical and pastoral poetry of the eighteenth century. Clare's view of human life as lived in close relationship with nature is presented in his poetry as a series of contrasts between the freer, socially more equal, open-field village of his childhood, and the enclosed, agriculturally "improved," and socially stratified village of his manhood; between the Eden of a wild nature untouched by human beings, and the fallen nature of fences, uprooted landmarks, and vanished grazing rights; between the aesthetic response to nature which loves it for what it is, and the scientific response which loves it for profit and social status. Further, as a self-educated poet in a land of illiterate laborers, Clare had difficulty resolving the tension between his temptation to idealize village life and his equally strong temptation to expose its squalid ignorance. One evidence of this is the fact that he wrote "The Shepherd's Calendar," a celebration of the beauty and activity of a village, in the same year that he wrote "The Parish," a brutally frank attack on its ignorance and cultural isolation. In his best poetry, Clare is able to see both realities as only a part of the truth.

A typical Clare poem of his pre-asylum years will seek above all concreteness in its imagery, and a structure designed to make the images reveal the maximum amount of meaning. Clare is a master at creating multiple levels of significance through what at first seems like an almost random collection of sights and sounds. A poem that well illustrates this technique is his unrhymed sonnet, "Gypsies." It is a poem which deftly combines Clare's love of rural life with his awareness of its darker side. He begins the poem, as he does so many others, with a sense of the mystery of nature: "The snow falls deep; the forest lies alone"; but he immediately introduces the theme of human suffering amid the beauty: "The boy goes hasty for his load of brakes/ Then thinks upon the fire and hurries back." The cold is beautiful but potentially deadly. Then we are in the gypsy camp where there are only bushes to break the wind, where "tainted mutton wastes upon the coals," and the scrawny dog squats nearby "And vainly waits the morsel thrown away." Clare's use of internal rhyme is very successful, as "tainted" and "vainly" resonate against each other in interesting ways. In a sense, the gypsies are "tainted" in the settled village society, and thus hope in vain for acceptance. Clare has provided hints of an attitude, then, while allowing the details to carry the implications. He seems to reject both the villagers' ethnic bigotry and the hopelessness of gypsy life: "'Tis thus they live—a picture to the place/ A quiet, pilfering, unprotected race." The seeming offhandedness of "'Tis thus they live" is acceptance and rejection, simultaneously, as the remaining line and a half so neatly demonstrate by balancing "quiet" against "pilfering" against "unprotected." The sudden rise from specific images to broad generalization at the end does not surprise the reader because the details have been so carefully chosen throughout. Clare refuses to idealize gypsy life just as he refuses to excuse the villagers for their prejudice. The sonnet as he uses it here retains most of the traditional Shakespearean form except for the lack of rhyme. It is all the more impressive because Clare encloses his argument in a description which values the gypsies for the beauty they add to life. This determination to see life for what it is and an equal determination not to allow its bitterness to defeat him or prevent him from seeing its beauty, is one of Clare's most admirable qualities as a poet and as a man.

The themes of Clare's poetry grow directly out of the ways of seeing human life and nature illustrated in "Gypsies." Perhaps the most important of his themes is the contrast between the village and landscape of the past and of the present. In making this contrast in his poetry, Clare is not simply engaging in private history-making which would leave modern readers uninterested because they occupy a space and a time far removed from Clare's. Rather, he is comparing two fundamentally different approaches to the relationship between human beings and the natural world. The choice between these two approaches is as crucially important today as it was then, and for this reason alone Clare's poetry has lost none of its cogency for the modern world.

In Clare's time enclosure of the land for purposes of agricultural improvement was the issue that divided people in rural areas. No Clare poem speaks more eloquently to what enclosure did, psychologically as well as physically, to village life and to him as a poet than "The Mores" (that is, moors). It is written in a familiar eighteenth century form and style: the locodescriptive poem in heroic couplets. Nevertheless, Clare handles it in original ways. The heroic couplet in the eighteenth century embodies the polished wit and rational completeness which characterized the view of life held by the Age of Reason. Clare's couplet has a slow, solemn movement which is equally as impressive, though far different in effect. At the beginning of the poem, for example, the same sense of mystery in primeval nature seen in "Gypsies" is present here, although that mystery is more obviously a part of the argument to be made: "Far spread the moorey ground a level scene/ Bespread with rush and one eternal green/ That never felt the rage of blundering plough." Here again, balance: the quietness of the preenclosure view *versus* a barely suppressed anger; nature's innocence and eternity against the "blundering" greed of human beings.

Clare's description is always visually precise and yet capable of entertaining several levels of meaning: "uncheckt shadows of green green brown and grey," where "uncheckt" means both "without limits" and "not in checkered patterns as enclosed fields are." Or, a few lines later we have "One mighty flat undwarfed by bush or tree/ Spread its faint shadow of immensity." Here, "flat" functions both as a noun and as a kind of suspended adjective: we pause in suspense at this unusual caesura, so that the way in which we read the line reinforces the idea that we cannot see the limits of this "faint shadow of immensity/ In the blue mist the (h)orisons edge surrounds." Human pride erupts into the poem, for "Inclosure came and trampled on the grave/ Of labours rights." From here to the end of the poem there is continual tension between longing for the old freedom and the reality of the new concern for boundaries, profits, and class distinctions. When these two value-systems begin to clash more directly in the poem, the descriptive style becomes harsher, befitting the new dispensation: "And sky bound mores in mangled garbs are left/ Like mighty giants of their limbs bereft." Everywhere there is a pettiness, a separation rather than a communion: "Fence now meets fence in owners little bounds . . ./ In little parcels little minds to please/ With men and flocks imprisoned ill at ease."

As the poem proceeds it becomes clearer that Clare is really talking about a failure of vision: "Each little tyrant with his little sign/ Shows where man claims earth glows no more divine." The problem with the human desire to dominate nature is finally that it destroys that which makes us most human. In Clare's view, then, beauty, freedom, open fields, and social harmony have been succeeded by ugliness, fences, and social antagonism. Under these circumstances, poetic creativity becomes as difficult as any other activity requiring vision. The moors "are vanished now with commons wild and gay/ As poets visions of lifes early day." The cumulative force of the couplets, the measured movement of the lines, the masterful control over the reader's "eye" as it moves over the landscape, all create an emotional impact which makes "The Mores" typical of Clare at his best in the descriptive-narrative poem.

Clare's poetry grew increasingly lyric and less narrative-descriptive as the years passed. As with John Keats, Clare was particularly interested in taking the sonnet in new directions. They both believed that the sonnet might function as a stanza form for longer poems. In Keats's case, the result was the great odes of 1819; in Clare's, the very different but impressive poems on animals of the mid-1830's. Clare's poems had always been filled with a variety of animal life, but these poems move to a new attitude toward nature, emphasizing its otherness from human beings. By a seeming paradox, they move also toward an increased empathy *with* nature. The paradox is resolved by seeing that it is precisely the alienation of wild nature from human society (especially of certain hunted animals) with which Clare could identify because he, too, felt thus cut off from human understanding. The actions of animals in and around nests, caves, and hollow trees fascinated him. These were places where relatively helpless creatures might hope to escape.

In the poem "Sand Martin," for example, the bird inhabits the "desolate face" of a wasted landscape far away from man where it flits about "an unfrequented sky." Clare seems to admire most the sand martin's ability to "accept" the desolation of its habitat because of the protection it affords. The speaker of the poem feels "a hermit joy/ To see thee circle round nor go beyond/ That lone heath and its melancholy pond." Clare knew that a person's roots and his resulting sense of place might make him part of a scene that could enervate his spirit; yet he might be unable to function in any other place. Clare is a pioneer in using the sonnet to center on a single, unified experience by ignoring the traditional octave-sestet break and using instead accumulation of detail to create meaning. Thus his early reading in the topographical poetry of the eighteenth century, with its emphasis on a collection of images moving toward a visual as well as an emotional climax, served him well when he wished to make his poetry express through details his anguish and sense of isolation. Meaning emerges in a Clare description almost in slow motion, and it is sometimes late in the poem before the reader realizes what power the accumulated detail has acquired.

Clare is one of the great lyric poets of the English language. His roots were in a culture which valued the ballad and the oral tale as art forms as well as sources of tradition. Clare himself was a lifelong collector of ballads and folk songs (noting down music as well as words), and he played the violin well. Many of his finest lyrics come from the 1830's and the asylum years, when the bulk of his output became lyric rather than narrative or descriptive. The good lyric can sometimes succeed in reaching the widest audience when it is most personal and "private." From the mid-1830's come four of Clare's best: "Remembrances," "Song's Eternity," "With Garments Flowing," and "Decay." A brief comparison of these four will serve to illustrate the command that Clare exercised over a variety of forms, moods, and themes in the lyric. In "Remembrances," Clare uses a device so simple and well-known—the stages of human life compared to the seasons of the year—that in the hands of a lesser poet it would become trite and shopworn. This ballad-like poem has octameter lines and a typical rhyme scheme of aaabcccddd; it is marvelously adapted to the leisurely memories of childhood which the poem treats. From the first line, "Summers pleasures they are gone like to visions every one," Clare manages to imbue the commonest scenes from the past with a haunting quality which the incantatory rhythm of the verse reinforces perfectly.

"Song's Eternity" is a very different kind of lyric. Instead of unusually long lines, it has unusually short ones: alternating lines of four beats and two. Rather than the expansiveness of the quasinarrative ballad, Clare offers the crisp conciseness of

> What is song's eternity?
> Come and see.
> Melodies of earth and sky.
> Here they be.
> Songs once sung to Adam's ears.
> Can it be? . . .
> Songs awakened with the spheres
> Alive.

It is Clare's frequently heard theme of the eternity of nature, which will provide the necessary stay against the confusion of modern life.

The third lyric, "With Garments Flowing," represents still another form and another purpose. It is a love lyric written in a meter often found in Clare: stanzas with alternating nine and eight syllables, all tetrameter, rhyming ababcdcd. It is more regular than the forms used in "Remembrances" and "Song's Eternity," and was probably chosen because he wanted the ballad-like stanza without its looseness and conversational tone, together with the conciseness and rhythm of "Song's Eternity" without the absolute regularity of that poem. The success of "With Garments Flowing" lies also in the metonymy of the garments of the lover's dress standing for the lover herself.

To the speaker in the poem she is the type of all that is beautiful. Yet in describing her Clare retains homely details of village life while avoiding the sentimentality that can threaten such an attempt.

Finally, "Decay" is another quite different kind of lyric, and equally successful. Clare wrote it apparently as a means of understanding what was happening to his poetic voice as a result of the move in 1832 to another village—as a way of regaining his poetic voice or at least of explaining its loss. He skillfully controls the reader's response through subtle variations in the rhyme scheme in the ten-line stanzas, as well as through modulations in the simple theme: "O poesy is on the wane/ I hardly know her face again," which acts as a kind of refrain throughout. Personification is also important in this poem: the sun is a "homeless ranger" that "pursues a naked weary way/ Unnoticed like a very stranger." The blend of the local and the universal, as is so often true in Clare's poetry, is here perfectly calculated to communicate disorientation in a coherent manner: "I often think that west is gone/ Oh cruel time to undeceive us." Time has taken away the visionary gleam: "The stream it is a naked stream/ . . . The sky hangs o'er a broken dream/ The bramble's dwindled to a bramble." The tone becomes more bitter, and the speaker more puzzled even while attaining a new understanding: "And why should passing shadows grieve us/ . . . And hope is but a fancy play/ And joy the art of true believing." Here the sarcasm and the grief somehow perfectly complement each other.

Clare's creativity followed a different pattern in the asylum years. Long periods of virtual poetic silence were followed by relatively brief times of sustained production. The dominant theme of his asylum poems is the assertion of his identity as a free man and as a poet. Indeed, Clare had always believed that freedom of the eye and of the mind were necessary preconditions of artistic creativity. His determination to be remembered as a poet decades after his work had been largely forgotten is probably responsible both for the quality of his asylum work and for the fact that madness did not completely engulf his mind any sooner than it did. Clare's first sustained asylum production was a continuation of George Gordon, Lord Byron's *Childe Harold's Pilgrimage*, written in 1841 under the delusion that he was Byron. While it was left unfinished, the work demonstrates that his descriptive and lyric talents were not only unimpaired but also still developing. It was, however, in the first few years of his confinement at Northampton Asylum (from 1842 to about 1848) that some of Clare's finest poems were written. Three of these may be examined briefly for the light they cast on the theme of self-identity and on his level of achievement in these years. In one, "Peasant Poet," Clare seems to sum up what his poetic life had been about, emphasizing, of course, simplicity and love of nature. His gift for juxtaposing images of ordinary things in order to achieve fresh meaning is undiminished: "the daisy-covered ground" immediately next to "the cloud-bedappled sky"; the sound of the brook leading the eye to the swallow "swimming by." This peasant poet of whom he speaks (clearly himself) was not a great achiever "in life's affairs." He was just two things: "A peasant in his daily cares/ The poet in his joy." It is a descriptive lyric containing the essence of his poetic credo: poetry as joy, transforming the face of daily life.

The second poem, "An Invite to Eternity," is Clare's most sustained attempt to define the perception of the insane mind; not to define it as a dictionary would, but to re-create for the reader its vision of the world—making the reader participate in it and so identify with it. Like so many of Clare's poems, whenever written, this one begins with an invitation—in this case to a "sweet maid" who is to travel with him through the landscape of madness. In the same sort of personification seen in "Decay," both the sun and the path have forgotten where they are to go. In this "strange death of life to be," what we see is inverted, made into its opposite: "Where stones will turn to flooding streams/ Where plains will rise like ocean waves." The swaying rhythm of the tetrameter lines creates an almost hypnotic effect. It is an existence without identity: being and nonbeing at the same time. In this twilight existence they will not know each other's face, and time itself will cease to exist: "The present mixed with reasons gone/ And past and present all as one." Knowing all this, he asks the maid, can her life be led "To join the living with the dead?" If so (and he seems to await her answer with the serenity of absolute knowledge), "Then trace thy footsteps on with me/ We're wed to one eternity." Logic, time, identity, and ordinary perception of the "real" have all been suspended, to be replaced by their opposites. The perfectly ordered form of the poem, its calm account of the horrors of irrationality, provide remarkable evidence of Clare's ability at times in the asylum to view his own insanity from outside, as it were. Perhaps more important, the poem demonstrates how much he was still a poet in control of his art.

The third poem is entitled simply, "I Am." If "Peasant Poet" sums up Clare's view of himself as poet, and "An Invite to Eternity" his view of himself as insane, "I Am" may be said to provide the essence of Clare as child of God. In the poem he creates a persona supremely tragic: the good man bereft of that which gave his life purpose, and left to experience the moment of self-understanding completely alone. The poem turns on the idea of existence without essence, and the first stanza reiterates the "I Am" four times in its six lines: since no one knows anything of me except that I exist, I become "the self-consumer of my woes." They have no outlet, they meet with no understanding. The tremendous psychological pressure that this would ordinarily create is somehow controlled and made to yield calm resignation rather than anger, as the speaker surveys "the vast shipwreck of my lifes esteems." Instead, in the third and final stanza we return to a familiar Clare theme: the Eden of nature. There, where there is neither man nor woman, only God, peace is at last possible: "Untroubling and untroubled where I lie/ The grass below, above, the vaulted sky." In Clare's fen country, the two essential facts had always been the moors and the sky—both flat, immense, bare, unchanging, losing themselves at the edge in mist and shadow.

## Major publication other than poetry
NONFICTION: *Sketches in the Life of John Clare, Written by Himself*, 1931.

## Bibliography

Barrell, John. *The Idea of Landscape and the Sense of Place*, 1972.

Crossan, Greg. *A Relish for Eternity*, 1976.

Dendurent, H. O. *John Clare: A Reference Guide*, 1978.

Grigson, Geoffrey. *Poems and Poets*, 1969.

Howard, William. *John Clare*, 1981.

Keith, W. J. *The Poetry of Nature*, 1980.

Murry, J. Middleton. *John Clare and Other Studies*, 1950.

Pinsky, Robert. "That Sweet Man, John Clare," in *The Rarer Action*, 1970.

Storey, Mark. *The Poetry of John Clare*, 1974.

Tibble, J. W., and Anne Tibble. *John Clare: A Life*, 1972.

Todd, Janet. *In Adam's Garden*, 1973.

*Mark Minor*

# ARTHUR HUGH CLOUGH

**Born:** Liverpool, England; January 1, 1819
**Died:** Florence, Italy; November 13, 1861

## Principal poems and collections

*The Bothie of Tober-na-Vuolich*, 1848 (first published as *Toper-na-Fuosich*); *Ambarvalia*, 1849 (with Thomas Burbridge); *Amours de Voyage* (published serially in the *Atlantic Monthly*, I, February-May, 1858); *Poems*, 1862 (Mrs. Clough, editor); *Mari Magno*, 1862 (written in 1861); *Dipsychus*, 1865 (written in 1850); *The Poems of A. H. Clough*, 1951 (H. F. Lowry, editor).

## Other literary forms

Arthur Hugh Clough, although primarily a poet, was also a distinguished essayist. Clough's essays tend to cluster around two topics—literary criticism, and social, especially religious, issues. His prose works appeared primarily in newspapers and periodicals. They have been collected in *The Poems and Prose Remains of Arthur Hugh Clough* (1869) and *Selected Prose Works of Arthur Hugh Clough* (1964).

## Achievements

Most assessments of Clough's achievements raise the question, "Why did he not achieve more?" This question originated with his contemporaries and reflects the social attitudes and professional expectations of Victorian times. A young man who was well-begun, that is, one who was graduated from Oxford or Cambridge, and who enjoyed the respect of his colleagues, was expected to rise to eminence in his profession. Clough began with these high expectations. Subsequently, however, he surrendered a fellowship at Oxford, took an administrative post at the University of London, became an examiner in the Education office, and, finally, an aide to Florence Nightingale. Contemporaries saw this path as a continual falling off. Furthermore, his real accomplishments in poetry occur in just over a single decade of his life. Perhaps a more generous way of assessing Clough's achievement is to concentrate on his creative work itself. In his writing one finds a ferocious intellectual honesty which, by its clarity of vision, allows subsequent generations to see more clearly what were the inner tensions of the reflective person in an age of religious, scientific, and political ferment. Clough is an articulate observer of the age which witnessed the rapid spread of evangelicalism, the sharp reaction against it by the Oxford movement, the open attacks on historic Christianity, and the fervent reply of a beleaguered orthodoxy. Moreover, he is not only an observer; but he is also a sympathetic participant drawn in painfully divergent directions by the conflicts of his times.

## Biography

When Arthur Hugh Clough was three years old, his family moved from Liverpool to Charleston, South Carolina. During the six years he spent in America, he lived under the constant influence of his mother's evangelical piety. In spite of a subsequent religious disillusionment, the concerns and temperament of the evangelical disposition marked Clough's poetry for the rest of his life.

In 1828 Clough was sent back to England for his education. In the following year, he entered Rugby and so fell under another of the dominant influences upon his life and work—namely, the family of the headmaster, Thomas Arnold. Arnold and his two sons Tom and Matthew (later the poet) fostered in Clough the ideals of a commitment to reason, rigorous self-discipline in pursuit of high goals, and a deep moral sobriety in contemplating public affairs. At Rugby, Clough was editor of the *Rugby Magazine* and head of the School House.

Clough won a prestigious scholarship to Balliol College, Oxford, which he entered in 1827. In 1841, he took a second-class degree, to the considerable surprise of friends who had expected more, and he was denied a fellowship in his own college after his graduation. Nevertheless, he was elected to a fellowship in Oriel College and so remained at Oxford, where he became one of the most popular tutors.

Throughout his years at Oxford, Clough had watched the progress of the Oxford movement. The polemical context of religious discussions on the Oxford campus at the time may have contributed to a growing skepticism, which culminated in Clough's resigning the Oriel Fellowship in 1848 as an act of conscience. He could not endorse the Thirty-nine Articles (the Creed of the Anglican Church), as Oxford dons were expected to do. The soul-searching struggle of his departure from Oxford may be intimated in his poem *The Bothie of Tober-na-Vuolich*, written shortly thereafter.

Clough was not "ruined" in English education, however, and in 1849, after a trip to Italy during which he witnessed the French suppression of Giuseppe Mazzini's Roman Republic, he became the principal of University Hall, University College, London. From the Italian trip came his *Amours de Voyage*. He returned to Italy the following year and, while there, began his long and perhaps best-known poem, *Dipsychus* (first published in *Letters and Remains*, 1865).

In 1852 Clough resigned his duties at University Hall in a dispute over the manner in which religious instruction should be administered and over his refusal to recruit actively students in this prototype of a modern university. He set sail for America, where he enjoyed some reputation for his *The Bothie of Tober-na-Vuolich*, and the favor of such American literary figures as Ralph Waldo Emerson, James Russell Lowell, Henry Wadsworth Longfellow, and Charles Eliot Norton. Nevertheless, he could not find a position which would

allow him an income sufficient to marry the girl he had left in England—
Blanche Smith. Thus, he returned to England when Thomas Carlyle secured
for him a position with the Education Office.

Clough and Blanche Smith were married in June, 1854, and for the remain-
ing seven years of his life he continued his rather routine work as a bureaucrat.
This employment, compounded by the increasing duties he performed for
Florence Nightingale, Blanche's cousin, crowded out his efforts at poetry.
This busy employment helps to account for the fact that Clough's most prolific
period of creativity was confined to a single decade of his life.

During 1859, Clough was stricken ill with scarlatina. Traveling about the
Continent in an effort to recover his health gave him opportunity to think of
poetry once again. He had written a good deal of the unfinished *Mari Magno*
(first published in *Poems*, 1862) when he died in Florence in 1861. He was
buried in the Protestant cemetery there, just four months after Elizabeth
Barrett Browning had been interred in the same place.

**Analysis**

Arthur Hugh Clough's poetry is the effort of a man reared in deep religious
faith to discover whether, following his apostasy, an honest skepticism could
produce high-minded contentments equal to those of the idealism he had
repudiated.

Although he wrote occasional poems throughout his life and published a
number in the school magazine at Rugby, Clough's career as a serious poet
extends only from 1848 to 1858, with a resurgence of activity in the last year
of his life, 1861. *The Bothie of Tober-na-Vuolich*, his first major work,
appeared at the end of a long year of soul-searching. Early in 1848 he had
resigned as tutor, and in October he resigned his fellowship at Oriel. In
November the poem appeared. It is a long account of a group of Oxford
scholars who retire to the Scottish highlands to read for examinations. The
most distinctive member of the party, Philip Hewson, is a freethinking radical
who falls in love three different times during the extended stay—the last time
with the girl who lives in the bothie (cottage) at Tober-na-Vuolich. Philip's
various personal experiences have a softening effect on his political views.
Early in the poem he makes a high-strung and doctrinaire attack on the
privileged classes, but the women he meets have to be dealt with as actual
and complex beings. When he finally falls in love with the peasant girl Elspie,
he comes to realize that his economic account of the peasantry is far too
simple to explain the living person. In the belief that Oxford scholasticism
is too far removed from the life of experience, Philip declines to return—for
reasons similar to those of the poet himself. Even Philip's skepticism now
seems to him too doctrinaire to account for the stress of his inner life, and
the poem ends with Philip and Elspie emigrating to New Zealand where he
"hewed and dug; subdued the earth and his spirit." Clough suggests that his

late skepticism might be as doctrinaire as his early faith, and he looks to the leavening of actual experience to moderate his own abstract scholasticism.

*The Bothie of Tober-na-Vuolich* is written in hexameters. This fact has produced a long-running controversy over the metrical effects of the poem. Wendell Harris has given a comprehensive account of the arguments (*Arthur Hugh Clough*, 1970). Clough's defenders—such as Matthew Arnold—believe that his use of hexameters gives his poem the primitive, homespun forcefulness which is also to be found in the poetry of classical antiquity—in the *Iliad* (c. 800 B.C.) for example: "So in the golden morning they parted and went to the westward." Critics of the poem believe that for a sustained work the meter, tending to "break down into anapests" (Harris), flows against the natural iambs of English narrative discourse. It falls somewhere between prose and poetry: "So in the cottage with Adam the pupils live together/ Duly remained, and read, and looked no more for Philip." If there is to be found a justification for the meter, it is in Clough's expectation that the rough-hewn meter would reinforce his theme: the rejection of doctrinaire scholasticism (and the modern poetic conventions) in favor of an experientially authenticated sense of love and social justice.

*Ambarvalia* appeared in January, 1849—only three months after *The Bothie of Tober-na-Vuolich*. *Ambarvalia* is a collection of poems on several topics. The title refers to an ancient Roman festival in which animals were sacrificed to ensure the fertility of the fields. By this title Clough may have intended to remove himself from a sectarian Christian ideal of the world and to evoke the image of a mythology at once more primitive and closer to nature. The leading poem of the collection implies this sort of skepticism; it is called "The Questioning Spirit." In it one human spirit confronts all the others with troubling questions, and they reply that they neither know nor need to know the solution to such rarefied philosophical problems. The poem is an attack on a mindless sort of orthodoxy: "Only with questionings pass I to and fro,/ Perplexing these that sleep, and in their folly/ imbreeding doubt and sceptic melancholy." That melancholy questioning, coupled with a persistent but vague hope which always attends his agnosticism, could be the theme of Clough's entire poetry. The poem "Why Should I Say I See the Things I See Not" is a well-nigh militant refusal to say that reality rests on things not manifest, "Unfit, unseen, unimagined, all unknown." The last of the twenty-nine poems in *Ambarvalia* asks the ancient question whether there actually are gods who treat human beings in the apparently shabby ways that fate seems to dictate. He answers his own question in this problematical way:

> If it is so let it be so
> And we will all agree so;
> But the plot has counterplot,
> It may be, and yet be not.

In 1850, Clough began his long poem *Dipsychus*. Although it did not appear (posthumously) until 1865 (indeed it was never truly finished), this poem has since become Clough's best-known work. It consists of fourteen scenes, an Epilogue, and four more scenes of a continuation. The poem is set in Venice. Its protagonist is Dipsychus, the divided soul, who is engaged in a lengthy dialogue with Spirit (who, as the reader later learns, is Mephistopheles). Some readers have believed that the Spirit is the projected voice of the skeptical "half" of Dipsychus' mind. A better reading seems to be that Dipsychus represents the mind torn between faith and doubt, and Spirit represents the distractions which would alleviate his inward tensions through the pleasures of everyday life: sex, wealth, the struggle for power, and the like. Dipsychus, however, does not want to be merely mollified; he wants to know the honest truth of the world.

*Dipsychus* is not only reminiscent of Johann Wolfgang von Goethe's *Faust* (1790-1832), but it also even challenges comparison. Goethe's poem has more action and pageantry, a grander scale and more subtle inquiry, but Clough's poem presents the issues with a bold forthrightness which marks the possibility of a clearly skeptical voice in Victorian society even before the publication of *On the Origin of Species* (1859). The clause "Christ is not risen" becomes a recurring refrain in the opening scenes. Spirit (Mephistopheles) replies that if such is the case, all of Dipsychus's metaphysics would be futile and he might as well console himself with the pleasures of the flesh:

> This lovely creature's glowing charms
> Are gross illusion, I don't doubt that;
> But when I pressed her in my arms
> I somehow didn't think about that.

Finally, Dipsychus, having succumbed to Spirit's temptation to "Enjoy the minute," despairs of a metaphysic which will give authenticity to his actions and resigns himself to live the common life. In the continuation, however, when he has lived long and become a successful Lord Chief Justice, he must face the woman he debauched thirty years earlier. He must face the fact that even if his actions seem not to be subject to the guidance of metaphysics, they nevertheless have consequences: "Once Pleasure and now Guilt." The poem ends with the inference that because actions have results, experience may after all generate meanings and values even when doctrinaire ideologies fail.

*Amours de Voyage* was written in 1849, although it did not appear publicly until 1858. In this poem Clough is still trying to make hexameters carry a rather plain narrative. Structurally, the poem is a series of letters, one group from Claude to Eustace describing his travels in Italy and his infatuation for an English girl he has encountered. The interspersed letters are from Georgiana Trevellyn to Louisa. Georgiana's letters are filled with girlish gossip and observations on political affairs, but such comments give way to an increasing preoccupation with the Trevellyns' new acquaintance—Claude. In postscripts to Georgiana's letters and then in a correspondence of her own, Mary Trevellyn describes first her contempt, then her aloofness, then her interest, then her obsession with Claude. Their first acquaintance, which left them at cross-purposes, gives way to real love for each other. Claude and Mary miss connections at various Continental watering places until Mary reports that she is returning to England, and the reader concludes that the protagonists have missed their chance for love, because Claude is going to Egypt.

The letters, however, are not only about an ironic love affair which never occurred; but they are also about the events which undermine other features of Claude's high-minded idealism. In this regard, *Amours de Voyage* is much like Friedrich Schiller's philosophical letters. Claude decides to leave Europe not merely because he cannot locate Mary, but also because "Rome will not suit me; the priests and soldiers possess it." The authoritarian spirit of European orthodoxy and the militant spirit of European politics offer no consolation to a young freethinker who sees that Europe is going to miss its chance for peace as he has missed his chance for love.

Clough worked little at poetry after 1858 until it became evident that his failing health was not yielding to treatment. At the time of his death he was hard at work on *Mari Magno*. The poem is a Chaucerian collection of tales told by travelers aboard a transatlantic ship bound for America, across the "great sea." The tales are told on six different nights of the voyage. The clergyman tells two, the lawyer two, an American one, the narrator one in his own voice, and the mate one.

At this late hour of his life, Clough's stories tell of love missed or nearly missed. The failure of idealized love and the necessity for going on with practical life are forced on the protagonists by impersonal chance, by odd coincidences, a too-late arrival at a rendezvous, a ship which leaves too soon. There is little searching here for the great idea, no return to the struggle for a secular metaphysic which will justify actions and values. Rather, there is merely a plaintive lament for a lost idealism that has no home in this pragmatic world, and a sad sense that even true hearts and high-minded spirits must come to grips with a world of unkept promises and missed appointments. A poignant longing for this hopeless idealism is balanced against the tranquillity which comes from a resignation to life as it is.

Clough's poetry, taken altogether, considers the common themes of love, faith, and learning, makes them vulnerable to the disillusionments of modern skepticism and then asks certain questions. First, does intellectual honesty necessarily erode the authority of these traditional ideals? Second, is there some new, coherent perception of the world (in *Dipsychus* he calls it a "Second Reverence") which will satisfy the demands of both a rigorous honesty and the spiritual needs which our ideals have traditionally satisfied? These questions make Clough a representative figure among the young intellectuals of mid-nineteenth century Europe. His friend Matthew Arnold described the dilemma of these persons as a struggle "between two worlds, one dead the other powerless to be born." Clough does seem to have acquired some tranquillity in the years following his marriage, and critics disagree whether he found it because he quit struggling, or because he discovered what he was looking for—a high-minded skepticism which was humane and satisfying. Perhaps the safest way to interpret his life and work is to affirm that their outward expressions suggest an inward acceptance complex enough to tantalize biographers, effectual enough to redeem Clough's sense of well-being.

## Major publications other than poetry

NONFICTION: *Letters and Remains*, 1865 (Mrs. Clough, editor); *Prose Remains*, 1888; *Selected Prose Works*, 1964 (B. B. Trawick, editor).

MISCELLANEOUS: *Poems and Prose Remains*, 1869 (Mrs. Clough, editor, 2 volumes).

## Bibliography

Bowers, Frederick. "Arthur Hugh Clough: Recent Revaluations," in *Humanities Association Bulletin* (Canada). XVI (Fall, 1965), pp. 17-26.

Chorley, Lady Katherine. *Arthur Hugh Clough: The Uncommitted Mind*, 1962.

Gollin, Richard, Walter E. Houghton, and Michael Timko. *Arthur Hugh Clough: A Descriptive Catalogue*, 1967.

Greenberger, Evelyn B. *Arthur Hugh Clough: The Growth of a Poet's Mind*, 1970.

Harris, Wendell V. *Arthur Hugh Clough*, 1970.

Houghton, Walter. *The Poetry of Clough*, 1963.

Timko, Michael. *Innocent Victorian: The Satiric Poetry of Arthur Hugh Clough*, 1966.

Veyriras, Paul. *Arthur Hugh Clough*, 1964.

*L. Robert Stevens*

# HARTLEY COLERIDGE

**Born:** Clevedon, England; September 19, 1796
**Died:** Grasmere, England; January 6, 1849

## Principal collections

*Poems, Songs, and Sonnets*, 1833; *Complete Poetical Works*, 1908 (R. Colles, editor); *New Poems*, 1942 (E. L. Griggs, editor).

## Other literary forms

Two volumes of *Essays and Marginalia*, edited by Hartley Coleridge's brother, Derwent, were issued in 1851. These constitute Hartley's most significant effort aside from poetry. At best, these essays and commentaries (chiefly on the plays of William Shakespeare) are impressionistic responses to literary texts. They are frequently reminiscent of the light and meandering essays of Leigh Hunt. A three-volume history entitled *Lives of Illustrious Worthies of Yorkshire* was completed by Hartley in 1833. Its interest is chiefly local and antiquarian.

Hartley also edited, with an introduction, the dramatic works of Philip Massinger and John Ford. His letters, edited by G. E. Griggs and E. L. Griggs, were published in 1936.

## Achievements

Suspended between the dying splendors of a defunct Romanticism and the alienated vision of the Victorians, Hartley Coleridge was fated to fulfill his destiny in a world devoid of spiritual guideposts, aesthetic touchstones, and moral certitudes. To be sure, the lingering fires of Romanticism continue to smolder in his verse with a certain pungency—and poignancy. Unlike his poetic forebears, however, he is utterly wanting in the confidence and self-possession necessary to carry through a large poetic design, and conspicuously lacking in the energy required to sustain an extended "criticism of life." On the other hand, Hartley Coleridge falls short of the troubled self-awareness of the mature Victorians: that intellectual toughness and resolution which allowed them, as in the case of Matthew Arnold and Alfred Tennyson, to face down their worst misgivings, or, as in the case of Robert Browning, to perceive those misgivings from the perspective of a comprehensive spiritual outlook.

Yet Coleridge's achievement is not, for that reason, to be derided and silently passed over. Notwithstanding the timidity of his muse and the diffidence of his vision, Hartley Coleridge's poetry has a remarkable bearing on the disinherited mind of the modern age. The modern reader will recognize in him a kindred spirit: a spirit fated to live through the moral blankness and mental vertigo of an age cut adrift from the old stabilities and headed for an even more uncertain future. The caution which Harold Bloom urges in any estimate of those writers who followed the age of D. H. Lawrence and T. S. Eliot has its relevance to the "post-Shelleyan school" of George Darley, Thomas Lovell Beddoes, John Clare, and Hartley Coleridge as well.

Given the general loss of bearings which afflicted virtually all (in Harold Bloom's words) of the "minor but inevitable poets" of Hartley Coleridge's generation and the constitutional weakness which Hartley inherited from the vacillating and bemused Samuel Taylor Coleridge, it must be allowed that, among the restricted nooks of his poetry, Hartley provides not only some lapidary specimens of the Petrarchan sonnet, but also, by virtue of his poetic witness to the times, an incipient sense of that gradual cooling of the universe, that loss of a divine radiance and light, which was to haunt and disturb several generations of his poetic descendants.

Moreover, it would be hard to dispute the claim of one critic that "after Shakespeare, Hartley Coleridge is our sweetest English sonneteer." The Victorian Age gave birth to a variety of sonnet sequences: Dante Gabriel Rossetti's, Elizabeth Barrett Browning's, George Meredith's. In comparison with Coleridge's, however, these seem alternately labored, shrill, or elaborately self-conscious. Coleridge's sonnets do not immediately call attention to themselves; they have neither the labored Latinity of Rossetti's nor the tremulous pathos of Browning's—but they do speak in a language which is invariably natural, restrained, and idiomatically English. In a word, Hartley Coleridge's virtues as an artist are fundamentally related to the understated clarity and eloquence of his compositions.

## Biography

The sense of vacillation and drift, of sensuous abandon to "the great god Whirl," which, for Irving Babbitt, has a necessary connection with the "infinite, indeterminate desire," of Romanticism, was both the cultural and patrimonial inheritance of Hartley Coleridge. It is not surprising that the weight of Romantic tradition should have inspired him with misgivings as to his own abilities and potential. That his paralysis—both as a man and a poet—was partial and not complete is, perhaps, the best that could be expected of one in his circumstances.

Hartley was the darling of his father, Samuel Taylor Coleridge, his uncle, Robert Southey, and his spiritual godfather, William Wordsworth. Given the Romantic celebration of childhood as the most privileged stage in a person's existence (and of Hartley as the most lucid example of that stage), it comes as no surprise that in the virtually posthumous existence that followed his puberty, Hartley was condemned to stagger amid the ruins of his lost innocence. It was not without some foresight that Wordsworth was to write of Hartley:

> O blessed Vision! happy Child!
> Thou art so exquisitely wild,
> I think of thee with many fears
> For what may be thy lot in future years.

These Romantic panegyrics on childhood take on a retrospective irony when one realizes that Hartley's proclivity to "wander like a breeze" (in the words which his father addressed to him as a child) had its origin in the lyrical overflowings of his august mentors.

As a child, Hartley lived in a make-believe kingdom fashioned by an imagination of extraordinary richness and fertility. It was the delight of both his father and his uncle to encourage and acclaim Hartley's exuberant myth-making and to foresee in these childish games the beginnings of a self-dedication to poetry. Yet, within a few years, this prepossessing child was to be described by Thomas Carlyle as "the strangest ghost of a human creature, with eyes that gleamed like two rainbows over a ruined world."

The seeds of that incipient ruin were sown at Oxford. After his failure to win the Newdigate prize for poetry, Hartley turned, as his father had before him, to the solace of an artificial escape. His addiction to alcohol, which began at this time, only served to aggravate an inveterate need to condemn himself. His short stature and chronic self-doubt contributed to his dismay in the presence of women, from whom he felt hopelessly estranged. After several attempts to support himself through writing and teaching, he eventually retired to the Lake District, where in the presence of sympathetic friends and on a patrimonial inheritance he was able to live in relative calm until his death.

It is not surprising that Samuel Taylor Coleridge should provide readers with the most accurate account of Hartley's afflictions, for, after all, his son's temperamental defects were, in a large degree, his own:

> If you can conceive, in connection with an excellent heart, sound religious principles, a mind constitutionally religious, and lastly, an active and powerful intellect—if you can conceive, I say, in connection with all these, not a mania, not a derangement, but an *idiocy* of will or rather of volition, you will have formed a tolerably correct conception of Hartley Coleridge.

A final estimate of Hartley the man, no less than Hartley the poet, requires, however, some modification. Hartley's social obtuseness and personal insecurity was related to a deeper distress; a feeling of cosmic homelessness and metaphysical unrest which gave him nothing "to hold fast," as Eliot remarked of Tennyson, "except his unique and unerring feeling for the sounds of words." The disquiet of living in a world in which one's beliefs and convictions seemed increasingly obsolete was as central to Hartley Coleridge's poetry as it was to his life.

**Analysis**

Apart from the sonnet, Hartley Coleridge's poetic legacy is of negligible value. There is one blank verse narrative, "Leonard and Susan," a fragmentary recasting of the Prometheus legend, and a legion of miscellaneous lyrics which share, as their common element, a preoccupation with unrequited love. The narrative is, unfortunately, wooden, predictable, and bathetic; the "Prometheus," despite occasional moments of lyric grace, lacks either an architectonic design or a clear thematic center; and the lyrics, with a few signal exceptions, repeat the familiar symptoms of Romantic nympholepsy (attachment, that is to say, to a woman at once phantasmal and beyond possession) without the insight that the best of the Romantics were able to glean from their doomed erotic idylls. The formerly much-anthologized "She is not fair to outward view" displays, for example, one unctuously resigned to a condition which reads like a caricature of courtly love: "Her very frowns are fairer far,/ Than smiles of other maidens are."

The sonnets, however, are of a more strenuous order. Though they frequently derive from some consecrated Romantic theme—the loss of childhood innocence, the transvaluation of traditional beliefs, the benevolence of natural law—they depart, with surprising candor, from the consoling resolutions one would expect from a Romantic poet. It is not, for example, "the glory and the dream," that spacious sense of an infinite present, which Coleridge laments with the passing of childhood, but rather the growing estrangement from the sense of right and wrong, of grateful dependence on a forgiving God, which comes with the compromises and insensibility of age. Similarly, it is not with a feeling of exhilaration and limitless adventure that Coleridge contemplates the loss of a stable and hierarchic system of values; on the contrary, a nagging and restless anxiety characterizes this poet's response to a universe which seems alien to the moral being of humanity. Finally, when he turns to nature, it is not to see a world in a grain of sand, but to question the possibility that any one particular grain should have its place or significance in some sacramental order or providential plan. The peculiar quality of these poems is that the tranquil accents and reassuring rhythms of the Wordsworthian sonnet are being used to express experiences which are anything but tranquil and reassuring. This disparity between the form of the poems and their content creates a sensation analogous to that which Tennyson achieves when, in *In Memoriam* (1850), he uses the traditional meters and repetitious patterns of the hymnal to express a feeling of utter abandonment and loss.

When seen from the perspective of Samuel Taylor Coleridge's poetic benedictions over his son's cradle, Hartley Coleridge's own musings over his childhood acquire a crushing poignancy. Indeed, the poet's retrospective responses to his father's paternal hopes underscore his own sense of poetic belatedness and spiritual failure—a failure which he consciously counterpoints with the serene domesticity of "Frost at Midnight" (1798) or the dreaming innocence of "The Nightingale." When Coleridge asks, "Whither is gone the wisdom and the power/ That ancient sages scatter'd with the notes/ Of thought-suggesting lyres," or "Youth, love, and mirth, what are they but the portion,/ Wherewith the Prodigal left his father's home?," one recognizes not only the crippling disenchantment of the failed Romantic but also the guilt-ridden conscience of the prodigal son. In short, Coleridge consciously echoes his father's poems only to reveal an irrevocable rift between the confident afflatus of the first Romantics and the exploded ideals of their descendants.

In "To a Deaf and Dumb Little Girl," Hartley Coleridge carries to a debilitating extreme the Romantic notion of the child's unconscious communion with the beautiful, the true, and the good. It may be recalled that in "It is a beauteous evening, calm and free," Wordsworth's child, though "untouched by solemn thought," dwells in unconscious harmony with "the Temple's inner shrine." In "Ode: Intimations of Immortality," the child, despite being "deaf and silent," is intrinsically attuned to "the eternal deep,/ Haunted for ever by the eternal mind." Coleridge's deaf-mute, who has obvious affinities with the children of Wordsworth's sonnet and "ode," is altogether withdrawn from the real world into a realm of abstract revery: "Herself in all, she lives in privacy." This privacy is absolute, unbridgeable, and potentially catatonic. Childhood, here, is less a state of innocence than it is of schizophrenic self-absorption; it is, in fact, the outward and visible emblem of the poet's own alienated consciousness—a consciousness that, "concentrated" in "solitary seeing," hopes to find in its own silent depths that power, "beauteous or sublime," which has apparently departed from the tangible world. Coleridge's parting comment on the afflicted child, "God must be with her in her solitude," is, indeed, a lame and irresolute counterpart to Wordsworth's ringing affirmations.

It is not, as one might expect, the child's ability to engage in a perpetual transformation of reality which Coleridge extolls, but rather the child's keen awareness of human suffering, his spiritual dependence, and need for consolation. Indeed, Coleridge's conception of childhood bears a clear and unmistakable likeness to the childhood of Gerard Manley Hopkins' Margaret. For both poets, childhood is a time of affliction as much as it is of transport, and, perhaps, more prodigal of anxiety than it is of bliss. Coleridge inverts the customary Romantic response to childhood and prefigures the Victorian emphasis on the child's intimation of mortality, of the blight man was born for. Hence, in one of several sonnets on his own childhood, Hartley Coleridge is not convulsed by the absence of those "hopes that faded when my head was gray," but rather by the diminution of "the pain I felt, the gushing tears/ I used to shed when I had gone astray."

Hartley Coleridge's personal and psychological sense of dispossession and disinheritance—of estrangement from those primal intuitions which give stability, purpose, and direction to one's life—has its cultural counterpart in that feeling of cosmic homelessness which possessed the minds of the post-Romantic age. Irving Babbitt has noticed a resemblance between Hartley Coleridge and Gérard de Nerval; the association is not fortuitous, for both poets were obsessed with the loss of ancient wisdom and disquieted by the moral wasteland of the modern world. Like Nerval's Aquitanian Prince in the abolished tower (whom Eliot evokes in *The Waste Land*, 1922, as a companion in his sense of loss), Coleridge is also in search of those abiding verities which no longer seemed to penetrate the desolate reaches of the post-Napoleonic era.

In sonnets such as "Let me not deem that I was made in vain," or "It were a state too terrible for man," Coleridge expresses the sheer panic that overcomes a man when he sees nothing higher than his own will and intelligence, nothing more assured than the sensuous flux of existence. Indeed, for Hartley Coleridge, the experience of dread in an age of unrestrained secularism is infinitely more shattering than the anxieties suffered by earlier man; for although pain and hardship were more extensive in less humanitarian times, a man was formerly capable of recognizing that "his path was trod/ By saints of old, who knew their way to God." The modern man can achieve no tragic catharsis of his ills and, in consequence, can only stare blindly into an almost certain oblivion. In this regard, the sonnet "Hope" represents the spirit of the age as an abandoned woman whose lover has been lost at sea. This sea, emblematic of a future which rushes from a past consigned to oblivion and plunges toward a void without comfort or hope, connects Coleridge with a later generation of Victorians who similarly brooded over the radical contingency of the human lot. That "inexhaustible note of langour, discontent, and homesickness," which Walter Pater detected in the poetry of Coleridge's father, has acquired even greater urgency in the sonnets of the forsaken son. Yet, even here, the ontological burden of Coleridge's theme fuses with the sense of abandonment by a father whose undisciplined will and philosophical abstraction left him little time or patience for the practical cares of paternity: "Yet can I not but mourn because he died/ That was my father, should have been my guide." Coleridge's vague and abstracted father imperceptibly blends with the image of a Deity whose word no longer resonates, whose rod no longer checks and reproves.

Seen from the perspective of Coleridge's later years, the solemn intonations of the elder Coleridge over his sleeping child inevitably give rise to mixed feelings. In "Frost at Midnight," the individual drops of water from the eaves are taken to be emblematic of individual life immersed in the passage of time. The image of the frost validates the poet's awareness of that one sacramental life which connects his own childhood with that of the sleeping infant by his side. Yet in a cruel reversal of his father's image, Hartley Coleridge's own fixity on the past has left him "still . . . a child, though I be old," the victim of an "untimely frost,/ That makes the labour of the soul to cease." Hartley

Coleridge inherited from the first Romantics a debilitating belief that one's significance and worth lies not in the constant reference of one's actions and thoughts to a firm ethical center, but in one's ability to dwell in an uninterrupted state of emotional gush. In his father's terms "we receive but what we give/ And in our life alone does Nature live." When the years of his emotional gush were past, it is not surprising that Hartley Coleridge should have confessed that "Time is my debtor for my years untold."

"Frost at Midnight" by Coleridge senior adumbrates one of the principal themes of nineteenth century poetry and may well serve as a starting point for any discussion of Hartley Coleridge's peculiar version of that theme. The Romantic poet does not circumvent the multitudinousness of being in order to attain the infinite or intuit the universal. Samuel Taylor Coleridge's ability to coalesce the individual drops of water which trickle from his cottage eaves into a sacramental emblem of that one life "within us and abroad" is, then, a moment of paradigmatic importance. It implies that the apprehension of a unified reality is available in an immediate and particular act of perception. This perception of the One in the Many and the Many in the One was to undergird countless Romantic effusions in the presence of small celandines, clouds, nightingales, cuckoos, and daffodils.

As the first spontaneous overflow of Romanticism waned, however, the ability to perceive the universal in the particular became increasingly problematic; indeed, the absence of a coherent cosmic order is a thematic touchstone of the Victorians. This progressive estrangement from a sense of fixed values provides the starting point for the lamentations of the early Victorians; in the latter half of the nineteenth century, however, what was once a subject of dolor and despair becomes a rallying call for dissipation and dispersal.

Where does Hartley Coleridge's poetry fit into this gradual and, at first, inconsolable response to the growing spirit of relativism? Notwithstanding an inveterate need to affirm that "Each drop counted in a storm of rain/ Hath its own mission," that "the very shadow of an insect's wing" shades and protects the drooping violet, Hartley Coleridge is continually possessed by the dread that "my Being was an accident," that crass casualty rather than divine dispensation directs the course of the Universe. His nature sonnets, for example, do not provide the occasion to utter encomiums on the benevolence of natural law, but to chart the inclemencies of an inhospitable world, the erratic deviation of a particular day, or moment in that day, from the constraint of a universal pattern. In a sonnet entitled "February 1st, 1842," the early signs of vernal promise are annulled by the fate of one "pining flow'ret." At the most, it may be vouchsafed "A sunbeam clear and kind" before it dies. The relation of this single blossom to the ensuing season is problematic; rather than bearing its part in the grand procession of nature, it is trod under by the march of irreversible events. In short, it possesses no clear and appointed role in the cosmic scheme; its death, therefore, seems wanton and without significance. Similarly, in the sonnet "September," the only unity to be found in the diversity of "Autumn's tincture manifold" is "a unity of grey" wherein "All things appear their tangible form to lose/ In ghostly vastness." The sacramental presence which in "Frost at Midnight" would allow the sleeping child, Hartley, to experience himself "in all things and all things in himself," becomes, in the post-Romantic dread of the awakened adult, a fellowship in dissolution and death. Coleridge's "September" is, as it were, a palinode to John Keats's "To Autumn" (a poem which also derives from "Frost at Midnight"). The ubiquitous sense of Being which pervades Keats's poem, which binds death and life, "mists" and "mellow fruitfulness," into the harmonious give-and-take of reconciled opposites, is replaced in Hartley Coleridge's sonnet by a soulless determinism. In a collateral poem, "On a calm day toward the close of the year," Coleridge traces the downward curve of a falling leaf. Its wavering, uncertain, and scarcely perceptible descent leads to the following reflection: "One might suppose that central gravity,/ Prime law of nature, were about to stop;/ Ne'er died a year with spirit so profound." The absence of a "central gravity" refers not only to the leaf's arrested progress to the ground but also to the absence of a "Divine Law," which grounds, sustains, and harmonizes the sensuous flux of existence and gives a permanent meaning to its transient effects and mutations.

The theme of defeated faith, implicit in so many of Hartley Coleridge's sonnets, reaches its apogee in one unexampled lyric: "The Deserted Church." The poet strays among one of those ruins of the Age of Faith, so dear to the heart of Romantic medievalists. "I looked within," claims the poet, "but all within was cold." A lone bell suspended in a dilapidated tower is all that is left of this crumbling edifice. The bell, "lowly swinging to and fro," is the auditory equivalent of the poet's lonely and irresolute faith; significantly, its former "merry peal" has given way to a "dull unfrequent knell."

## Major publications other than poetry

NONFICTION: *Lives of Illustrious Worthies of Yorkshire*, 1833; *Essays and Marginalia*, 1851 (Derwent Coleridge, editor).

## Bibliography
Bagehot, Walter. *Literary Studies*, 1879.
Blunden, Edmund. *Votive Tablets*, 1967.
Griggs, Earl Leslie. *Hartley Coleridge: His Life and Work*, 1929.
Hartman, Herbert. *Hartley Coleridge: Poet's Son and Poet*, 1931.
Pomeroy, Sister Mary Joseph. *The Poetry of Hartley Coleridge*, 1927.
Reeves, James. *Five Late Romantic Poets*, 1974.

*Stephen I. Gurney*

# SAMUEL TAYLOR COLERIDGE

**Born:** Ottery St. Mary, England; October 21, 1772
**Died:** Highgate, London, England; July 25, 1834

## Principal poems and collections

*Poems on Various Subjects*, 1796, 1797 (with Charles Lamb and Charles Lloyd); *A Sheet of Sonnets*, 1796 (with W. L. Bowles, Robert Southey, and others); *Lyrical Ballads*, 1798 (with William Wordsworth); *Dejection: An Ode*, 1802; *Christabel*, 1816; *Sibylline Leaves*, 1817; *The Complete Poetical Works of Samuel Taylor Coleridge*, 1912 (Ernest Hartley Coleridge, editor, 2 volumes).

## Other literary forms

Samuel Taylor Coleridge's original verse dramas—*The Fall of Robespierre* (1794, with Robert Southey), *Remorse* (1813, originally *Osorio*), and *Zapolya* (1817)—are of particular interest to readers of his poetry, as is *Wallenstein* (1800), his translation of two dramas by J. C. F. von Schiller. His major prose includes the contents of two periodicals, *The Watchman* (1796) and *The Friend* (1809-1810), two Lay Sermons, "The Statesman's Manual" (1816) and "A Lay Sermon" (1817), the *Biographia Literaria* (1817), "Essay on Method," originally published in *The Encyclopaedia Metropolitana*, and a series of metaphysical aphorisms, *Aids to Reflection* (1825). His lectures on politics, religion, literature, and philosophy have been collected in various editions, as have other short essays, unpublished manuscripts, letters, records of conversations (*Table Talk*), notebooks, and marginalia. These prose works share common interests with his poetry and suggest the philosophical context in which it should be read. Coleridge's literary criticism is particularly relevant to his poetry.

## Achievements

It is ironic that Coleridge has come to be known to the general reader primarily as a poet, for poetry was not his own primary interest and the poems with which his name is most strongly linked—*The Rime of the Ancient Mariner* (1798), "Kubla Khan," and *Christabel*—were products of a few months in a long literary career. He did not suffer a decline in poetic creativity; he simply turned his attention to political, metaphysical, and theological issues that were best treated in prose. That Coleridge is counted among the major poets of British Romanticism is, for this reason, all the more remarkable. For most poets, the handful of commonly anthologized poems is a scant representation of their output; for Coleridge, it is, in many instances, the sum of his accomplishment. His minor verse is often conventional and uninspired. His major poems, in contrast, speak with singular emotional and intellectual intensity in a surprising range of forms—from the symbolic fantasy of *The Rime of the Ancient Mariner* (which first appeared in *Lyrical Ballads*) to the autobiographical sincerity of the conversation poems—exerting an influence on subsequent poets far beyond what Coleridge himself anticipated.

## Biography

Samuel Taylor Coleridge was born October 21, 1772, in the Devonshire town of Ottery St. Mary, the youngest of ten children. His father, a clergyman and teacher, died in October, 1781, and the next year Coleridge was sent to school at Christ's Hospital, London. His friends at school included Charles Lamb, two years his junior, whose essay "Christ's Hospital Five-and-Thirty Years Ago" (1820) describes the two sides of Coleridge—the "poor friendless boy," far from his home, "alone among six hundred playmates"; the precocious scholar, "Logician, Metaphysician, Bard!," holding his auditors "entranced with imagination." Both characteristics—a deep sense of isolation and the effort to use learning and eloquence to overcome it—remained with Coleridge throughout his life.

He entered Cambridge in 1791, but never completed work for his university degree. Depressed by debts, he fled the university in December, 1793, and enlisted in the Light Dragoons under the name Silas Tompkyn Comberbache. Rescued by his brothers, he returned to Cambridge in April and resumed his studies. Two months later he met Robert Southey, with whom he soon made plans to establish a utopian community ("Pantisocracy") in America. Southey was engaged to marry Edith Fricker, and so it seemed appropriate for Coleridge to engage himself to her sister Sara. The project failed, but Coleridge, through his own sense of duty and Southey's insistence, married a woman he had never loved and with whom his relationship was soon to become strained.

As a married man, Coleridge had to leave the university and make a living for his wife and, in time, children—Hartley (1796-1849), Berkeley (1798-1799), Derwent (b. 1800), and Sara (1802-1852). Economic survival was, it turned out, possible only with the support of friends such as Thomas Poole and the publisher Joseph Cottle and, in 1798, a life annuity from Josiah and Tom Wedgewood. The early years of Coleridge's married life, in which he lived with his family at Nether Stowey, were the period of his closest relationship with the poet William Wordsworth. Inspired by Wordsworth, whom he in turn inspired—Coleridge wrote most of his major poetry. Together, the two men published *Lyrical Ballads* in 1798, the proceeds of which enabled them, along with Wordsworth's sister Dorothy, to spend the winter in Germany, where Coleridge studied metaphysics at the University of Göttingen.

Returning to England the following year, Coleridge met and fell deeply in love with Sara Hutchinson, a friend of Dorothy who later became Wordsworth's sister-in-law. This passion, which remained strong for many years, furthered Coleridge's estrangement from his wife, with whom he moved to

Keswick in the Lake District of England, in July, 1800, to be near the Words-worths at Grasmere. Coleridge's health had always been poor, and he had become addicted to opium, which, according to current medical practice, he had originally taken to relieve pain. Seeking a change of climate, he traveled to Malta and then Italy in 1804 to 1806. On his return, he and his wife "*determined* to part absolutely and finally," leaving Coleridge in custody of his sons Hartley and Derwent (Berkeley had died in 1799).

In 1808, Coleridge gave his first public lectures and in the next two years published the twenty-seven issues of *The Friend*. By now, he was a figure of national standing, but his private life remained in disarray. Sara Hutchinson, who had assisted him in preparing copy for *The Friend*, separated herself from him, and in 1810 he quarreled decisively with Wordsworth. (They were later reconciled, but the period of close friendship was over.) Six years later, after various unsuccessful attempts to cure himself of opium addiction and set his affairs in order, he put himself in the care of James Gillman, a physician living at Highgate, a northern suburb of London. Under Gillman's roof, Coleridge was once again able to work. He wrote the two Lay Sermons, "The Statesman's Manual" and "A Lay Sermon"; completed the *Biographia Literaria*, originally planned as an autobiographical introduction to *Sibylline Leaves* but ultimately two volumes in its own right; and revised the essays he had written for *The Friend*, including among them a version of the "Essay on Method" which he had composed for the first volume of *The Encyclopaedia Metropolitana*. He also resumed his public lectures on philosophy and literature and in time became a London celebrity, enthralling visitors with his conversation and gradually attracting a circle of disciples. Meanwhile, he worked at the *magnum opus* that was to synthesize his metaphysical and theological thought in a single intellectual system. This project, however, remained incomplete when Coleridge died at Highgate, July 25, 1834.

### Analysis

Samuel Taylor Coleridge's major poems turn on problems of self-esteem and identity. Exploring states of isolation and ineffectuality, they test strategies to overcome weakness without asserting its antithesis—a powerful self, secure in its own thoughts and utterances, the potency and independence of which Coleridge feared would only exacerbate his loneliness. His reluctance to assert his own abilities is evident in his habitual deprecation of his own poetry and hyperbolic praise of William Wordsworth's. It is evident as well in his best verse, which is either written in an unpretentious "conversational" tone or, when it is not, is carefully dissociated from his own voice and identity. Yet by means of these strategies, he is often able to assert indirectly or vicariously the strong self he otherwise repressed.

Writing to John Thelwall in 1796, Coleridge called the first of the conversation poems, "The Eolian Harp" (written in 1795), the "favorite of *my* poems." He originally published it, in 1796, with the indication "Composed August 20th, 1795, At Clevedon, Somersetshire," which dates at least some version of the text six weeks before his marriage to Sara Fricker. Since Sara plays a role in the poem, the exact date is crucial. "The Eolian Harp" is not, as it has been called, a "honeymoon" poem; rather, it anticipates a future in which Coleridge and Sara will sit together by their "Cot o'ergrown/ With white-flower'd Jasmin." Significantly, Sara remains silent throughout the poem; her only contribution is the "mild reproof" that "darts" from her "more serious eye," quelling the poet's intellectual daring. Yet this reproof is as imaginary as Sara's presence itself. At the climax of the poem, meditative thought gives way to the need for human response; tellingly, the response he imagines and therefore, one must assume, desires, is reproof.

"The Eolian Harp" establishes a structural pattern for the conversation poems as a group. Coleridge is, in effect, alone, "and the world *so* hush'd!/ The stilly murmur of the distant Sea/ Tells us of silence." The eolian harp in the window sounds in the breeze and reminds him of "the one Life within us and abroad,/ Which meets all motion and becomes its soul." This observation leads to the central question of the poem:

> And what if all of animated nature
> Be but organic Harps diversely fram'd,
> That tremble into thought, as o'er them sweeps
> Plastic and vast, one intellectual breeze,
> At once the Soul of each, and God of all?

Sara's glance dispells "These shapings of the unregenerate mind," but, of course, it is too late, since they have already been expressed in the poem. (Indeed, the letter to Thelwall makes it clear that it was this expression of pantheism, not its retraction, that made the poem dear to Coleridge.) For this reason, the conflict between two sides of Coleridge's thought—metaphysical speculation and orthodox Christianity—remains unresolved. If the poem is in any way disquieting, it is not because it exemplifies a failure of nerve, but because of the identifications it suggests between metaphysical speculation and the isolated self, religious orthodoxy and the conventions— down to the vines covering the cottage—of married life. Coleridge, in other words, does not imagine a wife who will love him all the more for his intellectual daring. Instead, he imagines one who will chastise him for the very qualities that make him an original thinker. To "possess/ Peace, and this Cot, and thee, heart-honour'd Maid!," Coleridge must acknowledge himself "A sinful and most miserable man,/ Wilder'd and dark." Happiness, as well as poetic closure, depends upon this acceptance of diminished self-esteem. Even so, by embedding an expression of intellectual strength within the context of domestic conventionality, Coleridge is able to achieve a degree of poetic authority otherwise absent in the final lines of the poem. The ability to renounce a powerful self is itself a gesture of power: the acceptance of loss becomes—as in other Romantic poems—a form of strength.

The structure of "The Eolian Harp" can be summarized as follows: a state of isolation (the more isolated for the presence of an unresponsive companion) gives way to meditation, which leads to the possibility of a self powerful through its association with an all-powerful force. This state of mind gives place to the acknowledgment of a human relationship dependent on the poet's recognition of his own inadequacy, the reward for which is a poetic voice with the authority to close the poem.

This pattern recurs in "This Lime-Tree Bower My Prison" (1797). The poem is addressed to Charles Lamb, but the "gentle-hearted Charles" of the text is really a surrogate for the figure of Wordsworth, whose loss Coleridge is unwilling to face head-on. Incapacitated by a burn—appropriately, his wife's fault—Coleridge is left alone seated in a clump of lime trees while his friends—Lamb and William and Dorothy Wordsworth—set off on a long walk through the countryside. They are, like Sara in "The Eolian Harp," there and yet not there: their presence in the poem intensifies Coleridge's sense of isolation. He follows them in his imagination, and the gesture itself becomes a means of connecting himself with them. Natural images of weakness, enclosure, and solitude give way to those of strength, expansion, and connection, and the tone of the poem shifts from speculation to assertion. In a climactic moment, he imagines his friends "gazing round/ On the wide landscape," until it achieves the transcendence of "such hues/ As veil the Almighty Spirit, when yet he makes/ Spirits perceive his presence."

As in "The Eolian Harp," the perception of an omnipotent force pervading the universe returns Coleridge to his present state, but with a new sense of his own being and his relationship with the friends to whom he addresses the poem. His own isolation is now seen as an end in itself. "Sometimes/ 'Tis well to be bereft of promised good," Coleridge argues, "That we may lift the soul, and contemplate/ With lively joy the joys we cannot share."

"Frost at Midnight," the finest of the conversation poems, replaces silent wife or absent friends with a sleeping child (Hartley—although he is not named in the text). Summer is replaced by winter; isolation is now a function of seasonal change itself. In this zero-world, "The Frost performs its secret ministry,/ Unhelped by any wind." The force that moved the eolian harp into sound is gone. The natural surroundings of the poem drift into nonexistence: "Sea, and hill, and wood,/ With all the numberless goings-on of life,/ Inaudible as dreams!" This is the nadir of self from which the poet reconstructs his being—first by perception of "dim sympathies" with the "low-burnt fire" before him; then by a process of recollection and predication. The "film" on the grate reminds Coleridge of his childhood at Christ's Hospital, where a similar image conveyed hopes of seeing someone from home and therefore a renewal of the conditions of his earlier life in Ottery St. Mary. Yet even in recollection, the bells of his "sweet birth-place" are most expressive not as a voice of the present moment, but as "articulate sounds of things to come!" The spell of the past was, in fact, a spell of the imagined future. The visitor he longed for turns out to be a version of the self of the poet, his "sister more beloved/ My play-mate when we both were clothed alike." The condition of loss that opens the poem cannot be filled by the presence of another human being; it is a fundamental emptiness in the self, which, Coleridge suggests, can never be filled, but only recognized as a necessary condition of adulthood. Yet this recognition of incompleteness is the poet's means of experiencing a sense of identity missing in the opening lines of the poem.

"Frost at Midnight" locates this sense of identity in Coleridge's own life. It is not a matter of metaphysical or religious belief, as it is in "The Eolian Harp" or "This Lime-Tree Bower My Prison," but a function of the self that recognizes its own coherence in time. This recognition enables him to speak to the "Dear Babe" who had been there all along, but had remained a piece of the setting and not a living human being. Like the friends of "This Lime-Tree Bower My Prison," who are projected exploring a landscape, the boy Hartley is imagined wandering "like a breeze/ By lakes and sandy shores." The static existence of the poet in the present moment is contrasted with the movement of a surrogate. This movement, however, is itself subordinated to the voice of the poet who can promise his son a happiness he himself has not known.

In all three poems, Coleridge achieves a voice that entails the recognition of his own loss—in acknowledging Sara's reproof or losing himself in the empathic construction of the experience of friend or son. The act entails a defeat of the self, but also a vicarious participation in powerful forces that reveal themselves in the working of the universe, and through this participation a partial triumph of the self over its own sense of inadequacy. In "Frost at Midnight," the surrogate figure of his son not only embodies a locomotor power denied the static speaker; but he is also, in his capacity to read the "language" uttered by God in the form of landscape, associated with absolute power itself.

Although written in a very different mode, *The Rime of the Ancient Mariner* centers on a similar experience of participation in supernatural power. At the core of the poem is, of course, the story of the Mariner who shoots the albatross and endures complete and devastating isolation from his fellowman. The poem, however, is not a direct narrative of these events; rather, it is a narrative of the Mariner's narrating them. The result of the extraordinary experience he has undergone is to make him an itinerant storyteller. It has given him a voice, but a voice grounded on his own incompleteness of self. He has returned to land, but remains homeless and without permanent human relationships. In this respect, *The Rime of the Ancient Mariner* is Coleridge's nightmare alternative to the conversation poem. As "conversations," they suggest the possibility of a relationship with his audience that can in part compensate for the inadequate human relationships described in the poem. The Mariner's story is a kind of conversation. He tells it to the Wedding-Guest he has singled out for that purpose, but the relationship between speaker and audience can scarcely be said to compensate for the Mariner's lack of human relationships. The Wedding-Guest is compelled to listen by the hypnotic power of the Mariner's "glittering eye." He "beats his breast" at the thought of the wedding from which he is being detained, and repeatedly expresses his fear of the Mariner. In the end, he registers no compassion for the man whose story he has just heard. He is too "stunned" for that—and the Mariner has left the stage without asking for applause. His audience is changed by the story—"A sadder and a wiser man,/ He rose the morrow morn"—but of this the Mariner can know nothing. Thus, the power of the Mariner's story to captivate and transform its audience simply furthers his alienation from his fellow human beings.

Structurally, the poem follows the three-stage pattern of the conversation poems. A state of isolation and immobility is succeeded by one in which the Mariner becomes the object of (and is thus associated with) powerful super-natural agencies, and this leads to the moralizing voice of the conclusion. Unlike the conversation poems, *The Rime of the Ancient Mariner* prefaces individual isolation with social isolation. The Mariner and his shipmates, in what has become one of the most familiar narratives in English literature, sail from Europe toward Cape Horn, where they are surrounded by a polar ice jam. An albatross appears and accepts food from the sailors; a fair wind springs up and they are able to resume their journey northward into the Pacific; the albatross follows them, "And every day, for food or play,/ Came to the mariner's hollo!"—until the Mariner, seemingly without reason, shoots the bird with his crossbow. Coleridge warned readers against allegorizing the poem, and it is fruitless to search for a specific identification for the albatross. What is important is the bird's gratuitous arrival and the Mariner's equally gratuitous crossbow shot. The polar ice that threatens the ship is nature at its most alien. Seen against that backdrop, the albatross seems relatively human; the mariners, accordingly, "hailed it in God's name"; "As if it had been a Christian soul." Like the "film" in "Frost at Midnight"—a poem in which crucial events are also set against a wintry backdrop—the bird offers them a means of bridging the gap between man and nature, self and nonself, through projecting human characteristics on a creature of the natural world. By shooting the albatross, the Mariner blocks this projection and thus traps both himself and his shipmates in a state of isolation.

The Mariner's act has no explicit motive because it is a function of human nature itself, but it is not merely a sign of original sin or congenital perversity. His narrative has until now been characterized by a remarkable passivity. Events simply happen. Even the ship's progress is characterized not by its own movement but by the changing position of the sun in the sky. The ice that surrounds the ship is only one element of a natural world that dominates the fate of the ship and its crew, and it is against this overwhelming dominance that the Mariner takes his crossbow shot. The gesture is an assertion of the human spirit against an essentially inhuman universe, aimed at the harmless albatross because aimed at the act of self-deceptive projection by which his shipmates attempt to mitigate their sense of isolation.

He is punished for this self-assertion—first, by the crewmen who blame him for the calm that follows and tie the albatross around his neck as a sign of guilt. It is only after this occurs that the Mariner, thirsty and guilt-ridden, perceives events that are explicitly supernatural and the second stage of his punishment begins. Yet the Mariner's isolation, even after his shipmates have died and left him alone on the becalmed ship, remains a consequence of his assertion of self against the natural world; and the turning point of the poem is equally his own doing. In the midst of the calm, the water had seemed abhorrently ugly: "slimy things did crawl with legs/ Upon the slimy sea," while "the water, like a witch's oils,/ Burnt green, and blue and white." Now, "bemocked" by moonlight, the same creatures are beautiful: "Blue, glossy green, and velvet black,/ They coiled and swam; and every track/ Was a flash of golden fire." In this perception of beauty, the Mariner explains, "A spring of love gushed from my heart,/ And I blessed them unaware." At the same moment, he is once again able to pray and the albatross falls from his neck into the sea. Prayer—the ability to voice his mind and feelings and, in so doing, relate them to a higher order of being— is a function of love, and love is a function of the apprehension of beauty. In blessing the water snakes, it should be noted, the Mariner has not returned to the viewpoint of his shipmates when they attributed human characteristics to the albatross. When he conceives of the snakes as "happy living things," he acknowledges a bond between all forms of organic life, but their beauty is not dependent on human projection.

Yet achieving this chastened vision does not end the Mariner's suffering. Not only must he endure an extension of his shipboard isolation, but also when, eventually, he returns to his native land, he is not granted reintegration into its society. The Hermit from whom he asks absolution demands quick answer to his own question, " 'What manner of man art thou?' " In response, the Mariner experiences a spasm of physical agony that forces him to tell the story of his adventures. The tale told, he is left free of pain—until such time as "That agony returns" and he is compelled to repeat the narrative: "That moment that his face I see,/ I know the man that must hear me:/ To him my tale I teach." The Mariner has become a poet—like Coleridge, a poet gifted with "strange power of speech" and plagued with somatic pain, with power to fix his auditors' attention and transform them into "sadder and wiser" men. Yet the price of this power is enormous. It entails not only the shipboard suffering of the Mariner, but also perpetual alienation from his fellow human beings. Telling his story is the only relationship allowed him, and he does not even fully understand the meaning of his narration. In the concluding lines of the poem, he attempts to draw a moral—

> He prayeth best, who loveth best
> All things both great and small;
> For the dear God who loveth us,
> He made and loveth all.

These words are not without bearing on the poem, but they overlook the extraordinary disproportion between the Mariner's crime and its punishment. Readers of the poem—as well as, one supposes, the Wedding-Guest—are more likely to question the benevolence of the "dear God who loveth us" than to perceive the Mariner's story as an illustration of God's love. Thus, the voice of moral authority that gave the conversation poems a means of closure is itself called into question. The soul that acknowledges its essential isolation in the universe can never hope for reintegration into society. The poet whose song is the tale of his own suffering can "stun" his reader, but can never achieve a lasting human relationship. His experience can be given the aesthetic coherence of narrative, but he can never connect the expressive significance of that narrative with his life as a whole.

It is in part the medium of the poem that allows Coleridge to face these bleak possibilities. Its ballad stanza and archaic diction, along with the marginal glosses added in 1815 to 1816, dissociate the text from its modern poet. Freed from an explicit identification with the Mariner, Coleridge is able both to explore implications of the poet's role that would have been difficult to face directly and to write about experiences for which there was no precedent in conventional meditative verse.

A similar strategy is associated with "Kubla Khan," which can be read as an alternative to *The Rime of the Ancient Mariner*. The poem, which was not published until 1816, nearly two decades after it was written, is Coleridge's most daring account of poetic inspiration and the special nature of the poet. In the poem, the poet's isolation is perceived not as weakness but strength. Even in 1816, the gesture of self-assertion was difficult for Coleridge, and he prefaced the poem with an account designed to diminish its significance. "Kubla Khan" was, he explained, "a psychological curiosity," the fragment of a longer poem he had composed in an opium-induced sleep, "if that indeed can be called composition in which all the images rose up before him as *things*, with a parallel production of the correspondent expressions, without any sensation or consciousness of effort." Waking, he began to write out the verses he had in this manner "composed," but was interrupted by a visitor, after whose departure he found he could no longer remember more than "the general purport of the vision" and a few "scattered lines and images."

The problem with this explanation is that "Kubla Khan" does not strike reader as a fragment. It is, as it stands, an entirely satisfactory whole. Moreover, the facts of Coleridge's Preface have themselves been called into question.

Just what was Coleridge trying to hide? The poem turns on an analogy between the act of an emperor and the act of a poet. Kubla Khan's "pleasure-dome" in Xanadu is more than a monarch's self-indulgence; symbolically, it attempts to arrest the process of life itself. His walls encircle "twice five miles of fertile ground," in the midst of which flows "Alph," the sacred river of life, but they control neither the source of the river nor its conclusion in the "lifeless ocean" to which it runs. The source is a "deep romantic chasm" that Coleridge associates with the violence of natural process, with human sexuality, and with the libidinal origins of poetry in the song of a "woman wailing for her demon-lovers." Kubla's pleasure-dome is "a miracle of rare device," but it can exert no lasting influence. The achievement of the most powerful Oriental despot is limited by the conditions of life, and even his attempt to order a limited space evokes "Ancestral voices prophesying war!"

In contrast, the achievement of the poet is not bounded by space and time and partakes of the dangerous potency of natural creativity itself. Yet the nature of inspiration is tricky. The speaker of the poem recollects a visionary "Abyssinian maid" playing a dulcimer, and it is the possibility of reviving "within me/ Her symphony and song" that holds out the hope of a corresponding creativity: "To such a deep delight 'twould win me,/ . . . I would build that dome in air, . . ." The poet's act is always secondary, never primary creativity. Even so, to re-create in poetry Kubla's achievement—without its liabilities—is to become a dangerous being. Like the Mariner, the inspired poet has "flashing eyes" that can cast a spell over his audience. His special nature may be the sign of an incomplete self—for inspiration depends on the possibility of recovering a lost recollection; nevertheless, it is a special nature that threatens to re-create the world in its own image.

Nowhere else is Coleridge so confident about his powers as a poet or writer. *Christabel*, written in the same period as *The Rime of the Ancient Mariner* and "Kubla Khan," remains a fascinating fragment. Like "Kubla Khan," it was not published until 1816. By then, the verse romances of Sir Walter Scott and George Gordon, Lord Byron had caught the public's attention, and among Coleridge's motives in publishing his poem was to lay claim to a poetic form he believed he had originated. More important, though, his decision to publish two parts of an incomplete narrative almost two decades after he had begun the poem was also a means of acknowledging that *Christabel* was and would remain unfinished.

To attribute its incompletion to Coleridge's procrastination evades the real question: Why did the poem itself preclude development? Various answers have been offered; the most convincing argue a conflict between the metaphysical or religious significance of Christabel—whose name conflates Christ and Abel—with the exigencies of the narrative structure in which she is placed. As Walter Jackson Bate explains it, the "problem of finding motives and actions for Christabel . . . had imposed an insupportable psychological burden on Coleridge." The problem that Coleridge fails to solve is the problem of depicting credible innocence. Christabel, the virgin who finds the mysterious Lady Geraldine in the forest and brings her home to the castle of her father, Sir Leoline, only to fall victim to Geraldine's sinister spell, is either hopelessly passive and merely a victim, or, if active, something less than entirely innocent. At the same time, Geraldine, who approaches her prey with "a stricken look," is potentially the more interesting character. Christabel is too much like the albatross in *The Rime of the Ancient Mariner*; Geraldine, too much like the Mariner himself, whose guilt changes him from a simple seaman to an archetype of human isolation and suffering. Christabel's name suggests that Coleridge had intended for her to play a sacrificial role; but by promising to reunite Sir Leoline with his childhood friend, Roland de Vaux of Tryermaine, whom she claims as her father, Geraldine, too, has a potentially positive function in the narrative. Whether or not her claim is true, it nevertheless initiates action that may lead to a reconciliation, not only between two long-separated friends, but also between Sir Leoline's death-obsessed maturity and the time in his youth when he was able to experience friendship. There is, therefore, a suggestion that Geraldine is able to effect the link between childhood and maturity, innocence and experience, of particular concern to Coleridge—and to other Romantic poets as well. If Christabel and Geraldine represent the passive and active sides of Coleridge, then his failure to complete the narrative is yet another example of his inability to synthesize his personality—or to allow one side to win out at the expense of the other.

A few other poems from 1797 to 1798 deserve mention. "The Nightingale" (1798), although less interesting than the other titles in the group, conforms to the general structure of the conversation poems and so confirms its importance. "Fears in Solitude" (1798) is at once a conversation poem and something more. Like the others, it begins in a state of isolation and ends with social reintegration; its median state of self-assertion, however, takes the form of a public political statement. The voice of the statement is often strident, but this quality is understandable in a poem written at a time when invasion by France was daily rumored. "Fears in Solitude" attacks British militarism, British materialism, and British patriotism. Yet it is itself deeply patriotic. "There lives nor form nor feeling in my soul," Coleridge acknowledges, "Unborrowed from my country"; and for this reason the poem is not a series of topical criticism, but an expression of the dilemma of a poet divided between moral judgment of and personal identification with his native land.

When Coleridge returned from Germany in the summer of 1799, his period of intense poetic creativity was over. The poems that he wrote in the remaining years of his life were written by a man who no longer thought of himself as a poet and who therefore treated poetry as a mode of expression rather than a calling. *Dejection: An Ode*, which Coleridge dated April 4, 1802, offers a rationale for this change and seems to have been written as a formal farewell to the possibility of a career as a poet. The poem's epigraph from the *Ballad of Sir Patrick Spence* and its concern with perception link it with *The Rime of the Ancient Mariner*; its use of the image of the eolian harp links it with the poem by that name and, by extension, with the free-associational style of the conversation poems as a group. Its tone and manner are also close to those of the conversation poems, but its designation as an ode suggests an effort to elevate it to the level of formal statement. At the same time, its recurrent addresses to an unnamed "Lady" (Sara Hutchinson) suggest that the poem was primarily intended for a specific rather than a general audience, for a reader with a special interest in the poet who will not expect the poem to describe a universal human experience. Thus, the poem is at once closely related to Coleridge's earlier verse and significantly different from it.

In keeping with the conversation-poem structure, *Dejection* begins in a mood of solitary contemplation. The poet ponders the moon and "the dull sobbing draft that moans and rakes/ Upon the strings of this Aeolian lute." Together, they portend a storm in the offing, and Coleridge hopes that the violence of the "slant night shower" may startle him from his depression. His state, he explains, is not merely grief; it is "A stifled, drowsy, unimpassioned grief,/ Which finds no natural outlet, no relief,/ In word, or sign, or tear." All modes of emotional expression are blocked: he is able to "see" the beauty of the natural world, but he cannot "feel" it, and thereby use it as a symbol for his own inner state. He has lost the ability to invest the "outward forms" of nature with passion and life because, by his account, his inner source of passion and life has dried up. This ability he calls "Joy"—"the spirit and the power,/ Which wedding Nature to us gives in dower/ A new Earth and new Heaven." The language of apocalypse identifies "Joy" with religious faith; the notion of language suggests a more general identification with the expressive mode of his earlier poetry and its ability to transform an ordinary situation into an especially meaningful event. To have no "outlet . . ./ In word" is to have lost the voice of that poetry; to make the observation within a poetic text is to suggest one more difference between *Dejection* and Coleridge's earlier poetry.

*Dejection* may seem like a restatement of the notion of a possible harmony—now lost—between nature and the human that was expressed in the earlier poetry. In fact, *Dejection* denies the grounds of the harmony advanced in the earlier poems. In "Frost at Midnight," for example, the "shapes and sounds" of the natural world are perceived as an "eternal language, which thy/ God utters." In "The Eolian Harp," man is conceptualized (tentatively) as only one of the media through which the eternal force expresses itself. *Dejection*, in contrast, identifies the source of "Joy" in man himself. In feeling the beauty of nature, "we in ourselves rejoice." While the earlier poems toyed with pantheism, this focus on the state of mind of the individual soul is squarely orthodox, but the religious conservatism of *Dejection* does not in itself explain the termination of Coleridge's poetic career.

Coleridge himself attributes this termination to his own self-consciousness. As he explains in *Dejection*, he had sought "by abstruse research to seal/ From my own nature all the natural man"; but this scientific analysis of the self got the better of him, and now his conscious mind is compelled to subject the whole of experience to its analytic scrutiny. Nothing now escapes the dominance of reason, and insofar as the power of Coleridge's greatest poetry lay in its capacity to dramatize or at least imagine a universe imbued with supernatural meaning, the power is lost. Theologically, this capacity can be associated with pantheism or the vaguely heterodox natural theology of the conversation poems; psychologically, its potency, derived from primal narcissism, is related to the animism given explicit form in the spirits who supervise the action in *The Rime of the Ancient Mariner*. The power of this poetry, it can be argued, lies in its ability to recapture a primitive human experience of the world. The psychological awareness that Coleridge gained by his own self-analysis made this primitive naïveté impossible. *Dejection* is thus potentially a poem celebrating the maturity of the intellect—its recognition that its earlier powerful experience of nature, even when attributed to a Christian deity, was a matter of projection and therefore a function of his need to associate himself with an objective expression of his own potency. If the poem is not celebratory, it is because the consequences of this recognition amount to an admission of the importance of his individual self at odds with Coleridge's need for social acceptance. At the same time, it deprives him of that powerful confirmation of self derived from the illusionary sense of harmony with the animistic forces of the natural world. *Dejection* should have been a poem about Coleridge's internalization of these forces and triumphant recognition of his own strength of mind. Instead, he acknowledges the illusion of animism without being able to internalize the psychic energy invested in the animistic vision.

In disavowing belief in a transcendental power inherent in Nature, Coleridge disavows the power of his own earlier poetry. *Dejection* lacks the ease and confidence of the conversation poems, and its structure is noticeably mechanical. The storm that ends *Dejection* replaces the voice of authority that defined their closure; but, despite being anticipated by the opening stanzas, it is a *deus ex machina* without organic connection with the intellectual and emotional themes of the poem. The wind may excite the poet and even cause a change in his mood, but, for reasons that the poem itself makes clear, it can effect no fundamental transformation of his being. Hence, it is simply unimportant; and to expect it to have greater effect is, in the words of "The Picture" (1802), to be a "Gentle Lunatic."

Having foregone "Gentle Lunacy," the best of Coleridge's later poetry speaks with an intense but entirely naturalistic sincerity. In poems such as "The Blossoming of the Solitary Date-Tree" (1805), "The Pains of Sleep" (1815), and "Work Without Hope" (1826), Coleridge makes no attempt to transform his poetic self into the vehicle for universal truth. He simply presents his feelings and thoughts to the reader. He complains about his condition, but there is no sense that the act of complaint, beyond getting something off his chest for the time being, can effect any significant alteration of the self. Other poems lack even this concern for the limited audience whom he might have expected to be concerned with his personal problems. Poems such as "Limbo" (1817) and "Ne Plus Ultra" (1826?) are notebook exercises in conceiving the inconceivable—in this case, the states of minimal being, in which even the Kantian categories of space and time are reduced to uncertain conceptions, and absolute negation, "The one permitted opposite of God!" With other poems written for a similar private purpose, they are remarkable for the expressive power of their condensed imagery and their capacity to actualize philosophical thought. Coleridge's mastery of language never deserted him.

The greatness of the half dozen or so poems on which his reputation is based derives, however, from more than mastery of language. It derives from a confidence in the power of language that Coleridge, for legitimate reasons, came to doubt. Those half dozen or so poems assume that Coleridge is not a great poet, but that the grounding medium of poetry, like the "eternal language" of nature, is itself great. The very fact of his achievement in 1797 to 1798 presented to him the possibility that it was Coleridge and not poetry in which greatness lay; and, given that possibility, Coleridge could no longer conceive of himself as a poet. He would continue to write, but in media in which it was the thought behind the prose, and not the thinker, that gave meaning to language.

**Major publications other than poetry**

PLAYS: *The Fall of Robespierre*, 1794 (with Robert Southey); *Remorse* 1813; *Zapolya*, 1817.

NONFICTION: *The Watchman*, 1796; *Wallenstein*, 1800 (translation of J. C. F. von Schiller's *The Piccolomini* and *The Death of Wallenstein*); *The Friend*, 1809-1810, 1818; "The Statesman's Manual," 1816; "A Lay Sermon," 1817; *Biographia Literaria*, 1817; *Aids to Reflection*, 1825.

**Bibliography**

Angus, Douglas. "The Theme of Love and Guilt in Coleridge's Three Major Poems," in *Journal of English and Germanic Philology*. LIX (October, 1960), pp. 655-668.

Barth, J. Robert, S. J. *The Symbolic Imagination: Coleridge and the Romantic*

*Tradition*, 1977.

Bate, Walter Jackson. *Coleridge*, 1968.

Chambers, E. K. *Samuel Taylor Coleridge: A Biographical Study*, 1938.

Mercer, Dorothy F. "The Symbolism of 'Kubla Khan,'" in *Journal of Aesthetics and Art Criticism*. XII (September, 1953), pp. 784-801.

Prickett, Stephen. *Coleridge and Wordsworth: The Poetry of Growth*, 1970.

Walsh, William. *Coleridge: The Work and the Relevance*, 1967.

Willey, Basil. *Samuel Taylor Coleridge*, 1972.

Yarlott, Geoffrey. *Coleridge & the Abyssinian Maid*, 1967.

*Frederick Kirchhoff*

# WILLIAM COLLINS

**Born:** Chichester, England; December 25, 1721
**Died:** Chichester, England; June 12, 1759

## Principal poems and collections

*Persian Eclogues*, 1742; *An Epistle: Verses Humbly Address'd to Sir Thomas Hanmer on His Edition of Shakespear's Works*, 1744; *Odes on Several Descriptive and Allegoric Subjects*, 1746 (dated 1747); *Ode on the Popular Superstitions of the Highlands of Scotland, Considered as the Subject of Poetry*, 1788 (written in 1749).

## Other literary forms

The form of William Collins' literary accomplishments was limited to poetry.

## Achievements

William Collins' achievements in poetry do not embody the results of careful observation of life, his best poems being descriptive and allegorical. His feelings were intense when he contemplated abstractions such as simplicity, an aesthetic ideal to which his ode gives subtle definition by means of description. His ability to think about abstractions and intellectual concepts in pictorial terms was Collins' most remarkable gift. A second gift was his ability to link every part of his poem to the next, so that the poem flows along in an unbroken stream.

His best work was done in the ode. Of the twelve such pieces published under the title *Odes on Several Descriptive and Allegorical Subjects* in 1746, three stand out for special effects. The "Ode on the Poetical Character" roughly approximates the true Pindaric ode, and, unlike Augustan forms, shows the poet to be an inspired creator and projects imagination as the prime essential of a true poet. "The Passions, an Ode for Music" is a pseudo-Pindaric ode in the tradition of John Dryden's "Alexander's Feast." Its richness of image and appropriate variety of movement have made it the poet's most popular piece. *An Ode on the Popular Superstitions of the Highlands of Scotland* is Collins' longest poem, containing his invention of the seventeen-line stanza of iambic pentameter ending with an Alexandrine. It was also the first significant attempt in English literature to concentrate on the romantic elements of Scottish legend and landscape.

Collins' themes are significant because they anticipate the interests of the early nineteenth century Romantic poets and thus the broad concerns found in modern poetry. Five themes are noteworthy. First, Collins is concerned with the role of imagination in poetry. He believes that imagination rather than reason, an Augustan concern, is the essential trait of the poet. Second, he is a critic of literature, one whose commentary is conditioned by his concern for the imagination. Third, Collins shows a strong interest in folklore and its relation to literature, anticipating Samuel Taylor Coleridge and William Wordsworth. Fourth, he often emphasizes patriotic and political themes, themes which promote ideas of freedom, liberty and justice, all special concerns of the early Romantic writers. Finally, Collins continually expresses concern for psychological issues in his poetry. All these themes are tied directly to the problem of imagination.

### Biography

William Collins was born at Chichester in Sussex in December, 1721. His early years seem to have been those of a favored child. Whether Collins attended a school or learned his first letters at home or under the tutelage of a local curate, he was well enough prepared by the time he was eleven to be admitted as a scholar to Winchester College. His years at Winchester were important. It was there that he made friendships with Joseph Warton, William Whitehead, and James Hampton, and studied mythology and legend in Homer and Vergil. He both wrote and published his first poems while at Winchester.

Some scholars believe that it was Warton's friendship and influence that led Collins to become interested in literature. The Warton family was thoroughly literary, and it is possible that Joseph's example first persuaded the youth from his Chichester home and encouraged him to begin cultivating his literary interests. In any case, Collins' literary powers developed while he was at Winchester. One of the poems which he wrote during these years, "Sonnet," was published in the *Gentlemen's Magazine* in October, 1739.

After completing his studies at Winchester, Collins was admitted to Queen's College, Oxford, on March 21, 1740. On July 29, 1741, he was appointed Demy of Magdalen College, allowing him some stipend, and in 1743 he took the Bachelor's degree and left Oxford. Before leaving college, he had published his *Persian Eclogues* and, although the work was published anonymously, the publication was Collins' first serious claim to public notice and ironically remained his chief popular accomplishment during his lifetime. While at Oxford, Collins also published *Verses Humbly Address'd to Sir Thomas Hanmer*, which, like *Persian Eclogues*, was well received. The book went into a second edition in 1744, which in itself might have been the inspiration that caused Collins to leave for London to try his hand at the literary life. He moved to the city for a brief period, but eventually settled in Richmond where he worked for a time and established new friendships, in particular one with James Thomson.

When Bonnie Prince Charles landed in Scotland in 1745 and sounds of war spread, Collins turned to writing patriotic verse. During the early part of 1746, Collins was working on his odes. Perhaps they had been in progress for some time; in any event, scholars are quite sure that by the summer of 1746 they were nearing the form in which they now exist. It may have been at this time that Collins traveled to the Guildford races, where he met Joseph Warton. In time they mutually decided to publish their poems. The publication of his *Odes* in 1746 was the high-water mark of Collins' life, even though he probably did not realize it at the time, primarily because the public took very little note of them. Scholars do not know what his reaction to this relative failure may have been, but they do know that he was engaged in various literary projects in 1747 and that he remained active in literary circles. The depressing malady to which Thomas Warton refers in one of his letters did not begin to afflict Collins until 1750 at the earliest.

Collins began disposing of his share of the family property in Chichester in 1749 and when he made his last trip there in October for final legalities he met John Home, beginning another fertile creative period in his life. By 1750 there were announcements that a new translation by Mr. William Collins of Torquato Tasso's *Jerusalem Delivered* (1575) would appear. Although no copy seems to exist, there is every reason to believe that Collins did translate the poem. After meeting Home, Collins also went on to write the famous ode on the superstitions of Scotland.

It must have been about the end of 1750 or in 1751 that Collins' illness began. Eventually he was committed to an insane asylum. Warton mentions that at Easter, 1751, Collins was "given over and supposed to be dying." Samuel Johnson's account is probably substantially accurate—except that he has him dying in 1756 rather than in 1759. No one since the eighteenth century has added to the knowledge of the last period of Collins' life.

**Analysis**

Although the heroic couplet had achieved its dominance by the time of William Collins, lyric poetry was still alive, albeit somewhat in reserve as a popular mode of expression. The lyric poet of the second quarter of the eighteenth century had available a number of traditional forms: the Pindaric ode for exalted subjects, the Horatian ode for a variety of urban and meditative themes, the elegy, and the song. A new type appeared, another type of "ode" which centered around a personified abstraction treated in a descriptive way. Borrowing from John Milton's style in "L'Allegro" and "Il Penseroso," the Wartons and Collins played a major role in developing this form.

Collins did not achieve fame with his odes during his lifetime, and perhaps this lack of recognition contributed to his early mental instability and eventual death at thirty-eight. His odes never attain warmth and personal intimacy, but they do achieve particular effects which are unsurpassed in eighteenth century poetry: pensive melody, emotionally charged landscape, vigorous allegory, and rich romanticism.

Collins, like his friends the Wartons, advocated concepts of poetry that would eventually dominate poetic thought by the turn of the nineteenth century. His belief that poetry should be freely imagined and passionately felt, that it should be blessed with *furor poesis*, puts him basically into the Wordsworthian camp. His formalism and abstraction, ties to his Augustan background, obviously hamper his style. Collins is much like Edwin Arlington Robinson's Miniver Cheevy, born out of time. He has one poetic foot in the past, but the other, much larger one, extends far into the future, since it would be some forty years after his death before the publication of William Wordsworth and Samuel Taylor Coleridge's *Lyrical Ballads* (1798), the recognized *locus classicus* of Romanticism. Collins has been compared with the early nineteenth century poet Percy Bysshe Shelley in his use of abstraction; in the work of both poets, personifications become real figures which help to express a delicate mood without recourse to great detail: "Spring with dewey fingers cold" and "Freedom a weeping hermit" illustrate the method well. This personification of natural phenomena in eighteenth century verse for the most part symbolizes affective states, where the allegorical figure sums up the meaning which the phenomenon has for the poet.

Collins does seem at times to strive for scholarly classicism. His mixture of classical and medieval sources illustrates his "two voices" long before Alfred, Lord Tennyson's metaphor and poems come into overt expression. He was the most free of all the early precursors of Romanticism, and his predominant concern was the spirit of beauty. Most critics compare Collins favorably with his contemporaries, especially with Thomas Gray, generally agreeing with William Hazlitt's assessment. Hazlitt argued that Collins possessed genuine inspiration, and that even though his work is marred by affectation and certain obscurities, "he also catches rich glimpses of the bowers of paradise."

Perhaps the best guide to Collins' attitude toward inspiration and imagination is his "Ode on the Poetical Character." Early in the ode, Collins asserts that the true poetical character is godlike, for the bard is one "prepared and bathed in heaven." Following this apotheosis, Collins pursues the idea by describing God's creation of the world as analogous to the poet's act of creation. A bit of sixteenth century pagan/Christian syncretism is reflected in his analogy: God was the original type of all poets and the contemporary poet imitates His divine power. Collins, however, adds allegorical layers to this analogy. He suggests that Fancy is a separate female entity, and not merely an attribute of God; and he adds the rather confusing metaphor of a girdle of poetic imagination.

Collins turns to the examples of John Milton and Edmund Spenser, suggesting that the true poet will find his voice in a kind of wedding of their diverse styles. One finds such a poet, according to stanza three, "high on some cliff . . . of prospect wild," accompanied by holy genie and surrounded by an Eden-like environment. In this ode there is a sense of a new aesthetic attitude that later comes to be described as "Romantic"; John Langhorne says that the ode is so wild it seems to have been written under the Romantic tyranny of the imagination.

The wedding of the styles of Spenser and Milton which results in this strong emotional verse can be related to Collins' earlier work entitled *Persian Eclogues*. He prefaces his eclogues with the statement that "The style of my countrymen is as naturally strong and nervous as that of an Arabian or Persian is rich and figurative." Spenser is a writer whom Collins associates with Persian genius because of his luxuriously expansive style. Following the contemporary attitude toward Hebraic poetry as being energetic but brief rather than copious, Collins thinks of Milton as an example. The fusion of these two styles results in rich, emotional verse.

*Persian Eclogues* was published in 1742 while Collins was at Oxford; but the individual eclogues had been written sometime between his birthday in 1738 and the winter of 1740. According to Joseph Warton, Collins wrote them at a time when he was studying Persian history. In Collins' time, exotic Eastern interests were becoming popular, and features of Oriental poetry had become fascinating to the post-Augustan generation. Thomas Rymer comments that fancy dominated Oriental verse, "wild, vast and unbridled." Obviously, such a style met with Collins' approval; the pretense that he was actually translating Persian poetry allowed him to attempt a rich elegance and wildness of thought, traits which became characteristic of his mature Romanticism.

Most critics agree that the eclogues contain little genuine Orientalism. In diction and structure they closely follow conventions of the eighteenth century pastoral, especially those of Alexander Pope. There are several significant differences, however, between Pope and Collins, the first of which is simply that Collins' setting is exotic, not English. Also, there is a difference in theme; although both writers follow the conventional emphasis on the power of time, Collins' tone is secular rather than Christian, as in Shelley's pastoral elegy "Adonais." Collins does not see the essence of pastoral as the recognition of man's fall and of modern man's desire to repudiate Adam and inherited sin. By using the seasons, Pope, for example, is able to trace man's decline from a golden age to an age of error, with a final eclogue showing the transforming power of Christ, who can bring the golden age back for all mankind. Collins does not use the seasons for his structure and he does not use the sacred closing eclogue. Rather, he suggests that the usable values of the past should be put into practice in contemporary society.

There is little borrowing in *Persian Eclogues* from other sources. The third eclogue may be a variation of a story of a King of Persia who, after witnessing the simple life of his peasant subjects, gives up his kingship for a time in order to live with shepherds. The King eventually returns to court with a favorite shepherd, who in turn longs continually for his rural home. This story appeared in Ambrose Phillips' periodical *The Free-Thinker* in 1719 and 1739, thus making it possible for Collins to have seen it.

Another poem reflecting Collins' orientation toward Romanticism is the 1746 "Ode to Liberty." The background for the ode is the War of the Austrian Succession. The war with France saw the city of Genoa fall prey to allied invasion because of Austrian occupation: Genoa is another example of the democratic fight for liberty, paralleling Austria's own William Tell who refused to bow to the dictatorial governor's demands. The "Ode to Liberty" suggests a desire for peace, implying throughout a great sympathy for those who suffer innocently. Collins' question in Strophe One, perhaps alluding to the exhortations of Tyrtaus to the Spartans in the Second Messenian War to fight with courage, stresses the disgrace of cowardice and the glory of patriotism. He also alludes to William Tell in Epode One, and his closing remarks suggest that England will welcome to its shores for peaceful play the dedicated youth who fought so bravely.

It is generally observed that the ode which expresses Collins' Romantic temperament at its best is one of his last works, originally entitled *Ode to a Friend on His Return*, but published posthumously in 1788 as *An Ode on the Popular Superstitions of the Highlands of Scotland*. The ode was addressed to a friend and fellow writer, John Home, who was leaving London after his failure to place one of his plays on the London stage.

The Romantic nature of the piece is seen in the opening lines as Collins asks his friend to rediscover a region inhabited by "Fairy People" and ruled by "Fancy." The ancient bards seem to rise in masque-like manner around Home, whose mind is "possest" by strange powers. The "matted hair with bough fantastic crown'd" enhances the supernatural mood that Collins establishes. Collins admonishes Home to make use of such forces in writing his plays. By employing supernatural tales such as are found in the folklore of Scotland, Collins says, the modern poet can partake of the visionary power found therein and share in its creative force. Probably the most alluring section of the ode is the story of the hapless swain caught up in the force of the kelpie's wrath. The swain is led astray by glimmering mazes that cheer his sight. These lights are actually the will-o'-the-wisps, a vision deluding and drawing him to the water monster, whose malignant design becomes obvious to the reader at this point. The poor swain becomes a passive, helpless wretch in the clutches of the evil kelpie. His death leads to his transformation into a supernatural being, unable to bridge the gap between his former and his present life.

In the closing lines, Collins invokes a natural environment that is sustained by supernatural traditions. The ode is undoubtedly a celebration of the new visionary source which would further liberate poetry in the Romantic period.

**Bibliography**
Abrams, M. H. *The Mirror and the Lamp*, 1953.
Camden, Carroll, ed. *Restoration and Eighteenth-Century Literature*, 1963.

Chapin, Chester. *Personification in Eighteenth-Century Poetry*, 1968.
Courthope, W. J. *A History of English Poetry*, 1962.
Grierson, Herbert, and J. C. Smith. *A Critical History of English Poetry*, 1967.
Hagstrum, Jean. *The Sister Arts*, 1958.
Jones, R. F. "Eclogue Types in English Poetry of the Eighteenth Century," in *Journal of English and Germanic Philology*. XXIV (1925), pp. 51-57.
Poole, Austin L. *Poems of Gray and Collins*, 1937.
Shuster, George N. *The English Ode from Milton to Keats*, 1964.
Sigworth, Oliver. *William Collins*, 1965.
Tillyard, E. M. W. *Essays Literary and Educational*, 1967.
Wendorf, Richard. *William Collins and Eighteenth-Century English Poetry*, 1981.

*John W. Crawford*

# WILLIAM CONGREVE

**Born:** Bardsey Grange, Yorkshire, England; January 24, 1670
**Died:** London, England; January 19, 1729

**Principal collection**
*Poems upon Several Occasions*, 1710.

**Other literary forms**
William Congreve's major works are his plays: four comedies, *The Old Bachelor* (1693); *The Double-Dealer* (1693); *Love for Love* (1695); and *The Way of the World* (1700); and one tragedy, *The Mourning Bride* (1697). Congreve also wrote criticism, *Amendments of Mr. Collier's False and Imperfect Citations* (1698); a novella, *Incognita* (1692); a masque, *The Judgement of Paris* (1701); and an opera, *Semele* (1707). Some of his letters were published in a collection edited by John Dennis (1696). His other miscellaneous writings include contributions to *The Gentleman's Journal* (1692-1694), an essay for *The Tatler* (February 13, 1711), and the "Dedication to John Dryden's *Dramatick Works*" (1717).

**Achievements**
In his own day Congreve had a considerable reputation as a poet. John Dryden, in his poem "To My Dear Friend Mr. Congreve," crowned him as his successor; and, as a political poet supporting William III, Congreve performed much the same function as Dryden did for Charles II and James II. Contemporary writers such as Jonathan Swift and the lesser known Charles Hopkins and William Dove praised Congreve's verse extravagantly. Almost all of this praise, however, stemmed from Congreve's reputation as a dramatist and from his pleasing personality. By the middle of the eighteenth century critics began looking at Congreve's poetry in isolation and harshly condemned it. In the nineteenth century Thomas Macaulay pronounced Congreve's poetry to be of little value and long forgotten, and Edmund Gosse concentrated on Congreve the man, giving no very favorable judgment. After such a great fall in Congreve's reputation, critical judgment of his poetry has settled: he is considered an elegant minor poet, whose real fame rests on his plays. His best poems are his light love songs and his witty prologues; his greatest contribution to poetry was his condemnation of the irregular Cowleyan Pindaric, a form which had led to much laxness and mediocrity in poetry.

**Biography**
William Congreve was born in Yorkshire but grew up in Ireland where his father served as an army lieutenant. Unlike many poets of his day, he belonged to the gentry: his grandfather was squire of Stretton Hall in Staffordshire.

Congreve attended Kilkenny College, where he is reported to have written his first poem, on the death of his headmaster's magpie. Swift was an older classmate of Congreve at Kilkenny and later at Trinity College, Dublin. After college, Congreve moved to London to study law but soon became entranced by the literary life. He frequented Will's coffeehouse, published a novel, and began writing odes and songs. His translations of Homer won Dryden's praise and friendship, and Dryden edited and then sponsored Congreve's first play, *The Old Bachelor*. During the play's run Congreve fell in love with the young actress Anne Bracegirdle, for whom he wrote many poems and the part of Millamant in *The Way of the World*. For his promise as a propagandist for William III, Congreve was given his first of a long series of political posts, Commissioner for Hackney Coaches; in gratitude, he produced the standard celebratory odes. *The Mourning Bride*, Congreve's only tragedy, was his greatest popular success, although he is most acclaimed now for *The Way of the World*, a relative failure in its own day.

After the less-than-rapturous reception of *The Way of the World*, suffering from increasing blindness and painful gout, Congreve declined to expend the enormous amount of energy and concentration needed to write plays. He continued to write verses on occasion and became a gentleman about town, friend of prominent writers, and gallant of Henrietta, Duchess of Marlborough. Although he stopped writing for the theater, his love for it never waned; in 1705 he became the director of the new Haymarket Theater. His government posts continued; in 1714 he was made Searcher of Customs and then Secretary to the Island of Jamaica, an office which gave him adequate income for the rest of his life. He died in 1729 and was buried in Westminster Abbey, where the Duchess was buried beside him a few years later.

**Analysis**

William Congreve's best poetry, like his plays, brings Restoration society to life: the intricacies of the courtship dance, and the war in the theaters between playwrights and critics. When Congreve strays from his own milieu into political propaganda, however, or makes attempts at the sublime, his poetry rarely rises above the mediocre.

Congreve's poems, particularly his songs, reveal the feelings of both partners in the courtship dance. His men are not confident and promiscuous Horners who accumulate conquest after conquest, but insecure young men who often have been hurt or discarded by women. One song, in anapests, mimics the headstrong impetuosity and lumbering clumsiness of a young man in love: "I Look'd, and I sigh'd, and I wish'd I cou'd speak." Another song, "The Reconciliation," reminds one of John Donne's "Go and Catch a Falling Star": a cynical young man insists that women prove ungrateful whenever men are true and claims that the joys women give are "few, short, and insincere." "Song," one of Congreve's best-known and most-liked poems, purportedly composed for Anne Bracegirdle, is written in the calm yet bittersweet manner of Sir Thomas Wyatt. A lover, remembering the past joys of his inconstant mistress, determines not to seek revenge but to be grateful for what has been. Many of Congreve's songs sound this same theme of a young man bemoaning his lost love.

Congreve's women fall into two categories: honorable women torn between their desire to love and be loved and their need to maintain their virtue, and inconstant women who leave heartbroken, hapless men in their wake. Congreve shows great sensitivity to the plight of women in the love-honor struggle of Restoration society. In "Song in Dialogue, For Two Women" the two women speakers decide whether or not to yield to their lovers' enticements. The first speaker claims she will but changes her mind after listening to the second. Both sing a chorus which acknowledges how quickly men can lose interest: "And granting Desire,/ We feed not the Fire,/ But make it more quickly expire." In another song Selinda is caught between her religious desire for purity and her secular desire to keep her lover: she runs to the church if he asks her favor yet cries when she thinks he will leave her. Selinda's lover wittily reveals the pressure put on a Restoration woman: "Wou'd she cou'd make of me a Saint,/ Or I of her a Sinner."

Like Alexander Pope, Congreve has his essay on women: three short poems on Amoret, Lesbia, and Doris. "Doris," which was much praised by Richard Steele, presents a fully-rounded picture of a promiscuous "Nymph of riper Age" who shines on various lovers in the night and quickly forgets them the next day. "Lesbia" describes a young man's discovery of the empty head of the idol he worships: the "trickling Nonsense" from her coral lips like balm heals his heart wounded by love. "Amoret" presents a contradictory young woman, who affects "to seem unaffected" and laughs at others for what she prizes in herself. A blind hypocrite, she does not see that "She is the Thing that she despises."

Congreve claimed to be a moralist, exposing the vice and folly of his society. He is indeed harsh in his condemnation of unfaithful, hypocritical wives. In his Epilogue to Thones Sontherne's *Oroonoko* (1695) he satirizes town ladies who profess to be Christian and virtuous yet despise their spouses and take their marriage vows lightly. Promiscuous single women may leave angry, unhappy men, but they do not undermine the foundations of society—marriage and family.

Congreve's prologues and epilogues, though less vigorous and daring than Dryden's, comment on the state of the theater and society through the use of witty imagery. His prologues are fitting appetizers for the feasts which follow. The Prologue to *The Old Bachelor* begins seriously, with an image that Congreve was to use on other occasions: the play as a battleground between critics and writers. The Prologue is the drum signaling the opening of the skirmishes. This Prologue, however, ends in a burlesque, with the pretty spokeswoman (Anne Bracegirdle) forgetting her lines, pleading with the audience to like the play, and running offstage in confusion.

Critics habitually drew the fire of Restoration playwrights, and Congreve regularly traded insults with them. The Epilogue to *The Old Bachelor* sandwiches a witty comparison of young women and playwrights in between the standard pleading to be approved and the standard insulting of the critics ("If he's an ass, he will be tried by's peers"). Once the end is gained, both women and playwrights are damned (discarded).

The Prologue to *The Double-Dealer* is more sophisticated, with fewer drops in tone. It compares the play to a Moorish infant, thrown by its father (the playwright) into the sea (the pit) to prove its legitimacy. The image serves Congreve well; he can describe the pit as tempestuous and call the critics sharks. The Epilogue to *The Double-Dealer* classifies the audience of the Restoration theater, critics all: the men of learning, the pit, the ladies, the beaux, the witlings, and the cits, each of whom has different exacting requirements for a successful play. The same theme recurs in Congreve's Epilogue to *Oroonoko*. The poet divides his time among the different tastes; his one foot wears the sock, the other the buskin, and in striving to please he is forced to hop in a single boot.

In addition to condemning the critics and the problems they create for authors, Congreve condemns the amateur playwrights who at the time were drowning the stage. He laments that the theater has become a church whose main activity is funerals, not christenings. In another witty metaphor, he tells the wits that Pegasus—that is, the art of writing—has tricks which take more to master than merely getting up and riding. He ridicules the lady playwrights in lines as good as Pope's in *The Dunciad* (1728-1743): "With the same Ease, and Negligence of Thought,/ The charming Play is writ, and Fringe is wrought." One important theme of Congreve is the hard task serious writers have, not in writing itself but in presenting their works, when they are assailed by ignorant critics and torpedoed by amateurish mishmash.

Jeremy Collier attacked Congreve's licentiousness in his "Short View of the Immorality and Profaneness of the English Stage," but Congreve blamed the audience for the type of plays which were popular. Reciting his "Epilogue at the Opening of the Queen's Theatre," Bracegirdle told the audience that the beaux may find it hard to spend one night without smutty jests, but she promises them soon "to your selves shew your dear selves again" and display "in bold Strokes the vicious Town." Congreve whirls in defensive fury against the pseudoreformers. In "Prologue, to the Court, on the Queen's Birthday," he claims that playwrights seek to war against vice and folly but reformers force the muse to assume the very forms she has been fighting. Reformers break the mirror (the plays) which reflect their own ignorance and malice. Congreve renounces the stage, saying his muse will now pursue the nobler tasks of painting the "Beauties of the Mind" and, by showing the court the virtues of one such as the Queen, "shame to Manners an incorrigible Town." He says he will remain a moralist although his means have changed. Unfortunately, when he praises the virtuous Queen, his lines lack the strength of the earlier diatribe: the only line in this prologue that matches the eloquence of his fury is one in which the muse "secretly Applauds, and silently Admires" the Queen.

When Congreve leaves writing for the stage or writing about the stage, his poetic powers by and large desert him and his claim of remaining a moralist is specious; it is hard to find any morality in "poet-laureate" praises. The only thing which redeems Congreve's laudatory verses to William and to Mary is his imagery, which leaps out from the sycophantic meanderings. In "To the King, on the Taking of Namure" Congreve admits that his proper sphere is singing simple love songs, but he underestimates his own abilities. His description of the battle of Namure rises above the commonplace, with its discordant consonants imitating the clash and clang of battle (before Pope's strictures on sound and sense) and his images of the earth in labor giving birth to the "dead Irruptions" and the air tormented by the cannon fire and smoke. Warlord man is shown to victimize nature.

On the other hand, nature befriends man when he is gentle. In "The Mourning Muse of Alexis, Lamenting the Death of Queen Mary," Congreve describes the beauty and peace of nature mourning Queen Mary: sable clouds adorn the chalk cliffs, bees deposit their honey on Mary's tomb, and glowworms light the dirges of fairies. The imagery is beautiful, but if one comes to the poem with the expectation that it will give solace, it is disappointingly silly.

Although the classical set pieces in Congreve's poems to King William are disastrous, the set piece in the irregular ode "On Mrs. Arabella Hunt, Singing" works well. Much like Pope's portrayal of dullness in *The Dunciad*, Congreve's mighty god Silence is wrapped in a melancholy thought, wreathed by mists and darkness, lulled by poppy vapors, and sitting on an "ancient" sigh. Silence is vanquished by the beauty of Hunt's singing, and her listeners are left in a state reminiscent of the lovers on John Keats's Grecian urn, "For ever to be dying so, yet never die."

Congreve's "A Hymn to Harmony, in Honour of St. Cecilia's Day, 1701" and Pope's "Ode for Musick, on St. Cecilia's Day," when compared, illustrate the difference between a great poet and a minor one. In both poems the authors describe the ability of music to soothe troubled minds. Congreve says that the muses with balmy sound assuage a wrathful and revengeful mind, while Pope turns the idea into a concrete image, personifying melancholy, sloth, and envy and showing rather than explaining the effect of music on them. Pope may have mined Congreve's ore for ideas, but he cut, polished, and presented the more beautiful gems.

Congreve's technical abilities never equal the power of his imagery. He squirms and struggles under the burden of rhyming. In order to achieve his rhymes, he often destroys his syntax or creates a jingle of sound rather than a flow. Even when he does find a rhyme, it frequently is only an eye-rhyme or a jarring approximation of a rhyme. Perhaps one reason that Congreve was able to create exquisite poetry in *The Mourning Bride*, lines which Samuel Johnson called "The most poetical paragraph" in the "whole mass of English poetry," is that he was not forced into rhyme and could write blank verse.

Like other writers who experiment in genres other than their major ones, Congreve does not repeat the brilliance of his plays in his poetry. Lacking technical virtuosity, flawed by absurd and frozen set pieces, and distinguished by no more than ordinary political praise, his poems nevertheless can sparkle with striking imagery and wit. Above all, Congreve's poems, with their views of the theater and of love and honor in Restoration society, add to the reader's understanding of his plays.

**Major publications other than poetry**
SHORT FICTION: *Incognita*, 1692.
PLAYS: *The Old Bachelor*, 1693; *The Double-Dealer*, 1693; *Love for Love*, 1695; *The Mourning Bride*, 1697; *The Way of the World*, 1700; *The Judgement of Paris*, 1701 (masque); *Semele*, 1707 (opera).
NONFICTION: *Amendments of Mr. Collier's False and Imperfect Citations*, 1698.

**Bibliography**
Hodges, John C. *William Congreve the Man*, 1941.
Johnson, Samuel. *Lives of the English Poets*, 1905. Edited by George Birkbeck Hill.
Novak, Maximillian E. *William Congreve*, 1971.
Taylor, D. C. *William Congreve*, 1931.

*Ann Willardson Engar*

# HENRY CONSTABLE

**Born:** Flamborough (?), England; 1562
**Died:** Liège, France; 1613

## Principal collections

*Diana*, 1592, 1594; *The Poems of Henry Constable*, 1960 (Joan Grundy, editor).

## Other literary forms

Henry Constable's other writings were political and religious prose works. While still a Protestant, he wrote a pamphlet called *A short vew of a large examination of Cardinall Allen his trayterous justification of Sir W. Stanley and Yorck* (c. 1588). This was an answer to a work of 1587 in which the Roman Catholic cardinal had justified the surrender of Daventer to the Spaniards by Stanley, one of Leicester's chief officers. Constable answered specific arguments of Allen's work with arguments based on justice and Protestant theology. He mocked the cardinal, implying that he was a "purple whore." He also wrote the *Examen pacifique de la doctrine des Huguenots* (1589, *The Catholike Moderator: Or, A Moderate Examination of the Doctrine of the Protestants*), published anonymously in Paris. The work was pro-Huguenot, but in it the author pretended to be a Catholic. It was translated into English in 1623. The work was an enlargement of a response that he wrote to another tract. Again, Constable was concerned with politics, theology, and justice, but he also indicated that he desired the union of the Protestant and Roman Catholic Churches. Constable was soon to become a Catholic. He wrote an unpublished theological work (c. 1596) that has been lost, and another work on English affairs (c. 1597). He is presumed to be the author or coauthor of an anonymous book in defense of King James's title in 1600, which was an answer to another work supporting Spain that was erroneously attributed to him. He also collaborated with Dr. W. Percy on a work against the Spanish and Jesuits in 1601. It is clear that Constable was deeply involved in the political and religious matters of his day. His religious interests were to affect greatly his life and his poetry, and he wrote an important group of religious sonnets after his conversion to Catholicism. As the prose works mentioned above showed his commitment to the Protestant cause, his religious sonnets showed his strong feelings for the Catholic faith.

## Achievements

In his best-known work, *Diana*, Constable wrote highly polished courtly sonnets. Some modern critics consider his undated Spiritual Sonnets, which appeared only in manuscript, to be superior to the *Diana* in their originality and strong sense of feeling. Both his secular and his religious poems, however, were sonnets of praise. His love of argument is evident in the logical patterns of his sonnets, particularly in his use of symmetrical antitheses, often with accompanying alliteration. The openings of many of his sonnets are striking, and he made use of clever conceits, including some of the extended Metaphysical variety that are memorable. His diction was simple and unaffected, though his style was marked by considerable repetition.

Although today he is considered to be a minor poet, he was regarded as a major talent by his contemporaries. He was one of the earliest of Elizabethan sonnet writers and helped to create the fashion. Many of his sonnets had been written before 1591, when Sir Philip Sidney's *Astrophel and Stella* was published. The *Diana* of 1592 was one of the earliest collections of sonnets. Samuel Daniel, the author of *Delia* (1592), may have been influenced by Constable rather than the other way around. William Shakespeare seems to have borrowed specific details from Constable, and Michael Drayton also showed Constable's influence. Francis Meres in *Palladis Tamia* (1598) praised him highly. Ben Jonson's "An Ode" (c. 1600) listed Constable with Homer, Ovid, Petrarch, Pierre de Ronsard and Sidney, and his name is mentioned in the company of excellent poets by Drayton and Gabriel Harvey. In the anonymous play *Returne from Parnassus* (c. 1600), he is spoken of as "Sweate Constable." Edmund Bolton in the *Hypercritica* (1618) termed Constable "a great master in the English Tongue, nor had any Gentleman of our Nation a more pure, quick, or higher Delivery of Conceit. . . ." The contemporary poet Alexander Montgomerie wrote a Scottish version of one of his poems, and a Latin translation of another is included in the *Poemata* (1607) of Dousa (Filius). After his own time, he was largely known until the nineteenth century, when his poetry was edited by W. C. Hazlitt and was included in anthologies of Elizabethan sonnets.

**Biography**

Henry Constable came from a line of distinguished ancestors on both his father's and his mother's side. The surname originated from the office of Constable in Chester, which had been held by members of his father's family since the time of William the Conqueror, although his father's branch of the family had settled in Yorkshire. The poet must have been born in 1562, since he was thirteen years old in 1575, and was presumably born at Flamborough. There is no information about his childhood. He attended St. John's College, Cambridge, his rank being recognized there by special distinctions. After receiving his bachelor's degree in 1579 or 1580 by a special grace, the reason not made clear, he was admitted to Lincoln's Inn on February 21, 1583. Later in the same year, a letter he wrote to his father indicates that he was with the English ambassador, Walsingham, in Scotland. Walsingham recommended the young Constable to the English ambassador in Paris, who was distantly related to Constable, and he became an emissary. He seems to have been a proponent of the Protestant cause at Paris, remaining there until 1585. He wrote indignantly about the actions of English Catholics in Paris, and he was recommended to Walsingham by Stafford as a good choice to help the Protestant Henry of Navarre stand firm in the face of Catholic arguments. After Constable left Paris, he traveled to Heidelberg, to Poland, to Italy, perhaps to Hamburg, and probably to the Low Countries. His pamphlet in answer to a work by Cardinal Allen was probably written in 1588.

It seems likely that Constable spent the years 1588 and 1589 at court, and he was said to have been a favorite of the Queen. He wrote sonnets, including ones to Penelope Rich, and was much in the company of Arabella Stuart. He was friendly with many Protestants of the Continent, including followers of Henry of Navarre. One of these, Claude d'Isle, Seigneur de Marivaux, sent several letters by James VI of Scotland to their destination by way of Constable. Another follower of Henry of Navarre and friend of Constable was Jean Hotman, who wished to see the Protestant and Roman Catholic Churches united. Constable was involved with him and others, including Penelope Rich, in an intrigue to obtain the favor of James VI for the Earl of Essex. Constable met with the King and assured him of his loyalty despite the fact that Arabella Stuart was the chief rival of James in his claims to the throne of England. The scheme was, however, not successful. Constable was at the Scottish court some weeks before October 21, 1589, when he returned to London. While at the Scottish court, he of course met the members of James's literary circle. In 1589, he also wrote the work defending the Huguenots in which he pretended to be a Catholic.

By 1590, Constable had decided to become a Roman Catholic. By the end of that year, all his secular sonnets had probably been written and collected. In 1591 he went to France with Essex on an expedition to assist Henry IV militarily. Not long afterward, however, he apparently joined the other side and publicly became a Catholic. His father was said to have died as a result. Constable wrote a letter to the Countess of Shrewsbury, protesting that if his safety in England were not assured, he would stay in France. After a trip to Rome, he remained in France, living in Paris, occasionally traveling to Rouen, Scotland, Rome, Antwerp, and Brussels. He was often in need of money, although he had an irregular pension from Henry IV. Although he was a Catholic exile, he did not support the claim of Spain to the throne of England. He supported instead the claim of James VI of Scotland, from whom Catholics at least hoped for tolerance. For several years Constable schemed to assure the safety of English Catholics, the return of England to the Roman Catholic church, and the union of Catholics and Protestants. He tried to use the influence of Henry IV to secure some toleration for Catholics in England; he was part of a plot to convert the Queen of Scots to Catholicism; and he tried to convert James IV as well. He wrote some theological and political pieces, and in 1600 he went to Rome to persuade the Pope to support him in another excursion to Scotland. The attempt failed.

Constable returned to England after James I became king in 1603 and was permitted to possess his family's lands. He hoped, with the help of others, to convert James I, but in 1604 he was committed to the Tower of London after some letters revealing the scheme had been seized in France and sent back to England, probably by the King of France. Released in a few months, Constable was confined to his house. Once more deprived of his inheritance, he became dependent on kinsmen. For the next few years he was in and out of prison, until in 1610 he was either banished or simply permitted to leave the country.

After Henry IV's death, Constable returned to France. He died at Liège in 1613 after going there to help convert a Protestant minister. He lay meditating on the crucifix for several days before he died, demonstrating the truth of the words he had written while imprisoned in the Tower of London: "whether I remayn in prison, or go out, I have learned to live alone with God."

**Analysis**

In his courtly sonnets, collected in the *Diana*, Henry Constable used the traditional conventions of the Petrarchan sonnet. He was also influenced by the French and Italian sonnets of his contemporaries, particularly Philippe Desportes. The title *Diana* is borrowed from Desportes' chief sonnet sequence, and the Italian headlines in the work (sonnetto primo and so on) reveal the Italian influence.

His most recent editor, Joan Grundy, considers the Todd manuscript of this work to be the closest thing to an authoritative text, having been assembled before Constable's departure from England from poems that had been written over a period of time. There is an elaborate framework divided into three parts; these parts are then further divided into groups of seven sonnets. Constable provided explanatory titles, some notes on numerical symbolism, and the disclaimer that the sonnets are "vayne poems." In all his sonnets, Constable used the Petrarchan sonnet form abba abba cde cde, with variations.

Many of the sonnets in the *Diana* are love poems. In the sonnet "To his Mistrisse," which begins, "Grace full of grace," he declares that although these verses include love complaints to others, he now loves only her. The last three lines play on the word "grace" again, vowing that he flies to God for grace that he may live in delight or never love again. Grace was a theological concept with varying interpretations, as well as being part of a noble address and a woman's name. L. I. Guiney in *Recusant Poets* (1939) speculated that the "Grace" might be Grace Talbot, youngest daughter of George Talbot, sixth Earl of Shrewsbury. The last sonnet in the manuscript is "To the diuine protection of the Ladie Arbella the author commendeth both his Graces honoure and his Muses aeternitye." Arabella Stuart was the granddaughter of the Countess of Shrewsbury. Constable's sonnet "To the Countesse of Shrewsburye vpon occasion of his dear Mistrisse whoe liu'd vnder her gouer[n]ment" (Part III, group 3, sonnet 2), indicates that he loved someone in her company. It is not even certain, however, whether the sonnet was written to the Countess or to the Dowager Countess. The Countess has also been suggested as a candidate for Constable's Diana, and even Mary, Queen of Scots has been mentioned because she was in the custody of the Dowager Countess at one time. Another possibility is Penelope Rich. The Harrington manuscript consists of twenty-one sonnets appearing under the title "Mr. Henry Constable's sonetes to the Lady Ritche, 1589." Penelope Rich had requested Constable in a letter to Hotman "qu'il ne soit plus amoureux." This lady was Philip Sidney's Stella and she was involved in political intrigue with Constable.

In Part I, sonnet 3 of group 1, which deals with the "variable affections" of love, Constable uses repetition to great effect, combining it with antithesis. The first, fifth, and ninth lines begin, "Thyne eye," and the second, sixth, and tenth lines begin, "Myne eye." Her eye, he declares, is the mirror where he sees his heart, and his eye is a window through which her eye may see his heart; there, he says, she may see herself painted in bloody colors. Her eye is the "pyle" or pointed tip of a dart, and his eye is the aiming-point she uses to hit his heart. "Myne eye thus helpes thyne eye to work my smarte." Her eye is a fire and his eye a river of tears, but the water cannot extinguish the flames, nor can the fire dry up the streams from his eye. Constable's technique in this poem is to proceed by a series of parallel and antithetical metaphors. Some of them are traditional, but "Thine eye the pyle" is presumably original, at least in English, since the *Oxford English Dictionary* cites this poem as the earliest example of the word's usage. Shakespeare is thought to have imitated lines 1-4 of this poem in his Sonnet XXIV. Constable's contemporary, Alexander Montgomerie, wrote a Scots version of the sonnet.

In the first sonnet of the second group, "An Exhortation to the reader to come and see his Mistrisse beautie," Constable combines repetition with hyperbole. He repeats the word "come" twice in both line 1 and line 6, while in the sestet, "millions" becomes the dominant note, being repeated in lines 9, 10, and 12. Here he uses hyperbole ingeniously to praise the subject of the poem, who is a wonder of nature. He exhorts the reader to come and see her in order to write about her so that the next generation will lament being born too late to see her. Everyone should come and write about her, he protests, for the time may be too short and men too few to write the history of her least part, even though they should write constantly and about nothing else. In the sestet, he declares that the millions who write about her are too few to praise one of her features, and can only write about one aspect of her eye, her lip, or her hand, such as "The light or blacke the tast or red the soft or white." This poem was inspired by Petrarch's Sonnet CCXLVIII.

While the first part of *Diana* is about the "variable affections of loue," Constable points out in his "The order of the booke" that the first seven poems are about the beginning of love, the second seven are in praise of his mistress, and the third seven concern specific events in his love experience. In the second sonnet of this third set, "Of his Mistrisse vpon occasion of her walking in a garden," he personifies some of the flowers, making the roses red because they blush for shame when they see her lips and the lilies white because they become pale with envy of her. He indicates his own love by stating that the violets take their color from the blood his heart has shed for her. In the sestet, she becomes a kind of nature goddess. All flowers take their "vertue" from her and their smells from her breath; the heat from her eyes warms the earth, and she manages to water it as well by making him cry. Shakespeare imitated the opening of this sonnet in *The Rape of Lucrece* (1594), lines 477-479.

In the second sonnet of that same set, "To his Ladies hand vpon occasion of her gloue which in her absence he kissed," Constable uses a traditional theme, for there were many French and Italian poems addressed to the lady's hand, and the theme going back to Petrarch's Sonnet CXCIX. The idea of the hand shooting out arrows was also traditional, but Constable goes on to compare his five wounds caused by her five ivory arrows (her fingers) with the Stigmata of St. Francis. This poem, then, uses remarkably specific religious imagery. The stigmata were the impressions of the five wounds of Christ that St. Francis received on his flesh. Constable uses contrasts cleverly here, declaring that St. Francis did not feel the wounds, while he (Constable) lives in torment, and that the wounds of St. Francis were in his hands and feet, while his own wounds are in his heart. The metaphor becomes an elaborate conceit, for if he is therefore a saint like St. Francis, the bow which shot the shafts is a relic, and thus her hand should be kissed. Her glove is a divine thing because it is the quiver of her arrows (the covering of her hand) and the shrine of a relic (her hand).

Constable's *Spiritual Sonnets* praise God and His saints rather than an earthly love. The sequence begins with three sonnets to God the Father, the Son, and the Holy Ghost. The one praising God the Father begins by declaring that His essence and His existence are the same, the terminology being derived from scholastic philosophy. The essence of a being was the nature of the being, and existence was the actuality of the being. God's nature was to exist, for He was contingent on no other cause. The next lines reflect the idea that the mind of God reflects God, and thus that the Son of God is the Image of God the Father. The doctrine is based on St. Paul's description in Hebrews of the Son as "being the brightness of his glory, and the express image of his person." Constable makes use of this material in the poem, saying that there is mutual love between Father and Son, as the sighs of lovers become one breath, while both breathe one spirit of equal deity, the Holy Ghost. That the Holy Ghost proceeds from both the Father and the Son was orthodox Catholic doctrine. Constable ends the poem by asking God the Father, who wishes to have the title of Father, to engrave his mind with heavenly knowledge so that it may become His Son's image (continuing the image figure but applying it to himself), and by praying that his heart may become the temple of the Spirit, thus neatly linking the abstract theological discussion of the early part of the sonnet with the individual experience of God.

"To God the Sonne," the middle sonnet, is less abstract. The poet addresses Christ as "Great Prynce of heaven," begotten of the King and of the Virgin Queen, descendant of King David. After this royal beginning, he contrasts the angels singing at His birth with the shepherds playing their pipes; likewise, Kings become as humble shepherds for Christ's sake. Heaven and earth, high and low estate, all have a claim to Christ's birth, for he was begotten in heaven, was of kingly race on his mother's side, and was poor. In "To God the Holy Ghost," Constable becomes more abstract and theological again by way of allegorical personification, likening the Holy Ghost in heaven to the love with which the Son and the Father kiss. He describes how the Holy Ghost took the shape of a dove and of fiery tongues, and asks the Holy Ghost to bestow upon his love of God His wings and His fire, so that he may appear a seraphim in His sight. The burning quality of the seraphim in theological writings, such as Dionysius' *Celestial Hierarchy*, is here in keeping with the fiery nature of the Holy Ghost, for Constable asks the Holy Ghost for his wings and fire, two qualities of the seraphim that he wants to possess. This trinity of poems has sources in such writers as St. Augustine and Thomas Aquinas, but each poem is a personal prayer addressed to an aspect of God.

In "To the Blessed Sacrament," Constable relates the red wine and white Eucharist of the communion service to the red blood and white body of Christ, the body pale because of the shedding of blood. Christ's body is now veiled in white to be received by Constable in the Eucharist, as though in His burial sheet, making Constable into a burial vault or monument for the corpse. He prays that the Christ whom he has received into his body in the Eucharist will appear to his soul, which is imprisoned in earth the way his forefathers were suspended in Limbo when Christ gave them light. He asks Christ to clear his thoughts and free him in a similar way from the flames of evil desire. The poem is a unified sequence of Metaphysical conceits.

In "To the Blessed Lady" (the first of his poems with that title), Constable speaks of the Virgin Mary as a Queen of Queens, born without original sin. God the Father provided His Spirit for her spouse, and she conceived His only Son, and so she was linked with the whole Trinity. Queens of this earth should no longer glory in their role, for much greater honor is due the queen "Who had your God, for father, spowse, & sonne." Constable here delights in the realization of Mary's multiple relationships with God, an intellectual concept that holds the element of surprise.

At the beginning of the first of Constable's four poems on Mary Magdalen, he alludes to the saint's legendary retiring to a penitential life in Provence, saying that "For few nyghtes solace in delitious bedd," she did penance "nak'd on nak'd rocke in desert cell" for thirty years. He speaks directly to her in the poem, saying that for each tear she shed, she has a sea of pleasure now. The poem develops through a series of contrasts. In one of his other poems to the same saint, he begins by saying that she can better declare to him the pleasures of heavenly love than someone who has never experienced any other loves, or than someone who is not a woman, for his soul will be like a woman once moved by lust, but then betrothed to God's Son. His body is "the garment of my spryght" in the daytime of his life, and death will bring "the nyght of my delyght." His soul will be "vncloth'd," and resting from labor, "clasped in the armes of God," will "inioye/ by sweete coniunction, everlastying ioye." The poem proceeds by a complicated sequence of analogies and contrasts: Mary Magdalen knew earthly love, knew heavenly love; his soul is like her, having experienced lust and spiritual love; in the day, his soul is covered with the garment of his body, but in the night of mystical union with God it will be naked.

In his sonnets Constable praises his subjects, both secular and religious, by comparisons (some traditional and some highly original and Metaphysical), and often by ironic contrasts expressed with grammatical parallelism. His wording is simple and there is much deliberate repetition. Through his carefully reasoned and highly-polished sonnets he communicates very well both his love of Diana and his love of God.

**Major publications other than poetry**

NONFICTION: *A short vew of a large examination of Cardinall Allen his trayterous justification of Sir W. Stanley and Yorck*, c. 1588; *Examen pacifique de la doctrine des Huguenots*, 1589 (*The Catholike Moderator: Or, A Moderate Examination of the Doctrine of the Protestants*).

**Bibliography**

Guiney, L. I. *Recusant Poets*, 1939.

Lee, Sidney. "Henry Constable," in *Dictionary of National Biography from the Beginning to 1900*, 1953. Edited by Leslie Stephen and Sidney Lee.

_____ , ed. *Elizabethan Sonnets: An English Garner*, 1964.

Wickes, George. "Henry Constable: Courtier Poet," in *Renaissance Papers*. April, 1956, pp. 102-107.

_____ . "Henry Constable, Poet and Courtier, 1562-1613," in *Biographical Studies*. II, no. 4 (1954), pp. 272-300.

# CID CORMAN

**Born:** Boston, Massachusetts; June 29, 1924

**Principal collections**

*subluna*, 1945; *A Thanksgiving Ecologue from Theocritus*, 1954; *The Precisions*, 1955; *The Responses*, 1956; *Stances and Distances*, 1957; *The Marches*, 1957; *A Table in Provenance*, 1958; *The Descent from Daimonji*, 1959; *For Sure*, 1959; *Sun Rock Man*, 1962; *In Good Time*, 1964; *In No Time*, 1964; *Nonce*, 1965; *For You*, 1966; *For Granted*, 1966; *Back Roads to Far Towns*, 1967 (translation); *Words for Each Other*, 1968; *& Without End*, 1968; *No More*, 1969; *Plight*, 1969; *Livingdying*, 1970; *Things*, 1971 (translation);*Out and Out*, 1972; *Leaves of Hypnos*, 1973; *Breathings*, 1974 (translation); $\stackrel{\circ}{\intercal}$, 1974; *Once and for All: Poems for William Bronk*, 1975; *Aegis*, 1982 (selected poems).

**Other literary forms**

Cid Corman's oeuvre is immense. In addition to his many volumes of poetry, he has published a large number of translations from the French, German, Italian, and Japanese. These have not only appeared as separate volumes, including the work of such diverse writers as Matsuo Bashō, Shimpei Kusano, René Char, Francis Ponge, and Phillippe Jaccottet, but also lie scattered throughout his books and magazine publications. These latter include a virtual pantheon of major writers, among them Eugenio Montale, Mario Luzi, René Daumal, Paul Celan, as well as many little-known European and Asian writers.

Corman has been equally prolific as an essayist and commentator on contemporary letters. Several of his essays have been published in *Word for Word: Essays on the Art of Language* (1977). Corman has, in addition, maintained an enormous literary and cultural correspondence with other writers and intellectuals.

**Achievements**

Among poets of his generation, no figure stands more at the center of both poetic activity and influence than Cid Corman. As poet, translator, and one of contemporary letters' most important editors, Corman has been generator, clearing house, arbitrator, and gadfly, presiding at one of the most fertile and creative periods of American poetry. Through his own poetry and through his still-active twenty-five-year editorship of *Origin* magazine, Corman has been a central reference point in the poetic battleground of the postwar years. *Origin*, which published William Carlos Williams, Louis Zukofsky, Charles Olson, Robert Creeley, Denise Levertov, and Robert Duncan, performed for its time what T. S. Eliot's *Criterion, The Dial,* and *The Literary Review* performed for theirs as major grounds of modern writing.

Both Corman's poetry and his translations, still in need of major critical attention, have been of great importance to younger writers. The essential lines of Corman's poetic style were established in his earliest books, and its simplicity of structure and depth of realization marked a maturity of stance that younger poets, in the ongoing literary ferment, have turned to as a kind of spiritual and intellectual benchmark. This early maturity, based on Corman's desire for a poetry that would not engage in the more self-indulgent (hence more popular) styles of writing of its time, claimed for poetry a philosophical sense of anonymity, a nonaggressive quality that seemed, given Corman's unique position, to be an eye in the center of the literary storm. This quality, evident in all of Corman's work, gives his voice a peculiarly important place among his contemporaries, for its tact and quiet come not out of diffidence but out of a difficult assuredness not often found in American literary life.

### Biography

The two major poles of Cid Corman's life have been the United States and Japan, specifically Boston and Kyoto. Close study of his work shows how it embodies both the tensions of urban American life, social and literary, and the qualities of philosophical serenity and complex identification with nature associated with the Orient. Corman was born in Boston and attended the Boston Latin School and then Tufts University, where he was graduated (Phi Beta Kappa) in 1945. He did graduate work at the University of Michigan, where he won a Hopwood Award in Poetry. Back in Boston, Corman ran what was to be the first of his "editorial" contributions to modern poetry, a weekly radio program on WMEX which presented the best of contemporary poets in the Boston area. In 1951, he began *Origin* magazine, which he has continued to publish to this day. A "Fulbright" to Paris and a year as an English instructor in Matera, Italy (the source for much of the material of Corman's early volumes of poetry), were the initial phases of Corman's voyaging away from America in order to discover and resolve the contradictions of literary self-exile. Such exile was, and is, Corman's major theme. After returning to the United States, Corman made the first of his trips to Kyoto, spent two years in San Francisco, and then returned to Kyoto, where he stayed for more than sixteen years.

In Kyoto Corman's work and influence flourished. There he not only wrote an enormous amount of poetry but also published in a simple and elegant format *Origin* magazine, sending it back to the United States for argument, discussion, and protest, as well as distribution. For Corman, the activity in Kyoto, along with the influence of the city's famous Zen teachers, made the Japanese city one of the necessary places of pilgrimage of American poetry.

To contemporary poets who visited or lived in Kyoto, such as Gary Snyder, Philip Whalen, and Clayton Eshleman, Corman's activities and, indeed, his physical presence in the coffee shop that he and his Japanese wife, Shizumi, ran, meant serious engagement and encounter with some of the strongest literary currents of the 1960's and 1970's.

In 1979, Corman returned to Boston, where he continues to write and edit both his own work and *Origin*, now in its fourth series.

**Analysis**

In one of his earliest books, *Sun Rock Man*, Cid Corman writes: "Already I feel breathless/ as if I have come too far,/ to find peace, to have found it." The thread linking more than thirty years of Corman's poetry, translation, and editorship is the quest back toward some deep original peace, some attempt to find a permanent home in exile. Corman's work is one long and moving dialectic, informed by his sense of having "come too far" and yet of being unable to return. The shifts, both technical and in terms of subject matter, that one discovers in his poems are like signposts pointing both forward and backward at once; they remind the reader that every act of creation has been one of decreation as well, that self-exile for Corman means also new territory.

In Corman's career, this new territory has meant, geographically, first Europe, then almost twenty years in Japan. One sees, in particular, the Japanese influence in the details of Corman's verse: his affinity for natural objects and the short, almost Oriental, tightness of his forms. Yet far more important has been the psychological and literary territory Corman has traversed. Psychically, this terrain embraces the open spaces of poetic activity, of "making it new" as chartered by such forebears as William Carlos Williams, Ezra Pound, and Louis Zukofsky. Like the poetry of these predecessors, Corman's work is a departure from the traditional verse conventions of its time; it is marked, as well, by a willingness to bear the immediate deflections of incident, encounter, or thought much as Williams' poetry submitted to the "local" or Zukofsky's to the dictates of the musical phrase. Corman's work can be said to seek its timelessness in its very moment. Thus his poems are spontaneous registers of isolation, of immersion in somewhat alien landscapes where both the native or local language and its cultural iconography are essentially mute; yet it is also immersion in that deeper awareness of world and people caught in the inarticulateness of their situations. In Corman much is characterized as silent, as unknowable. Rather than raiding the inarticulate, Corman's work attempts to come to terms with it, to construct a language that seems to represent a shared act of man and world.

Corman's earliest published poems, such as those in *Sun Rock Man*, attempt to render precisely these occasions of inarticulateness. In them, Corman employs an imagist or objectivist technique, which rigorously favors the recording eye over the conceptualizing mind. The poet is an agency or a recording instrument, and the abject poverty and hopelessness of Matera, an impoverished Italian hill town, is witnessed "objectively." Authorial control is maintained, as it were, only by the details to be selected. Poems such as "the dignities" or "Luna Park" operate under the force of Williams' "no ideas but in things," realized with an eye and ear for detail and tone that are compelling and satisfying; they seem to present an almost pure externality which speaks so eloquently and powerfully that comment is superfluous.

In the end, however, one feels that such poems may rely too heavily on their being a form of *exotica*, particularly when their occasion is almost solely the function of the poet's arrival on the scene. Indeed, the less formally accomplished poems of *Sun Rock Man* suggest a troubled and yet more fruitful ambivalence, for they sound the note which in Corman's career has its most significant distinction: a deepening capacity to express simultaneously the subjective and the objective terms of situations. As he says of his stay in Matera, "Nothing displaces us/ like our own intelligence."

This displacement, suggesting a leave-taking that is both poetic and physical, is the major theme of all of Corman's mature work. The exile is not simply one of banishment to strange lands but to a kind of Rilkean soul-work of facing out on the "speechlessness" of the world. Thus, in nearly all the poems after *Sun Rock Man*, the visual imagistic technique, while not abandoned, is forsworn in favor of rendering the physicality of voicing itself, in an attempt to say without inflation or rhetoric the meaning for the poet of such speechlessness.

Corman's poems often begin within an action, as though the poet finds himself surprised by circumstance into utterance. The prepositions or relational conjunctions, the statements containing continuous verb forms ("finding," "remembering," and so on) found at the head of many of Corman's poems are devices for signaling the organic connection between the active and changing content of the poet's situation and the arising of the poem. Rather than the "picture-making" or mimesis of the earlier poems (or of the more imagistically inclined poet), these poems are specifically linguistic occasions, not meant to hold the mirror up to nature but to sound it. Thus in one poem about a bell in *And Without End*, it is, as he puts it, "as if the/ air needed clearing,/ as if the sweet sound/ were a vanishing." The poem may be said to seek, like the sound of the bell, to have both its distinctness and its completeness, completeness in the sense that though sound is invisible and adds nothing visual to the picture, it permeates and thus colors everything within hearing. Such soundings have a tactful and nonjudgmental quality about them; there is, as in many other of Corman's poems, a Buddhistic or Zen-like sense of aesthetic appreciation that is, as the poem continues "so clear/ it hardly matters to say more than 'See if you can hear it'/ and 'it' is a bell."

Corman's poems have a way of establishing an equanimity or resting place for memory. They involve an uncovering effect, moving from an unspecified dramatic statement to a highly qualified core of meaning. This meaning often resides less in a particular line or statement than in the cumulative effect of passage through the poem. In a poem entitled "Back" (in ⚬̶), for example, a device similar to the "bell" sound of the poem discussed above utilizes repetition and variants of tone or phrase to advance and specify meaning. Generalized "man" becomes "me" "given to go on"; a "call/ summoning/ all plays on" until the "event" is so "taken to/ heart" that "heart at/ height flings out." The intelligence of the poem resolves itself not only ideationally but virtually at the level of the syllable (something Corman has learned well from Zukofsky and Olson), where each moment of development is anticipated musically. In Corman, the minims of speech are deployed much like the quavers of traditional song, as both accents and resistances to the plain meanings of words.

Such fine tuning informs all of Corman's work. The poems seem to draw attention to little more than their own process of realization, as though the form of thought that the poet engenders—though given as language—takes on the characteristics of a visual construct, something cleanly and sparingly drawn. Critics have referred to the "haiku-like" qualities of Corman's verse, but it is perhaps more accurate to note its peculiar transformation of imagistic technique into the realm of thought, as though the processes of the mind could be delineated as carefully as the leaf on a plum branch.

This confrontation with silence—since silence cannot respond, only evoke—becomes in Corman a form of self-realization, an embodying of poetic utterance which has its root in both estrangement and participation. The poet is at all costs trying to make a home in this homelessness, and the tension of his poetry is the attempt to give this silence its due:

> Don't make me laugh
> or I'll cry: that's the cry,
> Here me, my silence,
> in silence.

The key to such poetry is that both its solipsistic and playful qualities are embedded in the ironies of ambiguity and tone. There is something deeply comic and even lighthearted in Corman's address to a language-less world—comic in the very basic sense that seriousness and any heavy-handed desire to mean are always operative under the meaning-canceling sign of death. As Corman notes in one poem:

> in time go
> words also, however true
> Man's life is a conjuring
> finally nothing once more.

This air of "finally nothing" pervades Corman's most recent work, giving the sense of exile both ease and humor, transfiguring the past and its pains into a newer richness and balance. Here the self fully recognizes itself as a transparency, an agency which works on and gives voice to its interferences. Poetic tension comes out of the drama and new knowledge is gained in reconciliation with the modalities of the past. Thus, Corman writes:

> To bear back the lost
> is at all events
> much like entering
> the enemy's lines
> to plead for one's dead
> for burial.

Corman's poems seek out what the phenomenologists would call the "pre-objective world"; that is the world existing before overlaps of human concept and understanding. At the same time, they suggest that the self, about which it is easy to be glib, is no more easily grasped than that exterior world. The strength of the poetry derives from Corman's urge to pare down to that world, to reduce, to silence language to all but its essential qualities, to make it, as he says in "Morion," a poem about a gem which resembles an Arp sculpture: "Nothing extra,/ all edge and no edge./ solid heart. What one/ offers another."

Such poetry has the feel of a natural object; its spareness resists the desire to appropriate it, calling instead for tact and subtlety in response. Unlike much contemporary poetry, Corman's poems refuse to trade on present anxieties, refuse to be converted into a form of moral coinage—there is barely a word in these poems about the "big issues." Nevertheless, they insinuate themselves into one's moral consciousness by going to ground, by addressing the self at its most affective point, the economy of its own organization: "Doorways/ reveal my/ shadow and/ make me ask/ myself once/ more if this/ mask I wear/ of words keeps/ my body/ clear of breath."

This grounding acts like an Archimedean lever on ordinary notions of identity, and thus gives an astonishing capaciousness to the small forms which Corman so skillfully uses. One would almost want to claim for this poetry a ripple effect, or claim—and here its comparison to haiku is warranted—that it introduces an irruption into the quotidian while at the same time preserving the flavor of the quotidian intact. Such poetry does not easily lend itself to paraphrase or exegesis, nor are its larger incursions into consciousness as immediate as certain more fashionable confessional modes of writing.

This delayed effect and the fact that Corman's work is both large in bulk (he is one of the most prolific poets writing today) and scattered throughout many volumes and little-known magazines, accounts for the lack of a larger critical effort directed at his work. Another reason may be that his work, seen only fitfully, is regarded as only another part of the vast output of American lyricism.

Yet Corman, rightly perceived, is not a lyric poet at all, but, like Ezra Pound, a poet of the epic. It can be said of modern poetry that the lyric has overshadowed the epic, that given the alienated or fragmented sense of self which constitutes contemporary life, the narrative drive required for the epic form can no longer be sustained. One can also read much contemporary poetry as a counter-epic, celebrating, instead of a hero's overcoming obstacles, the hero's sense of loss, discovering, as with Eliot, the fragments to shore against the ruins. By contrast, Corman's poetry would intimate a third way, where the epic has merely gone interior, where the story's arc travels across and engages the adventures of consciousness. Surely Corman's poems might be letters home from such a voyage, reminders in their cumulative reconciliations of sight and sound, of place and identity, that self and world are indeed home for each other.

## Major publications other than poetry
NONFICTION: *William Bronk: An Essay*, 1976; *Word for Word: Essays on the Art of Language*, 1977.

## Bibliography
*Madrona*. III (December, 1975), special Corman issue.
Taggert, John. *A Bibliography of Works by Cid Corman*, 1975.

*Michael Heller*

# GREGORY CORSO

**Born:** New York, New York; March 26, 1930

## Principal poems and collections

*The Vestal Lady of Brattle, and Other Poems*, 1955; *Gasoline*, 1958; "Bomb," 1958; "Marriage," 1959; *The Happy Birthday of Death*, 1960; *Minutes to Go, with Others*, 1960; *Long Live Man*, 1962; *Selected Poems*, 1962; *The Mutation of the Spirit*, 1964; *There Is Yet Time to Run Back Through Life and Expiate All That's Been Sadly Done*, 1965; *Ten Times a Poem*, 1967; *Elegiac Feelings American*, 1970; *Herald of the Autochthonic Spirit*, 1981.

## Other literary forms

Although Gregory Corso has published mainly poetry, he has also written a short play, *In This Hung-up Age*, produced at Harvard University in 1955; a novel, *The American Express* (1961); and two film scripts: *Happy Death*, with Jay Socin, produced in New York in 1965; and *The Little Black Door on the Left*, included in a group of screenplays entitled *Pardon Me, Sir, But Is My Eye Hurting Your Elbow?* (1968). He has also written, with Anselm Hollo and Tom Raworth, a series of parodies, *The Minicab War*, published in London by the Matrix Press in 1961.

His poems have been translated into at least six languages and also appear on several recordings along with the works and conversations of other Beat poets such as Lawrence Ferlinghetti and Allen Ginsberg. An extensive interview, illustrated with photographs of Corso, as well as with several of his drawings, appeared in *Writings from Unmuzzled Ox Magazine* (1981). The *Unmuzzled Ox*, playfully self-identified as "a magazine of Pre-Anti-Post-Modernism," had published two previous Corso issues in the early 1970's (called *The Japanese Notebook Ox*), but this is the first reprint of an entire Corso issue (May, 1973) in book form.

## Achievements

Perhaps Corso's greatest contribution to the Beat movement specifically and American poetry generally lies in his role as a literary paradigm, so to speak, for the "New Bohemianism" appearing in America after World War II and through the 1950's. Corso, more than any of his contemporaries, lived the true Beat life. Brought up in the slums of New York City, with practically no formal education, Corso was, in the words of the poet-critic Kenneth Rexroth, "a genuine *naif*. A real wildman, with all the charm of a hoodlum . . . a wholesome Antonin Artaud."

Despite the fact that Corso never went beyond elementary school, he soon gained the reputation of being one of the most talented of the "Beat Generation" school of writers. Following the 1955 publication of *The Vestal Lady of Brattle, and Other Poems* and his meeting with Jack Kerouac, Allen Ginsberg, and Gary Snyder a year later, his poetry began to appear often in such publications as *Esquire, Partisan Review, Contact,* and the *Evergreen Review.*

In 1958, Lawrence Ferlinghetti first published Corso's famous "Bomb" poem as a broadside at his City Lights Bookshop in San Francisco, as well as the book *Gasoline* in the same year. After an extended tour of England, France, Germany, Italy, and Greece, Corso returned to the United States in 1961, finding himself viewed as a sort of *enfant terrible* of the Beat generation. During the following three years he was even hired to teach poetry for a term at New York State University at Buffalo on the basis of his reputation as a major figure in the Beat movement—a kind of John Keats or Percy Bysshe Shelley of American Bohemianism. In this context, he was awarded the Longview Foundation Award in 1959 for his poem "Marriage"; he also received the Poetry Foundation Award.

### Biography

Gregory Corso was born in New York City to poor Italian immigrant parents, Fortunato Samuel and Michelina (Colloni) Corso. His mother died when he was a child, and about this loss Corso has written: "I do not know how to accept love when love is given me. I needed that love when I was motherless young and never had it." His unhappy childhood was marked by his being sent to an orphanage at eleven and to the Children's Observation Ward at Bellevue when he was thirteen. At that time, Corso later wrote, "I was alone in the world—no mother and my father was at war . . . to exist I stole minor things and to sleep I slept on the rooftops and in the subway." In summarizing his thirteenth year, however, Corso insists that although he went "through a strange hell that year" of 1943, it is "such hells that give birth to the poet."

After three years on the streets of New York, having lived with five different foster parents, Corso was arrested with two friends while attempting to rob a store. Instead of being sent to a boy's reformatory, Corso was sentenced to three years at Clinton Prison, which, according to the poet, "proved to be one of the greatest things that ever happened to me." He even dedicated his second book of poems, *Gasoline,* "to the angels of Clinton Prison" who forced him to give up the often "silly consciousness of youth" to confront the world of men.

After being released from prison in 1950, Corso took on a number of short-term jobs, including working as a manual laborer from 1950 to 1951, becoming a reporter for the *Los Angeles Examiner* from 1951 to 1952 and sailing on Norwegian vessels as a merchant seaman from 1952 to 1953. He also spent some time in Mexico and in Cambridge, Massachusetts, where he was encouraged in his writing of poetry by an editor of the *Cambridge Review,* and where, with the support of several Harvard students, he published his first book of poetry, *The Vestal Lady of Brattle, and Other Poems*, 1955.

Between that time and his departure for Europe in 1959, Corso attracted widespread attention with a series of poetry readings he gave in the East and Midwest. In November, 1963, after returning from his European travels, he married Sally November. For Corso, the decade of the 1960's was marked by a divorce and more travel in Europe. After the publication of *The Happy Birthday of Death* in 1960, which included such celebrated poems as "Bomb," "Power," "Army," and the award-winning "Marriage," the work that he did in the following decade was very uneven, frequently bordering on flippancy and sentimentality, as in the poems comprising *Long Live Man* and *The Mutation of the Spirit*.

His most recent collections of poems, *Elegiac Feelings American* and *Herald of the Autochthonic Spirit*, were published a decade apart, appearing in 1970 and 1981, respectively. The increased intervals between offerings indicates a shift in Corso's attitude toward the relationship between the poet and his poems. During the salad days of the Beat movement, Corso took his cue from his contemporaries (notably Kerouac) by rejecting any mode of writing except pure spontaneity, but his later and current poems are much more carefully revised and tightly crafted works.

**Analysis**

Carolyn Gaiser, in 1961, wrote that "The mask that is most distinctly Gregory Corso's [is] the mask of the sophisticated child." Every display of spontaneity and mad perception in Gregory Corso's poetry, she contends, is "consciously and effectively designed." Because Corso's poetry has matured since Gaiser's comment, however, it is now possible to step back and view it in a broader context. From his early poems to his current work, one finds the recurring persona of the clown as an embodiment of the Dionysian force of emotion and spontaneity, as opposed to the Apollonian powers of order, clarity, and moderation. The clown's comedy, which has its root in the very fact of being "a poet in such a world as the world is today," ranges from the mischievous laughter of the child to the darker, often somber irony of the poet-in-the-world.

In an early collection, *Gasoline*, Corso solidifies his poetic identity in a directly autobiographical poem, "In the Fleeting Hand of Time." Here the poet casts his lot not with the Apollonian academics, who "lay forth sheepskin plans," but with life in the "all too real mafia streets." In another poem from this early collection, entitled "Birthplace Revisited," the poet captures what Allen Ginsberg refers to as "the inside sound of language alone" by virtually overturning the expected or commonplace. This brief poem opens with a mysterious figure wandering the lonely, dark street, seeking out the place where he was born. The figure resembles a character from a detective story—

in mouth, hat over eye, hand on gat"—but when he ... st flight of stairs, "Dirty Ears aims a knife at me . . . watches." This is not exactly the kind of image one ... the language of the standard-bearers of Corso's time, ... John Crowe Ransom. In fact, in an act of Dionysian ... a poem entitled "I Am 25," bluntly proclaims "I HATE ..."—especially those "who speak their youth in whispers." ... true Dionysian fashion, would like to gain the confidence ... an," insinuating himself into the sanctity of his home, and ... ir apology tongues/ and steal their poems."

... rk, *Long Live Man* (1962), he continues his Dionysian assault ... iterary conventions. The poem "After Reading 'In the Clear- ... ple, finds the speaker admitting that he likes the "Old Poet- ... rost better now that he knows he is "no Saturday Evening Post ... Nevertheless, Frost is "old, old" like Rome, and, says the poet, "You u... tedly think unwell of us/ but we are your natural children." What Corso intends is not to suggest that youth should respect age, but rather, as William Wordsworth wrote in "Ode: Intimations of Immortality," "the child is father to the man." For, as Corso points out in his urban poem, "A City Child's Day," the "Grownups do not go where children go/ At break of day their worlds split apart."

*The Happy Birthday of Death*, published two years before *Long Live Man*, presents the best example of Corso as Dionysian clown. In the lengthy ten-part poem entitled simply "Clown," Corso presents this persona more explicitly than he does in any other place when he asserts that "I myself am my own happy fool." The fool or the clown is the personification of the "pure poetry" of Arthur Rimbaud or Walt Whitman, rejecting the academic Apollonian style of the formalists. "I am an always clown," writes Corso, "and need not make grammatic Death's diameter."

Several of the poems of *The Happy Birthday of Death*, notably the award-winning "Marriage," offer critiques of respected institutions of bourgeois society. This poem, perhaps Corso's most popular, is structured around a central question: "Should I get married? Should I be good?" In a surrealistic feast of language-play, Corso contrasts the social ritual of marriage ("absurd rice and clanky cans and shoes," Niagara Falls honeymoons, cornball relatives) with the irrational and spontaneous phrases he inserts throughout the poem, such as "Flash Gordon soap," "Pie Glue," "Radio Belly! Cat Shovel!" and "Christmas Teeth." In opposition to the conformist regimentation of suburban life, the speaker contrives unconventional schemes, such as sneaking onto a neighbor's property late at night and "hanging pictures of Rimbaud on the lawnmower" or covering "his golf clubs with 1920 Norwegian books."

Two short poems in the earlier *Long Live Man*, viewed together, seem to foreshadow the approach Corso later used to criticize the institution of marriage and, still later, in his two most recent books, *Elegiac Feeling American* and *Herald of the Autochthonic Spirit*, to maintain his Dionysian critique of Apollonian standards. The first poem is entitled "Suburban Mad Song"; the second, "The Love of Two Seasons." The first asks how the wife will look at the husband after "the horns are still"—when the celebration is ended—"and marriage drops its quiet shoe." In other words, when the Dionysian passion of the first experiences become the frozen form—the institution—the once-happy couple "freeze right in their chairs/ troubled by the table." The only solution for such stasis, Corso seems to be saying in the other short poem, "The Love of Two Seasons," is "the aerial laughter [of] mischief."

In "The American Way," a long poem from *Elegiac Feeling American*, Corso worries that the prophetic force of Christ is becoming frozen by American civil religion. "They are frankensteining Christ," the poet says despairingly; "they are putting the fear of Christ in America" and "bringing their Christ to the stadiums." Christ, for Corso, is the pure force of reality, while religious institutions are merely perversions even as love between two people is a pure and sacred force, while marriage is profane. "If America falls," writes Corso, "It will be the blame of its educators preachers communicators alike."

The *Herald of the Autochthonic Spirit*, Corso's latest book, suggests that not only has the poet, now over fifty, not withered with age, but that he has mastered an ironic voice while maintaining his comic, childlike energy. In a simple poem, "When a Boy," remarks, first of all, how he "monitored the stairs/ alter'd the mass" in church, as opposed to the pleasure of summer camp when he "kissed the moon in a barrel of rain." Similarly, in the poem "Youthful Religious Experience" he tells how he found a dead cat when he was six years old and compassionately prayed for it, placing a cross on the animal. When he told this to the Sunday school teacher, she pulled his ears and told him to remove the cross. The old, Corso maintains, can never comprehend the eternally young.

The romantic—and Corso is certainly in the tradition of Keats and Shelley—sees the child as a pure, spontaneous Dionysian being; always naturally perceptive, always instinctively aware of sham, pretense, and deception. Such perception runs throughout American literature, from the character of Pearl in Nathaniel Hawthorne's *The Scarlet Letter* (1850), to the child who "went forth" in Walt Whitman, to Huckleberry Finn in Mark Twain's novel, to Holden Caulfield in J. D. Salinger's *The Catcher in the Rye* (1951). Similarly, in Corso's poetry the child (particularly the self of the poet's recollection) stands for pure Dionysian perception without the intervening deceptions of rules and conventions.

In "What the Child Sees," another poem included in his most recent publication, Corso depicts the child as "innocently contemptuous of the sight" of old age's foolishness. "There's rust on the old truths," Corso contends in

"For Homer," and "New lies don't smell as nice as new shoes." What the poet—like the child—perceives as pleasurable is the immediate, sensual experience, such as the smell of new shoes, not the abstractions of dried-up old lies. The sadness at the root of this pleasure, however, is a sadness that appears in much of Corso's poetry, evoked by the perennial reality of death. In a poem dedicated to one of his heroes, entitled "I Met This Guy Who Died," Corso writes about a drunken outing with his friend Jack Kerouac. Taken home to see Corso's newborn child, Kerouac moans: "Oh Gregory, You brought up something to die."

Corso is passionately concerned with the mystery of death, a theme that is more pervasive in his work than any other, with the exception of the pure experience of childhood. Indeed, the intermingling of these two motifs essentially characterizes the Dionysian spirit of Corso—as well as the art of the Beat generation in general. "How I love to probe life," Corso writes in an autobiographical essay. "That's what poetry is to me, a wondrous prober. . . . It's not the metre or measure of a line, a breath not 'law' music, but the assembly of great eye sounds placed into an inspired measured idea."

## Major publications other than poetry
NOVEL: *The American Express*, 1961.
FICTION: *The Minicab War*, 1961 (with Anselm Hollo and Tom Raworth).
PLAYS: *In This Hung-up Age*, 1955; *Happy Death*, 1965 (screenplay, with Jay Socin); *The Little Black Door on the Left*, 1968 (screenplay).
MISCELLANEOUS: *Writings from Unmuzzled Ox Magazine*, 1981.

## Bibliography
Cook, Bruce. *The Beat Generation*, 1971.
Glikes, Edwin. *Of Poetry and Power*, 1963.
Parkinson, Thomas. *A Casebook on the Beats*, 1961.
Nemerov, Howard. *Poets on Poetry*, 1966.
Wilson, Robert. *A Bibliography of Works by Corso*, 1966.

*Donald E. Winters, Jr.*

# CHARLES COTTON

**Born:** Beresford Hall, England; April 28, 1630
**Died:** London, England; February 16, 1687

**Principal poems and collections**

"An Elegie upon the Lord Hastings," 1649; *A Panegyrick to the King's Most Excellent Majesty*, 1660; "The Answer," 1661; *Scarronides: Or, Virgile Travestie*, 1664; *A Voyage to Ireland in Burlesque*, 1670; *Horace*, 1671 (translation of a play, with original lyric poetry); *Burlesque upon Burlesque*, 1675; "To my dear and most worthy Friend, Mr. Izaak Walton," 1675; "The Retirement," 1676; *The Wonders of the Peake*, 1681; *Poems on Several Occasions*, 1689; *Genuine Works*, 1715.

**Other literary forms**

Apart from his original poetry, Charles Cotton also published translations and burlesques (now of minor interest), books on planting and gaming, and a treatise on fly fishing that became part two of Izaak Walton's *The Compleat Angler* (1676). He is not known to have written fiction, essays, or pamphlets. As with most seventeenth century figures, there is no diary and not much correspondence. Consequently, information on Cotton's day-to-day life is sparse, and many of his poems (which circulated in manuscript) cannot be precisely dated.

**Achievements**

During his lifetime and throughout the eighteenth century, Cotton was known almost exclusively as a writer of burlesques and translations. His rendering of Michel de Montaigne into idiomatic English prose was particularly admired. Today, however, Cotton is esteemed as a congenial minor poet of the Restoration period who anticipated aspects of Romanticism in his verse and who collaborated belatedly with Walton to produce one of the most popular books in English literature. Yet Cotton is a significant landscape poet, a perceptive observer of rural life, an often graceful lyricist, and a distinguished regionalist.

Not until the Romantic period was Cotton taken seriously as an original versifier. Charles Lamb, a lover of old books, rediscovered Cotton's *Poems on Several Occasions* more than a century after their publication and quoted several of them delightedly in a letter of March 5, 1803. He selected four examples of Cotton's work to be included in Robert Southey's *Specimens of the Later English Poets* (1807): "Song. Montross," "The Litany," "The Retirement," and the "Morning" quatrain. William Wordsworth discussed, praised, and quoted Cotton's "Winter" quatrains in his famous Preface to the *Poems* of 1815. Samuel Taylor Coleridge extolled Cotton's *Poems on Several Occa-*

*sions* in *Biographia Literaria* (1817), Chapter XIX. Lamb, again, called special attention to Cotton's poem "The New Year" in his essay "New Year's Eve" (*Essays of Elia*, 1823), and with this, Cotton's poetic reputation was at its peak. Cotton lost favor during the Victorian years and proved less interesting to the earlier twentieth century than more complicated Metaphysical poets such as John Donne. Though holding a place in the literary history of seventeenth century England, Cotton has never been regarded as a major writer.

## Biography

Charles Cotton was born at Beresford Hall, Staffordshire, on April 28, 1630. The only child of Charles and Olive Stanhope Cotton, he was, like his father, a country squire with literary interests—and a Royalist. The English Civil War which began when he was twelve, inspired Cotton with a vision of worldwide chaos that he soon expressed in verse through descriptions of the adjacent Peak District scenery in Derbyshire. From about 1648 to 1655, young Charles was tutored by Ralph Rawson, who is mentioned in several of Cotton's early poems and who in turn addressed a poem to him. Cotton's first published poem was "An Elegie upon the Lord Hastings" (1649); Hastings had died the same year at the age of nineteen. Other poems lamenting Hasting's death were written by John Dryden, Robert Herrick, Andrew Marvell, John Denham, Sir Aston Cokayne, Alexander Brome, and John Bancroft. It cannot be said that Cotton's was the best. In 1651, he wrote another elegy, on Lord Derby, a Royalist who was captured after the Battle of Worcester and beheaded on October 15, 1651. His strong political feelings were made further apparent in "The Litany" and in "To Poet E____ W____ ," the latter castigating Edmund Waller for his servile obsequiousness in the face of the Cromwellian regime. Cotton wrote all of these potentially seditious poems as a young bachelor in his twenties. Like almost all his shorter verse, they remained unpublished during his lifetime.

Throughout the winter of 1655-1656 Cotton was in France. From there, he addressed several poems of amorous longing to Isabella Hutchinson ("Chloris"), whom he married on June 30, 1656, and who bore him nine children before her death in 1669. She may also have been the inspiration for "On Christmas-Day, 1659," which is the only one of Cotton's major poems to be concerned with orthodox religion. Its happy mood anticipated the impending restoration of the monarchy, which took place on May 29, 1660; Cotton then wrote *A Panegyrick to the King's Most Excellent Majesty*, celebrating a day that must have been as exhilarating to him as that of his own wedding.

For the next twenty-five years Cotton published the literary works (not all of them precisely datable) upon which his immediate reputation would rest. Thus, in 1661, "The Answer" (to Alexander Brome) celebrated that "dusty corner of the World" which Cotton called his own and the return of his humble Muse, which for the next few years manifested itself primarily in translations.

A prose translation of *The Moral Philosophy of the Stoicks* (1664), from the French of Guillaume Du Vair, preceded Cotton's famous *Scarronides*, a daringly bawdy verse burlesque of Vergil. Named for a previous French work (Paul Scarron's *Virgile travesti*, 1648), it became Cotton's most popular poem, which Samuel Pepys, among others, thought "extraordinary good" (*Diary*, March 2, 1664). To a modern critic such as James Sutherland, on the other hand, it seems nothing more than a "crude, sniggering, schoolboy denigration" of an immortal poet whom force-fed students of the classics were all too willing to disparage. Whatever its worth as literature, *Scarronides* remained central to Cotton's reputation until the nineteenth century. In 1666, however, he wrote the "Winter" quatrains, which were later to be praised by Wordsworth.

When his wife died in 1669, Cotton (who married again five years later) left Beresford Hall long enough to head a military expedition to Ireland, with his agreeable poetic narrative *A Voyage to Ireland in Burlesque* the only significant result. Consisting of three cantos of rhymed hexameters, *A Voyage to Ireland in Burlesque* is a good-hearted diary of travel vexations, candid and earthy. Cotton's translation of Pierre Corneille's drama *Horace* (1671), appearing the next year, included ten songs and choruses of his own, the largest body of Cotton's lyric poetry to be published in his lifetime. He was now at the height of his literary productivity. In 1674, Cotton published more translations from the French, including one of Blaize de Montluc, and an original work in prose, *The Compleat Gamester*, which was reprinted at frequent intervals for the next fifty years. *The Planters Manual* (1675), also an original prose, was less successful, being only a guide to successful horticulture. His next major success was a burlesque in verse of the Roman poet Lucian. Called *Burlesque upon Burlesque*, it was written in Hudibrastic tetrameter (imitating Samuel Butler). Having created a taste for such literary travesties with his earlier demolitions of Vergil, Cotton now replied to his own imitators by providing them with a further model from which to steal.

These were also the years of his close friendship with Izaak Walton, whose *The Compleat Angler* (1653, with innumerable later editions) had already influenced Cotton's *The Compleat Gamester* of 1674. That same year, Cotton built the famous fishing house in which his initials and Walton's were intertwined over the front door. He published one of his best poems, "To my dear and most worthy Friend, Mr. Izaak Walton," in the 1675 edition of Walton's *Lives* (of Donne, Richard Hooker, and George Herbert) after having written it three years earlier. When Walton's *The Compleat Angler* was next published (1676, fifth edition), it included a second part by Cotton, the treatise on fly fishing that is surely his best-known and most-read work today. Cotton's idyllic poem "The Retirement," published in the same volume, ends with Cotton's hope of living "sixty full years." He actually died just short of fifty-seven.

In 1678, the philosopher Thomas Hobbes published *De Mirabilibus Pecci*, a Latin poem extolling the already well-known wonders of the Peak District in Derbyshire, including caverns, springs, and a great house. Alongside the Latin in this edition there was an English translation "by a person of Quality" who may have been Cotton but probably was not. In any case, Hobbes's versified horseback journey through this anomalous landscape led Cotton to compose his longest poem, *The Wonders of the Peake*, published in 1681. The year of its appearance was also one of almost unbearable financial stress for Cotton, who had inherited a deeply entailed estate from his father (d. 1658) and could no longer cope with the accumulated debts. He was therefore obliged to sell Beresford Hall at auction. Fortunately, it was immediately purchased by his cousin John Beresford, who allowed Cotton to remain until his death six years later. It was thus an ebullient Cotton who cheerfully defied the severe winter of 1682-1683 in a "Burlesque upon the Great Frost," addressed of John Bradshaw. Much of his confinement was probably devoted to his translation of Montaigne (1685), which eighteenth century readers generally considered to be the most notable of all his works. Two memorable late poems were "To Astraea" (1686), addressed to Aphra Behn, the first professional woman author in England, and the "Angler's Ballad," which, with its reference to King James II (reigned 1685-1688), is usually regarded as Cotton's last. These and others were collected as *Poems on Several Occasions* in 1689, two years after Cotton's death, and the *Genuine Works* followed in 1715. Alexander Chalmers published "The Poems of Charles Cotton"—including almost all of his poetry—in *The Works of the English Poets* (1810), and Thomas Campbell included selections in *Specimens of the British Poets* (1819). There were no further substantial editions of Charles Cotton's poetry until the twentieth century.

**Analysis**

When Charles Cotton was twelve years old, Puritan insurgents overthrew the monarchy of Charles I and established a Presbyterian commonwealth in its place. During the last years of his life, James II sought to restore Roman Catholicism, and Cotton just missed seeing the Bloodless Revolution of 1688, which banished James to the Continent and returned the monarchy to Protestantism. Of these momentous events, Cotton had surprisingly little to say. While "The Litany," for example, is outspokenly anti-Cromwellian, it regards the Protector only as a vile nuisance, on a level with "ill wine" and "a domineering Spouse." Similarly, Cotton was even more predisposed to ignore the religious controversies of his time. Only "On Christmas Day, 1659" is, of all his works, significantly Christian; even in his several elegies, there is no specifically Christian consolation. Of the great subjects available to him, Cotton did little with politics (after 1651), very little with religion, and nothing with discovery or science.

Cotton's subjects are the traditionally Horatian ones of leisure, relaxation, friendship, love, and drinking, with some special attention in his case to the river Dove, fishing, his fellow poets, and the scenery of the Peak. He is also especially observant of rural life, so that many of his poems are designedly pastoral, including eclogues in which Cotton himself appears as a lovesick shepherd. When sadness intrudes upon these idyllic scenes, it is generally economic in origin: poverty is another of Cotton's themes, especially as it affects the literary life.

For all his love of retirement and solitude, Cotton was not a literary elitist. There are few barriers to the enjoyment of his poems, which are straightforwardly written in plain, colloquial English, as was thought appropriate to pastoral and the burlesque. Though influenced by his Metaphysical predecessors, John Donne especially, Cotton is more akin to Robert Herrick. Both Cotton and Herrick, for example, are observant regionalists particularly ready to celebrate the rewarding, if seemingly inconsequential, joys of rural life and of the milder emotions. Thus, Cotton generally prefers well-observed pastoral details and witty asides to complex imagery or erudite mythology. His contempt for classical learning was probably quite real. There is throughout Cotton's work a serene complacency regarding the adequacy of his own light-hearted perceptions and the healthiness of his instincts. While Romantic critics such as Charles Lamb appreciated the accuracy and vigor of Cotton's outlook, Victorians (such as the American James Russell Lowell) were frequently dismayed by his unapologetic "vulgarity" regarding bodily parts and functions.

A more serious objection to Cotton's verse is its apparent lack of substance. Without quite achieving the epigrammatic quotability of, for example, Richard Lovelace or Andrew Marvell, Cotton resembles both in his largely traditional thematic concerns. He writes most obviously to amuse himself, and sometimes to amuse, compliment, or insult others, but rarely to inspire deep feeling or thought. In several instances, his poems are overlong and drift into lower reaches of the imagination. In others, potentially fine lyrics are marred by inadequacies that a more serious poet would have been at pains to remove. Because poetry for Cotton was private and usually recreational, his work often lacks finality and polish. From a generic point of view, Cotton was most original in bringing to public notice the burlesque and the travel narrative as poetic forms. The other forms that he uses are generally conventional and had been used by his immediate predecessors. His lyrics, for example, are, in form, technique, and substance, largely unoriginal, except insofar as they are infused by a unique and engaging personality.

Ultimately, this personability is his greatest strength. Within his best poems (and his prose addition to Walton), Cotton is superbly himself, and nowhere more so than in "The Answer," a verse epistle to Alexander Brome, whose minor verse helped to reawaken Cotton's neglected Muse, which thrived on solitude. "No friends, no visitors, no company" were desired, "So that my solace [wrote Cotton] lies amongst my grounds,/ and my best companie's my horse and hounds." In a second epistle to Brome, also in heroic couplets, Cotton laments the neglected poet who "knows his lot is to be Poor." A related panegyric, "On the Excellent Poems of My Most Worthy Friend, Mr. Thomas Flatman" (another minor poet of the time), is Cotton's fullest statement of his own concept of poetry, which involves the balancing of old and new, judgment and wit, knowledge and feeling, naturalness and style, propriety and vigor. In many of his literary poems, however, Cotton denigrates his own poetic abilities and himself. If his burlesques are often mock-heroic, he is sometimes even antiheroic in his lyrics. Thus, in his "Epistle to John Bradshaw Esq.," Cotton describes his return to Beresford Hall after a four-month business trip to London. He remains

> The same dull Northern clod I was before,
> Gravely enquiring how Ewes are a Score,
> How the Hay-Harvest, and the Corn was got,
> And if or no there's like to be a Rot;
> Just the same Sot I was e'er I remov'd,
> Nor by my travel, nor the Court improv'd.

Cotton is at his best when most incorrigible.

*The Wonders of the Peake*, probably written two years earlier, is Cotton's longest original poem, being almost fifteen hundred lines of his favorite heroic couplets. In organization and substance it is straightforward, as the reader is led to visit each of the seven "wonders" (traditional before Cotton) in turn: Poole's Hole, a cave; St. Anne's Well, a spring; Tydes-well, another spring; Elden-Hole, a second cave; Mam-Tor, a disintegrating mountain; Peak Cavern ("Peake's-Arse"), the third and most important cave; and Chatsworth, seat of the Duke of Devonshire, a splendid mansion inexplicably situated in this wilderness of geological oddities. Although undistinguished as verse, the poem is of major historical significance as a journey poem, when examples in that genre were unusual, and as a then rare attempt to describe an uncultivated landscape in English verse.

Prior to the seventeenth century, landscape was generally neglected in British literature and art (consider William Shakespeare's plays). Only following the Restoration in 1660 did scenery in literature become increasingly common. Among the reasons for its popularity were the influence of Dutch landscape painting (with an Italian influence following somewhat later), the popularity of Vergil, the rise of Baconian science, and a new naturalism (as in the thought of Thomas Hobbes, whose Latin poem on the Peak preceded Cotton's English one). As Marjorie Hope Nicolson has shown (in her book *Mountain Gloom and Mountain Glory*, 1959), with some understandable oversimplification, Cotton is of special interest in the history of British landscape aesthetics because *The Wonders of the Peake* articulates so powerfully the genuine disgust, and yet interest, which irregular terrain such as that of

Derbyshire evoked. For Cotton, the limestone caverns of the Peak are both sexual and theological. They are also theaters of the imagination, wherein the mind is invited to transform ambiguously shaped dripstone formations into what it will. Cotton, in other words, substantially discovered the cavern imagery that many later poets, William Blake especially, would use in discussing the subconscious mind. Thus, Cotton was a precursor of eighteenth century landscape aesthetics and of Romantic landscape imagery.

Cotton's shorter poems, almost all of them published posthumously in 1689 from an uncertain text, are easily categorized (since they cannot be dated) into form and subject areas: poems of nature and the rural life, love poems, odes, elegies and epitaphs, epistles, epigrams, narratives, and burlesques and satires. The nature poems include "The Retirement"; sets of quatrains to morning, noon, evening, and night; various eclogues; and "Winter," which consists of fifty-three quatrains of tetrameter couplets full of the rural imagery and controlled understatement that Wordsworth admired; it is probably Cotton's best poem. The love poems include songs, odes, madrigals, sonnets, and a rondeau. Those addressed to "Chloris," his future wife, and others inspired by her (such as "The Separation") are among Cotton's finest works, reaching a depth of feeling that he seldom again achieved. Yet other poems by him addressed to or concerning women are crudely sensual and even misogynistic, if maliciously funny. Thus, "Resolution in Four Sonnets, of a Poetical Question put to me by a Friend, concerning four Rural Sisters" estimates the relative seductibility of each, while "To Aelia" (which begins "Poor antiquated slut, forbear") admonishes an overaged debauchee. Though Cotton wrote odes on many subjects, particularly love, he also composed a series of Pindaric ones on hope, melancholy, woman, beauty, contentment, poverty, and death. Those to hope, melancholy, and death are serious poetry reminiscent of Donne and Herbert. Some of his earliest poems were elegies; those still capable of moving modern readers were written in honor of his first wife ("Gods! are you just?") and of his fellow poet Richard Lovelace. Several of the epitaphs, like that on Robert Port, are long enough to compete with the elegies; that on M. H., a whore, is a macabre evocation of necrophilia and grief. The shorter epitaphs and Cotton's epigrams are generally ineffective. His narrative poems, such as those on Ireland and the Peak, grade into his epistles, as in "A Journey into the Peak. To Sir Aston Cockain." Finally, several of the odes and epistles are really drinking songs, as Cotton in his later years cheerfully faced the prospects of poverty and old age.

Despite its variety and excellence, Cotton's *Poems on Several Occasions* was little noticed in its own time, even though, as James Sutherland has suggested, it contained "more and better poetry . . . than is to be found in any other minor poet of the Restoration." By the time it appeared, naturalness and honesty were out of fashion, and Cavalier morality had been circumscribed. Though Cotton's burlesques continued to be read, his accomplishments in more important genres were almost totally forgotten until appreciative Romantic readers established a new assessment of Cotton that has since become the basis for his modern reputation.

## Major publications other than poetry

PLAY: *Horace*, 1671 (translation with original lyric poetry).

NONFICTION: *The Moral Philosophy of the Stoicks*, 1664 (translation); *The History of the Life of the Duke of Espernon*, 1670 (translation); *The Fair One of Tunis*, 1674 (translation); *The Commentaries of Messire Blaize de Montluc, Mareschal of France*, 1674 (translation); *The Compleat Gamester*, 1674; *The Planters Manual*, 1675; *The Compleat Angler, Part II*, 1676; *Essays of Michael Seigneur de Montaigne*, 1685 (translation); *Memoirs of the Sieur De Pontis*, 1694 (translation).

## Bibliography

Beresford, John, ed. *Poems of Charles Cotton, 1630-1687*, 1923.

Buxton, John, ed. *Poems of Charles Cotton*, 1958.

Heywood, G. G. P. *Charles Cotton and His River*, 1928.

Nicolson, Marjorie Hope. *Mountain Gloom and Mountain Glory*, 1959.

Sembower, C. J. *The Life and the Poetry of Charles Cotton*, 1911.

Sutherland, James. *English Literature of the Late Seventeenth Century*, 1969.

*Dennis R. Dean*

# ABRAHAM COWLEY

**Born:** London, England; 1618
**Died:** Chertsey, England; July 28, 1667

### Principal poems and collections

*Poetical Blossoms*, 1633; *The Mistress: Or, Several Copies of Love Verses*, 1647; *Poems*, 1656 (also published as *Miscellanies*); *Verses upon Several Occasions*, 1663; *Poemata Latina*, 1668.

### Other literary forms

From time to time, Abraham Cowley interrupted his poetic activity with bits of drama and prose. The former were light, immature attempts: a pastoral drama, *Love's Riddle* (1638); a Latin comedy entitled *Naufragium Joculare* (1638); another comedy, *The Guardian* (1641), hastily put together when Prince Charles passed through Cambridge, but rewritten in 1661 as *The Cutter of Coleman Street*. His serious prose is direct and concise, although the pieces tend to repeat the traditional Renaissance theme of solitude. His most notable prose work was a pamphlet on *A Proposition for the Advancement of Experimental Philosophy* (1661), which may have hastened the founding of the Royal Society.

### Achievements

Almost fifty years ago, the respected critic and literary historian Douglas Bush suggested that Abraham Cowley needed to be seen and understood as a man of his own age, rather than as an artist whose appeal is timeless. That statement may well be the key to assessing Cowley's achievement. During his own day, he secured a considerable reputation as a poet that endured well into the eighteenth century. Then, in 1779, Samuel Johnson issued, as the initial piece to what became *Lives of the Poets* (1779-1781), his *Life of Cowley*. With his usual rhetorical balance, Johnson described Cowley as a poet who had been "at one time too much praised and too much neglected at another." The London sage, through laborious comparison, classified his subject among the Metaphysical poets of the first half of the seventeenth century—a group that he could not always discuss in positive terms. Johnson, however, did single out Cowley as the best among the Metaphysicals and also the last of them. In general, Johnson praised the "Ode of Wit" (1668), turned a neutral ear toward the "Pindarique Odes" (1656), and evaluated the prose as possessing smooth and placid "equability." Cowley was all but forgotten during the nineteenth century, and not until after World War I, when critics such as Sir Herbert J. C. Grierson and T. S. Eliot began to rediscover Metaphysical verse, did his achievement begin to be understood.

Cowley is a transitional figure, a poet who tended to relinquish the emotional values of John Donne and George Herbert and grasp the edges of reason and wit. He was more versatile than the early Metaphysicals: he embraced the influence of Donne and Ben Jonson, relied upon the Pindaric form that would take hold in the eighteenth century, conceived of an experimental biblical epic in English (*Davideis*, 1656) well in advance of John Milton's major project, and demonstrated an open-mindedness that allowed him to write in support of Francis Bacon, Thomas Hobbes, and the Royal Society. Cowley's elegies on the deaths of William Hervey and Richard Crashaw are extremely frank poems of natural pain and loss, while at the same time the poet recognized the need for the human intellect to be aware of "Things Divine"—the dullness of the earthly as opposed to the reality of the heavenly.

Indeed, Cowley's versatile imagination ranged far and wide, and he easily adapted diverse subjects to fit his own purposes. Unlike the poets of the Restoration and the early eighteenth century who followed him, he ignored various current fashions and concentrated upon economy, unity, form, and imagination; he did not have to force the grotesque upon his readers, nor did he have to inundate them with a pretense of art. Cowley was a master at what Bishop Thomas Sprat termed, in 1668, "harmonious artistry." He turned his back upon wild and affected extravagance and embraced propriety and measure; he applied wit to matter, combined philosophy with charity and religion. Even when writing amorous verse, he took inspiration both from the courtier and from the scholar—the passion of the one and the wisdom of the other.

Perhaps Cowley's greatest achievement as a poet was that, even in retirement, he stood willing to consider the intellectual challenges of a new world, a world at the edge of scientific and political revolution. He seemed extremely sensitive to the need for the poem as a means for expressing the intellectual essence of that new world, yet he never forsook the Renaissance tradition in which he had been taught. Cowley gave to English poetry a sensible mixture of seriousness, learning, imagination, intelligence, and perception. Although he often wrestled with himself, caught between authority and reason, between the rational and the imaginative, between the rejected past and the uncertain future, he managed to control his art, to triumph over the uncertainty and confusion of his time. Through poetry, Cowley searched for order; through poetry he achieved order—classical, scientific, and religious order—in a world that had itself become worn from passion. The achievement of Cowley is that he showed his successors—especially the Augustans of the early eighteenth century—that a poet should seek and find new material and new methods without having to sever the strong cord of the past.

## Biography

Abraham Cowley was born in the parish of St. Michael le Quern, Cheapside, in London, sometime after July, 1618, the seventh child and fifth son (born posthumously) of Thomas Cowley, a stationer and grocer, who left £1000 to be divided among his seven children. His mother was Thomasine Berrye, to whom Thomas Cowley had pledged his faith sometime in 1581. The widow did the best she could to educate her children through her own devices, and then managed to send the boys off to more formal institutions. Thus, she obtained young Abraham's admission as a king's scholar at Westminster School, to which he proceeded armed with some acquaintance with Spenser. By the age of fifteen, he was already a published poet; his first collection of five pieces entitled *Poetical Blossoms* (1633) was followed by a second edition three years later. One of the poems, "Pyramus and Thisbe," some 226 lines long, had been written when he was ten; another, "Constantia and Philetus," was written during the poet's twelfth year.

Cowley's scholarly skills unfortunately did not keep pace with the development of his poetic muse. Apparently the boy balked at the drudgeries of learning grammar and languages; furthermore, his masters contended that his natural quickness made such study unnecessary. In the end, he failed to gain election to Cambridge in 1636 and had to wait until mid-June of the following year, at which time he became a scholar of Trinity College. Cambridge proved no deterrent to young Cowley's poetic bent; in 1638, he published a pastoral drama, *Love's Riddle*, written at least four years previously. Then, on February 2, 1638, members of Trinity College performed his Latin comedy, *Naufragium Joculare*, which he published shortly thereafter. After taking his B.A. in 1639, Cowley remained at Cambridge through 1642, by which time he had earned the M.A. The year before, when Prince Charles had passed through Cambridge, the young poet had hastily prepared for the occasion a comedy entitled *The Guardian*; the piece was acted a number of times prior to its publication in 1650 and it continued to be performed, privately, of course, during the Commonwealth and the suppression of the theaters.

Leaving Cambridge in 1643, Cowley continued to write poetry, principally at St. John's College, Oxford, where he had "retired" and become intimate with royalist leaders. Joining the family of Jermyn (later St. Albans), he followed the Queen to France in 1646, where he found a fellow poet, Richard Crashaw. The exiled court employed Cowley for a number of diplomatic services, particularly on missions to Jersey and Holland; other activities included transmitting a correspondence in cipher between Charles I and his Queen. During this period, several of Cowley's works appeared in London: a collection of poems entitled *The Mistress* (1647); and two satires, *The Four Ages of England: Or, The Iron Age* (1648) and *A Satyre Against Separatists* (1648). His poetic output was restricted, however, because his diplomatic work occupied all of his days and most of his evenings. In 1656, his employers sent him to England on what can only be termed an espionage mission under the guise of seeking retirement. He was arrested, but only because the authorities mistook him for someone else; released on bail, he remained under strict probation until Charles II reclaimed the throne of England in 1660.

For Cowley, however, the big event of 1656 was the publication of his most important collection, *Poems*—including the juvenile pieces, the elegies of Hervey and Crashaw, *The Mistress*, the "Pindaric Odes", and *Davideis*. The last item, an epic of four books (out of twelve that he had originally planned), actually belonged to the poet's Cambridge period, and Cowley finally admitted that he had abandoned plans to complete it. After the publication of the *Poems*, Cowley, still in the employ of the exiled royalists in France, suddenly took up the study of medicine—as a means of obscuring his espionage activities. Seemingly without difficulty, he earned his M.D. degree at Oxford in December, 1657, and then retired to Kent, where he studied and produced a Latin poem, "Plantarum Libri duo" (published in 1662). After the Restoration, Cowley's best poetry and prose appeared: "Ode upon the Blessed Restoration" (1660), *Vision Concerning His Late Pretended Highness, Cromwell the Wicked* (1661), *A Proposition for the Advancement of Experimental Philosophy* (1661), "Ode to the Royal Society" (1661), and *Verses upon Several Occasions* (1663).

Cowley's early employer, Jermyn, by then the Earl of St. Albans, helped to obtain for him some royal land at Chertsy, where he could spend the remainder of his days in easy retirement. There he settled in April, 1665. His health began to decline, however, and the fact that his tenants balked at paying their rents did little to improve his physical and emotional condition. In late July, 1667, after being outdoors longer than necessary, he caught a severe cold; he died on the 28th of that month. Cowley was buried with considerable ceremony in Westminster Abbey, near Geoffrey Chaucer and Edmund Spenser, and for the rest of the seventeenth century poets and critics continued to view him as the model of cultivated poetry.

### Analysis

Abraham Cowley launched his career as a serious poet at the age of fifteen, while still a student at Westminster School, with the publication of *Poetical Blossoms*. In fact, there is evidence that the volume had been prepared in some form at least two years earlier. At any rate, what appeared was a rather high level of poetic juvenilia, five pieces in which both sound and sense reflected an ability far beyond the poet's youth. The first, "Pyramus and Thisbe," 226 lines, does not differ too markedly from Ovid's tale, although Cowley's Venus seems overly malevolent and the (then) ten-year-old poet carried to extremes the desired but untasted joys of love. Otherwise, the piece evidences a sense of discipline and knowledge often reserved for the mature imagination, as young Cowley attempted to control his phrasing and his verse form. The second poem in the collection, "Constantia and Philetus," may serve as a companion to "Pyramus and Thisbe," although it is certainly no mere imitation. Cowley, now about twelve, again chose as his subject a tragic love story, keeping hold upon Venus, Cupid, and other deities. However, he shifted his setting from ancient Rome to the suburban surroundings of an Italian villa, there to unfold a rather conventional poetic narrative: two lovers, a rival favored by the parents, a sympathetic brother, and a dead heroine. He adorned the entire scene with amorous conceits and characters yearning for the beauties of the country and the consolations of nature.

In addition to the larger pieces, *Poetical Blossoms* contained an interesting trio of shorter efforts. In "A Dream of Elysium," Cowley, seemingly engaged in an exercise in poetic self-education, parades before a sleeping poet a host of classical favorites: Hyacinth, Narcissus, Apollo, Ovid, Homer, Cato, Leander, Hero, Portia, Brutus, Pyramus, Thisbe. The final two poems of the volume constitute the young writer's first attempts at what would become, for him, an important form—the occasional poem. Both pieces are elegies: one mourns the death of a public official, Dudley, Lord Carleton and Viscount Dorchester, who attended Westminster School, served as secretary of state, and died in Feburary, 1632; the other was occasioned by the death of Cowley's cousin, Richard Clerke, a student at Lincoln's Inn. Naturally, the two poems contain extravagant praises and lofty figures, no doubt reflecting what the boy had read in his favorite, Spenser, and had been taught by his masters. There are those who speculate that had Cowley died in adolescence, as Thomas Chatterton did in the next century, the verses of *Poetical Blossoms* would have sustained at least a very small poetic reputation in a very obscure niche of literary history. Cowley, however, despite a number of purely political distractions during his adult life, managed to extend his poetic talents beyond childhood exercises; and it is to the products of his maturity that one must turn for the comprehension and appreciation of his art.

Perhaps Cowley's most important contribution to poetry came in 1656 with the publication of his extensive collection, *Poems*, several additions to which he made during his lifetime. Of more than passing interest is the Preface to this volume, wherein Cowley attempts, by reference to his own personal situation, to explain the relationship between the poet and his environment. In 1656, he had little desire to write poetry, mainly because of the political instability of the moment, his own health, and his mental state. He admitted that a warlike, unstable, and even tragic age may be the best for the poet to write about, but it may also be the worst time in which to write. Living as he did, a stranger under surveillance in his own homeland, he felt restricted in his artistic endeavors. "The soul," he complained in the Preface, "must be filled with bright and delightful ideas when it undertakes to communicate delight to others, which is the main end of poesy." Thus, he had given serious thought to abandoning Puritan England for the obscurity of some plantation in the Americas, and the 1656 *Poems* was to be his legacy to a world for whose conflicts and confrontations he no longer had any concern.

The *Poems* contain four divisions: the "Miscellanies," including the

"Anacreontiques"; "The Mistress," a collection of love poems; "Pindarique Odes"; and the "Davideis," a heroic epic focusing upon the problems of the Old Testament king. In subsequent editions, Cowley and his editors added "Verses on Various Occasions" and "Several Discourses by Way of Essays in Prose and Verse." Cowley himself informed his readers that the *Miscellanies* constituted poems preserved from earlier folios (some even from his school days); unfortunately, he made no distinction between the poor efforts and those of quality. Thus, an immature ode, "Here's to thee, Dick," stands near the serious and moving elegy "On the Death of Mr. William Hervey," in which he conveys both universal meaning and personal tragedy and loss. Cowley, however, rarely allowed himself to travel the route of the strictly personal; for him, poetry required support from learning, from scholastic comparisons that did not always rise to poetical levels. The fine valedictory "To the Lord Falkland," which celebrates the friendship between two interesting but divergent personalities, is sprinkled with lofty scientific comparisons to display the order that reigns in the crowded mind of his hero. Indeed, there are moments in Cowley's elegies when the reader wonders if the poet was more interested in praising the virtues of science and learning than in mourning the loss of friends. Such high distractions, however, do not weaken the intensity of Cowley's sincerity.

*The Mistress*, originally published in 1647, comprises one hundred love poems, or, in Cowley's own terms, feigned addresses to some fair creature of the fancy. Almost apologetically, the poet explains in the prefatory remarks that all writers of verse, must at one time or another pay some service to Love, in order to prove themselves true to Love. Unfortunately, Cowley evidences difficulty in warming to the occasion, perhaps held back by the prevalent mood of Puritan strictness that then dominated the art. Thus, many of his physical and psychological images of Love come from traditions rather than from the heart: Love is an interchange of hearts, a flame, a worship, a river frozen by disdain. On the other hand, Cowley's original, nontraditional images and similes are often wildly incongruous, even unintentionally comical, and lacking in strange true feeling. Tears are made by smoke, but not by flame; the lover's heart bursts upon its object "Like a grenado shot into a magazine"; a love story cut into bark burns and withers the tree; a young lady's beauty changes from civil government to tyranny. Certainly, *The Mistress* reveals that Cowley could employ an obvious degree of playfulness in verse; he could counterfeit, with ease and ingenuity, a series of love adventures; he could sustain some semblance of unity in a seeming hodgepodge of romantic episodes; he could amuse his readers. For those of his age who took their love poetry seriously, however—for those who expected grace, warmth, tenderness, even truth—*The Mistress* must have been rather disappointing.

There is some confusion concerning the form of the "Pindarique Odes." Cowley may have wanted readers to believe that he was writing the true

Pindaric ode—strophe, antistrophe (alike in form) and epode (different in form from the first two divisions), with varying meter and verse lengths within a strophe, but nevertheless regular metrical schemes established for corresponding divisions. Actually, he created a new form, an irregular ode: he discarded the usual stanza patterns, varied the length of lines and the number of lines within the strophes, and varied the meter with shifts in emotional intensity. He obviously knew what he was doing and probably chose the title for the section to disguise a questionable innovation. In fact, he doubted (in the Preface) whether the form would be understood by most of his readers, even those acquainted with the principles of poetry. Nevertheless, he employed sudden and lengthy digressions, "unusual and bold" figures, and various and irregular numbers. Cowley's purpose throughout was to achieve a sense of harmony between what he viewed as the *liberty* of the ode and the moral *liberty* of life, the latter combining responsibility and freedom. Through moral liberty he hoped to find simplicity, retirement, and charm; the liberty of the ode, he thought, might allow for a greater participation in intellectual exercise.

In practice, the ode allowed Cowley the opportunity to subject his readers to a host of what he had termed "bold figures," images that would have occurred to no one other than he. Thus, on one occasion he asks his Muse to "rein her Pindaric Pegasus closely in," since the beast is "an unruly and a hardmouthed horse," At another time, the Muse appears in her chariot, with Eloquence, Wit, Memory, and Invention running by her side. Suddenly, Cowley stops the action to compare the Muse with the Creator and with the two worlds that they have created. Such comparisons, with their accompanying "bold" images, allowed the poet to display his learning, to set down explanatory notes of definition, explication, and interpretation—whether his readers needed them or not. As long as he could serve as his own explicator, there seemed no limit to his invention. Generally, though, Cowley's odes fall short of their intentions as *complete* pieces of poetry. The digressions—the instruments of the poet's new-found intellectual freedom—may strike and impress the reader momentarily, but they also distract and divert the attention from the main idea of the poem.

Not all of Cowley's odes fall short of the mark. He succeeded when his subject interested him enough to say something substantive about it. In both "To Mr. Hobbes" and "Brutus" he followed the serious thinkers of his time. The first poem finds him looking beyond the transitory troubles of the moment to a new day. The second allows him to observe Cromwell, the Caesar of his time and, like the conscientious royalist of the period, seek contemplation rather than action. He looks to history and philosophy to explain the evils of tyranny and to find parallels with other evils that eventually gave way to good. In the ode to Hobbes, Cowley finds solace in the fact that all ideas and concepts of permanent value must remain young and fresh forever. In the ode to Brutus, the poet discovers that odd events, evil men, and wretched actions are not themselves sufficient to destroy or even obscure Virtue. Again, the particular circumstances of the moment and his deep personal disappointment gave Cowley the conviction to express what he actually felt.

It is tempting to dismiss *Davideis* as another example of Cowley's juvenilia. Of the twelve books planned, only four were finished, and those were written while Cowley was still at Cambridge, By 1656, and perhaps even before, Cowley had lost his taste for the epic and determined not to finish it. If anything can be salvaged from *Davideis* it may be found in the Preface, where the poet makes an eloquent plea for sacred poetry. Cowley complains that for too long wit and eloquence have been wasted on the beggarly flattery of important persons, idolizing of foolish women, and senseless fables. The time has come, he announces, to recover poetry from the devil and restore it to the kingdom of God, to rescue it from the impure waters of Damascus and baptize it in the Jordan. Unfortunately, the epic that follows never rises to the elegance or merit of the prefatory prose. The poem simply sinks from its own weight. Cowley's Hell, for example, is a labyrinth of cosmic elements: caverns that breed rare metals; nests of infant, weeping winds; a complex court of mother waters. The journey there is indeed long and laborious, and the relationship between all of those cosmic details (gold, winds, voices, tides, and tidelessness) and Hell is never made clear. Cowley himself acknowledged the immaturity and weakness of the epic, but he also saw it as an adumbration of the poetic potential of biblical history. Eleven years after the publication of *Davideis* in the collected *Poems*, John Milton published *Paradise Lost*.

Cowley added to the collected editions of his poems as they were issued between 1656 and his death in 1667. As with the contents of the first edition, the pieces vary in quality. In "Hymn to Light," the poet manages to achieve a proper balance between his learning and his imagination. The reader senses that Cowley has actually observed the "winged arrows" shooting from the "golden quiver of the sky," the result of a long succession of fresh and bright dawns rising in the English countryside. Those very dawns seem to have frightened "sleep, the lazy owl of night," turning the face of "cloudy care" into a "gentle, beamy smile." During those blessed years of retirement, away from the unnatural complications and intrigues of the political world, Cowley turned more and more toward the beauty of nature as a source of pleasure. Although in "Hymn to Light" he labels light an offspring of chaos, its very beams embrace and enhance the charms and beauty of the world, while at the same time tempting the selfish and inconsiderate by shining upon valuable elements. Toward the end of the poem, he conceives of light as a "clear river" that pours forth its radiance from the vast ocean of the sky; it collects in pools and lakes when its course is opposed by some firm body—the earth, for example. Such a conceit may appear overly abstract and abstruse, but it is perhaps the most extreme figure of the poem, demonstrating the degree to which the mature Cowley had advanced beyond his juvenile epic endeavors.

There are critics who assert that with the "Ode to the Royal Society" (1667), Cowley rose to his highest level. That is debatable, but it is certainly his last important poem. The poem was written at the request of Cowley's friend, the diarist John Evelyn, who asked for a tribute to the Royal Society to complement the official history being undertaken by Thomas Sprat, Bishop of Rochester. The poem, published the same year as Sprat's *History of the Royal Society*, focused not so much upon the institution in question or even on science in general, but upon the evolution of philosophy, which Cowley placed into two chronological periods: before and after Francis Bacon. The poet dwells briefly on the constrictions of the early philosophies, which merely wandered among the labyrinths of endless discourse, with little or no positive effect upon mankind. Then follows an impassioned attack upon pure authority, which arrived at erroneous scientific and intellectual conclusions, and stubbornly clung to them. Cowley compares Francis Bacon, who, with his *Advancement of Learning* (1605), *Novum Organum* (1620), and *De Augmentis Scientiarum* (1623), had initiated a new age of philosophy, with Moses; men of intellect were led out of the barren wasteland of the past to the very borders of exalted wit. Only Bacon, maintains Cowley, was willing to act and capable of routing the ghostlike body of authority that had for so long misled people with its dead thoughts. The philosophers of the past were but mechanics, copiers of others' work; Bacon summoned the mind away from words, the mere pictures of thoughts, and redirected it toward objects, the proper focus of the mind. Thus, the poet paid tribute to the philosopher as the proper predecessor of the Royal Society; his investigations paved the way for the significant accomplishments of that institution. The immediate success of the poem may have been due in part to Cowley's personal ties with the Royal Society—particularly as a friend of both Sprat and Evelyn, and as the author of *A Proposition for the Advancement of Experimental Philosophy*. Those critics who have praised the piece for its pure poetic merit, however, have rightly identified it as the culmination of Cowley's contributions to the English ode.

Beginning with Joseph Addison's negative criticism (*The Spectator* 62, May, 1711) and extending through the critique in Samuel Johnson's *Lives of the Poets*, Cowley's reputation has endured the accusations of mixed wit and strained metaphysical conceits. Obviously, Addison and Johnson, even though they represent opposite chronological poles of the eighteenth century, were still too close to their subject to assess him objectively and to recognize him as a transitional figure. Cowley lived during the end of one intellectual age and the beginning of another. He belonged alongside John Donne, Richard Crashaw, George Herbert, Henry Vaughan, Thomas Traherne, and Andrew Marvell; he owed equal allegiance to the writers of the early Restoration, to such classicists as John Denham and Edmund Waller. Thus, his poetry reflects the traditions of one period and the freshness of another, the extravagances of youth and the freedom to combine ingenuity with reason and learning. Cowley also had the distinct advantage of a point of view resulting from the mastery of several positive sciences and of practically all of the literature of Europe. Knowledge, reflection, control, clear judgment: these he carried with him from the Puritan Revolution into the Restoration and then to his own retirement. He belonged to an age principally of learning and of prose; he wrote poetry with the sustained rhetorical and emotional force that often results in greatness. Unfortunately, his meteor merely approached greatness, flaring only for a brief moment on the literary horizon.

## Major publications other than poetry

PLAYS: *Love's Riddle*, 1638; *Naufragium Joculare*, 1638; *The Guardian*, 1641; *The Cutter of Coleman Street*, 1658.

NONFICTION: *A Proposition for the Advancement of Experimental Philosophy*, 1661; *Discourse by Way of Vision Concerning Oliver Cromwell*, 1661; *Several Discourses by Way of Essays in Prose and Verse*, 1668.

MISCELLANEOUS: *The Works of Mr. Abraham Cowley*, 1668, 1681, 1689, 1700, 1707-1708, 1710-1711.

## Bibliography

Hinman, Robert B. *Abraham Cowley's World of Order*, 1960.

Loiseau, Jean. *Abraham Cowley: Sa Vie, Son Oeuvre*, 1931.

───────────── . *Abraham Cowley's Reputation in England*, 1931.

McLean, Alvin H. *The Poetry of Variation: A Study of Abraham Cowley*, 1971.

Nethercot, Arther H. *Abraham Cowley. The Muse's Hannibal*, 1926.

Taaffe, James G. *Abraham Cowley*, 1972.

Trotter, David. *The Poetry of Abraham Cowley*, 1979.

Yarnall, Emma. *Abraham Cowley*, 1897.

*Samuel J. Rogal*

# MALCOLM COWLEY

**Born:** Belsano, Pennsylvania; August 24, 1898

**Principal collections**
*Blue Juniata*, 1929; *The Dry Season*, 1941; *Blue Juniata: Collected Poems*, 1968.

**Other literary forms**
Although Malcolm Cowley began his literary career as a poet, and has remained a practicing poet, critic of poetry, and adviser to scores of American poets for most of his more than sixty-year career, his literary reputation derives chiefly from his prose works, which include literary criticism and literary and cultural history as well as numerous essays and book reviews written for newspapers, magazines, and literary journals. Many of Cowley's critical essays are considered to be seminal studies of major American poets and novelists, such as Hart Crane, Ernest Hemingway, and William Faulkner. In addition, Cowley's major works of literary and cultural history, including *Exile's Return* (1934, 1951); *After the Genteel Tradition: American Writers 1910-1930* (1937, 1964); *The Literary Situation* (1954); *A Second Flowering: Works and Days of the Lost Generation* (1973); *—And I Worked at the Writer's Trade* (1978); and *The Dream of the Golden Mountains: Remembering the 1930s* (1980), have served as primary sources of information about the intellectual, social, political, and historical events and issues that shaped the aesthetic practices and the social and political beliefs of modern American writers. Cowley's published books range from pioneering translations of important novels and essays by French writers of the 1920's and 1930's, such as Maurice Barrès, Paul Valéry, Louis Aragon, and André Gide, to editions of the works of several of America's classic nineteenth century writers, such as Walt Whitman, *The Complete Poetry and Prose of Walt Whitman* (1948), and Nathaniel Hawthorne, *The Portable Hawthorne* (1948). His publications also include a volume analyzing the intellectual history of modern Western civilization, *Books That Changed Our Minds* (1939), and a historical study of the African slave trade, *Black Cargoes: A History of the Atlantic Slave Trade* (1962), written in collaboration with Daniel P. Mannix.

Cowley has edited anthologies of several of his contemporaries, editions that significantly contributed to expanding their audience and to establishing their literary reputations. The most notable of these were *The Portable Hemingway* (1944), *The Portable Faulkner* (1946), *The Stories of F. Scott Fitzgerald* (1950), and *Three Novels of F. Scott Fitzgerald: The Great Gatsby . . . Tender Is the Night . . . The Last Tycoon* (1953).

Cowley's literary journalism has been partially collected in two volumes,

*Think Back on Us: A Contemporary Chronicle of the 1930's* (1967), and *A Many Windowed House: Collected Essays on American Writers and American Writing* (1970). The only portion of Cowley's literary correspondence (most of which is housed in Chicago's Newberry Library) that has been published is a volume of letters, with explanatory narration, between Cowley and William Faulkner regarding their eighteen-year friendship, *The Faulkner-Cowley File: Letters and Memories, 1944-1962* (1968).

## Achievements

Cowley was formally honored by the American cultural and educational community relatively late in his career. His fellow writers honored him early and continuously, however, by both public recognition and private expression. Since a significant portion of his work is concerned with the writer in the modern world, in a way that James Atlas has described as almost unique in the history of American letters, Cowley has been an acknowledged leader and spokesman for the American literary community for fifty years. Consequently, many of Cowley's honors have been bestowed for his service to the profession of letters as much as for his individual achievements as a poet and writer.

In 1921 Cowley was granted an American Field Service Fellowship permitting him to spend two years in France studying at the University of Montpellier, an experience that was crucial in exposing him to the revolutionary ideas and practices of modern artists in France. In 1927 he received the Levinson Prize for poetry. In 1939 *Poetry* magazine awarded him the Harriet Monroe Memorial Prize. In 1946 he received a grant from the National Institute of Arts and Letters, and in 1967 the newly created National Endowment for the Arts gave Cowley a ten thousand-dollar award in recognition of his service to American letters. The Modern Language Association of America awarded Cowley its Hubbel Medal in 1978 for services to American literature. In 1980 the American Book Publishers Council voted Cowley its American Book Award in the autobiography category, paperback division, for —*And I Worked at the Writer's Trade.*

Cowley was elected to the National Institute of Arts and Letters in the early 1950's, and the Institute membership shortly thereafter honored him by twice electing him president, from 1956 to 1959 and from 1962 to 1965. Cowley was also elected to the senior body of the National Institute, the American Academy of Arts and Letters, and he served as chancellor of that body from 1967 to 1977. These tenures were periods in which Cowley helped to supervise the creation and granting of a number of prizes and monetary awards to scores of writers for both individual works of literature and for contributions to literature over entire careers. For more than forty years Cowley also served as an adviser, director, and vice-president of Yaddo, the private foundation that provides subsidized residence for writers and artists in Saratoga Springs,

New York.

Cowley served as a distinguished visiting professor at the University of Washington in Seattle in 1950; at Stanford University in 1956, 1959, 1960-1961, and 1965; at the University of Michigan in 1957; as Regents Professor at the University of California, Berkeley, in 1962; at Cornell University, 1964; at the University of Minnesota in 1971; and at the University of Warwick in England in 1973. He has been awarded honorary doctorates of literature by Franklin and Marshall College, 1961; Colby College, 1962; the University of Warwick, England, 1975; the University of New Haven, 1976; and Monmouth College, 1978.

Though Cowley began publishing more than six decades ago, his work remained uncollected until relatively late in his career. Yet his influence on other critics, academic scholars, poets, and novelists has been substantial. His essays written while serving as literary editor of *The New Republic* from 1929 until 1944 made Cowley one of the most widely read voices of literary and cultural analysis during the years of the Great Depression and World War II. In the postwar period academic scholars considered his writing to be a critical guide to American literature and American literary history in the entire first half of the twentieth century. When Robert Spiller, Willard Thorp, and Henry Seidel Canby began work on the now standard reference work *The Literary History of the United States* (1948-1953), they asked Cowley to write the sections concerning the social history of modern American authors and the influence of American literature on foreign nations.

As adviser to one of America's foremost publishing companies, the Viking Press, for more than thirty years, Cowley played a role in developing Viking's literary publications, including such ventures as the Viking Portable Library, the paperback Compass editions, the Viking Critical Editions, and the first significant publication in America of many new writers, among them authors such as Jack Kerouac, Ken Kesey, and Tillie Olson, as well as a number of poets, such as Donald Hall, Philip Booth, and A. D. Hope. In the late 1940's Cowley served on the committees that inaugurated the National Book Awards and the Bollingen Prize for Poetry, and in the early 1950's he helped to advise the Rockefeller Foundation on the funding of literary magazines.

Cowley's critical acumen concerning his own generation of writers was matched by his ability to recognize and sponsor other talented writers. He first published John Cheever and discussed his fiction with him for more than forty years. He promoted Nelson Algren from his first reading of his work in 1942 until Algren's death in 1981. In addition, a number of academic critics, such as John W. Aldridge, Michael Millgate, Larzer Ziff, and Philip Young, have attested to the influence Cowley had on their careers.

One of only a handful of American poets who have become successful literary journalists, historians, and critics, and whose prose work belongs to the canon of American literature, Cowley has gained a reputation as one of the most perceptive of modern literary analysts. He has been described as one of the most lucid English prose stylists of the twentieth century. Because of his belief in the cultural value and importance of poetry (indeed of all literature), Cowley sees the use of language, particularly by artists and journalists, as an expression of the moral character of society, and his analysis of modern writers and their history has been the distinctive achievement of his career.

## Biography

Malcolm Cowley was born on August 24, 1898, in the small farming village of Belsano in the Allegheny hills east of Pittsburgh. His father, William Cowley, was a homeopathic physician who maintained his office in a building in an older section of Pittsburgh. The family rented an apartment in the same building, so Cowley grew up in an urban business neighborhood with few children for companionship. The Cowley summer house in Belsano had been left to William Cowley by the poet's grandmother, and it was there that Cowley's mother, Josephine (Hutmacher) Cowley, took her only child to spend the summers while her husband worked in Pittsburgh. The farm community of Belsano and Cowley's experiences there during the long summers had a profound impact on his life and poetry. He was never comfortable in urban environments. Cowley's childhood was, like that of many writers, one of periodic solitude and long hours spent alone reading and imagining. Though he received most of his early schooling in Pittsburgh, Cowley was most comfortable in the farming community of Belsano.

He entered Harvard College in 1915 on a scholarship from the Harvard Club of Pittsburgh. There he made several important literary friendships, some of them with older poets such as S. Foster Damon, Conrad Aiken, and E. E. Cummings. These friends, themselves innovators in the modern poetry movement, introduced Cowley to the work of the nineteenth century French symbolists and to older New England poets such as Edwin Arlington Robinson and Amy Lowell, who was then a proponent of Imagism.

In the spring of 1917, Cowley volunteered for the American Field Service in France, and he served, like other Harvard writers such as Cummings, John Dos Passos, and Robert Hillyer, as part of the earliest group of Americans to see the battlefronts of World War I. Cowley drove a munitions truck for the French Army for six months, then returned to New York, where he lived for several months in Greenwich Village waiting to return to college. While living a life of poverty, and writing some poetry and book reviews to survive, he met and later married an older artist, Marguerite Frances Baird (Peggy), who was a confirmed bohemian painter divorced from her first husband, the New York poet Orrick Johns. Peggy Baird introduced Cowley to many older Greenwich Village artists, and to Clarence Britten, then literary editor of *The Dial*, who gave Cowley books for review and indirectly initiated his career in literary journalism.

Cowley returned to Harvard in September, 1919, and was graduated in the winter of 1920 after another absence spent in Army ROTC training. He had been elected president of *The Harvard Advocate* in the spring of 1918 and spent his last two college terms working to keep alive what little literary life there was at Harvard during the war years.

After college, Cowley returned to Greenwich Village, where he and Peggy lived a bohemian life again in a cheap tenement while Cowley worked as a copywriter for *Sweet's Architectural Catalogue*. He continued to do some freelance book reviewing and wrote poems and essays for magazines.

In July, 1921, Cowley went to France for two years. There he studied at the University of Montpellier and lived for short periods in Claude Monet's village of Giverney outside Paris. In Paris, his New York friend Matthew Josephson introduced him to the French Dadaist and surrealist writers and painters, and Cowley met most of the American expatriate writers who had gone to Europe after World War I to escape the conservative, sometimes reactionary political, aesthetic, and social ideas dominating American culture in the postwar years. In France, Cowley also worked as an editor and writer for two of the most famous "little magazines" of the expatriates in those years, *Broom* and *Secession*. While most of the American expatriates absorbed a good deal of the social, political, and aesthetic ideas of the modern European avant-garde art movement, Cowley rebelled against such ideas and began to defend the traditional aesthetic values of Western artistic realism and mimesis. His experiences in France resulted in his understanding of the aesthetic brilliance of the modern artistic revolution, but he became sharply critical of many of the modernist doctrines and practices.

When Cowley returned to New York in August, 1923, he embarked on a career that he hoped would emulate the ideal of a professional man of letters. In the latter half of the 1920's Cowley wrote poems, essays, and book reviews for a number of the most prominent literary journals and newspapers of the time, and translated books of French literature, some of which became bestsellers. Cowley was also the friend of a number of writers living near New York in the 1920's, such as Hart Crane, Allen Tate, Robert Penn Warren, and Katherine Anne Porter.

When Edmund Wilson retired as literary editor of *The New Republic* in the summer of 1929, he chose Cowley to succeed him. For sixteen years thereafter Cowley served in a job he loved, and exhausted himself in attempting to connect the world of literature and books with the world of politics, public affairs, and social history. His own poetry and prose of the time provide cultural historians with one of the best records of the tumultuous intellectual and political fervor of the Depression and World War II years.

After being forced to resign by Congressman Martin Dies in the spring of 1942 from his position as aide to Archibald MacLeish at the Roosevelt

Administration's Office of Facts and Figures, for allegedly being a "communist threat" to America because of his left-wing political sympathies during the Depression, Cowley retired from any active political involvement and moved to Sherman, Connecticut, where he had already remodeled an old barn. In the forty years since that time he has worked as a free-lance writer, editor, part-time college teacher, and adviser to the Viking Press, writing and editing the books that consolidated his reputation as one of the finest American literary critics and historians of the twentieth century.

In 1932 Cowley had divorced his first wife and married Muriel Maurer, with whom he has lived for the past fifty years. The Cowleys have a son, Robert, who has been a magazine and book editor in New York.

**Analysis**

To appreciate Malcolm Cowley's poetry, it is necessary to see it in relation to the major cultural movement of his time, usually described by historians as artistic or cultural modernism, or simply modernism. Modernism represented a radical break with the centuries-long traditions of Western humanistic, realistic art. The humanistic tradition was characterized by a belief that art has a moral and social function in the larger process of human civilization.

The theories and practice of modern artists developed in reaction to both the humanistic tradition of Western civilization and the profound changes in Western society that resulted from the rising prestige of science and technology, the industrial revolution, and the organized use of scientific knowledge and technology by modern financial capitalism. Characteristic ideas of modern art included a repudiation of any criteria except the aesthetic as a basis for judging art, and the contention that the artistic imagination is an essentially irrational, as opposed to rational, process that governs scientific investigation and ordinary human communication.

The complex and revolutionary impulse of modern art, its antinaturalist aesthetic, its repudiation of the traditions of Western art, the social alienation and rebellion of modern artists, and their profound hostility to modern society constituted an epochal change in art history. The sometimes confused and alienated psychology that they represented, together with the explosion of experimental forms that it produced, were manifested while Malcolm Cowley was beginning his literary career. His critical study of that historical epoch and its influence on modern American writers was the subject of his most famous book, *Exile's Return*. It was also the subject of his first published book of poetry, *Blue Juniata*.

When Cowley published *Blue Juniata* in 1929 the book was described by Allen Tate as an important historical record of the entire literary generation of the 1920's. *Blue Juniata* was published at the urging of Hart Crane, who wanted it organized to reflect the "emotional record" of its author in accord with the values of modern poetics. Instead, Cowley structured the book historically in five sections, each containing poems describing periods and places that Cowley experienced with his contemporaries. The sections include poems about his years of adolescence and World War I, the years of expatriate artists in France and Europe after the war, the migration to New York and the frenzied life of the Jazz Age, and a section of miscellaneous poems reflecting the poet's sense of upheaval in the decade of the 1920's. The book mirrors Cowley's private reaction to his time, and the time itself.

If the aesthetic of modern art was antinatural, the title section of *Blue Juniata* is filled with poems celebrating nature. The title is taken from a river in west-central Pennsylvania, the rural environment that Cowley loved but to which, like the childhood homes of Thomas Wolfe, Hemingway, Fitzgerald, and others of his generation, he could not "go home again."

Cowley's poems reflect the modern poetry movement in other ways. In the second section of the book, called "Adolescence," he reprints poems written during his bohemian days after the war. Poems such as "Kelly's Barroom" imitate the style of the French symbolist poet Jules Laforgue and his theme of youthful disillusionment. Laforgue had been recommended to younger American poets such as Cowley by Ezra Pound and T. S. Eliot, whose "The Love Song of J. Alfred Prufrock" was also derivative of Laforgue.

The third section of *Blue Juniata* consists of poems written in Europe, where many of Cowley's American friends had been influenced by the French Dadaist artists and by the international avant-garde centered in Paris and led by James Joyce, Marcel Proust, Pablo Picasso, and other European artists. Cowley's poems of those years include English versions of some of the great modern poems, such as Guillaume Apollinaire's "Marizibill," and an ironic poem undercutting a classical theme which he entitled "Mediterranean Beach." Such poems as "Valuta" satirize the exploitation by artists of postwar Europe's economic situation, while "Sunrise over the Heiterwand" hints at the political confusion of Pound, Eliot, and other symbolists. Another poem of Cowley's Paris years, "Château de Soupir: 1917," is a satire on Marcel Proust's monumental novel, *À la recherche du temps perdu* (1913-1927, *Remembrance of Things Past*). A poem entitled "Two Swans" is a commentary on the outlaw sensibility of Charles Baudelaire and later symbolists, who maintained that poetic beauty was to be found in the bizarre and criminal underworld.

Many of the poems of the fourth section of *Blue Juniata* ("The City of Anger, Poems: 1924-1928") are portraits of literary friends. In "The Narrow House," Cowley describes Kenneth Burke as a pastoral recluse of vast ambition and hopes who has husbanded his land in rebellion against the industrial age. Another remarkable poem, "The Flower in the Sea," portrays Hart Crane's obsession with the symbolist idea of the "Poète Maudit" and his fascination with the sea. It is a portrait whose prophecy Crane fulfilled several years later, when he committed suicide by jumping overboard in the Gulf of

Mexico. One poem, "Buy 300 Steel," satirizes Cowley's friend Matthew Josephson, who was forced to work at a job he hated as a stockbroker in the Roaring Twenties. Harold Loeb, an heir to a small portion of the Guggenheim copper fortune and the man who financed the avant-garde art magazine *Broom*, is described in Cowley's poem "Tumbling Mustard" as representing the frenzied energy of the artists of the 1920's. Allen Tate, with his taste for classical poetry and poetic styles, is addressed by Cowley in his sonnet "Towers of Song."

Even in his poems about New York, Cowley reveals a social consciousness that distinguished him from his peers. Two poems of the late 1920's, "The Lady from Harlem: In Memory of Florence Mills," and "For St. Bartholomew's Eve (August 23, 1927)," are overtly political, reacting to the injustices felt by liberal artists at famous trials in New York, as well as in Boston in 1927 where the anarchist immigrants Nicola Sacco and Bartolomeo Vanzetti were tried and executed. Many of Cowley's pastoral poems in *Blue Juniata* also imply a social theme. In several short narrative and descriptive poems, such as "Laurel Mountain," "Seven O'Clock," "Hickory Cove," "The Farm Died," and "Empty Barn, Dead Farm," Cowley's tone is elegiac, lamenting the declining farm communities of nineteenth century America displaced by the growing urban industrialization of the twentieth century. Two other poems, "The Hill Above the Mine" and "Mine No. 6" are stark descriptions of the ruin brought to Cowley's boyhood Pennsylvania by the greed of the mining industry. All those poems reflect Cowley's deep emotional attachment to the American landscape.

Though Cowley gave a more complete and analytical history of his literary generation in *Exile's Return*, *Blue Juniata* contains many of the themes and ideas that he later developed in that book. Indeed, the final poem of his collection, "The Urn," is a concise statement, in formal stanzas, of the central experience of the entire "Lost Generation," their experience of exile, uprootedness, and aching memory for a country of childhood which could never be regained in the modern world.

As a critical analyst of the Depression-era literature of social commitment and a historian of modern American literature, Cowley's major prose works are descriptive, analytical, and narrative. His deepest response to the literary and political culture of the Great Depression is revealed, however, in a slim volume of poems, his second collection, published in 1941.

*The Dry Season* contains seventeen poems, most of them written between 1935 and 1941. A few poems in the collection go back to the late 1920's, but had been omitted from *Blue Juniata*. These poems, such as "Tar Babies," which was originally published in the avant-garde magazine *transition* in 1928, satirize the decadent, often sexually aberrant behavior of the artistic culture of the 1920's. "The Eater of Darkness," a poem dedicated to Cowley's friend and early Dadaist enthusiast Robert Coates, describes the bizarre literary world of New York by presenting the Jazz Age in terms of *Alice's Adventures in Wonderland* (1865). The chaotic, sometimes destructive, rebel society of modern American art had been the theme of Coates's novel *Yesterday's Burden's* (1933), which Cowley cited in *Exile's Return* as evidence of the turn by American artists in the early 1930's from modernist art and social rebellion to social involvement.

The poetry of *The Dry Season* reveals the emotional history of Cowley's own social involvement. For example, two poems, "The Mother" and "The Firstborn," are autobiographical, written after the death of his mother. Both poems reveal a sense of guilt on the part of a son who felt unable to help his parents while they suffered, like millions of Americans, from deprivation. On a visit to Pittsburgh shortly before his mother's death, Cowley had been stunned to find that his father, a doctor unable to collect payment from most of his patients, had become a partial invalid and that his mother sometimes did not have enough to eat. The plight of his family reinforced his conviction that radical measures were needed to change the American economic structure. He also felt that writers and artists could find hope, a renewed sense of relevance, and a large audience if their art mirrored the human issues of their age.

His poems "The Last International" and "Tomorrow Morning" reflect the hopes and humanist faith that comprised Cowley's passionate response to the turmoil of the time. The imagery of "The Last International" alludes to Homer, Vergil, and Dante and their visions of hell. In Cowley's poem, however, the dead rise up to revolutionize contemporary life.

An important aspect of "Tomorrow Morning" is its intuitive recognition that radical politics and solidarity with the politically and economically disadvantaged required affiliation with political fringe groups that would taint artistic integrity, and would probably tragically fail to change historical conditions anyway. Given the evils of Fascism, and the economic chaos against which Cowley believed a coalition was necessary, the poem implies that artists have no choice but to work with all factions opposed to the reactionary forces and ideas of the time.

What Cowley was unprepared for was the enormity of human evil that Fascism revealed and that Soviet Communism initially masked from the often naïve writers of the 1930's. He was also surprised and hurt by the sometimes savage bitterness engendered among artists by the failed political hopes of the age. After observing the bitter factionalism of intellectuals in the late 1930's and suffering with his friends from vicious attacks by apologists for both Fascism and Communism, Cowley became disillusioned by his entire political experience. Poems such as "The End of the World," "Seven," "The Lost People," and "The Dry Season" metaphorically imply that the poet's heart, mind, and spirit are despondent, like stream beds in a drought, and he yearns for some answers in an age when all myths, all beliefs, and all values seem destroyed by man's terrible capacity for evil. Like W. H. Auden in his poem "New Year Letter" (1940), Cowley felt the political confusion of the late 1930's as a deep void, the collapse of humanistic hopes and ideals.

*The Dry Season* also contains a few poems written in the late 1930's that reveal Cowley's renewed love for the American landscape, pointing the way toward solace for his political disillusionment. "This Morning Robins," "Eight Melons," and "The Long Voyage" are pastoral lyrics celebrating spring and the late summer harvest when the abundance of nature provides men with sustenance to last through the "dry winter" of nature and the human heart: "Now the dark waters at the bow/ fold back, like earth against the plow;/ foam brightens like the dogwood now/ at home, in my own country." Cowley returned to the country in the 1940's, the country of American farmers and craftsmen, of small-town friendliness and the world of nature. He spent the remainder of his active literary career there defending the values in which he deeply believed.

When Cowley's collected poems were published in 1968, Kenneth Rexroth wrote in a review of the year's poetry that Cowley was an important American poet, somewhat overlooked because of his more famous peers and the brilliance of his prose.

The *Blue Juniata: Collected Poems* stands as a summary of Cowley's entire literary career. The book contains most of the poems from his two previous collections, with several changes of titles, some rearrangement of order, and minor revisions of content. Several previously uncollected poems are also included, while new poems from the 1950's and 1960's are collected in two final sections called "The Unsaved World" and "Another Country."

The book's structure is both thematic and historical, and it reveals the remarkable consistency of its author. The new work in the volume again reveals a writer with a strong satiric style and an acute sense of history. Poems such as "Ode in a Time of Crisis" and "The Enemy Within" are witty, ironic commentaries on the political paranoia and undemocratic practices of the McCarthy era in the early 1950's. With allusive irony, Cowley compares McCarthy's political tactics to another great scandal of American history, the Salem witchcraft trials.

Several of Cowley's finest poems of his late years are further meditations on his favorite theme, the relationship between man and nature. Poems such as "Natural History," a sequence in five parts, "The Living Water," a poem with echoes of the nature poetry of Henry David Thoreau and Ralph Waldo Emerson, and "Here with the Long Grass Rippling," perhaps Cowley's finest long poem (with clear allusions to Walt Whitman's "Song of Myself"), indicate again his almost religious feeling for the American landscape. "Here with the Long Grass Rippling" in particular embodies a recurring theme of the American poetic tradition, an undoctrinaire, noncreedal, yet mystical faith in the spiritual made manifest in the world of nature.

While modern artists often sought frantically, sometimes tragically, to revive a sense of myth, ritual, and religious emotion in the secular, materialistic culture of modernity, seeking impossible modes of escape from nature by means of art, Cowley's vision of the sacred value of the smallest insect or flower, and the interconnectedness of the natural environment with the culture of the world, reiterates his lifelong literary theme. Literature at its best is a mirror of human history and a moral criticism of contemporary society. The profound meditation of "Here with the Long Grass Rippling" also helps to explain Cowley's great analyses of the illustrious members of his own literary generation and his sensitive response to writers such as Faulkner, Hemingway, and Wolfe, and their affinities with nineteenth century America. Having himself been shaped by the revolutionary culture of modern art, Cowley journeyed backward to find his own beliefs best expressed by the radically democratic values of America's classic writers.

His collected poetry and prose thus describes the literary odyssey of modern American writers, many of whom were his closest friends. Those writers created a new aesthetic and a new ethic that was fundamentally shaped by their experience of modern art and politics. They also modified that art by their own "long voyages" back to rediscover their moral heritage in the art of Hawthorne, Whitman, and Thoreau. Cowley's "Lost Generation" began as symbolists in technique and temperament, but in the end they remained faithful to the great humanistic tradition of their nineteenth century forebears, who were, after all, as Cowley was one of the earliest to notice, America's first truly modern writers.

### Major publications other than poetry

NONFICTION: *Exile's Return*, 1934, 1951; *After the Genteel Tradition: American Writers 1910-1930*, 1937, 1964; *Books That Changed Our Minds*, 1939 (edited); *The Literary Situation*, 1954; *Black Cargoes: A History of the Atlantic Slave Trade*, 1962; *The Faulkner-Cowley File: Letters and Memories, 1944-1962*, 1966; *Think Back on Us: A Contemporary Chronicle of the 1930's*, 1967; *A Many Windowed House: Collected Essays on American Writers and American Writing*, 1970; *A Second Flowering: Works and Days of the Lost Generation*, 1973; *—And I Worked at the Writer's Trade*, 1978; *The Dream of the Golden Mountains: Remembering the 1930s*, 1980.

ANTHOLOGIES: *The Portable Hemingway*, 1944; *The Portable Faulkner*, 1946; *The Portable Hawthorne*, 1948; *The Stories of F. Scott Fitzgerald*, 1950; *Three Novels of F. Scott Fitzgerald: The Great Gatsby . . . Tender Is the Night . . . The Last Tycoon*, 1953.

MISCELLANEOUS: *The Complete Poetry and Prose of Walt Whitman*, 1948 (edited).

**Bibliography**

Core, George. "Malcolm Cowley," in *American Writers: A Collection of Literary Biographies*. Supplement II, Part I, pp. 135-156. Edited by A. Walton Litz.

Eisenberg, Diane U. *Malcolm Cowley: A Checklist of His Writings, 1916-1973*, 1975.

Kempf, James M. *Exiles and Establishmentarians: A Biographical-Historical Study of the Formative Years of Malcolm Cowley's Literary Career*, 1981.

——————— . "Cowley's Odyssey: Literature and Faith in the Thirties," in *The Sewanee Review*. LXXXIX (Winter, 1981), pp. 520-539.

Simpson, Lewis P. "Malcolm Cowley and the American Writer," in *The Sewanee Review*. LXXXIV (Spring, 1976), pp. 220-247.

Young, Philip. "For Malcolm Cowley: Critic, Poet, 1898-," in *The Southern Review*. IX (Autumn, 1973), pp. 778-795.

*James M. Kempf*

# WILLIAM COWPER

**Born:** Great Berkhamsted, England; November 26, 1731
**Died:** East Dereham, England; April 25, 1800

## Principal poems and collections

*Olney Hymns*, 1779 (with John Newton); *Poems*, 1782; *The Task*, 1785; *Completed Poetical Works*, 1907 (standard edition).

## Other literary forms

The *Olney Hymns* are now commonly studied as poems. Of the sixty-four hymns contributed to the volume by William Cowper, only a very few still appear in church hymnals. The hymn, however, while certainly kin to the poem, presents unique demands on the author and cannot be judged fairly by the same critical standards. The hymn must try to reflect universal Christian feelings on a level immediately recognizable to all the human souls and intellects that make up a congregation. It must be orthodox and express only the expected. It must be simple, and above all it must not reveal what is individual about the author. To the extent that Cowper's unique genius could not always be restrained by convention, he is not consistently as good a hymnist as Isaac Watts or Charles Wesley.

In the eighteenth century, the familiar letter became so artistically refined that modern literary scholars now regard it as a minor literary form. Cowper's collected correspondence fills four volumes (Wright edition, 1904) and treats an incredible range of subjects and themes with great insight, humor, and style. Literary historians regard him as one of the very finest letter writers in English.

## Achievements

Modern literary historians commonly assign Cowper to the ranks of the so-called pre-Romantics, and to be sure, his subjective voice, preference for the rural to the urban, and social concern are qualities more easily discernible in the poetry of the early nineteenth century than of the late eighteenth century. Cowper, however, was not attempting to create a literary movement. The poetry characteristic of his later years is clearly a perfection of themes and forms that occupied his attention from the first, and those early efforts are not radical departures from what is considered mainstream neoclassicism. Satire, mock-heroic, general nature description, all are present, but Cowper grew in his art and was not concerned that his growth made him into something a bit different.

Cowper's satires, for example, are notable for a measure of charity toward their subjects, charity which he saw was lacking in the satires of Alexander Pope and his contemporaries. Moreover, Cowper was greatly interested in poetic structure but also felt that the poetry of his age put too much emphasis on structure at the expense of real human personality. The canon of Cowper's work is of a very uneven quality, but his finest efforts, such as *The Task*, display an unobtrusive structure and identifiable human presence uncommon in the neoclassical age, and they are fine by the standards of any age. Perhaps his outstanding structural achievement is the conversational blank verse used in *The Task*. There is no more interesting development in that form between John Milton and William Wordsworth. Yet, while Cowper's critical reputation is quite good, he is not regarded as one of the major figures in English letters. The conventions of neoclassical poetry had been manipulated with greater skill by Pope, and the new directions suggested by Cowper would be very shortly perfected by Wordsworth. Thus, the achievement of Cowper, by no means insignificant, is somewhat obscured by the giants who surround him.

### Biography

William Cowper was born on November 26, 1731, in Great Berkhampsted, Hertfordshire, England. He was the fourth child of the Reverend Dr. John Cowper, rector of Great Berkhampstead, and Ann Donne. Both parents represented distinguished families. The Cowpers had distinguished themselves by loyalty to the Crown, and John Cowper's uncle, Sir William, had been created baron in 1706 and earl in 1718. The Donne's were of even nobler lineage and traced descent from Henry III. The famous seventeenth century poet, John Donne, was of the same illustrious family. John and Ann had seven children, but only William and their last child, also named John, survived infancy. Very shortly after the birth of John, Ann died; William was only six at the time.

Cowper's father appears to have been neither a cruel nor especially loving parent. Shortly after Ann's death, young William was sent away to school. This early separation from his parent—not unusual in upper-class households—seems to have affected the poet greatly, for, several years later, Cowper attacked the practice and the school system in general in a poem, *Tirocinium* (1785). While a student at Westminster, Cowper met his first love, his cousin Theodora. The affair was terminated in 1756, but it is commemorated in nineteen sentimental love poems addressed to Delia. Cowper suffered his first severe attack of depression in 1752. He was studying law at the time and was called to the bar in 1754. Although he had no great fondness for the profession, his family had thought it best that he have some livelihood.

In 1759, Cowper was appointed Commissioner of Bankrupts, a minor governmental post that paid very little. Out of the need for financial security, he applied for an appointment to the post of Clerk of the Journals of the House of Lords. When the incumbent clerk died, Cowper's appointment was put forward only to be challenged by supporters of another candidate. In 1763, Cowper learned that he would have to face an examination to determine the best applicant. This prospect greatly aggravated his already depressed state, and he experienced a severe mental breakdown during which he unsuccessfully attempted suicide. Clearly, he could not occupy a government post. The sense of rejection as a consequence of this realization joined with the recollection of his mother's death and the broken affair with Theodora led Cowper to imagine that his exile from normal human relationships was only God's sign to him that he was also excluded from the company of the blessed for all eternity.

Following an eighteen month residence in an asylum, Cowper moved to the country where he soon made the acquaintance of the Unwin family. He resided with that cheerful and cordial family in Huntingdon and then accompanied Mrs. Unwin in her move to the town of Olney following the sudden death of her husband. Here, Cowper met the revivalist minister John Newton, and, for a time, he enjoyed a useful and productive existence. He became interested in the problems of the poor and various charitable activities and joined with Newton in writing a collection of hymns which was later published as the *Olney Hymns*. In January, 1773, however, shortly before his planned marriage to the widowed Mrs. Unwin, Cowper again suffered a period of instability. Convinced by a terrifying dream that it was God's will, he once again attempted suicide. His failure only added to his distress, for now, sure that he had failed to obey God's command, he became utterly convinced of his damnation. Although he recovered from the 1773 breakdown, despair never left him.

Largely as a distraction, Cowper turned his attention to writing poetry, and in February, 1782, he published his first significant collection. The early 1780's were made happier for Cowper by his friendship with Lady Austin, who had taken up residence near Olney. It was at the suggestion of this good-humored lady that in July, 1783, he began his masterpiece, *The Task*. That poem provided the title for his next collection which appeared in 1785. Yet, whatever joy Cowper may have derived from the favorable public response to his new volume was soon erased by the death of Mrs. Unwin's son, William. This shock, plus the anxiety caused by moving from his beloved Olney to Weston, was more than Cowper could endure, and in 1787 he again lost his grip on reality.

Following his recovery, Cowper again turned to writing. He began a translation of Homer and addressed himself to social issues, especially the fight against slavery. For a few years at least he was able to reproduce the routine and uneventful living he had enjoyed at Olney. In December, 1791, however, Mrs. Unwin suffered a stroke; in May, 1792, she suffered another which rendered her immobile and speechless. She recovered somewhat, but the guilt Cowper felt at recalling how her life had been spent in his care, plunged him again into deep melancholy. His feelings are well expressed in "To Mary," written in the fall of 1793. Not even the satisfaction of his great poetic fame and an annual pension of three hundred pounds from George III could lift him from despair or silence the voices of eternal doom which came to him at night. On December 17, 1796, Mrs. Unwin died. "The Castaway," composed in 1799, is one of the bleakest poems in English and itself sufficient comment on the last three years of Cowper's life. On April 25, 1800, after a one-month struggle with edema, he died. A witness described his last facial expression as one of "holy surprise."

## Analysis

William Cowper's poetic achievement is marked by a tension between subjectivity and objectivity, a tension which, at its best, produces a unique poetry defying easy classification as either neoclassical or Romantic. Cowper wrote poetry to preserve his sanity. It was a way to distract himself from the terrible brooding on the inevitability of his damnation, and even when his gloom made it impossible to focus on subjects other than his own condition, at least the very act of writing, the mechanical business of finding rhymes or maintaining meter, defused the self-destructive potential of the messages of despair that crowded his dreams and came to him in the whisperings of mysterious voices. Because the poetry was not only by Cowper but also *for* Cowper, it displays a subjectivity uncommon in the neoclassical tradition. Although Cowper had his own opinions about poetry and disliked the formal, elegant couplet structure that dominated the verse of his day, he was not completely a rebel. Objectivity, Horatian humor, sentimentality, respect for the classics, the very qualities that define neoclassicism are all present in Cowper's verse. Unlike William Wordsworth, he never issued a manifesto to revolutionize poetry. Indeed, the level-headed detachment of the Horatian persona, so popular with Cowper's contemporaries, was a stance that he often tried to capture for the sake of his own mental stability. When Cowper manages a balance between the subjectivity that injects his own gentle humanity into a poem and the objectivity that allows universal significance, he is at his best.

One of Cowper's most famous poems illustrates the poet at less than his best when he manages almost fully to withhold his own personality and allows convention to structure his message. "On the Receipt of My Mother's Picture Out of Norfolk" was written in 1790, fifty-three years after his mother's death and only ten years before his own. The poem avoids the theme of death and rather focuses on the mother with the only tool available to it: convention. The poem begins with a reference to the power of art to immortalize, a theme which might have supported some interesting content. The poet then introduces yet another worthy theme: "And while that face renews my filial grief,/ Fancy shall weave a charm for my relief"; while the art of the picture kindles an old grief, the art of the poem will provide the balm. Neither theme, however, survives beyond the first few lines of the poem. Instead, Cowper turns to the popular conventions of eighteenth century verse to produce a proper comment on a dead mother.

The verse form is the heroic couplet, the dominant form of the age. The diction is formal because the neoclassical notion of decorum—words appropriately matched to the subject matter—demanded formality in the respectful approach of a child to a parent. Ann Cowper, the poet's mother, is unrecognizable in the poem; she has no individuality, no visual reality for the reader. Consistent with the neoclassical emphasis on the general and ideal rather than the particular and commonplace, Cowper creates a cloud of expected motherly virtues through which the face of Ann can be seen but dimly. Here it should be remembered, however, that the poet is reacting to a picture, an eighteenth century portrait, not to a tangible human being, and that portrait itself would have been an idealized representation reflective of the aesthetic principle voiced by Sir Joshua Reynolds: "The general idea constitutes real excellence. . . . Even in portraits, the grace, and, we may add, the likeness, consists more in taking the general air than in observing the exact similitude of feature."

The poem, then, does accurately treat its subject if that subject is indeed the portrait. Still, the treatment is for the most part a catalog of hackneyed images—"sweet smiles" and "dear eyes"—mixed with a few images that need more than originality to save them, such as the extended simile which likens the mother to "a gallant bark from Albion's coast" that "shoots into port at some well-havered isle," a rather unflattering analogy if the reader attempts to use it to help visualize the mother. The overall sentimentality of the poem is also no departure from neoclassical convention. Sentimentalism in all literary genres had emerged as a popular reaction to the great emphasis placed on reason by so many eighteenth century thinkers. The universe, it was held, is logical and ordered, and all nature, including human nature, is ultimately understandable by the human ability to reason. Sentimentalism answered this by calling attention to emotions and feelings. Humanity is not merely rational; there are finer qualities beyond the power of logic to comprehend. At its best, sentiment could add an element of emotion to reason and make a work more reflective of the real human psyche. At its worst, sentiment drowned reality in maudlin fictions and saccharine absurdities. Cowper's poem does not completely sink in the quagmire of sentimental syrup. It hangs on by the thread of an idea about the immortalizing power of art, a thread which is visible at the beginning and then again at the end but which for the greater part of the poem is lost in the swamp.

All of this is not to say that "On the Receipt of My Mother's Picture Out of Norfolk" is a bad poem. Indeed, it remains one of Cowper's most frequently anthologized works. If it is conventional, it is still worth studying as a good example of several aspects of the neoclassical tradition unknown to readers who name the age after Alexander Pope or Samuel Johnson. Cowper, however, was capable of doing better. The problem with the mother poem was that rather than writing about his mother he pretended to write about his own feelings and memories. The memories after so many years were probably dim, and he seems to have chosen to avoid an expression of his dark fears and utter isolation in favor of a conventional grieving son persona.

Cowper succeeds more fully when his reaction to a situation or event includes, but also goes beyond, the feelings most readers would experience when he injects enough of his purely subjective response to allow the reader to see a somewhat different but still believable dimension to what it is to be human. The loss of a mother is certainly an appropriate correlative to the emotions expressed in the poem. Moreover, the emotional response is certainly believable; it is not, however, unique. The loss of a seaman overboard during a storm is also an appropriate correlative to the emotions of the speaker in "The Castaway," but here Cowper does more than simply respond to a situation.

The episode of the seaman swept overboard in a storm, an account of which Cowper had read in George Anson's *Voyage* (1748) some years before writing the poem, is actually an extended metaphor for the poet's own condition. Interestingly, the analogy between poet and sailor is only briefly pointed out at the very beginning and again at the end of the poem. The metaphor, the story of the sailor, is for the most part presented with curious objectivity. The facts of the tragedy are all there: the storm, the struggles of the seaman, the futile attempts at rescue. There is also a respectable measure of grief in the subdued tone of the speaker; the reader, however, could not be misled by this seeming objectivity. It is at once apparent that the poem is really about the tragic fate of the poet, but it is precisely in this tension between the objective and subjective that the poem says so much. The effect of the long metaphor in keeping the poet's ego in the background is to illustrate that indeed the poet is an insignificant thing—a tiny, isolated being beyond the help of his fellows and the concern of his God. That curious objectivity is in fact the attitude of the universe toward Cowper. It does not seem to care, and it is not hostile. It has simply excluded Cowper from the scheme of things, a scheme which allows for the possibility of salvation for all humans.

The God in "The Castaway" seems strangely Deistic. He is unwilling to interfere with the predetermined operation of His universe; but unlike many of his contemporaries who viewed the universe with optimism, believing that if God was remote at least the system that He set in motion was good, Cowper sees no goodness in his own portion. In "The Castaway," Cowper can neither bless nor curse his fate, for any action would detract from the utter futility he wishes to convey. "The Castaway," then, is highly subjective. The poet is in no way suggesting that the fate of the metaphorical sailor describes the universal human condition. Indeed, humanity is on board the ship, which survives the storm. Cowper is talking about himself, but the air of objectivity in the presentation stresses the futility and isolation he wishes to convey. In other words, the structure of the poem contributes greatly to its message. What is Cowper in the eyes of God? He is no more than the minimal first-person intrusion in the sixty-six lines that constitute "The Castaway."

Cowper was a fine craftsman in the structuring of poems. His collected works clearly show a fondness for experimentation, and as is to be expected, some of those experiments were more successful than others. An interesting example is "The Poplar Field," a frequently anthologized lyric that deals with the fleeting glories of this world. Here, Cowper deliberately violates decorum and adopts a sprightly, heavily accented meter. The mere four feet to a line gallops the reader through musings on various reminders of mortality. The meter seems to mock the expected seriousness of the theme to produce a parody of melancholy landscape verse. The content of the poem consists, for the most part, of uninspired platitudes and clichés, but this is the necessary fodder for parody. A less generous reading might assert that parody is not an issue. The poem is rather a straightforward presentation of the joys of melancholy, the pleasures of the contemplative life. The meter is the vehicle for communicating the pleasure idea to the audience, and Cowper's "The Poplar Field" is really a direct descendant of John Milton's "Allegro." If this is the case, the trite content cannot be justified as fuel for a satiric fire and must be held to be just that: trite content. Perhaps, then, "The Poplar Field" is of the same family as "On the Receipt of My Mother's Picture Out of Norfolk": both poems suffer from the substitution of conventions for the presence of the real Cowper.

An experiment of unchallenged success is "The Diverting History of John Gilpin." Structure is everything in this delightful ballad about the misadventures of a linen draper on his twenty-year delayed honeymoon. The lively meter and rhyming quatrains are ideally suited to the rollicking humor of the piece. Gilpin, a rather bombastic but totally good-natured hero, has his adventure told by a narrator who is himself satirized by the deceptively careless method of his composition. It soon becomes clear that the poem is everything and that the narrator will not be stopped or the rhythm broken by such concerns as taking time to find an appropriate figure rather than a silly one or even by running out of content to fill the quatrain: "So like an arrow swift he flew,/ Shot by an archer strong;/ So did he fly—which brings me to/ The middle of my song." For Cowper, the poem lived up to its title; it seems to have diverted him indeed, for the reader familiar with Cowper's voice will look in vain for a trace of the brooding author of "The Castaway." Yet, beneath the funny story, the brilliant metrics, and the silly narrator, there is still the gentle poet who prefers to laugh with his characters rather than reduce them to the grotesque fools that populate so much of eighteenth century satire.

Despite the success of "The Diverting History of John Gilpin," Cowper has never been considered a leading satirist of the age. Satire, especially in the popular Horatian mode, must have had its attractions for him. The detached, witty observer who by choice leaves the herd to remark upon the foibles of humanity presented an ideal persona, but it was a stance that Cowper could seldom sustain. The satirist must appear objective; the folly must appear to be a genuine part of the target and not merely in the satirist's perception of the target. Cowper could maintain that kind of objectivity only when there was really nothing at stake. Poking fun at the world of John Gilpin is harmless, for there is no suggestion that the world is real beyond the confines of the poem. When the subject is real, however, Cowper cannot stand aside. He lacks wit, in the neoclassical sense of the word. Wit consisted of the genius needed to conceive the raw material of art and the acquired good taste to know how to arrange bits of that material into a unified whole. Wit did not allow for the subjective intrusion of the author's personal problems. Cowper's genius was so intertwined with his special mental condition that he could not remain detached, and when he tried, his acquired skill could only arrange conventions, substitutes for his unique raw material. Moreover, Cowper lacked the satirist's willingness to ridicule. He had nothing against humanity. The shipmates are guiltless in the tragedy of the castaway. Humanity, to be sure, has its delusions and vanities, but Cowper preferred the deflected blow to the sharp thrust.

*The Task* is Cowper's major achievement, and it is the satiric Cowper who introduces the work. His friend, Lady Austin, had suggested a sofa as an appropriate topic for a poem in blank verse. Of course, such a subject could only be addressed satirically, and Cowper elected the conventional form of mock-heroic. Specifically, he alluded to *The Aeneid* with "I sing the sofa" and thereby suggested that a modern Vergil would be hard pressed to find in eighteenth century society a topic deserving heroic treatment. Yet, the sofa is more than simply a mean subject, it is a quite appropriate symbol for sloth and luxury, the very qualities responsible for society's falling away from the truly heroic. Having called attention to the problem, there is little more for the sofa to do, except that it led Cowper to something worth saying, and he needed a structure less restrictive of his own involvement than the mock-heroic. So with a comment on how he prefers walks in the country to life on the sofa, Cowper shifts to an appreciation of nature theme and the *I* who had been the Vergilian persona of the satire suddenly becomes Cowper himself.

*The Task* is far too long a work for detailed analysis here. Its five thousand lines are divided into six parts: "The Sofa," "The Time-Piece," "The Garden," "The Winter Evening," "The Winter Morning Walk," and "The Winter Walk at Noon." The question of the overall unity of the work has probably attracted the greatest amount of critical attention. Cowper's own comments about the poem indicate that he was not aiming at tight thematic development; rather, the ideas were naturally suggested by immediately preceding ideas with the whole moving along with the ease of an intelligent but unplanned conversation.

Cowper's style, once the mock-heroic has been dropped, certainly suggests conversation. The diction is elegant but natural, quite different from the language of the other popular eighteenth century nature poet James Thomson, whose baroque language in *The Seasons* (1730) imitated the grand style of John Milton. Moreover, Cowper's blank verse avoids the end-stopped lines used by Thomson, which detracted from the conversational effect by their epigrammatic regularity. The deceptively artless ease of the poem with its several scenes, frequent digressions, and inclusion of highly personal material might easily lead the reader to conclude that the poet is recording a stream of consciousness with no central purpose or theme in mind. In fact, *The Task* is concerned with the need and search for balance in nature and human life. The sofa itself suggests the theme, for if it represents the scale tipping toward excessive luxury, there must somewhere in the range of experience be an ideal conditon against which such excesses can be recognized and measured.

The ultimate excess to which the sofa points is the city, London, which on a physical plane reveals squalor, corruption, and insanity; its spiritual reality is sin. The opposite side of the scale also has a spiritual and physical existence. Spiritually, this extreme is the untempered wrath of God, pure divine power; on the physical level, such power is reflected in disturbances in nature and the brutalism that is the alternative to civilization. The early books explore the extremes and present the rural countryside as perhaps the best balance. This balance is insecure, however, for intrusions of both natural and human turmoil bring constant disturbance. The latter parts of the poem demonstrate the futility of finding a secure position in the physical environment. For those who enjoy God's grace, conversion can clarify the balance and bring freedom and order. The final book reveals God as the ultimate source of harmony. In His infinite kindness and infinite sternness, the Father judges all and that judgment is perfection.

Among the landscape descriptions, character sketches, social criticism, and personal confessions, a unifying theme is perceptible if not obvious in *The Task*, and interestingly, it is the theme that best describes Cowper's life and art, the quest for a place of stability, a point of balance. In his art, he experimented to find his own voice, and he found it between the extremes of objectivity, toward which most art of his age tended, and the subjectivity that would characterize the art of the next generation. In the task of his life, he sought the balance of sanity, a quiet place of his own between the stress of urban society and the horror of being utterly alone, a castaway in a sea of despair. Tragically, he could not occupy that stable middle ground for very long; but in his best poetry, he created a remarkable sanity and said still-important things in a way that cannot easily be pigeon-holed as neoclassical or Romantic and in a way that is uniquely Cowper.

**Major publication other than poetry**
NONFICTION: *Correspondence, Arranged in Chronological Order*, 1904.

## Bibliography

Cecil, David. *The Stricken Deer*, 1929.
Free, William N. *William Cowper*, 1970.
Gilbert, Thomas. *William Cowper and the Eighteenth Century*, 1948.
Golden, Morris. *In Search of Stability*, 1960.
Hartley, Lodwick. *William Cowper: The Continuing Revaluation*, 1960.
_____ .*William Cowper: Humanitarian*, 1938.
Quinlan, Maurice. *William Cowper: A Critical Life*, 1970.
Ryskamp, Charles. *William Cowper of the Inner Temple, Esq., 1959.*

*William J. Heim*

# LOUIS OSBORNE COXE

**Born:** Manchester, New Hampshire; April 15, 1918

### Principal poems and collections

*The Sea Faring and Other Poems*, 1947; *The Second Man and Other Poems*, 1955; *The Wilderness and Other Poems*, 1958; *The Middle Passage*, 1960; *The Last Hero and Other Poems*, 1965 (includes translation); *Nikal Seyn and Decoration Day: A Poem and a Play*, 1966; *Passage: Selected Poems 1943-1978*, 1979.

### Other literary forms

In the manner of two of his famous teachers and later academic colleagues, R. P. Blackmur and Allen Tate, and several poets of his literary generation such as Randall Jarrell and Robert Lowell, Louis Osborne Coxe has produced distinguished art in a wide range of literary forms. For more than forty years he has demonstrated a technical virtuosity in numerous poetic forms, and in drama, literary criticism, and essays. He has also written a book-length critical biography of Edwin Arlington Robinson and translated poems of several modern French poets. A true man of letters, he has been an accomplished writer in almost every literary genre.

Coxe has written two significant works of drama. The first, *Billy Budd* (1951), was based on Herman Melville's novella. Written in collaboration with Robert Chapman, Coxe's version of Melville's story was begun in 1947 as a verse drama and was revised over a period of two years before being produced by the Experimental Theatre at New York's Lennox Hill Settlement House in 1949. During the next two years, the play was modified further while being adapted for Broadway. The finished prose version of the play, which ran on Broadway for four months in 1951 and which won praise from theater critics such as Brooks Atkinson of *The New York Times*, is the version Coxe and Chapman chose to retain. That version was published by Hill and Wang in 1962 in the *Spotlight Dramabooks* series of contemporary plays.

Coxe's second major work of drama, *Decoration Day* (1966), was published by Vanderbilt University Press as a companion piece to his narrative poem "Nikal Seyn." *Decoration Day* is a play about a retired Union Army general who is near the end of his life and about to retire from the presidency of a small college in Maine in 1914 on the eve of World War I. The technical complexity of *Decoration Day* reveals Coxe's mastery of theater conventions. It uses double characters and flashback sequences to interweave incidents from the historical past with the present circumstances of the main characters. The drama reflects Coxe's often unconventional utilization of older literary traditions and themes. The play (with allusions to Homer's *Iliad*) concerns the conflict between a soldier's sense of duty and his awareness that he will be called to serve in situations which are characterized by absurdity and the pointless waste of human lives.

The theme of duty in contemporary literature is unusual. Most modern writers have responded to the situation of modern war with a literature of revolt and an almost conventional response of "antiheroic" themes and black humor. Coxe's reassertion of the ideal of duty reveals much about his character. *Decoration Day* is a gesture of commemoration to his New England ancestors, those farmers, shopkeepers, and craftsmen who, without seeking the role of hero, nevertheless defended the ideals of American freedom and equality with noble sacrifice.

In a similar manner, much of his literary criticism pays tribute to unfashionable New England poets and novelists. The literary studies collected in *Enabling Acts: Selected Essays in Criticism* (1976) offer learned and astute defenses of artists such as James Gould Cozzens, Edwin Arlington Robinson, Edward Thomas, and Herman Melville. The book also includes a number of speculative essays on topics which have been major issues of aesthetic debate in twentieth century American literature, such as the relation between "History and Imagination," "Poetry and Religion," the nature of metaphor, and the diminished social status of poets in a modern industrial society. The essays in *Enabling Acts* were written over a period of three decades and published in a wide range of journals, from such national political papers as *The New Republic* and *The Nation* to prominent literary quarterlies such as *The Hudson Review*, *The Sewanee Review*, and *American Literature*.

One of Coxe's earliest essays was a critical defense of Edwin Arlington Robinson, a poet for whom he has a deep sympathy. In numerous essays, he has cited Robinson's example, and he published longer studies of Robinson in the University of Minnesota "Pamphlets on American Writers" series, *Edwin Arlington Robinson* (1962), and a book-length critical biography, *Edwin Arlington Robinson: The Life of Poetry* (1969). This latter volume was part of a series, "Pegasus American Authors," published by the Western Publishing Company of New York. It is one of the two or three best studies ever done of Robinson and reveals Coxe to be a critic of sympathetic intelligence with a clear and vibrant prose style and wide learning.

Coxe's translations of several French symbolist and modern poets, such as Charles Baudelaire, Guillaume Apollinaire, Jacques Prévert, and Raymond Queneau, were collected in a section of his book *The Last Hero and Other Poems* under the title, "Versions."

## Achievements

The formal recognition of Coxe's literary achievements reflects the diversity of his activities. Few contemporary American poets have reached a large public audience. Coxe is no exception. His reception by the educated audience of American readers and literary professionals, however, began early, upon publication of his first book of poems in 1947. After publication of the book, Coxe was awarded a Briggs-Copeland Fellowship by Harvard University for the 1948-1949 academic year.

The publication of his second book of poems in 1955 was followed by the award of a fellowship in writing sponsored by the *Sewanee Review* literary magazine. During the period of the fellowship, Coxe wrote a large part of his longest and perhaps most visually imaginative narrative poem, *The Middle Passage*. In 1962, Coxe was chosen for a Creative Arts Award by Brandeis University.

Coxe was honored for his general literary achievement in 1977 by the National Endowment for the Arts. In 1978 the American Academy of Poets selected him as one of its Prize poets.

While earning distinction as a poet, dramatist, and literary scholar, Coxe continued to work as an educator. He was twice selected by the Fulbright Commission as an outstanding teacher and given fellowships to teach American culture and literature in Ireland and France. During the academic year of 1959-1960, he taught at Trinity College, Dublin, and in 1970-1971, he served as Fulbright Professor at the Université de Provence, Aix-Marseille. Coxe also served as visiting professor and Fellow in Creative Writing at Princeton University from 1962 to 1963. Since 1955, he has been the Franklin Pierce Professor of English at Bowdoin College, Maine.

In a century in which American poetic styles and subject matter have been dramatically influenced by the experimental impulse of modern art, and by the Romantic sensibility of that movement, Coxe has quietly continued to write poetry in traditional forms. In particular he has kept alive the tradition of long narrative poetry which the great nineteenth century New England poets John Greenleaf Whittier and Henry Wadsworth Longfellow, and his fellow Maine poet Robinson, made a central part of American poetic history. Coxe has demonstrated in both poetic practice and critical essays the "storytelling" entertainment value and the educational virtues of narrative poetry.

With a moral conscience as acutely critical of the contradictions of New England's history as Robert Lowell's, Coxe has nevertheless expressed those aspects of modern life that reflect enduring values and transcend the evils of a particular historical era. In long narrative poems and in short lyrics, in commemorative verse and private tributes, Coxe has both criticized modern American life and celebrated the pleasures of living in modern times. His poems commemorate friends and teachers and the prosaic virtues of human community as well as his respect for men in history who have heroically faced their destiny.

Several of Coxe's major narrative poems stand as brilliant examples of his often-stated theme that the literary imagination in modern times can respond not only to the anguish of its circumstances but also to the plight of mankind in past history, from the American Indian wars of the eighteenth century and the moral scandal of American nineteenth century slave trading, to the terror and nobility of men in battle in World War II. Coxe is a poet for whom historical reality and the suffering and heroism of other human beings provoke the most powerful imaginative responses. In submerging his own personality so as to release his historical imagination, Coxe has kept alive the tradition of English narrative verse, a tradition that has produced many great poems, and one in which he has achieved his own most distinguished work.

## Biography

Louis Osborne Coxe was born on April 15, 1918, in Manchester, New Hampshire. His father, Charles Shearman Coxe, and his mother, Helen Eyre Osborne, both had deep roots in New England. Coxe's mother traced her lineage to 1640, and early in his life his family moved from Manchester to his mother's ancestral home of Salem, Massachusetts. For anyone with literary ambitions growing up in Salem, it was impossible to avoid the legacy of Melville, Nathaniel Hawthorne, and Ralph Waldo Emerson, those nineteenth century New England writers who provided American literature its shaping voice while awakening the nation to the morally ambiguous, contradictory nature of its historical past and values.

If New England was the first major influence on his art, two other experiences were equally important, college and the United States Navy. In the fall of 1936, after being graduated from St. Paul's preparatory school in Concord, New Hampshire, Coxe entered Princeton University, the college of several relatives, including an uncle, Howard Coxe, who was graduated with the Princeton class of 1920. Howard Coxe had been a fringe member of the important World War I era Princeton literary group that included F. Scott Fitzgerald, Edmund Wilson, and John Peale Bishop. He had gone to Paris in the 1920's as part of the famous postwar literary migration. For Coxe, an uncle involved in a literary career with such esteemed writers was a figure of compelling romantic interest.

The Princeton of the late 1930's seemed a much more forbidding environment and one which, given the circumstance of the Great Depression and the impending war, was hardly a place to encourage young writers. A constellation of circumstances, however, conspired to do just that by bringing together another group of writers that fostered the second major literary renaissance at Princeton in the twentieth century. In 1939, the Dean of Princeton, Christian Gauss, upon the recommendation of Professor Willard Thorp, brought Allen Tate to the college to organize and administer a program in creative writing. Tate inaugurated the program in the fall of 1939 and the next year brought R. P. Blackmur to be his assistant. Both men were influential critical analysts of modern writing as well as practicing poets and editors of literary magazines: Tate's *The Fugitive* was the organ of the southern Agrarian poets, while Blackmur had edited *The Hound and Horn*, a major journal of American modern writing in the late 1920's and early 1930's. Coxe was befriended by both men, and they were profound influences on his career. He has recalled that Blackmur's acute critical intelligence, his ability to demonstrate the "dense possibilities" of poetry, made a lasting impression on him. Thirty-five years after he first met Tate, and after serving as his colleague at the University of Minnesota from 1949 to 1955, Coxe dedicated his volume of critical essays, *Enabling Acts*, to him.

The Creative Arts Program at Princeton in the early 1940's became a breeding ground of talent that included Coxe's classmate, the poet William Meredith, and the men who later founded *The Hudson Review*, Frederick Morgan, William Arrowsmith, Joseph Bennet, and Robert Wise. With the connections to the larger literary world that Tate and Blackmur provided, Coxe began his literary career with high standards and respect for wide learning.

Two other teachers at Princeton had an even greater influence on Coxe. Professor E. D. H. Johnson, a specialist in Victorian literature, taught Coxe the history of the great Victorian poets and the way in which their narrative poetry subtly served as a bridge to literary modernism. Coxe dedicated his fourth book of poetry, the book-length narrative poem *The Middle Passage*, to Johnson.

Finally, the teacher who perhaps most lastingly influenced Coxe was Willard Thorp. A literary historian and pioneer Melville scholar, Thorp inaugurated the first program in American studies at Princeton in the late 1940's. While Tate and Blackmur were associated (often reductively so) with the so-called "New Criticism" which dominated the academic study of literature in America from the 1940's through the 1960's, Thorp's historical approach was based on a simple premise: an artist and his work could not be separated from the cultural history that surrounded him. Social and political as well as historical, religious, psychological, biographical, and ideological influences were important elements in the understanding of a writer's work. The intense study of American writers such as Hawthorne, Melville, and Emerson, and their relationship to American culture, which Thorp, Van Wyck Brooks, F. O. Matthiessen, and others inaugurated in the late 1930's, exploded in the 1940's and was a principal component of Coxe's literary education. His extraordinary interest in history and literature was fired by Thorp's teaching, and in gratitude Coxe dedicated his first book of poetry to him.

When World War II began, Coxe was called to service. In June, 1942, he began four years of service as a naval officer, most of which took place in the bloody battles of the Pacific. Coxe commanded two different patrol craft, the U.S.S. *PC 549* and the U.S.S. *PC 1195*. As in the case of James Dickey, Randall Jarrell, and James Jones, the experience of World War II became a central subject of his writing. However vicious a war it was, Coxe also saw in the behavior of the American sailors and soldiers a nobility recalling older literary themes. America's last just and unambiguous war, a war upon which the fate of the Western world hinged, World War II provided Coxe with one of his greatest and recurring subjects. It was to be the central experience of his life.

In 1946, Coxe married Edith Winsor. They have three sons and one daughter and live in Brunswick, Maine, where he continues to teach at Bowdoin College.

### Analysis

Like all good critics, Louis Osborne Coxe has written about other writers with insight while revealing his own aesthetic values. Three issues pervade his critical work. In a number of essays, Coxe displays antipathy to the styles, aesthetic theories, and social themes of modern writers. In particular, he has quarreled with the symbolist theory of metaphor and the cult of subjective, often drug- or alcohol-induced "derangement of the senses" which poets such as Arthur Rimbaud, Hart Crane, and numerous other modern writers have followed in search of literary creativity. The evasion of social involvement by modern writers, and what Coxe has called the romantic quest to subordinate the world to the sensibility of a single mind, led to occasionally great art, he once wrote, but also to "mechanical, destructive, and obscurantist elements that always threaten a symbolist work." The strange and often inaccessibly private iconography and eccentric forms of modern art have nevertheless been the dominant aesthetic expression of the twentieth century. That fact helps to explain Coxe's unease with the art of his time.

He has often criticized modern fiction and poetry for following the example of Henry James, James Joyce, Marcel Proust, and Ezra Pound by creating a literature of stylistic digression, baroque embellishment, and abandonment of traditional forms. One Coxe essay, in defense of narrative poetry, urges writers to rediscover the direct and action-oriented style of narrative verse, a literary mode, he argues (perhaps naïvely), that could make literature once more accessible to modern audiences. In an essay discussing the relation of poetry to religion, Coxe argues that much modern poetry reveals the presence of religious sensibility in modern times, but that this artistic sensibility lacks adequate social forms in which to express itself. Similarly, in a long essay analyzing the relation between history and the literary imagination, Coxe writes that dreams and fantasies, the subject of much post-Romantic art, are only a fraction of the subject matter available for poetry. Poetry should "wrestle with possibilities and facts, with natural laws and human nature, always recognizing that there may be more-or-less than meets the eye."

The "religion of humanity," the complex reality of mankind, is the subject of Coxe's own art and the one he values most. The writers he admires, such as George Bernard Shaw, William Shakespeare, James Gould Cozzens, Robert Frost, E. E. Cummings, and Edwin Arlington Robinson represent for him artists who understand the temptations of fantasy as well as the possibility of material limitations. They are writers, however, who always direct the reader to "the source of art and metaphor," the world of nature and human reality. For Coxe, the great writers are always moralists, not by virtue of didactic statement but by their careful "rendering" of complex human existence, "from which art cannot escape." Those writers who provide the customs, forms, and "mastery of reality" that enable one to live in human history, and who teach how to confront death and life, love and war, sadness and joy; in short, all the elements of human life: these are the writers he praises. He seems to have applied that dictum to his own writing, for he judges art as moral to the degree it teaches one how to live, "to be wise" so as to survive in, not escape from, the human condition.

Published by Henry Holt and Company, *The Sea Faring and Other Poems* contains forty-one poems. Though not entirely arranged by theme, three subjects dominate the book. As expected for a poet who spent World War II at sea, the volume contains a preponderance of poems about war. Coxe's war poems are of two types: two longer narrative poems, the title poem and "Epistle to Oahu," open and close the volume. In between are a number of shorter poems describing scenes and aspects of the Navy. The other two groups of poems concern New England writers and the poet's private response to experience.

"The Sea Faring" is a long narrative poem that re-creates the visual and auditory scene of naval ships in convoy traveling quietly through ocean waters en route to battle. The omnipresence of death and the movement of the ships toward war are understated in the poem, not only because they create the initial setting of the entire book, but also because Coxe felt admiration for the spectacle of naval armadas. Neither the tone of the poem nor its narration, however, obscures the poet's awareness of the destructive consequences of war or the moral culpability of men unleashed to kill, "We are a weary vessel with a housekeeper's chores/ To do to keep us slick for enmity." Yet, the poem recalls images of men working harmoniously and the smells, sights, and sounds of an enterprise larger than individuals, "things certainly to be remembered of war." Those images stick in Coxe's memory and temper his emotional anguish at the loss of lives. One brief scene midway through the poem describes the narrator's return after the war to a peaceful college campus where the quiet, cultured civility of university life appears to have proceeded untouched by the violence of World War II. This "impossible return" gives meaning to the rest of the poem. The palpable barbarity of militaristic Fascism in World War II and the need to defeat that enemy move Coxe to see men at war as seafarers venturing forth in search of "trouble" so that civility can survive at home.

Many of the short poems of *The Sea Faring and Other Poems* such as "Convoy," "Lookout," "Gunners Mate," "Liberty Party," "Ships Cook," and

"Pin-Up Girl," communicate specific experiences of World War II naval life. They also reveal Coxe's imaginative link between the events of his generation and the seemingly perennial voyages of New England seafarers, from the lobsterman who exchanges his fishing traps for gunnery duty to the "liberty" that Herman Melville's characters in *White-Jacket* (1850) took a century before.

Several poems, such as "For M. E. S. Before D-Day," "Discharge," and "V-J Day," reveal a complex emotional response to the end of battle and death. In several elegiac poems, Coxe also pays tribute to those sailors who did not make it home: "Dead Marine," "Sea Elegy," and "Epistle to Oahu" contain stark images of bloated bodies floating in water and the carnage of rotting men on Pacific island shores, the littered products of now silent guns. These poems, however, do not simply lament the dead. Particularly in "Epistle to Oahu," Coxe attempts to give a historical meaning to the dead soldiers by showing that the living understand their sacrifice. The death of friends is a "vulnerable beauty/ Risking all hurt on enterprise." The survivors, the poem's narrator argues, suffer too, with the spirit of fallen comrades and images of their graves on scattered Pacific islands impressed forever on their memory. The image that will symbolize for him the dead of war, he declares, is the peaceful image of Hawaii's Oahu island valleys, where "troubled" conscience now sees earthly gardens. Those islands of the mind are the memorial Coxe offers for his friends and other Americans who died so that the living could flourish in earthly gardens of love.

*The Sea Faring and Other Poems* is not a one-note book, however. Love lyrics such as "For M. B. and F. W.," "For Asher Hinds," "Little River," "Slow Movement," and "Miami Beach" display a formal stanzaic and metrical precision and a disciplined intelligence which recall the English Metaphysical poets. The personal lyrics in the volume also include memoirs of youth, as in the poem "Recess," and of family and friends.

New England too, and its great literary "seafarers," is the subject of a final group of poems in the book. Poems about Jones Very, Melville, Hawthorne, and Ambrose Bierce indicate Coxe's interest in the cultural past of New England and its historical contradictions. The poems on Hawthorne and Melville demonstrate Coxe's awareness of the new literary scholarship on those writers, for he saw them as artists wracked by moral conscience and critical of simplistic transcendental mysticism and American optimism. His portrait of Jones Very criticizes the "crackpot" visions of a writer who lost touch with reality.

At the end of the war, with time for reflection, Coxe spent several years on a poetic journey of investigation into the region that had bred him. The chief subject of *The Second Man and Other Poems* is New England, although it was published by the University of Minnesota Press, written largely while Coxe taught at Minnesota, and dedicated to one of the great scholars of that university, Samuel Holt Monk.

"New England: A Memory" is one of Coxe's finest metrical performances. In four sections, the poet recalls scenes of childhood in Salem and Boston, his father's house, and Gallows Hill, the scene of the infamous Salem witchcraft hangings of September 22, 1692. In several dramatic monologues in the manner of Robert Browning and Edgar Lee Masters, Coxe gives voice to Salem and New England legends. "Samuel Sewall" is about the only man involved in the witchcraft trials who later admitted guilt and possible wrongdoing. "Hannah Dustin" presents a legendary New England woman of Haverhill, Massachusetts, who was kidnaped by marauding Indians with her one-week-old baby on March 15, 1697. In revenge for the murder of her baby, Dustin killed and scalped ten sleeping Indians before escaping. "Samuel McIntire" concerns the most famous architect of Salem's revolutionary period, and there are several meditations on the Civil War dead, including "Union Soldier" and "Civil War Dead, Memorial Hall."

A few poems in *The Second Man and Other Poems*, "Carrier Pilot," "Passage," and "Islands," demonstrate that Coxe's memory was still haunted by his war experience. One new aspect of the book is the expression of a formal religious sensibility. "Magnetic Pole, True Pole," "Aubade," "Nuns on Shipboard," "The Navigator Contemplates Heaven," and the book's title poem, preceded by an epigraph from the book of I Corinthians, reveal a densely allusive poet using natural and naval metaphors to affirm orthodox Christian values.

Coxe's World War II experience seems to have strengthened his faith in Christianity. Poems such as "Death Watch," "Elegy for a Child," "Children at the Beach," and "For a Nativity" reveal anguish at the death of loved ones, and yet a poet who can celebrate the joy of children at play and the miracle of birth. These poems imply that Coxe found in Christian doctrine a profound analysis of human existence with its cycles of death and rebirth, suffering and joy.

Another theme connects a final group of poems. Coxe once argued that nature is the source of metaphor. In *The Second Man and Other Poems*, he included several lyrics illustrating his point. "Haying" echoes the pastoral poems of Andrew Marvell and Robert Frost. A religious sensibility remains evident but is overwhelmed by the poet's exuberance at summer's beauty. Poems such as "Thaw," for example ("Thaw is the movement of the heart,") and "Autumn," "Watching Water," "Lament," and "Marsh Hawk," use natural analogues to communicate human emotion, from the lust of youth to the instinctual behavior of hunters. All these poems celebrate nature as a symbol of spiritual order.

Coxe moved back to New England in 1955. At Brunswick, he was close to Maine's forests, a land still untouched by freeways, suburbs, and franchised food stores. The title poem of *The Wilderness and Other Poems* is a poetic evocation of Colonial America. It describes two French Canadian Jesuits who bribe Indians to attack English settlements to help regain New England for Catholicism. Coxe's poem portrays the tragic consequences of their unrealistic missionary zeal and search for martyrdom. It also communicates his sympathy for the Indians who were unwittingly caught in the French and Indian wars, the natives who lost their land.

"The Wilderness" concludes with an exhortation to love, despite the terrible follies to which mankind is subject. Poems such as "Lent" and "Pentecost" show Coxe's continuing preoccupation with devotional poetry in the manner of the Elizabethans.

A number of poems in *The Wilderness and Other Poems*, however, emphasize a somewhat different theme. Many, such as "End of the Road," express a reverence for natural reality and the more traditional American poetic theme of the spiritual made manifest in nature.

The major new emphasis of the book derives from numerous poems sounding another great American literary theme, the humanist faith in man's wisdom, courage, and dignity in knowingly confronting his tragic destiny. "Place with Skyrockets," "The Old Ones," and "Northwest Wind" remind readers of what Coxe's poetry so often dramatizes, mankind's immense capacity for evil and his tragic fate. Coxe's description of human waste and ignorance, however, is tempered by other poems, such as "The Glen" and "Hero's Winter," that admonish men to search within themselves to find strength and to make their history meaningful: "Man must do his part/ . . . and own/ Abounding grace in promise kept and trees new-grown." His fine poem "For My Son's Birthday" continues this theme by acknowledging that adults can do little to make life easier for children. The least they can do is pass on wisdom gained from the crucible of experience. Awareness of the human condition, "sorrow's here, too late for gain," must not paralyze men and blind them to the need to confront their fate with dignity and heroism:

> Do what you must: the time is in your eyes.
> Fear nothing the world tells you, nor my words . . .
> And live in joy. Set free the dead and kill . . .
> Old ground or new, slaves to the end, but free.

The University of Chicago Press published *The Middle Passage* in 1960, demonstrating the virtue of American cultural pluralism. One of the finest achievements of postwar American poetry, it is the longest, most compelling narrative of Coxe's career. The book was beautifully bound and a collaborator, Gobin Stair, wrote the text in flowing script, photographically reproduced. He also did haunting illustrations based on Coxe's description of African slaves brutally transported to the Americas on the "middle passage" of slave ships.

The source of Coxe's poem was *The Adventures of an African Slaver, Being the True Account of the Life of Theodore Canot . . . As Told in the Year 1854 to Brantz Mayer*. Published in America in 1928 with an Introduction by Malcolm Cowley, the Canot book told the story of a Salem sailor who became involved in the slave trade. Coxe's poem re-creates in sordid, visually stunning, lean narrative action the journey of a Salem whaling ship, ironically named the "Happy Delivery," which, midway in voyage, learns its true destination is the African Gold Coast and its cargo, slaves.

As the poem begins, Canot, an apothecary apprentice from Salem, is hired by two Salem shipowners, Bliss and Crane, as medical officer. Canot gradually degenerates, becoming captain after first drugging, then murdering Captain Ames. In seven sections, the poem traces the journey of human slaving and moral corruption. At occasional points, the narrator speaks from a later perspective describing Canot as old and returning to Salem to die, penniless but without remorse for his past, which included the death of more than half of his first slave cargo and the starvation and sexual abuse of his black mistress.

New England's moral corruption because of capitalist greed is a major theme of Coxe's poem. The dark history of his Salem ancestors rode heavily on his conscience, and the poem unsparingly evokes the action and drama of a foul epoch of American history. Like Joseph Conrad's *Heart of Darkness* (1902), Coxe's poem is not simply an indictment of nineteenth century mercantilism and racism. It retells the fall of man, who in every age wrestles with his Manichaean spirit.

Human heroism and wisdom—these are old themes in Western literature, yet enduring ones. The title of Coxe's fifth book of verse, *The Last Hero and Other Poems*, does not refer to a contemporary hero. Rather, it refers to a sequence of six poems that begin the book and concern Western literature's first hero, Homer's Odysseus. Like Alfred, Lord Tennyson, Coxe finds the myth of Odysseus and the values he embodied a source of wisdom for his own age. Courage, faithfulness to family, intelligence, adaptability, and the ability to endure a hostile fate—these are traits Coxe values for the modern age.

Other heroes in the book demonstrate a similar integrity, though often in a quiet way. "In Memory of C. H. P., M.D." is a memorial to a dead physician friend in whom Coxe saw the finest traits of human compassion, dedication, and perseverance. "E. A. Robinson: Head Tide, October 1963" ruminates on a writer Coxe saw as heroic in his courage to confront despair and literary neglect while remaining faithful to his human responsibilities.

Several poems in *The Last Hero and Other Poems* revive Coxe's great theme of World War II. "On Seeing Films of the War," "Unknown Soldiers," "Breaking the Barrier," and the book's concluding poem, "The Strait," reveal a poet's sensitive intelligence connecting current circumstances to images and memories of the past, while indirectly comparing modern warfare and its inhuman consequences with the moral lessons learned (and too often forgotten) from history. "The Strait" in particular dramatizes the naval battle of February 27, 1942, known as the Battle of the Java Sea, in which a Japanese fleet destroyed a confused, ill-prepared Allied naval squadron attempting to defend Dutch Indonesia.

Meditative poems on English and Irish history constitute another group of poems in the volume, poems written while Coxe was teaching in Dublin in 1960. Still another group of poems represents further explorations of human psychology and man's response to nature. *The Last Hero and Other Poems* is a rewarding collection, demonstrating perhaps more than any of his books Coxe's practice of poetry disciplined by wide learning and acute intelligence.

Eleven years before the publication of *Nikal Seyn*, Coxe wrote a brief dramatic monologue about a nineteenth century British soldier who became famous in Victorian England for his role in suppressing the Sepoy Mutiny in colonial India. "General John Nicholson" portrayed him as the ruthless, iron-willed soldier of historical accounts.

Nicholson appears to have fascinated Coxe. The mutiny was a dark episode in British history. Angered by religious and cultural imperialism and military stupidity, Indian soldiers mutinied near the cities of Meerut, Delhi, and Lucknow in the summer of 1857. They slaughtered men, women, and children, raising fears that all Europeans in India were endangered. The episode was documented for English audiences by books, diaries, and news dispatches. The importance of the event is indicated by the interest of Karl Marx and Friedrich Engels, who compiled a book about the uprising as evidence of growing anticolonial rebellion.

Nicholson's legend grew because his native troops saw him as godlike. They nicknamed him Nikal Seyn. In August and September of 1857, he led four thousand men over scorched desert terrain and finally liberated Delhi. Before being killed in battle, he cut men in half with his sword, hung Indians indiscriminately, and in an earlier action blew apart forty disarmed mutineers by launching them alive from cannon.

"Nikal Seyn" recounts the historical facts of this story but from the viewpoint of a ninety-year-old Irish Catholic Ulsterman telling an American scholar about his life with Nicholson years before. In the new poem, Coxe describes Nicholson as far from godlike, vulnerably human, the victim of circumstances, the bigotry of his age, and arrogance. At the poem's end, readers learn the narrator's young wife, sexually attracted to the General, had once gone to his room and asked to sleep with him. The poem ends with Nicholson dying, remorsefully asking the narrator about the demands women and country make on man's soul, and, ambiguously, asking forgiveness for the affair and for his brutal past.

This harrowing story has another resonance. Coxe was in Ireland in 1960 and heard the voices of Catholic dissidence and Protestant bigotry. He has his narrator long for an earlier "heroic" age in which revenge and lawlessness were acceptable. The sectarian fanaticism of modern Northern Ireland, the poem hints, repeats the irrational hatred and barbarity that erupted in India in 1857.

Coxe's volume, *Passages*, includes a representative sampling of poems from a richly creative career spanning thirty-five years. A selection from each of his books is included, illustrating his three great subjects: poems of nature and private experience, war, and New England history.

More than half the book is consumed by the reprinting, this time in typeface, of *The Middle Passage*. The volume also includes a number of new poems written during the previous decade in which natural scenes evoke the peaceful, quiet landscape of Maine. These poems represent a slight departure for Coxe. For a poet of so many violent poetic narratives, the new lyrics in *Passage* represent a relatively content spirit. Poems such as "God's Country," "New Year's Eve," "Anniversary," "On the Border," "Loyalist Graveyard, Acadia," and "Four Songs from Five Plays" convey an insistent preoccupation with contemporary America and a celebration of Maine's natural landscape. The voices from the historical past which haunted Coxe seem quieted:

> And the time changes, takes a departure west
> into other quadrants where the hunter ghosts
> travel the painted woods making up fires.
> We go east, back of the known past
> that comes round again making the country fair.

Coxe's poetic journey has been a violent one, like America's historical journey. That he finds peace at its end is a sign that a major American poet yet has hope for his country.

**Major publications other than poetry**
  PLAYS: *Billy Budd*, 1951 (with Robert Chapman); *Decoration Day*, 1966.
  NONFICTION: *Edwin Arlington Robinson*, 1962; *Edwin Arlington Robinson: The Life of Poetry*, 1969; *Enabling Acts: Selected Essays in Criticism*, 1976.

**Bibliography**
Fraser, Russell. "R. P. Blackmur at Princeton," in *The Sewanee Review*. LXXXIX (Fall, 1981), pp. 540-559.
Johnson, E. D. H. "Louis Coxe," in *The Princeton University Library Chronicle*. XXV (Autumn, 1963), pp. 11-20.
McGovern, Robert. "Louis Coxe: Misplaced Poet," in *The Hollins Critic*. XVII, no. 2 (1980), pp. 1-17.
Thorp, Willard. "Allen Tate at Princeton," in *The Princeton University Library Chronicle*. IV (Autumn, 1979), pp. 1-21.

*James M. Kempf*

# GEORGE CRABBE

**Born:** Aldeburgh, England; December 24, 1754
**Died:** Trowbridge, England; February 3, 1832

**Principal poems and collections**
*Inebriety*, 1775; *The Candidate*, 1780; *The Library*, 1781; *The Village*, 1783; *The News-Paper*, 1785; *Poems*, 1807; *The Borough*, 1810; *Tales in Verse*, 1812; *Tales of the Hall*, 1819; *Posthumous Tales*, 1834.

**Other literary forms**
Of George Crabbe's writings in forms other than verse, little has survived. Extant are critical prose prefaces to various of his published verse collections, a treatise on "The Natural History of the Vale of Belvoir" which appeared in 1795, an autobiographical sketch published anonymously in *The New Monthly Magazine* in 1816, a selection of his sermons published posthumously in 1850, and certain of his letters, journals, and notebook entries which have been published in varying formats throughout the years since his death. With the exception of several of the critical prefaces, particularly that which accompanies *Tales in Verse*, and portions of the letters and journal entries, these do not shed significant light on Crabbe's poetic accomplishments. In the period 1801-1802, Crabbe is known to have written and subsequently burned three novels and an extensive prose treatise on botany.

**Achievements**
The problem of assessing Crabbe's achievements as a poet has proved a difficult one from the start. It vexed Crabbe's contemporaries and continues in some measure to vex scholars today. To a large extent this may be caused by the difficulties in classification. His works bridge the gap between neoclassicism and Romanticism and on separate occasions—or even simultaneously—display characteristics of both movements. As the bewildering variety of labels which have been applied to Crabbe indicate, the multifaceted nature of his canon defies easy categorization. He has been termed a realist, a naturalist, an Augustan, a romantic, a sociological novelist in verse, a psychological dramatist, a social critic, a poetic practitioner of the scientific method, a didactic moralist, a social historian, a "Dutch painter," and a human camera. Such labels, often supportable when applied to selected portions of Crabbe's work, do not appear useful in describing his total achievement. Nevertheless, it is upon such restricted interpretations that estimations of Crabbe have frequently been built. While attesting to his artistic versatility and providing a focal point for isolated instances of detailed analysis and appreciation, the result has been in large part detrimental to the establishment of a sound critical tradition with respect to Crabbe, for readers of all types—

and especially the critics—are most often reluctant to give serious consideration to an artist who cannot be conveniently classified.

Crabbe's earliest literary productions were clearly derivative, most often fashionable satires and other forms in the Augustan mode, but after the appearance of *The Village* one begins to find such terms as "original," "unique," and "inventive" being consistently applied to him. Dr. Samuel Johnson, who read *The Village* in manuscript, praised it as "original, vigorous, and elegant." The sensation surrounding the publication of *The Village* proved to be a mixed blessing, for while it won Crabbe many admirers it also served to fix him in the popular imagination as an antipastoralist and as the "poet of the poor," tags which are misleading and inaccurate when applied to a large part of his work. Crabbe's art showed consistent development throughout his long writing career, particularly in the progressively sophisticated manner in which he articulated his main form, narrative verse. He experimented frequently with narrative techniques and with innovative framing concepts for his collections of verse tales and is often credited with having influenced such writers of prose fiction as Jane Austen and Thomas Hardy. On the other hand, he remained doggedly faithful to that stalwart of eighteenth century prosody, the heroic couplet, departing from it only rarely in his more than sixty-five thousand lines of published verse. Following the appearance of *The Village*, Crabbe's reputation continued to grow, despite a twenty-two-year hiatus in his publishing career, finally declining in his later years largely as a result of the predominant influence of romantic literary tastes. In his time, he was praised highly by Dr. Johnson, Sir Walter Scott, Lord Byron, and even William Wordsworth, with whom he had little in common in either taste or technique; his most consistent and eloquent champion, however, was Francis Jeffrey, the formidable critic of *The Edinburgh Review*. His harshest critics, on the other hand, were Samuel Taylor Coleridge and William Hazlitt, both of whom found him significantly deficient in "imagination" (as the Romantics were prone to define that term) owing to his meticulous attention to realistic detail. The high estimation of Crabbe's achievements drifted slowly downward throughout the course of the nineteenth century but began to revive in the twentieth century with largely favorable critical reassessments by such figures as E. M. Forster, F. L. Lucas, and F. R. Leavis. In recent years, his work has been the subject of several extended critical studies, and, while it is doubtful that he will ever be awarded a place among the highest ranking English poets, it appears certain that he is again being accorded some of the critical and popular esteem in which he once was held.

## Biography

George Crabbe was born on Christmas Eve, December 24, 1754, in Aldeburgh (or, as it was then known, Aldborough), Suffolk, the eldest son of the local collector of salt duties, who early recognized the intellectual potential of his son and endeavored to provide educational opportunities for him beyond those normally accessible to one in his station. Once a busy and prosperous seaport, Aldeburgh had dwindled in size and importance by the middle of the eighteenth century and contained a populace whose general poverty, ignorance, and ill-nature was matched by the isolated, inhospitable conditions of a seacoast plagued by tempestuous weather and surrounded by a dreary countryside consisting largely of salt marshes, heaths, and tidal flats. Crabbe's early experiences in this setting left a lasting impression: throughout his life Aldeburgh retained a strong hold on his imagination. This strange mixture of fascination and repugnance formed the basis for a large number of the characters and settings which are possibly the most striking features of his poetry.

Between the ages of eight and thirteen, Crabbe's father arranged for him to attend grammar schools in Bungay and Stowmarket, both in Norfolk, where he received the foundations of a classical education and is known to have made his first attempts at composing doggerel verse. Unable to continue financing his son's education, and having determined that the field of medicine would be the most suitable to his son's talents and inclinations, the elder Crabbe in 1768 engaged for George to be bound as an apprentice to an apothecary and surgeon at Wickhambrook, near Bury St. Edmund's, in Suffolk. Used more as a farm hand than as a surgical apprentice, young Crabbe was exceedingly unhappy there and, in 1771, was removed by his father to a more favorable situation in Woodbridge, Suffolk. These were to prove relatively happy years, for, though he seems to have shown no great interest in his medical studies, life in Woodbridge was an agreeable contrast to what he had known in Aldeburgh and Wickhambrook. It was also during this period that he met and courted his future wife, Sarah Elmy, and saw his first poem of any consequence, *Inebriety* (1775), appear in print.

In the summer of 1775, his apprenticeship over, Crabbe returned to Aldeburgh, and, after a period of uncertainty during which he worked as a common laborer on the docks (much to the dismay of his father), he finally began to practice his profession late in the year. The next four years were particularly frustrating and unhappy ones for the young doctor: it is clear that he never had any real confidence in his abilities as a physician and that he felt himself to be surrounded by people who did not appreciate him and to whom he felt in every way superior. His practice was unsuccessful and his continuing poverty made it appear doubtful whether he would ever find himself in a position financially stable enough to marry his beloved Sarah. Thus, in early 1780, he abandoned his practice, borrowed five pounds from a local philanthropist, and journeyed to London to take his chances as a poet. Although he would never again return to the profession of medicine, the years spent in training and practice were not entirely wasted ones, for they are undoubtedly responsible for such often-noted features of his poetry as his minute attention to detail and his fascination with aberrant psychological states.

London did not treat Crabbe kindly. Although he did manage to publish *The Candidate*, a dull, unreadable poem, his attempts to secure patronage were singularly unsuccessful, and his increasingly desperate financial state brought him to the point where, by early 1781, he was threatened with debtor's prison. At this propitious moment he found the patron he had been seeking, the influential statesman Edmund Burke, who eased his financial straits, helped him find publishers for his poetry, and introduced him to such eminent figures of the day as Sir Joshua Reynolds, Charles James Fox, and Dr. Johnson. It was Burke also who convinced Crabbe to take holy orders in the Anglican Church and who used his influence to get the young poet ordained, which occurred in 1782. Burke then secured for him a position which allowed him to pursue his duties as a clergyman while at the same time leaving sufficient leisure to write poetry.

His financial worries finally over, his career set, Crabbe entered a largely productive and happy phase in his life. He and Sarah were married in 1783, and over the years Crabbe was assigned to various livings in Suffolk and Leicestershire. In the early 1790's, the deaths of several of their children affected Sarah's mental state in a way that would become progressively more desperate until her death in 1813. At about the same time Crabbe began to suffer from vertigo and digestive ailments. Opium was prescribed, and he continued to use the drug for the remainder of his life. For these and perhaps other reasons, he published no poetry for a period of twenty-two years, though he is known to have continued writing poems and other literary works, the majority of which he ultimately destroyed. Crabbe's literary reemergence in 1807 marked the beginning of his most significant period of poetic production, culminating in the 1819 publication of *Tales of the Hall*. Following Sarah's death, he assumed the livings at Trowbridge, in Wiltshire, where he passed the remaining years of his life as a celebrated member of his community, taking occasional trips to London and Suffolk to visit old friends. Though he never remarried, he maintained a lively correspondence with admiring female readers in several parts of the British Isles. Crabbe died in the rectory at Trowbridge on February 3, 1832.

**Analysis**

No critical assessment of George Crabbe's work has ever isolated his essence more precisely than do the words he himself provided in the concluding lines of Letter I of *The Borough*:

> Of sea or river, of a quay or street,
> The best description must be incomplete;
> But when a happier theme succeeds, and when

Men are our subjects and the deeds of men;
Then may we find the Muse in happier style,
And we may sometimes sigh and sometimes smile.

Any reader who has generously sampled Crabbe's work would likely agree with the point suggested here: it is indeed people and their actions that form the central focus in the majority of his poems. Crabbe was, above all else, a narrative poet, and in the estimation of some critics second only to Geoffrey Chaucer. Paradoxically, however, his reputation in his own day (and to some extent even in the present) was not primarily based on that fact. Rather, he was seen as a painter in words—a master of highly particularized visual imagery who conjured up vivid landscapes and interior settings, most often for the purpose of emphasizing the sordid and brutal elements of existence. Though people might be present in these scenes, they were generally seen as little more than corollary features to the inanimate components dominating the whole (such as the famous description of the aged shepherd in the poorhouse found in Book I of *The Village*). Hence, Sir Walter Scott's well-known epithet, "nature's sternest poet" ("nature" in the nineteenth century sense of the term), has come to epitomize the predominant attitude toward Crabbe as a poet. That view is indeed unfortunate, for the narrowness of its emphasis ignores the very features of Crabbe's work upon which his surest claim to significance might be built. Missing in this approach, for example, is any notion of the richness and diversity of Crabbe's humor, surely one of his most delightful features. Furthermore, such a limited view fails to note the increasingly optimistic tone of Crabbe's work, in its progress from *The Village* to *Tales of the Hall*. Most important, however, the opinion reverses what surely must be the proper emphasis when considering Crabbe's poetry as a whole: people, rather than merely serving to enhance Crabbe's realistic descriptions, are in fact the subject and center of his concern. Nature and external detail, while present to a significant degree in his poetry, exist primarily to illuminate his fascination with character.

If any one reason might be cited for the disproportionate emphasis given to Crabbe's descriptive and pessimistic qualities, it would most likely be the influence of *The Village*. This poem, a sensation in its own day and still the most consistently anthologized of Crabbe's works, paints an unrelentingly bleak picture of human existence in a manner which is essentially descriptive and which makes extensive use of external detail. These same concerns and techniques may also be seen to operate in large portions of Crabbe's next two major works, *The Parish Register* and *The Borough*. In all of these, the influence of Crabbe's early life, and especially his perceptions of his native town of Aldeburgh, form the controlling focus. At the same time, however, as early as *The Village* itself, and certainly in the works which follow it, the perceptive reader can note Crabbe's increasing interest in character and nar-

ration. By the time *Tales in Verse* was published the mode had become completely narrative and continued to be so throughout the poet's writing career.
Moreover, a concomitant softening of the hard lines presented in Crabbe's
early poetry becomes increasingly evident as he moved more and more in the
direction of a psychological and sociological examination of the factors necessary for successful human interaction. True, social criticism, human suffering, and the stultifying effects of an inhospitable environment are factors
which never disappear entirely from Crabbe's writings. As time goes on,
however, they retreat significantly from their earlier position of predominance
and assume no more than their proportionate role in what Jeffrey referred
to as "the pattern of Crabbe's arabesque."

With a canon as large as Crabbe's, it is perhaps to be expected that a
remarkably large and diverse array of themes and motifs may be cataloged
when examining his work as a whole. Nevertheless, certain patterns recur
frequently enough in dynamic variation so as to be considered dominant.
Proceeding, as they invariably do, from an intense interest in character and
in human interaction, they are all rich in psychological and sociological
insights. Chief among them are the problems of moral isolation, of the influence of relatives upon young minds, of success and failure in matters of love,
courtship and marriage, and of the search for reconciliation as an antidote
to bitterness and estrangement. To watch these thematic concerns grow in
texture and complexity as Crabbe explores them in a succession of tales is
one of the pleasures of reading a generous and representative selection of his
works. Of no less interest is the process of experimentation and refinement
by which Crabbe first discovers and then seeks to perfect the stylistic and
structural mechanisms best suited to his characteristic narrative voice.

From the moment of its first appearance in 1783 to the present, the most
immediate response of critics and general readers alike has been to see *The
Village* as a poem written in response to Oliver Goldsmith's *The Deserted
Village* (1770), published thirteen years earlier. This is certainly understandable. The respective titles invite such comparison, and Crabbe himself explicitly alludes to Goldsmith's poem on several occasions. Furthermore, it is
apparent to even the most casual reader that Crabbe's Aldeburgh (for most
assuredly it is Aldeburgh that forms the model for *The Village*) is in every
conceivable way the very antithesis of Goldsmith's Auburn. While all this is
true, the notion of Crabbe's poem as a simple rebuttal of Goldsmith is far
too limiting; rather, it should be seen as a poem which constitutes in large
part a reaction against the entire eighteenth century literary convention which
governs Goldsmith's poem. The term antipastoral is a convenient label to use
here, but only if one keeps in mind the fact that Crabbe's bias against the
pastoral mode is somewhat specialized. It is not classical pastoralism which
Crabbe objects to, or even its manifestations in earlier English poetry, but
rather the manner in which, in the eighteenth century, poets and public alike

had irrationally come to accept the conventions of pastoral description as constituting accurate and useful representations of rural life. If it is somewhat difficult to understand the tone of outrage which underlies the cutting edge of Crabbe's realism in this poem, it is perhaps because most modern readers, unlike Crabbe, have been spared the effusions of countless minor poets, most of them deservedly now forgotten, whose celebrations of the joys of pastoral rusticity filled the "poet's corner" of many a fashionable eighteenth century magazine. It is to them that he speaks when he says: "Yes, thus the Muses sing of happy swains,/ Because the Muses never knew their pains." Crabbe knew their pains; he had felt many of them himself, perhaps too many to assure his own objectivity. For, whatever the merits of seeing *The Village* as a realistic rejoinder to an artificial and decadent literary tradition, one must always remember that Crabbe's brand of realism may at times in itself be somewhat suspect by virtue of the conscious and unconscious prejudices he bears toward his subject matter.

*The Village* consists of two parts—Books I and II—but it is Book I which has always commanded the greatest interest. This portion of the poem is dominated by a number of descriptive set pieces, perhaps the most frequently quoted passages in all of Crabbe's works. The first of these, and the one which perhaps best epitomizes the poem's uncompromisingly harsh view of rural life, concerns the countryside which surrounds the village—the coastline and adjoining heaths. It is a bleak, barren, forbidding prospect which Crabbe presents, a landscape inhospitable to man and barely capable of sustaining life of any sort. Images of decay and sickness, of despair, of almost anthropomorphic hostility pervade the descriptions, chiefly of vegetation, of this isolated sector of the East Anglian seacoast. Almost imperceptibly, Crabbe moves from this dominant sense of place to his initial, tentative descriptions of the inhabitants, the first of many instances in his poetry where people and physical setting are juxtaposed in meaningful counterpoint.

The next of the famous set pieces in the poem is a description of the village poorhouse, the vividness and intensity of which so struck Crabbe's contemporaries that the language they frequently used to discuss it is of a sort most generally reserved for discussions of painting. Several modern commentators have argued that in this section of the poem Crabbe is functioning primarily as a social critic, calling into question, among other things, the prevailing Poor Laws and their administration in local parishes. This may be so; nevertheless, it is again the pure descriptive vividness of this scene which remains its most memorable feature. The details relating to the exterior and interior of the building form a backdrop to the cataloging of its miserable inhabitants. Again, the predominant images are of decay, oppressiveness, and despair. Amid these scenes of not-so-quiet desperation, Crabbe gives particular attention to one inhabitant of the poorhouse, an old shepherd, worn out, useless, lodged there to pine away his days in loneliness and frustration. Perhaps nowhere else in the poem does Crabbe so brutally and cynically mock the pastoral ideal. Book I ends with vicious satirical portraits of the doctor and priest who, paid by the parish to attend to the needs of the inhabitants of the poorhouse, openly and contemptuously neglect their duties.

Book II is considerably less successful in its execution, primarily owing to a lack of consistency in tone and format. Crabbe begins by intimating that he wishes to soften his harsh picture of village life by showing some of its gentler moments; soon, however, this degenerates into a description and condemnation of the drunkenness of the villagers, a subject that he had previously explored in the youthful *Inebriety*. Even more disturbing, however, is the poem's conclusion, which takes the form of an unrelated and lengthy eulogy on Lord Robert Manners, late younger brother of the Duke of Rutland, the man whom Crabbe was currently serving as private chaplain.

Although it is probably his best-known work and contains some of his finest descriptive writing, *The Village* is hardly Crabbe's most representative poem. In his treatment of the aged shepherd, in the satiric portraits of the doctor and priest, one may sense the embryonic forms of the distinctive narrative voice which would ultimately come to dominate his poetry; before this manifested itself, however, a number of years had intervened.

With the exception of *The News-Paper*, a lukewarm satire on the periodical press very much in the Augustan mode, Crabbe published no poetry in the period between the appearance of *The Village* in 1783 and the release of the collection, *Poems*, in 1807. That he was not artistically inactive during this period, however, is evidenced by the vigor and diversity of the poems found in the 1807 volume, and there is ample reason to lament the many efforts in manuscript he is known to have destroyed at this time. In addition to his previously published works, the 1807 *Poems* contained a number of commendable new efforts, including "The Birth of Flattery," "The Hall of Justice," and the provocative "Sir Eustace Grey." All of these works show Crabbe experimenting with various narrative techniques. The star attraction of the new collection, however, was a much longer poem entitled *The Parish Register*.

Readers who enjoyed the angry, debunking tone of Crabbe's antipastoralism in *The Village* were probably delighted by the first several hundred lines of *The Parish Register*, which seem to signal a continuation of the same interests. "Since vice the world subdued and waters drown'd,/ Auburn and Eden can no more be found," Crabbe notes wryly, and then proceeds to unveil a number of highly particularized descriptions, the most memorable of which outlines in vivid and often disgusting detail the vice and squalor of a poor village street. If anything, Crabbe appears to be well on his way to outdoing his previous efforts in this vein. At this point, however, the poem suddenly takes a new tack and begins to present a series of narratives which in the aggregate constitute its dominant feature.

The plan of *The Parish Register* is, in essence, simple and ingenious. A narrative voice is created by Crabbe; it is that of the parish priest of a small village who, at year's end, reviews the records in his church register and comments in varying fashion on the real-life stories which lie behind the cold names and dates. The poem has three divisions—"Baptisms," "Marriages," and "Burials"—and in each the loquacious speaker presents a number of narratives ranging in length and complexity from simple vignettes of a few lines to more ambitious efforts resembling full-blown tales. Generally, the best narratives are found in "Baptisms" and "Burials," particularly in the latter. Two stories of chief interest in the "Baptisms" section are that of Lucy, the daughter of a proud and wealthy miller, who conceives a child out of wedlock, is ostracized by her father and the community, and slowly goes mad, and that of Richard Monday, a foundling brought up and abused in the village poorhouse, who leaves the village to become an enormous success in the world and on his deathbed leaves only a pittance to his native town. "Burials" contains a number of memorable portraits, including those of the prudent, matriarchal Widow Goe, and of old Sexton Dibble, who managed to outlive the five parsons he successively served. The most interesting, however, are the stories of Robin Dingley and Roger Cuff. In the first of these, Robin, a poor but contented man, becomes the victim of a clever attorney who leads him to place all his hopes on the possibility of a rich inheritance; when these are dashed, the loss drives him crazy and makes him a wanderer for life. The acuteness of Crabbe's psychological perceptions are noteworthy in this story, one of the first of a number of tales in which he explores the bases of aberrant behavior. Borrowing certain motifs from older folk tales, the story of Roger Cuff tells of a young man who has a falling out with his kin, goes off to sea, and years later, having made his fortune, returns disguised as a beggar to test the moral fiber of the surviving members of his family. Refused by the closest of them, he shares his wealth with an unpretentious distant relative who lives as a reclusive hermit in the forest. Years later, in "The Family of Love," one of the stories from his posthumous collection of tales, Crabbe returned to this theme but with significant alterations.

In *The Parish Register* one can observe Crabbe in the process of discovering his considerable talents as a writer of narrative verse. His experimentations with frame, point of view, dialogue and character interaction, and a host of other practical and thematic considerations, point the way toward more sophisticated efforts yet to come. Even as he was finishing this poem, he was hard at work on a far more ambitious undertaking, *The Borough*.

One of Crabbe's longest poems—approximately eight thousand lines—*The Borough* is also one of his most perplexing and in many ways his least successful effort when considered as a whole. Within its vast scope, however, there are isolated instances of writing which rank among the poet's best. As in *The Village* and *The Parish Register*, the subject of Crabbe's third major poem is once again a thinly disguised Aldeburgh. This time, however, the scale is much more ambitious, for, as he makes clear in his lengthy prose preface and in the opening section of the poem, the aim of *The Borough* is nothing less than complete description: all aspects of the town, its buildings, trades and professions, public institutions, social activities, and inhabitants are to be revealed. Naturally, the scheme is so grandiose as to preclude its complete achievement, but the efforts which Crabbe makes in pursuing it are in themselves somewhat remarkable. The result, unfortunately, sometimes seems more akin to social history than to poetry. In structure, the poem is epistolary, consisting of a series of twenty-four verse letters written by a resident of the borough to a friend in a far distant part of the country who has requested a description of the place. Among them are some of the dullest pieces of writing in Crabbe's entire canon, including the letters on "Elections," "The Hospital and Governors," and "Schools." Paradoxically, however, this same ponderous framework yields some of Crabbe's finest narrative pieces.

Letters XIX to XXII, collectively entitled "The Poor of the Borough," provide the most fully developed narratives found in Crabbe's work to this point. They are, in essence, short stories in verse, each one focusing on a different character type and probing the psychological dimensions of motivation and consequence. "Ellen Orford" (Letter XX), a story in which Crabbe broadens his narrative technique by having Ellen tell a large part of her own history, is an account of cumulative personal tragedy, borne stoically by a woman whose essential goodness and faith in God enable her to rise above what Hamlet termed "the slings and arrows of outrageous fortune." No such inspirational note is provided in "Abel Keene" (Letter XXI), in which a pious man is seduced into abandoning his faith, the process ending in despair and suicide. A fascinating study of self-deception and its disastrous results is presented in "The Parish Clerk" (Letter XIX), which tells the story of Jachin, the spiritually proud clerk of the parish who feels he is above sin and alienates everyone with his smug sanctimony. Tempted by his poverty and secure in the rationalizations he has constructed for his conduct, as well as in the foolproof method he has devised for its implementation, Jachin begins to steal from the collection plate during services. Eventually caught and publicly disgraced, he goes the way of many of Crabbe's moral outcasts, retreating from the society of men to blend into the bleakness of the surrounding countryside, where his mental and physical energies are gradually dissipated and death comes as a welcome relief.

By most accounts the finest story in *The Borough*, perhaps the best in all of Crabbe's canon, is "Peter Grimes" (Letter XXII), upon which Benjamin Britten based his well-known opera. The tale has so many remarkable features—its implicit attack on the abuses of the apprentice system, its subtle articulation of the notion that the ultimate responsibility for deviant behavior may rest within the society which fosters it, its powerful juxtapositions of external description and interior states of mind, and its surprisingly modern probing of the psychological bases of child abuse—that it is difficult to isolate any one of them as the key factor in assessing the impact it has had upon most readers. A misanthropic fisherman who lives on the fringes of his community, Peter Grimes emerged from a childhood in which he irrationally hated the father who loved him. As an adult, he acquires and successively destroys three young orphans from London who are bound to him as apprentices. The townspeople, aware of what is occurring, turn their backs on what they view as none of their business ("Grimes is at his exercise," they say when the cries of his victims are heard in the town's streets), until the death of the third boy proves to be more than they can ignore. Although they cannot legally punish him—nothing can be proved conclusively—Grimes is forbidden to take any more apprentices and is ostracized by the community. He withdraws into the desolation of the tidal flats and salt marshes surrounding his village and there, brooding alone under the hot sun, he becomes possessed by wild and persistent visions of his father and the murdered apprentices, who dance on the waters and beckon him to join them in their element. His mind shattered, he sinks to death in an agony of terror and desperation. "Peter Grimes" is a story of considerable power, owing in large part to Crabbe's masterful conception of the title character, who, like William Shakespeare's Iago and Herman Melville's Claggart, taxes the limits of critical understanding.

Despite the ponderous framing device employed by Crabbe in *The Borough*, it is possible in the narrative portions of that poem to see him working toward the use of a narrator who is to a certain degree effaced, as well as toward an occasional reliance on multiple points of view. In *Tales in Verse*, which appeared in 1812, he continued those trends and abandoned, temporarily, the use of any sort of framing device. Here, in his first collection of poetry devoted entirely to narrative themes, Crabbe presents a series of twenty-one discrete verse tales in which, as he notes in his preface, "the attempt at union therefore has been relinquished, and these relations are submitted to the public, connected by no other circumstance than their being the productions of the same author, and devoted to the same purpose, the entertainment of his readers." Ironically, what Crabbe himself half-apologetically presented as a loose compendium of disparate elements may, in fact, be his most thoroughly integrated work, for there is one factor that the vast majority of the individual tales share in common: they are, in large part, variations from every conceivable point of view on the themes of love, courtship, and marriage.

In the collection, *Tales in Verse*, Crabbe presents a number of his most memorable stories. One useful method of approaching the collection is to distinguish between those tales in which two persons have successfully found the basis for compatibility, avoiding the numerous pitfalls which at any point in the love-courtship-marriage continuum can destroy the entire process, and those in which the reverse has occurred. Thus, in the latter category may be grouped such tales as "Procrastination" (IV), "The Patron" (V), "The Mother" (VIII), "Squire Thomas: Or, The Precipitate Choice" (XII), and "Resentment"(XVII), while the former is represented by "The Parting Hour" (II), "The Frank Courtship" (VI), "The Widow's Tale" (VII), "Arabella" (IX),"The Lover's Journey" (X), "Jesse and Colin" (XIII), "The Confidant" (XVI), and "The Wager" (XVIII). Myriad influences may affect the delicate balance of the relationships explored in these tales, ensuring their ultimate success or failure; but two situations recur in a variety of forms. In the first of them, Crabbe explores the power, for better or for worse, that a third person may exert on a couple's life. The influence may range from a healthy one, as in the case of the emancipated aunt in "The Frank Courtship," to that which is destructive, as in "The Mother." In other situations, the influence may present an obstacle which must be overcome and resolved in order that the relationship may achieve its true potential, as is demonstrated in "The Confidant." The other recurring situation, one which came to be a dominant motif in Crabbe's remaining work, is the need to seek out and establish the compassionate basis of understanding which must ultimately be the cornerstone of any successful, lasting human relationship. Frequently this is seen in the context of a major disrupting incident in a couple's life which tests the ability of one of them to display the qualities of forgiveness and understanding necessary to keep the relationship alive. The opposite effects of this type of situation are presented, respectively, in "Resentment" and "The Confidant," as well as in certain other of the tales.

Beyond its thematic articulations, which are at once perceptive and sophisticated, "The Frank Courtship" is a tale which commands attention by virtue of its tone and stylistic qualities. Perhaps nowhere else in Crabbe is dialogue used to such delightful effect as in the courting scene between Sybil and her young suitor, Josiah; it is a piece of dramatic interchange which in the sharpness and vivacity of language reminds one of the best of Shakespeare's romantic comedies. Further, the optimistic, at times almost playful, tone of this composition may be cited as one of several memorable instances in Crabbe which serve to balance the elements of somberness and pessimism most frequently ascribed to him.

In *Tales in Verse*, while not abandoning his interests in individual psychological observation, Crabbe moved strongly in the direction of exploring the dynamics of social interaction between people. This interest carried over strongly into his next major production, *Tales of the Hall*. One of the features most immediately apparent in *Tales of the Hall* is the author's return to the use of a comprehensive framing device for the presentation of a number of separate tales. Crabbe has integrated within the controlling frame of his new collection the same sort of thematic cohesiveness which serves to connect the individual narratives of *Tales in Verse*. Again, the great majority of the various tales (here called "Books") represent diverse angles of vision from which to observe the many features inherent in the love-courtship-marriage syndrome. As if to emphasize his desire to pursue these studies from as many angles as possible, Crabbe further complicates his design by experimenting freely with multiple points of view and with other structural complexities in certain of the tales.

The frame itself is of considerable interest and, in its complex pattern of development, has led more than one critic to the conclusion that *Tales of the Hall* may justifiably be termed a novel in verse. As outlined in "The Hall" (I) and the several books which immediately succeed it, the collection is bound by the story of two half-brothers, George and Richard, who after long separation have come together on a somewhat experimental basis to see what, if anything, they might have in common. Here, on the elder brother George's recently purchased estate (the Hall) they spend some weeks together, gradually wearing away the reserve and potential misunderstandings which at various points threaten to disturb the growing bond between their vastly differing personalities. In the course of this process, they tell tales of various sorts, some concerning themselves, others about people they have known in the past or have recently met in the surrounding area, and are frequently joined by a third companion and narrator, the local vicar. As the various tales unfold, the story of George and Richard itself develops in texture and complexity, resolving itself amicably, if somewhat flatly, in the final book. If the overall form of *Tales of the Hall* may be compared to that of the novel, however, it also bears certain affinities in substance to the type of long autobiographical poem which was proving increasingly popular among poets during this period (as, for example, those of Wordsworth and Byron). A convincing case might be made for seeing George and Richard—and to a certain extent even Jacques, the vicar—as varying projections of Crabbe's own conceptualized self-image.

The quality of the individual stories of *Tales of the Hall* is perhaps more uneven than that of *Tales in Verse*. The best of the stories, however, are definitely of a very high order. One is "Smugglers and Poachers" (XXI), an intricately plotted tale which, in addition to evidencing Crabbe's ongoing concern with social injustices, provides in its depiction of the emnity between the brothers James and Robert a bitter and dramatic counterpoint to the happier circumstances of the brothers found in the frame tale. Estrangement and failure in matters of love continue to find expression, as in the powerfully tragic "Ruth" (V) or the more philosophical "Lady Barbara: Or, The Ghost" (XVI); but on the whole, the tone of this collection is more consistently optimistic than in any of Crabbe's previous efforts and the note of forgiveness and reconciliation which dominates a number of the tales continues a trend first noticed in *Tales in Verse*. Two tales which illustrate this rather well are "William Bailey" (XIX) and the structurally complex "Sir Owen Dale" (XII), both of which feature central characters who ultimately come to realize that the errors of the past cannot be allowed to poison the present forever. If there is a moral lesson to be drawn from the essentially nondidactic poetry of the later Crabbe, it is surely this point.

Two years after Crabbe's death there appeared the most complete edition of his poetry available up to that time. Edited by his son, and including as its final volume the highly readable biographical account of his father's life, the *Poetical Works* of 1834 featured a number of poems never published by Crabbe during his lifetime, many of which were obviously still in a state of manuscript revision at the time of his death. Of chief interest among them is the group known collectively as *Posthumous Tales*.

Actually, the twenty-two tales which constitute this final collection of narrative verse fall into two groups. Tales VI through XXII represent what may be described as draft versions of a new collection of poems which Crabbe had tentatively entitled *The Farewell and Return*. Crabbe's organizing principle in the collection posits a situation in which a young man leaves his native town and returns many years later to find it immensely changed. Each tale is divided into two basic parts, the first of which provides a description of a person or thing at the time of the narrator's departure, while the second involves an updating on the part of a friend whom the narrator encounters upon his return. The concept, while ingenious in nature and serving to demonstrate Crabbe's continuing preoccupation with the problem of narrative frames, is far from successful; the individual tales often resolve themselves into a depressingly predictable series of variations on the theme of destructive mutability. These evident shortcomings should not be judged too harshly, however, since it is reasonable to assume that, given the chance for suitable revision, Crabbe would ultimately have rendered the collection consistent with the quality of his previous work. One tale from *The Farewell and Return* group, "The Boat Race" (XVIII), is deserving of special mention, if only by virtue of its splendidly effective description of a sudden storm on the river and its disastrous effects.

In some respects the best narratives in the *Posthumous Tales* are found in the five unrelated tales which begin the collection, including the delightful "Silford Hall: Or, The Happy Day" (I), a highly autobiographical account of an impressionable young lad's sense of wonder and delight on receiving a guided tour of an aristocrat's palatial estate. Also of significant interest is "The Family of Love" (II), a tale in many ways reminiscent of the account of Roger Cuff found in *The Parish Register*, but with the significant difference that the central character of this later narrative finds it within himself to forgive his erring kin, reestablishing the bond of human understanding he could so easily and irrevocably destroy. In this contrasting treatment of an earlier theme, one can again gauge the distance which Crabbe has traveled in his attitude toward the potential for social fulfillment.

In the last analysis, one cannot escape the conclusion that there is a certain amount of unevenness in Crabbe's work, perhaps enough to justify his exclusion from the first rank of English poets. His occasional difficulty in blending new characters into a narrative, his sometimes annoying penchant for wordy digressiveness, his periodic lapses in tone and in the handling of dialogue, even those infrequent examples of "bad lines" which his nineteenth century detractors so loved to quote—all these and perhaps others as well might be charged to him as observable defects in technique. To dwell too long and too hard on these factors, however, is to miss the true essence of Crabbe, and to a large degree his power. In his relentless scrutiny of psychological and sociological themes, from the dark, brooding malevolence of "Peter Grimes" to the delicate social harmonies of "The Frank Courtship" and the frame of *Tales of the Hall*, one can clearly see the elements which link him securely to such widely divergent masters of English storytelling as Emily Brontë and Jane Austen. Oliver Sigworth, a recent commentator on Crabbe, strikes the proper balance when he notes that "We may wish for various perfections which Crabbe did not attain, but, unique as he is, some may be happy in those which he possessed."

**Major publication other than poetry**
NONFICTION: "The Natural History of the Vale of Belvoir," 1795.

**Bibliography**
Bareham, Terrence. *George Crabbe*, 1977.
Blackburne, Neville. *The Restless Ocean*, 1972.
Chamberlain, Robert L. *George Crabbe*, 1964.
Haddakin, Lilian. *The Poetry of Crabbe*, 1955.
Hatch, Ronald B. *Crabbe's Arabesque: Social Drama in the Poetry of George Crabbe*, 1976.
Huchon, René. *George Crabbe and His Times, 1754-1832*, 1968.
Nelson, Beth. *George Crabbe and the Progress of Eighteenth-Century Narrative Verse*, 1976.
New, Peter. *George Crabbe's Poetry*, 1976.
Pollard, Arthur, ed. *Crabbe: The Critical Heritage*, 1972.
Sigworth, Oliver F. *Nature's Sternest Painter: Five Essays on the Poetry of George Crabbe*, 1965.

*Richard E. Meyer*

# HART CRANE

**Born:** Garrettsville, Ohio; July 21, 1899
**Died:** Gulf of Mexico; April 27, 1932

**Principal poem and collections**
*White Buildings*, 1926; *The Bridge*, 1930; *Collected Poems*, 1933 (Waldo Frank, editor).

**Other literary forms**
Hart Crane's principal literary production was poetry. Other writings include reviews, several essays on literature, and two essays on poetry: "General Aims and Theories" and "Modern Poetry." Several volumes of his letters have been published, including those between Crane and the critic Yvor Winters and Crane's letters to his family and friends.

**Achievements**
Crane is acknowledged to be a fine lyric poet whose language is daring, opulent, and sometimes magnificent. Although complaints about the difficulty and obscurity of his poetry persist, the poems are not pure glittering surface. When Harriet Monroe, editor of *Poetry*, challenged metaphors of his such as the "calyx of death's bounty" in "At Melville's Tomb," Crane demonstrated the sense within the figure.

Crane is significant, moreover, in being a particularly modern poet. He wrote that poets had to be able to deal with the machine as naturally and casually as earlier poets had treated sheep and trees and cathedrals. His aim was to portray the effects of modern life on people's sensibilities. In his poetry Crane caught the frenzied rhythms and idioms of the jazz age.

Crane's stature also rests on his having created a sustained long poem, *The Bridge*. Early critics looking for a classical epic deplored the poem's seeming lack of narrative structure. Some critics also objected to Crane's joining the party of Walt Whitman at a time when Whitman and optimism were in disfavor. Later critics, however, have seen *The Bridge* as one of the great poems in modern American literature. They find in it a more Romantic structure, the structure of the poet's consciousness or the structure of human consciousness.

**Biography**
Harold Hart Crane's parents were Grace Hart, a Chicago beauty, and C. A. (Clarence Authur) Crane, a self-made businessman who became a successful candy manufacturer. An only child, Crane felt that he was made the battleground of his parents' conflicts. When Crane was fifteen years old, a family trip to his grandmother's Caribbean plantation, the Isle of Pines, erupted in

quarreling. Crane subsequently made two suicide attempts.

When he was seventeen, Crane went to New York to become a poet, not to prepare to enter college as his father thought. In the next several years Crane alternated between living in Cleveland and New York, working at low-paying jobs, primarily in advertising, jobs that drained his energy for writing poetry. Crane received little financial support from his father, who wanted Crane to commit himself to a business career. In 1917, siding with his mother in a family argument, Harold Crane began using the name Hart Crane.

In this period Crane's poems were being published in "little" magazines. To stimulate his creativity, Crane often relied on drink and music, a habit that led him to later problems with alcohol. (His poem "The Wine Menagerie" pays tribute to the connection he found between intoxication and poetic vision.) Crane's homosexual life-style, which involved him in brawls and run-ins with the police, also provided him the experience of love.

"For the Marriage of Faustus and Helen" was published in 1923, a break-through for Crane, who previously had written only short lyrics. Poor and often unemployed, he applied in 1925 for a grant from Otto Kahn, a financier and patron of the arts. Crane received money to help support him while he worked on *The Bridge*, a poem which was to be a synthesis of the American identity. The next summer Crane wrote a major part of his masterwork at his grandmother's plantation on the Isle of Pines, Cuba. In 1926 a collection of his poetry, *White Buildings*, was published.

Crane's stormy family life continued. In 1928, in California, after helping to nurse his sick grandmother, Crane had a final quarrel with his mother, Grace, and they never saw each other again. Shortly thereafter Crane received a legacy from his grandmother Hart's estate and he traveled to London and Paris. There he met Harry and Caresse Crosby, who offered to publish *The Bridge* in a special edition. In 1930 in Paris and then in New York *The Bridge* was published.

That winter Crane was reconciled with his father. A few months later in 1931 Crane received a fellowship from the Guggenheim Foundation. He spent a year in Mexico preparing to write a poetic drama on the conquest of Mexico. The year was marked by drinking sprees and trouble with the police for brawling and homosexuality. After traveling back briefly to Ohio for his father's funeral, Crane returned to Mexico.

At the end of his stay in Mexico, Crane had a close relationship with Peggy Cowley, who was being divorced from Malcolm Cowley. The two had plans to be married, but Crane had fits of despondency, fears about his difficulty with writing, and anxieties about the quality of his latest poem, "The Broken Tower." After a suicide attempt that Crane feared would attract police attention, he and Peggy Cowley set sail for New York on the *Orizaba*. A stop at Havana in which Crane and Cowley lost track of each other was followed by a night on board ship during which Crane went on a violent drinking spree and was robbed and beaten. The next day at noon Crane jumped overboard from the deck of the *Orizaba* and was never found.

**Analysis**

Hart Crane's characteristic mode of poetry is visionary transformation. His language is that of transformation aimed at a reality beyond the surface of consciousness. Crane called the technique that subtly converts one image into another the "logic of metaphor." Like that of the French symbolist poets— Charles Baudelaire, Arthur Rimbaud, Jules Laforgue, and Paul Verlaine— Crane's language is often vivid and obscure, a "jeweled" style that juxtaposes apparently alien entities. It is a poetry of indirection, not naming but suggesting objects or using them for an evocation of mood, for their magic suggestiveness. Sometimes choosing words for their music or texture, Crane employs the technique of synaesthesia, the correspondence between different sense modalities. Symbolists such as Crane, intuiting a correspondence between the material world and spiritual realities, aim to elicit a response beyond the level of ordinary consciousness.

Influenced by T. S. Eliot (but wanting to counteract the pessimism of the early Eliot), Crane used ironic mythological, religious, and literary echoes interspersed with snatches of banal conversation and lines from popular songs and slang. His method of achieving various perspectives almost simultaneously by the juxtaposition of such unlikely elements has been called "cubist." The tension between his cubist and symbolist methods and his Whitmanian sentiments accounts for the unique quality of Crane's style.

Crane's poetry uses visionary transformations in an attempt to encompass the modern experience. In *The Bridge*, historical figures such as Christopher Columbus, legendary characters such as Rip Van Winkle, and mythic figures such as Maquokeeta (the consort of Pocahontas) are made part of the poet's consciousness, associated with personal memories of his childhood and with scenes of modern urban soullessness. The modern scene is transmuted by the elements, which provide a standard of value and a range of alternatives. In "For the Marriage of Faustus and Helen" the classic figure of Helen of Troy is brought together with the Renaissance figure of Dr. Faustus, and the two figures with their complex contexts bring a new perspective to the streetcar, the nightclub, and the aerial battle they visit in Crane's poem. Crane learned from the Symbolists that an image can become symbolic within a private context, calling up a dense network of meanings, emotions, and associations. Such images, unlike traditional symbols, draw on the cumulative force of the poet's personal associations—his personal "language"—rather than on the common cultural heritage. Crane's poetry fuses such personal symbols with traditional symbols from the sweep of Western culture.

"For the Marriage of Faustus and Helen," a poem of almost 140 lines, is Crane's first long poem. It is a marraige song for Faustus, the poet in search of spiritual fulfillment, and Helen, a figure of ideal beauty. The poem begins, however, in the tawdry modern world with the mind fettered by artificial distinctions and smothered with the trivial: stock quotations, baseball scores, and office memos. "Smutty wings" in the first stanza becomes "sparrow wings" in the second as evening brings freedom from the strictures of the office.

The poet enters his experience by getting lost, forgetting his streetcar fare and forgetting to get a transfer. Between green and pink advertisements he sees Helen's eyes across the aisle from him, half laughing. The poet wants to touch her hands as a sign of love. Helen offers him words, inspiring his poetry. The poet's promise of love makes Helen ecstatic, and, like a Romantic poet, the modern poet dedicates his vision to her praise.

The setting of the next section is a rooftop nightclub with dancers cavorting to jazz played by black musicians. The scene of wild revelry is Dionysian. The abandon of the dancers is contrasted with the passivity of relatives, sitting home in rocking chairs. The poet invites the reader to experience a fortunate fall "downstairs" into sensual abandon. ("National Winter Garden" in *The Bridge* presents a much more somber and sordid version of the fall.) Here the scene is a fallen world where people titter at death. The flapper who is the incarnation of Helen in the fallen realm should not be frowned on, however; even though it is "guilty song," sensual love, that she inspires, she is young and still retains some of the innocence of the ideal Helen.

The scene changes again in the third section, with the poet addressing a fighter pilot as an emissary of death (a problem that Crane would explore again in *The Bridge*). Crane treats war and the desecration of the heavens as the ultimate problem for the poet who would love the world and see beauty in it. It is not only eternity and abstract beauty that the poet praises but also the years, and beauty in and out of time, to which the bleeding hands of the poet pray. More advanced than business or religion, the imagination of the poet reaches beyond despair.

*The Bridge*, a poem of more than twelve hundred lines, is Crane's masterwork, comparable to T. S. Eliot's *The Waste Land* (1922) and William Carlos Williams' *Paterson* (1946-1951). Although it is not a classical epic because it is not a narrative, the poem's seriousness and magnitude are reflected in its theme: the poet tries to find in himself and in America the possibility of the redemption of love and vision. Crane wanted the poem to be not an expression of narrow nationalism but a synthesis of the spiritual reality of America.

The central symbol of the poem is the Brooklyn Bridge, a product of contemporary technology that seemed in its beauty to embody man's aspirations for transcendence. In the poem the bridge is seen as a musical instrument, a harp; as the whitest flower, the anemone; as a ship, a woman, a world. In a letter to Otto Kahn, his patron, Crane said that the bridge symbolizes "consciousness spanning time and space." It is a figure of power in repose, a quality that Crane ascribes in the poem to God. The bridge also symbolizes all that joins and unifies, as the bridge unites the material and the spiritual in its existence.

"To Brooklyn Bridge," the proem, is an invocation to the bridge, in which the central opposition of the poem is sketched out—the life-giving spirituality of the bridge versus the deadening influence of the materialistic, commercial city. The freedom of the soaring seagull in the sky is contrasted with the destructive compulsion of the "bedlamite" who jumps from the bridge, amid the jeering onlookers. The poet asks the bridge to "lend a myth to God," to be the means of belief and transcendence in the city that seems to have no ideals and nothing in which to believe.

In the next section, "Ave Maria," Crane goes back to the beginnings of America and to an age of faith, to Columbus after his discovery. Journeying back to Spain, Columbus meditates that he will tell the Queen and her court that he is bringing back "Cathay." He will announce his discovery of a new reality, something that the poet accomplishes in his journey into history and myth. (In this section the sea acts as a bridge between the two continents.) Columbus' dedication has its counterweight, however, in Fernando, Isabella's husband, who anticipates a "delirium of jewels." Even in the discovery of America the motive for its exploitation was present.

The next section of the poem, "Powhatan's Daughter," includes five sections. The first part, "The Harbor Dawn," is set in the present, with the sounds of fog horns, trucks passing, and stevedores yelling—back by the Brooklyn Bridge but enshrouded in fog. The blurring of sights and sounds by fog and water is in preparation for a blurring of time and space for a visionary journey with the poet. In the sanctuary of his room by the bridge or in his dream, the poet has an experience of love, in which his beloved is portrayed in mythic terms. Her eyes drink the dawn, and there is a forest in her hair. The mythic past lives in the present, or at least in the love of the poet.

The next section, "Van Winkle," shifts abruptly with the mention of macadam roads that leap across the country and seem to take the poet back to his childhood as well as to figures in American history that he learned about in school: Francisco Pizarro, Hernando Cortez, Priscilla Alden, Captain John Smith, and Rip Van Winkle. Van Winkle, who was legendary rather than historical, was a man out of time, displaced, because he refused to grow up. Here Van Winkle forgets the office hours and the pay and so ends up sweeping a tenement. He can get only menial work in a commercial society that demands a dedication to materialistic values. Rip has a different, uncommercial vision. He looks at Broadway and sees a springtime daisy chain. Instead of the lifeless city, he sees a beautiful natural world.

Lines about Van Winkle are interspersed with memories of the poet's own childhood. The memories pick up equivalents for recurring symbols of the poem—the eagle for space and the snake for time. The poet remembers stoning garter snakes that "flashed back" at him. Instead of eagles, his space figures were paper airplanes, launched into the air.

Mythic journeys often involve the search for the father or the mother as a part of the search for identity. Crane introduces a possible need for that search in recounting two memories of disjunction from his parents: a glimpse of his father whipping him with a lilac switch and a more subtle denial by his mother, who once "almost" brought him a smile from church and then withheld it. Together with the smile, the mother seems to be withholding her approval and love. The final image of the section is of Rip, ready for a streetcar ride, warned that it is getting late. It is time for the journey to continue.

"The River" begins with a jumble of sounds, fragments of conversations—perhaps on the streetcar—mention of commercial products such as Tintex and Japalac, and slogans from advertising, with fragments slapped against one another, making no sense. A misplaced faith links "SCIENCE—COMMERCE and the HOLYGHOST." Unlike the sermons in stones that William Shakespeare's world could find, the slogans and jingles are meaningless.

From the streetcar the scene switches to a magnificent train, the Twentieth Century Limited, roaring cross-country. The poem focuses on the hoboes who ride the rails and who, like Van Winkle, refuse to grow up. The men who did grow up, however, killed the last bear in the Dakotas and strung telegraph wires across the mountain streams. Those who want progress and a world of "whistles, wire, and steam" have a different time-sense from that of the wanderers. Although people like the poet's father would call the hoboes useless clods, the wanderers sense some truth and know the body of the land as alive and beautiful. In that knowledge they are like the poet who knows the land "bare"—intimately—and loves her. The eagle of space and the serpent of time appear, adorning the body of the beloved land, but the old gods need to be propitiated because the iron of modern civilization (and especially of the railroad) has split and broken the land and the mythic faith.

The train seems now to follow the river or to become the river. Everyone becomes part of the river, that is timeless because eternal; lost in the river, each one becomes his father's father. The poet and the poem are not only traveling across the country but are journeying back into time as well. Affirming again the possibility of love, the river whose one will is to flow is united with the Gulf in passion.

In "The Dance," the poet returns to the time of Indian greatness, the time of Pocahontas. The poet imagines himself an Indian, initiated into the world view of the brave, at home in nature, speeding over streams in his canoe. He salutes Maquokeeta, the medicine man and priest. He commands Maquokeeta to dance man back to the tribal morning, to a time of harmony between man and nature when he had power even over rainbows, sky bridges. Maquokeeta is named the snake that lives before and beyond, the serpent Time itself. The time that he creates in his dance is the time of mythic wholeness. Pocahontas, the earth, is his eternal bride, and in the dance he possesses her; time and space are made one. The poet has become one with Maquokeeta by calling him up and participating imaginatively in the dance.

The next section, "Indiana," a transitional one, is a letdown of poetic energy and drama. The verse is more prosaic and the rhymes seem strained. The explicit function of the piece is to have the national spirit passed from the Indian to the white settlers in a continuation of American history. It also chronicles the parting of a mother from a son, who is now to be independent, (an important struggle in Crane's own life). The mother's pleas and clinging continue to the end of the section and almost beyond, binding the son by his pledge. Unwilling to let go, she begs for remembrance, naming the young man "stranger," "son," and finally "my friend." The relationship of friend, however, seems more request than fact, and nothing is related from the son's point of view.

Once the poet has succeeded in getting away, in the "Cutty Sark" section, his verse returns to the energy and style of "The River" and earlier sections. The narrator is again the poet, introducing a tall, eerie sailor he has met in a South Street bar. Like the hoboes and perhaps like the poet, the sailor is an outcast. (In various ways he resembles Herman Melville's Captain Ahab and Samuel Taylor Coleridge's Ancient Mariner.) Like the hoboes in "The River," this sailor has a different sense of time from that of the commercial city. Instead of being tuned to the cycles of nature, the sailor's time-sense has been disturbed by the expanse of Arctic white, eternity itself. The sailor, who says he cannot live on land any more, is almost run down by a truck as he tries to cross the street, a sign of the break between the inarticulate, prophetic sailor and the cynical city.

The poet starts walking across the Brooklyn Bridge to get home, and his thoughts are still filled with memories of the clipper ships, related to the bridge in shape by being called "parabolas." Just as Ferdinand's greed was part of Columbus' discovery of America, part of the motive for the sailing ships was "sweet opium" and the tea the imperial British sought. The poet's experience and the American experience are still a mixture of the ideal and the sordid.

"Cape Hatteras" is a substantial section of almost 250 lines. It begins with a primitive setting, with a dinosaur sinking into the ground and coastal mountains rising out of the land. In contrast to the impersonal geological processes, the poet, who has been wandering through time and space, tells the reader that he has returned home to eat an apple and to read Walt Whitman. From Marseille and Bombay, he is going home to America, to the body of Pocahontas and the sweetness of the land under the "derricks, chimneys," and "tunnels." He is returning to try to get a perspective on the exotic experiences he has had.

Next, the poet contemplates the infinity of space that is not subjugated by time and the actions of man, even though modern man can know space by "an engine in a cloud." The poet invokes Whitman and asks if infinity was the same when Whitman walked on the beach in communion with the sea. The poet's answer is that Whitman's vision lives even in the stock-market society of the present and in the free paths into the future. Opposed to Whitman's vision, however, is the fallen world of the machine, a demonic world of unleashed power. The din and the violence of slapping belts and frogs's eyes that suddenly appear, vulnerable in the midst of such uncontrolled machinery, make the world a nightmare, an apocalyptic vision. The dance of the machines is a devilish parody of the heavenly, creative dance of the poet as the Indian priest, and America as Pocahontas.

The poet presents the scene of the Wright brothers at Kitty Hawk with their silver biplane, praising their daring but deploring the use of the invention for war. A demonic image that is parallel to the later image of the bridge as an anemone is the grenade as a flower with "screaming petals." Such terrible power is rationalized with theories as destructive as hail to the fertile earth. Imaginative vision cannot control the machines that have splintered space, even as the iron railroad split the land. The poet reminds the pilot that at the great speed of the airplane, the pilot has no time to consider what doom he is causing: he is intoxicated with space. The pilot's real mission is to join the edges of infinity, to bring them together in a loving union, to conjugate them. The poet follows his warning with a scene of the fighter pilot's destruction. Hit by a shell, the plane spirals down in a dance of death, and all that bravery becomes "mashed and shapeless debris."

If the fighter pilot represents a false relationship with space and infinity, Whitman is a figure with the right relationship, one whose vision of the earth and its renewal makes possible a new brotherhood. Whitman makes himself a living bridge between the sky and man through song. Whitman is also chief mourner of the men lost in wars, from the Civil War to Crane's time.

The next part of "Cape Hatteras" reads like a Romantic poet's declaration of his awakening to the beauty and inspiration of nature in its rhapsodic description of flowers and of heights that the poet has climbed. The declaration is followed by an apostrophe to Whitman as the awakener of the poet. Whitman is named his poetic master, the bread of angels in a eucharistic sense, and the one who began work on the Bridge, the myth or imaginative construction that the poet is here creating. In Whitman the poet seems to have claimed his poetic father: he says that Whitman's vision has passed into his hands.

In the next section, "Three Songs," the poet tries to work through his relationship with the feminine. In the first song, "Southern Cross," he says that he yearns for a relationship that would be heavenly, ideal, and also real.

(He pictures night and the constellation of the Southern Cross.) What he has found, however, is not Woman, nameless and ideal, but Eve and Magdalene, fallen women, and a Venus who is subhuman and apelike. All the women lead to one grave, to death. The poet seems to feel disgust at the physical being of woman. He next pictures woman as a ship. Like the Ancient Mariner in Coleridge's poem, he is revolted by the generative (physical-sexual) nature of the sea. In Crane's poem, however, it is the feminine ship that is pictured as promiscuous, defiled by the masculine sea. The feminine also has qualities of a sea monster that can sting man. The Southern Cross, the poet's idealization of the feminine, drops below the horizon at dawn and what is left is woman's innumerable spawn, evidence of her indiscriminate sexuality.

The next song, "National Winter Garden," may seem to be a continuation of the poet's disgust with women, but it is different in being given an actual, rather than an archetypal, setting. The scene is a striptease in a burlesque show. The stripper's dance is a vulgar parody of sexuality and another parody of the creative, ecstatic dance of the Indian Priest-poet and Pocahontas. The burlesque queen awakens sexual appetite, but she is only pretending to have youth and beauty. Her pearls and snake ring are also fake, and the poet, who is waiting for someone else, runs away from the final "spasm." Here, however, the poet can make a reconciliation with Magdalene, with feminine sexuality, admitting its finality. Both men and women are physical and sexual; their natures are inescapable. If a woman is an agent of death, she is also an agent of birth. If each man dies alone in sexual union with her, he is also somehow born back into life, into his own sexual nature.

A third song for woman is "Virginia." The woman, Mary, is young, child-like, and possibly innocent. The poet seems to be using echoes of a popular song. Mary is working on Saturday at an office tower. She is seen in chivalric terms; the poet is serenading her, and she is at least temporarily inaccessible. Flowers are blooming and bells are ringing, even if they are "popcorn bells." Like Rapunzel in the fairy tale, Mary is asked to let down her golden hair. All seems light and graceful (even though in the fairy tale the prince pays for his courtship with Rapunzel with a period of wandering in the forest, blinded). At the end of the song the poet calls the girl "Cathedral Mary," sanctifying her, perhaps ironically.

In "Quaker Hill" the tone changes from the light, playful tone of the previous song. The section begins with a diatribe against weekenders descending on the countryside. Self-absorbed, they are out of tune with nature. They also have a distorted relation with time, being eager to buy as an expensive antique a cheap old deal table whose finish is being eaten by woodlice. The poet says that time will make strange neighbors.

Meditating on time as a destroyer, the poet asks where his kinsmen, his spiritual fathers are. To find his heritage, he has to look past the "scalped Yankees" to the mythic world of the Indians and accept his "sundered parentage." The poet says that men must come down from the hawk's to the worm's viewpoint and take on their tongues not the eucharist but the dust of mortality.

This humiliation is associated with the artist's abject position in modern society. Emily Dickinson and Isadora Duncan are introduced as examples of artists scorned in their day, and the only consolation the poet offers is that pain teaches patience. He asserts that patience will keep the artist from despair, implying that time will vindicate him. The section closes with a motif that is parallel to the fall of the fighter pilot to shapeless debris. Like the plane spiraling down, a leaf breaks off from a tree and descends in a whirling motion, but the leaf is part of a natural cycle, and the poet has put his faith in time and nature.

The scene shifts back to the city in the next section, "The Tunnel." The natural world is left behind, and the poet is in the center of the gawdy theater district. References to hell, death, and "tabloid crime-sheets" make the area a wasteland. The subway, the fastest way home, is a descent into hell. The traveler cannot look himself in the eye without being startled and afraid. The sound of the subway is a monotone, but fragments of conversation are lewdly suggestive. The subway riders are the walking dead, living on like hair and fingernails on a corpse, yet "swinging" goes on persistently "somehow any-how." The sounds of the subway make a phonograph of hell that plays within the poet's brain. This labyrinth of sound even rewinds itself; from this hell there is no exit. Love is a "burnt match." In "For the Marriage of Faustus and Helen," the flapper, the modern embodiment of beauty, was like a skater in the skies. Here the discarded match is skating in the pool of a urinal.

Suddenly the poet sees a disembodied head swinging from a subway strap. The apparition, figure of the artist scorned and destroyed by his society, is Edgar Allan Poe. Poe's eyes are seen below the dandruff and the toothpaste ads. In this banal setting death reaches out through Poe to the poet. At this point the subway comes to a dead stop. A sight of escape is momentary, and then the train descends for the final dive under the river.

As the train lurches forward again, the poet sees a "wop washerwoman." In the midst of the inferno there is a positive figure of a woman. Although she is not a discoverer like Columbus, her work has dignity: she cleans the city at night. A maternal figure, she brings home to her children her eyes and hands, Crane's symbols of vision and love. A victim like Poe and the poet, the cleaning woman is bandaged. Other birth imagery here is demonic: a day being born is immediately slaughtered. The poet's greatest agony is that in this nightmare he failed to preserve a song.

In his great agony the poet feels the train start to ascend. Both the poet and the train are, like Lazarus, resurrected. They are returning to the natural world above ground. His vocation renewed, the poet can affirm the everlasting word. Once above ground again the poet is at the river bank, ready to turn to the bridge.

With the poet resurrected, "Atlantis"—the final section of the poem—is a song of deliverance. It is an ecstatic paean to the bridge, seen as music, light, love, joy, and inspiration. More dynamic than the music of the spheres, the music of the bridge creates a divinity. It is a myth that kills death: it gives death its utter wound, just by its light, its unshadow. By the myth of the bridge the cities are endowed with ripe fields. They have become natural, organic, and fruitful. The bridge is the city's "glittering pledge" forever. It is the Answerer of all questions. In the poet's vision and in the poem it is unutterably beautiful.

"Atlantis" acts as a synthesis, subsuming earlier motifs such as stars, seagulls, cities, the river, the flower, grass, history and myth, circles and spirals. The question "Is it Cathay?" links the end of *The Bridge* with Columbus' discovery of America in the beginning, not in a mood of anxiety but in wonder at an America transfigured. The final two lines bring together time and space— the serpent and the eagle—with the music and radiance and energy of the bridge transcendent.

**Major publications other than poetry**
NONFICTION: *The Letters of Hart Crane*, 1952 (Brom Weber, editor).
MISCELLANEOUS: *The Complete Poems and Selected Letters and Prose of Hart Crane*, 1966 (Brom Weber, editor).

**Bibliography**
Butterfield, R. W. *The Broken Arc: A Study of Hart Crane*, 1969.
Dembo, L. S. *Hart Crane's Sanscrit Charge*, 1960.
Hazo, Samuel. *Hart Crane*, 1963.
Horton, Philip. *Hart Crane: The Life of an American Poet*, 1937.
Leibowitz, Herbert. *Hart Crane*, 1968.
Lewis, R. W. B. *The Poetry of Hart Crane: A Critical Study*, 1967.
Paul, Sherman. *Hart's Bridge*, 1972.
Unterecker, John. *Voyager: A Life of Hart Crane*, 1969.
Uroff, M. D. *Hart Crane: The Patterns of His Poetry*, 1974.
Weber, Brom. *Hart Crane: A Biographical and Critical Study*, 1948.

*Kate Begnal*

# STEPHEN CRANE

**Born:** Newark, New Jersey; November 1, 1871
**Died:** Badenweiler, Germany; June 5, 1900

## Principal collections
*The Black Riders*, 1895; *A Souvenir and a Medley*, 1896; *War Is Kind*, 1899.

## Other literary forms
Stephen Crane is best known as a novelist and short-story writer, and deservedly so. His first novel, *Maggie: A Girl of the Streets* (1893) was an early and almost pure example of naturalistic fiction. About the time of his twenty-fourth birthday, *The Red Badge of Courage* (1895) made him famous. Of his other novels—*George's Mother* (1896), *The Third Violet* (1897), *Active Service* (1899), and *The O'Ruddy* (1903, with Robert Barr), only *The Monster* (1899), which is a novella, may lay claim to greatness. Of the scores of tales, sketches, and journalistic pieces that verge on fiction, the best are "The Reluctant Voyagers" (1893), "The Open Boat," "The Bride Comes to Yellow Sky," "Death and the Child," and "The Blue Hotel" (all in 1898). Of Crane's dramatic efforts, there is *The Ghost* (1899, with Henry James) performed in a room at Crane's home in England. According to one contemporary review, the play was a mixture of "farce, comedy, opera, and burlesque." His only other play is a slight closet drama called *The Blood of the Martyr* (1898?). He once suggested collaborating with Joseph Conrad on a play, but Conrad demurred.

## Achievements
As one of the first impressionistic writers—Joseph Conrad called him "The Impressionist"—Crane was among the first to express in writing a new way of looking at the world. Impressionism grew out of scientific discoveries that showed how human physiology, particularly that of the eyes, determines the way everything in the universe, everything outside the individual body and mind, is seen. People do not see the world as it is, yet the mind and eye collaborate to interpret what is for Crane, at least, a chaotic universe as fundamentally unified, coherent, and explainable. The delusion is compounded when human beings get together, for then they tend to create even grander fabrications, such as religion and history. Although Crane is also seen as one of the first American naturalistic writers, a symbolist, an imagist, and even a nihilist, the achievements which justify these labels all derive from his impressionistic view of the world.

Crane's major achievement, both as a fiction writer and a poet, is that he so unflinchingly fought his way through established assumptions about the way life is. He is the logical end of a long line of American Puritans and transcendentalists who believed in the individual pursuit of truth. The great and perhaps fitting irony of such logic is that Crane repudiated the truths in which his predecessors believed. In his fiction, he uses the old genres, but his impressionistic style denies their validity; in his poetry he attacks tradition directly, in part through what he says and in part by how he says it. Rejecting everything conventional about poetry in his day—rhyme, rhythm, conventional images, "safe" metaphors that never shocked Victorian sensibilities—Crane ends by denying things much more important: nationalism, patriotism, the greatness of individual and collective man, the existence of supernatural powers which care and protect and guide. In his best fiction and occasionally in his poetry, Crane faces squarely the horror of a meaningless universe, although he was unable to build a new and positive vision on the rubble of the old.

**Biography**

Born in a Methodist parsonage in Newark, New Jersey, Stephen Crane was the fourteenth and last child of a minister whose family had been in America for more than two centuries. On his mother's side, almost every male was a minister; one became a bishop. By the time his father died in 1880, Crane had lived in several places in New York and New Jersey and had been thoroughly indoctrinated in the faith he was soon to reject. Also around that time, he wrote his first poem, "I'd Rather Have—." His first short story, "Uncle Jake and the Bell Handle," was written in 1885, and the same year he enrolled in Pennington Seminary, where he stayed until 1887. Between 1888 and 1891, he intermittently attended Claverack College, the Hudson River Institute, Lafayette College, and Syracuse University. He was never graduated from any of these schools, preferring baseball to study. In 1892, the New York *Tribune* published many of his New York City sketches and over a dozen Sullivan County tales. Having apparently forgotten Miss Helen Trent, his first love, he fell in love with one Mrs. Lily Brandon Munroe. That year, too, the mechanics union took exception to his article on their annual fete, which resulted in Crane's brother, Townley, being fired from the *Tribune*.

In 1893, Crane published at his own expense an early version of *Maggie*. William Dean Howells introduced him to Emily Dickinson's poetry, and in the next year he met Hamlin Garland. Also in 1894, the Philadelphia *Press* published an abridged version of *The Red Badge of Courage*.

The year 1895 is notable for three things: during the first half of the year he traveled in the West, where he met Willa Cather, and in Mexico for the Bachellor Syndicate; *The Black Riders* was published in May; and *The Red Badge of Courage* appeared in October. By December, he was famous, having just turned twenty-four. In 1896, he published *The Little Regiment* and fell in love with Cora Stewart (Howorth), whom he never married but with whom he lived for the rest of his life.

In January, 1897, on the way to report the insurgency in Cuba, he was shipwrecked off the Florida coast. Four months later he was in Greece reporting on the Greco-Turkish War. Moving back to England, he became friendly with Joseph Conrad, Henry James, Harold Frederic, H. G. Wells, and others. During that year, he wrote most of his great short stories: "The Open Boat," "The Bride Comes to Yellow Sky," and "The Blue Hotel."

Never very healthy, Crane began to weaken in 1898 as a result of malaria, which he contracted in Cuba while reporting on the Spanish-American War. By 1899, Crane was back in England and living well above his means. Although he published *War Is Kind*, *Active Service*, and *The Monster and Other Stories*, he continued to fall more deeply in debt. By 1900, he was hopelessly debt-ridden and fatally ill. Exhausted from overwork, intestinal tuberculosis, malaria, and a will to experience life almost unmatched in literary history, Crane died, not yet twenty-nine years old. He left behind works that fill ten sizable volumes.

## Analysis

Stephen Crane's poetry, like his life and fiction, consists almost entirely of "enormous repudiations." Filled with vivid animism, startling metaphors, strident naturalism, and bitter nihilism, the poetry repudiates the God of Crane's father, the natural order seen as benevolent by the Romantics and transcendentalists, the brotherhood of man in any areas except sin and blind conformity, the rightness and glory of war, the possibility of justice, the grandeur of love, even man's ability to perceive a modicum of truth clearly. Repudiation is fundamental to his poetry. He rejects rhyme, among other things, and in doing so he anticipates Ezra Pound, Carl Sandburg, and Wallace Stevens, whose poetry came to fruition only in the twentieth century. Crane often went further than these poets by eschewing the rhythms that had defined lyric and narrative verse for more than two thousand years.

Crane never referred to his work as "poetry"; he almost invariably referred to his "lines." Once, however, he alluded to the didactic, nearly therapeutic, nature of his poems by calling them "pills." Unlike the fiction, which is often hauntingly and ironically lyrical, the poetry consciously strives for what Crane called a "tongue of wood." This tongue produced a sound which jarred against the ears of his contemporaries, and for the most part, as Crane himself observed, "in truth it was lamentable." Although Crane managed to avoid writing in the rhymed and metered style that filled the poetry libraries of his day, the cost to the quality of his lines was great. For example, few poets with Crane's credentials could write the following without knowing just how lamentable it was: "Now let me crunch you/ With the full weight of affrighted love."

While he was seldom this guilty of what Pound later called "emotional slither," Crane nevertheless failed, most of the time, to re-create and liberate in his poetry the intensity of his thought and emotion. Love, for example, is sometimes a biological trap and sometimes a vehicle for defying the Protestant ethic that damned those caught in love's sensuality. As a trap, love can even descend to a pathological fetishism, producing some of Crane's most "lamentable" lines: "I weep and gnash/ And I love the little shoe/ The little, little shoe." On the other hand, as a way of throwing down a gauntlet before accepted Protestant belief, it can produce some of Crane's most beautiful lines. "Should the wide world roll away," depicts a love so enthralling and encompassing that the speaker denies any need for the other props that support mankind. The poem flies in the face of convention by adding sex to Huck Finn's decision to "go to Hell" rather than betray Jim: "Neither God nor man nor place to stand/ Would be to me essential/ If thou and thy white arms were there/ And the fall to doom a long way."

Not always so summarily dismissed, God appears in a score or more of the poems as himself, Nature, or some other metaphor. It could even be said that God manifests three different faces: as God the Father, he is malevolent and capricious; as God the Son, he is kindly and pitying; as the Holy Ghost, he is indifferent. "A man said to the universe," Crane's most anthologized poem, depicts a God who responds to man's insistent cry for recognition ("Sir, I exist!") by both acknowledging the "fact" and refusing to be bound by any "sense of obligation" as a result of it. God is similarly indifferent in "God fashioned the ship of the world carefully." Only here the indifference is more clearly deistic: Once the world was made, God went bowling.

A kindly God appears in the second stanza of "The livid lightnings flashed in the clouds" as "whispers in the heart" and as "melodies,/ Distant, sighing, like faintest breath." A pitying God appears obliquely as Christ in a Spanish-American War poem called "The Battle Hymn." He is a sacrifice not only of God (the "Father of the Never-Ending Circles"), but also to God from the jingoistic war spirit of American patriots during that "splendid little war." In "There was One I met upon the road," where man is presented to God as a mass of sin, God's response is to look "With kinder eyes" and say, "poor soul." Conversely, if the poem is read ironically—that is, if God is taken as the creator of sin—then the God of this poem is not pitying, but rather, cruel and malevolent.

Most often, God is malevolent and unyielding, hateful and unworthy of worship. In many poems, man looks at him with "grim hatred," as a capricious dealer of death, a denier of man's suffering, a bully, and a firm upholder of the Darwinian belief in the survival of the fittest. In "To the Maiden" and "The Ocean said to me once," God is Nature, but still basically malevolent, instructing the seeker in the latter poem to tell a nearby woman that her lover has been "laid/ In a cool hall" with a "wealth of golden sand." In the next stanza, she is also to be told that her lover's hand will be heaped with corpses "Until he stands like a child/ With surplus of toys."

Since Crane also heaps bitter abuse upon the Church, it sometimes remains unclear as to whether the God that Crane depicts as malevolent is Crane's God or whether it is God as seen by the Church. In a number of poems, the Church is viewed as the betrayer of the New Testament God of compassion. Everywhere, "figures robed in black" are revealed as hypocritical and evil: "You say you are holy," "With eye and with gesture," "There was a great cathedral," "Walking in the sky," "Two or three angels," "A row of thick pillars," "If you would seek a friend among men," and a host of others bitterly accuse the Church of irrelevance. As Crane sees it, the Church not only fails to help man live on this planet, this "space-lost bulb," as he calls it in "The Blue Hotel," but also actively makes life more difficult.

Another of man's beliefs pilloried by Crane is brotherhood. The "subtle battle brotherhood" which fails to keep Henry Fleming from running away in *The Red Badge of Courage* becomes a banal and damnable conformity in the poetry. "'Think as I think,' said a man" is a short piece in which the speaker chooses instead to "be a toad." Patriotism is a collective "falsity," a "godly vice" that "makes us slaves." The rather good poem, "When a people reach the top of a hill" is one long irony against "the blue battalions" of collective action. Responding to a question about mob courage, Crane once wrote in a letter: "The mob? The mob has no courage. That is the chatter of clubs and writers." In his poetry, as elsewhere, Crane shared the nineteenth century's fear of the mob. The only brotherhood that exists in Crane's poetry is a brotherhood of sin, as shown in "I stood upon a high place."

Although the most obviously insane use of the mob occurs in war, and although Crane made his reputation on war fiction, war as a theme does not loom very large in his poetry. "I suppose I ought to be thankful to 'The Red Badge,'" Crane wrote, "But I am much fonder of my little book of poems, 'The Black Riders.'" *The Black Riders*, Crane thought, was "about life in general," while *The Red Badge of Courage* is a "mere episode in life." Aside from a few poems which allude to the Spanish-American War, war is more generalized, as in the poem beginning "There exists the eternal face of conflict."

The theme of injustice ranges among the poems from the yellow journalism of American newspapers in Crane's day to the cosmic injustice of God to man. In all cases, Crane is bitterly insistent that justice simply does not exist. One particular injustice, however, overshadows all others: the injustice of wealth. Wealth as wealth is not questioned, but rather what it seems to do to people who have it and to those who do not. Charity, for example, is "a lie." It is given by "bigoted men of a moment" as food that "turns into a yoke." The recipients are expected "to vanish/ Grateful because of full mouths." Yet, the poem warns the charitable that their turn will come: "— Wait—/ Await your turn." Only once in the ten volumes of his collected works does Crane complain about his poverty, and even then he does so in self-mockery, choosing a Chaucerian "complaint to his purse." The wealthy are "fat asses," "too well-dressed to protest against infamy." Successful men are "complacent, smiling," and "stand heavily on the dead."

The major theme of Crane's poetry, as Milne Holton's *Cylinder of Vision* (1972) has shown about the fiction, is man's utter inability to perceive the truth and his amazing willingness to believe that he does indeed see it. For Crane, the world is chaotic, and all man's beliefs about God and nations, about religions and history, are almost entirely delusory. He never resolves, for example, the conflict between the malevolent and the pitying God, choosing instead to let it stand in several two-stanza poems in which one stanza describes God the beast and the other the God of compassion. "When a people reach the top of a hill" is read by Daniel Hoffman as praise of the American nation and the triumph of man over fate, but it may also be read ironically as an exposure of utter delusion. Everywhere in the poetry, there are "gardens lying at impossible distances." In one poem, "A man saw a ball of gold in the sky," Crane uses his characteristic cosmic point of view to allow the man to climb into the sky only to find the gold ball made of clay. When he returns, the man finds the ball again made of gold: "By the heavens, it was a ball of gold." Misperception can involve delusion, as in "I saw a man pursuing the horizon," and monumental egotism, as in "I looked here," which takes William Shakespeare's "My mistress' eyes are nothing like the sun" another step by saying that her real beauty is irrelevant since he perceives her as beautiful. In another poem, Crane says it more directly. In the thirteen lines of "If you would seek a friend among men," the speaker notes seven times that all one needs to know about people is that they are "crying their wares." As with most of Crane's poetry, this theme can be traced to the Bible: All is vanity.

Ultimately, Crane's poetry is a protest against the conditions of life and against the lies man tells himself to make life tolerable. That protest sustained his brief poetic career, although in time, he did become less angry with God for not existing, or at least for not paying attention. Crane is modern in the sense that, like most modern poets, he rejected both the theism and the humanism of the nineteenth century; but he lived too soon to benefit from the experiments of others who were also soon to reject them.

**Major publications other than poetry**

NOVELS: *Maggie: A Girl of the Streets*, 1893; *The Red Badge of Courage*, 1895; *George's Mother*, 1896; *The Third Violet*, 1897; *Active Service*, 1899; *The O'Ruddy*, 1903 (with Robert Barr).

SHORT FICTION: *The Little Regiment*, 1896; *The Open Boat and Other Tales of Adventure*, 1898; *The Monster and Other Stories*, 1899; *Whilomville Stories*, 1900; *Wounds in the Rain*, 1900.

PLAYS: *The Blood of the Martyr*, 1898?, 1940; *The Ghost*, 1899 (with Henry James).

NONFICTION: *The Great Battles of the World*, 1901.

**Bibliography**

Beer, Thomas. *Stephen Crane: A Study in American Letters*, 1923.
Berryman, John. *Stephen Crane*, 1950.
Hoffman, Daniel G. *The Poetry of Stephen Crane*, 1957.
Katz, Joseph, ed. *The Poems of Stephen Crane: A Critical Edition*, 1966.
Stallman, Robert. *Stephen Crane: A Biography*, 1968.

*Chester L. Wolford*

# RICHARD CRASHAW

**Born:** London, England; c. 1612
**Died:** Loreto, Italy; August 21, 1649

**Principal collections**
*Epigrammatum Sacrorum Liber*, 1634; *Steps to the Temple*, 1646, 1648; *Carmen Deo Nostro*, 1652.

**Other literary forms**
Richard Crashaw wrote primarily religious poetry reflecting the life of Christ and the symbols of Christianity.

**Achievements**
Crashaw occupies his niche in literary history as a sort of maverick Metaphysical whose poetry, although displaying many of the techniques and characteristics of John Donne and George Herbert, is unique in its baroque flamboyance and its strong Roman Catholic sensibilities.

A poet of fluctuating popularity, Crashaw has had his work treated as decadent Metaphysical poetry, as an outstanding example of ornate wit, as conventional Catholic devotion, and as intensely personal expression. His poems are longer and more elaborate than those of his model George Herbert, although his themes are narrower in focus. Crashaw is sometimes ranked with Donne and Herbert as a "major" Metaphysical poet; alternately, he is linked with such significant but "minor" writers as Abraham Cowley and Henry Vaughan.

In his intense rendering of Counter-Reformation Roman Catholic spirituality, as well as in his use of powerful visual experiences, Crashaw is distinctive. His poetry, widely popular in his own day, continued to attract readers and critical appreciation through the end of the seventeenth century and early in the eighteenth; it waned with the pre-Romantics and their successors and received relatively little notice until early in the twentieth century, when a host of major critics rediscovered religious poetry.

**Biography**
The only child of William Crashaw, Richard Crashaw was born in London in either 1612 or 1613. His mother died when he was an infant; William Crashaw's second wife, Elizabeth, died when Richard was seven.

William Crashaw, Anglican divine, seems an unlikely parent for one of England's most famous converts to Roman Catholicism. Staunchly Low Church (some say Puritan) in his theology and in his life-style, the elder Crashaw devoted his life to preaching and writing, partly against the Laudian or High Church excesses in the Church of England but principally against what he perceived as the far greater dangers of the Church of Rome itself. In his efforts to know the full strength of the enemy, William Crashaw amassed an impressive collection of "Romish" writings; the critic can only speculate what effect these works, as well as his father's convictions, may have had on the spiritual development of Richard Crashaw.

After two years at London's famed Charterhouse School with its austere regime and classical curriculum, Crashaw was admitted, in 1631, to Pembroke College at Cambridge. He would receive his B.A. in 1634 and his M.A. in 1638. He came to Pembroke with something of a reputation as a poet, a reputation which grew steadily as he produced Latin and Greek epigrams as well as English models, translations of the Psalms, and various occasional verses. These works form the basis of his 1634 publication, *Epigrammatum Sacrorum Liber*, the only work Crashaw himself would see through the printing process.

In 1635, Crashaw was appointed to a fellowship at Peterhouse College and sometime shortly thereafter was ordained to the Anglican priesthood. At Peterhouse he was in direct contact with a circle of Laudian churchmen whose devotion, emphasis on liturgical ceremony and propriety, and reverence marked another step in Crashaw's eventual spiritual journey to Rome. During this period between 1635 and 1643 Crashaw also learned Spanish and Italian, moving with ease into the reading of the Spanish mystics, among them Teresa of Avila and John of the Cross, as well as the rich tradition of Italian devotional literature. This material would strongly influence his later poetry, to the extent that his work is sometimes described as continental rather than English.

Another significant event of the Peterhouse years was Crashaw's acquaintance with the community at Little Gidding, the religious retreat founded by George Herbert's friend Nicholas Ferrar. At Little Gidding, daily communal prayers and other religious observances were prescribed and orderly; the ancient church building was restored by the community to a Laudian elegance; the sanctuary fittings were rich and reverent. Although Ferrar and his followers steadfastly maintained their allegiance to Canterbury, the community was sometimes criticized as Papist.

These same criticisms were being levied at Peterhouse, where John Cosin, Master of Peterhouse and a friend of Crashaw, was restoring and adorning the college chapel with equal devotion. Reports of the candles, incense, and crucifixes at Peterhouse continued to arouse Puritan suspicions; in the early 1640's Cosin, along with Crashaw, was censured for "popish doctrine." In 1643 Parliament, goaded by the growing Puritan forces, forbade all altar ornaments as well as all pictures of saints. In these early years of the Civil Wars, Cosin, Crashaw, and four others were formally expelled from their Fellowships and forced to depart.

The last six years of Crashaw's life, the key years of his conversion and the flowering of his poetry, are difficult to trace with any certainty. In 1644, he wrote from Leyden, speaking of his poverty and his loneliness. He may have revisited England, probably only for a short period. At some point he made the acquaintance of Queen Henrietta Maria who, as a devout Catholic, took up his cause in a letter to Pope Innocent. Somewhere in his physical and spiritual travels, Crashaw decided—or discerned a call—to commit himself to Roman Catholicism; this central experience cannot be dated. He continued to write, completing the poems his editor would entitle *Steps to the Temple* (a humble compliment to George Herbert's *The Temple*, 1633), revising many of his earlier poems, and working on the pieces which would form his last volume, *Carmen Deo Nostro*.

Crashaw spent time in Rome and in Paris, absorbing the rich art of these cities as well as their expressions of Catholicism. In Paris, he was befriended by the poet Abraham Cowley who, appalled at his friend's physical condition, obtained care and financial assistance for him. Back in Rome, Crashaw was appointed to the service of a cardinal and subsequently was sent to Loreto, the house where, according to Catholic tradition, the Virgin Mary received word of the Annunciation. Crashaw had barely reached this Marian shrine when he fell ill; he died August 21, 1649.

### Analysis

Richard Crashaw's poetry may be divided into three groups of unequal significance for the scholar: the early epigrams, the secular poetry, and the religious poetry. The early epigrams and translations are studied, meticulous, and often occasional. The 178 Latin epigrams in *Epigrammatum Sacrorum Liber* show the influence of Martial and other classical writers. Crashaw also uses biblical motifs, particularly for his several English epigrams, displaying in his treatment of these themes an example of the close reading which will underlie his later work.

As a book of poetry, these early pieces are significant for the discipline they reveal and for their fascination with wordplay—puns, quips, repetitions, conceits—which Crashaw will later elevate to such exuberance. They are finger exercises, and if they lack the genius of John Milton's college ventures, they nevertheless suggest later greatness.

Crashaw's second body of verse, the secular or nonsacred poetry, comprises much of the work found in *Delights of the Muses*, the volume appended to and published with *Steps to the Temple*. In that volume, Crashaw displays the Donnean Metaphysical, writing poems with titles such as "Wishes. To His (Supposed) Mistress," "A Picture Sent to a Friend," "Venus Putting on Mars His Armor," and "Loves Horoscope." Witty, polished, urbane, these poems show an accomplished and sophisticated writer delighting in the possibilities of English poetry. Intensely visual, these poems often select a single image and elaborate it in a manner reminiscent of the earlier emblem tradition. The classical tradition is still strong but the metrics are clearly English.

Although the poems in *Delights of the Muses* are often Donne-like in their wit, there is a certain reticence to them. The robust speaker of Donne's *Songs and Sonnets* (1633) is absent in Crashaw; there is relatively little use of the personal pronoun and none of the speechlike abruptness which makes so many of Donne's poems memorable. The meter is usually highly regular, most often iambic tetrameter or pentameter, and the cadences are smooth. There is an unsubstantiated tradition that Crashaw was a trained musician; these poems would support that claim.

From time to time there is a baffling half-revelation, for example in the two-line "On Marriage," when the speaker declares that he would "be married, but I'd have no wife,/ I would be married to the single life." Whether this is witty posturing, cynical disclaimer, or an honest account of his own state (Crashaw never married), the reader cannot tell. Crashaw's work would appear in anthologies even if he had written only the secular poetry, but his name would definitely be in smaller type. The poet himself spent far less effort in revising these secular poems, suggesting that he too considered them of secondary importance.

Turning to Crashaw's major works, those rich poems which he wrote and revised for the collections that would become *Steps to the Temple* and *Carmen Deo Nostro*, one is confronted with a lavish, even bewildering, highly sensuous, celebration of the Christianity which so fired the poet. If Donne argues with God in his holy sonnets and Herbert prays through *The Temple*, then Crashaw contemplates and exclaims. Apparently gifted with mystical experiences even in the midst of his English tradition, Crashaw's mode of prayer is much more akin to that of Teresa of Avila than to the Book of Common Prayer. Like Teresa, who said that she could meditate for hours on the opening two words of the Lord's Prayer, Crashaw, confronted by the mysteries of Christ's life, death, and resurrection, meditates, celebrates, sorrows, refines, ponders, *sees*. Faced with mystery, he expresses it in paradox and strains to reconcile the opposites. Christianity does, after all, continually join flesh and spirit, God and Man, justice and mercy, life and death. Crashaw's poetry does the same: it reveals rather than persuades. Unlike Henry Vaughan and especially Thomas Traherne, whose religious poetry is almost unflaggingly optimistic, Crashaw focuses on both the joys and sufferings of Christianity and more on the sufferings of Christ and the Virgin Mary, although he involves himself in the joyous mysteries of Christianity as well.

"In the Holy Nativity of Our Lord," one of his best-known, most tightly written poems, makes a most appropriate introduction to the poet. Starting with the paradox of the revelation of Christ's birth to humble shepherds, Crashaw structures his hymn in a series of dualities and paradoxes: "Loves noone" meets "Natures night," frost is replaced by flowers, a tiny manger provides a bed for "this huge birth" of God who becomes man. The dualities in the poem are underscored by the shepherds themselves, classically named

Tityrus and Thursis, who alternate verses and sing the chorus together.

The contrasts lead to the central question of the hymn, where to find a "fit" bed for the infant Jesus. When the "whitest sheets of snow" prove pure but too cold and the "rosie fleece" of angels' wings is warm but cannot "passe for pure," the shepherds return to the nativity scene to discover that the Christ Child has vividly and dramatically reached his own solution:

> See see, how soone his new-bloom'd cheeke
> Twixt's mother's brests is gone to bed.
> Sweet choice (said I!) no way but so
> Not to lye cold, yet sleep in snow.

The paradox is resolved in the person of the Virgin-Mother, Mary; the "I" of the shepherds becomes the "we" of all the faithful; the celebration of "Eternitie shut in a span/ Summer in winter, day in night,/ Heaven in Earth and god in man" ends in a full chorus, followed by an anthem of liturgical joy.

Several traits elevate this poem well above the countless conventional, albeit sincere, Nativity poems of this period. The central image is vivid and personal; the Christ Child is presented not as King but as nursing infant. Crashaw brilliantly takes the biblical motif of the Son of Man, who has no place to lay his head, and transforms it into image. The poem moves gracefully from opening question to resolution, celebrating that resolution and concluding with the offering: "at last . . . our selves become our owne best sacrifice." It is a poem of liturgical color: the images of white and gold which weave through the stanzas are reminiscent of the vestments worn for the Christmas liturgy as well as the sunrise of Christmas day.

One of Crashaw's simpler poems because of its traditional subject matter, "In the Holy Nativity of Our Lord" exemplifies the gifts of the poet. Crashaw is a worker with color: gold and silver, red and crimson and scarlet, and blinding white fill the poems along with modifiers such as "bright," "rosy," "radiant," and a score of others. The poet is highly conscious of textures and surfaces, forever describing his images as "soft," "rough," "slippery." Predominantly Anglo-Saxon in his diction (his most repeated nouns are monosyllables—"die," "birth," "sun," "flame," "heart," "eyes"), Crashaw betrays his early fondness for Latin in some of his favorite adjectives: "immortal," "triumphant," "illustrious," and "supernatural." He alliterates constantly, playing with vowel and consonant sounds to achieve unity of tone as well as musical qualities.

Ironically, Crashaw's most characteristic gifts as a poet, particularly his enthusiasm for the refined and elaborate image, are responsible for some of his most-criticized efforts. Of these, the most famous is "Sainte Mary Magdalen or The Weeper," a long poem commemorating the legend of Mary Magdalene, the sinner forgiven by Jesus, who, according to tradition, wept

tears of repentance for many years. The motif is a beloved one in the seventeenth century; poems celebrating (and recommending) tears abound, often
with Mary Magdalene, St. Peter, or another grieving Christian as the focal
point. Crashaw's poem is really not about Mary Magdalene at all; rather it
is about the tears themselves which, after falling from Mary Magdalene's eyes,
follow a circuitous, thirty-seven stanza route, develop a speech of their own,
and finally go up to heaven to meet "a worthy object, Our Lords Feet." In
between his opening salutation of Magdalene's eyes ("Ever bubling things!
Thawing crystall! Snowy hills!) and the final image of Jesus, Crashaw scatters
images and conceits with such abandon as to bewilder the unwary. Some of
these conceits are richly apt: Magdalene is "pretious prodigall! Faire spendthrift of thy self!" Others (and there are many more of these) are extravagant,
incredible, even ludicrous:

> And now where e're he strayes
> ...........................................................
> He's follow'd by two faithfull fountaines,
> Two walking Bathes; two weeping motions;
> Portable and compendious Oceans.

"The Weeper" has been cited as the prime example of all that is bad, even
bathetic, in Crashaw, and surely the twentieth century reader, accustomed
to a leaner poetic style and certainly to a less visible religious expression,
confronts major problems. These can be partially alleviated, however, with
at least some considerations of the traditions out of which Crashaw is writing.
He is, in a sense, doing in "The Weeper" what Teresa of Avila is doing with
the Lord's Prayer: he is taking a single image and pondering it at length,
refining and embroidering and elaborating the object of his meditation until
it reaches a conclusion.

Crashaw is also influenced by the Christian tradition of litanies. A litany
is a long series of short prayers, each one a single phrase or epithet, often
recited by a priest with responses ("pray for us" or "have mercy on us") from
the congregation. A litany does what the poem does: it presents aspect after
aspect of the holy person or mystery so that the faithful may, in some sense,
*see*. The petitions of a litany are not related to one another but to the person
or mystery they are celebrating: the Virgin Mary, for example, is called Ark
of the Covenant, Morning Star, Mystical Rose, Tower of Ivory, not because
these phrases have any relationship to one another, but because they are
figures or conceits of her. Depending on one's scriptural background or perhaps spiritual disposition, some phrases suggest more devotion than others.

Much has been said of Crashaw's affinities with the movement in art called
baroque—that richly decorative aesthetic which suggests tension, opposites
pulling at each other, extravagant gestures and ornate detail, which somehow
connotes a sense of unworldliness or otherness. "The Weeper," in its maze

of images and conceits, suggests that within it lies a significant truth which the reader cannot follow but at which he can only guess. The poem is perhaps less baroque than some of Crashaw's other works but it has that same energy, tension, and movement.

Finally, one might consider the fact that the poem celebrates Mary Magdalene, who wept repeatedly, even for years. The poem, too, celebrates repeatedly, with a focus on image after image, indeed perhaps doing the very thing it celebrates. Like Mary Magdalene, the poem reverences the Lord again and again. Read in this sense, "The Weeper" may well be a hieroglyph, the term used by Joseph Summers to describe George Herbert's poetry (*George Herbert: His Religion and Art*, 1954).

All of the above is not intended as a defense of "The Weeper" so much as an attempt to view Crashaw in his contexts. Like many of the mystics, he has little need for discursive structure, preferring instead the intuitive, associative mode for communicating his experiences. If some images are banal, they are still a part of his contemplation and they stay in the poem. It is an unfamiliar aesthetic but not one without some validity. It is worth noting that nearly all Crashaw's numerous revisions of his poetry are toward length; he rarely discarded and never shortened.

As a Roman Catholic, Crashaw was more free than his Church of England contemporaries to consider the lives of the saints. Although the biblical Mary Magdalene and the Virgin Mary were appropriate for the devotions of at least High Church Anglicans, saints such as Teresa of Avila were less so, even though Teresa's works had appeared in English as early as 1611 and would surely have been familiar to devout readers. It is not known whether William Crashaw possessed a copy of Teresa's classic *The Interior Castle* (1583); if he did, and if he preached against it, there is an intriguing poetic justice in his son's selection of Teresa for his richest poems. The two St. Teresa poems rank among Crashaw's finest.

The poems contrast as well as match; "A Hymn to the Name and Honor of the Admirable Saint Teresa" is a legend or story made into a lesson, whereas "The Flaming Heart" is a meditation upon an image, possibly, as Louis Martz (in *The Wit of Love*, 1969) suggests, the painting by the Antwerp artist Gerhard Seghers, or perhaps the more famous Bernini statue in the Coronaro Chapel, St. Maria della Vittoria, Rome. Crashaw could have seen either representation, and he may well have seen both.

"A Hymn to the Name and Honor of the Admirable Saint Teresa" begins with the story of the child Teresa who, wanting martyrdom and heaven for her faith, persuades her little brother to go off with her in search of the Moors who will, she hopes, put them to death. The poet, meditating on the greatness of heart in the six-year-old Teresa, is both witty and moving when he breaks in, "Sweet, not so fast!" A richer, more demanding martyrdom awaits the adult Teresa; she will be called to the contemplative life, reform the Carmelite order, write magnificent works, and give herself totally to the love of God. Dying to self in the most ancient tradition, she will indeed be a spiritual martyr. The poem combines, in the richest Metaphysical tradition, intellect and emotion, tough demands and profoundly intuitive responses. Teresa is not free to choose her martyrdom any more than were the first Christians; she can only respond to the choice that God makes for her.

In the poem, Crashaw is working in the best tradition of Anglican preaching as well as with Roman Catholic sensitivity. He begins with a story, an exemplum, with good clear narrative, aphorisms ("'Tis Love, not years nor limbs, that can/ Make the Martyr, or the man"), vivid drama, and a totally believable picture of the child Teresa and her ardent love of God. The regular tetrameter lines with their aabb rhymes move the story gracefully, even inevitably, along. Then, with "not so fast," the poet moves into a new vein altogether, summoning back Teresa—and the reader—to contemplate what giving oneself to God really means. The poetry moves from narrative to lyrical, intuitive expression and is filled with images, exclamations, and apostrophes. Instead of martyrdom as a child, Teresa will face numerous mystical deaths, which will prepare her for the final death which brings total union with the Lord; these mystical deaths "Shall all at last dye into one,/ And melt thy soules sweet mansion." The diction becomes 'more and more simple as the concepts underneath the poetry become increasingly mystical. The poem concludes in a dazzling combination of Anglican neatness ("decorum") and Roman Catholic transcendence: the one who wishes to see Jesus "must learne in life to dye like Thee." The poem is simultaneously a meditation upon a holy life and a lyrical celebration of one who was chosen by God to live totally for him. The women in Crashaw's poetry, whether the Virgin Mary, Magdalene, Teresa, or even that "not impossible she" of the poem to "His (Supposed) Mistress," are all great souled, larger than life, intensely vivid, and visual. Later, Crashaw would write "An Apologie" for the hymn as "Having been writt when the author was yet among the protestantes"; one wonders whether its discursive, even preachy, tone is a manifestation of this state of mind. Surely, the poem needs no "apologie."

In the second Teresa poem, "The Flaming Heart," Crashaw keeps his tetrameter rhymed couplets but adopts a totally different stance, moving from story-with-lesson to contemplation. The thirteenth century theologian Thomas Aquinas defines contemplation as simultaneously knowing and loving one of the divine mysteries, and the poem illustrates that definition. The speaker is gazing at a picture or statue of Teresa in which she is visited by a seraphim, a celestial being, who, holding a burning dart, prepares to transfix the saint. The scene is taken from Teresa's own journal account of her divine revelations and translates the momentary interior apprehension into external narration. Teresa's language is explicitly sexual; the cherub with the dart, the piercing, the pain followed by ecstatic joy, all of these are a part of that long tradition which uses the language of physical love for God's encounters with his people. It is the language of Donne's holy sonnets. Catholic artists, directed by the Council of Trent to make the mysteries of faith more vivid for believers, are drawn to this incident; it is not surprising that the newly converted Crashaw, already enamored of image and mystery, would be drawn to the story of Teresa, another "not impossible she."

"The Flaming Heart" welcomes "you that come as friends" almost as though the readers are pilgrims to the church where the image is displayed. The faithful viewers are, however, immediately corrected by the wit of the speaker; although "they say" that one figure is the seraphim and the other is Teresa, the speaker assumes the role of correcting guide, asking, "be ruled by me." The figures must be reversed; the saint is the seraphim.

With that flashing insight, "Read HIM for her and her for him," the poet moves into the entire burden of the long poem, constantly juxtaposing Teresa and the seraph, celebrating her angelic virtues and total love of God, casting the seraph in the role of a "rivalled lover" who needs to veil his face, singing praise of the "flaming heart" of Teresa which is so afire with love. The couplets race in their eagerness to show this instant, moving from abstract to concrete, from Teresa to the seraph. The colors are rich here, crimson, golden, and fiery; the sense of pain becoming joy is almost tangible; the transcendence of the moment breaks out of the visual representation as the speaker also moves out of time and space and into the world of mystical prayer. The closing lines, perhaps Crashaw's most intense and most often cited, are litany, prayer, celebration, vision.

**Bibliography**
Bertonasco, Marc. *Crashaw and the Baroque*, 1971.
Low, Anthony. *Love's Architecture: Devotional Modes in Seventeenth-Century English Poetry*, 1978.
Martz, Louis. *The Wit of Love*, 1969.
Parrish, Paul. *Richard Crashaw*, 1980.
Williams, George Walton. *Image and Symbol in the Sacred Poetry of Richard Crashaw*, 1963.

*Katherine Hanley, C.S.J.*

# ROBERT CREELEY

**Born:** Arlington, Massachusetts; May 21, 1926

## Principal collections

*Le Fou*, 1952; *The Kind of Act Of*, 1953; *The Immoral Proposition*, 1953;
*All That Is Lovely in Men*, 1955; *If You*, 1956; *The Whip*, 1957; *A Form of
Women*, 1959; *For Love: Poems 1950-1960*, 1962; *Words*, 1967; *Pieces*, 1969;
*The Charm*, 1969; *A Day Book*, 1972; *Thirty Things*, 1974; *Away*, 1976;
*Selected Poems*, 1976; *Hello*, 1978; *Later*, 1979; *Echoes*, 1982.

## Other literary forms

Robert Creeley has published fiction, including short stories collected in
*The Gold Diggers and Other Stories* (1965) and a novel, *The Island* (1963).
Many of his essays, introductions, and reviews are collected in *A Quick
Graph: Collected Notes & Essays* (1970, Donald Allen, editor), and interviews
in which he articulates his poetics are assembled in *Contexts of Poetry: Inter-
views 1961-1971* (1973). Creeley's complete correspondence with Charles
Olson, edited by George F. Butterick, is currently being published; to date,
four volumes have been issued.

## Achievements

Creeley's poetry articulates or, better, enacts, with an extraordinary precision both of words and of rhythms, day-to-day life with respect not to its
paraphernalia, its accoutrements, its events in the journalistic sense, but to
the self's experience of itself, of the other (other people, the external physical
world), of time, space, place, and words. It is personal without being private.
It renders the quality and dynamics of emotions of intense interpersonal
interaction, especially that of men and women in love, though also of friendships. It explores the problematic situation of consciousness, which must be
always inside a mind and within a present, both of which are always inexorably,
irrevocably leaving themselves behind. It seeks to discover and make apparent—through wordplay, unusual word order and wording (especially involving
ellipsis), and other devices—the nature of language, including the thingliness
of words. It is a verse that probes limits of thought and language in an activity
set in motion by both ethical and epistemological concerns.

## Biography

Robert White Creeley, the son of Dr. Oscar Slate Creeley, a distinguished
physician who died when Robert was four, and Genevieve Jules Creeley, was
reared on a farm in West Acton, Massachusetts. There are numerous references to the West Acton farmhouse in his poetry. His mother worked as a

public health nurse to support him and his older sister, Helen. Growing up in a household of women and living in rural New England both helped to shape Creeley's sensibility, developing his sensitivity to the nuances of interpersonal relationships and encouraging an economy in the use of words and a responsiveness to the sheer particularity of things. Besides the death of his father, another early loss affected him: at four, he lost his left eye as a result of an accident two years earlier, and as a child wearing a glass eye he was vulnerable among other children. A sense of vulnerability is a conspicuous characteristic of Creeley's poetry.

Creeley attended Holderness School, a small private high school in Plymouth, New Hampshire. There, he manifested an interest in writing, working on all the school publications and serving as editor-in-chief of the literary magazine. Vying with this interest, however, was a love of animals that led him to consider studying veterinary medicine.

In 1943, he entered Harvard, but World War II disrupted his education, and after less than two years he left the university to serve for a year as an ambulance driver with the American Field Service in India. After returning to the United States in late 1945, he married Ann MacKinnon and moved with her to Provincetown, Massachusetts, at the time an artists' colony. They lived on a trust fund of hers, and Creeley reentered Harvard, commuting to his classes by boat. After his war experience, he felt dissociated from American values and generally unsettled. He was drinking regularly on the boat from Provincetown; academic life at Harvard did not seem to afford what he was confusedly seeking, and he ultimately left without a degree in the last semester of his senior year.

From 1948 to 1951, the Creeleys tried subsistence farming, but the farm, in a beautiful location near Littleton, New Hampshire, was rundown, making it too expensive to maintain. From his rural isolation, however, Creeley made contacts that would be extremely important to his own poetic career and to contemporary American poetry. He began correspondence with Cid Corman, and also wrote to a number of other poets soliciting manuscripts for an alternative literary magazine he and a friend were endeavoring to start. That project proved abortive, but much of the material he collected was later incorporated in the first issue of Corman's *Origin*, the first magazine to provide an outlet for poets in what was emerging as the Ezra Pound-William Carlos Williams-Charles Olson tradition. The attempt to collect material for the magazine also led to the beginning of what would become a voluminous and tremendously important correspondence with Olson. It was in letters between Creeley and Olson that the notion of Projective Verse (as opposed to writing in closed forms), elaborated in a seminal essay of Olson's, was worked out.

When their farming venture in New Hampshire proved impracticable, the Creeleys, now with two sons, tried living in France (where a daughter was born) for a year and a half in 1951 and 1952; then, from 1952 to 1955, on the

Spanish island of Mallorca, the latter experience providing much of the material for Creeley's novel *The Island*. During his time on Mallorca, Creeley started his own press, The Divers Press, and, at the instigation of Olson, then heading Black Mountain College, began the *Black Mountain Review*. Published for seven issues between 1954 and 1957, it provided an outlet for a wide range of new writing and was perhaps the most important little magazine of its time. Creeley also went to Black Mountain College to teach during this period. (Olson was later instrumental in his being awarded a B.A. degree from Black Mountain.) In 1955, he and Ann were divorced.

In 1956, Creeley spent some time in San Francisco, where he met Allen Ginsberg, with whom he had been corresponding, and other beat poets, whom he featured in the final issue of *Black Mountain Review*. He then settled in Albuquerque, New Mexico, where he taught at a boys' school; met Bobbie Hall, a visual artist, whom he married in 1957; and began work on an M.A. at the University of New Mexico (he received the degree in 1960). From 1959 to 1961, he lived in Guatemala, working as a tutor on a *finca* (plantation) there. His work was included in Donald Hall's controversial and influential anthology of nontraditional verse by young American poets, *New American Poetry: 1945-1960*, published in 1960, and in the early 1960's, beginning with the publication of his poems of the 1950's by Scribner's, his reputation as a poet began to spread beyond the readership of little magazines and small press publications. During the 1960's and 1970's, he taught at the University of New Mexico, the University of British Columbia, San Francisco State College, and the State University of New York at Buffalo.

The publication of his *Selected Poems* in 1976 made a sampling of his work accessible in one volume. That year also saw the end of his and Bobbie's twenty-year marriage, which was also often an artistic collaboration. In 1977, he married Penelope Highton, of New Zealand. *The Collected Poems of Robert Creeley, 1945-1975*, is forthcoming from the University of California Press.

## Analysis

Robert Creeley's poetry is immediately remarkable for its spareness, its tautness. Its imagery is drawn from a repertoire of common natural and man-made objects and phenomena, named with minimal elaboration: light, dark, sun, moon, water, grass, window, door, table, chair, and such. Its verse is short-line free verse; the short lines are often enjambed, frequently violently, producing a jerky, syncopated movement (Creeley himself has indicated the influence of jazz on the movement of his verse). A stanzaic format of couplets, tercets, or quatrains that may or may not reflect the grammatical structure of the text is common, giving the poems an orderly appearance on the page. Poems that trace the curve of an evolving emotional situation involving a man and a woman constitutes the longest poems in Creeley's oeuvre of generally short lyric poetry.

*For Love* collects Creeley's poetry of the 1950's, a body of work that includes diverse modes—the jingling rhythms and concrete if nonsensical events of nursery rhymes, the delicacy and sensuousness of Elizabethan song, the jazzy rhythms and colorful diction of contemporary street talk, as well as the groping movement and simple diction of Creeley's most characteristic voice. Irony, generally self-directed, is often the dominant tone of these poems, especially the earlier ones in the first two of the book's three sections. The earliest of these poems reflect the influence of Charles Olson directly in that the text is arranged on the page in Olson's manner, with indentations, spacing between words, and line-grouping registering the pacing and pauses of the poet's speech in his composition by field. "Le Fou," dedicated to Olson, "who plots, then, the lines/ talking, taking, always the beat from/ the breath," is a well-known example. In this poem, Creeley interweaves two utterances, one speaking of movement in a figurative sense, the other of a literal movement in some vehicle, by using the device of an unclosed parenthesis, which Olson had learned from E. E. Cummings. Creeley also creates a visual image of movement by stepping his lines diagonally down across the page. Olson's technique serves in these poems as a vehicle for the expression of preoccupations that are already very much Creeley's own. Thus, in "Le Fou" he writes, "I mean, graces come slowly,/ it is that way." A sense of slowness, arduousness, in the achievement of grace (an achievement always transitory) pervades Creeley's mature poetry and is manifested there particularly in the breaking of the flow of speech into short lines, often enjambed.

After the first few poems of *For Love*, Creeley turns from Olson-like arrangements of the text on the page to stanzaic formats, grouping short lines in couplets, tercets, and quatrains, the stanza divisions sometimes, sometimes not, coinciding with syntactical and logical divisions of the text. There is often a songlike quality to these poems (and he often entitles them "Song")— besides stanzaic forms, he employs repetition (sometimes refrains) and often diction and/ or imagery suggestive of folk or art song.

In "A Form of Women," songlike features are used in part as an instrument of irony, but also more subtly. This poem is the first of several key love poems in *For Love*; these poems are longer than the majority (which are very short) and articulate a complex emotion or developing emotional experience. "A Form of Women" is an address to the beloved in the form of closed quatrains of short, end-stopped lines; the language is simple in diction and syntax, with much parallelism and verbal repetition. Rather than being a detailed realistic setting, the highly personal experience articulated in the poem is furnished with the elemental figures of moonlight and darkness. The speaker introduces himself in a rhymed first stanza that contains a vague, childlike image of dread. By the fifth stanza he has come down to a stark statement of the occurrence that is troubling him: "I could not touch you./ I wanted very much to/ touch you/ but could not." Reflecting on this failure, he meditates (in stanza seven): "My face is my own./ My hands are my own. My mouth is my own/ but I am not." The final line of that quatrain is ambiguous; it can be read as an ellipsis of "I am not my own" or as a statement that "I do not exist." Both readings seem plausible as expressions of the speaker's sense of himself in the aftermath of his failure to touch. By the conclusion of the poem, the elemental imagery of moonlight and darkness and the songlike repetitions come to intensify and universalize the personal emotion.

Such a symbolic landscape as that of the moon and trees and darkness in "A Form of Women" is also found in "The Door," a long poem dedicated to Robert Duncan that is in the penultimate position in the 1956-1958 section of *For Love* ("A Form of Women" is the second poem in that section). There a door opening onto a wood or garden in which there is a "Lady" who symbolizes the object of desire that the speaker would pursue. More often, however, any description of setting at all is absent, this being one of the characteristics that has earned Creeley's poetry the epithet "minimalist." "Goodbye" is such a minimalist poem; it is strikingly spare in language, with very simple diction and very short sentences and presentational fragments, and within its short length of four tercets of short lines, it has frequent repetition. Like "A Form of Women," it is concerned with a failure to achieve contact in a relationship; it differs in having its minimal narration in the third person, and in that the failure to turn toward the other is the woman's. The device of repetition here functions to give insistence to the presentation and to convey a sense of stasis and paralysis.

There is a narrative movement traceable through the lyric poems of *For Love*, from marital breakdown to entrance into, and gradual establishment of, a new love relationship. "The Rain" in section three is one of the poems that present the emergence of the new relationship and one of the many poems that exhibit Creeley's skill at articulating elusive subjective states that have rarely been represented in literature. The first four of the six quatrains of the poem articulate the speaker's response to a rain and his dissatisfaction with that response. In the first stanza a sense of the rain's persistence is conveyed by repetition: "All night the sound had/ come back again,/ and again falls/ this quiet, persistent rain." After this initial bit of description, the speaker asks abruptly, "What am I to myself/ that must be remembered,/ insisted upon/ so often?" The abruptness seems to reflect the movement of his thought and conveys an intensity of reaction against his feeling of being locked in self-absorption. A further question, elaborating on the first, runs from the end of the second stanza over the next two stanzas; the speaker wants the rain to have some meaning for him other than what it does, "something not so insistent," and wonders if it ever will. The fifth stanza brings another abrupt rhetorical swerve, from questions addressed to himself to an address to his love, bidding her to "Be for me, like rain,/ the getting out //

of the tiredness, the fatuousness, the semi-/ lust of intentional indifference."
With the turn from introspection to the other, the rain changes for him to the
positive power that he had despaired of its becoming. Again, the rhetorical
abruptness seems to mime the movement of the speaker's thought—in this
case, the unpredictable and alogical way the mind can move beyond what was
an impasse a moment before.

The image of rain is again associated with release and with love in "The
Rose," a poem late in section three, dedicated to Bobbie. "The Rose" is a
narrative poem, but it differs from most narrative poetry in presenting more
a sequence of emotional states than a sequence of events. It is in the third
person, with a "she" and a "he" as its characters. The language is generally
simple in diction and syntax, with frequent repetition, and the text is arranged
in quatrains, mostly closed, of very short lines. Like "The Rain," "The Rose"
begins in unease and moves to an expansive resolution. At the beginning of
the poem, the woman is walking up and down, and the man, apparently
judging her to be restless, speaks bitterly: "'Did you want/ to go, then why/
don't you.'" In the third stanza, "She went"; in the fourth, "He follows."
What happens then? The narrator does not tell the reader, but instead asks,
"Where do they walk now?/ Do they talk now[?]" The place where they are
is not described, but called "that other place/ grown monstrous." The implication here seems to be that mere literal description would be inadequate to
convey what was essential to the experience. From whatever initial dissension
and alienation, the man and woman eventually come to a recovery through
a revelation of sorts, a revelation of her nature to him, which is presented
in terms of the rose as symbol: "There roses, here roses,/ flowers, a pose of/
nature, her/ nature has disclosed to him." Whether or not there are actual
roses in an external landscape is irrelevant to the inner experience that Creeley
chooses as the subject of his tale. In the final three stanzas the language and
verse change, a single long sentence (the main clause preceded by a lengthy
subordinate clause), with the highest incidence of repetition in the poem,
running over the three quatrains, in sharp contrast to the short sentences of
the rest of the poem. The repetition imparts a sense of heightened intensity,
and the flow of the long sentence gives the reader a sense of relief from the
constriction of the clipped sentences and closed stanzas, a sensation apparently
corresponding to the emotional release experienced by the man and woman
in their reconciliation.

Closing the book is the title poem, again dedicated to Bobbie, an address
to the beloved in sixteen quatrains. It is a stumbling, halting address, in which
the poet wrestles with his own inability, in the present of the poem, to say
what he has earlier been anxious to say. "Yesterday I wanted to/ speak of
it," he begins; then, finding himself balked, asks, "Today, what is it that/ is
finally so helpless, // different, despairs of its own/ statement[?]" He begins
a sentence with "If the moon did not. . ." (ellipsis is Creeley's) but imme-

diately breaks off and revises that start: "no, if you did not." Leaving the verb of this subordinate clause without an object, he rushes ahead to a main clause, "I wouldn't either," but then proceeds to question what that missing object is: "but/ what would I not // do[?]" Utterance could scarcely be more unsure of itself. The stumbling quality of the text is intensified by the way it is divided into lines and stanzas; there is frequent strong enjambment, between as well as within stanzas, and the short lines are often broken by syntactical boundaries, these features producing a by-fits-and-starts movement. By the end of the fifth stanza, the poet has come no closer to the utterance he had felt ready to make "yesterday": "That is love yesterday/ or tomorrow, not/ now."

The poem continues to struggle toward an expression, a solution, in the now. The poet feels he cannot eat what the beloved has given him because he has "not earned it," then questions the appropriateness of thinking of love in such terms: "Must/ I think of everything/ as earned." He feels himself sunk in "tedium,/ despair, . . ./ self-regard." By the tenth stanza, even the sense of having had something to say seems to have dissipated, as the poet turns to the beloved to ask, "Love, what do I think/ to say." Nor is the beloved herself a definite, stable *other* to receive his address; his questioning turns to examine what it is he is addressing: "What have you become to ask,/ what have I made you into[?]" From this nadir of utter uncertainty, he begins to climb upward with an acknowledgment of the fact of want as the basis of all utterance: "Nothing says anything/ but that which it wishes/ would come true." In the fourteenth stanza, he is finally able to "begin . . . now," having finally "stumble[d] into" the possibility. Thus, the end of the book announces itself as a beginning, and the beginning made is an elliptical utterance: For you // also (also) // some time beyond place, or/ place beyond time, no/ mind left to // say anything at all." If "Nothing says anything/ but that which it wishes/ would come true," this may be taken as a wish that the beloved may reach, with him (that seems to be the insistent implication of the repeated "also"), a state beyond time, place, mind, and the necessity of speech. The poem and the book close with the final sentence, "Into the company of love/ it all returns." There is no specific antecedent for "it," so the reference seems inclusive, and the statement seems to affirm the possibility of transcendence through love.

"It is all a rhythm," runs the first line of "The Rhythm," the first poem in *Words*, and the reader will do well to take this assertion as an indication that he or she will be rewarded for attentiveness to the rhythms Creeley creates by his syntax and his lineation. The concern with rhythm is explicit as well as implicit in this collection, invoked sometimes as "measure," sometimes in the images of walking and dancing (see "Walking," "Quick-Step," and "The Measure" in Part I and "Dancing" in Part II). Flux is recognized and accepted as intrinsic to all experience; rhythm, patterned motion in time, is seen not only as a crucial property of verse, but also as a fundamental property of life.

A poem called "Song" early in the book, exemplifies these concerns and their embodiment in the poetry of *Words*. The text is arranged in three quatrains of very short lines (two to four syllables, one to two stresses); grammatically, it is a single, complex but highly elliptical sentence, consisting entirely of nominal and adjectival phrases, with no finite verbs. The first stanza (elliptically) a "measure": "The grit/ of things,/ a measure/ resistant—." The stanza ends with a dash for punctuation, and the nominal construction that comprises all of stanza two and runs over into the last stanza seems to be in apposition to "the grit of things," an elaboration of that concept. This elaboration forces a revision, an extension, of the usual understanding of "things" as concrete objects, for the first noun in apposition is "times"— "times walk-/ ing, talk-/ ing, telling/ lies." The enjambments that split the participles "walking" and "talking" and, as it were, momentarily cover up the object of "telling," to surprise the reader with it when he or she rounds to the beginning of the next line, give a kinesthetic experience of "resistance." If the usual understanding of "things" is stretched by finding "times" in apposition to it, likewise the usual understanding of "times" is challenged by the implied designation of the various times enumerated in stanza two as "places," through a noun phrase coordinate with "times. . .": "and // all the other/ places." "Thing," "time," "place" are treated equally as designations of instances of experience, which are experiences of/in all of them. These instances are, in the words of the last phrase of the poem "no/ one ever/ quite the same."

What Creeley proposes as "a measure," then, is antithetical in its properties to the measures people are accustomed to using, units of uniform size. The form of his verse can thus be understood as in accord with his sense of the nature of experience: his lines are not measured in the "equal" units of traditional feet but are divided in response to the particular words that come to constitute the poem at hand.

"The Rocks," the second poem in *Words*, uses rocks as a metaphor for thought—"the/ rocks of thought // which displace,/ dropped in/ the water, // much else"—and finds in water the substance of life and love, introducing a thematic opposition that is central to the book and, in water, one of its principal positive images. The third poem, "Water," begins with "blue sky/ that // water will/ never make," begins with the limitations or imperfections of water but then turns to "sing" (praise) "broken water's/ forms" as identified with "mind's form" and "love's/ error." Rocks are again associated with thought, given a negative valuation relative to the flux of experience, in "'I Keep to Myself Such Measures. . .'" later in Part I: "The mind/ fast as it goes, loses // pace, puts in place of it/ like rocks simple markers." In "A Birthday," a poem apparently to Bobbie Creeley near the end of the book, a reconciliation with the unstoppable ongoingness of things is expressed in terms of a turning to water: "I had thought/ a moment of stasis/ possible," says the speaker, but he has found that "dripping" is the "condition" of the "beauty" that comes from being "one by one" with the beloved.

*Words* includes several longer poems—"The Dream," "Anger," and "Distance" in Part I and "The World" and "Enough" in Part II—that continue the exploration, begun in "The Rose" and "For Love," of the dynamics of emotions, especially in a love relationship. "The Dream," a poem in five sections, narrates a painful dream with remarkable fidelity to the truths and possibilities of dream-reality, so different from waking reality. In this dream of himself and his mother, the poet *is* both himself and his mother, the latter seen principally as her hair; he both attacks and hurts his mother *and* suffers her pain. Meditating on the dream in section three, he sees it as reflecting the situation in which men generally find themselves *vis-à-vis* women: men are "empty of/ all but themselves," "lonely"; turning from their emptiness and loneliness, the poet finds himself become "my mother hating/ myself." Not only do the boundaries of self dissolve in this poem, in accord with dream-reality, but also the poet, awake, is profoundly disoriented and uncertain of the very sorts of things people generally assume without question. In section five, he is unsure whether he "dreamed/ the dream more/ than thinking," and in the closing passage he addresses a "you," pleading, "Don't/ go. Away./ If this is where we are."

Similarly, in the narrative and meditative poem "Anger," the reality represented is one in which the normally assumed integrity of the self is dissolved. A narration in the third person of an outbreak of anger between a man and a woman occupies the first of the poem's six sections. The style here functions expressionistically. The poem opens with a series of extremely short declarative sentences, running from the first tercet—"The time is./ The air seems a cover,/ the room is quiet"—to the fourth, where the pace suddenly accelerates with a presentation, "a truck through the walls," followed by a string of modifiers. The acceleration of pace seems to mime the surge of emotion in the man, for the truck with its sudden glare of headlights and roar of motor apparently precipitates his rage. The violence of his reaction is conveyed by the abruptness of the very short declarative sentence, "He/ hated it," that follows the relatively elaborate passage on the truck. The anger itself is presented mainly in figurative language; his face becomes a "moon . . . // of black light," which in turn becomes an image of what life suddenly is for him, "black," "an open/ hole of horror," which becomes "a hole // for anger" into which he descends. Here there is none of the usual narrative clarity of who did and said what: he is suddenly "between them," "she" and "the other," "the other" being himself. After the expressionistic narrative of the first section, Creeley abandons the third person: section two is in the first person, section three in the third—apparently an address of the poet to himself. Section four begins with an address to "my face" and continues in the first person. Creeley expresses the sense of being locked in himself, a subjective state he often renders in his poems. Here the sentence enacts an escape from this entrapment even as it asserts it to be the case: the poet says he sees "my/ eye locked in/ self sight, not // the world . . ." but then continues, "but the close // breathing beside/ me I reach out/ for, feel. . . ." There is a psychological realism to this ungrammatical slide from one sense of self-in-the-world to another. Section five picks up the narrative thread with "After," after the fight that, it now appears, is to be taken as having gone on all night; there is a feeling "as if/ the sun had // been wrong to return," but nevertheless a "relief." In the two tercets that constitute the final section, the poet, as "we," seems again to address himself as "you," with an epigrammatic analysis of what went wrong—"All you say you want/ to do to yourself you do/ to someone else as yourself"—and a wondering what will finally become of this "you."

"The World" is similar to "The Dream" and "Anger" in being a narrative of a night. The poet addresses his love, recalling a night when it seemed her dead brother came and leaned over them in bed while she slept. This is no ghost story in the sense of one told for mere thrills. The ghost that the speaker sees as his wife's "grey lost tired bewildered/ brother, unused, untaken—/ hated by love" gives him a sense that he himself, not the brother, is an intruder. Creeley's poem is concerned with his sense of people's holds on one another, his doubts about one's rights to another's love.

Unlike "The Dream," "Anger," and "The World," neither "Distance" nor "Enough" deals with a single dramatic situation. Both are meditative lyrics, and both are concerned, like so many of Creeley's poems, with the problem of distance between the self and the beloved. "Distance" is a difficult poem because of its abrupt transitions, shifts in tense, and extremely elliptical language. The overall movement is from the speaker's want—it begins, "Hadn't I been/ aching, for you"—through uncertain groping—"But what // were you, where,/ . . . I/ was always // thinking"—and a sense of dislocation—"where are/ you, am I happy,/ is this car // mine"—to a feeling of being interpenetrated by others, of their answering his want—"pushing/ the flesh aside,/ they step in-/ to my own."

The complex meditation of "Enough" is divided into eight parts. It is concerned both with the poet's relation with his wife and with the role of words. He begins with words and the possibility they represent of "speak[ing]/ of what has happened," which is prerequisite to reaching understanding and achieving a basis for going on. Over the whole poem, the generally very short lines, often broken by punctuation, give a sense of the difficulty of finding words. Through words, he recalls meeting Bobbie for the first time and articulates his sense of "never/ having left after that,/ not to my own mind." He records that the ensuing years together brought "some happy days/ but some bitter // and sad." In the first four parts of the poem, he tries, falteringly, to reach across the distance between himself, locked in his own mind, and the woman he addresses. Words have sometimes been a way for him to possess her body, to see it, to "dance" for her, but they can fail to go from his mind to her consciousness. In part three, he feels himself in "an ocean of vagueness," "try[ing] to feel/ where you are." In part four the distance reaches its greatest extent; instead of making contact with the other person, the speaker is alone in his own mind, in a fantasy of "obscene bodies/ twisting." Part five begins to climb up from this nadir, the words themselves making the way out, word by tentative word: "One/ by one/ the form // comes." Part six ponders the fact that the speaker and the "you" he addresses are necessarily one here, the other there, "In two/ places." Part seven opens abruptly with the harsh image, "Your body is a garbage can," made more emphatic by the fact that a clause is given complete in a single line, longer than the norm, instead of being broken over two or more lines. The speaker does not stop with this one way of looking at the woman's body, however, but goes on to see it also as "a white/ softness . . . that has/ its own // place time/ after time." The acceptance of and respect for her separateness implicit here is made explicit in the "vow" of part eight (two epigrammatic couplets) to "respect" her body. At the poem's end, this necessary separateness of persons is no longer seen as an alienating distance: the poet can "vow to yours to be/ enough, enough, enough" ("yours" is ambiguous, certainly referring to the woman's body, but also inviting a reading of a more inclusive reference).

The form of *Pieces* is strikingly unique. The "pieces" are mostly in verse, with the lines usually short and arranged in short stanzas (couplets, tercets, quatrains), some in prose. In the Scribner's edition, the pieces are not isolated on single pages; they follow one another with different degrees of separation. A single dot is the slightest degree; a row of three dots suggests a stronger boundary. Pieces marked off from what precedes them by either of these symbols may be titled or untitled. Titles are usually entirely in capital letters. The result of this form of presentation is that the pieces seem to various degrees to assert their autonomy, to various degrees to be submerged in, to be pieces of, a larger whole—or, more accurately, of a larger piece. This form implies a skepticism about the pretense to completeness of the conventional poem.

In these pieces, Creeley often meditates on the nature of the self's experience of the world and the problem of its knowledge of the other. Language is, of course, a principal means of one's knowing and experiencing the world and other people, and it is often the particular focus of Creeley's meditations. The first piece in the book contemplates the wonder and paradoxicality of "a sentence/ which // began 'it was,'" which, despite the tense of its verb, is uttered and heard or written and read in "a present" and becomes "a presence," which itself has duration, goes along in time, "saying/ something/ as it goes," coming to a period at the end. Interestingly, this little meditation itself contains no sentence, but is carried out in two presentational fragments—placing the phenomenon considered immediately before the reader, as full predications would not—arranged in four tercets of short lines. Later in the book, a piece insists on the value of the sheer fact of "saying something," as opposed to writing in order to say some predetermined thing: "Never write/ to say more/ than saying/ something." Creeley sees value as inhering in the process of interaction with the language (which is in part a process of discovery of meaning) rather than in the imposition of an intended meaning on the language. A horizontal rule separates these four lines from the other five lines of the piece, which proclaim a related value—the sensuous pleasure to be found in words regardless of what they are saying: "Words/ are/ pleasure./ All/ words." In giving the reader one word at a time, those five lines invite him to hold the words one at a time in the eye and/or the ear, on the tongue, and savor their full vowels, their liquids, their written (printed) forms.

In one tiny piece, Creeley draws attention to two so-called function words, two of the little words that are normally scarcely perceived as words, let alone in the manner Creeley would have words perceived. He does this by constructing phrases in which each word modifies a repetition of itself: "Not from not/ but in in." In their first occurrences, "not" and "in" perform their respective functions of negation and prepositional relation, and the reader naturally directs his attention ahead toward the anticipated nouns—until he finds in their places "not" and "in" again, this time referring (as they do in this sentence) to "the word 'not'" and "the word 'in.'" This time he is forced to notice those little words as he likely has not done before. Creeley also draws attention to the peculiarities, the humor revealed upon scrutiny, of another kind of language the details of which are generally ignored—colloquial speech. He does this by transcribing bits of it broken into lines so as to impede taking it all in at once, as in these two pieces: "What she says she wants/ she wants she says." "Oh no you/ don't, do you?"

Creeley sees language as changing in time and varying with social and cultural groups, and he accordingly sees the poet as having to find a language and form appropriate to his particular place and time—which will initially be met with hostility by those whose notion of poetry is based on the poetry of another era or culture. This situation is addressed directly in the satirical piece called "Diction." After alluding to "The grand time when the words/ were fit for human allegation, // . . . and the lids fit," the poem speaks of "the wind [that] blew through it," and the reaction to this "wind" by "they," who said "in hostile, little voices:/ 'It's changed, it's not the same!'" In another piece, Creeley simply presents the condition in which he sees the language as coming to him: "Late, the words, late/ the form of them, al- // ready past what they were/ fit for." The words he has at his disposal are "late" in that they have been used by previous generations of speakers and writers; their forms, too, are "late," in that they have altered through history in accord with various sound shifts. They are "past what they were fit for," because the same things said over and over in the same way lose impact. At the same time, they are all ready for further uses, different from their old ones: Creeley's violent enjambment, splitting the word "already" between its first and second syllables, allows him to say two true things at once by a pun that is both playful and serious.

Another piece addresses the problem of "what words in/ time make of things." Creeley offers a facetious example: "Mr./ Warner came from a small/ town in the middle mid-/ eastern Atlantic states." His comment on this kind of language, "That—in time—displaces/ all else might be said of/ him," indicates the kind of conscience that underlies his own unconventional but precise ways of talking about things.

Besides language, Creeley's meditations in *Pieces* often focus on other aspects of the experience of consciousness. The sense of enclosure in the self, which is expressed in his earlier poetry, is also articulated here. One of the early pieces considers "Inside/ and out," calling them "impossible locations." In the middle couplets of the poem, the line-divisions give the reader a kinesthetic sense of the problematical transition between these locations: "reaching in/ from out- // side, out/ from in- // side." What one has to mediate between inside and out, Creeley gives the reader in a presentation constituting the final couplet: "one/ hand." Invited initially to contemplate an impossibility, the reader is left to contemplate that which transcends, however imperfectly, the impossibility—as much a wonder as any of the normally neglected things to which Creeley draws attention.

The problem of self's entrapment in itself is considered with specific reference to interpersonal relations and as complicated by the passage of time, in a piece where the speaker says in the first tercet (of two): "I cannot see you/ there for what you/ thought you were." The problem in relations between separate selves is not simply that of reaching out from inside, but of reaching another's "inside" from one's own. If the concern is to penetrate to the other's inside as it was at some time in the past, the difficulty is increased by the faultiness of memory and the fact that both the self and the other have gone on changing in the interim: "The faded memories/ myself enclose/ passing too." Creeley's economy of expression here gives the two tercets a tremendous density of meaning, while the neatness of the form invites the reader to contemplate that meaning at length.

Besides such short, dense meditations on aspects of the experience of consciousness, there is a series of pieces, under the title "NUMBERS," that deal with each of the numerals, one through nine and zero. These use the numbers in various ways, some serious, some playful. Creeley presents associations that the number in question has for him (the first poem for "Four" begins, "This number for me/ is comfort, a secure/ fact of things."), reflects on numbers in terms of people (thus a little piece for "One" is the couplet, "You are not/ me, nor I you," and a piece for "Two" says scrupulously, "What you wanted/ I felt, or felt I felt"), engages in verbal play, or contemplates a number in quite abstract terms. *Pieces* also includes a long narrative poem, "The Finger," derived from a drug experience. It is similar to "The Door" in *For Love* in having an archetypal female figure instead of a realistic one, and similar to "The Dream" in *Words* in rendering a reality other than everyday waking reality.

Creeley's later collections generally follow the form of *Pieces*, with an increasing autobiographical emphasis: fragmentary notations together with more or less fully crystallized poems, all closely connected to the day-to-day life of the poet, as opposed to a collection of autonomous lyrics. *A Day Book*, the dust-jacket of which pictures calendar pages (Tuesday, November 19, 1968, on the front; Friday, June 11, 1971, on the back) consists of two parts: the first, undated prose journal entries; the second, entitled "In London," poetry, with the pieces (as in *Pieces*) set off to various degrees—some titled; some untitled with the first words set in capitals; and within both of these kinds of pieces, sections separated by elipses.

*Hello* is a poetic journal covering two months from February 29 to May 3, 1976, during which Creeley traveled in New Zealand, Australia, the Philippines, Malaysia, Hong Kong, Japan, and Korea. After the frequent abstractness of the language and subject matter of *Pieces*, these poems and verse fragments stay generally close to physical sensation and personal emotional experience (an emphasis that will continue in *Later*), though they often continue to reflect Creeley's acute awareness of the difference between the external world (whatever that is) and his sensory and mental experience of it (which is all the knowledge of it one can have). The book is not scenic in the manner typical of a travelogue, however, for Creeley tends to perceive the same elemental things—light, water—in the South Pacific as he does at home. Memories and a sense of time's having passed and of his own aging enter often into Creeley's poems in *Hello*. What begins as an observation or series of observations of the place in which he finds himself will shift to a reflection on his mortality or move by association to memories. In this book, he allows his emotional vulnerability to be apparent; the period covered by the journal is that of his breakup with his wife Bobbie. The poetry here (as is appropriate to its nature as a verse journal) is more nakedly personal than previously. Several pieces show him groping for a way to continue in his life. "Later," one of these, is not (as many of the pieces in *Hello* are) a simple journal notation in verse, but a tightly constructed poem. Its seven tercets of short lines, heavily syncopated and repetitive, mime in their movement the uncertain feeling about for a way forward that they describe, the poet's persisting (in the words of the poem's ending) "in waiting, for that way // to be the way I can/ still let go, still want, and/ still let go, and want to."

The rather long poem "Cebu" exemplifies many of the essential features of the book as a whole. Although a potentially autonomous poem, not a notation dependent on the context of the rest of the journal, it passes from one image or idea to another by mental association and is looser in the ordering of its material and more casual in tone than is the case with Creeley's earlier long poems. The greater looseness is reflected in the use of a somewhat longer line than Creeley's usual very short one (the lines are arranged in couplets, often open). Observation of a detention home and a prison along the route from the airport reminds the poet of a picture he had seen of a new prison in Chicago that was a high rise "looking like a modern hotel." This in turn brings to mind high-rise housing for the poor in Singapore. Talking about high rises leads to an assertion of his own preference for staying close to the ground, and thence back to the place in which he finds himself, its housing, "open-sided, thatched roofed," which he likes. As he continues, though, it is not the lowness of this native housing that becomes the focus of his meditation, but its fragility, as if it were built for ephemerality. He approves this readiness to "be gone in a flash,/ or molder more slowly/ back into humus," and applies the example to his own human life, admitting to being "scared" sometimes of dying and wishfully thinking of his life as an exception to the processes to which all life is subject. "It isn't," he knows, and he knows that likewise "some of those // bananas are already rotten,/ and no doubt there are vacant // falling-down houses, and boats/ with holes in their bottoms" ("boats filling/ the channel" and "banana trees," as well as native houses, are things noted earlier in the poem, so the loose associative movement does pick up at least some of the threads it introduces). He accedes to this decay and his part in it, declaring his willingness to "let what/ world I do have to be the world." Turning his attention outward again to the present place in which he is writing, "this room," he is reminded by the air conditioner of the American southwest and more specifically of his mother-in-law's in Albuquerque. In a breathless sentence that keeps extending itself beyond all expectation, his mother-in-law is swept into the embrace of the poet's global feeling that has been generated in the course of the poem itself, now brought to an expansive, affirmative conclusion: "and I wonder what she's doing // today, and if she's happy there,/ as I am here, with these green // walls, and the lights on, and/ finally loving everything I know." Though few of the poems in *Hello* arrive at such a pitch of affirmation, they typically proceed as "Cebu" does, by association, taking the poet to initially unforeseen conclusions, though those conclusions may be questions and irresolution.

In *Later*, some of Creeley's concerns have been intensified by aging and loss. The experience of time passing—of the diurnal cycle of light and dark, of the seasonal cycle with its changes and returns of weathers, but also of linear time, of what is gone without prospect of return—and of memory, as it problematically recovers the gone things of the past and impinges on the experience of the present, is now acutely felt and registered and reflected upon in the poems. The poet mulls over the question of the sources and cure of human unhappiness and the question of what is ultimately of value to a human being in the world. The first three poems of the book—"Myself," "This World," and "The House"—constitute a closely linked series of meditations, their linkage being pointed up by their sharing the same stanzaic form (quatrains), and announce the book's principal themes and images. The self of "Myself" defines itself at once as older and as now knowing to be impossible what a younger self felt possible, but as nevertheless still wanting (that word so common in Creeley's earlier poetry) "to know/ why, human, men/ and women are // so torn, so lost,/ why hopes cannot/ find better world/ than this." The poem closes by quoting from Percy Bysshe Shelley: "'And for the morn/ of truth they feigned, // deep night/ Caught them ere evening. . . .'" The opening lines of the second poem then take up the imagery of morning and evening, day and night, light and dark, that will run through the whole book, in what seems a reply to Shelley: "If night's the harder,/ closer time, days/ come." This poem then moves through description of a day on the beach, with the changes in air and water, to raise at its end two questions: "What then/ will be lost, // recovered./ What/ matters as one/ in this world?" These questions are the dominant concerns of the poems that follow.

In the third poem, "The House," the speaker, confronted by an old restaurant in ruins, begins to take them up, urging an effort to bring to and hold in mind the past of the place, the "myriad people" of that past, and expressing confidence in the possibility of "put[ting] it all right" again. The vision of the old building put right becomes the first of a series of images of interior spaces in the book—small, simple, warm enclosures for human activity and interaction that seem to be presented as images of what matters and that seem to represent what the poet finds to be valuable (see particularly "La Conca," "Place," "The Table," "Later (9)," "If I Had My Way"). Together with the human house, the human "song" is affirmed as achievable (the present poem itself an instance) and valuable. In the course of the book, the notion of the song (or story) as a thing of human value reappears and is elaborated upon, with the insistence that the value inheres not in the singer or teller, but in the song or story, that the making of songs and stories is a common activity, not an activity of an elite (see especially "Childish" and "Reflections"). This is reflected in the use Creeley makes of street language and the language of popular songs—not for color, but as vehicles of wisdom as authentic as any. The commonality of the experience of life, the equality of every human man or woman with every other in the world, is a reiterated theme of the book.

The title poem of the book is a sequence of ten poems constituting an intensive examination of what is lost, what can be recovered, what can be held to and affirmed as valuable. The sense of loss reaches its greatest intensity in "Later (6)," where a dog apparently owned years before by the speaker becomes an emblem for all that is irrevocably lost: "After all/ these years, //

no dog's coming home/ again . . . your voice not the one/ used to call him home." Not only has the dog died, but its owner has moved toward his own death. In "Later (9)," an attic room becomes an emblem of what can be held and valued, both in physical actuality and in memory: "Sitting up here in/ newly constituted // attic room . . . thinking of old attic, // West Acton farmhouse,/ same treasures here." "I've come as far,/ as high, as I'll go," says the speaker looking out at the words "KISS ME. I love you" chalked on a facing wall and at an old horse chestnut "gather[ing] strength to face winter." He declares himself to be after "man-made/ endurance," such as is exemplified by the room in which he finds himself, of which he asks, "Where finally else/ in the world come to rest. . . ?" He does not see it as a retreat, but as a place of presences: "There's more always here // than just me, in this room,/ this attic, apartment, // this house, this world." The final poem of the sequence celebrates life that in a present "feels place in the physical // with others,/ . . . finds a home/ on earth."

The "rest" achieved in the concluding poems of the "Later" sequence is temporary, however, and the principal concern of the remainder of the book is with the difficulty of undertaking, in the words of "If I Had My Way," "to begin again // again." The final poem, "Prayer to Hermes," asks, "must I forever/ walk on, *walk on*—/ as I have and/ as I can?" and concludes by proclaiming the poet's spiritual brotherhood with Hermes in the drive of one who "*will* find heaven in hell,/ . . . and *will* tell of itself/ all, *all* in the world," implying that he will find it in himself to continue and that his continuance will be through his inexhaustible and irresistible impulse to poetry.

### Major publications other than poetry
NOVEL: *The Island*, 1963.

SHORT FICTION: *The Gold Diggers and Other Stories*, 1965.

NONFICTION: *A Quick Graph: Collected Notes & Essays*, 1970 (Donald Allen, editor); *Contexts of Poetry: Interviews 1961-1971*, 1973.

### Bibliography
Bacon, Terry R. "Closure in Robert Creeley's Poetry," in *Modern Poetry Studies*. VIII (1977), pp. 227-247.

Edelberg, Cynthia Dubin. *Robert Creeley's Poetry: A Critical Introduction*, 1978.

Ford, Arthur L. *Robert Creeley*, 1978.

Oberg, Arthur. "Robert Creeley: And the Power to Tell *Is* Glory," in *Ohio Review*. XVIII, no. 1 (1977), pp. 79-97.

Spanos, William V., ed. "Robert Creeley: A Gathering," a special issue of *Boundary 2*. VI, no. 3, and VII, no. 1, combined (1978).

*Eleanor von Auw Berry*

# COUNTÉE CULLEN

**Born:** New York, New York; May 30, 1903
**Died:** New York, New York; January 9, 1946

## Principal collections

*Color*, 1925; *Copper Sun*, 1927; *The Ballad of the Brown Girl: An Old Ballad Retold*, 1927; *The Black Christ, and Other Poems*, 1929; *The Medea, and Some Poems*, 1935; *The Lost Zoo (a Rhyme for the Young, But Not Too Young)*, 1940; *On These I Stand: An Anthology of the Best Poems of Countée Cullen*, 1947.

## Other literary forms

Countée Cullen wrote nearly as much prose as he did poetry. While serving from 1926 through most of 1928 as literary editor of *Opportunity*, a magazine vehicle for the National Urban League, Cullen wrote several articles, including book reviews, and a series of topical essays for a column called "The Dark Tower" about figures and events involved in the Harlem Renaissance. He also wrote many stories for children, most of which are collected in *My Lives and How I Lost Them* (1942), the "autobiography" of Cullen's own pet, Christopher Cat, who had allegedly reached his ninth life. Earlier, in 1932, the poet had tried his hand at a novel, publishing it as *One Way to Heaven*. In addition to articles, reviews, stories, and a novel, the poet translated, or collaborated in the writing of, three plays, one of them being a musical. Cullen translated Euripedes' *Medea* (1935) for the volume by the same name; in 1942, Virgil Thomson set to music the seven verse choruses from Cullen's translation. With Owen Dodson, Cullen wrote the one-act play *The Third Fourth of July*, which appeared posthumously in 1946. The musical was produced at the Martin Beck Theater on Broadway where it ran for 113 performances; this production also introduced Pearl Bailey as the character Butterfly.

## Achievements

Cullen's literary accomplishments were many. While he was a student at DeWitt Clinton High School, New York City, he published his first poems and made numerous and regular contributions to the high school literary magazine. From DeWitt, whose other distinguished graduates include Lionel Trilling and James Baldwin, Cullen went to New York University. There he distinguished himself by becoming a member of Phi Beta Kappa and in the same year, 1925, by publishing *Color*, his first collection of poems. In June, 1926, the poet took his second degree, an M.A. in English literature from Harvard. In December, 1926, *Color* was awarded the first Harmon Gold Award for literature, which carried with it a cash award of five hundred dollars. Just before publication in 1927 of his second book, *Copper Sun*, Cullen received a Guggenheim Fellowship for a year's study and writing in France. While in France, he worked on improving his French conversation by engaging a private tutor and his knowledge of French literature by enrolling in courses at the Sorbonne. Out of this experience came *The Black Christ, and Other Poems*. In 1944, the poet was offered the chair of Creative Literature at Nashville's Fisk University, but he refused in order to continue his teaching at the Frederick Douglass Junior High in New York City.

## Biography

Despite his several trips abroad, Countée Porter Cullen lived most of his life in New York City, spending his childhood years with his grandmother. When he reached adolescence, he was adopted by the Reverend and Mrs. Frederick A. Cullen; Reverend Cullen was minister of the Salem Methodist Episcopal Church of Harlem. The years spent with the Cullens in the Methodist parsonage made a lasting impression on the young poet; although he experienced periods of intense questioning, Cullen appears never to have discarded his belief in Christianity.

During his undergraduate years at New York University, the young poet became heavily involved with figures of the Harlem Renaissance; among these Harlem literati were Zora Neale Hurston, Langston Hughes, Carl Van Vechten (a white writer who treated black themes), and Wallace Thurman. After the appearance of *Color* in 1925 and the receipt of his Harvard M.A. in June, 1926, Cullen assumed the position of literary editor of *Opportunity*. At the end of October, 1926, he wrote one of the most important of his "Dark Tower" essays about the appearance of that great treasure of the Harlem Renaissance, the short-lived, but first black literary and art quarterly, *Fire* (issued only once). He contributed one of his best poems, "From the Dark Tower," to *Fire*. About the solitary issue, Cullen wrote that it held great significance for black American culture, because it represented "a brave and beautiful attempt to meet our need for an all-literary and artistic medium of expression."

On April 10, 1928, Cullen married Nina Yolande DuBois, daughter of one of the most powerful figures of twentieth century black American culture, W. E. B. DuBois; the two were appropriately married at Salem Methodist Episcopal Church. This star-crossed union proved to be of short duration, however; while Cullen was in Paris on his Guggenheim Fellowship, Yolande was granted a decree of divorce. The marriage had not lasted two years. Much of Cullen's poetry deals with disappointment in love, and one senses that the poet was himself often disappointed in such matters.

In 1940, however, after Cullen had taught for several years at the Frederick Douglass Junior High School of New York, he married a second time; on this occasion he chose Ida Mae Roberson, whom he had known for ten years.

Ida Mae represented to the poet the ideal woman; she was intelligent, loyal, and empathetic, if not as beautiful and well-connected as his former wife.

When Cullen died of uremic poisoning on January 9, 1946, only forty-three years old, the New York newspapers devoted several columns to detailing his career, and praising him for his distinguished literary accomplishments. Yet in recent years, Houston A. Baker has deplored (in *A Many-Colored Coat of Dreams: The Poetry of Countée Cullen*, 1974) the fact that to date no collection of Cullen's poetry has been published since the posthumous *On These I Stand* (1947); nor have any of his previously published volumes been reprinted. Indeed, many volumes of this important Harlem Renaissance poet can be read today only in rare book rooms of university libraries.

**Analysis**

In his scholarly book of 1937, *Negro Poetry and Drama*, Sterling A. Brown, whose poems and essays continue to exert formidable influence on black American culture, remarked that Countée Cullen's poetry is "the most polished lyricism of modern Negro poetry." About his own poetry and poetry in general, Cullen himself observed: "good poetry is a lofty thought beautifully expressed. Poetry should not be too intellectual. It should deal more, I think, with the emotions." In this definition of "good poetry," Cullen reflects his declared, constant aspiration to transcend his color and to strike a universal chord. Yet the perceptive poet, novelist, essayist and critic James Weldon Johnson asserted that the best of Cullen's poetry "is motivated by race. He is always seeking to free himself and his art from these bonds." The tension prevalent in Cullen's poems, then, is between the objective of transcendence—to reach the universal, to enter the "mainstream"—and his ineluctable return to the predicament his race faces in a white world. This tension causes him, on the one hand, to demonstrate a paramount example of T. S. Eliot's "tradition and the individual talent" and, on the other, to embody the black aesthetic (as articulated during the Harlem Renaissance); in his best poems, he achieves both. Transcending the bonds of race and country, he produces poetry which looks to the literature and ideas of the past while it identifies its creator as an original artist; yet, at the same time, he celebrates his African heritage, dramatizes black heroism, and reveals the reality of being black in a hostile world.

"Yet Do I Marvel," perhaps Cullen's most famous single poem, displays the poet during one of his most intensely lyrical, personal moments; yet this poem also illustrates his reverence for tradition. The sonnet, essentially Shakespearean in rhyme scheme, is actually Petrarchan in its internal form. The Petrarchan form is even suggested in the rhyme scheme; the first two quatrains rhyme abab, cdcd in perfect accord with the Shakespearean scheme. The next six lines, however, break the expected pattern of yet another quatrain in the same scheme; instead of efef followed by a couplet gg, the poem adopts the scheme ee ff gg. While retaining the concluding couplet (gg), the other two (eeff) combine with the final couplet, suggesting the Petrarchan structure of the sestet. The poem is essentially divided, then, into the octave, wherein the problem is stated, and the sestet, in which some sort of resolution is attempted.

Analysis of the poem's content shows that Cullen chooses the internal form of the Petrarchan sonnet but retains a measure of the Shakespearean form for dramatic effect. The first eight lines of the poem express by means of antiphrastic statements or ironic declaratives that the poem's speaker doubts God's goodness and benevolent intent, especially in His creation of certain limited beings. The poem begins with the assertion that "I doubt not God is good, well-meaning, kind" and then proceeds to reveal that the speaker actually believes just the opposite to be true; that is, he actually says, "I do doubt God is good." For God has created the "little buried mole" to continue blind and "flesh that mirrors Him" to "some day die." Then the persona cites two illustrations of cruel, irremediable predicaments from classical mythology, those of Tantalus and Sisyphus. These mythological figures are traditional examples: Tantalus, the man who suffers eternal denial of that which he seeks; and Sisyphus, the man who suffers the eternal drudgery of being forced to toil endlessly again and again only to lose his objective each time he thinks he has won it.

The illustration of the mole and the man who must die rehearses the existential pathos of twentieth century men estranged from God and thrust into a hostile universe. What appeared to be naïve affirmations of God's goodness become penetrating questions which reveal Cullen himself in a moment of intense doubt. This attitude of contention with God closely resembles that expressed by Gerard Manley Hopkins in his sonnet "Thou Art Indeed Just, Lord." The probing questions, combined with the apparent resolve to believe, are indeed close; one might suggest that Cullen has adapted Hopkins' struggle for certainty to the black predicament, the real subject of Cullen's poem. The predicaments of Tantalus and Sisyphus (anticipating Albert Camus' later essay) comment on a personal problem, one close to home for Cullen himself. The notion of men struggling eternally toward a goal, thinking they have achieved it but having it torn from them, articulates the plight of black artists in America. In keeping with the form of the Petrarchan sonnet, the ninth line constitutes the *volta* or turn toward some sort of resolution. From ironic questioning, the persona moves to direct statement, even to a degree of affirmation. "Inscrutable His ways are," the speaker declares, to a mere human being who is too preoccupied with the vicissitudes of his mundane existence to grasp "What awful brain compels His awful hand," this last line echoing William Blake's "The Tyger." The apparent resolution becomes clouded by the poem's striking final couplet: "Yet do I marvel at this curious thing:/ To make a poet black, and bid him sing!"

The doubt remains; nothing is finally resolved. The plight of the black poet becomes identical with that of Tantalus and Sisyphus. Like these figures from classical mythology, the black poet is, in the contemporary, nonmythological world, forced to struggle endlessly toward a goal he will never, as the poem suggests, be allowed to reach. Cullen has effectively combined the Petrarchan and the Shakespearean sonnet forms; the sestet's first four lines function as an apparent resolution of the problem advanced by the octave. The concluding couplet, however, recalling the Shakespearean device of concentrating the entire poem's comment within the final two lines, restates the problem of the octave by maintaining that, in the case of a black poet, God has created the supreme irony. In "Yet Do I Marvel," Cullen has succeeded in making an intensely personal statement; as James Johnson suggested, this poem "is motivated by race." Nevertheless, not only race is at work here. Rather than selecting a more modern form, perhaps free verse, the poet employs the sonent tradition in a surprising and effective way, and he also shows his regard for tradition by citing mythological figures and by summoning up Blake.

Cullen displays his regard for tradition in many other poems. "The Medusa," for example, by its very title celebrates once again the classical tradition; in this piece, another sonnet, the poet suggests that the face of a woman who rejected him has the malign power of the Medusa. In an epitaph, a favorite form of Cullen, he celebrates the poetry of John Keats, whose "singing lips that cold death kissed/ Have seared his own with flame." Keats was Cullen's avowed favorite poet, and Cullen celebrates him in yet a second poem, "To John Keats, Poet at Spring Time." As suggested by Cullen's definition of poetry, it was Keats's concern for beauty which attracted him: "in spite of all men say/ Of Beauty, you have felt her most."

Beauty and classical mythology were not the only elements of tradition which Cullen revered. Indeed, he forcefully celebrated his own African heritage, exemplifying the first of the tenets of the black aesthetic. *Heritage* represents his most concentrated effort to reclaim his African roots. This 128-line lyric opens as the persona longs for the song of "wild barbaric birds/ Goading massive jungle herds" from which through no fault of his own he has been removed for three centuries. He then articulates Johnson's observation that this poet is ever "seeking to free himself and his art" from the bonds of this heritage. The poem's speaker remarks that, although he crams his thumbs against his ears, and keeps them there, "Great drums" always throb "through the air." This duplicity of mind and action force upon him a sense of "distress, and joy allied." Despite this distress, he continues to conjure up in his mind's eye "cats/ Crouching in the river reeds," "Silver snakes," and "the savage measures of/ Jungle boys and girls in love." The rain has a particularly dramatic effect on him; "While its primal measures drip," a distant, resonant voice beckons him to "'Strip!/ Off this new exuberance./ Come and dance the Lover's Dance!'" Out of this experience of recollection and reclaiming his past comes the urge to "fashion dark gods" and, finally, even to dare "to give You [the one God]/ Dark despairing features."

The intense need expressed here, to see God as literally black, predicts the long narrative poem of 1929, *The Black Christ*. This poem, perhaps more than any other of Cullen's poems, represents his attempt to portray black heroism, the second tenet of the black aesthetic. Briefly the poem tells the tale of Jim, a young black man who comes to believe it is inevitable that he will suffer death at the hands of an angry lynch mob. Miraculously, after the inevitable lynching has indeed occurred, the young man appears to his younger brother and mother, much as Jesus of Nazareth, according to the gospels, appeared before his disciples. Chirst has essentially transformed himself into black Jim. Although the poem contains such faults as a main character who speaks in dialect at one point and waxes eloquent at another, and one speech by Jim who, pursued by the mob, speaks so long that he cannot possibly escape (of course one may argue that he was doomed from the start), it has moments of artistic brilliance.

Jim "was handsome in a way/ Night is after a long, hot day." He could never bend his spirit to the white man's demands: "my blood's too hot to knuckle." Like Richard Wright's Bigger Thomas, Jim was a man of action whose deeds "let loose/ The pent-up torrent of abuse," which clamored in his younger brother "for release." Toward the middle of the poem, Jim's brother, the narrator, describes Jim, after the older brother has become tipsy with drink, as "Spring's gayest cavalier"; this occurs "in the dim/ Half-light" of the evening. At the end, "Spring's gayest cavalier" has become the black Christ, Spring's radiant sacrifice, suggesting that "Half-light" reveals only selective truths, those one may be inclined to believe are true because of one's human limitations, whereas God's total light reveals absolute truth unfettered. Following this suggestion, the image "Spring's gayest cavalier" becomes even more fecund. The word cavalier calls up another poem by Hopkins, "The Windhover," which is dedicated to Christ. In this poem, the speaker addresses Christ with the exclamation, "O my chevalier!" Both cavalier and chevalier have their origins in the same Latin word, *caballarius*. Since Cullen knew both French and Latin and since Hopkins' poems had been published in 1918, it is reasonable to suggest a more than coincidental connection. At any rate, "Spring's gayest cavalier" embodies an example of effective foreshadowing.

Just before the mob seizes Jim, the narrator maintains that "The air about him shaped a crown/ Of light, or so it seemed to me," similar to the nimbus so often appearing in medieval paintings of Christ, the holy family, the disciples, and the saints. The narrator describes the seizure itself in an epic simile of nine lines. When Jim has been lynched, the younger brother exclaims, "My Lycidas was dead. There swung/ In all his glory, lusty, young,/ My Jonathan, my Patrocles." Here Cullen brings together the works of John Milton, the Bible, and Homer into one image which appears to syncretize them all. Clearly, the poet is attempting to construct in Jim a hero of cosmic proportions while at the same time managing to unify, if only for a moment, four grand traditions: the English, the biblical, the classical, and of course, the black American.

While *The Black Christ* dramatizes black heroism, it also suggests what it means to be black in a hostile, white world. Not all the black experience, however, is tainted with such unspeakable horror. In "Harlem Wine," Cullen reveals how blacks overcome their pain and rebellious inclinations through the medium of music. The blues, a totally black cultural phenomenon, "hurtle flesh and bone past fear/ Down alleyways of dreams." Indeed the wine of Harlem can its "joy compute/ with blithe, ecstatic hips." The ballad stanza of this poem's three quatrains rocks with rhythm, repeating Cullen's immensely successful performance in another long narrative poem, *The Ballad of the Brown Girl*.

Although not as notable a rhythmic performance as "Harlem Wine" or *The Ballad of the Brown Girl*, "From the Dark Tower" is, nevertheless, a remarkable poem. It contains a profound expression of the black experience. Important to a reading of the poem is the fact that the Dark Tower was an actual place located on New York's 136th Street in the heart of Harlem; poets and artists of the Harlem Renaissance often gathered there to discuss their writings and their art. Perhaps this poem grew out of one of those gatherings. The poem is more identifiably a Petrarchan or Italian sonnet than "Yet Do I Marvel"; as prescribed by the form, the octave is arranged into two quatrains, each rhyming abbaabba, while the sestet rhymes ccddee. The rhyme scheme of the sestet closely resembles that in "Yet Do I Marvel."

The octave of "From the Dark Tower" states the poem's problem in an unconventional, perhaps surprising manner, by means of a series of threats. The first threat introduces the conceit of planting, to which the poem returns in its last pair of couplets. The poet begins, "We shall not always plant while others reap/ The golden increment of bursting fruit." The planting conceit suggests almost immediately the image of slaves working the fields of a Southern plantation. Conjuring up this memory of the antebellum South, but then asserting by use of the future tense, "We *shall* not," that nothing has changed—that is, that the white world has relegated twentieth century blacks to their former status as slaves, not even as good as second class citizens— Cullen strikes a minor chord of deep, poignant bitterness felt by many contemporary blacks. Yet what these blacks produce with their planting is richly fertile, a "bursting fruit"; the problem is that "others reap" this "golden increment." The poet's threat promises that this tide of gross, unjust rapine will soon turn against its perpetrators.

The next few lines compound this initial threat with others. These same oppressed people will not forever bow "abject and mute" to such treatment by a people who have shown by their oppression that they are the inferiors of their victims. "Not everlastingly" will these victims "beguile" this evil race "with mellow flute"; the reader can readily picture scenes of supposedly contented, dancing "Darkies" and ostensibly happy minstrel men. "We were not made eternally to weep" declares the poet in the last line of the octave. This line constitutes the *volta* or turning point in the poem. All the bitterness and resentment implied in the preceding lines are exposed here. An oppressed people simply will not shed tears forever; sorrow and self-pity inevitably turn to anger and rebellion.

The first four lines of the sestet state cases in defense of the octave's propositions that this oppressed people, now identified by the comparisons made in these lines as the black race, is "no less lovely being dark." The poet returns subtly to his planting conceit by citing the case of flowers which "cannot bloom at all/ In light, but crumple, piteous, and fall." From the infinite heavens to finite flowers of earth Cullen takes his reader, grasping universal and particular significance for his people and thereby restoring and bolstering their pride and sense of worth.

Then follow the piercing, deep-felt last lines: "So, in the dark we hide the heart that bleeds,/ And wait, and tend our agonizing seeds." As with "Yet Do I Marvel," Cullen has effectively combined the structures of the Petrarchan and Shakespearean sonnets by concluding his poem with this trenchant, succinct couplet. The planting conceit, however, has altered dramatically. What has been "golden increment" for white oppressors will yet surely prove the "bursting fruit" of "agonizing seeds." The poem represents, then, a sort of revolutionary predeclaration of independence. This "document" first states the offenses sustained by the downtrodden, next asserts their worth and significance as human beings, and finally argues that the black people will "wait" until an appropriate time to reveal their agony through rebellion. Cullen has here predicted the anger of James Baldwin's *The Fire Next Time* (1963) and the rhetoric of the Black Armageddon, a more recent literary movement led by such poets as Imamu Amiri Baraka, Sonia Sanchez, and Nikki Giovanni.

Whereas these contemporary figures of the Black Armageddon movement almost invariably select unconventional forms in which to express their rebellion, Cullen demonstrated his respect for tradition in voicing his parallel feelings. Although Cullen's work ably displays his knowledge of the traditions of the Western world, from Homer to Keats (and even Edna St. Vincent Millay), it equally enunciates his empathy with black Americans in its celebration of the black aesthetic. At the same time that his poetry incorporates classicism and English Romanticism, it affirms his black heritage and the black American experience. Cullen neither denies his responsibility to his race nor disavows his commitment to transcend his particular circumstances.

**Major publications other than poetry**
NOVEL: *One Way to Heaven*, 1932.
PLAY: *The Third Fourth of July*, 1946.
CHILDREN'S LITERATURE: *My Lives and How I Lost Them*, 1942.
MISCELLANEOUS: *Caroling Dusk*, 1927 (edited).

**Bibliography**
Baker, Houston A., Jr. *A Many-Colored Coat of Dreams: The Poetry of Countée Cullen*, 1974.
Brown, Sterling A. *Negro Poetry and Drama*, 1937.
Collier, Eugenia W. "I Do Not Marvel, Countée Cullen," in *Modern Black Poets: A Collection of Critical Essays*, 1973. Edited by Donald B. Gibson.
Davis, Arthur P. "The Alien-and-Exile Theme in Countée Cullen's Racial Poems," in *Phylon*. XIV (1953), pp. 390-400.
Daniel, Walter C. "Countée Cullen as Literary Critic," in *College Language Association Journal*. XIV (1971), pp. 281-290.
Emanuel, James H., and Theodore L. Gross. "Countee Cullen," in *Dark Symphony: Negro Literature in America*, 1968. Edited by James H. Emanuel and Theodore L. Gross.
Fergusen, Blanche E. *Countée Cullen and the Negro Renaissance*, 1966.
Johnson, James Weldon. *The Book of American Negro Poetry*, 1931.
Perry, Margaret. *A Bio-Bibliography of Countée P. Cullen: 1903-1946*, 1971.
Turner, Darwin. *In a Minor Chord*, 1971.
Whitlow, Roger. *Black American Literature: A Critical History*, 1973.
Woodruff, Bertram L. "The Poetic Philosophy of Countée Cullen," in *Phylon*. I (1940), pp. 213-223.

*John C. Shields*

# E. E. CUMMINGS

**Born:** Cambridge, Massachusetts; October 14, 1894
**Died:** North Conway, New Hampshire; September 3, 1962

**Principal collections**
*Tulips and Chimneys*, 1923; *&*, 1925; *XLI Poems*, 1925; *Is 5*, 1926; *W: Seventy New Poems*, 1931; *No Thanks*, 1935; *1/20 Poems*, 1936; *Collected Poems*, 1938; *50 Poems*, 1940; *1 x 1*, 1944; *Xiape*, 1950; *Poems, 1923-1954*, 1954; *95 Poems*, 1958; *One Hundred Selected Poems*, 1959; *Selected Poems*, 1960; *73 Poems*, 1963; *E. E. Cummings: A Selection of Poems*, 1965; *Complete Poems, 1913-1962*, 1968.

**Other literary forms**
In addition to poetry, E. E. Cummings also published two long prose narratives, *The Enormous Room* (1922) and *Eimi* (1933); a translation from the French of *The Red Front*, by Louis Aragon (1933); a long play, *Him* (1927); two short plays, *Anthropos: The Future of Art* (1944) and *Santa Claus: A Morality* (1946); a ballet, *Tom* (1935); a collection of his own drawings in charcoal, ink, oil, pastels, and watercolor, *CIOPW* (1931); his autobiographical Harvard lectures, *i: six nonlectures* (1953); and a collection of his wife's photographs with captions by Cummings, *Adventures in Value* (1962).

Of these, *The Enormous Room* and *Eimi* are of particular interest because of their contributions to Cummings' critical reputation and to his development as an artist. The former is the poet's account of his three-month confinement in a French concentration camp in 1917. It was hailed upon its appearance as a significant firsthand account of the war and has become one of the classic records of World War I. It is also significant in that it is Cummings' first book, and, although prose, it reflects the same kinds of linguistic experimentation and innovation apparent in his poetry. Also reflecting his stylistic innovations is *Eimi*, Cummings' account of a trip to Russia, which has a topical vitality similar to the war experiences. The major themes of the critical response to Cummings' poetry, which developed in the 1920's, were implicit in the responses to *The Enormous Room*. Those themes, explicit by 1933, also helped to shape the criticism of *Eimi*.

Similar to the two prose narratives, *Him*, a long, expressionistic drama, is also representative of Cummings' development and of his critical reputation. Experimental and distinctive, the drama was produced in 1928 by the Provincetown Players. In the program notes, Cummings cautioned the audience against trying to understand the play. Instead, he advised the audience to "let it try to understand you." As with the poetry and the prose, there were outraged cries claiming that the play was unintelligible, although there was also an affirmation of the lyrical originality and intensity of the play. The recognition of Cummings' lyrical talents was gradually to replace the often angry rejections of his work because of its eccentricity.

Stylistically distinctive and therefore important in any full assessment of his achievement is the collection of Cummings' presentations as the annual Charles Eliot Norton Lecturer in Poetry at Harvard, *i: six nonlectures*. Of immediate interest, however, is the autobiographical content of the lectures. Lecture One is entitled "my parents" and contains poetic and affectionate sketches of his mother and father; Lecture Two is entitled "their son." The final four, less pointedly autobiographical in the usual sense of the word, are an exploration of the relationship between the poet's values and his sense of personal identity, between what he believes and what he is.

**Achievements**

Cummings is not usually included in the first rank of modernist poets, which always begins with T. S. Eliot, William Butler Yeats, and Ezra Pound and is, more often than not, rounded out with Wallace Stevens and William Carlos Williams. Two aspects of his career, however, give his achievement a great deal of significance. First, he was on the cutting edge of the modernist, experimental movement in verse. Pound, at the center of that movement, was dedicated to restoring value and integrity to the word by breaking the mold of the past, and in that cause, he evangelically admonished the poets of his generation to "make it new." Although a disciple of no one, Cummings led the assault on conventional verse, pushing experimentation to extremes and beyond with his peculiarly distinctive typography and his unconventional syntax, grammar, and punctuation. Although he paid the price of such experimentation, which brought charges of superficiality and unintelligibility, he served the modernist movement well by helping to educate an audience for the innovations in verse and prose of the second and third decades of the century.

Second, Cummings was not only a leading experimenter in an age of experimentation but also an intense lyric poet and an effective satirist. As a lyricist, he celebrated those experiences, values, and attitudes which lyric poets of all times have celebrated; and high on his list was love—sexual, romantic, and ideal or transcendental. His love poetry often reminds readers of Renaissance poets because of its subject matter, diction, and imagery. He is often bawdy, often sentimental, sometimes concrete, sometimes abstract, but almost always intense. Many of his lyrics express a childlike joy before nature and the natural state; he also celebrated personal relationships, particularly in his well-known tributes to his father and mother.

As a satirist, Cummings' principal target is man *en masse*. This thrust is the opposite of the celebration of individuality, a principal subject of his lyricism. In poems with a military setting, he satirically attacks not the military but the submergence of the individual into the mass which the military often brings about. He attacks the same submergence in poems that seem to be attacking modern advertising or salesmen. Neither, however, is the real object of his scorn; it is not modern advertising but the mass mind of the mass market which it engenders that he lashes out at in several of his most effective satiric pieces.

Cummings celebrates love, spontaneity, individuality, and a childlike wonder before nature. He attacks conformity, the mass mind, progress, and hypocrisy. His greatest achievement is that in an age of experimentation in verse, and in an age defensive and self-conscious about feeling, he fashioned a personal, highly idiosyncratic style which at its best provided him with effective vehicles for some of the finest lyric and satiric poetry of the modernist period.

## Biography

Edward Estlin Cummings, who preferred to be known as e. e. cummings (sans capital letters), was born in Cambridge, Massachusetts, on October 14, 1894, the first of two children born to Edward Cummings and Rebecca Harwell Clarke. His father was a Harvard graduate and lecturer, an ordained Unitarian minister, and pastor of the South Congregational Church from 1909 to 1925. Cummings received his degree *magna cum laude* from Harvard in 1915 and a Harvard M.A. the following year. A landmark in his career came in 1952 when he returned to Harvard to deliver the Charles Eliot Norton Lectures. Subsequently published as *i: six nonlectures*, all of which are highly personal and autobiographical, the first is of particular interest because of its affectionate, idealized portraits of his parents.

Cummings went to France in 1917 to join Norton Harje's Ambulance Corps. A combination of unfortunate and nearly ludicrous events led to his incarceration by the French authorities on suspicion of disloyalty. He and a friend were confined in a concentration camp at La Ferté Macé from late September through December, 1917. That experience is the subject matter of Cummings' first book, *The Enormous Room*, which has come to be regarded as a classic account of personal experience in World War I. Although prose, it launched the poet's career and, because of its style, set the tone and, implicitly, some of the basic themes that were to characterize the responses to his poetry for the next two decades. Before 1922, Cummings had published poems in the *Harvard Monthly*, in *The Dial*, and six poems in *Eight Harvard Poets*, but it was *The Enormous Room* that began his critical reputation. His first book of poems, *Tulips and Chimneys*, was published in 1923.

In 1923, Cummings moved to Patchin Place in New York City and lived there, spending the summers at his family's place in New Hampshire, until his death in 1962. Cummings traveled to Russia in 1931 and converted that experience into the second of his two major prose works, *Eimi*, 1933. In 1932, he married Marion Morehouse, a model, actress, and photographer. It was his third marriage and it survived. She died in 1969. The three decades Cummings spent with Marion and the nearly four decades at Patchin Place deserve emphasis in a biographical sketch because they provide a perspective that brings some balance to the poet's reputation as a bohemian *enfant terrible*. Although he never lost the cutting edge of his capacity to shock, he lived a relatively settled life devoted to painting and writing poetry.

In addition to the Charles Eliot Norton Lectureship, among the honors and awards he received were the Dial Award in 1925 for "distinguished service to American letters"; two Guggenheim Fellowships, in 1933 and 1951; and a special citation by National Book Awards in 1955 for *Poems, 1923-1954*. In 1957, he received the Bollingen Prize in Poetry and the Boston Arts Festival Award.

**Analysis**

Since E. E. Cummings rarely used titles, all those poems without titles will be identified by reference to the Index of First Lines in *Complete Poems, 1913-1962*. An analysis of Cummings' poetry turns, for the most part, upon judgments about his innovative, highly idiosyncratic versification. Some of Cummings' critics have thought his techniques to be not only cheap and shallow tricks but also ultimately nonpoetic. There was, from the early stages of his career, general agreement about his potential as a lyric and satiric poet. As that career developed through his middle and late periods, negative criticism of his verse diminished as affirmation grew. Although there always will be dissenting voices, the consensus for some time has been that his innovative verse techniques and his lyric and satiric talents were successfully blended in the best of his work.

Cummings wrote both free verse and conventional verse, particularly in the form of quatrains and sonnets. He also imposed on conventional verse the combination of typographical eccentricities and grammatical and syntactical permutations which constitute his distinctive hallmark. There is a considerable range between his most extreme free-verse poems, where the hallmark is superimposed, and his most conventional sonnets, where the hallmark is barely discernible. An example of the extreme is his "grasshopper" poem, "r-p-o-p-h-e-s-s-a-g-r," which is at the same time a masterpiece and a failure. The poem is a masterful blending of form and content, an achievement that might be described as pure technique becoming pure form. It fails as a poem, however, to move the reader or to matter very much except as a witty display of pyrotechnics. Its achievement, nevertheless, is a considerable one, and it serves as a useful model of one kind of poem for which Cummings is best known.

"r-p-o-p-h-e-s-s-a-g-r" is structurally a free-verse poem in which Cummings employs many of his distinctive typographical devices. The word "grasshopper" occurs four times in the poem, its letters jumbled beyond recognition the first three times. The grasshopper's leap, capturing the essence of grass-hoppers, brings its name into proper arrangement. Cummings also uses parentheses to break up words and to signal recombinations of letters and syllables resulting in conventional spelling, syntax, and meaning. At the literal and figurative center of the poem is the word "leaps," which links the first two versions of the word "grasshopper" to the final two, culminating in the resolution of the proper arrangement of letters. Cummings' diagonal typography for the word "leaps" is intended to render spatially, in the visual terms of a painter, the conceptual meaning of the word.

A poem of even less substance than "grasshopper," and therefore illustratively useful in the same way, is the "leaf-falling" poem "l(a." The four words of the poem, "a," "leaf," "falls," and "loneliness," are arranged along a vertical line with two or three letters or characters on each horizontal line, except for the final five of "iness." Thus, the poem begins with "l(a," with the rest of the poem directly below, two or three letters at a time, spaced out to suggest two triplets, set off by an opening, an intervening, and a closing single line. The use of the two parentheses, setting off "a leaf falls," actually helps in the reading of the poem. To the extent that the slender column of letters on the relatively vast whiteness of the page visually complements the theme of the poem, human loneliness engendered by the cyclical dying of the natural world in the fall of the year, Cummings has again succeeded in an effective union of form and content.

Other examples of this kind of verse are poems depicting a black, ragtime piano player ("ta"), a sunset ("stinging"), and a thunderstorm ("n(o)w/the." The arrangement on the page of the portrait of the piano player is very much like that of "loneliness," as is the second half of the poem depicting a sunset by the sea. Cummings attempts in the thunderstorm poem to create visual effects to complement the conceptual meaning of the words "lightening" and "thunder." In one line, he states that the world "iS Slapped:with;liGhtninG"; thunder in the poems appears as "THuNdeR." These five poems represent some of Cummings' more effective uses of several of his most representative devices, particularly eccentric typography and spatial arrangement intended to create special visual effects. Often successful, these same devices at times fail completely, merely producing involved semantic puzzles hardly worth the effort necessary to solve them. More important, however, is the fact that the same features of versification exemplified by these poems of relatively little substance are to be found in his very best lyric and satiric poetry, the best of which stands between the highly eccentric versification of "r-p-o-p-h-e-s-s-a-g-r"and his relatively conventional uses of the sonnet form.

Cummings wrote many sonnets. A convenient sampling of his uses of the form is to be found in *Is 5*, which begins with five sonnets and closes with five. The first five are portraits or sketches of prostitutes and are among the few Cummings poems with titles; in this example, the respective names of each of the women. The subject matter of the final five sonnets of the collection, in sharp contrast to the portraits, is romantic love, and this set is more conventional than the portraits of the prostitutes. Cummings' best lyric poetry tends to be his more conventional verse: a comparative reading of the second and the tenth sonnets of *Is 5* will illustrate Cummings' mastery of conventional lyric forms.

Three observations can be made about the second sonnet of *Is 5*, the portrait of Mame ("Mame") and the tenth ("if I have made, my lady, intricate"). First, the former is a portrait of a prostitute, while the latter is addressed to "my lady." Second, Mame speaks in a Brooklyn dialect, such as "duh woild," "some noive," and "dat baby." What little quoted speech there is in "if I have made, my lady, intricate" is not dialect and would not be obtrusive in a Renaissance sonnet. Third, Mame's sonnet is relatively loose structurally, while my lady's is one of Cummings' most conventional. The loose structure of the former results largely from the dramatic presentation, particularly as it calls for the use of fragmented speech in dialect. Both sonnets are conventional syntactically, grammatically, and typographically. Formally and thematically, "if I have made, my lady, intricate" stands in dramatic contrast to "r-p-o-p-h-e-s-s-a-g-r." The sonnet is one of Cummings' better lyric poems, the best of which make use of the formal eccentricities of "r-p-o-p-h-e-s-s-a-g-r" in the poet's successful blending of traditional subject matter with his personally distinctive, modern verse forms.

Cummings' principal lyric subject matter is his celebration of romantic, sexual, and transcendental love and of the beauty, physical and spiritual, of lovers. A good example of a successful blend of his distinctive versification with a traditional lyric subject is "(ponder,darling,these busted statues." Formally, the poem might be thought as standing near the middle of the range defined by the extremes of "r-p-o-p-h-e-s-s-a-g-r" and "if I have made, my lady, intricate." As such, it represents well the characteristics of Cummings' poetry. The blend of versification with a traditional subject is effective because of the appropriateness of the fragmented verse to the imagery of broken statuary and architectural ruins and of both to the poem's *carpe diem* theme.

The most obvious aspect of Cummings' distinctive verse is typographical, his sparse and erratic use of capitals and of parentheses. These particular details function in this poem of lyric substance to further understanding. Two sets of parentheses clearly delineate the three sections of the poem, the first and last being enclosed by them. The capitalization gives emphasis to the "Greediest Paws" of time and to the all-important "Horizontal" business. In addition to the typography, two examples of Cummings' manipulation of syntax also contribute to understanding his style: verse paragraphs three and six. As with the typography, the unconventional syntax contributes to the unmistakable distinctiveness of Cummings' verse without in any way impeding the reader's comprehension and hence appreciation of the poem.

The poem "(ponder,darling,these busted statues" is the modern poets' address to the perennially coy mistress. As in Andrew Marvell's poem "To His Coy Mistress" (1650), the woman is asked to consider the mutability of all things and urged, since time passes irrevocably, to get on with meaningful "horizontal" business. Marvell's plea turns on his images of the grave and the desert of eternity. Cummings, the quintessential modern, stands with the woman among the architectural ruins of a past that must be not so much denied as ignored, or, at least, turned away from. Although it is a lesser poem than T. S. Eliot's *The Waste Land* (1922), it shares with that landmark of the modernist period the fragmented artifacts of the past. More important, Cummings, like Eliot, is addressing the fundamental question of their time: What does one do in the midst of such ruins? Cummings' answer, "make love," is direct, obvious, and highly ironic; it is not simply flippant and clever. The poet's urgent request to get on with the important horizontal business is one of the most traditional lyric responses to the overt awareness of mortality, one of man's principal talismans down through the centuries against the certainty of death.

"somewhere i have never travelled,gladly beyond" and "you shall above all things be glad and young" provide good examples of Cummings' celebration of transcendental love. It should be noted that the categories, physical or sexual love and transcendental love, are not mutually exclusive. That is, nothing in "(ponder,darling,these busted statues" precludes the possibility that the lovers see something in each other deeper and more enduring than sex. On the other hand, it would be foolish to deny the sexual suggestiveness of the imagery of "somewhere i have never travelled,gladly beyond."

The poem "since feeling is first" is an explicit celebration of feeling, the wellspring of all lyricism. Examples of his affirmation of spontaneity, of nature, and of the natural and the childlike selves can be found in "when god lets my body be," "i thank You God for most this amazing," "in Just-," and "O sweet spontaneous." Cummings' intense tribute to his father, "my father moved through dooms of love," and his slight but moving poem for his mother, "if there are any heavens my mother will(all by herself)have," extend the range of lyric subject matter to include filial affection. "anyone lived in a pretty how town" is Cummings' allegorical "everyman" which has a poignancy similar to that of Thornton Wilder's *Our Town* (1938).

These poems provide examples of Cummings' principal lyric subject matter. They also constitute a group useful for studying the formal variety found in some of his best poetry. Two of them, the poem on his father and "anyone lived in a pretty how town," are fairly conventional quatrains given a twist by Cummings' characteristic grammatical distortion: the parts of speech exchange roles. For example, the father moves "through griefs of joy" and sings "desire into begin." Everyman of "anyone lived in a pretty how town" "sang his didn't" and "danced his did." In general, the key to this special vocabulary, here and in other poems, is that the present, immediate, concrete, and spontaneous are being affirmed, while their opposites are being rejected. "Is" is superior to "was." The "dooms of feel" are to be celebrated; the "pomp of must and shall" scorned. In addition to these examples of Cummings' quatrains, this group also contains another of his fairly conventional sonnets, "i thank You God for most this amazing," and several free verse poems, including "in Just-," and "O sweet spontaneous." As a group, they illustrate and support the generalization stated earlier that Cummings makes the most effective use of his distinctive devices in his more substantive lyric poetry.

Because satirists use lyricism to intensify their satirical thrusts, there is often no hard line between satiric and lyric poetry. The distinction for Cummings in particular is more a matter of emphasis than a clear-cut distinction. Because so much of his poetry is primarily satirical, however, it is profitable to consider several appropriate examples. It is also instructive to note that, as with his best lyric poetry, his best satiric pieces are those characterized by an effective blending of his distinctive devices with the resources of traditional verse. An excellent example of such blending and of the use of lyric intensity for satiric purposes is "i sing of Olaf glad and big."

The poem looks and even sounds like free verse. It is, however, an intricately constructed set of interlocking quatrains and couplets in four-stress lines. The loosening of what sounds like very regular verse is effected by the spacing on the page and by the counterpoint of sentence or sense structure against the verse structure. That tension between verse and sense is intensified by the characteristic use of parentheses and syntactical inversions. As in "(ponder,darling,these busted statues," the parentheses are used conventionally for humorous asides, as when readers are told that colonel left the scene "hurriedly to shave," and for emphasis, as in the passages on Olaf's knees and Christ's mercy. The syntactical inversions effectively provide emphasis and hardly impede understanding. The hyphenating of the word "object-or" catches the genius of Cummings' style at its best. The poem is about a conscientious objector who becomes an "object" in the hands of his fellow soldiers.

The satire is directed not at the military or against war, but at the lockstep, group mentality which, although fostered particularly by the military, may be found in the highly organized structures of all institutions: corporate, religious, academic. For Cummings, affirmation of the bravery of the individual places heavy emphasis on "individual," and it is the group, crowd, or gang that is being indicted. The irony of the closing lines strongly suggests that the military is but the protective arm of the nation or culture locked into value systems symbolized by abstractions such as the nation's "blueeyed pride." Olaf, blond and blue-eyed, fits the abstraction and hence his culpability is compounded. He was "blonder," however (that is nearer the ideal of bravery and of manhood), than most and willing to pay lip service to the ideal, while others lose themselves in the false security of the crowd.

Two other satires set in the context of war but directed at more fundamental targets are "my sweet old etcetera" and "plato told." The first satirizes, in a light vein, attitudes very close to those of the soldiers of "i sing of Olaf glad and big." Aunts, sister, mother, and father all think war is glorious, while the soldier, who describes them, lies in the muddy trenches, thereby refuting the grandiose notions of those safe and comfortable at home. "plato told" comes closest to being an indictment of war, but its focus is really on the obtuseness of "him," on his failure to understand what everyone has been telling him, which is that war is hell. All three of these "war" poems satirize a failure to see reality.

"POEM, OR BEAUTY HURTS MR. VINAL," one of Cummings' few titled poems, is a harsh but clever indictment of modern advertising and, implicitly, of the culture from which it derives. Cummings piles up actual lines from advertisements for garters, gum, shirt collars, drawers, Kodaks, and laxatives juxtaposed with fragments of lines from "America the Beautiful" and fragmented allusions to Robert Browning in the sixth verse paragraph. The poem makes fun of the glibness and excessive claims of advertising but then takes a turn toward the end to focus on Cummings' primary satiric target: men and woman, "gelded" or "spaded," who have allowed themselves to be manipulated into anonymous units of the "market." Cummings makes the same point in one of his harshest sonnets, "a salesman is an it that stinks Excuse." Almost savage in tone, the poem once again links various seemingly incongruous activities in terms of the marketplace: the selling of "hate condoms education . . . democracy." The focus of Cummings' attack shifts from its ostensible targets—the military, advertising, and a salesman to processes which rob people of their individuality and freedom of choice.

Cummings' innovative genius as a versifier, excessive in many of the lesser poems, is modified and restrained in his poems of substance, effecting in many of them happy unions of form and content. He is, as a result, a modernist poet of consequence.

## Major publications other than poetry

NOVEL: *The Enormous Room*, 1922.

PLAYS: *Him*, 1927; *Tom: A Ballet*, 1935; *Anthropos: The Future of Art*, 1944; *Santa Claus: A Morality*, 1946.

NONFICTION: *Eimi*, 1933; *i: six nonlectures*, 1953.

MISCELLANEOUS: *CIOPW*, 1931; *Adventures in Value*, 1962.

## Bibliography

Baum, S. V. *E. E. Cummings and the Critics*, 1962.
Friedman, Norman. *e. e. cummings: The Art of His Poetry*, 1967.

_____ . *e. e. cummings: The Growth of a Writer*, 1964.
Marks, Barry A. *E. E. Cummings*, 1964.
Norman, Charles. *E. E. Cummings: The Magic Maker*, 1964.

*Lloyd N. Dendinger*

# CYNEWULF

**Born:** Unknown. Flourished 775-825.


**Principal poems**
*The Fates of the Apostles*; *Juliana*; *Elene*; *Christ II (Ascension)*.

Cynewulf's name is known to students of Old English poetry because, in the conclusions of the four poems which can with certainty be attributed to him, he "signed" his name in runic letters. The name, however, was not deciphered until 1840. Cynewulf did not write his name directly, but wove the runes into the concluding meditations of his poems, so that they can be read not only as letters spelling his name, but also as symbols representing words that form part of the poetry. This riddling device—with both personal and poetic purposes—is typical of Cynewulf's poetry, which often applies devices used in earlier heroic and secular poetry to his meditative religious verse.

Cynewulf's four poems are extant in two of the four major manuscript collections of Old English poetry, both copied around the year 1000 in the West Saxon dialect. The Exeter Book, now in the Exeter Cathedral Library, contains *Christ II* and *Juliana*; the Vercelli Book, located in the northern Italian cathedral library of Vercelli, includes *The Fates of the Apostles* and *Elene*. Nineteenth century scholars, driven by the rare discovery of a poet's name from a period of general anonymity, attributed all the religious verse in these two manuscripts to Cynewulf. Just as Caedmon was considered to be the author of the poems dealing with Old Testament subjects extant in the Junius manuscript, so Cynewulf became the author of the saints' lives and allegorical poetry of the Exeter and Vercelli manuscripts. Only *Beowulf*, found in the fourth major manuscript, escaped being attributed with confidence to Cynewulf.

This poetry does in some respects share stylistic and thematic features with the four poems of Cynewulf. The two *Guthlac* poems ("A" and "B") treat the life and death of the eighth century hermit Saint Guthlac. Like *Juliana*, Cynewulf's account of the martyrdom of Saint Juliana, these poems deal with a saint who was challenged and harassed by demons. Guthlac is a Mercian saint associated with Croyland Abbey in Lincolnshire, an area perhaps connected with Cynewulf. Furthermore, *Guthlac B*, based on the Latin *Vita Guthlaci* by Felix of Croyland, shares several stylistic devices with the "signed" poems. Since in the Exeter Book its conclusion is missing, it is possible that it may have closed with a passage containing Cynewulf's name.

Also stylistically related to Cynewulf's poetry is *The Dream of the Rood*. Found not only in the Vercelli Book but also in fragments inscribed in runes on the Ruthwell Cross (located in southwest Scotland), this dream vision shares certain descriptive passages with *Elene*. Whereas *Elene* describes Constantine's conversion and Saint Helena's discovery of the cross, *The Dream of the Rood* concentrates on Christ's Crucifixion; nevertheless, both share a devotion to the glorious cross of victory. Now usually dated earlier than Cynewulf's poetry, *The Dream of the Rood* has been called one of the greatest religious lyrics in the English language. It certainly is the best of the "Cynewulfian group," those poems associated with, but not now attributed to, Cynewulf.

The other poems attributed by nineteenth century scholars to Cynewulf share fewer stylistic and thematic elements with the four signed poems. *Andreas*, a saint's legend based on the apocryphal Latin *Acts of Saints Andrew and Matthew*, was long tied to *The Fates of the Apostles*, a summary description of the deaths of Christ's disciples. Since *The Fates of the Apostles*—considered to be an epilogue to *Andreas*, which precedes it in the Vercelli Book—contained the runic signature, scholars reasoned that *Andreas* must also be by Cynewulf. Similarly, *Christ I (Advent)* and *Christ III (Last Judgment)* were attributed to Cynewulf before critical analysis subdivided *Christ* into three distinct poems. Although the three may be thematically related and perhaps were even brought together by Cynewulf, only *Christ II* (lines 441-866) concludes with the runic signature. It is a meditation on, and explication of, the significance of Christ's Ascension. *Christ I*, a series of antiphons for use in Vespers during the week preceding Christmas, is, according to Claes Schaar, "fairly close to Cynewulf's poetry," whereas *Christ III*, a rather uneven picture of the Last Judgment and the terrors awaiting the sinful, is definitely not by Cynewulf. *The Phoenix*, an allegorical treatment of Christ's Resurrection; *Physiologus*, a series of allegorized interpretations of natural history, and *Wulf and Eadwacer*, once understood as a riddle containing Cynewulf's name, are today not associated with Cynewulf.

Nineteenth century understanding of the Cynewulf canon had a certain balance and symmetry which is attractive. If Caedmon dealt with the epic themes of the Old Testament, Cynewulf emphasized themes more exclusively Christian: allegories of salvation, events in the life of Christ, and the stories of the early martyrs. This poetry spanned Christian history from Palestine in the first century to England in the eighth; from Christ's birth (*Christ I*) to his death (*The Dream of the Rood*), Resurrection (*The Phoenix*), and Ascension (*Christ II*); from the foundation of the church by the first missionaries (*The Fates of the Apostles* and *Andreas*), to the suffering of the martyrs (*Juliana*), the official recognition of Christianity by the Empire (*Elene*), and the continuity of the tradition of the hermit saint in England (*Guthlac*). This broad survey of Christian history not unexpectedly concluded with a description of the Last Judgment (*Christ III*).

The analyses of S. K. Das and Schaar in the 1940's, however, have limited Cynewulf's canon to the four poems containing his name, leaving one to wonder whether even these rather varied and differing works would have survived the complex and thorough stylistic and linguistic analyses if they had not concluded with a runic signature. Resembling the effect of higher criticism of the Bible, Old English scholarship has reduced Cynewulf from being the author of a large and diverse body of verse to being the composer of 2,600 lines: *The Fates of the Apostles* (122 lines), *Juliana* (731 lines), *Elene* (1,321 lines), and *Christ II* (426 lines).

## Other literary forms

Cynewulf's known literary works remain the four poems attributed to him in the Exeter Book and the Vercelli Book.

## Achievements

Since the discovery of his name in the nineteenth century, Cynewulf's reputation, like the size of his canon, has fluctuated widely. Certainly, a prolific poet who could count *The Dream of the Rood* among his works would deserve much respect, but the Cynewulf of the four signed poems has not fared so well. Scholars have always shown great interest in Cynewulf, primarily because of his runic signatures. Daniel Calder is probably right in suggesting that critical assessment of the poet has suffered "from the need to make him more important than he is." General histories and surveys of Old English poetry, for example, devote much space to this poet with a name, but have been essentially unimpressed by the poetry itself. Some have seen it as a diluted version of the earlier heroic style, a breakdown of technique, and the end of a great tradition. Commenting on *The Fates of the Apostles* in his recent history of medieval poetry, Derek Pearsall states that the poem "has the characteristic nerveless orthodoxy of treatment which prompts one to think of Cynewulf's poems in turn as the final product of a declining old age." Even the editors of Cynewulf have not been admiring. Rosemary Woolf, editor of *Juliana*, sees the poem as bringing "Old English poetry into a blind alley." What is not certain in these and numerous other such assessments of Cynewulf is the extent to which they reflect the quality of his poetry or the critic's preference for the heroic style of earlier English poetry. The modern distaste for the hagiographic subject matter and overt didacticism of these Christian poems may also account for Cynewulf's bad notices.

More recent studies approaching Cynewulf's poems within the contexts of Christian exegesis, hagiography, and iconography, however, have signaled a general reevaluation of the poems. *Elene* and *Christ II* have been especially praised. Scholars have been impressed by the "sophisticated handling" of patristic motifs in *Christ II* and the "beauty of intellectual form" of *Elene*. Comparisons of Cynewulf's poems with religious pictorial art have been especially popular. *Juliana* has been compared to an icon, *Christ* to a triptych, and *Elene* to panels on a church wall. To judge these poems against Aristotelian and nineteenth century expectations of realism is as foolish as judging a Byzantine icon or a complex design in the *Book of Kells* against Renaissance expectations of linear perspective and verisimilitude in art.

As helpful as these new approaches to the structure and characters of Cynewulf's narratives are, the poems remain to be appreciated and analyzed as poetry. Clearly, poetry was very important to Cynewulf. His runic signatures may reflect his desire to elicit prayers, but they also imply that he believed the poems deserved reward. As a recent study notes, whereas the earlier oral poets (the scops) probably saw their poetry as common property, Cynewulf's signatures and requests for prayers suggest "that he believed that he had a permanent claim on his work" (Barbara Raw, *The Art and Background of Old English Poetry*, 1978).

In *Christ II*, Cynewulf includes poetry and song among the gifts that Christ bestows on man. Thus, the composition of poetry itself is considered a pious act, the development of God-given talent, the manipulation of secular technique for religious purposes. Certainly, Cynewulf so manipulated Anglo-Saxon poetic technique. In his poetry, he borrows and adapts formulaic phrases, standard motifs, and established kennings (elaborate and traditional metaphors such as "swan-road" for "sea"). He continues the tradition of alliterative and accentual verse, dividing the poetic line into two half lines containing two stresses each. These half lines are joined by alliteration, the pattern of which varies from line to line but is generally controlled by the sound of the first stressed syllable in the second half line. The pattern of stressed and unstressed syllables also varies, allowing the poet a variety of rhythmic effects.

Cynewulf's poetry does differ in many respects from the earlier heroic poetry and even from the religious verse formerly attributed to Caedmon. On occasion, Cynewulf experiments with rhyme—something very unusual in Old English, as is also his use of runes. Some of the differences may be caused by Cynewulf's dependence on Latin texts, although detailed studies of his use of sources suggest that Cynewulf actually improved and clarified the syntax of his originals. His style has been described as "classic." Cynewulf's verse is also "looser," "lighter," and more varied rhythmically, developing a great number of secondary stresses. In contrast to the elevated tone of *Beowulf* (c. 1000), it is more conversational. Some consider this effect prosaic, the end of a poetic tradition, but more recently, Raw has explained the style as a deliberate attempt at informality, an effort to follow Augustine's advice to express Christian themes in a simple style. Cynewulf does vary his style according to his subject, from meditation to set descriptive passages and formal debates. In his introduction to *Anglo-Saxon Poetry* (1954), R. K. Gordon states that "Cynewulf is as deliberate and conscious an artist as Tennyson." Such an estimate may be overstated, but Cynewulf does deserve attention as a poet and not merely as a "monastic craftsman" with a name.

## Biography

The discovery of Cynewulf's name has not meant the discovery of a biography for the poet. Working from a name deciphered from runes, scholars have made tortuous attempts to discover a Cynewulf in historical records who could be identified as the poet. Candidates have included Cenwulf, an abbot of Peterborough (died 1006), Cynewulf, a bishop of Lindisfarne (c. 780), and Cynewulf, a priest of Dunwich (c. 803). None of these identifications has been accepted, and scholars are left with what meager data can be deduced from the four poems. Based on the poetry's subject matter, dependence on Latin sources, and relationship to the liturgical calendar, scholars assume he was a literate poet, a cleric, and probably a monk. Based on dialect and linguistic analysis, Cynewulf is usually dated around the turn of the eighth and ninth centuries and placed within the broad area of the Anglian dialect, in northern and eastern England. Since the runes twice give the poet's name as "Cynewulf" and twice as "Cynwulf," suggesting a variation of spelling not known in texts from the north, scholars have further limited the dialect to Mercian. This conclusion is supported by the rhyming passages in *Elene* and *Christ II*, which are most effective when the Mercian, rather than the manuscript's West Saxon, dialect is followed.

The evidence nevertheless remains scanty. Elaborate arguments based on what the "I" persona says in the poems have suggested that Cynewulf was a wandering minstrel or that he led a riotous and sinful life until, through conversion, he became a religious poet. Such arguments misunderstand the traditions of the elegiac wanderer in Old English poetry and conventional Christian humility motifs. Like other attempts to deal with the unknown poet rather than with his known poetry, they are fruitless. As Daniel Calder concludes, after surveying what little is known,

> Barring the discovery of wholly new evidence, the pursuit of Cynewulf's identity and the spinning out of a biography remain idle tasks. He emerges from the anonymity of Anglo-Saxon poetry long enough to sign his name and then disappear again into that great obscurity he shares with all the other scops who left no trace.

## Analysis

Cynewulf's four poems vary in length, subject, complexity, and style, yet they may be characterized as sharing similar source materials, purposes, and themes. All four are essentially didactic Christian poems, based on Latin prose originals, probably composed with the liturgical calendar in mind, and perhaps to be read as poetic meditations accompanying other monastic readings. The poems are didactic and specifically Christian in that their major purpose is to teach or celebrate significant events of salvation history. The four reflect a variety of Latin originals and specific types of monastic readings, meditative practice, and exegetical thought. In *The Fates of the Apostles*,

Cynewulf notes that he borrowed from many holy books, and he clearly takes pride in his knowledge and use of the "authorities" throughout his work.

Thematically, Cynewulf's poems reflect an interest also typical of his time and of monastic literature, the cosmic conflict between the forces of good and evil. This conflict is portrayed in both human and supernatural terms, sometimes in brief summaries of Christian suffering, sometimes in long debates and complaints. To highlight this conflict, Cynewulf establishes polarities of good and evil. The devil and his cohorts are clearly opposed to Christ and his faithful. Emperors and the wealthy persecute martyrs and the poor, and the headstrong Jews oppose the reasonable Christians. Idols contrast with Christian worship; lust attacks virginity; the law cannot conquer grace.

Characters are either black or white, symbols of good or evil rather than individuals. While imprisoned, Juliana is suddenly visited by a demon pretending to be an angel. Her suitor, who in the Latin sources is merely a pragmatic Roman official, is portrayed by Cynewulf as a champion of paganism. There must be no hesitation, no sense that characters may have a divided mind. When the actors in this cosmic drama do change, they do not develop characters but flip from one extreme to another, as if shifting masks. In *Elene*, Judas shifts from being a miracle-working Christian bishop. Paralleling the career of Saul in the New Testament, whose conversion from persecutor to persecuted is signaled by a change of his name to Paul, Judas' name is changed to Cyriacus. As in the New Testament, which lies behind Cynewulf's Latin sources, there definitely is no place for the lukewarm.

Cynewulf's poems draw on the recorded victories of the faithful in the past to teach Christians in the present to uphold their inheritance of truth. This didactic purpose is accomplished by two means: Cynewulf portrays past events as types or symbols which can be applied to contemporary Christians, and he inserts personal comments in the conclusions of his poems, confessing his own need to follow the examples of the past and to repent in the present. As in the past Christ gave power to the saints to withstand the forces of Satan, so in the continuing battle between good and evil, he gives power to overcome temptation. The monastic communities, which understood themselves to be the inheritors of the tradition begun by the martyrs, will likewise conquer evil. The cosmic battle, given personal application, is made urgent by the concluding meditations on the transitory nature of the world, on the Last Judgment, and on the joys of heaven. In the future, contemporary events will be judged according to their place in the battle lines, and those joining the forces of Christianity will be appropriately rewarded.

Basically a catalog listing the missionary activities and deaths of Christ's twelve apostles, *The Fates of the Apostles* is based on various Latin historical martyrologies, perhaps on a version of the *Breviarium Apostolorum* (The Breviary of the Apostles). Its brief accounts of the early Christian missionaries may have been intended for reading during November to celebrate the martyred saints. Of Cynewulf's four poems, *The Fates of the Apostles* is considered as "the least effective" and "inferior" by several critics. Such evaluations probably reflect modern contempt not only for the poem's subject but also for its form. Yet to the Anglo-Saxon Christian community, sharing strong missionary impulses, interested in converting pagans, and claiming to be both historically and universally established, the poem's subject is a proclamation of legitimacy. Its form, furthermore, would not seem odd in an age when Christian chronicles were often composed in poetry and the poet was caretaker of the community's memory. Such catalogs have an honorable parentage both in the Old and New Testaments and in classical literature—in the catalogs of Homer, for example.

More appreciative critics have sought through elaborate numerical and grammatical analysis to complicate the poem, to see it as more than a simple catalog, as mannered, mystical, and even ironic. Yet, what seems most obvious about *The Fates of the Apostles* is its simplicity of purpose and structure. It establishes in the clearest possible outline the conflict between good and evil: Christian heroes, courageously obeying Christ's command to go into all nations, preach to the heathen, and suffer martyrdom. These deeds are related to the poet, his world, and his heavenly goals through the poem's prologue and epilogue.

Mentioning each of the twelve apostles in turn, Cynewulf follows a simple pattern with appropriate variations: "We have heard how X taught the people in, or journeyed to, Y and died at the hands of Z." The specific acts are introduced by a personal comment on the poet's own weariness and similarly conclude with a personal request that those who hear the poem will pray to the apostles for him. Then follows the runic signature, which inverts the spelling of his name to read "FWULCYN." The runes are woven as a riddle into a meditation on the mutability of earthly joy and wealth. The poet then refers to himself as a wanderer—a motif of long standing in Christian thought, which rejects this world as a home—and concludes with a reminder of the true home of all Christians, Heaven.

*Juliana* is a classic saint's life. Based on a Latin prose life, perhaps Saint Bede's *Martyrology* (c. 700) or one of Saint Bede's sources, the poem narrates the various human and devilish tortures and temptations withstood by Saint Juliana, who died about 305-311 and whose martyrdom is celebrated in the Christian calendar on February 16. Like *The Fates of the Apostles*, *Juliana* has not fared well with critics. To Stanley Greenfield, for example, it is "the least impressive as poetry of the Cynewulf group" (*Critical History of Old English Literature*, 1965). In contrast to the *The Fates of the Apostles* it is a lengthy and somewhat repetitive account (even though lacking approximately 130 lines) of the suffering not of numerous saints but of a single martyr.

The conflict between the opposing forces of good and evil is again drawn through stark contrasts. Juliana's suitor, Eleusius, is portrayed as possessing stores of treasure, representing earthly nobility and power. Repeatedly characterized by his wealth, he is the choice of Juliana's father, who tells the virgin that Eleusius is better, nobler, and wealthier than she, thus deserving her love. In contrast, Juliana's heart is set on a different bridegroom, the noble ruler of Heaven, possessing eternal wealth and divine power. As in the traditional love triangle of romance—what Northrop Frye calls "the secular scripture"—the father is enraged by his daughter's intransigence and gives her over to her enemies. Here, however, the love triangle leads to supernatural conflict, as Juliana contrasts her Lord with Eleusius' devils. After forcing a long confession from a demon, "the enemy of the soul," and suffering numerous torments, Juliana is killed. Eleusius, driven mad by the ordeal of dealing with a martyr, is drowned, along with his companions.

The narrative concludes by describing the hellish destiny of Eleusius and his supporters, using the language of heroic poetry to deny the rewards traditionally given to the Germanic *comitatus* (the heroic band of warriors) by its chieftain. It is as if Cynewulf uses the heroic style to condemn an old heroism and to substitute a new Christian heroism, not based on violent deeds but on faithful suffering, for the destiny of Eleusius and the pagans is contrasted to the destiny of Juliana, whose martyred body is the occasion of joy in her native Nicomedia, and continuing glory for Christians. This continuity is then extended by Cynewulf to the present when he asks for aid from Saint Juliana in his own preparation for death. Weaving his name into a meditation on death—here using three groups of runes, "CYN," "EWU," "LF"—the poet again requests prayers from those who read his poem and asks that the ruler of Heaven stand by him at the final judgment.

Also in the tradition of the saint's legend, *Elene* spins a more complicated narrative than does *Juliana*. Based on a version of the *Inventio Sanctae Crucis* similar to the *Acta Cyriaci*, it relates the discovery of the true cross by Saint Helena, the mother of Constantine. This event is celebrated in the liturgical calendar on May 3. *Elene* is generally considered to be Cynewulf's finest poem; its description of the glorious cross gleaming in the sky is often compared with the imagery of *The Dream of the Rood*. *Elene*'s popularity may also be the result of its development of several passages in the heroic style, including Elene's sea journey and Constantine's war against the Huns. Using the vigorous language of battle poetry, Cynewulf here develops the motif of the beasts of battle: the raven, eagle, and wolf that traditionally frequent Old English poetic battles.

Nevertheless, *Elene*'s basic theme is Christian, and although it borrows epic devices, the poem's main subject is conversion. It describes three miraculous conversions related to the discovery of the cross: Constantine's conversion following his vision of the cross; Judas' conversion leading to the discovery of the cross; and, the conversion of the Jews after the discovery of the nails used to crucify Christ. In relating these conversions, the poem may strike modern readers as inexplicable and even offensive. The suffering of the Christian martyr memorialized in *Juliana* becomes here the militancy of the Christian emperor. The cross becomes the banner of war, and the nails of the cross, hammered by Roman soldiers into the flesh of Christ, become amulets for the bridle of the Roman emperor, assuring that he will vanquish all. Similarly, in contrast to the protagonist of *Juliana*, Elene represents imperial power and can force her beliefs on others. Thus she has Judas cast into a cistern for seven days until he acknowledges the truth of Christianity. In Cynewulf's black-and-white view of salvation history, Elene is on the side of right, whereas the Jews, cursed for rejecting Christ, deserve humiliation and punishment.

An unsympathetic approach to *Elene*, however, misunderstands both the Christian background of the poem and its development of characters as types. The figure of Judas, particularly, needs careful attention. The poem introduces him after Elene asks to see the wisest among the Jews. Groups of three thousand, then one thousand, and finally five hundred wise men are rejected by Elene before Judas, "the one skilled in speeches," is found. The whole process resembles the Old Testament account of Abraham's bargaining with Jehovah over Sodom (Genesis 18:23-33), reducing the number of the righteous to Lot and his family. Judas shares features with Lot, for, like him, he has ancient parentage and familial ties to the righteous, yet represents a doomed people. He knows the truth of Christianity from his father; furthermore, his brother was Stephen, the first Christian martyr. He refuses, however, to accept what he knows. Like his namesake, Judas Iscariot, the most despised Jew in Christian history, he rejects Christ until driven to admit the truth by Elene. Then his role is reversed, a point emphasized by the demon who appears in the poem to complain of Christian interference in the designs of evil. This new Judas—like Christ, the new Adam—provides the way to salvation through the cross. By converting to Christianity and using his wisdom to discover the cross, Judas Cyriacus saves not only himself, but also the Jewish people, whom medieval Christians believed would ultimately be converted to Christianity.

Other characters in *Elene* are similarly given typological significance. Constantine is associated with Christ and Elene with *ecclesia*, the victorious Christian Church. The confrontation between Judas and Elene thus symbolizes a standard doctrinal topic of Christian apologetic and polemical literature: the confrontation between *synagoga* and *ecclasia*, the law of Judaism and the grace of Christ. The confrontation is settled by the elevation of the cross, the visible token of Christ's redemptive act and a disastrous defeat for the devil.

Like the missionary activities of the apostles and the martyrdom of the saints, however, this confrontation is only one of a series of battles in the larger war between good and evil. It remains for the individual to take sides in the war, to join forces with *ecclasia*, as Cynewulf emphasizes in his conclusion. In a passage developing internal rhymes, he relates his own conversion from sin to the cross. The poet takes the past event and gives it personal application, for his own conversion associates him with the three conversions of the narrative. Then, after weaving his name in runes into a meditation on the mutability of this world, Cynewulf describes doomsday and the respective rewards of the righteous and evil. This concluding radical perspective explains the militancy of the Christian emperor, the conversion of the Jews, and the poet's own dedication to the cross.

Unlike Cynewulf's other poems, *Christ II* deals not with Christian saints but with a key event in the life of Christ, the Ascension. Rather than drawing from legendary sources, it closely parallels the last part of Pope Gregory's homily on the Ascension (homily 29), with some additions based on Saint Bede's *On the Lord's Ascension* (c. 700) and monastic readings for Ascensiontide. Although Claes Schaar believed that in *Christ II* "the poet is somewhat overwhelmed by the rhetoric of Gregory," others have praised Cynewulf's "masterful reworking" of the homily. Daniel Calder, comparing Cynewulf's treatment of Gregory to Gregory's treatment of the Bible, notes that the poet "takes liberties with Gregory's text" to arrive at the truth concerning the Ascension, sometimes expanding, other times rearranging, his Latin source.

The result is an imaginative exposition of the significance of the Ascension combining Christian allegory and exegesis with Germanic poetic techniques. The description of Christ's six leaps in his role as mankind's savior, from incarnation to Ascension, allegorically develops the exegesis of the Song of Solomon and establishes the Ascension as the final necessary step in the long process of man's salvation. Christ, "the famous Prince," leaves his band of retainers on earth (the disciples) and goes to join the band of angels in Heaven. The disciples, like the wanderers of Old English elegiac poetry, are overwhelmed by the loss of their leader, whereas the angels raise a song of joy and triumph. Yet, the apostles are not left helpless, for Christ bestows gifts on mankind, including not only the spiritual gifts of wisdom, poetry, and teaching, but also the physical gifts of victory in battle and seafaring.

Even the description of Christ's glorious Ascension, however, is understood in the context of the cosmic battle between good and evil. Christ is welcomed to Heaven by a song praising his harrowing of hell, his victory against the "ancient foes." In another passage experimenting with internal rhyme, Cynewulf establishes the significance of Christ's act, which makes possible man's choice between salvation and damnation. The passage, reflecting the poet's pronounced dualism, contrasts Heaven and hell, light and dark, majesty and doom, glory and torment.

Later, Cynewulf relates Christ's six redemptive leaps to man's need to leap by holy deeds to the rewards of Heaven. The Father of Heaven will help man overcome sin and will protect his faithful against the attacks of fiends in the cosmic battle. The importance of such reliance on Christ is underscored in the poem's conclusion, Cynewulf's elaborate treatment of doomsday. Introduced by his own confession of sin and fear of judgment, it includes the runic signature woven into the description of terror facing the worldly man before the almighty judge.

Thus, as in *The Fates of the Apostles*, *Juliana*, and *Elene*, Cynewulf in *Christ II* ties the events of Christian history, developed from his Latin sources, to his contemporary world through personal confession. The poems all teach a basic concept underlying the Christian liturgy and its understanding of sacred time: the close relationship between the past, present, and future. The victories of the past in the struggle between good and evil symbolized by the ministry of Christ and the lives of the saints must be repeated in the present by the individual Christian, for in the future all will face the judgment of God.

**Bibliography**

Calder, Daniel G. *Cynewulf*, 1981.

Krapp, George Philip, ed. *The Vercelli Book*, 1932.

Krapp, George Philip, and Elliott Van Kirk Dobbie, eds. *Exeter Book*, 1936.

Schaar, Claes. *Critical Studies in the Cynewulf Group*, 1949.

Sisam, Kenneth. "Cynewulf and His Poetry," in *Proceedings of the British Academy*. XVIII (1934), pp. 303-331.

*Richard Kenneth Emmerson*

# SAMUEL DANIEL

**Born:** Taunton, England; 1562(?)
**Died:** Beckington, England; October, 1619

## Principal poems and collections

*Delia*, 1592; *The Complaint of Rosamond*, 1592; *The First Fowre Bookes of the Civile Warres Between the Two Houses of Lancaster and Yorke*, 1595, enlarged in 1599 and 1601; *Poeticall Essayes*, 1599; *The Works of Samuel Daniel*, 1601; *Certaine Small Poems*, 1605; *Songs for the Lute, Viol and Voice*, 1606.

## Other literary forms

In 1594, for the third edition of *Delia*—which bore the title *Delia and Rosamond augmented*—Samuel Daniel included a play, *Cleopatra*, which was written in the "Senecan mode." Actually, the author entered the piece in the Stationers' Register as early as October 19, 1593, and dedicated it to his patron, Mary Herbert, Countess of Pembroke (1561-1621), the sister of Sir Philip Sidney. He stated that he wrote it at her request and as a companion to her own translation of the French playwright Robert Gainier's *Tragedy of Antonie* (1592). Six years later, Daniel began another play, three acts of a tragedy based on the story of Philotas, taken from Quintus Curtius, Justin, and Plutarch's *Life of Alexander*. Originally, he had intended the play to be acted at Bath during the Christmas season by certain gentlemen's sons; however, his printers urged him to complete other projects, and *The Tragedy of Philotas* was not completed and published until 1605. Daniel dedicated the work to Prince Henry, complaining that the public favor extended to him during the reign of Elizabeth had not been carried over to that of James I.

*The Tragedy of Philotas* caused Daniel some problems at Court, principally because suspicion arose that Philotas was actually a representation of the late Earl of Essex. Such a conclusion meant that the author was trying to apologize for or to defend Essex's rebellion of 1601. Thus, the nobles summoned Daniel before them requesting him to explain his meaning; upon doing so, he was nevertheless reprimanded. In 1607, Daniel published a "corrected" edition of *The Tragedy of Philotas*, with an "apology" denying that his play warranted the aspersions that had been cast upon it. Finally, the poet published, in 1618, a prose *Collection of the Historie of England*, from the beginnings of English history to the end of Edward III's reign (1377), a work that had occupied him for a number of years and which was undertaken with royal patronage.

## Achievements

Daniel's reputation has suffered the misfortune of history, the poet having lived and written during an age of literary giants. In a sense, he lies buried beneath the weight of Edmund Spenser, William Shakespeare, John Lyly,

Sir Philip Sidney, Michael Drayton, Thomas Campion, and Ben Jonson. The existence of those personages was not itself sufficient to relegate Daniel to the second rank of poets; rather, the writer's own attitudes toward poetry and the state of the world contributed to his eventual position in the literary history of the later Elizabethan period. On the surface, Daniel appears as an intelligent and thoughtful poet, gifted with imagination and literary eloquence. No one has ever questioned his dedication to the craft of poetry, as he labored to write and then to polish his verse. He embraced all of the virtues associated with the best practitioners of his art: patience to correct and revise, and sensitivity to criticism. Those very virtues, however, restricted both his artistic and personal advancements. He was by nature reluctant to burst forth upon the world. Incessant labor and untiring revision became a refuge for his hesitancy and uncertainty, and he spent much time, both in and outside his poetry, reflecting upon and developing a variety of viewpoints.

Nevertheless, that hesitancy and uncertainty, as observed from a distance of almost three centuries, may well constitute the essence of Daniel's achievement as a poet. He never saw himself other than as a poet called upon to write poetry. With that purpose in mind, he sought perfection, although he fully recognized the impossibility of ever rising to that state. For example, he revised *The Complaint of Rosamond* five times and *Delia* on four occasions, while *Musophilus: Or, A Defence of Poesie* was altered substantially from its first appearance in 1599 through editions of 1601, 1602, 1607, 1611, and 1623— so often, in fact, that he almost ruined the piece. Still, the revisions reveal Daniel at work, striving to improve the verbal melodies of his lines, repairing what he thought were technical blemishes, purging the Elizabethan idiom from his language, seeking conciseness at almost any cost. Indeed, in discussing these revisions and alterations, a modern editor of Daniel's poetry has referred to the writer as "something of a neo-classicist born before his time," particularly in reference to his passion for accuracy.

Daniel may have been somewhat intimidated by his contemporaries, but he certainly could stand foremost among them in terms of his patriotism— the eagerness and sincerity with which he expressed his love for his country. Patriotism was a mark of the times; still, the careful reader of his poems will readily observe that he availed himself of every opportunity to support England. In his *The First Fowre Bookes of the Civile Warres Between the Two Houses of Lancaster and York*, for example, he extols the virtues of the Talbots, dukes of Shrewsbury, and of Prince Henry at Agincourt with a passion equal to Shakespeare's history plays; he blames a French woman by the name of Margaret for the murder of Henry IV's youngest son, the Duke of Humphrey; he cries out to Neptune as god of the sea and protector of his nation to shut out ungodly wiles, vile impieties, and all variety of corruption in order to keep England "meere English." Such expression, however, is not limited to patriotism for the sake of mere nationalism; indeed, Daniel recognized all aspects and varieties of patriotic virtue: the courage of the Welsh bowmen and the fortitude and religious conviction of Sir William Wallace, the principal champion of Scotland's independence. Kings are also given their due, as Daniel describes Edward I, a generous prince and Christian warrior who shed his blood for England's greatness. Richard Coeur de Lion (Richard I), on the other hand, and from a more objective point of view, is depicted as having found himself caught up in his campaigns against Philip II of France in an unjust and unprofitable war, deceiving both the world and himself.

Daniel's dedication to England can be related directly to his love of the past. In that respect, he stood equal to a select band among his contemporaries, principally Sidney and Spenser. He rose in anger at allusions by others to the vaunted infallibility of the Greeks and Romans. Such proclamations, he maintained, were but passions that clouded sound men's judgments and caused them to lose respect for the traditions of their own nations. Thus, as in *Musophilus*, Daniel sought out those times that, free from classical ornamentation and deformity, fashioned the wonderful architecture of England. Standing, regretfully, before Stonehenge, he sees it as a vague symbol of the nation's birth: "The misery of darke forgetfulnesse." Similarly, he looks back upon an early day to a peaceful and devout world, in which men of learning lived in a cloistered security. What happened to that cloister? It was a bubble of illusion, burst from without by printing presses which spread controversy and by gunpowder which destroyed the ancient form and discipline of medieval warfare.

In the final analysis, however, Daniel must be seen as a poet of the Renaissance whose imagination grew out of Renaissance ideals of action—to pursue learning and to reconcile the ideal of action with that of culture. Such poetry, particularly in *Musophilus*, became prophecy in which Daniel looked to a new world that would continue to emphasize the civilization of times past. In that new world, the poet (perhaps Daniel himself) rises to considerable heights when he explicates the fine qualities of that former age. Like his contemporaries, Shakespeare and Spenser, Daniel represented the true Elizabethan poet because, as did all true Elizabethans, he tried very hard to transcend the boundaries of his age. "The Starres, that have most glorie," he wrote, "have no rest."

## Biography

Although the exact date and place of Samuel Daniel's birth remain unknown, he was probably born near Taunton, in north Somerset, in late 1562 or early 1563, the son of John Daniel, a music master. A younger brother, John, became a musician of some reputation, having earned a bachelor of music degree in 1604 from Christ Church College, Oxford, after which he published twenty songs entitled *Songs for the Lute, Viol and Voice*—with words by his poet-brother. A third brother, also named John, engaged himself in the service of the Earl of Essex. He was later fined and imprisoned for having embezzled certain of Essex's letters to his wife and, in 1601, for conspiring with one Peter Bales to blackmail the countess.

Samuel Daniel entered Magdalen Hall, Oxford, in 1581, at the age of nineteen as a commoner. However, he did not remain quite long enough to earn a degree; after about three years, he found English poetry, history, and translation more to his liking than the stricter disciplines of logic and philosophy. Thus, in 1585 he published his first book, a translation of a tract on devices, or crests, entitled *Imprese*, by Paolo Giovo, Bishop of Nocera. By 1586 he had obtained a position with Lord Stafford, Elizabeth's ambassador to France; in September of that year, he was found at Rye in the company of an Italian doctor, Julio Marino. If one is to trust the 1594 sonnet collection, *Delia* (numbers 47 and 48), Daniel had spent almost two years in Italy—either from 1584 to 1586, or at some period prior to 1589. Shortly after 1590, the poet became tutor to William Herbert, third Earl of Pembroke, son of Sir Philip Sidney's sister, Mary, and the patron of Shakespeare. Thus, Daniel took up residence at Wilton, near Salisbury, the seat of the Pembrokes.

The real attraction for Daniel at Wilton was not his pupil, but the boy's mother, Mary Herbert, Countess of Pembroke. A woman of excellent literary taste and of distinctive literary talent, she had married Henry Herbert in 1577 and became the most famous patroness of literature in her time, bestowing her favors and encouragement upon Spenser, Ben Jonson, Shakespeare, her brother Philip Sidney, and, of course, Daniel. Despite such support for his work, however, Daniel first appeared before the world without his consent or even foreknowledge. At the end of the 1591 edition of Sidney's *Astrophel and Stella*, the printer (or editor) attached twenty-seven of Daniel's sonnets; what really bothered him, however, was the fact that the pieces contained typographical errors which offended his sense of correctness. He countered by issuing, in February, 1592, his volume of *Delia*, with fifty sonnets dedicated to the Countess of Pembroke. The volume was well received, with the result that Daniel published a new edition later the same year (with four new sonnets and *The Complaint of Rosamond*, a long narrative poem) and a third edition in 1594. In the latter collection, he replaced the prose dedication to the Countess of Pembroke with a sonnet, added a number of sonnets and deleted others, enlarged *The Complaint of Rosamond* by twenty-three stanzas, and included his Senecan tragedy, *Cleopatra*.

Daniel's reputation grew and attracted Spenser's attention, the epic poet thinking highly of him and encouraging him to write tragedy. Daniel was not interested in such projects, however; instead, he produced a long historical poem, *The First Fowre Bookes of the Civile Warres Between the Two Houses of Lancaster and Yorke*; on the model of Lucan's ancient *Pharsalia*. For the next five years (1595-1599), Daniel published nothing new, principally because he was busily engaged at Skipton, Yorkshire, in tutoring Anne Clifford, daughter of the Countess of Cumberland, then eleven years of age. He enjoyed the relationship with the family, but felt restricted by the work that kept him from writing poetry—especially the completion of his *Civile Warres*. Nevertheless, he managed to wrench himself free long enough to compose, in 1599, his poem *Musophilus* and a verse *Letter from Octavia to Marcus Antonius*. Two years later he published the first collected edition of his works, *Poeticall Essayes*. That was followed by a complete edition later in 1601, *The Works of Samuel Daniel*.

There are those who would maintain that, upon Spenser's death in 1599, Daniel succeeded him as poet laureate of England. However, before Ben Jonson received his patent and pension in February, 1616, the official position of poet laureate did not really exist. True, Spenser had received £50 a year from Queen Elizabeth, but that sum signified informal royal recognition rather than payment for a distinct position or office. Although Daniel occupied no formal position as a poet, he visited often at Court early in the reign of James I, where friends received him well. Further, Daniel had determined to be one of the first to congratulate James on the king's arrival in England; thus, he sent him *A Panegyricke Congratulatorie* while he traveled toward London. In 1602, the poet had dedicated a sonnet to "Her Sacred Majestie," Queen Anne. With his political fences fairly secure, he turned his attention to *The Tragedy of Philotas* (1605).

Daniel spent the better part of his later years reviewing his early poetry, preparing editions of his works, and writing second-rate entertainments for Court festivities: *The Vision of the Twelve Goddesses* (1604), *The Queenes Arcadia* (1605), *Tethys Festival: Or, The Queenes Wake* (1610), and *Hymens Triumph* (1615), the last piece to be published by Daniel during his lifetime. Such efforts yielded some reward, for he received the appointment of inspector of the children of the Queen's revels, a post that he gave over to his brother John in 1619. In 1607, the poet served as a groom of the Queen's privie chamber, which meant a stipend of £60 a year. He had moved out of London in 1603 and rented a farm in Wiltshire, near Devizes. There, in June, 1618, he wrote his last poem "To the Right Reverend Father in God, James Montague, Lord Bishop of Winchester," Dean of the Chapel and a member of the Privy Council, the purpose of which was to console the cleric during his sickness. Daniel himself died in October, 1619.

### Analysis

Perhaps the most sensible point at which to begin an analysis of Samuel Daniel's poetry is the commentary of his contemporaries. The poets of his day saw considerable quality in his work. Francis Meres, a rector, schoolmaster, and literary reviewer, believed that in the *Delia* sonnets, Daniel captured the matchless beauty of his titled subject, while the individual's passion rose at the reading of the distressed Rosamond's death. Meres also found the

*Civile Warres* to be equal to Lucan's *Pharsalia*. The lyric poet and writer of romances, Thomas Lodge, gave him the highest praise for invention and choice of language, while Thomas Carew, one of Ben Jonson's principal disciples, labeled him the English Lucan. Daniel's rhyme caught the attention of the Scots pamphleteer and versifier, William Drummond of Hawthornden, who believed it second to none, and a number of lesser poetic lights during the reigns of Elizabeth and James I heaped praise upon Daniel's sharp conceits, pure English, and choice of words. There were, of course, a like number of detractors, foremost among them being Ben Jonson, the dramatist John Marston, and Michael Drayton, who claimed that Daniel was only a historian in verse who should have written prose rather than poetry. Interestingly, the judgments of Daniel's contemporaries, both positive and unfavorable, were not too far off the mark.

Daniel reached the height of his stature as a poet with the publication of his sonnet sequence, *Delia*, and its apparent companion piece, the long narrative poem *The Complaint of Rosamond*. Although the poet, by 1592, might have been expected to demonstrate some evidence of having been influenced by Sir Philip Sidney and his sister, the Countess of Pembroke, *Delia*, in particular, differs significantly from *Astrophel and Stella*. The former contains little of the drama and personal tension found in Sidney's sequence, but it has considerably more melody and clear imagery. The majority of the sonnets follow the English (or Shakespearean) pattern, with three quatrains and a final couplet. Unlike those of Shakespeare, however, the poems lack any bursts of emotional surge or lift. Instead, Daniel clung to this pure diction, serene rhythms, and sparkling clarity that allowed his reader, to see, without difficulty, such objects as a clear-eyed rector of a holy hill, a modest maid decked with the blush of honor, and the green paths of youth and love. True, the sonnets are supposed to reflect the passionate love adventures of the poet's youth; obviously, however, time, a series of careful revisions for later editions, and the quiet and placid nature of maturity created a unified series of sober, restrained, and meditated utterances. There are a number of interesting biographical and source problems surrounding *Delia*, particularly the identity of the lady of the title and accusations of plagarism from several French sonneteers; these remain debates of a speculative nature and ought not to detract from the true poetic force of the complete sequence.

*The Complaint of Rosamond* first appeared in 1592, bound with the authorized edition of *Delia*. Thus, scholars have quickly labeled it a companion to the sonnets, although it might be more accurately termed a transition. On one hand, its style and content relate it to *Delia*; but it also moves in the opposite direction, toward the serious, contemplative tone of later poems. In 106 seven-line stanzas, Daniel relates the story of Rosamond Clifford, mistress of Henry II; but the poet does not forget entirely the Delia of his sonnets. The ghost of Rosamond, while pleading with the poet to attempt to relate her narrative, apologizes for intruding upon his own private griefs. However, the spirit strongly suggests that Delia's heart may be moved by evidence of poetic sympathy for one of her sex—namely, Rosamond. Before vanishing, the ghost appeals to Delia for a sigh to help her pass to a sweet Elysian rest. Thus, Daniel finds himself alone with his own sorrows concerning the errors of his youth. In another context, the despondent Rosamond reflects upon the cruelty of isolating beauty from the admiration of the world. She points to the beautiful women who come to town to display their loveliness— all except Delia, who has been left in a remote part of the country. *The Complaint of Rosamond* demonstrates the skill with which Daniel could construct a long narrative poem containing both story and moral, uncluttered with social, religious, or political complications. In *The Complaint of Rosamond*, he concentrated almost exclusively on the theme of personal tragedy and the contrast between exaltation and misery. Such concentration permitted him to develop a character, write a story reflecting universal melancholy, and place both in a context appropriate to and worthy of the term *complaint*.

Daniel's *Cleopatra* is a carefully formed Senecan tragedy in alternate rhyme, justifiably dismissed as drama but not sufficiently appreciated for its poetry. The play, which focuses mainly on events subsequent to Anthony's death, was dwarfed by Shakespeare's *Antony and Cleopatra* (1606-1607), which swept all rivals from the field. Nevertheless, Daniel's *Cleopatra* can be appreciated as literature. It contains an abundance of human feeling from which the reader may derive dramatic and poetic pleasure; further, its form and diction have been compared with that of Shakespeare's *Antony and Cleopatra* and John Dryden's *All for Love* (1678). Daniel concentrates his attention on Cleopatra to examine her at a moment of significant crisis, to view her from various perspectives. For example, he weaves into his verse-drama a number of seemingly peripheral scenes that function as comments on Cleopatra's resolve to die. Such scenes—Arius saving Philostratus from death, Philostratus being ashamed of clinging to life so eagerly in time of national disaster—place the story of individual persons into the larger, more important context of politics and society. Certainly there is much to observe in the conflict between Cleopatra as queen and as mother. Daniel, however, does not lose sight of the "higher" moral issues: pride and riot out of control, government and citizens overcome by impiety and false security, and the entire society wallowing in what he terms "fat-fed pleasure."

Certainly, the historical and political issues in *Cleopatra* helped to establish Daniel's interest in those areas, and he never lost sight of his mission to give the world a memorable historical epic. Thus, almost exactly a year after entering *Cleopatra* in the Stationers Register, the poet issued the initial version of his *Civile Warres*. After almost fifteen years of labor, beginning in 1594, Daniel managed to produce eight books amounting to about seven thousand ottava rima lines. The work began with Richard II in 1377 and was supposed to end with the marriage of Henry VII to Elizabeth of York in January, 1486, but the poet fell slightly short of the mark and arrived only at 1464 and the marriage of Edward IV and Lady Elizabeth Grey. Although it would be a disservice to Daniel's motives to term the project a mistake, it may well have been too ambitious an undertaking for one who was not a fully committed historian. Daniel set out to versify the truth, not to write a poem; he hoped that the result would serve all of his countrymen, a national epic that seemed right for the time. Unfortunately, his contemporaries viewed the *Civile Warres* as a verse chronicle, not as an epic poem. In fact, Ben Jonson complained that Daniel had written a poetic commentary on the civil wars, but had failed to include a single battle—a comment that was more figurative than factual.

Actually, the problems arising from the project were not entirely of Daniel's own making. He originally intended to establish himself as a legitimate epic poet and a loyal subject of Elizabeth by anchoring the *Civile Warres* to Tudor myth and history. Although the blood factions of the nation produced a bloody war, good eventually came from the evil. Elizabeth would serve as a symbol of peace following the civil strife, thus inspiring poets to record and comment upon the events. By 1609, however, prior to completing the final book of the *Civile Warres*, Daniel found himself without a subject: Elizabeth was dead. He had by that time, however, directed his attention to other forms of historical writing, especially prose, and he simply lost interest in the epic, as well as in the historical period he was attempting to versify.

History was not the only study to capture Daniel's interest and muse. His *Poeticall Essayes* of 1599 contain one of his most characteristic poems, *Musophilus*. It is certainly a very personal piece, yet it stands as a fine example of the verse dialogue. On the personal level, the poet contends that he must develop and defend his own art, not only for the benefit of those who are contemptuous of it but also to reestablish his faith in himself and in the career of letters to which he has dedicated himself. That personal level, then, dictates the structure of the poem. Philocosmus, the unlettered man of action, confronts Musophilus, the defender of culture and of all learning. Daniel maintained that the idea for the poem was his—from his own heart—but there are clear connections to Count Baldassare Castiglione's *Il Cortegiano* (translated into English in 1561). At any rate, Philocosmus (like the French) reflects the great heresy of knowing only the nobility of arms; he ignores and also abhors letters, and considers learned men rascals. Such thinking is of course countered with the idea of letters being profitable and necessary for life and culture. The mind, therefore, enters the contest against materialism and narrow utilitarianism in order to preserve reverence. Daniel seriously believed that religious innovation and reform would eventually alter all priorities—the good as well as the bad—thus eradicating the sacred traditions of religion. In other words, in defending poetry and learning, the lines of *Musophilus* clearly echo the poet's fear of the scientific spirit, of an arrogance wherein men strive to talk rather than to worship. The ideal for Daniel was for humility and modesty to accompany knowledge and learning.

Daniel's career as a poet must be viewed in two stages. In his early period, the poet committed himself to pageantry and the patriotism of Elizabethan England. He sought to glorify his nation, applying his imagination to its ideals and achievements. As he matured, however—as his experiences widened and his intellect developed and deepened—he learned how to control the complex combination of poetry and history. Further, he learned about the language of poetry. Once in command of the poet's art, of language, he began to understand the conflicts in which all Elizabethan poets engaged: confidence in and concern for the ability to write poetry; dedication to the notion of England, but doubt of the events of history; trust in beauty, but skepticism about surface materialism. Still, with all of these conflicts, Daniel managed to succeed as a poet because, in the end, he appealed to custom and nature, both of which provided him "wings" to carry him "not out of his course, but as it were beyond his power to a faire happier flights."

**Major publications other than poetry**
PLAYS: *Cleopatra*, 1594; *The Tragedy of Philotas*, 1605.

NONFICTION: *The Defence of Ryme*, 1603; *The Collection of the Historie of England*, 1618.

MISCELLANEOUS: *The Complete Works in Verse and Prose of Samuel Daniel*, 1885-1896, 1963 (Alexander B. Grosart, editor, 5 volumes).

**Bibliography**
Butrick, Lyle H., ed. *"The Queenes Arcadia" by Samuel Daniel*, 1968.
Harner, James L. *Samuel Daniel and Michael Drayton: A Reference Guide*, 1980.
Himelick, Raymond, ed. *Samuel Daniel's "Musophilus"*, 1965.
Johnson, Marsue M. *The Well-Rimed Daniel: An Examination of "Delia" and "A Defence of Ryme"*, 1965.
Leavenworth, Russell E . *Daniel's "Cleopatra": A Critical Study*, 1974.
Michel, Laurence, ed. *"The Tragedy of Philotas" by Samuel Daniel*, 1949.
Rees, Joan. *Samuel Daniel: A Critical and Biographical Study*, 1964.
Seronsy, Cecil. *Samuel Daniel*, 1967.

*Samuel J. Rogal*

# GEORGE DARLEY

**Born:** Dublin, Ireland; 1795
**Died:** London, England; November 23, 1845

## Principal collections

*Errors of Ecstasie: A Dramatic Poem with Other Poems*, 1822; *Nepenthe*, 1835; *Poems of the Late George Darley*, 1890; *The Complete Poetical Works of George Darley*, 1908 (Ramsey Colles, editor).

## Other literary forms

George Darley was what today might be called a literary hack. The profession of writer in the early nineteenth century was a precarious one, and Darley tried his hand at most of the popular literary forms of his time. Although his work was usually unsigned, in keeping with the tradition of anonymous reviewing and publishing at the time, Darley can be credited with lyrical dramas, or masques, in the Elizabethan style, and a large number of reviews of art exhibits and current plays. His major literary works include a series of "dramatic" poems, *Sylvia, or The May Queen: A Lyrical Drama* (1827); and two tragedies: *Thomas à Becket: A Dramatic Chronicle in Five Acts* (1840) and *Ethelstan, or The Battle of Branaburgh: A Dramatic Chronicle in Five Acts* (1844). The titles of Darley's dramatic pieces suggest that they were written to be publicly staged, but none ever made it to the theater. Finally, the letters of George Darley should be noted as a highly valuable commentary on the life of a professional writer at a critical phase in English literature. Darley's letters, even more than his various essays on literature and art, provide a useful series of insights into the events and problems of the time. In spite of Darley's shy disposition, he met many of the most famous poets and critics of his time, read widely in the literature of his day, and was a fair commentator on many pressing social issues. It should be noted that Darley spent his last five years writing scientific textbooks for the use of students of secondary age. He may also have written a *Life of Virgil*, which is ascribed to him in the British Museum Catalog.

## Achievements

Darley never attained the recognition for his poetry and dramatic works that he earnestly sought throughout most of his adult life, although he pretended to be indifferent to the poetic fame that invariably eluded him, and demanded that his friends be unsparing of his feelings in making their comments on his work. In truth, his poetry was seldom reviewed or even noticed by anyone outside the immediate circle of his friends. Even today it is difficult to find references to his ideas or to his poetry in anything but the most exhaustive surveys of English Romanticism. Still, within the circle of Darley's friends, he was regarded as something of a poetic genius—the poet who would bring forth a new era of poetry. Charles Lamb, Thomas Beddoes, and John Clare were enthusiastic readers of his work and did their best to secure attention from the critical reviews. Even the proverbially churlish Thomas Carlyle remarked that Darley was one of the few poets of his day who really understood the spirit of Elizabethan tragedy, to the extent of being able to imitate it with any kind of success. Yet Darley never achieved more than a marginal place among the English poets of the early nineteenth century.

It was only some forty years after his death that readers took up Darley's poetry with interest. Part of this interest derived from the Celtic renaissance, but part also derived from Darley's ultimate claims to be read as a good minor poet.

**Biography**

George Darley was born in Dublin, Ireland, in 1795. He was the oldest of seven children of Arthur and Mary Darley. His parents were of the upper class, who for unknown reasons went to America for an extended visit when Darley was about three. The boy was reared by his grandfather, and he always referred to this period of his life as the "sunshine of the breast." At this time in his life Darley acquired an extreme stammer, so severe that even in his later years his closest friends could scarcely make out what he was saying. The stammer may have been important in determining his later career as a poet, and it partly accounts for one of the most common themes in the poetry: the isolation of the poet.

In 1815 Darley entered Trinity College, Dublin. He apparently made few friends there and, curiously, never mentioned the school in his later correspondence. The stammer interfered with his examinations, but he received his degree in 1820 and immediately left for London. Despite his speech defect and chronic shyness, Darley made friends with a number of writers who were emerging in the 1820's. His friends encouraged his work, and the letters he exchanged with such poets as Clare and Beddoes reveal their high regard for his work.

Darley spent almost ten years in London working at various literary and scientific projects, but late in 1830 he determined to go to France. He wrote occasional essays on art for the *Athenaeum* and (perhaps) another journal entitled, *The Original*, but there are few records of his life in Paris or his tours to Italy. It is significant, however, that several members of the Darley family were, for a while, reunited. The older brothers toured Italy together, and later Germany. He had always been sickly and generally poor, but he was a good tourist, and the letters from this period are among his best.

Darley continued to review books on various subjects for the *Athenaeum*, earning a reputation for extreme severity. He adopted the role in his private life of a vivacious and often bitter critic; he died in November, 1845 having never revisited Ireland, which constituted the one subject that was above criticism.

**Analysis**

George Darley's best poetry is the work of a man seeking escape from the world. The sorrows of his life, his poverty and his lack of recognition, are for the most part not present in his poetry. Many of his poems are about love, beautiful women, and the death of innocent women. This preoccupation suggests one of the more common Romantic motifs: the separation between a desirable realm of creativity and fertility and the sterile existence of the poet's life. In Darley's love poems there is a continuing search for perfection— the perfect woman, the perfect love. These poems show the influence of the Cavalier poet Thomas Carew, and it might be noted that one of Darley's most successful poems ("It Is Not Beauty I Demand") was published in the *London Magazine* with the name Carew appended to it. The fraud was not discovered until much later, after Francis Palgrave had included the poem in *The Golden Treasury*.

The women in Darley's poems are not the sentimental idols of so much nineteenth century love poetry, yet these lyrics are marred by Darley's frequent use of Elizabethan clichés: lips as red as roses, breasts as white as snow, hair as golden as the sun. In setting and theme as well, Darley's love poems are excessively conventional.

In his nature poetry Darley was able to achieve a more authentic style and tone. His early years in the Irish countryside had given him an almost pantheistic appreciation of nature as the ultimate source of comfort; many of his nature poems border on a kind of religious veneration. It is nature that comforts man, not the Church; it is nature that speaks with an "unerring voice" and will, if attended to, provide man with the lessons in morality that he requires.

"A Country Sunday," one of Darley's finest nature poems, illustrates this idea of God-in-nature. The poem, given its reference to Sunday, is curiously barren of any directly religious references. It is the sun that gives joy and the wind that serves as the vehicle of prayer. Nature serves as the great link between man's sordid existence and heaven.

In several of the lyric poems the themes of nature and love are fused. "It Is Not Beauty I Demand"—Darley's one assuredly great poem—illustrates the blending of nature and love, though the intent of the poet is to raise human love to a level beyond anything that might be found in nature. Darley's method is to use many of the standard phrases about women's beauty ("a crystal brow"; "starry eyes"; "lips that seem on roses fed") in a series of ten rapidly moving quatrains, with eight beats to each line, and a simple rhyme scheme of abab cdcd through the whole of the poem. The quatrains move rapidly, in part because Darley uses the syntax and diction of one who is speaking directly to his reader.

In "It Is Not Beauty I Demand" the natural beauties of the perfect woman are rejected as mere ornaments, or "gauds." In the fourth stanza, Darley breaks from the Cavalier tradition of "all for love" and inserts a fairly traditional moral into the poem. Thus, the red lips are rejected because they lead to destruction, like the red coral "beneath the ocean stream" upon which the "adventurer" perishes. The same moral argument is continued in the following stanzas, in which the white cheeks of the woman are rejected because they incite "hot youths to fields of blood." Even the greatest symbol of female beauty—"Helen's breast"—is rejected because Helen's beauty provoked war and suffering.

Darley's ideal woman would be a companion, a comforter, one with "a tender heart" and "loyal mind." Despite Darley's obvious affinities in this poem with Thomas Carew and other Cavalier poets, the poem represents a rejection of the Cavalier ideals of going off to battle to prove one's love and honor; it also represents a challenge to the rich sensuality of much Romantic poetry. With its emphasis on the intellectual virtues of women and the pleasures of companionship (versus sex), "It Is Not Beauty I Demand" is ultimately an affirmation of the ideals of love and marriage associated with the Victorians.

Some mention might be made of Darley's two tragedies, which in spite of their obvious failure as stage plays represent his most sustained creative effort. Darley had always been an enthusiastic reader of William Shakespeare and other Elizabethan dramatists; one of the most striking themes in his dramatic reviews was the death of tragedy in his own time. He was especially sickened by the rise and popularity of domestic tragedy; he reviewed one of the most popular tragedies of his time (*Ion*) in an almost savage manner for its sentimentality. Darley was not able to reverse the tendencies of Victorian playwrighting, but his two tragedies, *Thomas à Becket* and *Ethelstan*, whatever their shortcomings as plays, illustrate what he though a tragedy ought to be. He invoked the Elizabethan ideal of a man in high place who is brought to his death through his own error and the malice of others. Darley, however, was not able to write dialogue, and his characters are much given to lengthy histrionic speeches. In many instances, the speeches cover entire scenes. As far as the plays have merit, they serve to illustrate the Victorian preoccupation with the "great man." Darley's heroes and villains are indeed on the heroic scale; but they lack credibility and the blank verse is frequently bathetic.

Darley's lyrics, his only lasting achievement, have a genuine but limited appeal. His speech impediment, aloofness, and chronic shyness seemed to have forced him into a career that would serve as a natural release to his emotions. In his poetry, Darley created a world of fantasy, of benevolent nature and beautiful maidens, an ordered universe that the poet never found in real life.

**Major publications other than poetry**

PLAYS: *Sylvia, or The May Queen: A Lyrical Drama*, 1827; *Thomas à Becket: A Dramatic Chronicle in Five Acts*, 1840; *Ethelstan, or The Battle of Branaburgh: A Dramatic Chronicle in Five Acts*, 1844.

NONFICTION: *The Life and Letters of George Darley*, 1928 (Claude Abbott, editor of letters).

**Bibliography**

Abbott, Claude. *The Life and Letters of George Darley*, 1928.

Colles, Ramsay, ed. "Introduction," in *The Complete Poetical Works of George Darley*, 1908.

Lange, Donald. "George Darley," in *Review of English Studies*. XXVII (1976), pp. 437-445.

*John R. Griffin*

# SIR WILLIAM DAVENANT

**Born:** Oxford, England; February, 1606
**Died:** London, England; April 7, 1668

### Principal collections

*Madagascar: With Other Poems*, 1638; *Gondibert*, 1651 (unfinished); *The Shorter Poems and Songs from the Plays and Masques*, 1972 (A. M. Gibbs, editor).

### Other literary forms

Although he produced a considerable body of lyric and epic poetry, the bulk of Sir William Davenant's literary work was designed for the stage. His early dramas, heavily indebted to William Shakespeare and Ben Jonson, included the tragedy *The Cruel Brother* (1627), the comedies *The Wits* (1633) and *News from Plymouth* (1635), and the pastoral romance *The Platonic Lovers* (1636). In the mid-1630's he began writing masques; the best and most elaborate of these, *Britannia Triumphans* (1638), was done in collaboration with Inigo Jones. *Salmacidia Spolia* (1640), also with Jones, was the last masque in which Charles I performed. After the Civil War, Davenant produced a series of dramatic entertainments, comprising a mixture of set speeches, scenes, and musical interludes, designed to circumvent the Puritan prohibition of conventional drama. The first was *The First Days Entertainment at Rutland House* (1656). In more sophisticated pieces on heroic themes, *The Siege of Rhodes* (1656) and *The Cruelty of the Spaniards in Peru* (1658), Davenant collaborated with such composers as Henry Lawes and Matthew Locke to create the English opera. After the Restoration he devoted much of his time to rewriting William Shakespeare, and in 1667 produced in collaboration with John Dryden an immensely popular comic travesty of *The Tempest*.

### Achievements

Davenant's lyric poetry, although essentially derivative from John Donne, Ben Jonson, and the Cavalier mode, is both skillful and varied. Davenant's longest poem, the unfinished *Gondibert*, is competent but undistinguished in its artistry. Nevertheless, it is of major importance when considered in conjunction with *The Preface to Gondibert with An Answer by Mr. Hobbes*. *Gondibert* was one of the first neoclassical poems. Here Davenant advocates such neoclassical precepts as the importance of restraint in metaphor, image, and sentiment; the use of the balanced, closed line; and the importance of probability. His popularization of neoclassical decorum and his development of the opera and the heroic drama are Sir William Davenant's major achievements.

**Biography**

Sir William Davenant, or D'Avenant, as he styled himself in later years, lived a life which seems to cry out to be the subject of a historical novel. Born into the middle class, destined to be a tradesman, he rose to become one of the most honored poets and playwrights of his day, a general in the army of Charles I, a successful diplomat, and the friend and companion of some of the most glamorous men and women of his age.

John Davenant, a vintner, was mayor of Oxford in 1606, the year of his son William's birth. Shakespeare was supposedly a regular visitor at the Davenant tavern and was reputed to be the boy's actual father, a rumor that the young poet actively fostered. Intended for apprenticeship to a London merchant, Davenant, at his father's death in 1622, was instead preferred to the powerful Duchess of Richmond as a page. At the Duke of Richmond's death in 1624, Davenant took service with Fulke Greville, Lord Brooke, opening even further the doors of patronage and preferment. The elder poet was an early supporter of his talent and by 1627 Davenant was a working playwright with his first tragedy, *The Cruel Brother*, licensed for performance. New plays followed quickly, but in 1630 Davenant fell silent for several years, the victim, it is believed, of a nearly fatal case of syphilis, an illness which cost him his nose. By 1633, however, Davenant had returned to the stage, writing a number of successful plays, gaining a reputation as a poet, and in the later years of the decade, achieving great success as a writer of court masques. In 1638, he was named poet laureate.

Davenant served with distinction in the Bishop's Wars of 1640 and was later implicated in the First Army Plot against Parliament. When the Civil War broke out, he served under the Duke of Newcastle as Lieutenant-General of Ordinance and later fought with the King's army, being knighted in 1642 at the seige of Gloucester. In the later years of the war, he specialized in procuring arms and ammunition, making several dangerous trips to the Continent. Eventually, upon the collapse of the Royalist cause, he fled to France and became one of Queen Henrietta-Maria's most trusted servants.

In France, Davenant began the collaboration with Thomas Hobbes which was to be instrumental in the development of neoclassical theory. In 1650, they published *The Preface to Gondibert with An Answer by Mr. Hobbes*. Meanwhile, Davenant was appointed Governor of Maryland by the exiled Charles II, but his ship to the new world was captured by privateers commissioned by Parliament. He spent the next two years in prison. Although released in 1652, at John Milton's intervention according to one tradition, Davenant spent the next few years in poverty and was again arrested, for debt, in 1654.

In 1656 Davenant returned to writing for the stage and, in his attempt to circumvent Puritan restrictions, developed the rambling art form which was the direct ancestor of both modern opera and Dryden's heroic drama. His career for the next few years was a series of successes, although he has been accused of selling out to the Puritan government. After the Restoration his popularity continued, but he was never reinstated in his laureateship. Charles II frequently attended his plays and at the time of his death on April 7, 1668, Davenant was one of the two most successful theater managers in London.

**Analysis**

Sir William Davenant began his career as a versatile, technically competent poet, adept at producing *à la mode* verse guaranteed to please his patrons. His shorter works, many of them clearly bearing the stamp of John Donne's or Ben Jonson's influence, cover the entire range of forms fashionable in Caroline England: odes, satires, panegyrics, songs, and occasional poems. His themes were essentially what one would expect from a man destined to become poet laureate: the heroism of Prince Rupert and the King, the importance of friendship and the good life, the nobility of any number of aristocrats, and the beauty of a variety of noble ladies, especially the Queen. As a lyric poet, Davenant was a competent craftsman, one of the best of that "mob of gentlemen who wrote with ease" and who surrounded Charles I. In later years, however, he became a trailblazer and his heroic poem, *Gondibert*, taken in conjunction with its *The Preface to Gondibert*, is one of the most important poems of the middle years of the seventeenth century.

Although many of his early verses had appeared in poetic miscellanies or editions of his or others' plays, the first collection of Davenant's poems to be printed was *Madagascar: With Other Poems* in 1638. It consisted of the long (446-line) title poem and forty-two shorter pieces, including poems addressed to the King and Queen, to aristocrats such as the Duchess of Buckingham and the Earls of Portland and Rutland, and to friends such as Endymion Porter, Henry Jermyn, and Thomas Carew. Also present are satiric works, several poems commemorating deaths, including William Shakespeare's, Ben Jonson's, and a false rumor of Davenant's own, and a number of prologues, epilogues, and songs from plays. The volume opens with commendatory verses from Porter, John Suckling, Carew, and William Habington.

Like Michael Drayton's "To the Virginian Voyage" of 1606, Davenant's "Madagascar" is a patriotic poem designed to stir Englishmen to great deeds of exploration and conquest. Whereas Drayton's poem is occasional— although three voyages were undertaken to Virginia in the year the work appeared—Davenant's piece honors a nonevent, Prince Rupert's proposed but never attempted expedition to South Africa, a voyage which his uncle Charles I eventually forbade and which Rupert's mother compared to an adventure of Don Quixote.

As the poem opens, Davenant recounts his soul's dream journey south to the tropics where he beholds Rupert, his "mighty Uncles Trident" in hand, disembarking on the island of Madagascar with an army. The natives immediately surrender, awed as much by Rupert's beauty as by his military prowess. Other Europeans, perhaps Spaniards, also invade, and each side chooses two champions to determine ownership of the island by single combat. The English champions, for whom "The God-like *Sidney* was a Type," are Davenant's friends Porter and Jermyn. Their conflict is recounted in typically "high, immortall verse," charged with elaborate conceits. The English champions are victorious but the treacherous Spaniards renege on their vow to surrender, thus proving the justice of the English claim and providing Davenant with material for further elaborately depicted battle scenes. Eventually, Rupert is proclaimed "The first true Monarch of the *Golden Isle*" and Madagascar's great riches are described at length, its value to the English crown confirmed. Exhausted, the poet's soul returns to his body.

At bottom, the Madagascar proposal was not very well thought out and when it was submitted to the East India Company, that body responded with what Davenant's biographer, A. H. Nethercot, calls "diplomatic caution," essentially refusing to have anything to do with it. Virtually all of Charles I's advisers pointed out the impossibility of the project, and Archbishop Laud even went so far as to offer Rupert a bishopric to replace his supposed governorship. Thus, the historical background lends to the poem a faint air of the ridiculous. Perhaps realizing this, Davenant concluded it with a whimsical description of himself, twirling a chain of office, growing goutish, sitting on the island's judicial bench. The poem's intent, however, is clear. With an eye toward the main chance of preferment, the soon-to-be poet laureate was quite obviously cultivating Rupert, the rising young star of the Caroline court.

Many of the poems which Davenant addressed to individual courtiers and noblemen, such as the typically if somewhat simplemindedly Jonsonian "To the King on New-years day 1630," are occasional verse. This poem begins by praising Charles I as a ruler who teaches by example, and by offering him all the joy inherent in such standard Cavalier touchstones as "Youth . . . Wine, and Wealth." It continues by wishing the King and the nation, first, peace, but peace "not compass'd by/ Expensive Treaties but a Victorie," and, second, a successful Parliament, one consisting of "such who can obey./ . . . not rebell." These veiled references to recent and only partially successful treaties with France and Spain and to Charles's dissolving of Parliament in March of 1629, typify Davenant's method and belief with regards to politics. He was essentially a "yes-man," defending Charles I's actions without reservation, or, if differing at all with the King's policy, arguing on the side of action, the side of victory without compromise.

Other poems in the volume include "Elizium, To the Duchess of Buckingham," which begins by describing one of those Arcadian utopias of friendship, love, and beauty so popular with Cavalier poets, and finishes by eulogizing the dead Duke of Buckingham; "A Journey into Worcestershire," a mock travelogue of the sort popularly used to satirize the foibles and follies of country bumpkins, Puritans, and the author and his friends; "Jeffereidos," a satire recounting the kidnaping of Jeffery Hudson, the Queen's dwarf; and a pastoral lament, "Written When Colonel Goring Was Believ'd to be Slaine," in which two swains, Porter and Jermyn, again bemoan Goring's supposed death, juxtaposing fairly standard pastoral and heroic references to Achilles, Hector, and Elizium with references to Columbus and Magellan, and a complex, Donne-like nautical conceit. References to ships, compasses, charts, and exploration appear over and over again in Davenant's work. Indeed the nautical world is his favorite source of metaphors.

Between 1660 and 1663 Davenant published three short panegyric poems, *To His Excellency the Lord General Monck* (1660), *Upon His Sacred Majestie's Return to His Dominions* (1660), and *To the King's Most Sacred Majesty* (1663). These are minor pieces, very much the sort of thing every other poet of the day was writing. They were republished in the 1673 *Works* along with *Poems on Several Occasions*, a volume of Davenant's short pieces which had been intended for separate publication in 1657, but which had never seen print. *Poems on Several Occasions* includes the long (624-line) *To the Earl of Orrey*, an elaborate panegyric written in the 1650's. Davenant praises Orrey, a noted statesman and soldier who was later to be instrumental in restoring Charles II to the throne, in an elaborate conceit in which the poet is an explorer sailing the marvelous coastline of the Earl's genius.

There are fifty shorter pieces in *Poems on Several Occasions*, some of them dating from the 1630's; most of them, like the *Madagascar* poems, are easily classifiable as occasional pieces, lyrics, and satires. Perhaps the finest verses in *Poems on Several Occasions* are the short lyrics. Davenant's "The Lark now leaves his watry Nest" is a lovely compliment, more Elizabethan than anything else, in which the standard metaphor of the lady's awakening being like the sun's rising is handled with uncommon grace. Another lyric, "Endimion Porter and Olivia," contemplates the fate of lovers after death and the danger of their being separated.

Davenant is remembered today primarily as the author of *Gondibert*. This heroic poem relates the maneuverings and martial engagements involved in establishing the successor to the aging Aribert, eighth century King of the Lombards. The King's heir is the beautiful Rhodalind, and the King wishes her to wed the Duke Gondibert, a knight who equals her in excellence. Unfortunately, the immoral but otherwise extremely capable Prince Oswald also aspires to the Princess' hand and will fight to gain it. Oswald's followers are all hardened veterans of many campaigns. Gondibert's, by contrast, are mere youths, brave, but inexperienced, and devout worshipers at the shrine of Love.

One day Oswald and his troops ambush Gondibert while he is returning from the hunt. Disdaining to take advantage of his superior numbers, the Prince offers to meet the Duke in single combat. Soon the several leaders of the two factions are similarly engaged and Davenant describes the battle in great detail and with considerable relish. Oswald and his men are noble foes, but because virtue and Gondibert must triumph, Oswald is killed. As was the case in the duel in "Madagascar," which clearly served as a thematic, though not a stylistic, rough sketch for the heroics of *Gondibert*, the defeated faction refuses to abide by its leader's promise and attacks the Duke's small party. Gondibert, wounded, nonetheless defeats them, and, although they have already proved doubly treacherous, gallantly lets them depart.

The poem goes on to relate the hero's recovery from his wounds at the palace of Astragon, a scientist-philosopher modeled on Sir Francis Bacon or Sir William Gilbert. While Civil War is brewing, Gondibert dallies with Astragon's daughter, Birtha, and falls in love with her shortly before discovering that he has been proclaimed fiancé to Rhodalind. Soon after, the work breaks off. Although he lived another seventeen years, Davenant never returned to it.

*Gondibert*'s importance lies not so much in its innate excellence as in the theory behind it. In its own day it provoked both controversy and ridicule. The poem was praised by Thomas Hobbes, who had something of a stake in it, and by both Edmund Waller and Abraham Cowley; but the more common reaction was highly negative. Some, like John Denham, were reduced to obscenities.

In the all-important *The Preface to Gondibert*, Davenant argues that Homer, despite his greatness, erred when he introduced the supernatural into poetry. It is acceptable, for example, for the poet to petition his Muse metaphorically, when it is clear that he is really speaking to what Davenant calls his "rationall Spirit," but it is not acceptable for the poet to treat the Muse as a person in her own right. Vergil is similarly at fault and, even more so, Torquato Tasso and Edmund Spenser, the great modern heroic poets, because they as Christians should know better. Davenant generally follows his own advice in *Gondibert*, grounding his characters' actions not in motivation provided by meddling deities, but in the desire for power, martial exercise, and love. He does, however, include an enchantress in the poem, and has the Duke give Birtha a magic emerald which will change color if he is unfaithful.

Davenant saw the heroic poem as, at least in part, a didactic tool and resolved to display characters who exemplified active Christian virtues, although his conflicting desire to promote the Cavalier virtue of martial prowess occasionally led him to extremes. To convey the moral message and to please the reader were for Davenant the first requirements of the heroic poem, and anything standing in the way was to be condemned. Thus, Spenser could be faulted for his archaic language, complex stanzas, and obscure allegories. Davenant's own language is lofty but contemporary, his stanza a simple four-line iambic pentameter, rhyming abab.

Davenant was attempting to define and put to use what is now thought of as the neoclassical poetic. Breaking with his own early use of the metaphysical manner, he emphasized decorum, arguing against extremes, whether of language, sentiment, metaphor, or wit, and insisting on the superiority of the familiar and the real. With Hobbes's aid Davenant set out to develop an active poetic which repudiated all use of the supernatural even in epic or heroic forms, and which insisted on a rationalist approach to human nature. The word "wit" had meant something very different to Donne from what it was to mean to Alexander Pope, and it was in Davenant's *The Preface to Gondibert* that many of the arguments were first expounded which were eventually to lead to that change.

**Major publications other than poetry**
PLAYS: *The Cruel Brother*, 1627; *The Wits*, 1633; *Love and Honour*, 1634; *News from Plymouth*, 1635; *The Platonic Lovers*, 1636; *The Unfortunate Lovers*, 1638; *Britannia Triumphans*, 1638 (masque); *Salmacidia Spolia*, 1640 (masque); *The First Days Entertainment at Rutland House*, 1656; *The Siege of Rhodes*, 1656; *The Cruelty of the Spaniards in Peru*, 1658; *The Playhouse to be Let*, 1659; *The Tempest*, 1667 (adaptation, with John Dryden).
NONFICTION: *The Preface to Gondibert with An Answer by Mr. Hobbes*, 1650 (with Thomas Hobbes).
MISCELLANEOUS: *Works*, 1673, 1968.

**Bibliography**
Dowlin, Cornell M. *Sir William Davenant's Gondibert, Its Preface, and Hobbes's Answer: A Study in English Neoclassicism*, 1934.
Harbage, Alfred. *Sir William Davenant: Poet Venturer*, 1935.
Nethercot, A. H. *Sir William D'Avenant: Poet Laureate and Playwright-Manager*, 1938.

*Michael M. Levy*

# SIR JOHN DAVIES

**Born:** Chicksgrove, England; 1569
**Died:** London, England; December 7, 1626

## Principal poems and collections

"The Epithalamion of the Muses," c. 1594; *Epigrames*, 1595-1599; *Orchestra: Or, A Poem of Dauncing*, 1596, 1622; *Nosce Teipsum: This Oracle expounded in two elegies*, 1599; *Hymnes of Astraea*, 1599; *A Contention betwixt a Widdowe, and a Maide*, presented in 1602; *Twelve Wonders of the World*, presented in 1602 or 1603; *The Poems of Sir John Davies*, 1975 (Robert Krueger, editor).

## Other literary forms

Throughout his literary career, Sir John Davies published various nonfiction prose works, including a history of Ireland and a political commentary.

## Achievements

Davies' reputation as a poet has shifted radically, depending on the taste of the reading public. His epigrams and occasional poems were very popular with his contemporaries; they survive in numerous manuscript copies. *Nosce Teipsum*, his long philosophical poem, went through five editions during his lifetime. Reprinted first by Nahum Tate in 1697, it went through several more editions and remained very popular in the eighteenth century. Alexander Pope paid Davies the compliment of imitating him, and Samuel Johnson praised his skill at arguing in verse. Samuel Taylor Coleridge, in *Biographia Literaria* (1817) adapts three stanzas from *Nosce Teipsum* to explain how the poetic imagination functions. In the modern era, Davies has attracted the favorable attention of poets such as T. S. Eliot and Theodore Roethke, but has fared less well in academic scholarship.

In his very influential work *The Elizabethan World Picture* (1943), E. M. W. Tillyard identified Davies as a principal intellectual spokesman for the Elizabethan "world picture" and described his verse as "typically Elizabethan." This approach to his poetry established Davies as a poet who should be read for his ideas, for the insights he offered regarding the Elizabethan mind. Davies' modern editor, Robert Krueger, takes precisely this position when he concludes his critical introduction to the standard edition with the following statement: "Davies will never again be read for profit or pleasure; his readers will always be students of the Elizabethan world" (*The Poems of Sir John Davies*).

While it would be foolhardy to conclude that Davies is a greatly underestimated "poet's poet," the major works of a poet who has continued to receive such favorable commentary from other practicing poets should not be dismissed as mediocre. His place in political history is assured: he served as Attorney General of Ireland under James I and assisted in planning the "Plantation of Ulster." His literary achievements are more difficult to assess: popular in his own day as the author of *Nosce Teipsum*, his long philosophical poem, and of salacious, satirical epigrams, Davies is now mostly remembered for his *Orchestra*.

## Biography

John Davies was born in 1569, just five years after William Shakespeare and two years before John Donne. His life belongs as much to the Jacobean as to the Elizabethan period. He probably became interested in writing epigrams while he was attending Winchester School. This preparatory school produced a large number of important epigrammatists, including John Owen, Thomas Bastard, and John Hoskins, as well as Davies. After spending some time at Oxford, Davies attended New Inn, an Inn of Chancery associated with the Inns of Court, before entering the Middle Temple and formally beginning his study of the law. Located near the theaters, the Inns of Court, the four important law schools in London, attracted many young men with literary as well as legal interests. Sir Francis Bacon studied at Gray's Inn, John Donne at Lincoln's Inn, and Sir Walter Raleigh and John Marston at the Middle Temple.

In the fall of 1592, Davies visited the University of Leiden, arriving a week after William Fleetwood and Richard Martin, his fellow students at the Middle Temple. William Camden, one of the leading English antiquarians, wrote a letter introducing Davies to Paul Merula, a distinguished Dutch jurist. The trip may have been partially motivated by the need to improve Fleetwood's image with the Middle Temple Benchers. He and Richard Martin were expelled on February 11, 1592, for their "misdemeanours and abuses to the Masters and Benchers." Davies was probably involved in the Candlemas disturbances, but he and Robert Jacob, a lifelong friend, were given the milder penalty of merely being excluded from commons.

By 1594 Davies had apparently been presented at court by Charles Blount, Lord Mountjoy, who, along with Sir Thomas Egerton, is described as Davies' patron in all of the manuscript sources for his biography. Queen Elizabeth had Davies sworn her servant-in-ordinary and encouraged him in his studies at the Middle Temple. He then served as part of the embassy to Scotland for the christening of Prince Henry at Stirling Castle on October 30, 1594.

On July 4, 1595, Davies was "called to the degree of the Utter Bar with the assent of all the Masters of the Bench." Since his admission to the Bar came after the minimum seven years of residence and since he was called with the permission of all the Masters of the Bench, not merely by a particular reader, he must have distinguished himself as a particularly brilliant student. Much of his best poetry was written during this period. By 1595 he had probably written *Nosce Teipsum*, which he did not publish until 1599, and most of his epigrams. In 1596 he published the first printed version of *Orchestra*, an encomium of dancing, to which he attached a dedicatory sonnet to Richard Martin, addressing him as his dearest friend.

On February 9, 1598, Davies entered the Middle Temple Dining Hall while the Benchers were seated decorously at the table, preparing for the practice court and other exercises which followed dinner. Davies walked immediately to the table where Richard Martin was seated and broke a bastinado over his head. Before leaving, he drew his rapier and brandished it above his head. For this flagrant violation of legal decorum, he was expelled on February 10 "never to return." No entirely satisfactory explanation for this attack has been proposed.

In *John Marston of the Middle Temple* (1969), Philip Finkelpearl speculated that the attack was related to a satiric reference to Davies' descent from a tanner which was made during the Christmas revels at the Middle Temple. Richard Martin played the Prince d'Amour, the central figure in the festivities, but it was Matagonius, the prince's poet, who was responsible for the satire against Davies. The incident occurred on December 27, 1597, so long before Davies' attack on Martin that it is difficult to believe that the two events were closely related. Whatever the provocation, it must have seemed significant to Davies, so much so, that he was willing to risk his promising legal future for public revenge.

After his expulsion Davies may have spent some time at Oxford. By 1601 he was serving in the House of Commons as a representative from Corfe Castle, Dorset. During the debate over monopolies, a raging controversy in this Parliament, he advocated that the House of Commons proceed to pass a bill canceling the monopolies or patents. The Queen's loyal supporters vigorously recommended that the House humbly petition her to redress their grievances, since granting monopolies was part of her royal prerogative. Sir Robert Cecil singled Davies out for a special reprimand. Martin also served in the Parliament of 1601 and also opposed monopolies; his active support of Davies' position suggests that the reconciliation between the two men may have been genuine. Davies' own outspoken demeanor is the more surprising because he had been readmitted to the Middle Temple only about a month before the debate.

After James came to the throne of England, Davies was appointed first Solicitor General and then Attorney General of Ireland. After receiving a knighthood in 1603, the first concrete evidence of his progress up the social ladder occurred in 1609 when he married Lady Eleanor Audeley, the daughter of George Touchet, Lord Audeley, later the Earl of Castlehaven. By 1612, Davies had been created a sergeant-at-law, and by 1613 he was well enough off financially to be listed as one of the chief adventurers in a list of investors in the Virginia Company. In 1612 he published his major prose work, a history of Ireland entitled *Discoverie of the True Causes why Ireland was never entirely Subdued, nor brought under Obedience of the Crowne of England*.

However socially advantageous Davies' marriage was, it cannot have been very pleasant. Lady Eleanor's brother, Mervyn Touchet, the second Earl of Castlehaven, was criminally insane. He was sentenced to death for unnatural offenses after a notorious trial in the House of Lords; Charles I temporarily improved the moral image of the aristocracy by allowing the execution to take place. Lady Eleanor herself was a religious fanatic who believed that she was the prophet Daniel reincarnated. The truth was supposedly revealed to her in anagrams which she explicated in incoherent prophecies. By her own report, three years before the end, she foresaw Davies' death and donned her mourning garments from that moment: "when about three days before his sudden death, before all his servants and his friends at the table, gave him pass to take his long sleep, by him thus put off, 'I pray weep not while I am alive, and I will give you leave to laugh when I am dead'" (*The Lady Eleanor Her Appeal*, 1646). Lady Eleanor did not mourn, but she had little reason to laugh after Davies' death. She remarried Sir Archibald Douglas in three months, but he neglected and finally deserted her. He also burned her manuscripts, and she prophesied that he, like Davies, would suffer for it. According to her reports, while taking communion he was struck dumb so that he could only make sounds like a beast. He apparently left England.

The above facts are significant for a critical analysis of the surviving biographical materials and manuscript verse of Davies. His daughter Lucy married Ferdinando Hastings and became the Countess of Huntingdon. Since her uncle was criminally insane and her mother's self-righteous fanaticism verged on madness, she would naturally want to present her father as morally upright and be sure that he was remembered for his solemn philosophical poetry and weighty prose. If the "licentious" sonnets first printed in the Clare Howard edition of Davies' *Poems* (1941) had been left among Davies' papers instead of in the library at Trinity College, Dublin, it is unlikely that either Lucy or her son Theophilus would have printed them. In his biographical notes on Davies, which survive in manuscript in the Hastings Collection at the Henry E. Huntington Library, Theophilus describes each of Davies' political appointments in detail, alludes to royal favors, and devotes several paragraphs to a description of Lucy Davies' dowry: Sir John's poetry is never mentioned.

**Analysis**

Sir John Davies' minor poetry falls into three general classes: dramatic entertainments written for court ceremonies or celebrations, occasional poems which he sent to prominent people, and satires commenting on a literary fashion or topical scandal. Of the entertainments which can be clearly attributed to Davies, the most important are "The Epithalamion of the Muses," presented at the wedding of Elizabeth Vere, daughter of Edward Vere, Earl of Oxford, to William Stanley, Earl of Derby, and preserved in the common-place book of Leweston Fitzjames of the Middle Temple; *A Contention betwixt a Widdowe, and a Maide* presented at the home of Sir Robert Cecil on December 6, 1602, in honor of Queen Elizabeth; and *Twelve Wonders of the World*, twelve poems in rhymed couplets which were apparently inscribed on a dozen trenchers which Davies presented to the Lord Treasurer on New Year's Day in 1602 or 1603. John Maynard set the *Twelve Wonders of the World* to music in 1611.

Davies' occasional poems were addressed to influential people such as Henry Percy, Earl of Northumberland; Sir Thomas Egerton, Lord Chancellor of England; Sir Edward Coke, Attorney General; as well as King James and Queen Anne. His "Gulling Sonnets" belong to the third class of topical poetry. In these sonnets Davies mocks the conventions of the Petrarchan sonnet sequences which were popular in the 1590's. These particular poems survived only in manuscript accompanied by a dedication to Sir Anthony Cooke. They must have been written between 1596, when Cooke was knighted, and 1604, when he died. An internal reference to *Zepheria* (1597), an anonymous sonnet sequence, suggests that they were completed by 1598. *Zepheria* was probably written by a young law student since it contains an awkward combination of learned legal terms and Petrarchan images.

In his nineteenth century Victorian edition of Davies' works, Alexander Grosart supplied a commentary on Davies which unfortunately has dominated twentieth century critical opinion of the poet's major works. *Orchestra*, a dialogue between Penelope and one of her wooers, is, according to Grosart, a *jeu d'esprit* which Davies tossed off in his youth. Grosart insisted that Davies' most valuable work was *Nosce Teipsum* and that the chief merit of this exhaustive compendium of knowledge about the soul and immortality was its originality. Responding to Grosart's claim, twentieth century academic scholarship on Davies has largely consisted of arguments that Davies' ideas derive from Plato, Aristotle, Pierre de la Primaudaye, Philippe du Plessis-Mornay, and Michel de Montaigne.

Underlying the approach to Davies which Grosart initiated is the assumption that a sixteenth century writer would have aimed at or even particularly valued originality. Davies, however, belonged to an age which suspected novelty, valued intellectual tradition, and sought to imitate poetic models rather than to express personal feelings. Poets consciously modeled themselves on previous poets. Edmund Spenser, who hoped to win the title of the English Vergil, began by writing pastorals just as his Latin master had done.

T. S. Eliot, in what remains the best critical appreciation of Davies' works, calls attention to his metrical virtuosity, his clarity and purity of diction, and his independence of thought. In shifting the critical issue from originality to independence of thought, Eliot demonstrates historical as well as literary insight. While Davies' ideas on the soul and immortality are not original, one should not expect them to be. His synthesis of many diverse sources shows intellectual independence.

Each of Davies' major poems has to be assessed in relation to other works in that particular genre. He consciously works with certain established poetic conventions. His *Nosce Teipsum* should be examined in relation to other long philosophical poems, such as Lucretius' *De rerum natura* (c. 60 B.C., *On the Nature of Things*), Aonio Paleario's *De immortalitate animae* (1536), Samuel Daniel's *Musophilus* (1599), and Fulke Greville's poetic treatises. *Orchestra* belongs to the genre of mythological wooing poems, which were later given the name *epyllia*, or minor epics. In writing *Orchestra*, Davies did not set out to write a poem about the Elizabethan world view; he suggests that *Orchestra* relates a wooing episode that Homer forgot to include in the *Odyssey* (c. 800 B.C.) because he wants his readers to associate the poem with other amatory poems popular in England in the 1590's. Of these, two of the most popular were Christopher Marlowe's *Hero and Leander* (1598) and Shakespeare's *Venus and Adonis* (1593). *Orchestra*, however, lacks the sensuality of these two poems and seems to resemble the more philosophical efforts in the genre, such as Michael Drayton's *Endimion and Phoebe* (1595) and George Chapman's *Ovids Banquet of Sense* (1595). The *Hymnes of Astraea* belong to a genre treated with disdain by most modern scholars. They are acrostic lyrics intended as an Accession Day tribute to Queen Elizabeth. Like the many entertainments written to praise Elizabeth's beauty or her purity, they are intended as courtly compliments and should be approached as artful "trifles," excellent in their kind.

Finally, it is important to emphasize that Davies was a man of ideas. His poems are intended to delight, but also to teach and to inform. Critics who associate poetry with the expression of feelings or the description of scenery may find his verse less immediately accessible. He thrived on formal restraints; to appreciate his poetry requires a sensitivity to the technical difficulties of writing verse. It also requires that the reader accept verse in which, in T. S. Eliot's words, "thought is not exploited for the sake of feeling; it is pursued for its own sake."

Davies' *Epigrames* appeared without a date and with a title page reading "At Middleburgh." No satisfactory explanation has been offered for the post-humous combination of Christopher Marlowe's translation of Ovid's *Elegies* with Davies' *Epigrames*. It is unlikely that the first edition was a piracy because Epigrams 47 and 48, which balance 1 and 2 in the printed text, seem to have been written specifically for the printed edition; they are absent from all four of the most important manuscripts. Although some of the epigrams may have dated from his school days, the majority were probably written between 1594 and 1595.

The poems are obviously modeled on Martial's epigrams, but Davies supplies details of sixteenth-century English life. In "Meditations of a Gull," he

describes a young gentleman consumed by "melancholy," a young man uninterested in politics who wears a cloak and a "great black feather." He is
clearly describing the *type* of young man who pretends to be an intellectual,
rather than a specific caricature. Davies, in fact, claims that his epigrams tax
under "a peculiar name,/ A generall vice, which merits publick blame." In
June, 1599, the Bishop of London and the Archbishop of Canterbury ordered
that "Davyes Epigrams and Marlowe's Elegyes" be burned. Since they seem
less obscene than other works so condemned, it may be that one of the
epigrams contained a libelous allusion unrecognizable today. Practice in this
genre, which requires condensation and lucidity, assisted Davies in developing
talents which he demonstrated more forcefully in *Nosce Teipsum* and *Orchestra*, but the *Epigrames* still have some interest because of the clever way in
which they mirror life in sixteenth century London.

*Nosce Teipsum: This Oracle expounded in two elegies*, was first printed in
1599, approximately one year after Davies was expelled from the Middle
Temple. The poem has frequently been described as an attempt on Davies'
part to "repair his fortunes with his pen," thus assuming that Davies wrote
it to show that he repented his assault on Martin and that he had completed
his reformation. The poem contains what could be interpreted as an autobiographical reference: affliction is described as having taken the narrator by
the ear to teach him a lesson. There is substantial evidence, however, that
the poem was begun long before Davies attacked Martin and that it was
revised over a period of several years.

The question of literary form has received little attention in discussions of
*Nosce Teipsum*, but an understanding of the nature of the poem's form and
structure is crucial. First, the argument, or organization of ideas, does not
define the form. It is impossible to outline *Nosce Teipsum* thematically without
reaching the conclusion that the poem is a loosely organized compendium of
Elizabethan knowledge. The second elegy, for example, defines the soul in
relation to the body, but then discusses the origin of the soul, the fall of man,
and free will, before considering the way in which the powers of the soul are
actually exercised in the body. The fall of man is discussed at the beginning
of the first elegy and then examined again in stanzas 138-186 of the second
elegy. Second, the poem is divided into two elegies of very different lengths,
forty-five stanzas in the first and 436 in the second. In the second elegy a
description of the soul requires 273 stanzas with arguments for immortality
requiring another 163 stanzas. Davies could have divided the second elegy
into two separate sections; that he did not do so requires some consideration.

The relationship between the two elegies is suggested by the general title
of the work, not by the separate titles of the two elegies: *Nosce Teipsum:
This Oracle expounded in two elegies*. The emphasis should be upon "oracle,"
not upon the broad tradition of self-knowledge. The first elegy, "Of Humane
Knowledge," is a riddle which presents the dilemmas that individuals expe-

rience in attempting to acquire self-knowledge. Both biblical and classical illustrations are used because the riddle of self-knowledge puzzles Christians as well as pagans. The second elegy represents a solution to the riddle, and it is structured as a classical oration. Davies' structure reverses the procedure of the classical oracle in which a relatively clear question led to an enigmatic answer. Influenced by the Renaissance concept of the "oracle" as an obscure riddle, Davies intends the first elegy to represent the question put to the deity in the ancient oracles; it concludes with an enigmatic statement of man's nature. The second elegy presents a clear and straightforward answer to that enigmatic statement. The relationship between the two elegies explains why the form of *Nosce Teipsum* required a break between the two poems.

The second elegy uses the seven-part format of a classical oration, following the divisions of Thomas Wilson, the sixteenth century rhetorician, rather than the six sections recommended by Cicero. The "entrance" (stanzas 1-21) invokes divine light, showing the poet's need for divine assistance by summarizing the diversity of opinions about the soul (7-15). The "narration" (22-174) consists of two parts: a definition (22-100) and a history (101-174). The soul is defined as a spirit separate from the body; then, the history of how the soul and body were created is summarized. The "proposition" (175-189) answers the questions: why the soul is related to the body, in what manner it is related to the body, and how the soul exercises her powers in the body. The answers summarize the major themes of the "history," "definition," and "division." Davies uses the "division" (190-269) literally to divide the faculties of the soul and their functions; traditionally, the division explained the disposition of the material. The arguments for the immortality of the soul are presented as the "confirmation" (274-357); the refutation of arguments against the immortality of the soul follows in the "confutation" (358-420). In the "conclusion" (421-436) Davies links the two main subjects, the soul and immortality, and then admonishes his own soul to be humble. This admonition parallels the invocation to divine light presented in the entrance.

Brilliantly using the resources of rhetoric, Davies takes the reader from darkness and ambiguity in the first elegy to light and clarity as the answer to the riddle is discovered. The vision of man as a "*proud* and yet a *wretched* thing" at the end of the first elegy is corrected in the Acclamation which precedes the arguments for immortality in the second elegy:

> O! What a lively life, what heavenly poer,
> What spreading vertue, what a sparkling fire!
> How great, how plentifull, how rich a dower
> Dost Thou within this dying flesh inspire!

Davies' most engaging poem, and probably his most interesting for the modern reader, is *Orchestra*, an encomium of dancing set within a Homeric frame. The poem is supposed to relate a dialogue between Penelope, Queen of Ithaca, and Antinous, one of the disorderly suitors who wants to marry Penelope. Antinous invites Penelope to dance, but she refuses, calling dancing "this new rage." He responds with a lengthy defense of dancing, its antiquity and order.

Davies successfully achieves an exuberant combination of fancy and learning by using the structure, imagery, and setting to suggest multiple levels of meaning. These levels overlap and reinforce one another, but they can be generally distinguished as philosophical, political, and aesthetic. On a philosophical level, the poem is an extended hyperbole which views the macrocosm and microcosm united in the universal dance of life. Davies, however, treats this traditional idea playfully as well as seriously. When he extends the central image of a dancing cosmos to include the description of the veins of the earth as dancing "saphire streames," and to include the personification of Echo, the "prattling" daughter of the air, as an imperfect dancer, the reader becomes keenly aware of the poet's artifice. One is amused by these unconventional extensions of the traditional metaphor, but one does not question its basic validity. The aesthetic effect that Davies achieves is to render the tone playful without undercutting the seriousness of the message.

Similarly, Davies interweaves the themes of love and beauty in ways which enrich the philosophical and aesthetic overtones of the poem. Love is described as the father of dancing and also functions as a major figure in the poem. Stanzas 28-76 are devoted to Antinous' description of Love's speeches and actions, and Love, disguised as a page, presents Antinous with the magic mirror which reflects an idealized view of Elizabeth and her court (stanzas 109-126). In stanzas 98-108 love also becomes the central issue in the dialogue between Penelope and Antinous. She attacks Love as "of every ill the hatefull Father vile" (stanza 98), supporting this charge with mythological examples (stanzas 99-100). She concludes with a rejection of both dancing and love in stanza 101: "Unhappy may they prove,/ That sitting free, will either daunce or love." Antinous replies by distinguishing mischievous Lust from that "true Love" who invented dancing, tuned the world's harmony, and linked men in "sweet societie." In stanzas 105-108, Antinous argues that Love dances in Penelope: her beauty is "but a daunce where Love hath us'd/ His finer cunning, and more curious art." As E. M. W. Tillyard has suggested, these stanzas allude to the Platonic ladder in which the lover is first attracted to the physical beauty of his mistress and then to her spiritual beauty and virtue; he is led up the ladder to the point at which he values virtue for its own sake. In stanza 108, the imagined vision of Penelope's virtues dancing a round dance in her soul almost puts Antinous into a trance.

The philosophical and aesthetic levels are closely related. Not only is Penelope's beauty described as a dance in which Love has used his "more curious art," but Love's dance in Penelope is also developed by artistic illustrations: Love dances in her fingers when she weaves her web (stanza 106) or when she plays "any silver-sounding instrument" (stanza 107). This type of aesthetic statement is set forth quite overtly in the poem, but there are also two digressions from the central action which function aesthetically to symbolize the entire poem: (1) Antinous reports a long speech which the god Love delivered to disorderly men and women in order to persuade them to dance. This persuasion to dance, stanzas 29-60, is a rhetorical set piece; it is unrelated to the main action, Antinous' persuasion of Penelope to dance, and yet it mirrors it. Love's speech is a macrocosmic parallel to the microcosm in which Antinous is wooing Penelope. (2) Near the conclusion of the poem (stanzas 109-126), in the second digression, Antinous summons Love disguised as a page boy to bring a magic mirror which reflects a vision of Elizabeth's court in which the sovereign moon is surrounded by dancing stars. The heavenly bodies and the court, or body politic, are united in harmonious order. Each of the above digressions comments upon the poem and underlines Davies' political intentions.

Queen Elizabeth was in her sixties when *Orchestra* was written, but she was surrounded by suitors who wished to be named as her successor. The contemporary political situation offered a close parallel to the Homeric setting, but Davies could not afford to make the comparisons too explicit. He merely hints that his own Queen Elizabeth, like Queen Penelope, is reluctant to participate in the orderly movement of the universe by assuring for a transfer of power (stanzas 60, 57-58). In the first digression, Antinous parallels Love, the god, who is attempting to persuade the disorderly men and women to learn to dance; by implication, Penelope parallels them.

The mirror, like the rhetorical set piece, symbolizes in miniature the poem. Davies' *Orchestra*, like the mirror, has displayed the timeless and ideal forms of order in the macrocosm and the microcosm. It has shown the past by describing Antinous' wooing of Penelope and hinted at the rejection of order in Penelope's refusal. The poem, like the mirror, also shows the present by describing the Queen surrounded by her courtiers as the moon surrounded by the stars, but there is no provision for the future. At the end of the poem, the reader does not know whether Queen Penelope will finally accept the invitation to dance and in so doing assure order throughout the macrocosm and microcosm. The invocation to Urania in stanza 127 is addressed to a "Prophetesse divine," not to the muse of heavenly love. This invocation, which follows the invocation in stanza 123 so closely, emphasizes that the poet cannot prophesy the future. He has shown the past, present, and the timeless ideal, but it is up to the Queen to provide for the future.

The epic trappings, in which the disorderly Antinous of the *Odyssey* becomes a spokesman for order, invite the reader to make parallels, but they are handled so playfully that *Orchestra* could, if need arose, masquerade as a simple wooing poem. The poem invites, but does not require a political interpretation. *Orchestra* is constructed so that it could pass as a *jeu d'esprit* or as a celebration of honor climaxing in a compliment to the Queen, but it was intended as Davies' "pithie exhortation" to Elizabeth to settle the succession so that an orderly transfer of power would be assured after her death.

Three versions of *Orchestra* have survived, and in each, Davies' handling of the conclusion reflects his views about the contemporary political situation. The only surviving manuscript of the poem (LF) is preserved in Leweston Fitzjames' commonplace book (Bodleian Library Add. MS. B. 97. fols. 258-38). LF contains only 113 stanzas of the first printed version: 1-108 plus 131. An entry in the Stationers' Register in 1594 suggests that LF preserves an early version composed in 1593-1594, a time when the publication of Father Robert Parsons' *Conference About the Next Succession to the Crown of England* had made the subject of the succession dangerous to discuss. The LF version omits the magic mirror sequence so that no celebration of order in the body politic is included in the poem.

The first printed version is entitled *Orchestra: Or, A Poeme of Dauncing. Iudicially prooving the true observation of time and measure, in the Authenticall and laudable use of Dauncing.* This version consists of stanzas 1-131. Probably to render the political implications less explicit, Davies added stanzas 109-126, the mirror sequence, to the already complete manuscript version before he published the poem in 1596.

The final version of the poem appeared in 1622, nearly twenty years after the succession had been peacefully settled. The 1622 version substitutes a dedication to Prince Charles for the earlier one to Richard Martin, who had died a few years earlier. Stanzas 127-131, which contain veiled allusions to poets popular in the 1590's, are omitted. Following stanza 126 there is the curious note: "Here are wanting some stanzas describing Queen Elizabeth. Then follow these." Ironically, the five new stanzas (132-136) contain a description of Queen Elizabeth. The printer seems to have confused these stanzas in manuscript and not known where to insert them; to conceal his confusion he added a note suggesting that something had been left out and merely printed the stanzas at the end of the text. These technical bibliographical issues are discussed in articles listed below in the bibliography.

When the stanzas are reordered and inserted in the appropriate places, it is clear that in this version Davies did intend to suggest that Queen Penelope accepted the invitation to dance. The invocation to Urania is omitted, and the poem concludes with stanza 126. Davies, looking back nostalgically on the Elizabethan court of his youth, suggests that Elizabeth's reign was indeed England's Golden Age.

*Hymnes of Astraea*, twenty-six acrostic lyrics, celebrate Queen Elizabeth as Astraea, the just virgin, who left the earth after the end of the Golden Age; these hymns suggest that the English Virgin Queen is an embodiment of Astraea who has returned to usher in the golden age of England. The number twenty-six was associated with the astrological sign of the constellation

Virgo, and Virgo, in turn, was associated with Astraea, the just virgin. In *Orchestra* Davies indicated that "the fairest sight that ever shall be seene" would occur when "sixe and twenty hundreth yeeres are past" (stanza 121). This reference demonstrates his awareness of the Virgo-Astraea tradition and his desire to associate it with Elizabeth, who, by deciding the succession question, could bring a new golden age to England.

*Hymnes of Astraea* is an artful and brilliantly sustained tour de force. Each of the twenty-six acrostic lyrics contains sixteen lines divided into stanzas of five, five, and six. In all twenty-six Davies follows a regular rhyme pattern of aabab ccdcd in the first two stanzas, with occasional variations from the dominant pattern of eefggf in the third stanzas. The meter is predominantly iambic tetrameter. *Hymnes of Astraea* was entered in the Stationers' Register on November 17, 1599, the Queen's Accession Day. Intended as an Accession Day tribute, the initial letters of the lines read downward spell the royal name: ELISABETHA REGINA.

## Major publications other than poetry

NONFICTION: *Discoverie of the True Causes why Ireland was never entirely Subdued, nor brought under Obedience of the Crowne of England, until the beginning of His Majesties happie raigne*, 1612; *Le Premer Report des Cases et Matters en Ley*, 1615; *Abridgement* of Sir Edward Coke's *Reports*, 1651; *The Question concerning Impositions, Tonnage, Poundage, Prizage, Customs*, 1656.

## Bibliography

Brink, J. R. "The Composition Date of Sir John Davies' *Nosce Teipsum*," in *The Huntington Library Quarterly*. XXXVII (1973), pp. 19-32.

——————— . "The Rhetorical Structure of Sir John Davies' *Nosce Teipsum*," in *Yearbook of English Studies*. IV (1974), pp. 52-61.

——————— . "Sir John Davies' *Orchestra*: Political Symbolism and Textual Revision," in *Durham University Journal*. LXXII (1980), pp. 195-201.

——————— . "The 1622 Edition of Sir John Davies' *Orchestra*," in *The Library*. XXX (1975), pp. 25-33.

Sanderson, James L. *Sir John Davies*, 1975.

Wilkes, G. A. "The Poetry of Sir John Davies," in *The Huntington Library Quarterly*. XXV (1962), pp. 283-298.

Yates, Frances. "Elizabeth as Astraea," in *Journal of the Warburg and Courtauld Institutes*. X (1947), pp. 27-82.

*Jeanie R. Brink*

# CECIL DAY LEWIS

**Born:** Balintubber, Ireland; April 27, 1904
**Died:** London, England; May 22, 1972

**Principal poems and collections**
*Beechen Vigil and Other Poems*, 1925; *Country Comets*, 1928; *Transitional Poem*, 1929; *From Feathers to Iron*, 1931; *The Magnetic Mountain*, 1933; *Collected Poems, 1929-1933*, 1935; *A Time to Dance and Other Poems*, 1935; *Noah and the Waters*, 1936; *Overtures to Death and Other Poems*, 1938; *Poems in Wartime*, 1940; *Selected Poems*, 1940; *Georgics*, 1940 (translation); *Word over All*, 1943; *Short Is the Time: Poems, 1936-1943*, 1945; *Cemetery by the Sea*, 1947 (translation); *Poems, 1943-1947*, 1948; *Collected Poems, 1929-1936*, 1948; *Selected Poems*, 1951; *The Aeneid*, 1952 (translation); *An Italian Visit*, 1953; *Collected Poems*, 1954; *The Newborn: D.M.B., 29th April 1957*, 1957; *Pegasus and Other Poems*, 1957; *The Gate and Other Poems*, 1962; *Eclogues*, 1963 (translation); *Requiem for the Living*, 1964; *A Marriage Song for Albert and Barbara*, 1965; *The Room and Other Poems*, 1965; *Day Lewis: Selections from His Poetry*, 1967 (Patric Dickinson, editor); *Selected Poems*, 1967; *The Abbey That Refused to Die: A Poem*, 1967; *The Whispering Roots*, 1970; *The Poems, 1925-1972*, 1977 (Ian Parsons, editor).

**Other literary forms**
Cecil Day Lewis' fiction can easily be placed into three categories, the first being the novels published prior to World War II: *The Friendly Tree* (1936), *Starting Point* (1937), and *Child of Misfortune* (1939). Then, under the pseudonym of Nicholas Blake, he became a significant contributor to the popular genre of detective fiction. Finally, there are two pieces of juvenile fiction.

Day Lewis' output was, however, not confined to fiction and poetry. He also produced a large body of literary criticism, editorial projects, and translations.

**Achievements**
Cecil Day Lewis was the most conscientious poet laureate in England's history—even surpassing Alfred, Lord Tennyson in his conception of the laureate's responsibilities. During his tenure, from 1968 until his death in 1972, a period in which he suffered from illness, Day Lewis produced a lengthy list of poems on national and topical themes, a majority of which stand on their own poetic merits, as opposed to personal and shallow tributes to specific royal personages. Indeed, during his period as the nation's laureate, Day Lewis underscored his own importance as a contributor to English poetry, as one who understood and accepted the tradition of English poetry and significantly enlarged upon it.

Day Lewis' poetic achievement was marked by a flexible attitude toward the political and social temper of his times. He never withdrew to some private shelter to ponder future poetical-political courses of action or to brood over loss or misfortune. On the contrary, he viewed poetry as being exceedingly public and the poet as being the property of that public. Thus, he tried to share himself and his work with as many people as possible through books of and about poetry for children, through lectures and radio broadcasts about poetry, and through societies and festivals for advancing the general state of the poetic art. Particularly in the later stages of his career when he served as laureate, Day Lewis spent almost as much time writing and talking *about* poetry as he did creating poems. His appointment, in 1951, as Professor of Poetry at Oxford allowed him, still further, to perform a distinct service to his art.

Finally, Day Lewis' achievement may be observed in the nature of his own work as a representation of what may conveniently be termed the poetry of the mid-twentieth century. The poetry of Cecil Day Lewis indeed represents the conflict within the modern poet of that period, a conflict between the old and the new. In *A Hope for Poetry* (1934), he elaborated upon that conflict as a confrontation between the idea of the poet forging ahead to shape a new society and a new society shaping artists in its own image.

Such poems as "The Conflict," "The Double Vision," "Marriage of Two," "The Misfit," and "The Neurotic" capture effectively the degrees of uncertainty that Day Lewis sensed about people of his place and time. He understood well the old injustices that prompted, in turn, men and women to perform new injustices against one another. For him, poetry served society by asking questions about those conflicts, by probing moral problems for answers to some very difficult questions. In the act of poetic questioning, he sought not only a personal answer, but also one that would best serve the social good.

## Biography

Cecil Day Lewis was born in 1904 at Ballintubber, Queen's County, in Ireland, where his father, the Reverend F. C. Day-Lewis, served as a curate. His mother, Kathleen Blake Squires, claimed distant relationship to Oliver Goldsmith, while the poet himself once reported a connection between his grandmother and the family of William Butler Yeats. The original name of the paternal family had been, simply, Day; the family later acquired the Lewis and then carried both names in hyphenated form. However, the poet discarded the hyphen for the purpose of practicing what he termed, in his autobiographical *The Buried Day* (1960), "inverted snobbery."

In 1907, when Day Lewis was only three years of age, the family severed its Irish connection and moved to England; by age six, the youngster had achieved some competence as a writer of verse. His pursuit of formal learning took him first to Sherborne School (Dorsetshire), then to Wadham College, Oxford, where he developed a particular interest in Latin poetry. He published *Beechen Vigil and Other Poems* while still an undergraduate, and spent the years between his departure from Oxford and the onset of World War II writing poetry and teaching English in a number of public schools in England and Scotland: Summer Fields, Oxford (1927-1928); Larchfield, Helensburgh, on the Firth of Clyde (1928-1930)—where he was succeeded by W. H. Auden; and Cheltenham College, Gloucestershire (1930-1935). With the publication of *Collected Poems, 1929-1933* and *A Question of Proof* (1935, the first detective story by Nicholas Blake), Day Lewis abandoned pedagogy for full-time authorship, although he would return to teaching and lecturing on a far more sophisticated level after World War II.

During the war, the poet worked for the Ministry of Information, after which he received a number of prestigious academic appointments: Clark Lecturer, Cambridge (1946); Warton Lecturer, British Academy, London (1951); Professor of Poetry, Oxford (1951-1956); Byron Lecturer, University of Nottingham (1952); Chancellor Dunning Lecturer, Queen's University, Kingston, Ontario (1954); Sidgwick Lecturer, University of Cambridge (1956); Norton Professor of Poetry, Harvard (1964-1965); and Compton Lecturer, University of Hull (1968). Day Lewis also served as director of the publishing house of Chatto and Windus, London, from 1954 until his death, as well as being a member of the Arts Council of Great Britain from 1962 to 1967. His most significant appointment and honor came in 1968, when he succeeded John Masefield (who died on May 12, 1967) as Poet Laureate of England. Although the list of candidates was never published, speculation as to his competition focused upon such names as Richard Church, Robert Graves, Edmund Blunden, and W. H. Auden. The last named had, by then, however, become an American citizen, while the first three poets were all more than seventy years of age. As matters turned out, Day Lewis' tenure as Laureate lasted only four years.

The poet's first marriage was to Constance Mary King in 1928; upon their divorce in 1951, he married Jill Balcon. His last residence was at Crooms Hill, outside London and west of Greenwich Park. After his death on May 22, 1972, Day Lewis' body was transferred for burial at Stinsford, Dorsetshire (one mile east of Dorchester), where he lies today, close to the remains of Thomas Hardy, whom he greatly admired.

**Analysis**

During his Oxford years and the period of his preparatory school teaching, Cecil Day Lewis published his first volumes of poetry: *Beechen Vigil and Other Poems*, followed by *Country Comets*. Both constitute a high level of juvenile verse, the products of a student who had studied much about poets and poetry, but who had learned little about life and had experienced even less. The two books demonstrate, however, that, prior to the age of twenty-five, Day Lewis had essentially mastered the craft of poetry. Further, the two volumes established that for him, a book of verse would emerge as a unified, thematic whole rather than merely as a collection of miscellaneous pieces.

The poet's earliest conflicts arose out of his inability to distinguish clearly the old values of his present and past worlds from the newly emerging ones of the present and the future. In two poems, for example, "Juvenilia" and "Sketches for a Portrait," the young man of privileged and comfortably secure economic class confronts a fundamental social problem: whether to continue to accept without question or challenge, the comfortable conventions of his class, or to look beyond both the class and the comforts in an attempt to understand and then to identify with the problems of people who exist totally outside his sphere of experience and values. Day Lewis inserts into the poetic environment high garden walls that protect the young man's neatly manicured lawn from the grime of the outside, but, certainly, the day must come when the dirt will filter through the wall and smudge the laurel. Then what?

The answers to that question did not come quickly or easily. Instead, in three separate volumes, Day Lewis portrayed the complexity of human experience as it unfolded in several stages. The first, entitled *Transitional Poem*, represents a form of self-analysis wherein the poet initially rejected the romantic nature worship of the preceding century as no solution to what he perceived as the mind's "own forked speculation." At twenty-five, Day Lewis had little or no sympathy for those among his contemporaries who appeared as "intellectual Quixotes," propagandizing abstract values and superficial critical criteria. As a poet he sought, instead, to harness the chaos of a disordered world and beget a new age built upon the "crest of things," upon the commonplace "household stuff, stone walls, mountains and trees/ [that] Placard the day with certainties." Further, the word of the artist, of the twentieth century poet, cannot be allowed, like the Word of God, to stand remote and free from actuality. Instead, poetry must return to life: "Wrenching a stony song from a scant acre/ The Word still justifies its Maker."

Two years later, in 1931, Day Lewis continued his spiritual self-analysis in *From Feathers to Iron*. The title of the piece came from an observation by John Keats: "We take but three steps from feathers to iron," in reference to the maturation process from a theoretical perception of life to an actual understanding of human existence. In this series of lyric poems, Day Lewis considered the theme of experience within the context of marriage and parenthood. Love, he maintained, cannot endure without the presence of children; two years seems the limit for the love of husband and wife to be "marooned on self-sufficiency," and thus new dimensions must be added to the union. The poems in the volume concern fertility, the passion and the pain involved with the anguish of birth, and the hope that fatherhood may end what the poet terms the "indeterminate quarrel between a fevered head and a cold heart." The narrator of the volume occupies the long period of expectation with poems to both mother and child, while the final days seem to him "numb with crisis, cramped with waiting"; after man and wife have, together, explored the extremes of pain and fear, deliverance finally arrives and the multifaceted experience draws to a close. Day Lewis may well have been the first to attempt, in verse, a serious analysis of marriage as it relates to birth and parenthood, placing it squarely within the context of the modern world, in the midst of its complexities and technological by-products.

Careful readers may sense, in the final of the three works—*The Magnetic Mountain*—the influences of Gerard Manley Hopkins and W. H. Auden. Day Lewis divided the piece into four major sections, the beginning being especially reminiscent of Hopkins' "The Windhover." The poet invokes a "kestrel joy, O hoverer in wind," as he searches 'beyond the railheads of reason" for a "magnetic mountain," for truth. He proposes to follow his friends—Auden and Rex Warner—along the political path toward truth, where, in the second section, he surveys some politically reactionary types: a clinging mother, a conventional schoolmaster, a priest, and a "domestic" man. Then, in the third section, Day Lewis exposes what he believes to be the real enemies of progress: the flattering spell of love, popular education and information, the "religion" of science, and false romantic ideals. The poem ends with a series of lyrics extolling a social effort governed by the duality of twentieth century man—as soarer ("windhover") and as an earthbound creature. Criticism of *The Magnetic Mountain* focuses upon the issue of influence; some critics maintain that it contains too much of Auden's political and social thought, not enough of Hopkins' language and rhythm, and even less of Day Lewis' own voice.

Although the emphasis in *Transitional Poem, From Feathers to Iron*, and *The Magnetic Mountain* may appear social and spiritual, the political implications of the three volumes should not be ignored. Scholars generally have been attentive to the political philosophy of the early, prewar poetry of Day Lewis, particularly in the light of the poet's interest, in company with a number of his intellectual and artistic contemporaries, in Communism as the principal healing agent for an economically and politically sick world. Day Lewis' excursions along the highways of Marxist philosophy, however, do not provide an adequate background needed to evaluate his work of the 1930's. Certainly a knowledge of his Communist sympathies helps to clarify certain attitudes and methods, particularly his bullying tone or even outright contempt toward middle-class men and women in pursuit of little else beyond their contented, individualistic careers. Nevertheless, standing steadily behind the signposts of political ideology can be seen the beauty and the momentum created by the language of poetry—*not* by the language of politics. Poetically, the pieces depend very little on their topical content, especially now, fifty years or so after the specific events have faded into the clouds of history. To his credit,

Day Lewis remained a poet and held fast to the principles of his art—as did Auden and Stephen Spender, and as did George Orwell in his fiction. Although Day Lewis tried his hand at political pamphleteering, especially when his passions gained the upper hand, he could not function for very long in that capacity.

Once Day Lewis had turned away from politics, his poetry reaped considerable artistic profit from force and economy. During the 1930's, the young poet struggled to find some use for the dominant images of the modern world, especially for modern industry and transportation. Similarly, he appeared uncomfortable, sometimes overly aggressive, in his attempts to find a place for the serenities of nature amidst the noise and the movement generated by his political themes. After 1939, however, even with the coming of world conflict, Day Lewis seemed eager to turn toward nature, to write as a true child of the provinces, as one who delighted in plowed fields, elevated tracts of land, and cloud formations, in air and in landscape; as one who sought to inject a positive spirit into his poetry after so many years of despair, disillusionment, and political frustration. "For me there is no dismay," he announced in *Word over All*, seemingly struck "Dumb as a rooted rock" by the tragedy of world events. Nevertheless, despite his unveiled Georgian mood, he could still communicate with a nation at war, declaring, in "The Assertion," that "Now is the time we assert/ To their face that men are love. . . ." Again, in "Lidice," he recognized the complexity and the composition of humanity, the good and the evil that existed everywhere and at all times, and he understood that "The pangs we felt from . . . atrocious hurt/ Promise a time when the killer shall see/ His sword is aimed at his own naked heart."

In *From Feathers to Iron* and *The Magnetic Mountain*, despite certain inclinations toward themes of social unrest, political upheaval, and general radicalism, Day Lewis rarely lost sight of the form and function of lyric poetry, of the beauty and the rhythm of poetic language. Both during and after the war, he intensified his mastery of and reliance upon the love song, especially those tender poems in which he attempted to trace the effect of love on the personality, as in "The Lighted House" and "The Album." With his change in thematic emphasis came, of course, certain regrets, particularly over having lost the wildness, the excitement, the rapture of youth. Thus, in "The Rebuke," the love song serves well as a means of asking some penetrating questions about "the sparks at random," the "spendthrift fire, the holy fire"; all that has passed without having left its proper, natural effect, and it is now too late to do anything about it. Day Lewis' lyric poetry is firmly in the tradition of Richard Lovelace, Andrew Marvell, and Alfred, Lord Tennyson; during his later years, he never really strayed far from those models.

The most ambitious and impressive volume of Day Lewis' poetry appeared in 1953 under the title *An Italian Visit*. The book consists of a long work divided into seven parts: "Dialogue at the Airport," "Flight to Italy," "A Letter from Rome," "Bus to Florence," "Florence: Works of Art," "Elegy Before Death: At Settignano," and "The Homeward Prospect." In this work Day Lewis has changed his poetic mood from an austere evangelizing spirit to an acceptance of a lighter, more genial mode of existence. He describes those who flowered in the 1930's as "an odd lot," "sceptical yet susceptible,/ Dour though enthusiastic." The poem is an intellectual travel book, a voyage of discovery not only of scenes and cities but also of the latent faculties of the traveler's mind and heart. Day Lewis' traveler, however, is a composite of three people who, in turn, reflect three aspects of the poet's own personality: Tom's concern is for the present, and Dick looks to the past; Harry, on the other hand, focuses upon neither, but searches the future for the truth. Tom takes his pleasure in the immediate moment as he seeks to gratify the senses through "The real, royal, vulgar pageant—/ Time flying like confetti or twirled in rosettes." Dick, the scholar, thinker, artist, and lover of the perfect, evaluates the present through the supreme achievements of the past ("Reaching across generations to find the parent stock"), while Harry—a sociologist, rationalist, brooder upon the human condition, and seeker of reality under appearances—sees the world as a "provocative, charming/ Strip-tease universe."

At the conclusion of the holiday, each traveler returns to England after having experienced a different Italy: Tom returns "enriched," Dick "sobered," and Harry "lightened." Two sections of the poem, "Florence: Works of Art" and "Elegy Before Death: At Settignano," stand apart from the five. In the former, Day Lewis seems to have had a grand time practicing parodies of the styles of Thomas Hardy, W. B. Yeats, Robert Frost, W. H. Auden, and Dylan Thomas—all poets whom he enthusiastically endorsed and admired. The "Settignano" section is a stark contrast, a profoundly moving meditation on the subjects of love, time, and mortality. The ark of love embarks through a "pinprick of doubt into the dark," wherein "a whole life is drained off," while in "Rhadamanthine" moments lovers find "a chance to make our flux/ Stand and deliver its holy spark." Merely a quick glance at the first and second generation Romantic poets of the nineteenth century reveals how well Day Lewis has extended the conventions of meditative verse and has done so without any perverse effort at originality for its own sake. For him, the traditions still hold.

Perhaps the most appealing human quality of Day Lewis' poetry is his natural hesitancy and inconsistency. Throughout his literary career, marked by political, social, and philosophical sampling and experimentation, he never once embraced the banner of unwavering certainty—the standard of false intellectual pride. He was, indeed, a poet of several points of view who spoke—as in *An Italian Visit*—in and through several voices, a modest thinker and artist who needed to work within a poetic tradition.

In the postwar poems and beyond, Day Lewis seemed to find his tradition. He came to understand what may be termed his "Englishness," his need for skeptical inquiry into himself and his world. That tradition bred and nurtured such authors as Robert Burns, William Barnes, and Thomas Hardy. Day Lewis had learned, from Hopkins and especially from Hardy, that the poet did not have to obligate himself to the smart and the fashionable; he had learned that the poet's responsibility rested upon the freedom to create his own personal atmosphere of seriousness and charm. After he cast off the restrictive mantle of fashionable radicalism, after he endured the tragedy of world war, Day Lewis found his freedom, his tradition, and his own poetic voice.

## Major publications other than poetry

NOVELS: *A Question of Proof*, 1935; *The Friendly Tree*, 1936; *Starting Point*, 1937; *Child of Misfortune*, 1939; *Malice in Wonderland*, 1940; *The Case of the Abominable Snowman*, 1941; *Minute for Murder*, 1947; *A Tangled Web*, 1956; *The Deadly Joker*, 1963; *The Private Wound*, 1968.

PLAY: *Noah and the Waters*, 1945.

NONFICTION: *A Hope for Poetry*, 1934; *Revolution in Writing*, 1935; *The Poetic Image*, 1947; *The Colloquial Element in English Poetry*, 1947; *The Poet's Task*, 1951; *The Poet's Way of Knowledge*, 1957; *The Buried Day*, 1960; *The Lyric Impulse*, 1965; *A Need for Poetry?*, 1968.

## Bibliography

Bullough, Geoffrey. *The Trend of Modern Poetry*, 1949.
Daiches, David. *Poetry and the Modern World*, 1969.
Dyment, Clifford. *C. Day Lewis*, 1955.
Hopkins, Kenneth. *The Poets Laureate*, 1966.
Riddel, Joseph N. *C. Day Lewis*, 1971.
Stanford, Derek. *Stephen Spender, Louis MacNeice, Cecil Day Lewis: A Critical Essay*, 1969.

*Samuel J. Rogal*

# THOMAS DEKKER

**Born:** London, England; c. 1572
**Died:** Clerkenwell(?), London, England; August, 1632 (?)

**Principal works**

*Old Fortunatus*, 1599 (play and poetry); *The Shoemaker's Holiday*, 1599 (play and poetry); *The Wonderful Year*, 1603 (prose and poetry); *The Honest Whore, Part I*, 1604 (with Thomas Middleton, play and poetry); *The Honest Whore, Part II*, c. 1605 (play and poetry); *The Double PP*, 1605 (prose and poetry); *Lanthorn and Candlelight*, 1608 (prose and poetry); *Dekker His Dream*, 1620 (prose and poetry); *The Virgin Martyr*, c. 1620 (with Philip Massinger, play and poetry); *The Witch of Edmonton*, 1621 (with Samuel Rowley and John Ford, play and poetry); *The Sun's Darling*, 1624 (with John Ford, play and poetry).

**Other literary forms**

Thomas Dekker was a prolific author. Although his canon is not easily fixed because of works presumed to be lost, disputed authorship, and revised editions, the sheer number of his publications is impressive. Dekker was primarily a dramatist. By himself he composed more than twenty plays, and he collaborated on as many as forty; more than half of these are not extant today. His plays come in all the genres that theater-hungry Elizabethans loved to devour: city comedies, history plays, classical romances, and domestic tragedies. Additionally, Dekker published about twenty-five prose tracts and pamphlets which catered to a variety of popular tastes: descriptions of London's low-life, collections of humorous and scandalous stories, and jeremiads on the nation's sins and its impending punishment at the hands of an angry God. Dekker found time between writing for the theater and the printing press to compose complimentary verses upon other poets' works and to twice prepare interludes, sketches, and songs for the pageants honoring the Lord Mayor of London.

The best edition of the plays, *The Dramatic Works of Thomas Dekker* (1953-1961), is edited by Fredson Bowers in four volumes. Those tracts dealing with the calamities befalling Stuart London are represented in *The Plague Pamphlets of Thomas Dekker* (1925, F. P. Wilson, editor). The bulk of Dekker's prose and verse is collected in the occasionally unreliable *Non-Dramatic Works of Thomas Dekker* (1884-1885, Alexander B. Grosart, editor, 4 volumes). A more readable and more judicious sampling of the tales and sketches is found in *Thomas Dekker: Selected Prose Writings* (1968, E. D. Pendry, editor).

**Achievements**

A writer such as Dekker, so prolific—almost prodigal—in output, necessarily produces a lot of chaff with his wheat. His plays often lack tightly knit plots and carefully proportioned form; his prose works, especially those satirizing the moral lapses of contemporaries, sometimes belabor the point. Two literary virtues, however, continue to endear Dekker to readers, virtues common to both plays and pamphlets, to both verse and prose.

First, Dekker is always a wordsmith of the highest rank. Although Ben Jonson complained of Dekker and his collaborators that "It's the bane and torment of our ears/ To hear the discords of those jangled rhymers," hardly any reader or critic since has shared the opinion. Since the seventeenth century, Dekker has been universally acknowledged as a gifted poet whose lyrical ability stands out in an age well-stocked with good lyric poets. Charles Lamb's famous pronouncement that Dekker had "poetry for everything" sums up the commonplace modern attitude. Not only Dekker's verse in the plays, however, but also his prose deserves to be called poetic. Dekker's language, whatever its form, is characterized by frequent sound effects, varied diction, and attention to rhythm. Thoroughly at home with Renaissance habits of decorative rhetoric, Dekker seemingly thought in poetry and thus wrote it naturally, effortlessly, and continually.

Second, Dekker's heart is always in the right place. His sympathetically drawn characters seem to come alive as he portrays the people, sights, and events of Elizabethan London. Dekker is often compared with Geoffrey Chaucer and William Shakespeare for his sense of the *comédie humaine*, for knowing the heights and depths of human experience and for still finding something to care about afterward. Dekker's keen observations of life underlie his sharp sense of society's incongruities—and give spice to his portrait gallery of gentlemen, ladies, shoemakers, and tradesmen caught up in the Elizabethan outburst of ambition for gold and glory.

**Biography**

Very few specifics of Thomas Dekker's life are known. He was probably born in 1572, although this date is conjectural. He may have served as a tradesman's apprentice or a sailor before beginning (in 1595?) to write plays for companies of actors. By playwriting and pamphleteering he kept himself alive for the next thirty-seven years. The date of his marriage is uncertain, but it is known that his wife Mary died in 1616. Dekker lived his life almost completely in London, first in Cripplegate and later in Clerkenwell. He was imprisoned for debt on three occasions and once for recusancy. Presumably the Thomas Dekker who was buried in August, 1632, in Clerkenwell parish was Thomas Dekker, playwright and pamphleteer.

Although Dekker's personal life is mostly subject to conjecture, his professional career can be more closely followed. It revolves around three intertwining themes: the dramatic collaborations, the pamphlets, and a life-long struggle against poverty. No one knows how Dekker's career started, but by

1598, he was writing plays alone or jointly for Philip Henslowe. Henslowe owned and managed the Rose Theatre, where he commissioned writers to compose plays for his prime tenants, an acting company called the Lord Admiral's Men. In 1598 alone, Dekker had a hand in fifteen plays (all now lost) which Henslowe commissioned. The sheer quantity indicates how audiences must have clamored for new productions, and some of the titles indicate the taste of the age for popularizations of history (*The First Civil Wars in France*), reworkings of classical tales (*Hannibal and Hermes*), and current stories of eccentric persons or scandalous events (*Black Batman of the North*). All of the plays on which Dekker worked had catchy titles: *The Roaring Girl* (c. 1610), *The Honest Whore*, *The Witch of Edmonton*, *Match Me in London* (c. 1613), to name a few.

As early as 1600, Dekker was writing for companies other than the Lord Admiral's Men. In the course of his career he would write for the leading acting companies of the time: the Children of St. Paul's, the Prince's Men, the Palsgrave's Men, and the Players of the Revels. More varied than his employers were his collaborators: as a young man Dekker worked with Michael Drayton, Ben Jonson, George Chapman, Henry Chettle, and even William Shakespeare. When he returned to the theater as an older man, the new young scriptwriters—a veritable "Who's Who" of Jacobean dramatists, including John Ford, Samuel Rowley, John Marston, Philip Massinger, and John Webster—worked with him.

Since his employers and collaborators changed so often, it is not surprising that at least once the intense dramatic rivalry characteristic of the age embroiled Dekker in controversy. In 1600, he was drafted into the brief but vitriolic "War of the Theatres" which had begun in the previous year when Marston satirized Jonson as a boorish and presumptuous poet. Jonson returned the compliment by poking fun at Marston in two plays and tried to anticipate a Marston-Dekker rejoinder with a third play, *Poetaster* (1601), which compares them to "screaming grasshoppers held by the wings." Marston and Dekker retaliated with *Satiromastix* (1601), an amalgam of tragic, comic, and tragicomic plots, portraying Jonson as a slow-witted and slow-working poet for hire.

In 1603, Dekker was forced to find another line of work when an outbreak of the plague closed the theaters. He produced a pamphlet, *The Wonderful Year*, which recounted the death of the Queen, Elizabeth I, the accession of James I, and the coming of the disease that scourged mankind's folly. In the next six years, Dekker published more than a dozen pamphlets designed to capitalize on readers' interest in current events and the city's criminal sub-culture. In his pamphlets, as in his plays, Dekker provides a panorama of cutpurses, pimps, courtesans, apprentices, and similar types; he paints scenes of busy streets and records the sounds of loud voices, creaking carriages, and thumped pots. Dekker's purpose is not that of the local colorist who preserves such scenes simply because they typify a time and place. Rather, his interest is that of the moralist who sees the side of city life that the upper classes would like to ignore and that the academics shrug off as part of the necessary order of things.

Dekker himself knew this low world intimately—at least he never seems to have gotten into the higher. Unlike his fellow writers Jonson and Shakespeare or the actor Edward Alleyn, Dekker could not or did not take advantage of the aristocracy's interest in the theater to secure for himself consistent patronage and financial stability. Playwriting seems to have brought Dekker only a few pounds per play: despite his prodigious outburst of fifteen collaborations in 1598, he was arrested for debt that year and the next. Fourteen years later, while both publishing pamphlets and writing plays, Dekker was again imprisoned for debt at the King's Bench, a prison notorious for its mismanagement. He remained in debtors' prison for six or seven years (1613-1619).

No wonder, then, that money is one of Dekker's favorite themes and gold one image to which he devotes loving attention. He neither worships the almighty guinea nor scorns sinful lucre. On the one hand, Dekker likes money: his best characters make shrewd but kindly use of the stuff; they work, and their labor supports them. He sometimes sees even confidence games as offshoots of a healthy capitalistic impulse. Old Fortunatus' claim, "Gold is the strength, the sinnewes of the world,/ The Health, the soule, the beautie most divine," may be misguided, but Dekker understands the impulse. He forgives prodigals easily. On the other hand, Dekker expects generosity from moneymakers. Even virtuous persons who do not use their wealth well come to bad ends; those who refuse to help the needy he assigns to the coldest regions of hell. According to E. D. Pendry in *Thomas Dekker: Selected Prose Writings*, the use of money is for Dekker an index of morality: virtue flows from its proper use and vice from its improper.

The last decade of Dekker's life was a repetition of the previous three. He wrote for the theater, published pamphlets, and teetered on the edge of debt. Though his life was hard and his social rank was low, Dekker generally wrote as if his literary trade was, like the shoemaker's, a truly gentle craft.

**Analysis**

Most of Thomas Dekker's best poetry is found in his plays; unfortunately, since most of his plays were collaborations, it is often difficult to assign particular poetic passages to Dekker, and perhaps even harder to assign the larger poetic designs to him. He is, however, generally credited with most of the poetry in *Old Fortunatus* and *The Honest Whore, Parts I* and *II*. He wrote the delightfully poetic *The Shoemaker's Holiday* almost unaided. Mother Sawyer's eloquent poetry in *The Witch of Edmonton* so closely resembles portions of his long pamphlet-poem, *Dekker His Dream*, as to make it all but certainly his. Songs and verses occupy varying proportions of his journalistic works, from a few lines in *The Wonderful Year*, to several songs in *Lanthorn and Candlelight*, to most of *The Double PP*. In all his plays, verse comprises a significant part of the dialogue.

While the quality of thought and care in organization vary from work to work and almost from line to line in a given work, the quality of the sound rarely falters. According to George Price in *Thomas Dekker* (1969), one poem long attributed to Dekker, *Canaan's Calamitie* (1598), has been excluded from the canon largely because of the inferior music of its verse. Critics often attach words such as "sweet," "lovely," "gentle," and "compassionate" to Dekker's most popular passages, and the adjectives seem to cover both sound and theme in works such as *Old Fortunatus* and *The Shoemaker's Holiday*.

An old-fashioned production in its own day, *Old Fortunatus* weaves a morality pageant in which the goddess Fortune and her attendants witness a power struggle between Virtue and Vice with a loose chronicle play about a man to whom Fortune grants a choice. Instead of health, strength, knowledge, and wisdom, old Fortunatus chooses riches. His wealth and native cunning enable him to steal knowledge (in the form of a magic hat). After Fortune claims the old man's life, his sons Ampedo and Andelocia, inheriting his magic purse and hat and make no better use of them than their father had done. Greedy Andelocia abducts a princess, plays assorted pranks at various courts, and ends up strangled by equally greedy courtiers; virtuous Ampedo wrings his hands, eventually burns the magic hat, and dies in the stocks, unmourned even by Virtue. Structurally, *Old Fortunatus* has the odd elegance of medieval drama. Fortune, Virtue, and Vice enter the human world five times, usually with song and emblematic show designed to judge men or to point out the choices open to them.

The play's allegorical pageantry demanded elaborate costuming and equally elaborate verse, ranging from songs in varied meters and tones to dialogues that are often more incantation than blank verse speech:

> *Kings*: Accursed Queen of chaunces, damned sorceresse.
> *The Rest*: Most pow'rfull Queen of chaunce, dread soveraignesse.
> *Fortune*: . . . [*To the Kings*] curse on: your cries to me are Musicke
> And fill the sacred rondure of mine eares
> With tunes more sweet than moving of the Spheres:
> Curse on.

Most of the chronicle play which is interwoven with the morality pageant employs blank verse liberally sprinkled with prose passages and rhymed couplets. Renaissance notions of decorum set forth rather clear-cut rules governing the use of prose and poetry. An iambic pentameter line was considered the best medium for tragedy and for kings' and nobles' speeches in comedy. Madmen, clowns, and letter-readers in tragedy and lower-class characters in comedy can speak prose. Dekker refines these guidelines. He uses prose for musing aloud, for French and Irish dialects, for talking to servants, and for expressing disappointment or depression: the sons mourn their dead father and have their most violent quarrel in prose. Dekker keys form to mood much as a modern songwriter does when he inserts a spoken passage into the lyrics. Even Dekker's prose, however, is textured like poetry; except for the lack of iambic pentameter rhythm, prose passages are virtually indistinguishable from verse. Typical are the lilting rhythms of the following passage (one of the cruelest in the play): "I was about to cast my little little self into a great love trance for him, fearing his hart was flint, but since I see 'tis pure virgin wax, he shall melt his belly full."

Sound itself is the subject of much comment in the play. Dekker's natural gift for pleasing rhythms, his knack for combining the gentler consonant sounds with higher frequency vowels, and his ear for slightly varied repetitions all combine to make *Old Fortunatus* strikingly beautiful poetry.

The fame of *Old Fortunatus*, however, rests on more than its sound. Dekker's imagery deserves the praise it consistently gets. The Princess's heartless line is one of many that connect melting with the play's values—love, fire, gold, and the sun—in ways that suggest both the purification of dross through the melting process and the fate of rich Crassus. Other images connect the silver moon and stars with music, and both precious metals with an earth producing fruit-laden trees that men use wisely or unwisely. The allegorical figures with their emblematic actions and costumes would heighten the effectiveness of such imagery for a viewing audience, just as hearing the poetry greatly magnifies its impact over silent reading.

In *The Shoemaker's Holiday*, Dekker shows a more sophisticated use of poetry. As in *Old Fortunatus*, he shifts between poetry and prose, depending somewhat on the characters' social class but more on mood, so that in a given scene a character can slip from prose to poetry and back while those around him remain in their normal métier. In the earlier play, however, he made little attempt to connect certain characters with certain sounds or images. In *The Shoemaker's Holiday*, characters have their own peculiar music.

The play combines three plots. In the first, Rowland Lacy disguises himself as Hans, a Dutch shoemaker, in order to avoid being shipped off to war in France, far from his beloved Rose Otley. His uncle, the Earl of Lincoln, and her father, Sir Roger Otley, oppose the love match. In the second, the shoemaker Rafe leaves his young wife Jane to do his country's bidding; later, lamed and supposed dead, he returns to find Jane missing. He rediscovers her just in time to stop her marriage to the rich but shallow Hammon. In the third, master shoemaker Simon Eyre, the employer of Lacy, Rafe, and a crew of journeymen and apprentices, rises by common sense and enthusiastic shop management to become London's merriest Lord Mayor.

Two relatively minor characters illustrate Dekker's poetic sense. The Earl of Lincoln, despite his blank verse, speaks less poetically than most of the other characters, and Eyre's journeyman, Firke, despite his freer prose rhythms, speaks much of the best poetry. Lincoln's decasyllables in the opening scene, for example, summarize Lacy's situation with few rhetorical figures:

> 'Twas now almost a year since he requested
> To travel countries for experiences.
> I furnished him with coin, bills of exchange,
> Letters of credit, men to wait on him.

Lincoln's speech is not absolutely unpoetic. Its rhythm is varied, quickened by added syllables and made natural by inverted feet—but that is all. Lincoln has a prosaic mind; to him Lacy's love is mere nuisance, a mild threat to the family name. Dishonest about his own motives, he presumes that others are likewise motivated by self-interest. Thus, when he speaks, his words slip easily off the tongue, but rarely figure forth the imaginative connections between things that Dekker's other characters display.

By contrast, Firke's lines have more of poetry's verbal texture than does most modern free verse. Asked the whereabouts of the eloped Rose and Lacy, he answers in a pastiche of poetic allusions and a pun on the gold coin that Elizabethans called angels: "No point: shall I betray my brother? no, shall I prove *Judas* to Hans? no, shall I crie treason to my corporation? no, I shall be firkt and yerkt then, but give me your angell, your angell shall tel you." The passage shouts an emphatic dance rhythm, forcefully repeats the focal "no, shall I," employs assonance ("*Judas* to *Hans*"), alliteration ("betray my brother"), and rhyme ("treason to my corporation" and "firkt and yerkt"). It speeds along, then slows to a perfectly cadenced close. The speaker, a boisterous, rowdy, practical joker, is always ready to burst into song, or something so close as to be indistinguishable from song.

Dekker gives these minor characters distinctive poetic voices. To the major characters he gives individualizing linguistic habits. Bluff Simon Eyre's trick of repeating himself would be maddening in a less kindly fellow. He is the only character capable of speaking prose to the king. Hammon, suitor both to Rose and Jane, speaks courtly compliment in light, rhymed couplets in which vows about "life" and "wife" play too heavy a part. Though he enjoys the banter of stychomithic verse, his images are stuffily conventional. As well-born characters, Lacy and Rose naturally speak blank verse. Lacy's voice, however, turns to a quick prose dialect when he is disguised as Hans; Rose occasionally startles by slipping out of her romantic preoccupations into a few lines of practical yet polished prose.

Perhaps the play's best poetry is that which Dekker gives to shoemaker Rafe and seamstress Jane. Surrounded by shopkeepers and unaccustomed to courtly compliment, these two must invent their own poetic images and rhythms. "I will not greeve you,/ With hopes to taste fruite, which will never fall," says Jane to Hammon. Hearing of Rafe's death, she dismisses her persistent suitor with lines remarkable for homespun grace. Rafe, in turn, gives the entire play its thematic unity in two passages which raise shoemaking from a craft to a communal act of love. As he leaves for France, Rafe gives Jane a parting gift: not the jewels and rings that rich men present their wives, but a pair of shoes "cut out by *Hodge*, Sticht by my fellow *Firke*, seam'd by my selfe,/ Made up and pinckt, with letters for thy name." The shoes are the epitome of the shoemaker's art, and they are individually Jane's. Dekker returns to the image at a pivotal point after Rafe comes home from the war. The shoes, now old and needing replacement, lead Rafe to reunion with the missing Jane. His homely poetry, the most original in a play full of original language, is more touching than preposterous:

> . . . this shoe I durst be sworne
> Once covered the instep of my *Jane*:
> This is her size, her breadth, thus trod my love,
> These true love knots I prickt, I hold my life,
> By this old shoe I shall find out my wife.

The simple language fits Rafe as well as the shoe fits Jane. In *The Shoemaker's Holiday*, craftsmen know their work as confidently as the master wordsmith Dekker knows his characters' individual voices.

Critics generally agree that the play is Dekker's poetic masterpiece. His other plays contain excellent poetry, nicely tuned to suit persona in sound, mood, and imagery, but none has the range and grace of *The Shoemaker's Holiday*. Of special interest to the student of Dekker's verse are two speeches in *The Honest Whore* plays. In Part I, Hippolito's furious diatribe against whoredom is a virtual monologue, rising in a hundred lines to a fine crescendo, which deserves careful metrical and figural analysis. Its counterpart in Part II, Bellafront's long argument against her former profession, deserves similar attention.

Dekker's pamphlets continue the habit of mixing prose and verse; most of them contain some poetry, if only in the rhymed couplets signifying closure. As early as 1603, in *The Wonderful Year*, he was writing essentially dramatic poetry. In that pamphlet, he includes two poems supposed to be the Prologue and a summary of the action of a play—the "play" of England's reaction to Elizabeth I's death. The poetic section ends with three short epigrams of a deliberately homespun sort. *Lanthorn and Candlelight* further reflects the dramatic in Dekker's poetry. In the opening chapter, poems are couched in cant, a special thieves' jargon. "To cant" means "to sing" but since "canters" are strange, they sing strangely: "Enough! With boozy cove maund nase,/ Tower the patring cove in the darkman case." Dekker includes both a "Canter's Dictionary" (largely plagiarized) and "Englished" translations. His habit of using dramatic voices in poetry finds a logical conclusion in such songs.

Poetry is sporadic in most of Dekker's pamphlets; in *The Double PP* and *Dekker His Dream*, however, it dominates. The former alternates sections of prose and poetry in an exhibition of English nationalism as complete as Simon Eyre's. In an elaborate rhetorical figure, Dekker presents ten kinds of papists as ten chivalric shields attacked by ten well-armed classes of English Protestants. The generally shallow but occasionally penetrating stereotypes show the influence of the current fad for Overburian Characters.

*Dekker His Dream* is a much better poem. Published shortly after his release from seven years in debtor's prison, the work is ostensibly autobiographical. Dekker claims to relate a dream he had after almost seven years of imprisonment in an enchanted cave. Using lines of rhymed iambic pentameter that vary with his subject in tone and tempo, Dekker describes the last day of the world, the final judgment, heaven and hell. Periodically he interrupts the narrative to justify his vision by quoting in prose from scripture or church authorities.

Structurally, *Dekker His Dream* is among his best works, building slowly to a climactic conclusion in which Dekker turns out to be, as William Blake said of John Milton, "of the devil's party." The poem begins with covert reminders of what Dekker himself has recently suffered, then moves vividly through the tale of Earth's destruction. Calmly, it relates the majestic coming of Christ and the harmonious rewards given the good, then turns rather quickly to hell. (In fact, Christ and Heaven occupy eight of Dekker's fifty-two pages.) Like Dante, Dekker secures permission to walk among the damned; he finds a two-part hell. In the first, the cold region, he sees the "rich dogs" who refused to help the poor and sick. Tormented by whips, diseases, snakes, and salamanders, they react with "Yels, teeth-gnashing, chattering, shivering." Then he moves into the traditional fires to find the drunkards, gamblers, adulterers, and gluttons—"millions" of them, whipped and stung with their own longings and with the "worme of conscience." Among them is a young man cursing God and proclaiming loudly as the whips descend that he does not deserve eternal punishment. Dekker gives him a perfectly logical defense: he had only thirty years of life, fifteen of which were spent asleep, five more in childishness, and some at least in good deeds. Nature had given him little—drops of gall from her left breast instead of milk—and his sins were small. His lengthy defense contains some of Dekker's best images and rhythms; it is interrupted by a booming angelic voice which shouts about justice until the rest of the damned, angered, outshout it, waking the poet. Dekker, hands shaking from the experience, concludes that, reading the world, "I found Here worse Devils than are in Hell."

The dream vision has been largely misinterpreted, but close study of the quality of the imagery and the proportions of the whole indicate that Dekker was indeed leading his readers to question the justice shouted by the avenging angel. It is a subtly and effectively composed poem, deserving more attention than it has had.

## Major publications other than poetry

PLAYS: *Old Fortunatus*, 1599 (play and poetry); *The Shoemaker's Holiday*, 1599 (play and poetry); *Patient Grissell*, 1600 (with Henry Chettle and William Haughton); *Satiromastix*, 1601; *Sir Thomas Wyatt*, 1602; *The Honest Whore, Part I*, 1604 (with Thomas Middleton, play and poetry); *Westward Ho!*, 1604 (with John Webster); *The Honest Whore, Part II*, c. 1695 (play and poetry); *Northward Ho!*, 1605 (with John Webster); *The Whore of Babylon*, c. 1606; *The Roaring Girl*, c. 1610 (with Thomas Middleton); *If It Be Not Good, the Devil Is In It*, c. 1611; *Match Me in London*, c. 1613; *The Virgin Martyr*, c. 1620 (with Philip Massinger, play and poetry); *The Witch of Edmonton*, 1621 (with John Ford and Samuel Rowley, play and poetry); *The Wonder of a Kingdom*, 1623 (with John Day); *The Sun's Darling*, 1624 (with John Ford, play and poetry); *The Noble Soldier*, 1631 (with John Day and Samuel Rowley).

MISCELLANEOUS: *The Magnificent Entertainment*, 1603 (with Ben Jonson and Thomas Middleton); *The Wonderful Year*, 1603 (prose and poetry); *The Double PP*, 1605 (prose and poetry); *The Seven Deadly Sins of London*, 1606; *News from Hell*, 1606; *The Bellman of London*, 1608; *Lanthorn and Candle-light*, 1608 (prose and poetry); *The Gull's Hornbook*, 1609; *Dekker His Dream*, 1620 (prose and poetry); *Penny-Wise and Proud-Foolish*, 1630.

## Bibliography

Conover, James H. *Thomas Dekker: An Analysis of Dramatic Structure*, 1969.
Ellis-Fermor, Una. "Dekker," in *The Jacobean Drama*, 1968.
Hunt, Mary L. *Thomas Dekker*, 1964.
Price, George R. *Thomas Dekker*, 1969.

*Robert M. Otten*
*Elizabeth Spalding Otten*

# WALTER DE LA MARE

**Born:** Charlton, Kent, England; April 25, 1873
**Died:** Twickenham, Middlesex, England; June 22, 1956

## Principal collections

*Songs of Childhood*, 1902; *Poems*, 1906; *The Listeners and Other Poems*, 1912; *A Child's Day: A Book of Rhymes*, 1912; *Peacock Pie: A Book of Rhymes*, 1913; *The Sunken Garden and Other Poems*, 1917; *Motley and Other Poems*, 1918; *Flora: A Book of Drawings*, 1919; *Poems 1901 to 1918*, 1920; *Story and Rhyme*, 1921; *The Veil and Other Poems*, 1921; *Down-Adown-Derry: A Book of Fairy Poems*, 1922; *Thus Her Tale*, 1923; *A Ballad of Christmas*, 1924; *Stuff and Nonsense and So On*, 1927; *Self to Self*, 1928; *The Snowdrop*, 1929; *Poems for Children*, 1930; *News*, 1930; *Lucy*, 1931; *Old Rhymes and New*, 1932; *The Fleeting and Other Poems*, 1933; *Poems 1919 to 1934*, 1935; *This Year, Next Year*, 1937; *Memory and Other Poems*, 1938; *Haunted*, 1939; *Bells and Grass*, 1941; *Collected Poems*, 1941; *Collected Rhymes and Verses*, 1944; *The Burning-Glass and Other Poems*, 1945; *The Traveller*, 1946; *Rhymes and Verses: Collected Poems for Young People*, 1947; *Inward Companion*, 1950; *Winged Chariot*, 1951; *O Lovely England and Other Poems*, 1953; *The Complete Poems*, 1969.

## Other literary forms

Walter de la Mare was a prolific author of fiction and nonfiction as well as poetry. His novels include modern adult fiction, such as *Memoirs of a Midget* (1921), and fiction for children, such as *The Three Mulla-Mulgars* (1910). His short stories fit into a variety of traditional genres; many are tales of the supernatural. The interests which manifest themselves in the poetry and fiction are more explicitly revealed in de la Mare's essays and his work as an editor. Not much given to analysis, as a critic he was primarily an appreciator and interpreter, much as he was as a poet. Of the anthologies he edited, *Behold, This Dreamer!* (1939) is perhaps the most revealing of the influences that de la Mare particularly valued in his work as a poet.

## Achievements

De la Mare was one of the most popular poets of his time. Since his death his reputation has faded. His verse sometimes sounds too romantic for the sensibilities of a modern audience. Yet, his children's verse remains in print, and the best of his adult poetry remains standard for inclusion in anthologies of twentieth century English poets. The present moderate eclipse of the popularity of his poetry is probably temporary, because his best verse has those iconoclastic qualities that make such poets as William Blake stand out from ordinary poets.

De La Mare's sensibility is deeply rooted in the Romanticism of the nineteenth century, and, like the works of Rudyard Kipling and George Bernard Shaw, his writings often seem reminiscent of the Victorian Age. Nevertheless, his subjects were from the twentieth century, and the resultant mixture of contemporary realism and Romantic style make him special among major poets. Of the various poetic modes represented in his works, the lyric was the one with which de la Mare had his greatest artistic success; he ranks among the best lyric poets in the English language, and he may be the best English lyric poet of his era. In his mastery of poetic form and metaphor, de la Mare compares favorably with the best the English language has to offer.

His blend of romance and realism, of the supernatural with the commonplace, inspired poets of his day. The term *delamarian* was coined sometime during de la Mare's middle years, and it is still used to identify works that employ techniques that are best represented by his work. The coinage of such a term is evidence of the esteem in which de la Mare was held by many of his contemporaries, and of the unique blend of form and ideas that makes him one of the twentieth century's best poets.

**Biography**

No full-length biography of Walter de la Mare has as yet been published. He was, by the few published accounts of those who knew him, a quiet and unremarkable man. One can reasonably infer from the absence of autobiographical material from an otherwise prolific writer that he was a private man. He seems to have lived his adventures through his writing, and his primary interests seem to have been of the intellect and the spirit.

He was born in 1873 to James Edward de la Mare and Lucy Sophia Browning de la Mare, a Scot. He attended St. Paul's Cathedral Choir School. While in school he founded and edited *The Choiristers' Journal*, a school magazine. In 1890, Walter de la Mare entered the employ of the Anglo-American Oil Company, where he served as bookkeeper until 1908. During these years he wrote essays, stories, and poetry, which appeared in various magazines, including *Black and White* and *The Sketch*. In 1902, *Songs of Childhood*, his first book—and one of his most lastingly popular—was published. There he used the pseudonym "Walter Ramal." Then, after using it also for his novel *Henry Brocken* in 1904, he dropped it. He married Constance Elfrida Igpen in 1899, with whom he had two sons and two daughters. She died in 1943.

De la Mare's employment at the Anglo-American Oil Company ended in 1908, when he was granted a Civil List pension of one hundred pounds a year. Thus encouraged, he embarked on a life of letters during which he produced poetry, short stories, essays, and one play, and edited volumes of poetry and essays. These many works reveal something of de la Mare's intellect, if not of his character. They reveal a preoccupation with inspiration and dreams, an irritation with Freudians and psychologists in general (they were too simplistic in their analyses, he believed), a love of romance, and a love for the child in people. The works reveal a complex mind that, curiously, preferred appreciation to analysis and observation to explanation.

## Analysis

The poetry of Walter de la Mare falls superficially into two groups: poetry for children and poetry for adults. This obvious and misleading division is unfortunate, however, because many readers have come to think of de la Mare as principally an author for children. Much of his poetry is intended for an adult readership; that which is meant for children is complex enough in theme to satisfy demanding adult readers. Much misunderstanding of the nature of de la Mare's poetry comes from its childlike response to the world. De la Mare distinguishes between the typically childlike and adult imagination. Children, he contends, view the world subjectively, making and remaking reality according to their egocentered desires. Adults are more analytical and tend to dissociate themselves from reality; they try to observe reality objectively. De la Mare prefers the childlike view, an inductive rather than deductive understanding of the world. Reality, he believes, is revealed through inspiration, an essentially subjective aspect of human imagination. The modern vogue of discussions of "higher planes of reality" would have had little meaning for de la Mare, but he would approve the notion that there is a reality beyond that which can be objectively observed. Time and nature are tyrants who rule mankind. Their effects can be observed, but they in themselves cannot. To understand the reality of time and nature, the poet uses his imaginative insight. In pursuit of such insight, de la Mare studied dreams; as a poet he strove to describe the world as if observing it while in a waking dream. He attempted to observe as he imagined a child might observe, and because childhood involves a continual discovery of both the physical reality and the spiritual reality of nature, de la Mare's poetry is alive with discovery, wonder, and—as discovery often brings—disappointment with the imperfections of the world.

De la Mare's interest in childlike inspiration led him to write poetry for children. His respect for childlike imagination is reflected in the absence of condescension in his children's verse. In fact, most of it resembles that which he wrote for adults, although his diction is at a level that children can understand. All the major concerns of de la Mare's intellectual life are expressed in his children's verse; in "The Old King" (1922), for example, he discusses death. The "old King of Cumberland" awakens in surprise and looks about his room for what had disturbed him, but all seems normal until he touches his chest "where now no surging restless beat/ Its long tale told." The King's heart has stopped and he is terrified. The whole of the poem is expressed in a manner which children can comprehend, and de la Mare makes three important points: that death is a fact, that there is a reality beyond death, and that death is dreamlike. He never means to frighten his young readers; rather, he means for them to understand. For example, in "Now, Dear Me!" (1912), he describes a fearsome ghost: "A-glowering with/ A chalk-white face/ Out of some dim/ And dismal place." The ghost turns out to be Elizabeth Ann, a child very much alive, done up to frighten her nurse. Children are invited to laugh at the very real fears that their imaginations can create.

A child is unlikely to miss the implied respect for his mind when he reads poetry that clearly states de la Mare's point of view on a subject of moral substance. "Hi!" (1930) is a lyric which presents a hunter's killing an animal: "Nevermore to peep again, creep again, leap again,/ Eat or sleep or drink again, Oh, what fun!" De la Mare's dismay at the killing of wildlife is clear, as is his effort to speak of an important matter to his young readership. Wildlife plays an important role in his poetry. Bears and elephants and other animals are shown as friendly to children. When Elizabeth Ann takes a bath in "Little Birds Bathe" (1912), her tub is invaded by a "Seal and Walrus/ And Polar Bear." A host of other animals join them, from alligators to swans to pumas. Her bath sounds fun, and the poem is as cheerful a depiction of bathing and imagination as one could hope to read. In "Who Really?" (1930), bears and bees share a natural antagonism and similarity—they are both thieves. In "The Holly" (1930), the poet describes the natural beauty of the holly tree. Repeatedly, he depicts nature as other than frightening; it can be awesome, but a child's imagination can render it knowable.

The supernatural and dreams are significant aspects of de la Mare's poetry for youngsters. His verse spans topics from Christianity to pagan mysticism. In "Eden" (1930), he discusses the fall of humanity from God's grace and its effect on all of nature. When the sin of humanity leads to the Great Flood, trees and animals suffer the consequences. Thus, the banishment of Adam and Eve is bewailed by the nightingale. The notion that the fates of Humanity and Nature are linked is unmistakable. Pagan mysticism in the forms of fairies and elves is common children's fare. Typical of de la Mare's respect for his young audience, he offers uncommon fairies. In "The Double" (1922), a fairy child joins a young dancer in a garden. The fairy is at once a reflection of the dancer and a part of the plants in the garden; it is at once substantial and incapable of leaving faintest marks of its footsteps. The poem is a sad evocation of childlike imagination; the fairy child disappears beyond recalling. Fairies and their kin are evocations of the natural world; they respond to people when people respond to nature. They are ephemeral, as much the products of imagination and dreams as of tradition and myth. "The World of Dream" (1912) takes poetic tradition and uses it to portray a child's view of sleep. When dreaming, one often seems to be floating on air or water; death is often described similarly. De la Mare takes his sleeping child on a ride in a boat equipped with "elphin lanterns," a boat with "hundreds of passengers." The misty world of sleep sounds peaceful and much like death.

The connecting of sleep and death is common in literature, yet death is not a customary topic intended for children. Although de la Mare writes for children, he spares them none of the topics that he deems important. Death is a part of nature; it is something that, as "Eden" shows, was brought into nature by mankind. Death is not inherently evil, although killing can be. In de la Mare's poetry, dreams and death are often linked, and he commonly uses dreams to reveal a truer reality than is found in the nondreaming world. Thus, death itself is not meant to be evil or even exceptionally awful. Even so, de la Mare did perceive evil in the world, and children are not spared its presence in his poetry. Evil is not trivialized for the sake of youthful readers. The poet shows children being punished for naughty behavior, as in "This Little Morsel of Morsels Here" (1912), but he does not lay the heavy burden of evil on the filching of gingery sweets: bears can misbehave and so can children. Naughtiness is natural, although undesirable. True evil is profound. It can be personified as a "handsome hunting man" in "Hi!" or as the actions of a child slashing his toy sword through the grasses of a meadow in "The Massacre" (1906). The actions seem innocent, but the child imagines heads lopped off and "dead about my feet." Nature in the form of sunlight and air recoils in horror from the imaginary deeds that in a child foreshadow the potential evil of adulthood.

Most of de la Mare's verse was directed at an adult audience. While his poetry for children reveals the bare forms of his poetic interests, it is primarily cheerful, concentrating on sympathetically helping children to use their imaginations; his adult poetry is more somber and even more mystical. The most famous of de la Mare's poems perhaps best exemplifies his characteristic blending of dreams, the supernatural, and the childlike imagination. "The Listeners" (1912) was once memorized by thousands of schoolchildren; it puzzled and enthralled de la Mare's contemporaries, and it is likely to survive the test of time, retaining its mystical and symbolic power.

In "The Listeners," a Traveller knocks at the door of a house that is at once empty and filled with "a host of phantom listeners." The Traveller smites the door and is answered only by echoes in empty hallways. He repeatedly calls, "Is anybody there?" and listens for replies. Even though no one answers, the Traveller senses the presence of the listeners: "And he felt in his heart their strangeness,/ Their stillness answering his cry." The Traveller strikes the door again and cries out, "Tell them I came, and no one answered,/ That I kept my word." The listeners who lurk in "the shadowiness of the still house" listen to him mount his horse and ride away. Throughout the poem, *silence* is as palpable as sound, and at its conclusion *silence* remains a part of the listeners' house. The poem exhibits the salient traits of most of de la Mare's poetry. Its tone, subject, and events all seem part of a dream, yet it is populated by mundane physical details: a horse dining on grass, the Traveller's "grey eyes," and a "dark stair." The poem's effect is mystification and strangeness; its appeal is emotional, rather than intellectual. The theme of *others* who are near-human beings but cannot be seen nor heard is important to an understanding of de la Mare's work. Humanity is surrounded by spirits and fairies in his poetry. The listeners might be spirits of the dead or of the supernatural world; they might be otherworldly memories of the presences of those who dwelt in the house. Their nature is ambiguous because human experience of the spiritual is usually ambiguous.

The Traveller himself offers another context besides the supernatural. He senses the listeners and speaks to them. His purpose is at once specific and general; he comes to fulfill a promise, but the circumstances under which the promise was made and the people to whom it was made are never presented, leaving ambiguity instead of specifics. The Traveller's purpose is general enough to represent general human purpose; the Traveller is symbolic of all people. The theme of life as a journey marks much of de la Mare's most evocative work, and the idea of humanity as an aggregate of individual travelers is an important part of de la Mare's poetic vision. The Traveller represents people, and the listeners, too, can be people. In a sense, all people are both travellers and listeners, and often communication between people can be vague and uncertain. Often people's purposes are as mysterious to others as is that of the Traveller. Often people are as distant from the lives of others as the listeners are from the Traveller. Typical of much of de la Mare's poetry, "The Listeners" allows multiple readings.

The eerie dream quality of "The Listeners" reflects de la Mare's understanding of the world. A theme that is found from his earliest to his latest poetry is that of reality as dream. The supernatural world can be more substantial than the world of common experience; dreams are at once reflective of how everyday reality compares with the more valid reality of the spirit and are connections between the natural and supernatural. Human beings are parts of both worlds because of their spiritual natures. In "Haunted" (1939), a persona—the poem's speaker—fears "Life, which ever in at window stares." His fear originates in the uncertainty of life: "You say, *This is.* The soul cries, *Only seems.*" What the conscious mind perceives as real the spirit understands as insubstantial. The persona notes "And who, when sleeping, finds unreal his dreams?" Dreams can seem to be real, and thus earthly life can seem to be all there is to existence. Yet in each person is a soul, a part of the supernatural world, and the soul perceives the danger and the reality beyond ordinary physical sensation. In "Haunted," the dangers lie in "the Fiend with his goods," who can turn a seemingly mundane activity into a spiritual threat. Those who inhabit the supernatural world have their own purposes, and human beings can miss seeing those purposes.

Even de la Mare's poetic depictions of contemporary life is imbued with his conception of humanity's mixed relationships with the commonplace and the otherworldly. "The Slum Child" (1933), for example, evokes with carefully selected detail the dreary, unnatural life of an urban child growing up in poverty. The poem features one of de la Mare's favorite topics, children, and one of the fundamental themes of his poetry, that nature is an important part of human experience. The youngster in "The Slum Child" suffers from lack of exposure to nature. The child lives in a world of stone, "lean-faced girls and boys," and beggary. De la Mare employs irony to convey the unnaturalness of the slum childhood, as when his speaker uses the word "harboured": "What evil, and filth, and poverty,/ In childhood harboured me." The best that can be said about childhood in a slum is that it is miserable.

A reader could interpret "The Slum Child" as simply a poem of social protest. De la Mare's love of children is well known, and his dismay at the abuse of children in the slum environment is clearly portrayed in the poem. Such a reading, however, would have to ignore the poem's last four stanzas. The poem is spiritual and consistent with de la Mare's emphasis on emotional rather than intellectual impact on his readers. He notes that within the child, "Some hidden one made mock of groans,/ Found living bread in stones." The depiction of slum life elicits anger, sadness, and feelings of hopelessness; yet the child's life is not hopeless. The poem's speaker, as an adult, looks back at his own youthful face and "I search its restless eyes,/ And, from those woe-flecked depths, at me/ Looks back through all its misery/ A self beyond surmise." The soul exists beyond the body. Even in the horrible slum one can find hope in one's spirit, which exists in the cosmos as well as in the tiny microcosm of everyday life. Like most of de la Mare's best poetry, "The Slum Child" is complex; it expresses de La Mare's horror of the child's life, and it reveals the inherent hopefulness of his belief in the supernatural.

The notion of the relative unimportance of the physical in relation to the spiritual is another theme that unifies de la Mare's poetry, from his first publications to his last. In one of his best poems, "The Traveller" (1945), this theme is symbolically presented. The Traveller himself is Everyman, and his journey is the journey that all people must take through life. The Traveller begins his journey at Titicaca, in the land of the Incas, and travels into strange places with alien landscapes. Throughout, de la Mare creates marvelously beautiful images. In the beginning, the Traveller gazes at "a vast plateau, smooth as porphyry,/ Its huge curve gradual as a woman's breast." He rides his Arabian horse onto the plateau, the surface of which is "Branched veins of sanguine in a milk-pale stone," becoming "Like night-blue porcelain." His journey takes him over "A vitreous region, like a sea asleep,/ Crystalline, convex, tideless and congealed." Eventually, the Traveller reaches "an immeasurable well/ Of lustrous crystal motionless black/ Deeped on. As he gazed . . ./ It seemed to him a presence there gazed back."

In a poem that purports to represent symbolically the life not only of each human being but of each earthly creature as well, such particular descriptions as the foregoing can be mystifying. "The Traveller" is a mixture of the implicit and the explicit. The poem's protagonist explicitly sees animals following him on his journey; he explicitly ages; he explicitly contemplates the meaning of his life: "Could Earth itself a living creature be,/ And he its transitory parasite?" As Henry Charles Duffin points out in his *Walter de la Mare: A Study of His Poetry* (1949), the poem's Earth is alive; it is an eye, and the Traveller traverses its ball and iris to its pupil, the "well." Throughout his life, from youthful determination to middle-aged contemplation to aged despair, the Traveller is watched. "Even the little ant . . . conscious may be of occult puissance near"; even, the poem states, the smallest of creatures can feel the living presence of the Earth.

Some critics have emphasized the despair in the poem; the divine may be too remote from humanity and humanity too small to be noticed. Doris Ross McCrosson, in *Walter de la Mare* (1966), is a notable advocate of de la Mare's despair and uncertainty about the existence and possible nature of God. Others, such as Victoria Sackville-West in "Walter de la Mare and 'The Traveller,'" *Proceedings of the British Academy* (1953), find an affirmation of faith in the poem. Typical of much of de la Mare's introspective poetry, "The Traveller" depicts pain and frustration as parts of living; and, typical of the poetry, Earth, nature, and each human being have spiritual aspects that can defy evil.

De la Mare wrote more than a thousand poems over more than half a century. In any such body of work, written during a long lifetime, one can rightly expect to find much diversity in subject and tone. De la Mare's work is no exception. Although he was a lyric poet all his life, his work shifted from short poems to long ones, and his prosody increased in complexity. To read the body of de la Mare's poetry is to experience a mind of diverse and passionate interests, with some of those interests unifying the whole of the poet's verse. De la Mare was a careful craftsman whose verse rhythms can disturb and delight wherever the content of a poem dictates. He loved children and strove to experience the world like a child, inductively. He saw the world of everyday experience as only part of a greater universe; he believed in spirits and a supernatural world. He saw great value in nature, even if it could be indifferent to human suffering.

These beliefs and passions enliven de la Mare's work, forming a background that colors all of his poems. If his poetry may be said to deliver a particular message, it is one which is at once simple and complex in its implications, like his verse: people are partly spiritual and thus should never be indifferent to evil, should love innocence, and should understand that each person is greater than he appears.

**Major publications other than poetry**

NOVELS: *Henry Brocken*, 1904; *The Return*, 1910; *The Three Mulla-Mulgars*, 1910 (reprinted as *The Three Royal Monkeys: Or, The Three Mulla-Mulgars*,

1935); *Memoirs of a Midget*, 1921; *At First Sight: A Novel*, 1928.

SHORT FICTION: *Story and Rhyme: A Selection*, 1921; *The Riddle and Other Stories*, 1923; *Ding Dong Bell*, 1924; *Broomsticks and Other Tales*, 1925; *Miss Jemima*, 1925; *Readings*, 1925-1926 (2 volumes); *The Connoisseur and Other Tales*, 1926; *Told Again: Traditional Tales*, 1927; *Old Joe*, 1927; *On the Edge*, 1930; *Seven Short Stories*, 1931; *The Lord Fish*, 1933; *The Wind Blows Over*, 1936; *The Nap and Other Stories*, 1936; *Animal Stories*, 1939; *The Picnic*, 1941; *The Best Stories of Walter de la Mare*, 1942; *The Old Lion and Other Stories*, 1942; *The Magic Jacket and Other Stories*, 1943; *The Scarecrow and Other Stories*, 1945; *The Dutch Cheese and Other Stories*, 1946; *Collected Stories for Children*, 1947; *A Beginning and Other Stories*, 1955; *Ghost Stories*, 1956.

PLAY: *Crossings: A Fairy Play*, 1921.

NONFICTION: *Rupert Brooke and the Intellectual Imagination*, 1919; *The Printing of Poetry*, 1931; *Lewis Carroll*, 1932; *Poetry in Prose*, 1936; *Pleasures and Speculations*, 1940; *Chardin, J.B.S. 1699-1779*, 1948; *Private View*, 1953.

ANTHOLOGIES: *Come Hither*, 1923; *The Shakespeare Songs*, 1929; *Stories from the Bible*, 1930; *Christina Rossetti's Poems*, 1930; *Desert Islands and Robinson Crusoe*, 1930; *Early One Morning in the Spring*, 1935; *Animal Stories*, 1939; *Behold, This Dreamer!*, 1939; *Love*, 1943.

**Bibliography**

Blunden, Edmund, et al. *Tribute to Walter de la Mare on His 75th Birthday*, 1948.

Brain, Russell. *Tea with Walter de la Mare*, 1957.

Chesterton, G. K. "Walter de la Mare," in *Fortnightly Review*. (July, 1932), pp. 47-53.

Clark, Leonard. "A Handlist of the Writings in Book Form (1902-1953) of Walter de la Mare," in *Studies in Bibliography*, 1953.

Duffin, Henry Charles. *Walter de la Mare: A Study of His Poetry*, 1970.

Hopkins, Kenneth. *Walter de la Mare*, 1957.

McCrosson, Doris Ross. *Walter de la Mare*, 1966.

Mégroz, R. L. *Walter de la Mare: A Biography and Critical Study*, 1972.

Reid, Forrest. *Walter de la Mare: A Critical Study*, 1970.

Richards, I. A. "Walter de la Mare," in *The New Republic*. (January, 31, 1976), pp. 31-33.

*Kirk H. Beetz*

# THOMAS DELONEY

**Born:** Norwich(?), England; c. 1543
**Died:** London(?), England; c. 1600

**Principal poems and collections**
 *Canaan's Calamitie: Or, The dolefull destruction of faire Jerusalem*, 1589; *Strange Histories*, 1602; *The Garland of Good Will*, 1631.

**Other literary forms**
 Thomas Deloney's modern reputation rests almost entirely on his four Elizabethan novels, all written during the last three years of his life. Ony two of these novels are listed in the Stationers' Register, *The Pleasant History of John Winchcomb in His Younger Years Called Jack of Newbury* on March 7, 1597, and *The Gentle Craft* on October 19, 1597. Although no conclusive evidence exists to date the other two, it is likely that *Thomas of Reading: Or, The Six Worthy Yeomen of the West* was the second novel published, coming sometime during the summer of 1597. The final work, *The Gentle Craft, Part 2*, was probably published early in 1598.

**Achievements**
 Deloney came upon the literary scene when, as a silk weaver, he began to write popular ballads in 1586. By 1592, he was well known enough in "the yarking up of Ballads" to attract the attention of Robert Greene and Gabriel Harvey, both of whom condemned him as a common balladmonger. Contemporary writers of the time generally slandered ballad writers including Deloney because street ballads were not much accepted by critics as a valid literary genre.
 Such published criticism does not, however, accurately reflect Deloney's early reputation as a poet. The middle-class Englishman, for whom Deloney wrote, bought and read Deloney's ballads in such quantity as to make him recognized as the "general" of the ballad makers. Unlike the balladmonger Autolycus in William Shakespeare's *The Winter's Tale* (1610-1611), Deloney does not write of "How a usuer's wife was brought to bed of twenty money bags at a burden, and how she longed to eat adders' heads and toads carbonadoes" and other such strange and sensational topics. Although he did not write of strange pigs and deformed human beings, he was often tarred with the same brush as those who did. The fact is that Deloney was one of a handful of ballad writers whose works were commercially very successful.
 Had Deloney's literary activities gone no further than his ballads or the longer *Canaans Calamitie*, his name would be merely a footnote to literary history, along with the names of William Elderton, Laurence Price, Martin Parker, and the some two hundred other Renaissance ballad writers who are known by name. Ballad writing for Deloney, however, was only a step in his

career. By writing ballads he could experiment with literary devices while he earned his livelihood as a silk weaver. Deloney was not alone in his endeavors, for most of the great writers of the time wrote a ballad or two. The ballads were chiefly literary exercises for Deloney, but some of them have merit which raises them above other time-bound street ballads.

## Biography

No documents have yet been uncovered which explain who Thomas Deloney's parents were, how extensive his education was, whom he married, or how many children he fathered. There remains neither a portrait of Deloney nor a description of his physical appearance. What is known of him is gleaned from scanty entries in the Stationers' Register, from remarks made about him by his contemporaries, and, most important, from his works. With the broad outline of the puzzle of Deloney's life thus sketched, the missing parts may be supplied by inference or speculation based on a general knowledge of middle-class life in Elizabethan England.

Deloney's death date can be set at 1600 with some certainty, for Will Kemp, the famous comic actor, reported in 1600 that Deloney had recently "dyed poorely . . . and was honestly buried." The date of his birth, however, is a matter of considerable speculation. The *Dictionary of National Biography* gives 1543, and several later dictionaries and encyclopedias have concurred; but in fact there is no evidence to establish the correctness of the date.

The place of Deloney's birth is also a matter of speculation. His earliest broadside ballad, "The Lamentation of Beccles," was published in Norwich. In addition, his name is probably of French ancestry, and many of his writings show an anti-Catholic bias. Both of these facts also suggest that Deloney lived in Norwich, for many of the Flemish and Huguenot Protestants who fled their homelands to escape religious persecution during the fifteenth and sixteenth centuries settled in Norwich. Although Deloney's first known literary venture, *A Declaration made by the Archbishop of Collen upon the Deede of his Mariage* (1583), was published in London, there is a great deal of evidence to tie Deloney to Norwich in the early part of his life.

Wherever he might have spent his childhood, Deloney's ability to use English clearly and effectively, his knowledge of Latin and French, his borrowings from contemporary literature, and his allusions to history and classical literature all suggest that he had a good basic education. It is clear that the early part of Deloney's adult life was spent as an artisan, a silk weaver, for several contemporary references refer to him as such. Many of his works show him to be a willing, if not actually a hired, spokesman for the clothiers of England. An early indication of Deloney as a writer comes with the publication of his aforementioned translation of the Latin pieces concerning the Archbishop of Collen's marriage. In 1586, he published the broadside ballad "The Lamentation of Beccles."

During the next six years, it appears, Deloney turned out so many ballads that upon the death of William Elderton, the famous London balladeer, he inherited the title "King of the Ballad Writers." From 1596 to 1600, he probably continued to write ballads, for Will Kemp in 1600 referred to him as "the great ballad maker, T. D., alias Thomas Deloney." Far more important, in the last four years of his life he published four novels, and from them the strength of his reputation as a significant writer is derived.

**Analysis**

Although Thomas Deloney is known to modern students of literature primarily as a prose writer, among his contemporaries his fame was as a ballad writer. Street ballads, drawing on the popularity of the folk ballad, were published in broadside form and sung by minstrels wandering from town to town for people interested in tales of old romance or history and stories of the latest fire, robbery, trial, or execution. The majority of Deloney's poems are in the ballad form and in the journalistic tradition.

The range of subjects in Deloney's ballads is wide: political, historical, social, religious, moral, and romantic. Fulfilling the common man's desire for the latest news, Deloney rushed into print with a ballad on the great fire that destroyed Beccles, a market town in Suffolk. Another ballad recounts the English capture of a Spanish galleon in 1588. At least five of his ballads deal with other contemporary events of interest to a public who had no newspapers to inform them of the details. Deloney's historical ballads are drawn from the chronicle histories, which appealed to the nationalistic Elizabethan's interest in his country's development. Ballads covering important events in the lives of kings, queens, and popular personalities of the day both informed and entertained a large audience. Social questions were considered in such ballads as "The Scarcity of Corn" and "The Lamentation of Mr. Pages Wife." "Virtuous Queen Judith" and "Truth and Ignorance" dealt with religious questions, and "Salomans good Houswife" and "Repent, England, Repent" examined moral questions. The Elizabethan interest in medieval romance which Deloney was later to exploit in several of his prose works was first dealt with in the ballads. "The Death of Rosamond," "Lancelot du Lake," "Patient Grissel," and "The Spanish Lady's Love" are only a few of the romances that Deloney served up in the popular medium to an attentive public. In short, the same subjects that the dramatists of the time used to appeal to the groundlings were used by Deloney to attract attention to his ballads. Although the themes often overlap in any particular ballad, Deloney's ballads fall naturally into three categories: journalistic, historical, and romantic. The longer poem, *Canaans Calamitie*, although containing both some good and some bad elements of ballads, is different in several respects from them.

As a balladist, Deloney's purpose was almost certainly to cater to public taste and interest, and as a result many of his poems sing of contemporary events. While the public was his master, however, none of Deloney's journalistic ballads pander to the crudest tastes; none is on subjects of merely sensational appeal.

England's struggles against the Spanish gave Deloney grist enough for his mill. For example, "The Happie obtaining of the Great Galleazzo," published in London in 1588, probably shortly after the battle, is primarily a song of national pride and praise celebrating a battle with the Spanish Armada on July 21, 1588. Like many Elizabethan pamphlets on the subject, Deloney's ballad is largely propaganda. England is "Noble England" and the enemy the "false Spaniards," who come to torture, rape, murder, and pillage the peaceful English, and of course "to deprive our noble Queene,/ both of her life and crowne." According to Deloney, the major reason for English victory is that whereas the Spanish trusted in force and the Pope, the English trusted in God. Deloney's love of heroism, however, will not allow God full credit for the defeat of the satanic Spanish. He plays up the strength of the enemy ("Great is their number,/ of ships upon the sea"), the magnificence of their ships ("That like a bulwarke on the sea,/ did seeme to each mans eye"), and the excellence of their equipment ("their provision wonderfull"). In the face of overpowering superiority, the English fought "coragiously," capturing one ship and sinking another.

The poem does contain some specific facts. The English had met the superior Spanish fleet at Plymouth, and in the ensuing battle the galleon commanded by Don Pedro de Valdez was captured. The ballad then follows the battle across the channel to Calais, where another Spanish ship was damaged and looted by the English. Deloney details such scenes as the execution of Don Hugo de Moncaldo, commander of the second ship (shot "through his braines"), the foaming sea ("Died and staind like scarlet red"), and the stores captured by the English ("Cannons" and "bread-corne wine and meat").

The immense amount of extant literature on the Spanish threat and the English victory is a measure of their importance to the English; and surely Deloney must have had little trouble finding an audience for his versified reports. More significant to a modern audience, however, is that the emotions of fear and exhilaration which sparked ancient songs of battle give these ballads a vitality born of justifiable pride in true heroism.

Probably the best of the journalistic poems is the one with the most troublesome subject. "The Lamentation of Mr. Pages Wife," about a woman sentenced to die for the murder of her husband, could have descended into sentimentality of the worst sort; but it did not. Apparently based on an actual incident in 1590, the ballad presents a moving analysis of the motives and regrets of the young Mrs. Ulalia Page of Plymouth, who, along with her lover, George Strangwidge, murdered Mr. Page.

Ulalia Page's lament is not merely that she must die while yet young.

Although she admits her guilt, she nevertheless argues that parents who force a daughter to marry against her will are also at fault. In a plot suggestive of the Romeo and Juliet theme, Ulalia had fallen in love with George Strangwidge. Her father, however, matched her with the old but wealthy Mr. Page; and thus Ulalia faces an unpleasant life with a man she detests. Ulalia pleads not to be sold to old Page:

> On knees I prayde they would not me constraine;
> With teares I cryde their purpose to refraine;
> With sighes and sobbes I did them often move,
> I might not wed whereas I could not love.

Her prayers are in vain, for she is indeed married to him. Although old Page was a decent enough man ("Cause knew I none I should despise him so"), he was not young Strangwidge, and to Ulalia he appeared to be a monster. Deloney is able to evoke sympathy for the desperate young woman who is in a state of near panic. She expresses her anguish and fear, in four end-stopped lines, suggesting the halting speech and excited breathing of the doomed woman. The stanza ends with an effective metonymy:

> My closen eies could not his sight abide:
> My tender youth did lothe his aged side:
> Scant could I taste the meate whereon he fed:
> My legges did lothe to lodge within his bed.

"The Lamentation of Mr. Pages Wife" is successful primarily because it possesses a degree of unity not often seen in street ballads, because it does not exploit the sensational aspects of adultery and murder, and because the emotions and motives of Ulalia are carefully analyzed. It is true that Deloney tacks on the usual moral ("And now, sweete Lord! forgive me my misdeedes") and the usual prayer for the Queen ("Lord! bless our Queene with long and happy life"). These are standard elements in all of Deloney's journalistic ballads, whether the primary subjects be the burning of a town or the report that "cruell whippes" to be used by the Spaniards against English men and women have been found on captured Spanish ships. The emphasis in "The Lamentation of Mr. Pages Wife," however, is upon the heartsick young woman whose life was made miserable by greedy parents and an unnatural social custom which allowed women to be treated as chattel.

The importance of history, especially English history, to Elizabethans is evidenced by the great interest in chronicle histories and in historical drama, poetry, and prose fiction which flourished during the period. Raphael Holinshed's monumental histories of England, Scotland, and Ireland became the standard works used by Shakespeare and others who found the material a fertile source for literature. It is no wonder that Deloney, drawing heavily upon Holinshed's histories, exploited both the general acceptance of works on historical subjects and the public's desire to know more about former kings, queens, and important events in the history of their emerging nation. There are seventeen ballads by Deloney about people and events of past history, more than on any other subject. Topics range from kings and queens and their paramours to commoners such as Wat Tyler and Jack Straw, from important events in English history to the story of Lady Godiva's famous ride.

Most of the ballads dealing with famous kings and queens are little more than narrative prose paraphrased in meter. Deloney experimented with several types of meter in his history ballads, the meter probably dictated more by the popular tune he had in mind than by the requirements of his material. Most of the ballads are set in logical stanzas of from five to ten lines each, but some, like "Wat Tyler and Jack Straw," have no stanza breaks. The rhythm is usually iambic, even when normal syntax has to be mutilated ("The Bishop of *Hereford* ill may be fare,/ he wrote us a letter for subtitltie rare"), but at times the rhythm all but disappears into simple prose: "Thus the dissembling Queene did seeke to hide,/ the heinous act by her owne meanes effected."

When dealing with material from the chronicles, Deloney displayed little passion for his subject. The fact that he wrote four ballads on the deposition of Edward II suggests that he had some interest in the subject; but the ballads themselves are mere rehearsals of the events. In the first of the four, "A Song of Queene Isabel," the narrator explains that Isabel, separated from her husband by the interference of the powerful Spencers, travels to France and Germany to seek help in taking the throne away from Edward. With help from a German knight, she returns to England and defeats her husband. The Spencers are hanged, the King imprisoned, and the young prince put on the throne. The narrative emphasizes Queen Isabel, but there is no explanation of the conflict between Edward and Isabel which drove her to rebellion. Isabel turns for aid to her brother, the King of France, who first agrees to help and next refuses to allow any Frenchman to support her. Deloney does not explain the sudden reversal or its effect upon Isabel, except to note that "This alteration did greatly grieue the Queene." Isabel seems to be the heroine of the first ballad, although it is not clear why Edward is a villain.

In the other ballads on the subject—"The Imprisonment of Edward the Second," "Of King Edward the Second, Being Poysoned," and "The Lamentation of Matreuers and Gurney"—Isabel is shown to be a dissembling, cruel woman, for she has her imprisoned husband tortured and killed and then compounds her villainy by banishing the men who, at her behest, have murdered him. What Isabel's motives are for her transition from wronged wife to villain are not clear. She has no Mortimer in the ballads to woo her away from faithful service to Edward as she does in Christopher Marlowe's *Edward II*—nor a Gaveston to envy, nor an accomplice to murder the King.

Others of Deloney's ballads dealing with past history show a similar lack of interest in both story and craftsmanship. Whether he is writing of King Edward, King John, Henry I, or Henry II, or of some famous event in English history, Deloney appears content to hammer the prose narrative into some sort of verse as rapidly as possible. Even when he chooses the popular tale of Lady Godiva's famous ride, a story which offers many opportunities for praise of English female resoluteness and beauty for analysis of male-female sexual behavior, or for lewd jest, Deloney merely takes the story as he has found it in the chronicles and sings it "To the Tune of Prince Arthur died at Ludlow."

In short, like most poets, Deloney is more effective when he is writing about people and events close to him. He can do little more with kings and queens than copy their exploits from the chronicles. The one time he attempted to portray a historical character familiarly—Queen Elizabeth talking to common people in "On the Want of Corn"—the Lord Mayor of London sought to arrest him for demeaning the Queen. But when he wrote about the people he knew—the common people—and about topics that excited him, he created ballads that were at times specific, well developed, and perceptive.

Along with contemporary events and subjects from past history, the Elizabethan citizen eagerly craved stories of chivalric romance. The popularity of stories about aristocratic ladies brought low by circumstance, of noble young men conducting courtly romances, of knights, shepherds, kings, queens, and even an occasional commoner having dangerous, exciting, and morally uplifting adventures can be seen in the ready acceptance of such prose romances as *A Discourse of the Adventures Passed by Master F. J.* (1573), by George Gascoigne; *Euphues* (1578-1580), by John Lyly; *Pandosto* (1588), by Robert Greene; *Arcadia* (1590), by Sir Philip Sidney; and *Rosalynde. Euphues Golden Legacie* (1590), by Thomas Lodge. *Euphues* was so popular during the sixteenth century that it appeared in thirteen editions between 1578 and 1597. Shakespeare, of course, borrowed the plots of *Rosalynde* and *Pandosto* for his *As You Like It* (1598) and *Pericles* (1608-1609). Indeed, the chivalric romance accounted for a large part of the output of early English printing presses.

The audience for romance was ordinarily made up of lords and ladies who could best identify with the heroes and heroines, the settings, and the language of the narratives. Lyly's *Euphues*, an "anatomy of wit" rather than an exciting action story, is more of an escape from simple, idiomatic prose than an escape from everyday life, and as such, it surely appealed more to courtiers, who could use a handbook of witty conversation, than to the common man, who would probably give up in despair, being unable to figure out who was doing what to whom. In the second half of the sixteenth century, however, tales of chivalry found their way into literature written for less sophisticated readers. The old tales began to show up in chapbooks and broadside ballads.

Deloney used elements of the romance in most of his ballads, whether his primary purpose was to report a contemporary news item, to recount a historical event, or to create a religious or moral exemplum. His historical ballad on King Edgar emphasizes neither the unprovincial temper of this Anglo-Saxon king nor the literary revival resulting from the establishment of English monasticism during his reign. Deloney's "New Song of King Edgar" tells "how he was deprived of a Lady, which he loved, by a knight of his court." Even those ballads which spin a romantic tale usually have some connection with history or legend.

"The Spanish Lady's Love" is one of Deloney's more successful romantic poems. A Spanish lady has fallen in love with her English captor, and when he is ordered home to England, she declares her love:

> Thou has set this present day,
>     my body free:
> But my heart in prison strong,
>     remains with thee.

The noble Englishman tries graciously to persuade her that a soldier's life would not suit her, that he could not afford to maintain her, and that she should marry a Spaniard, but throughout all his objections, the Spanish lady remains constant in her love for him. When the Englishman finally admits that he has a wife in England, the Spanish lady immediately ceases her suit even though she cannot stop loving him.

The subjects of Deloney's ballads were usually dignified enough to attract the attention of judicious readers. Poets such as Sir Philip Sidney and George Gascoigne wrote romantic poems, and Samuel Daniel and Michael Drayton wrote historical poems on subjects similar to Deloney's. These poets, however, writing for a more select audience, were able to use metrical and stanzaic patterns inappropriate for the balladeer. Deloney, clearly writing for the bourgeoisie, fitted his words and music to the eyes and ears of his audience. The public expected the ballads to be sung to familiar tunes, and as a result Deloney delivered his stories to the tune of "the hunt is up" or "Flying Fame" or "Prince Arthur died at Ludlow" or even "My Valentine." While such restrictions might have reined the wit of a better poet, Deloney was successful in his own way.

Whether Deloney ever had ambitions to achieve a poetic reputation beyond ballad-making is ultimately unanswerable, but his refusal to use merely sensational events for his ballads seems to elevate him at least above the Autolycuses of his day. On one occasion Deloney left ballads entirely, to try his hand at a longer poem of dignified style and matter.

In *Canaans Calamitie*, Deloney tells the story of the destruction of Jerusalem by the Roman Titus in A.D. 74, using as sources *de Bello Judaico* (c.

A.D. 75) by Flavius Josephus and *Christes Teares over Jerusalem* (1593) by Thomas Nashe. The poem, which has more than twelve hundred lines, uses a six-line stanza which had become popular for use in Ovidian mythological-erotic poems. In 1589, Thomas Lodge used the verse form in *Schillaes Metamorphosis*, and Shakespeare used it in *Venus and Adonis* (1593). Edmund Spenser also employed the pattern in the First Eclogue in *The Shepheardes Calender* (1579). The six lines are of iambic pentameter, rhyming ababcc. Deloney's most ambitious poem attempts to tell a significant story in a form befitting its moral importance, and in some respects it is successful. There is a clear narrative that includes an understandable conflict, a crisis, and a denouement. The action in the narrative is detailed and generally relevant, and descriptions of characters, setting, and motives are usually, although not always, detailed. His purpose in *Canaans Calamitie* is clearly stated in the note "To the Gentlemen Readers health":

> . . . in reading this Historie, you shall see how soone their state was changed, and the great plagues that followed their pevish and hatefull pride: by whose wofull fall, God graunt vs and all Christians to take example, lest following them in the like sinne, we feele the like smart.

The story of Canaan's calamity suited Deloney well, as it did Nashe and several ministers of their time, as an allegory of Elizabethan England. The vices of the inhabitants of Jerusalem, which brought down God's wrath upon their heads, were alien to the social tradition of England up to the time of Deloney. The Jews' placing of individual desires above the brotherhood of man was, to the medieval and early Renaissance Englishman, a characteristic of beasts, not men. Traditionally, communities and, later, the trade guilds fostered the concept of "the public good." Medieval society was communal in nature. The sick were visited, the destitute were cared for, and the dead were buried by the community. This social theory was, however, beginning to be displaced during the last few decades of the sixteenth century because of changing economic conditions. The advancement of the private person marked a new and often frightening departure from the codes of social behavior of the past. Many writers, including Robert Greene, Thomas Nashe, and the dramatists Thomas Dekker, Thomas Middleton, Philip Massinger, Thomas Heywood, and (especially) Ben Jonson satirized and condemned the selfishness and greed which were destroying the traditional social morality of England.

Deloney, writing during a period of great economic upheaval and change, doubtless saw in the story of the fall of Jerusalem an allegory for his time. Perhaps the most obvious parallel was found in the story of the famine. Overpopulation, migration to the cities, and the enclosing of agricultural fields for sheep pasturage put a serious strain on the ability of English farmers to raise enough grain to feed the population. Substandard harvests, which occurred from time to time throughout the sixteenth century, caused serious food shortages in London and the larger cities. Harvests were especially bad in the 1590's when Deloney was writing *Canaans Calamitie*. He exhorts his readers to "take example" from the story of the Jews, "lest following them in the like sinne, we feele the like smart." Focusing upon the injustices visited upon a Jewish woman, Miriam, and her son, Deloney alludes to the sins of his own time, hoping through pity and fear to instruct his audience in the dangers of violating the traditional social morals which he believes had made England great.

In *Canaans Calamitie*, Deloney turns to a theme he had used in "The Lamentation of Beccles" and several other ballads to show how sin against God's law will bring disorder and therefore suffering. In the longer poem, with its freer form, Deloney is able to draw a more detailed, more thorough, picture of his view of Elizabethan life and the sins that he believed would bring the downfall of man. Occasionally, in trying to present the real destruction of Jerusalem which was brought about by the Jews themselves, Deloney follows Nashe's lead and his own journalistic bent, thus becoming more sensational than his purposes required. Although Thomas Deloney is still in some respects "the great ballad maker, T. D.," parts of *Canaans Calamitie* show unmistakable signs of a maturing writer.

**Major publications other than poetry**
NOVELS: *Jack of Newbury* 1597; *Thomas of Reading*, c. 1597; *The Gentle Craft*, 1597; *The Gentle Craft, Part 2*, c. 1598.

**Bibliography**
Chevalley, Abel. *Thomas Deloney: Le Roman des métiers au temps de Shake-speare*, 1926.
Lawlis, Merritt E. *Apology for the Middle Class*, 1960.
Powys, Llewelyn. "Thomas Deloney," in *Virginia Quarterly Review*. IX (1933), pp. 578-594.
Reuter, Ole. "Some Aspects of Thomas Deloney's Prose Style," in *Neuphilologische Mitteilungen*. LXXVII (1976), pp. 599-607.
Rollins, Hyder E. "The Black-Letter Broadside Ballad," in PMLA. XXXIV (1919), pp. 258-339.
Sievers, Richard. "Thomas Deloney: Eine Studie über Balladenlitteratur der Shakspere Zeit," in *Palaestra*. XXXVI (1904), pp. 1-146.
Wright, Eugene P. *Thomas Deloney*, 1981.

*Eugene P. Wright*

# JAMES DICKEY

**Born:** Atlanta, Georgia; February 2, 1923

### Principal poems and collections

*Into the Stone and Other Poems*, 1960; *Drowning with Others*, 1962; *Helmets*, 1964; *Two Poems of the Air*, 1964; *Buckdancer's Choice*, 1965; *Poems 1957-1967*, 1967; *The Eye-Beaters, Blood, Victory, Madness, Buckhead and Mercy*, 1970; *Exchanges*, 1971; *Jericho: The South Beheld*, 1974 (prose poem); *The Zodiac*, 1976; *God's Images*, 1977 (prose poem); *Tucky the Hunter*, 1978; *In Pursuit of the Grey Soul*, 1978; *The Enemy from Eden*, 1978; *Head-Deep in Strange Sounds*, 1979; *The Strength of Fields*, 1979; *Puella*, 1982.

### Other literary forms

James Dickey has always viewed his poetry as "the center of the creative wheel," insisting that everything else he has written—including a novel, a screenplay, a television adaptation, four books of literary criticism, two books of rather poetic prose—is secondary to that. He is correct: his poetry is his major literary contribution, and the major themes of his novel *Deliverance* (1970) and of his coffee-table books, *Jericho: The South Beheld* and *God's Images*, are offshoots from those found in his poems. Even the critical ideas in his collections of reviews and critical essays—*The Suspect in Poetry* (1964), *Babel to Byzantium* (1968), *Self-Interviews* (1970), *Sorties* (1971)—come largely from his own poetic practice.

Nevertheless, it is important to acknowledge the popular and commercial success of his prose. His novel *Deliverance*, ambivalently reviewed by many of the same critics who had had only praise for his poetry, was on the best-seller list for several months, and it achieved near cult status with white-water enthusiasts and dedicated cliff-climbers. In the 1980's it is more highly regarded, and more often the subject of critical articles, than it was in the 1970's. His prose poem on the southern landscape, *Jericho: The South Beheld*, deserves notice in any account of recent commercial publishing as a stunning commercial success by an unlikely combination—a poet, an artist, and a publishing firm known far better for its popular magazines than for its literary endeavors.

It is debatable whether Dickey's prose has won an audience for his poetry, but, clearly, knowledge of the prose should make the poetry more accessible. Many of his poems are concerned with "deliverance," the theme of his novel, or with "beholding" nature, the theme of *Jericho: The South Beheld*. Few poets have left a clearer impression of their critical judgments and creative intentions, or as detailed a description of why and how individual poems were written, than Dickey has done in his critical prose. When his prose is read along with his poetry, it is clear that Dickey is an important postmodernist, reacting against the impersonality of modernism, placing stress not only on his literary works but also on the man who created them.

## Achievements

Dickey should not be regarded, as one major critic declared him to be, solely as a romantic advocate of "the more life school," even though his contributions have been important to the neoromanticism that came in vogue about 1957-1959 with the advent of confessional poetry and the Beat movement. Dickey, as poetry editor of *The Sewanee Review*, was a strong advocate of new directions in poetry, but at the same time he deplored the excesses of confessionalism and the Beat movement. To Dickey, then as now, technique and language mattered, and he stressed the importance of transcendence, not sensationalism, or the ordinariness of ordinary life. Dickey's contributions to postmodernism, as a critic and as a poet, have consistently been efforts to escape the limitations of the ordinary self, while retaining the formal control necessary for that oneness of form and content that the formalists had extolled. He sought to escape the pure dullness of ordinary life by such devices as empathetic exchange of identity, the use of archetypes (his "big forms"), surrealistic encounters set against landscape (his "country surrealism"), exploiting a narrative sense, and employing a distinctive voice or persona.

## Biography

Although James Dickey is Southern born and bred, he has never been regarded as distinctively Southern as an older generation of Vanderbilt poets and critics—John Crowe Ransom, Allen Tate, Robert Penn Warren—were. Instead, his work seems to be not of any particular school or region, or traceable to any specific influences. In his neoromanticism, however, he is in some ways simliar to a poet he admired, Theodore Roethke.

Dickey was born on February 2, 1923, in Atlanta, Georgia. At North Fulton High School, he was far more interested in athletics and in carpentry than in literature. In the fall of 1941 he entered Clemson Agricultural College (now Clemson University), not out of any interest in agriculture but to play football. At the end of the football season, and as an aftermath of Pearl Harbor, he left Clemson for the Army Air Corps.

Dickey has only a handful of war poems, even though his combat experience was extensive—more than one hundred missions in the South Pacific before his discharge in 1946. He returned to civilian life with a newly acquired interest in poetry, transferring to a university with a stronger tradition of literary studies, Vanderbilt University, and substituting track for football. While at Vanderbilt he "read a good deal" in the works of the Vanderbilt Agrarians, he has said, without ever thinking of himself as "a latter-day Agrarian."

Next to literature the strongest influence was his study of anthropology, which aroused in him a fascination with the outlook of primitive tribes. That outlook seemed to provide a lost perspective for civilized man that Dickey often seeks to recapture in his poetry. Even though Dickey has never acknowledged it, the formalism of former Vanderbiltians, the New Criticism of Ransom, Tate, Cleanth Brooks, and Warren, also undoubtedly influenced his work. Monroe K. Spears, then at Vanderbilt, convinced him that he had talent as a writer as well as a fine critical mind and should devote himself to literature rather than to science or engineering.

Dickey was graduated from Vanderbilt *magna cum laude* in 1950, received his M.A. degree in 1951, married a nursing graduate of Vanderbilt, Maxine Syerson, and accepted a teaching position at Rice Institute. He hoped, with further publication of his poetry, to move from the teaching of freshman composition and introductory literature courses to creative writing. Disappointingly, his responsibilities were primarily teaching freshman composition, and, when a public reading of a poem called "The Father's Body" led to controversy, he resigned from his position rather than give a public apology.

In April, 1956, at the age of thirty-three, Dickey began a new career as copywriter with a New York advertising firm, with responsibility for the Coca Cola account. For the next six years, writing advertising copy by day and poetry by night, Dickey was able to publish two volumes of poetry, *Into the Stone and Other Poems* and *Drowning with Others*. A Guggenheim Fellowship in 1962 permitted him a second year in Europe to write more poetry; he decided to leave advertising and risk all writing poetry full time. Dickey became a visiting Poet-in-Residence at Reed College (1963-1964), at San Fernando Valley State College (1964-1965), and at the University of Wisconsin (1966). He received his first major recognition in 1966 when he was awarded the National Book Award for *Buckdancer's Choice*. This was followed by his appointment as consultant in Poetry at the Library of Congress (1966-1968). The publication of *Poems 1957-1967* revealed just how remarkable his achievements during a decade of writing poetry had been. The consensus was that Dickey was the new major poet on the American literary scene. As a result of this critical recognition he received what he had long sought, an appointment to a university as poet-in-residence and teacher of creative writing. He joined the University of South Carolina faculty as Carolina Professor of English.

Dickey's career has been versatile and his life-style on occasion flamboyant, paralleling his conviction that the poet should be capable of finding within himself many different selves to serve as the personae of his poems. Dickey's career as an aviator, advertising writer, poet, novelist, and screenwriter, his frequent *macho* pose (athlete, hunter with bow and arrow), and occasional boisterous behavior as a lecturer, have created a legend that has attracted as much attention to the poet as to the poetry. None of this is surprising. If T. S. Eliot as the chief poet and critic of modernism sought to take the poet out of his poetry, Dickey, as an important critic and poet of postmodernism, has always sought to return the poet to a recognizable relationship with his poetry.

In 1976, following the death of his wife Maxine, he married Dorothy Dodson and lives a somewhat less public life, lecturing more infrequently, writing poetry, and teaching in Columbia, South Carolina.

## Analysis

James Dickey's first collection of poetry, *Into the Stone and Other Poems*, was only a modest one-third of a Scribner's *The Poets of Today* volume. Only five poems were based on his war experiences; the majority stressed nature as the force from which knowledge of life and death may be gained. The poems were largely affirmative, written from the perspective of a grateful survivor of war who owed his birth to the death of an older brother. There is a tension in the early poems between gratitude for life and a sense of guilt for being the one who survived.

Though he was never an admirer of T. S. Eliot's theory of impersonality in poetry, Dickey, when necessary, could find his own objective correlatives for personal feelings. In "The String" he makes use of the family pastime of performing tricks with string as the narrative base of his poem, inventing the fiction that his dead brother Eugene was a child who performed the family tricks. Consequently, his brother lives on as a link in a continuity reaffirmed when Dickey passes on the string tricks from the dead brother, whose place he took, to his own son.

In another early poem, "The Performance," one of his best, Dickey uses a similar device to structure a poem about another nonsurvivor. Donald Armstrong was his close friend in the service, a flyer both "happy-go-lucky and daring," who crash-landed while strafing in the Philippines: he was captured by the Japanese and beheaded the next day. Since no other information about his death was available, Dickey imagines Donald Armstrong transcending his ordinary limitations in a last performance before his death. At the air base Donald Armstrong had tried, but always failed, to achieve a perfect handstand. Dickey imagines that just as the executioner's sword is posed to strike off his head, Donald Armstrong, in the most extreme of human situations, achieves perfectly the handstand he had always failed to perform for his friends. This poem illustrates Dickey's use of personal experience, drawing on memory as a narrative base for lyric perceptions; it also illustrates his belief in the artistic prerogative of "making" a different view of the truth "from the official version that God made or the world made." He recalls that it was his English teacher at Vanderbilt, Monroe K. Spears, who alerted him to the possibility that a poet may lie creatively and transcend ordinary experiences. It was Spears's advice that gave Dickey his most important theme—transcendence.

Another means of achieving transcendence is to use the "big forms" of nature, and to move beyond the literal toward the archetypal and the mythological. In "The Vegetable King" an ordinary householder sleeps outside in early spring, and in a dream he is transformed into the sacrificial vegetable king whose Orphic dismemberment is necessary for the creation of spring. He sees everything from a perspective that becomes characteristic of Dickey's poetry, from beyond the ordinary human world. Upon waking, he cannot distinguish between dream and reality, between literal truth and the truth his subconscious has yielded.

In his next volume of poetry, *Drowning with Others*, Dickey utilizes another device to escape the ordinary self, "his way of exchange," a temporary empathetic escape from one's own personality. In "A Dog Sleeping on My Feet" the narrator watches his dog asleep, feet moving as he presumably dreams of a fox hunt, and experiences through his imagination the excitement of the chase. The escape is only temporary; there must always be a return to the human state, but with the difference that having known "the other" makes.

In a similar poem, "Listening to the Foxhounds," Dickey finds his narrative in the eccentric structure of the Appalachian fox hunt. The dogs do the work; the men sit leisurely around the fireside and drink, listening for the sounds of their dogs pursuing the fox. A hunter without a dog has the liberty that the persona here enjoys, identifying with the pursued fox, sharing the excitement of the escape as the fox leaps into the safety of his den.

The climactic poem in Dickey's imaginative exchanges with animals, "The Heaven of Animals," is a vision of a pastoral heaven, one appropriate for animals. He draws on the Platonic idea of heaven as a continuation of the finer moments on earth, not the biblical heaven where animals are deprived of the pleasures of the hunt. In this heaven the hunted is still hunted, the hunter still hunts, but there is a difference: although the thrill of the hunt remains, the hunted animal is not killed, but will rise and walk again.

"The Owl King," one of Dickey's most complex poems, carries forward his desire to see from a perspective beyond the ordinary. The narration is handled by three different voices, the father of a blind child, a mythical Owl King, and the blind child, who is taken up into the Owl's tree and there, as in fairy tales, is metamorphosized: though blind, he is taught to see.

In "The Hospital Window" Dickey returns to his family as subject, but here he explores the theme of transcendence of personal limitations and fears. He has just come down from the hospital room, where his father lies dying of cancer. While by his father's bedside, the son found himself unable to say what he should have said. From the street below, he looks up into the flame of the sunlight reflected from the hospital window and imagines a wave from his father. This gesture is taken as an attempt to communicate a hope of survival in the face of the immediate dangers both face—the father from cancer, the son from the swirling traffic through which he seeks to maneuver on the street below.

To Dickey, transcendence is no more than a temporary exchange of identity, a brief escape that can give life meaning. Transcendence is not even always possible for Dickey's personae, who must, on occasion, remain prisoners of their natural state and limitations. In "The Lifeguard," transcendence is only a fantasy; the reality is the human situation in which man is a prisoner, and from which there is no escape. The lifeguard at a boys' camp is aware that the young campers believe he has transcendent powers, yet he dives repeatedly and cannot find a boy who has drowned. Having failed, he cannot face the children. Retreating into hiding, he can transcend his human limitations only through fantasies that grant him the ability to perform miracles, even walk on water like Christ, and raise this child from the dead. His dream is false, but Dickey works into this poem some of the compassion that he admired in Randall Jarrell's poetry.

The title of his third book of poems, *Helmets*, would suggest a return to the war, but the poems are much more varied than that. He does use his war experience for "Drinking from a Helmet," a poem on the theme of the survivor, utilizing here the exchange of identity between a living survivor and a dead nonsurvivor, the wearer of the abandoned helmet. Drinking from the dead man's helmet, he dedicates himself to a life forever conditioned by the grace of his escape from the fate that befell the nonsurvivor, and he promises to pay tribute by looking up the brother of the dead man.

Dickey also reveals in this volume an unexpected facility for the comic, for the hyperbole characteristic of the humor of the old Southwest. In "Kudzu" he explores the mythical dimensions of the Japanese import, which does too well what it was imported into the South to do—grow on eroded land, devouring (Dickey imagines) hogs, cows, even houses. "Cherrylog Road" is one of Dickey's most popular ventures into the comic. He has said that he captured in the poem something of the quality of *The Adventures of Huckleberry Finn*, funny and yet innocent. The boy, fearful of his father's wrath, arrives on his motorcycle for a tryst in an unlikely place, the back of a junked automobile, in the company of snakes, turtles, roaches, mice, and toads.

Dickey also includes in *Helmets* a poem about social injustice, "A Folk Singer of the Thirties," an account of a folksinger crucified on a boxcar by railroad detectives. He shows compassion for the man crucified; but, writing from the perspective of the 1960's, he is aware of the folksinger both as a voice of conscience for the impoverished during the 1930's and as a performer corruptible by wealth during the vogue of the folksinger in the 1960's.

*Buckdancer's Choice* is still the critics' choice as Dickey's best volume of poetry during his decade of prolific creativity. It won the National Book Award for Poetry for 1965. In "The Shark's Parlor," Dickey combines comedy and a *rite de passage* narrative about two boys who, in their innocence, take on more than they can handle—a huge shark which, before it disappears into

the depths from which it had come, destroys a house. The boys have challenged the power of a primordial force.

The title poem, "Buckdancer's Choice," is a further contribution to Dickey's
major theme of attempted transcendence of human limitations. It is once
more a family poem, this time a tribute to his mother, who gave him life in
spite of her angina pectoris. She lies an invalid, still fending off death by
whistling the old "buck and wing" dancer's tune from the minstrel show. In
a second family poem, "The Celebration," Dickey joins a crowd at an amuse-
ment park and unexpectedly encounters his parents, walking as lovers,
unaware that they are being observed by their son. His perspective is mock-
voyeuristic, yet loving, as he observes these two silhouetted against the background of the rise and fall of the wheels of the carnival. They transcend "the
faint sleep" of the old, to which their son had relegated them, with an unexpected energy that has "all and nothing" to do with him. Their love created
him, and yet he cannot share the love that his parents feel for each other.

Dickey does discuss in *Buckdancer's Choice* issues current in the 1960's,
but he has his own indirect version. He is more interested in writing a good
poem than in any specific social or political issue. In "Slave Quarters," he
places himself in the plight of a slave owner who, because of the mores of
his society, cannot acknowledge the son that his lust in the slave quarters
produced, although he is permitted to own that son.

"The Firebombing" is Dickey's attempt to assume the guilt he should feel
for the World War II night firebombing of Tokyo, in which he participated.
Then he was insulated by the closed cockpit, the altitude of his plane, and
more than twenty years of urban comforts back in America, and Dickey now
confesses that it is impossible for him to acknowledge what he did. Dickey's
later nonparticipation in protests over the war in Vietnam and his inability
to accept his guilt in this poem led to an attack on Dickey by fellow poet
Robert Bly. Dickey's reply made it clear that he believed that official protest
poetry could not be anything but bad and that he was interested only in
writing good poems. "The Firebombing" is one of his best poems, expressing
pragmatically only what other aviators also had reported about their feelings
of detachment. If Dickey cannot accept guilt, he does manage to conjure up
an image suggesting the horror of what he has done. He depicts a victim
standing at his threshold with its "ears crackling off" like "powdery leaves,"
crumbling into nothingness.

In "Falling," the title poem of the last section of *Poems 1957-1967*, Dickey
is primarily interested in the contrast between actual clock time and the lived
time of the terrified stewardess as she falls from her plane to her death.
Dickey grants himself access to her thoughts, but he also stays detached
enough to analyze her emotions, ranging from a desire for rescue by the
acrobatics of daring sky divers to a brief, vain hope of falling somehow into
water on the plains of Kansas. No such transcendence is possible. What is

possible is something she is able to do herself, to accept her death and to remove her clothes to prepare ritualistically for her entry into earth and to create a mystery for the farm boys below.

Dickey is also interested in a description of the landscape below from the birdlike perspective of the plummeting stewardess. In still another poem in this section, "Reincarnations II," he uses the perspective of a sea bird, ungainly in its feathered body, still possessed by memories of its former human existence but beginning to experience the thrills of flight. This perspective is the point of view for Dickey's picture of the landscape of the South in *Jericho: The South Beheld*. It permits a panoramic view, utilizing "the big forms" of nature that help his poetry to transcend the ordinary. It may, if he wishes, allow a touch of surrealism, which he describes in "The Sheep Child" as "the great grassy world from both sides."

In "The Firebombing," "Falling," "The Sheep Child," and the long poem "May Day Sermon to the Women of Gilmer County, Georgia, by a Woman Preacher Leaving the Baptist Church," Dickey is at his creative peak, exploring new themes and experimenting with new forms such as the "split line," a long line broken up into phrasal units. The strong narrative thrust that Dickey was able to infuse into his earlier poems with their simple declarative sentences is maintained in "Falling" and in "May Day Sermon"; the poems are dramatic and, at the same time, excellent psychological analyses. "May Day Sermon" explores the eroticism that underlies the woman preacher's religious fundamentalism. She narrates with an intense interest what would not be expected to interest her—the youthful exploits of young lovers like the two Dickey has described in "Cherrylog Road"—and what ought not to interest her—the punishments inflicted on a daughter by her vengeful father, who severely flogs her for her sexual transgressions. What is exposed is the preacher's growing desire to leave the Baptist Church for a more primitive, vital, and natural form of religion.

With Dickey's next book, *The Eye-Beaters, Blood, Victory, Madness, Buckhead and Mercy*, many critics feel that something was lost that he has not yet regained: his affirmative attitude even when face-to-face with primitive and destructive forces, and the balance between his neoromantic themes and tight formal control. In this new volume he seemed to be preoccupied with physical decline, with madness and death; he even tended toward the confessional, an attitude he had always deplored. His insistence on a narrative base, real or surreal, for his lyric perceptions had been dropped for a loose associational structure. This apparently came about out of his desire to reach a larger audience and to touch people more directly.

Dickey's inventiveness, his expansive imagination, had been another strength of his poetry. He had used his prerogative of "creative lying" effectively to project transcendence of the ordinary and to imagine a surrealism beyond realism. In his more recent work he occasionally substitutes rhetorical devices for dramatic tension, and has even attempted the kind of public poems he had previously declined to write. "The Strength of Fields" is a poem written for the inauguration of his fellow Georgian and an admirer of his poetry, President Jimmy Carter, and "Apollo I and II" was written as part of his coverage of the Apollo flights for *Life* magazine. Yet there are fine moments in Dickey's recent poetry. The climax of the Apollo poems is the magical moment when the Apollo astronauts come out from the dark of the moon back into the light of the sun again and "behold/ the blue planet. . . ." Dickey as a poet of transcendence and an advocate of beholding knows that this is one of the great transcendent moments in the history of mankind.

In "The Eye-Beaters," Dickey seizes upon the bruises near the eyes of blind children in a home in Indiana. He is told that the bruises are self-inflicted, the result of blows to the eyes to produce the illusion of sight. This fact is so painful to him that he tries to transcend it by imagining them achieving a vision out of their pain, perhaps creative images like those pictures of the good hunt left behind in dark prehistoric caves by primitive artists also driven by instinct to bring something from the world of light into their dark world. There is, however, a difference. Previously, when Dickey imagined transcendent acts—Donald Armstrong's gesture or his father's wave from the hospital window—he tried to convince his reader that it might have happened. Here he confesses that he has imagined something that his own reason cannot accept; it is simply a fantasy of a compassionate mind to preserve its own sanity in the presence of a painful reality. The poet who used to convince his reader that he had projected himself totally, if temporarily, has seemingly become a believer in the Cartesian split: reason sees the truth; imagination lies.

Dickey's long poem *The Zodiac*, written in imitation of a poem by the Dutch poet Hendrik Marman, has some fine moments. The idea of relating himself to home, Amsterdam, and, beyond that, through the signs of the zodiac, to the universe, undoubtedly appealed to Dickey's imagination. Many of Dickey's contemporaries have imitated the work of other poets, and Dickey has written similar imitations of poems by his friend the Russian poet Andrei Voznesensky. He does well in conveying the character and desires of the drunken Dutch poet. Unfortunately, he undermines the authority of his persona by introducing an omniscient narrator whose purpose seems to be to destroy the reliability and believability of the Dutch sailor.

Dickey has written good short poems in the 1970's that hold promise for the future. "Pine," in *The Eye-Beaters, Blood, Victory, Madness, Buckhead and Mercy* demonstrates Dickey's command of sensuous descriptive details; "Madness," in the same volume, provides a vivid account of an uncanny vision which madness lends a rabid dog. Several of Dickey's lyrics in his tribute to the youthful femininity, *Puella*, reveal much of the old lyric grace. Dickey is a good lyric poet, a good narrative poet, a dramatic conveyor of states of consciousness when ordinary experience is transcended. He is not a very good confessional poet. He is at his best when his imagination roams free while his good critical sense maintains sufficient formal control. As a literary "triple threat"—poet, novelist, literary critic—he has made important contributions to postmodernism. His first important book of reviews and critical essays, *Babel to Byzantium*, clearly explains his intentions. Every good poet today, he says, needs his vision of his own "Byzantium." Dickey has had his, though he has not always held to it with perfect consistency. At its most impressive, his "Byzantium" provides his urbanized modern reader with a near-surrealistic view of the "grassy world from both sides," the human and the "other." James Dickey has written enough good poems with vision and with control to be one of the major American poets to emerge since 1950.

**Major publications other than poetry**
NOVEL: *Deliverance*, 1970.
NONFICTION: *The Suspect in Poetry*, 1964; *Spinning the Crystal Ball*, 1967, *Babel to Byzantium: Poets and Poetry Now*, 1968; *Metaphor as Pure Adventure*, 1968; *Self-Interviews*, 1970; *Sorties: Journal and New Essays*, 1971.

**Bibliography**
Ashley, Franklin, ed. *James Dickey: A Checklist*, 1971.
Calhoun, Richard J., ed. *James Dickey: The Expansive Imagination*, 1973.
Elledge, Jim, comp. *James Dickey: A Bibliography, 1947-1974*, 1979.
Glancy, Eileen K., ed. *James Dickey: The Critic as Poet: An Annotated Bibliography with an Introductory Essay*, 1971.
Lieberman, Laurence, ed. *The Achievement of James Dickey*, 1968.

*Richard J. Calhoun*

# EMILY DICKINSON

**Born:** Amherst, Massachusetts; December 10, 1830
**Died:** Amherst, Massachusetts; May 15, 1886

## Principal collections

*The Poems of Emily Dickinson*, 1955 (Thomas H. Johnson, editor, 3 volumes); *The Complete Poems of Emily Dickinson*, 1960 (Thomas H. Johnson, editor).

During her lifetime, only seven of Emily Dickinson's poems were published, most of them edited to make them more conventional. After Dickinson's death, her sister Lavinia discovered about nine hundred poems, over half of the 1,775 poems that now compose the Dickinson canon. She took these to a family friend, Mrs. Mabel Loomis Todd, who, with Dickinson's friend Thomas Wentworth Higginson, published 115 of the poems in 1890. Together they published a second group of 166 in 1891, and Mrs. Todd alone edited a third series in 1896. Unfortunately, Mrs. Todd and Col. Higginson continued the practice of revision that had begun with the first seven published poems, smoothing the rhymes and meter, revising the diction, and generally regularizing the poetry.

In 1914, Dickinson's niece, Martha Dickinson Bianchi, published the first of several volumes of the poetry she was to edit. Although she was more scrupulous about preserving Dickinson's language and intent, several editorial problems persisted, and the body of Dickinson's poetry remained fragmented and often altered. In 1950, the Dickinson literary estate was given to Harvard University, and Thomas H. Johnson began his work of editing, arranging, and presenting the text. In 1955, he produced the variorum edition, 1,775 poems arranged in an attempt at chronological order, given such evidence as handwriting changes and incorporation of the poems in letters, and including all variations of the poems. In 1960, he chose one form of each poem as the final version and published the resulting collection as *The Complete Poems*. Johnson's text and numbering system are accepted as the standard. His job was thorough, diligent, and imaginative. This is not to say, however, that his decisions about dates or choices among variants must be taken as final. Many scholars have other opinions, and since Dickinson herself apparently did not make final choices, there is no reason to accept every decision Johnson made.

## Other literary forms

In addition to her poetry, Emily Dickinson left behind voluminous correspondence. Because she was so rarely out of Amherst—and in her later life so rarely left her house—much of her contact with others took place through letters, many of which include poems. Like her poetry, the letters are witty, epigrammatic, and often enigmatic. They are available in *The Letters of Emily Dickinson* (1958, Thomas H. Johnson and Theodora Ward, editors, 3 volumes).

## Achievements

As surely as William Faulkner and Ernest Hemingway, different as they were, brought American fiction into the twentieth century, so Walt Whitman and Emily Dickinson brought about a revolution in American poetry. By the mid-nineteenth century, American lyric poetry had matured to an evenly polished state. Edgar Allan Poe, Ralph Waldo Emerson, and Herman Melville were creating poetry of both power and precision, but poetry in this country was still hampered by certain limiting assumptions about the nature of literary language, about the value of regular rhythm, meter, and rhyme, and about imagery as ornamental rather than organic. Were the medium not to become sterile and conventionalized, poets had to expand the possibilities of the form.

Into this situation came Dickinson and Whitman, poets who—except in their commitment to writing a personalized poetry unlike anything the century had thus far read—differ as widely as do Faulkner and Hemingway. Whitman rid himself of the limitations of regular meter entirely. Identifying with the common man, Whitman attempted to make him a hero who could encompass the universe. He was a poet of the open road; Whitman journeyed along, accumulating experience and attempting to unite himself with the world around him. For him, life was dynamic and progressive. Dickinson, however, was the poet of exclusion, of the shut door. She accepted the limitations of rhyme and meter, and worked endless variations on one basic pattern, exploring the nuances that the framework would allow. No democrat, she constructed for herself a set of aristocratic images; she was queen and empress. No traveler, she stayed at home to examine small fragments of the world she knew. For Dickinson life was kinesthetic; she recorded the impressions of experience on her nerves and on her soul. Rather than being linear and progressive, it was circular: "My business is circumference," she wrote, and she often described the arcs and circles of experience. As carefully as Whitman defined himself by inclusion, Dickinson defined herself and her experience by exclusion, by what she was not. Whitman was a poet of explanation; Dickinson, having rejected expansion, exploited suggestion.

Different as they were, however, they are America's greatest lyric poets. Although Dickinson was barely understood or appreciated in her own lifetime, she now seems a central figure—at once firmly in a tradition and, at the same time, a breaker of tradition, a revolutionary who freed American poetry for modern thought and technique.

## Biography

"Renunciation is a piercing virtue," wrote Emily Dickinson, and her life can be seen as a series of renunciations. Born in 1830 of a prominent Amherst family, she rarely left the town, except for time spent in Boston and trips to Washington and Philadelphia. She attended the Amherst Academy and Mount Holyoke Female Seminary. Although she was witty and popular, she set herself apart from the other girls by her refusal to be converted to the conventional Christianity of the town. Her life was marked by a circle of close friends and of family: a stern and humorless father, a mother who suffered a long period of illness and whom Emily took care of; her sister Lavinia, who likewise never married and remained in the family home; and her brother Austin, who married Sue Gilbert Dickinson and whose forceful personality, like that of his wife, affected the family while Emily Dickinson lived, and whose affair with Mrs. Todd, the editor of the poems, precipitated family squabbles that affected their publication.

Additionally, there was a series of men—for it almost seems that Dickinson took what she called her "preceptors" one at a time—who formed a sort of emotional resource for her. The first of these was Samuel Bowles, the editor of the neighboring Springfield, Massachusetts, *Republican*, which published some of her poetry. Charles Wadsworth was the minister of a Philadelphia church; a preacher famous for his eloquence, he preached one Sunday when Dickinson was in Philadelphia, and afterward they corresponded for several years. In 1862, however, he and his family moved from Philadelphia to the West Coast. Dickinson immediately sent four of her poems to Thomas Wentworth Higginson, at the *Atlantic Monthly*, for his advice, and they began a long friendship; although Higginson was never convinced that Dickinson was a finished poet, he was a continuing mentor. Finally, late in life, Dickinson met Judge Otis Lord, and for a time it seemed as if they were to be married; this was her one explicitly romantic friendship, but the marriage never took place. There were also less intense friendships with women, particularly Mabel Todd, who, despite her important role in Dickinson's life, never actually met her, and with the writer Helen Hunt Jackson, one of the few to accept Dickinson's poetry as it was written.

The nature of the relationships with the "preceptors" and their effect on the poetry is a matter of much controversy. It is complicated by three famous and emotional "Master" letters which Dickinson wrote between 1858 and 1862 (the dates are partly conjectural). Who the master was, is uncertain. For Johnson, Dickinson's editor, the great influence was Wadsworth, and although their relationship was always geographically distant, it was he who was the great love, his moving to California the emotional crisis that occasioned the great flood-years of poetry—366 poems in 1862 alone, according to Johnson. For Richard B. Sewall, author of the standard biography, Bowles was the master.

Whatever the case, it is true that after 1862, Dickinson rarely left her house, except for a necessary visit to Boston where she was treated for eye trouble. She wore white dresses and with more and more frequency refused to see visitors, usually remaining upstairs, listening to the conversations and entering, if at all, by calling down the stairs or by sending in poems or other tokens of her participation. She became known as the "Myth of Amherst," and from this image is drawn the popular notion of the eccentric old maid that persists in the imagination of many of her readers today. Yet it is clear that whatever the limits of her actual experience, Dickinson lived life on the emotional level with great intensity. Her poetry is dense with vividly rendered emotions and observations, and she transformed the paucity of her outward life into the richness of her inner life.

Richard Wilbur has suggested that Dickinson suffered three great deprivations in her life: of a lover, of publication and fame, and of a God in whom she could believe. Although she often questioned a world in which such deprivations were necessary, she more frequently compensated, as Wilbur believes, by calling her "privation good, rendering it positive by renunciation." That she lived in a world of distances, solitude, and renunciation her biography makes clear; that she turned that absence into beauty is the testimony of her poetry.

## Analysis

One of Emily Dickinson's poems (#1129) begins, "Tell all the Truth but tell it slant," and the oblique and often enigmatic rendering of Truth is the theme of Dickinson's poetry. Its motifs often recur: love, death, poetry, beauty, nature, immortality, the self; but such abstractions do not indicate the broad and rich changes that Dickinson obliquely rings on the truths she tells.

Dickinson's truth is, in the broadest sense, a religious truth. Formally, her poetry plays endless variations on the Protestant hymn meters that she knew from her youthful experiences in church. Her reading in contemporary poetry was limited, and the form she knew best was the iambic of hymns: common meter (with its alternating tetrameter and trimeter lines), long meter (four lines of tetrameter), and short meter (four of trimeter) became the framework of her poetry. That static form, however, could not contain the energy of her work, and the rhythms and rhymes are varied, upset, and broken to accommodate the feeling of her lines. The predictable patterns of hymns were not for Dickinson, who delighted in off-rhyme, consonance, and, less frequently, eye-rhyme.

Dickinson is a religious poet more than formally, but her thematic sense of religion lies not in her assurance, but in her continual questioning of God, in her attempt to define his nature and that of his world. Although she is always a poet of definition, straightforward definition was too direct for her: "The Riddle we can guess/ We speedily despise," she wrote. Her works often begin, "It was not" or "It was like," with the poem being an oblique attempt to define the "it." "I like to see it lap the Miles" (#585) is a typical Dickinson riddle poem. Like many, it begins with "it," a pronoun without an antecedent, so that the reader must join in the process of discovery and definition. The riddle is based on an extended metaphor; the answer to the riddle, a train, is compared to a horse; but in the poem both tenor (train) and vehicle (horse) are unstated. Meanwhile, what begins with an almost cloying tone, the train as an animal lapping and licking, moves through subtle gradations of attitude until the train stops at the end "docile and omnipotent." This juxtaposition of incongruous adjectives, like the coupling of unlikely adjective and noun, is another of Dickinson's favorite devices; just as the movement of the poem has been from the animal's (and train's) tame friendliness to its assertive power, so these adjectives crystallize the paradox.

"It sifts from Leaden Sieves" (#311), another riddle poem, also begins with an undefined "it," and again the movement of the poem and its description of the powerfully effacing strength of the snow, which is the subject of the poem and the answer to the riddle, is from apparently innocent beauty through detailed strength to a quietly understated dread. The emotional movement in the famous riddle poem "A Route of Evanescence" (#1463) is less striking, since the poet maintains the same awed appreciation of the hummingbird from beginning to end; but the source of that awe likewise moves from the bird's ephemeral beauty to its power.

Riddling becomes less straightforward, but no less central, in such a representative Dickinson poem as "It was not Death, for I stood up" (#510), in which many of her themes and techniques appear. The first third of the poem, two stanzas of the six, suggest what the "it" is not: death, night, frost, or fire. Each is presented in a couplet, but even in those pairs of lines, Dickinson manages to disconcert her reader. It is not death, for the persona is standing upright, the difference between life and death reduced to one of posture. Nor is it night, for the bells are chiming noon—but Dickinson's image for that fact is also unnatural. The bells are mouths, their clappers tongues, which are "Put out"; personification here does not have the effect of making the bells more human, but of making them grotesque, breaking down as it does the barriers between such normally discrete worlds as the mechanical and the human, a distinction that Dickinson often dissolves. Moreover, the notion of the bells sticking out their tongues suggests their contemptuous attitude toward man. In stanza two, it is not frost because hot winds are crawling on the persona's flesh. The hackneyed phrase is reversed, so it is not coolness, but heat that makes flesh crawl, and not the flesh itself that crawls, but the winds upon it; nor is it fire, for the persona's marble feet "Could keep a Chancel, cool." Again, the persona is dehumanized, now grotesquely marble. While accomplishing this, Dickinson has also begun her inclusion of sense-data, pervasive in the first part of the poem, so that the confrontation is not only intellectual and emotional but physical as well.

The second third of the poem changes the proportions. Although the experience is not actually any of the four things she has mentioned above, it is like them all; but now death, the first, is given seven lines, night three, frost only two, and fire is squeezed out altogether. It is like death because she has, after all, seen figures arranged like her own; now her life is "shaven,/ And fitted to a frame." It is like night when everything that "ticked"—again mechanical imagery for a natural phenomenon—has stopped, and like frosts, which in early autumn morns "Repeal the Beating Ground." Her vocabulary startles once more: the ground beats with life, but the frost can void it; "repeal" suggests the law, but nature's laws are here completely nullified.

Finally, in the last stanza, the metaphor shifts completely, and the experience is compared to something new: drowning at sea. It is "stopless" but "cool"; the agony that so often marks Dickinson's poetry may be appropriate to the persona, but nothing around her, neither people nor nature, seems to note it. Most important, there is neither chance nor means of rescue; there is no report of land. Any of these conditions would justify despair, but for the poet, this climactic experience is so chaotic that even despair is not justified, for there is no word of land to despair of reaching.

Thus, one sees many of Dickinson's typical devices at work: the tightly patterned form, based on an undefined subject, the riddle-like puzzle of defining that subject, the shifting of mood from apparent observation to horror, the grotesque images couched in emotionally distant language. All this delineates that experience, that confrontation—with God, with nature, with the self, with one's own mind—which is the center of Dickinson's best poetry. Whether her work looks inward or outward, the subject matter is a confrontation leading to awareness, and part of the terror is that for Dickinson there is never any mediating middle ground; she confronts herself in relation to an abyss beyond. There is no society, no community to make that experience palatable in any but the most grotesque sense of the word, the awful tasting of uncontrollable fear.

Dickinson often questions the nature of the universe; she senses that God is present only in one's awareness of his absence. She shares Robert Frost's notion that God has tricked man, but while for Frost God's trick is in the nature of creation, for Dickinson it is equally in God's refusal to answer our riddles about that creation. She writes of the "eclipse" of God, and for Dickinson, it is God himself who has caused the obscurity. The customary movement in her explicitly religious poetry is from apparent affirmation to resounding doubt. Poem #338 begins with the line "I know that He exists." While Dickinson rarely uses periods even at the end of her poems, here the first line ends with one: a short and complete affirmation of God's existence, but an affirmation that remains unqualified for only that one line. God is not omnipresent, but exists "Somewhere—in Silence"; Dickinson then offers a justification for God's absence: his life is so fine that he has hidden it from humans who are unworthy. The second stanza offers two more justifications: he is playing with people, and one will be that much happier at the blissful surprise one has earned. Yet the play, in typical Dickinson fashion, is a "fond Ambush," and both the juxtaposition of incongruous words and the reader's understanding that only villains engage in ambush indicate how quickly and how brutally the tone of the poem is changing.

The last half begins with "But," and indeed 256 of Dickinson's poems, nearly fifteen percent, have a coordinate conjunction as the first word of the middle line: a hinge that links the deceptive movement of the first half with the oblique realization that takes place in the second. The lines of poem #338 then become heavily alliterative, slowing the reader with closely linked, plosive *p*'s before she begins the final question: "Should the glee—glaze—/ In Death's—stiff—stare." The quasisubjunctive, another consistent poetic stance in Dickinson, cannot mask the fact that there is no open possibility here, for death must come, the glee will glaze. Then the fun—it is God's fun of which she writes—will look too expensive, the jest will "Have crawled too far!" Although the last sentence is in the form of a question, the poem closes with an end mark stronger than the opening period, an exclamation point which leaves no doubt as to the tone the poem takes.

This same movement appears in Dickinson's other overtly religious poems. Poem #501 ("This World is not Conclusion.") likewise begins with a clear statement followed by a period and then moves rapidly toward doubt. Here God is a "Species" who "stands beyond." Men are shown as baffled by the riddle of the universe, grasping at any "twig of Evidence." Man asks "a Vane, the way," indicating the inconstancy of that on which man relies and punning on "in vain." Whatever answer man receives is only a narcotic, which "cannot still the Tooth/ That nibbles at the soul." Again, in "It's easy to invent a Life" (#724), God seems to be playing with man, and although the poem begins with man's birth as God's invention, it ends with death as God's simply "leaving out a Man." In poem #1601, "Of God we ask one favor," the favor requested is that he forgive man, but it is clear that humans do not know for what they ask forgiveness and, as in Frost's "Forgive, O Lord," it is clear that the greater crime is not man's but God's. In "I never lost as much but twice" (#49), an early but accomplished work, God is "Burglar! Banker— Father!" robbing the poet, making her poor.

One large group of Dickinson's poems, of which these are only a sample, suggests her sense of religious deprivation. Her transformation of the meter and rhythm of hymns into her own songs combines with the overt questioning of the ultimate meaning of her existence to make her work religious. As much, however, as Dickinson pretends to justify the ways of her "eclipsed" God to man, that justification never lasts. If God is Father, he is also Burglar. If God in his omnipotence finds it easy to invent a life, in his caprice he finds it just as easy to leave one out.

Dickinson just as persistently questions nature, which was for her an equivocal manifestation of God's power and whims. Although there are occasional poems in which her experience of nature is exuberant ("I taste a liquor never brewed," for example, #214), in most of her work the experience is one of terror. A synecdochist rather than a symbolist, she describes and confronts a part of nature, that scene representing the whole. For her nineteenth century opposite, Whitman, the world was one of possibilities, of romantic venturing forth to project oneself onto the world and form an organic relationship with it. For Dickinson, the human and the natural give way to the inorganic; nature is, if like a clock, not so in its perfect design and workings, but in its likeliness to wind down and stop.

"I started Early—Took my Dog" (#520) is characteristic in its treatment of nature, although uncharacteristic in the romantic venturing forth of the persona. For the first third of the poem, she seems to be in control: she starts early, takes her pet, and visits the sea. The sea is treated with conventional and rather pretty metaphor; it is a house with a basement full of mermaids. Even here, however, is a suggestion that something is amiss: the frigates extend "Hempen Hands"; the ropes that moor the ships are characteristically personified, but the substitution of "hempen" for the similar sounding and expected "helpin'" (the missing *g* itself a delusive familiarity) suggests that the hands will entwine, not aid, the poet. As so often in Dickinson, the natural world seems to be staring at her, as if she is the chief actor in an unfolding drama, and suddenly, with the coordinate conjunction "but," the action begins. The sea is personified as a man who would attack her. She flees. He pursues, reaching higher and higher on her clothes, until finally she achieves the solid ground, and the sea, like a docile and omnipotent train, unconcerned but "Mighty," bows and withdraws, his power there for another day.

Whenever Dickinson looks at nature, the moment becomes a confrontation. Although she is superficially within the Puritan tradition of observing nature and reading its message, Dickinson differs not only in the chilling message that she reads, but also because nature refuses to remain passive; it is not simply an open book to be read—for books remain themselves—but active and aggressive; personification suggests its assertive malevolence. In #348 ("I dreaded that first Robin, so"), the initial part of the poem describes the poet's fear: spring is horrible; it shouts, mangles, and pierces. What Dickinson finally manages is merely a peace with spring; she makes herself "Queen of Calvary," and in deference to that, nature salutes her and leaves her alone.

The same accommodation with nature occurs in #986, "A narrow Fellow in the Grass," where the subject, a snake that she encounters, is first made to seem familiar and harmless. Then the poet suggests that she has made her peace with "Several of Nature's People," and she feels for them "a transport/ Of cordiality," although one expects a more ecstatic noun than cordiality after a sense of transport. Dickinson concludes with a potent description of her true feelings about the snake, "Zero at the Bone," a phrase which well reflects her emotion during most confrontations, internal or external.

One of Dickinson's finest poems, #1624 ("Apparently with no surprise"), a poem from late in her career, unites her attitudes toward nature and God. Even as Frost does in "Design," Dickinson examines one destructive scene in nature and uses it to represent a larger pattern; with Frost, too, she sees two possibilities for both microcosm and macrocosm: accident or dark design.

The first two lines of her short poem describe the "happy Flower." The personified flower is unsurprised by its sudden death: "The Frost beheads it at its play—/ In accidental power—/ The blonde Assassin passes on—." In common with many American writers, she reverses the conventional association of white with purity; here the killer, the frost, is blonde. While she suggests that the power may be accidental, in itself not a consoling thought, the two lines framing that assertion severely modify it, for beheading is rarely accidental; nor do assassins attain their power by chance.

Whichever the case, accident or design, there is finally little significant difference, for nothing in the world pays attention to what has happened. "The Sun proceeds unmoved," an unusual pun, since unmoved has the triple meaning of unconcerned, stationary, and without a prime mover; it measures off the time for a God who does approve.

Thus, when Dickinson turns her vision outward, she looks at essential reality translated, often appallingly, into human terms. The alternative vision for Dickinson is inward, at her own self, and despite the claims of her imperial language, what she sees there is just as chaotic and chilling as what she sees without. "The Soul selects her own Society," she writes (#303), and she makes that society a "divine Majority." "I'm Nobody," another Dickinson poem begins (#288); but in her poetry the explicit movement is from no one to someone, from the self as beggar to the self as monarch: empress or queen. Out of the deprivation of her small society, out of the renunciation of present pleasures, she makes a majority that fills her world with aristocratic presence. Yet, for all that affirmation, the poems that look directly inward suggest something more; her assurance is ambiguously modified, her boasting bravado is dissipated.

Occasionally, Dickinson's poetry justifies her internal confusion in conventional terms. Poem #435, "Much Madness is divinest Sense," makes the familiar assertion that, although the common majority have enough power to label nonconformists as insane and dangerous, often what appears as madness is sense, "divinest Sense—/ To a discerning Eye." Usually, however, her poetry of the mind is more unsettling, her understanding more personal. "I Felt a Funeral, in my Brain" (#280) and "'Twas like a Maelstrom, with a notch" (#414), employing the drowning imagery of "It was not Death," are the most piercing of Dickinson's poems about the death of reason, the chaotic confrontation with the instability within. They also indicate the central ambiguity that these poems present, for the metaphor that Dickinson favors for the death of reason is literal, physical death: the tenor, insanity; the vehicle, death. Yet one is never quite sure whether it might not be the other way around: the central subject death; the metaphoric vehicle, the death of reason. Through this uncertainty, these poems achieve a double-edged vitality, a shifting of idea and vehicle, foreground and background.

The awareness of one's tenuous grasp on his own reason seems clearest in

"I felt a Funeral, in my Brain," for there the funeral is explicitly "in," although not necessarily "of," the speaker's brain. The metaphor is developed through a series of comparisons with the funeral rites, each introduced by "and," each arriving with increasing haste. At first the monotony of the mourners' tread almost causes sense to break through, but instead the mind reacts by going numb. Evenutally the funeral metaphor gives way to that of a shipwreck—on the surface, an illogical shift, but given the movement of the poem, a continuation of the sense of confusion and abandonment. The last stanza returns to the dominant metaphor, presenting a rapid series of events, the first of which is "a Plank in Reason" breaking, plunging the persona—and the reader—back into the funeral imagery of a coffin dropping into a grave. The poem concludes with "And Finished knowing—then," an ambiguous finish suggesting both the end of her life and of her reasoning, thus fusing the two halves of the metaphor. These two readings of the last line do not exhaust its possibilities, for there is another way to read it: the speaker finished with "knowing" not as a gerund object, but as the participial modifier, so that even at the moment of her death, she dies knowing. Since for Dickinson awareness is the most chilling of experiences, it is an appropriately horrible alternative: not the end of knowing, but the end while knowing.

Death is not merely metaphorical for Dickinson; it is the greatest subject of her work. Perhaps her finest lyrics are on this topic, which she surveyed with a style at once laconic and acute, a tone of quiet terror conveyed through understatement and indirection. Her power arises from the tension between her formal and tonal control and the emotional intensity of what she writes. She approaches death from two perspectives, adopts two stances: the persona as the grieving onlooker, atempting to continue with life; her own faith tested by the experience of watching another die; and the persona as the dying person.

In such poems as "How many times these low feet staggered" (#187), where the dead person has "soldered mouth," and "There's been a Death, in the Opposite House" (#389), where the windows of the house open like "a Pod," the description of death is mechanical, as if a machine has simply stopped. The reaction of the onlookers is first bewilderment, then the undertaking of necessary duties, and finally an awful silence in which they are alone with their realization of what has occurred. Poem #1100 ("The last Night that She lived") best illustrates all of these attitudes. It oscillates between the quietly dying person—whose death is gentle, on a common night, who "mentioned—and forgot," who "struggled scarce—/ Consented"—and those, equally quiet but less capable of giving consent, who watch the death occur. First there is the conventional idea that they who watch see life differently: death becomes a great light that italicizes events. Yet as the poem continues with the onlookers' random comings and goings and their feelings of guilt over continuing to live, there is little sense that their awareness is complete. After the death, Dickinson provides one stanza, neatly summarizing the final understanding: "And We—We placed the Hair," the repeated pronoun, the little gasp for breath and hint of self-dramatization, fills part of the time with what must be done. Then there is nothing left to do or to be said: "And then an awful leisure was/ Belief to regulate." The strange linking of "awful" with "leisure," the disruption of syntax at the line break, and the notion that the best belief can do is regulate leisure, all suggest in two lines the confusion and disruption for those who remain alive.

By consensus the greatest of all Dickinson poems, "Because I could not stop for Death" (#712) explores death from the second perspective, as do such poems as "I Heard a Fly buzz—when I died" (#465) and "I died for Beauty" (#449), in which one who has died for beauty and one who has died for truth agree, with John Keats, that truth and beauty are the same—the poet adding the ironic commentary that their equality lies in the fact that the names of both are being covered up by moss.

"Because I could not stop for Death" unites love and death, for death comes to the persona in the form of a gentleman caller. Her reaction is neither haste to meet him, nor displeasure at his arrival. She has time to put away her "labor and . . . leisure"; he is civil. The only hint in the first two stanzas of what is really occurring is the presence of Immortality, and yet that presence, although not unnoticed, is as yet unfelt by the persona. The third stanza brings the customary metaphor of life as a journey and the convention of one's life passing before his eyes as he dies: from youth, through maturity, to sunset. Here, however, two of the images work against the surface calm: the children out for recess do not play, but strive; the grain is said to be gazing. "Grazing" might be the expected word, although even that would be somewhat out of place, but "gazing" both creates unfulfilled aural expectations and gives the sense of the persona as only one actor in a drama that many are watching.

Again, as is common in Dickinson, the poem is hinged by a coordinate conjunction in the exact middle. This time the conjunction is "Or," as the speaker realizes not that she is passing the sun, but that "He passed us." The metaphoric journey through life continues; it is now night, but the emotions have changed from the calm of control to fright. The speaker's "Zero at the Bone" is literal, for her clothing, frilly and light, while appropriate for a wedding, is not so for the funeral that is occurring. The final stop—for, like the first two stanzas, the last two are motionless—is before the grave, "a House that seemed/ A Swelling of the Ground." The swelling ground also suggests pregnancy, but this earth bears death, not life. The last stanza comments that even though the persona has been dead for centuries, all that time seems shorter than the one moment of realization of where her journey must ultimately end. Death, Dickinson's essential metaphor and subject, is seen in terms of a moment of confrontation. Absence thus becomes the major presence, confusion the major ordering principle.

Dickinson's poetry is at times sentimental, the extended metaphors occasionally too cute, the riddling tone sometimes too coy. Like any poet, that is, she has limitations; and because her poetry is so consistent throughout her life, those limitations may be more obvious than in a poet who changes more noticeably. They do not, however, diminish her stature. If she found her place in American literature only decades after her death, it is a place she will not forfeit. Her importance is, of course, partly historical: with Whitman she changed the shape and direction of American poetry, creating and fulfilling poetic potentials that make her a poet beyond her century. Her importance, however, is much greater than that. The intensity with which she converted emotional loss and intellectual questioning into art, the wit and energy of her work, mark the body of her poetry as among the finest America has yet produced.

**Major publication other than poetry**
NONFICTION: *The Letters of Emily Dickinson*, 1958 (Thomas H. Johnson and Theodora Ward, editors, 3 volumes).

**Bibliography**
Anderson, Charles. *Emily Dickinson's Poetry: Stairway of Surprise*, 1960.
Chase, Richard. *Emily Dickinson*, 1951.
Gelpi, Albert J. *Emily Dickinson: The Mind of the Poet*, 1965.
Griffith, Clark. *The Long Shadow: Emily Dickinson's Tragic Poetry*, 1964.
Johnson, Thomas H. *Emily Dickinson: An Interpretive Biography*, 1955.
Leyda, Jay. *The Years and Hours of Emily Dickinson*, 1960.
MacLeish, Archibald, et al. *Emily Dickinson: Three Views*, 1959.
Sewall, Richard B. *The Life of Emily Dickinson*, 1974.
Ward, Theodora. *The Capsule of the Mind: Chapters in the Life of Emily Dickinson*, 1968.
Whicher, George F. *This Was a Poet: A Critical Biography of Emily Dickinson*, 1939.

*Howard Faulkner*

# RICHARD WATSON DIXON

**Born:** Islington, England; May 5, 1833
**Died:** Warkworth, England; January 23, 1900

## Principal collections

*The Sicilian Vespers*, 1852; *Christ's Company and Other Poems*, 1861; *St. John on Patmos*, 1863; *Historical Odes and Other Poems*, 1864; *Mano*, 1883; *Odes and Eclogues*, 1884; *Lyrical Poems*, 1887; *The Story of Eudocia and Her Brothers*, 1888; *Songs and Odes*, 1896; *Last Poems*, 1905; *Poems by the Late Canon Richard Watson Dixon*, 1909.

## Other literary forms

Richard Watson Dixon's lifework was his *History of the Church of England from the Abolition of the Roman Jurisdiction* (1878-1900, 6 volumes). He also published a biography of his father, *The Life of James Dixon, D.D., Wesleyan Minister* (1874). His important correspondence with Gerard Manley Hopkins, in which there is much discussion of poetic theory, has been collected in *The Correspondence of Gerard Manley Hopkins and R. W. Dixon* (1935, Claude Colleer Abbott, editor).

## Achievements

Dixon published eight volumes of poetry in his lifetime and two additional volumes were published after his death. He also wrote a massive history of the separation of the Anglican Church from the Roman Catholic Church. He is remembered today, however, because he was part of two widely different literary circles or movements. He was not the central force of either circle, but he was one of the contributory followers of both the Pre-Raphaelite movement and the literary circle of Gerard Manley Hopkins (1844-1889). Dixon attended King Edward VI School at Birmingham from 1847 to 1852. There he became a friend of Edward Burne-Jones (1833-1898), later to become a famous painter and designer. Dixon and Burne-Jones went to Oxford where they formed "The Set" of young artists, including William Morris (1834-1896). Later "The Set" came under the leadership of Dante Gabriel Rossetti (1828-1882). This association of undergraduates constituted the core of the Pre-Raphaelite movement in art and literature. Although the Pre-Raphaelite position is not clearly defined, in general its adherents felt that painting had been degenerating since the time of Raphael (1483-1520). They especially rejected the ideal of academic art codified in the *Fifteen Discourses* (1769-1790) of Sir Joshua Reynolds (1723-1792). The Pre-Raphaelite painters demanded emotional sincerity. Their paintings were typically anecdotal, symbolic, and moralistic, used raw or bright colors, showed intense concern for minute detail, and attempted to render with fidelity exactly what the eye could see in a scene. Under the influence of "The Set," Dixon apparently studied art and helped to paint the murals in the debating hall at the Oxford Union; these murals are now destroyed, but in the 1850's they were a milestone in the development of the Pre-Raphaelite movement. "The Set" broke up after Dixon's college years because it had been motivated in part by a religious fervor which few members sustained. Burne-Jones and Morris abandoned their youthful aspirations toward a churchly career, while Dixon was ordained in the Church of England in 1858 and served well as a minister for the rest of his life. Nevertheless, he remains one of the formative forces in the literature of the Pre-Raphaelite movement.

In his maturity, Dixon became a member of an even more distinguished literary circle. The poet Gerard Manley Hopkins is generally considered to be one of the major forces in the development of modernism in literature. In 1878, Hopkins, who was a Jesuit priest, wrote to Dixon reminding him that he had once been a teacher in Hopkins' school. Hopkins also expressed his admiration for Dixon's poetry. From that letter a warm friendship developed between the two men, recorded in their published letters, *The Correspondence of Gerard Manley Hopkins and R. W. Dixon*. At the age of forty-five, Dixon found himself once more in the inner circle of a set of highly original writers: Hopkins and his associates, Robert Bridges (1844-1930), and Coventry Patmore (1823-1896). If modern readers recognize Dixon's name, it is probably as a member of Hopkins' literary circle. His letters to Hopkins are a veritable poet's workshop of close criticism and commentary on the process of writing.

## Biography

Richard Watson Dixon was born in 1833, the eldest son of James Dixon, a Wesleyan minister, whose biography the son wrote in 1874. Life in a large family, constantly moving from one preaching circuit to another, was not easy. Moreover, James Dixon preached in the industrial north of England among the slums and poverty of Liverpool, Sheffield, Manchester, and Birmingham. In 1847, the boy was enrolled in Birmingham's King Edward VI School, a stern, demanding, pious institution. He had never before attended school and was caned for his backwardness. He appears to have been a shy, kindly, mild-tempered person. His admiration for the poetry of John Keats appears in his poem *The Sicilian Vespers*, which won a school prize and was published in 1852. From Birmingham, Dixon matriculated at Pembroke College, Oxford, in 1851. With Burne-Jones, Morris, and others, he formed "The Set" which became a wellspring of the Pre-Raphaelite movement. "The Set" admired Gothic art, architecture, and John Ruskin's "Of the Nature of the Gothic." Dixon contributed to the Pre-Raphaelite journal founded by his companions, *The Oxford and Cambridge Magazine*. He also is said to have worked on the Oxford Union murals in 1857. In 1858, he took Holy Orders in the Anglican

Church and was ordained to the curacy of St. Mary-the-Less, Lambeth. From that time until his death, Dixon's main daily work was that of a simple minister caring for his flock and pursuing his daily duties, but throughout this period he wrote poetry and his massive history of the founding of the Anglican Church. He held a variety of minor positions in the church and spent a short term in 1861 as assistant master of Highgate School, where Gerard Manley Hopkins was then a student. From 1868 to 1875 he was minor canon and honorary librarian of Carlisle Cathedral. He then served an eight-year term as vicar of Hayton before moving to the vicarage of Warkworth in Northumberland, a position he held until his death in 1900.

Dixon's volumes of poetry fall into two groups. The first group was published between 1852 and 1864. After a twenty-year gap, a second group of five volumes appeared between 1883 and 1896. These later volumes were produced after Hopkins and Dixon had become correspondents and are therefore of special interest for the modern reader because they illuminate the detailed references to poetic theory contained in the Dixon/Hopkins letters.

### Analysis

*Mano* is Richard Watson Dixon's longest work, a narrative poem of some 5,500 lines. It is written in terza rima, the stanza of *La Divina Commedia* (c. 1320, *The Divine Comedy*) of Dante Alighieri (1265-1321). It employs archaic words and expressions and creates a fictional world of chivalry and courtly love, reminiscent of *The Faerie Queene* (1590-1596) by Edmund Spenser (1552-1599). Although the setting of *Mano* involves portentous dreams and miraculous events, it lacks the allegorical system underlying Spenser's work. The setting is France and Italy in the year 1000—the first millenium of the Christian era. The story is told by the monk Fergant and proceeds by wandering digressions in the manner of a medieval chronicle. The medieval trappings of this work are typical of Pre-Raphaelite poetry, as in William Morris' *The Defence of Guenevere and Other Poems* (1858). Although the poem does not adhere closely to a unified plot, the skeleton of the narrative is clear. Its basis is the pattern of the quest. The knight, Mano, is of unknown parentage. He is sent from France to Rome, where he is ordered to deliver the Lady Diantha to her father, after which he returns to France. On the way he has many encounters in battle and in love which test his heroic virtue. At the end of the story he learns who his father was. Such a quest pattern is common to many narratives, from Homer's *Odyssey* (c. 800 B.C.) to novels of the present day such as E. L. Doctorow's *Loon Lake* (1979). *Mano* has a tragic, or falling, plot: Mano is highly esteemed and prosperous at the beginning of the story, but is betrayed and burned at the stake at its conclusion. The cause of his downfall is misplaced love, the irony of Eros.

*Mano* is unlike the poetry of Gerard Manley Hopkins in that it is a long narrative written in iambic pentameter lines, with many slack or unstressed syllables introduced merely to fill out the iambic measure. Hopkins characteristically pruned all unnecessary syllables from his lines and created his craggy "sprung" rhythms that sound quite unlike the flowing lines of *Mano*. Dixon's poem, however, might have fascinated Hopkins with its archaic and unusual vocabulary. Its chivalric medievalizing theme, too, conforms to some of the framing ideas in Hopkins' poems, as in his sonnet "The Windhover." As a Jesuit priest, Hopkins thought of himself as a knight of Christ, so the courtly chivalry and religious references in *Mano* might have interested him as well.

When Hopkins first wrote to Dixon on June 4, 1878, he mentioned that as a schoolboy he had learned of Dixon's volume of poetry, *Christ's Company and Other Poems*. Hopkins says that he copied out three poems from that book so that he should always have them by him: "St. Paul," "St. John," and "Love's Consolation." There are thirty-six poems in all in *Christ's Company and Other Poems*, the first five of them making up the cycle *Christ's Company and Other Poems:* "St. Paul," "St. John," "St. Peter," "Mary Magdalene," and "The Holy Mother at the Cross." This set of poems is of high quality and compares favorably with the dramatic monologues of Robert Browning (1812-1889). "St. Paul," the opening poem, is an epistle or dramatic monologue supposedly written by the Roman Gallio, an official in Achaia, to his brother Seneca, the stoic philosopher. Like the dramatic monologues of Browning, this poem externalizes a mental conflict. Gallio is an educated man and knows the consolation of philosophy, but he has been strangely unsettled by a prisoner who was brought before him for judgment, a certain Paul, who told him of the new Christian faith. Indirectly, Gallio's lack of satisfaction in his pagan world view appears in his letter to his brother back in Rome. The second poem in *Christ's Company and Other Poems*, also singled out for praise by Hopkins, is a dramatic monologue spoken by St. John, who tells in sixty-four stanzas of his mystical visions. The most striking of these involves a fight between a snake and a gecko, or lizard. He also tells of Christ appearing as a courtly knight to his maiden, of a magical island where angels and archangels sing, and of the coming woe of Jerusalem. The third poem in the cycle, "St. Peter," is a dramatic monologue in which Peter regrets his denial of Christ on the eve of the crucifixion. "Mary Magdalene" is a rather sensual Pre-Raphaelite portrait of Mary at prayer. "The Holy Mother at the Cross," the final poem, describes the Mother of Christ standing at the foot of the cross; it makes an extended comparison between the cross and a flowering tree bearing a blood-red blossom.

The thirty-one other poems in *Christ's Company and Other Poems* are of varying quality. Hopkins singled out "Love's Consolation" to copy into his personal notebook. It is a long poem of about five hundred lines in iambic pentameter couplets, spoken as a dramatic monologue by a "Monk of Osney-ford." Throughout the poem there is a symbolic reference to the thorn tree, which is said to be evergreen and to bear blood-red berries among its leaves of thorn. On the theological level, this tree refers to Christ's cross, as in "The Holy Mother at the Cross." On the secular level, it refers to the convention of courtly love, which is by nature painful and wounding. The poet's advice appears to be to accept the pain of life and "live on bravely." Erotic and Christian love are analogous in this work.

A number of the other poems are similar to *Mano* in that they treat chivalric or courtly subjects; among these are "The Crusader's Monument" and "Romance." "A Nun's Story" is a murder mystery: Lady Catherine's rejected lover, Guido, kills her bridegroom, Lorenzo, and drives her into the cloister. Several other poems use the traditional ballad form to treat courtly love and war.

A few of these poems can stand with the best writing of the Victorian era. For example, "Proserpine" begins in rhymed iambic pentameter couplets to describe the ancient worship of the goddess of fertility. In a nightmarish, blighted landscape, where "dragon earth" falls in "labyrinthine toils" into a volcanic cave, "savage men, autochthonic" celebrate the ritual of ancient Demeter and Persephone. With rising urgency, the poem quotes the priest's song, invoking the blood of a black sacrificial bull to cause the earth to bloom once more in springtime. To a modern reader, a poem such as this lays bare the link between courtly love and Christian sacrifice as the main topics in Dixon's poetry. Both are displacements of a fertility myth of the kind explored in Jessie L. Weston's *From Ritual to Romance* (1920), and incorporated in *The Waste Land* (1922) of T. S. Eliot (1888-1965). Much of Hopkins' poetry, too, celebrates the fertility of nature and the vivifying sacrifice of Christ.

Dixon's *Historical Odes and Other Poems* was dedicated to his friend, the painter Edward Burne-Jones, and contains twenty-seven poems varying in length from some twenty lines to several long pieces of nearly a thousand lines. These poems repeat the concerns of *Mano* and *Christ's Company and Other Poems*. Several tell stories of courtly, fatal love. "Concealment: The Story of a Gentleman of Dauphiny" traces the unfortunate love of a knight for his lady, La Belle. "Perversity: The Story of Ermolai" is a typical "crossed lovers" plot. Several other poems deal with stories from classical literature. "The Birth of Apollo" is a powerful work, as is "Orpheus," which depicts his unhappy love for Eurydice. Three of the poems in *Historical Odes and Other Poems* continue the cycle of *Christ's Company and Other Poems*. "Legion" describes the experience of the man cleansed of evil spirits by Christ. "St. Thomas in India" is a dramatic monologue spoken by St. Thomas, who is confronted by pagan worship. It is an impressive rendering of St. Thomas' psychological stress, revulsion, and disorientation. "Joseph of Arimathea and Nicodemus" is a dialogue between the man who received Christ's body from the cross and Nicodemus, a Jewish leader who had defended Christ before the Sanhedrin. The complete cycle of *Christ's Company and Other Poems* thus consists of eight poems dealing with people who had direct contact with

Christ. It deserves a prominent place in the Victorian anthology.

The *Historical Odes* in the volume are four long poems: "Wellington," "Marlborough," "John Franklin," and "Havelock's March." Dixon devoted much of his energy to historical prose, writing a biography of his father and a massive history of the foundation of the Anglican Church. The historical poems in this volume examine men who really lived, not mythological figures or fictional courtly knights. What connects the historical, biographical studies to his knightly fictions is Dixon's concern for the nature of heroism. Wellington and Marlborough are of interest to him because they are modern knights. Their lives are a model of chivalric heroism. John Franklin, perhaps not so well-known to modern readers, was an English seaman who died in arctic exploration. "Havelock's March" tells the story of the British army unit which fought its way to the relief of besieged Lucknow. These poems reveal a Victorian pride in Empire and militarism which is not palatable to modern American readers. For Dixon, however, the code of conduct exhibited by Wellington, Marlborough, and Franklin manifests in modern dress the courtly ideal of Mano, which in turn is based on the moral authority of Christ's company, the true Christian, gentle knight.

*St. John on Patmos* is a long poem in iambic pentameter couplets describing the mystical visions or revelations of St. John. It is similar to *Christ's Company and Other Poems* in its forceful depiction of the impact of early Christianity. St. John sees whirling, wrathful prophecies of the struggle between the Dragon, who is the false prophet, and true Christianity. He sees three cities and three women. Sodom is equated with Jerusalem and represented as a shameless woman. Babylon stands for Rome and a destructive witch. The New Jerusalem, however, is the glorious future structure of the Church and it is compared to a spotless bride.

*Odes and Eclogues* contains a group of longer poems on classical stories, such as Cephalus and Procris, Apollo Pythius, an attractive study of the monster Polyphemus, and a set of shorter nature songs in which a simple emotion is projected onto a natural scene. "To a Bramble in Winter" is typical of this kind of romantic sentiment. The speaker sees a decrepit bramble bush in winter and asks what it was like in full summertime. He contrasts the youthful vigor of the plant and its then thoughtless joy with its present decayed condition. *Lyrical Poems* is dedicated to Gerard Manley Hopkins and is a continuation of the topics explored in the earlier *Odes and Eclogues*, but with a noticeable increase in poetic power. Classical stories include "Ulysses and Calypso" and "Mercury." Romantic nature poetry receives some careful thought in "Nature and Man," in which the poet asks how human emotions and man's environment interact. Since Dixon served as a vicar in parishes in the English Lake District, his references to local geography in this poem invite a comparison between his view of nature and that of William Wordsworth (1770-1850).

Dixon's poetry shows the influence of the Pre-Raphaelites in its descriptive and medievalizing passages. He sees an analogy between the true courtesy of a knight and the ideal of Christian sacrifice and, in turn, a reflection of Christian love in worldly love. He writes interesting dramatic monologues which introduce eccentric points of view and unreliable narration. For example, Fergant in *Mano* implies attitudes which are not the same as the normative values in the work as a whole. In this respect, Dixon is exploring the modernist tendencies in the work of such better-known contemporaries as Robert Browning. The psychodrama of several of the poems in *Christ's Company and Other Poems* exploits such potentialities of the monologue. Like many of the great Victorians, he had an immense interest in Roman and ancient Greek literature and built many of his poems on themes and situations derived from classical texts. His letters to Gerard Manley Hopkins show how much effort Dixon spent on the techniques of writing poetry: the verse forms, the metrical patterning, and the vocabulary. Probably this technician's skill and care attracted Hopkins to Dixon's work more than his subjects and stories, although both men were deeply involved in Christian, classical, and Romantic intellectual and emotional world views. Dixon's vocabulary must have fascinated Hopkins by its archaic and unusual words and phrases. Although some of Dixon's poetry deserves more attention than it has received, he will remain best known as one of literature's great reflectors, receiving and sharpening the spark of originality of his friends.

**Major publications other than poetry**

NONFICTION: *History of the Church of England from the Abolition of the Roman Jurisdiction*, 1878-1900 (6 volumes); *The Life of James Dixon, D.D., Wesleyan Minister*, 1874; *An Essay on the Maintenance of the Church of England*, 1874; *The Monastic Comperta*, 1879; *Seven Sermons*, 1888; *A Sermon*, 1897; *The Correspondence of Gerard Manley Hopkins and R. W. Dixon*, 1935 (Claude Colleer Abbott, editor).

**Bibliography**

Sambrook, James. *A Poet Hidden: The Life of Richard Watson Dixon, 1833-1900*, 1962.

Summerfield, H. "The Lyric Poetry of R. W. Dixon (1833-1900)," in *Trivium*. V (1970), pp. 57-71.

*Todd K. Bender*

# JOHN DONNE

**Born:** London, England; 1572
**Died:** London, England; March 31, 1631

## Principal collections

*An Anatomy of the World: The First Anniversary*, 1611; *Of the Progress of the Soule: The Second Anniversary*, 1612; *Poems by J. D.: With Elegies on the Authors Death*, 1633, 1635, 1639, 1649, 1650, 1654, 1669.

## Other literary forms

Although John Donne is known today chiefly as a lyric poet, the posthumous volume *Poems by J. D.*, which includes the lyrics, represents only a small part of his literary output. Donne was famous in his own age mainly as a preacher; in fact, he was probably the most popular preacher of an age when preaching held the same fascination for the general public that the cinema has today. Various sermons of Donne's were published during his lifetime, and several collections were published in the following decades. Without a commitment to Donne's religious values, few today would want to read through many of his sermons—grand as their style is. Donne must, however, be credited with the careful articulation of the parts of his sermons, which create a resounding unity of theme; and his control of prose rhythm and his ingenious imagery retain their power, even if modern readers are no longer disposed to see the majesty of God mirrored in such writing.

Excerpts from Donne's sermons thus have a continuing vitality for general readers in a way that excerpts from the sermons of, for example, Lancelot Andrewes cannot. In the early seventeenth century, Andrewes had been the most popular preacher before Donne, and, as Bishop of Winchester, he held a more important position. He also had a greater reputation as a stylist, but for modern readers, Andrewes carries to an extreme the baroque fashion of "crumbling a text" (analyzing in minute detail). The sermons of Andrewes are now unreadable without special training in theology and classical languages. On the other hand, though also writing for an educated audience with a serious interest in divinity, Donne wears his scholarship more easily and can still be read by the general student without special preparation. His sermon to the Virginia Company is the first sermon in English to make a missionary appeal.

The single most famous of Donne's sermons was his last. *Death's Duell* (1632), preached before King Charles on February 25, 1631, is a profound meditation on mortality. Man's mortality is always a major theme with Donne, but here he reaches a new eloquence. Full of startling imagery, the sermon takes as its theme the paradox that life is death and death is life—although Christ's death delivers mankind from death. When this last sermon of Donne's was published, Henry King, Bishop of Chichester, remarked that "as he exceeded others at first so at last he exceeded himself."

A work of similar theme but published by Donne in his own lifetime is the *Devotions upon Emergent Occasions* (1624). Composed, as R. C. Bald has shown, with extreme rapidity during a serious illness and convalescence in 1623, this work is based on the structured meditational technique of St. Francis de Sales, involving the sensuous evocation of scenes, although, as Thomas F. Van Laan has suggested, the work is perhaps also influenced by the *Spiritual Exercises* (1548) of St. Ignatius Loyola. It is divided into twenty-three sections, each consisting of a meditation, an expostulation, and a prayer. The work is an artfully constructed whole of sustained emotional power, but the meditations have achieved a special fame with their vivid evocations of the theme that sickness brings man closer to God by putting him in touch with his frailty and mortality. Various meditations from the *Devotions upon Emergent Occasions* present famous pictures of the tolling of the death knell, of the body as a microcosm, and of the curious medical practices of the day, for example, the application of live pigeons to Donne's feet to try to draw the vapors of fever from his head. By this last practice, Donne discovers that he is his own executioner since the vapors are believed to be the consequence of his melancholy, and this is no more than the studiousness required of him by his calling as a preacher. While in past centuries most readers found the work's self-consciousness and introspection alienating, the contemporary sensibility finds these characteristics especially congenial. The three meditations on the tolling of the bells have, in particular, provided titles and catchphrases for popular writers.

A posthumously published early study of mortality by Donne is *Essayes in Divinity* (1651). The *Essayes in Divinity*, written in a knotty, baroque style, is a collection of curiously impersonal considerations of the Creation and of the deliverance of the Israelites from bondage in Egypt. The work shows none of the fire of the sermons and of the *Devotions upon Emergent Occasions*. A very different sort of contemplation of mortality is provided in *Biathanatos* (1646). The casuistical reasoning perhaps shows evidence of Donne's Jesuit background. The same approach to logic and a similar iconoclasm are apparent in *Juvenilia: Or, Certain Paradoxes and Problems* (1633; the first complete version was, however, not published until 1923).

The earliest of Donne's publications were two works of religious controversy of a more serious nature. These works also show Donne's Jesuit background, but in them, he is reacting against his upbringing and presenting a case for Anglican moderation in the face of Roman Catholic—and especially Jesuit—pretensions. *Pseudo-Martyr* (1610) was written at the explicit request of King James, according to Donne's first biographer, Izaak Walton. Here and throughout his subsequent career, Donne is a strongly committed Erastian, seeing the Church as properly subordinate in this world to secular authority.

The other of these early works of controversy, *Ignatius His Conclave* (1611), which appeared in Latin as well as English, is still amusing to modern readers who are unlikely to come to it with quite the strong partisan feeling of its original audience.

### Achievements

Donne was a remarkably influential poet in his day. Despite the fact that it was only after his death that a substantial body of his poetry was published, the elegies and satires (and to a lesser extent the divine poems and the songs and sonnets) had already created a new poetic mode during Donne's lifetime as a result of circulating in manuscript. Thomas Carew, in a memorial elegy published in the first edition of Donne's poems, described him as ruling the "universal monarchy of wit." The poetry of the School of Donne was usually characterized in its own day by its "strong lines." This characterization seems to have meant that Donne and his followers were to be distinguished from the Sons of Ben, the poets influenced by Ben Jonson, chiefly by their experiments with rough meter and conversational syntax; Jonson, however, was also—somewhat confusingly—praised for strong lines. Donne's own characteristic metrics involve lines densely packed with syllables. He makes great use not only of syncope (dropping of an unstressed vowel within a word) and elision (dropping of an unstressed vowel at the juncture between words) but also of a device almost unique to Donne among English poets—synaloepha (speeding up of adjacent vowels at the juncture between words with no actual dropping). By hindsight Donne, Edward Lord Herbert of Cherbury, Henry King, George Herbert, John Cleveland, Richard Crashaw, Abraham Cowley, Henry Vaughan, Andrew Marvell, and others of the School of Donne share not only strong lines but also a common fund of imagery. Eschewing for the most part classical allusions, these poets turned to the imagery of everyday life and of the new learning in science and philosophy.

In the middle of the seventeenth century there occurred what T. S. Eliot has memorably described as a "dissociation of sensibility," after which it became increasingly difficult to see Donne's secular and religious values as part of a consistent whole. The beginnings of this attitude were already apparent in Donne's own day; in a letter, for example, he describes *Biathanatos* as the work not of Dr. Donne but of the youthful Jack Donne. Toward the end of the century, the change of perspective is complete when John Dryden describes Donne unsympathetically as one who "perplexes the Minds of the Fair Sex with nice Speculations of philosophy." The Restoration and the eighteenth century had lost Donne's sense of religious commitment and thus scrutinized a style in isolation from the content it intended to express. Donne's poetry was condemned as artificial, and his reputation disappeared almost overnight.

This was the situation when Samuel Johnson wrote the famous strictures on Donne in his "Life of Cowley." That these remarks occur in the *Life of Cowley* is perhaps a commentary on the fallen stature of the earlier poets: Donne did not himself merit individual treatment in *Lives of the Poets* (1779-1781). Conceding that to write like Donne "it was at least necessary to read and think," Johnson describes the wit of the School of Donne—accurately enough—as the "discovery of occult resemblances in things apparently unlike." While many readers of the earlier seventeenth century and of the twentieth century would consider the description high praise, for Johnson it was a condemnation. For him, the "most heterogeneous ideas are yoked by violence together." Johnson popularized the term "Metaphysical poetry" for this yoking; the term had, however, been used earlier, even in Donne's own day.

Donne's stature and influence in the twentieth century are equal to his great stature and wide influence in the seventeenth, but the attitude represented by Johnson remained the norm for the centuries between. Donne's current prestige is based on values different from those that accounted for his prestige in his own day. The seventeenth century took its religion seriously but understood religion as part of the whole fabric of life. Donne's stature as a preacher was for this reason part of his prestige as a poet. In addition, the fact that he wrote love poetry and sometimes used graphic erotic imagery did not in his own day seem incongruous with his calling as a preacher.

The twentieth century has not, of course, recovered the intense religiosity of the early seventeenth century, but what Eliot, Ezra Pound, and other poets of their circle had discovered in the 1920's was an aestheticism as intense as this religiosity. Their values naturally led them to praise lyric poetry in preference to epic and to prize intensity of emotion in literary work of all kinds. They disparaged the poetry of John Milton because it was an expression of ideas rather than of feeling and offered Donne as a model and a more appropriate great author for the period. The restoration of Donne's prestige was remarkably complete; but, paradoxically, precisely because the triumph of Donne was so complete, the denigration of Milton never quite occurred. The values that Eliot and others praised in Donne were looked for—and discovered—in Milton as well.

While fifty years ago Donne was perhaps a more exciting figure than he is today, because to appreciate him meant to throw over the eighteenth and nineteenth century allegiance to Milton as the great poet of the language, Donne's stature as a major figure is now assured. Contemporary scholarly opinion has, however, been moving inevitably toward seeing the divine poems as the capstone of his career. Scholarly opinion has, in fact, moved beyond Eliot's position and come to value literary works simply because they have religious content, since intensity of feeling will surely be found in a poetry of religious commitment. This is not a way of appreciating Donne and the Metaphysicals that would have been understood in the seventeenth century.

## Biography

Born in St. Nicholas Olave Parish, London, sometime between January 24 and June 19, 1572, John Donne came from a Welsh paternal line (originally Dwn) with some claim to gentility. His father, however, was an ironmonger, although important enough to serve as warden of his professional guild. On his mother's side, Donne's connections were distinguished both for their intellectual attainments and their recusancy—that is, allegiance to the Church of Rome in the face of the Elizabethan Church Settlement. Donne's maternal grandfather was the epigrammatist and playwright John Heywood. A great-grandfather, John Rastell, was a minor playwright. Two of Donne's uncles were Jesuits who died in exile for their faith, as did his great-uncle Judge William Rastell; and another great-uncle, the monk Thomas Heywood, was executed, having been caught saying mass. Finally, a great-grandmother was the sister of Sir Thomas More, whose skull Donne inherited and very characteristically kept as a *memento mori*. Donne's brother, Henry, died in prison, where he had been sent for harboring a seminary priest; and Donne justifiably said in *Pseudo-Martyr* that no family had suffered more for the Roman Church.

His father died while Donne was still in infancy. His mother married twice more. The step-father of Donne's youth was a prominent physician. At first educated at home by Roman Catholic tutors, in 1584, Donne and his younger brother, Henry, were admitted to Hart Hall, Oxford. While they were a precocious twelve and eleven at the time, they were entered in the register as even younger in order to circumvent the requirement that students of sixteen and over subscribe to the Oath of Supremacy. Donne spent probably three years at Oxford altogether.

Although records are lacking for the next period of Donne's life, one hypothesis is that he spent some of this time in travel abroad. With his brother, Donne eventually took up residence at the Inns of Court to prepare for a legal career. Unsettled in these career plans by the arrest and death of Henry, Donne began serious study of the relative claims of the Angelican and Roman Churches and finally abandoned the study of law entirely.

In 1596, he participated in the Earl of Essex's military expedition to Cadiz. Donne's affability and his growing reputation as a poet—sustained by the private circulation of some of his elegies and lyrics—recommended him to a son of Sir Thomas Egerton who had also participated in the sack of Cadiz; and Egerton, who was Lord Keeper, was persuaded to appoint Donne as his secretary. In this position and also in Parliament, where he served briefly in 1601, he had many opportunities to meet people of note, and he improved his reputation as a poet by composing satires and occasional poems as well as additional lyrics.

In 1601, Donne was already in his late twenties, and, during Christmastide, he contracted a secret marriage with Anne More, the sixteen-year-old niece of Lady Egerton. Since the marriage was contrary to her father's wishes, Donne was imprisoned for his offense; he also permanently lost his position as Egerton's secretary, and the couple were forced to live for several years on the charity of friends and relations. A comment made at the time, sometimes attributed to Donne himself, was, "John Donne, Anne Donne, Undone."

Although his career hopes had been dashed by the impetuous marriage, his winning personality and poetic skill won for him new friends in high places. He traveled abroad with Sir Walter Chute in 1605; he became a member of the salon of Lucy, Countess of Bedford; and he even attracted the attention of King James, who saw what a useful ornament Donne would be to the Church and urged him to take orders. Not completely resolved in his conscience to do so, Donne, for a considerable time, temporized. Yet, his activity during this period led him inevitably toward this step. A substantial body of Donne's religious verse was written during this period and sent to Magdalen Herbert, mother of George Herbert and Lord Herbert of Cherbury. Finally, he committed himself to seeking advancement within the Angelican Church with the publication of *Pseudo-Martyr*, a work of religious controversy on a problem strongly vexing the King—the refusal of Roman Catholics to subscribe to the Oath of Allegiance. Thereafter, the King refused to consider Donne for any post outside the Church. In 1610, Oxford University awarded an honorary master's degree to Donne, who had been prevented by his former religion from taking an undergraduate degree.

Having composed the *Anniversaries* under the patronage of Sir Robert Drury of Hawsted, he accompanied Sir Robert to Paris and then to Frankfort. After the return of the party to England in 1612, Donne and his family resided with Sir Robert. Although he continued to write occasional verse, Donne had definitely decided to take orders. Having prepared himself through further study, he was ordained early in 1615, and numerous avenues for advancement immediately became available to him. The King made him a royal chaplain. Cambridge awarded him the degree of Doctor of Divinity by royal command. Lincoln's Inn appointed him Reader in Divinity to the Society. In addition, he was able to turn down offers of fourteen country livings in his first year as a priest, while accepting two. The one blight on his early years as a priest was the death of his wife in 1617. In 1619, Donne took time out from his regular duties to serve as chaplain accompanying Lord Doncaster on an embassy to Germany.

Donne's fame as a preacher had been immediate, and it continued to grow each year. As Walton reports, even his friends were surprised by the continuous growth of his pulpit eloquence after such a striking beginning. Such genius received its proper setting in 1621 when Donne was appointed Dean of St. Paul's Cathedral. The position was also a lucrative one, and the Dean's residence was as large as an episcopal palace.

The winter of 1623-1624 was a particularly eventful time in Donne's life. Having contracted relapsing fever, he was on the verge of death, but with characteristic dedication—and also characteristic self-consciousness—he kept a meticulous record of his illness as an aid to devotion. The resulting work, *Devotions upon Emergent Occasions*, was published almost immediately. During the same period, Donne's daughter, Constance, married the aging Elizabethan actor Edward Alleyn, founder of Dulwich College. From circumstances surrounding the wedding, the publishing history of *Devotions upon Emergent Occasions* has been reconstructed. It now seems clear that Donne composed this highly structured work in just a few weeks while still physically incapacitated.

In 1624, he took on additional duties as Vicar of St. Dunstan's-in-the-West. After the death of King James in the following year, Donne was chosen to preach the first sermon before the new king. This and other sermons were printed at the request of King Charles. Also printed was his memorial sermon for Lady Danvers, as Magdalen Herbert had become.

Even when Donne again became gravely ill in 1629, he would not stop preaching. Ever conscious of his mortality during these last months, he sat for a portrait wearing his shroud. When he delivered his last sermon on Ash Wednesday in 1631, it was the famous *Death's Duell*. Walton gives a vivid account of the writing and preaching of this sermon during Donne's last illness, and some of the sermon's special urgency is perhaps explained by the fact that the king's household called it Donne's own funeral sermon. Indeed, a few weeks later, on March 31, 1631, he died, having been preceded only a few months before by his aged mother.

**Analysis**

The traditional dichotomy between Jack Donne and Dr. Donne, despite John Donne's own authority for it, is essentially false. In the seventeenth century context, the work of Donne constitutes a fundamental unity. Conventional wisdom may expect devotional poetry from a divine and feel a certain uneasiness when faced with love poetry, but such a view misses the point in two different ways. On the one hand, Donne's love poetry is philosophical in its nature and characterized by a texture of religious imagery; and, on the other hand, his devotional poetry makes unexpected, bold use of erotic imagery. What Donne presents is two sides of a consistent vision of the world and of the mortality of man.

In the nineteenth century, when Donne's poetry did occasionally attract some attention from the discerning, it was not for the lyrics but for the satires. The satirical mode seemed the most congenial use that Donne had found for his paradoxical style. This had also been the attitude of the eighteenth century, which, however, valued metrical euphony too highly to accept even the satires. In fact, Alexander Pope tried to rescue Donne for the eighteenth century by the curious expedient of "translating" his satires into verse, that is, by regularizing them. In addition to replacing Donne's strong lines and surprising caesurae with regular meter, Pope, as Addison C. Bross has shown, puts ideas into climactic sequence, makes particulars follow generalizations, groups similar images together, and untangles syntax. In other words, he homogenizes the works.

While today Donne's lyrics are preferred to his satires, the satires are regarded as artistically effective in their original form, although this artistry is of a different order from that of the lyrics. Sherry Zivley has shown that the imagery of the satires works in a somewhat different way from that of the imagery of the lyrics, where diverse images simply succeed one another. With images accumulated from a similarly wide range of sources, the satires build a thematic center. N. J. C. Andreasen has gone even further, discerning in the body of the satires a thematic unity. Andreasen sees Donne as having created a single persona for the satires, one who consistently deplores the encroaching materialism of the seventeenth century.

Satire III on religion ("Kind pity chokes my spleen") is undoubtedly the most famous of the satires. Using related images to picture men as engaging in a kind of courtship of the truth, the poem provides a defense of moderation and of a common ground between the competing churches of the post-Reformation world. Although written in the period of Donne's transition from the Roman Catholic Church to the Anglican, the poem rejects both of these, along with the Lutheran and the Calvinist Churches, and calls on men to put their trust in God and not in those who unjustly claim authority from God for churches of their own devising.

In addition to the fully developed satires, Donne wrote a small number of very brief epigrams. These mere witticisms are often on classical subjects and therefore without the occasional focus that turns Ben Jonson's epigrams into genuine poetry. This is the only place where Donne makes any substantial use of classical allusion.

In his own day, Donne's most popular poems were probably his elegies. While in modern usage the term *elegy* is applied only to a memorial poem, Donne's elegies derive their form from a classical tradition that uses the term, as well, for poetry of love complaint written in couplets. Generally longer than the more famous songs and sonnets, the elegies are written on the model of Ovid's *Amores (Loves)*. Twenty or more such poems have been attributed to Donne, but several of these are demonstrably not his. On the basis of manuscript evidence, Dame Helen Gardner has suggested that Donne intended fourteen poems to stand as a thematically unified Book of Elegies and that "The Autumnal" (Elegy IX), which has a different manuscript history, and "The Dream" (Elegy X), which is not in couplets, although authentic poems by Donne, do not form a part of it.

Elegy IX, "The Autumnal," is a praise of older women as more seasonable to the appetite because the uncontrollable fires of their youth have passed. There is a long tradition that this poem was specially written for Magdalen Herbert. If so, it is particularly daring since, although not a seduction poem, it is frankly erotic in its praise; inasmuch as Magdalen Herbert did take as her second husband a much younger man, however, it may be supposed that she would have appreciated the general recognition that sexual attractiveness and interest can endure and even ripen. On the other hand, the poem's praises are not without qualification. The persona admires autumnal beauty, but he can see nothing attractive in the truly aged, whom he rejects as death's heads from which the teeth have been scattered to various places—to the vexation of their souls since the teeth will have to be gathered together again for the resurrection of the body at the Last Judgment. Thus the poem shows Donne's typical combination of eroticism and contemplation of mortality in a mode of grotesque humor.

In Elegy XIX, "To His Mistress Going to Bed," the persona enthusiastically directs his mistress in her undressing. Aroused, he uses his hands to full advantage to explore her body. In a famous passage, he compares his amazement to that of someone discovering a new land. He next directs her to bare her body to him as fully as she would to the midwife. This graphic request is followed by the poem's closing couplet, in which the persona points out that he is naked already to show his mistress the way and thus poignantly reveals that he is only hoping for such lasciviousness from her and not already having his wanton way. Even this poem uses religious imagery—most clearly and most daringly when it advocates a woman's baring of her body to her lover by analogy with the baring of the soul before God. In an influential explication, Clay Hunt suggests that Donne is, in fact, ridiculing the Neoplatonic school of love that could seriously advance such an analogy. If so, Donne is clearly having it both ways and making the analogy available for its own sake as well.

The songs and sonnets, as the other love poems are usually called, although no sonnets in the conventional sense are included, show an imaginative variety of verse forms. They are particularly famous for their dramatic, conversational opening lines. In addition, these poems are a great storehouse of the kind of verbal ambiguity that William Empson has shown the modern world how to admire.

In "The Canonization," the persona justifies his love affair in explicitly sacred terms by explaining that his relationship with his beloved makes the two of them saints of love. John A. Clair has shown how the structure of "The Canonization" follows the five stages of the process of canonization in the Roman Catholic Church during the Renaissance: proof of sanctity, recognition of heroic virtue, demonstration of miracles, examination of relics and writings, and declaration of worthiness of veneration. The poem is thus addressed to a devil's advocate who refuses to see the holiness of erotic love.

It is this devil's advocate in love who is asked to hold his tongue, in the famous first line. "The Canonization" illustrates Donne's typical use of ambiguity as well as paradox, not as merely decorative wit, but to reveal deepest meanings. William H. Machett suggests that, for example, when the lovers in this poem become a "piece of chronicle," the word *piece* is a triple pun meaning masterpiece, fragment, and fortress. There is also a much more obvious meaning—piece of artillery—a meaning that interacts with the title to give a richer texture to the whole poem: the poem is not only about the making of saints of love; but it is also about the warfare between this idea and conventional notions of sex and religion. Consequently, yet another meaning of *piece* comes into play, the sexual.

"The Flea" is a seduction poem. Like many of the songs and sonnets, it takes the form of a logical argument making full use of the casuistries and indeed sophistries of the dialectic of Peter Ramus. In the first of the poem's three stanzas the persona asks the lady to contemplate a flea he has discerned upon her person. Since his blood and hers are mingled in the flea that has in succession bitten each of them, the mingling of the bloods that takes place during intercourse (as was then believed) has already occurred. In the second stanza the persona cautions the lady not to kill the flea. By joining their bloods the flea has become the place of their joining in marriage, so for her to kill the flea would be to murder him and also to commit both suicide and sacrilege. In the last stanza, the persona discovers that the lady has ignored his argument and killed the flea, but he is ready with another argument. When the lady triumphantly points out that they have survived this death of the flea, surely she is also showing how false her fears of sex are, since sex involves no greater loss of blood and no greater death. Implicit in these last lines is the traditional pun on "death," which was the popular term for sexual climax. The pun and the poem as a whole illustrate Donne's characteristic mingling of the sacred and the profane. It should be noted that a love poem on the subject of the lady's fleas was not an original idea with Donne, but the usual treatment of the subject was as an erotic fantasy. Donne's originality is precisely in his use of the subject for dialectic and in the restraint he shows in ending the poem before the lady capitulates, in fact without indicating whether she does.

"The Ecstasy," the longest of the songs and sonnets, has, for a lyric, attracted a remarkable range of divergent interpretations. The poem is about spiritual love and intermingling as the culmination of physical love, but some critics have seen the Neoplatonism, or spiritualizing of love, as quite serious, while others have insisted that it is merely a patently sophistical ploy of the persona to convince his mistress that, since they are one soul, the physical consummation of their love is harmless, appropriate, inevitable. If the critics who see who see "The Ecstasy" as a seduction poem are right, the conclusion is even more salacious than they have supposed, since it calls on the addressee to examine the lovers closely for the evidence of true love when they have given themselves over to their bodies—in other words, to watch them make love. In fact, the poem, like so many of Donne's, is quite content to be theological and erotic by turns—beginning with its very title, a term used of both religious experience and sexual experience. That the perfect soul brought into being by the union of the lovers should combine the flesh and spirit eternally is an understandable religious hope and also a good sexual fantasy. In this way, the poem illustrates Donne's philosophy of love. Although not all his poems use this theme, Donne has, in fact, a unique ability for his day to perceive love as experienced by equals.

Another famous poem of love between equals is "A Valediction: Forbidding Mourning." The poem rushes through a dazzling spectrum of imagery in just the way deplored by Samuel Johnson. In addition, in the *Life of Cowley* Johnson singles out the poem for his ultimate condemnation, saying that in the extended metaphor of the last three stanzas "it may be doubted whether absurdity or ingenuity has the better claim." During the present century, ingenuity has once again become respectable in poetry, and modern readers come with more sympathy than Johnson did to this famous extended metaphor, or conceit, comparing lovers who have to suffer a temporary separation to a pair of pencil compasses. Even the improbability of the image—which Johnson castigated as absurdity—has been given a context by modern scholarship. W. A. Murray, for example, has shown that the circle with a dot in the center, which is inscribed by the compasses reflecting the lovers who are separated yet joined, is, in fact, the alchemical symbol for gold, mentioned elsewhere in the poem and a traditional symbol of perfection. More ingeniously, John Freccero has seen Donne's compasses as inscribing not simply a circle but, as they close, a spiral. The spiral has some history of use in describing the motion of the planets. Since the spiral is also a conventional symbol of humanity, this spiral reading helps readers see in "A Valediction: Forbidding Mourning" Donne's characteristic balance of the celestial and the personal.

In fact, Donne's inclusiveness is even wider than it is usually assumed to be. He collapses not only physical and spiritual but also male and female. Donne has the unusual perspicacity to make the persona of "Break of Day" explicitly female, and although no critic has made the point before, there is nothing to prevent seeing a similar female persona in "A Valediction: Forbidding Mourning." Such a reading has the advantage of introducing some erotic puns in the compass conceit as the man (the fixed center in this reading) harkens after his beloved as she roams and then grows erect when she returns to him. More important, such a reading makes further sense out of the image of a circle inscribed by compasses. The circle is a traditional symbol of woman, and woman's life is traditionally completed—or, as the poem puts it, made just—with a man at the center. Since the circle is a natural sexual image for woman, in this reading, the poem illustrates the practical sex as well as the theoretical sociology behind its imagery as the lover's firmness makes the woman's circle taut. An objection that might be made to this reading is that the poem's various references to parting show that it is the speaker who is going away. While a woman of the seventeenth century would be unlikely to do extensive traveling apart from her lover (or even in his company), a woman may have to part as well as a man, and lovers might well think of themselves as roaming the world when kept apart only by the daily round of pedestrian business. There is no more reason in the poem for believing that the absent one will literally roam than for believing that this absent one will literally run.

While Walton assigns this poem to the occasion of Donne's trip to France with Sir Robert Drury in 1611, the apocryphal nature of Walton's story is sufficiently indicated by the fact that it does not appear until the 1675 version of his *Life of Donne*. This dating would, at the least, make "A Valediction: Forbidding Mourning" extremely late for the songs and sonnets. Nevertheless, were the poem occasioned by Donne's preparation to travel to France in 1611, reading it as spoken by a woman would still be appropriate, since Donne prepared for this trip by sending his wife and children to stay with relatives on the Isle of Wight several months before he was himself able to embark. In addition, a general knowledge of how poets work suggests that a lyric inspired by a specific occasion is seldom in every particular a document congruent with the poet's actual experience. Perhaps the poem finally says that a woman can make a virtue of necessary separation as well as a man can.

Among the songs and sonnets are a few poems that seem to have been written for patrons. Since Twickenham is the seat of the Earls of Bedford, "Twickenham Garden" is assumed to have been written for Lucy, Countess of Bedford. According to the poem, the garden is a refuge like Eden, but the persona admits that with him the serpent has been let in. He wishes he were instead an aphrodisiac plant or fountain more properly at home in the place. In the last stanza, he seems to become such a fountain, but he is disappointed to discover that all the lovers who visit the garden are false. The poem ends— perhaps rather curiously for a patronage poem—with the obscure paradox that the only true woman is the one whose truth is killing.

A similar depersonalization characterizes the riddling poem "A Nocturnal upon St. Lucy's Day, Being the Shortest Day." While the ironies of darkness and light and of the changing movement of time (*Lucy* means light, but her day provides less of it than any other) would have recommended the subject to Donne anyway, it must have been an additional stimulus that this astronomically significant day was the saint's day of one of his patronesses. Clarence H. Miller, seeing the poem as unique among the songs and sonnets in describing the union with the lady as exclusively sacred without any admixture of the profane, relates the poem to the liturgy for St. Lucy's Day. In the body of the poem, however, the persona sees himself as the epitaph for light, as every dead thing. Finally, he becomes St. Lucy's Day itself—for the purpose of providing lovers with a longer nighttime for lust. Despite a certain bitterness or at least coarseness of tone, the poem is usually seen as a lament for the Countess' death (1627); the death of Donne's wife, however, has also been suggested, although Anne More has no special association with St. Lucy and his love for her could not have been exclusively spiritual. Richard E. Hughes has considered the occasion of the poem from a different point of view and usefully suggested that, though commemorating the Countess of Bedford, the poem is not an improbably late lyric for the songs and sonnets but a lament from an earlier period for the loss of the Countess' friendship. If the tone is considered in the least charitable light, the poem might even be read as an accusation of patronage withdrawn.

The familiar letter came into its own as a genre during the seventeenth century, and collections even began to be published. About two hundred of Donne's letters survive. This is a larger number than for any other figure of the English Renaissance except Sir Francis Bacon, and Bacon's correspondence includes many letters written in his official capacity. Since the familiar letter had only begun to surface as a genre, much of the impersonality and formality of earlier letter writing persist in Donne's correspondence. Donne's son was a rather casual editor, and in light of the sometimes general nature of Donne's letters, the date and intended recipient of many remain unknown. One curiosity of this period of epistolary transition is the verse letter. Almost forty of Donne's letters are written in verse. Some of these are true occasional poems datable from internal evidence, but many are of a more general, philosophical nature.

The most famous of the verse letters are "The Storm" and "The Calm," the first certainly and the second probably addressed to Christopher Brooke. Traditionally, shipwrecks and other dangers of the sea are used to illustrate the unpredictability of fortune in men's lives, but, as B. F. Nellist has shown, Donne does not follow this convention; instead, he teaches that frustration and despair are to be accepted as part of man's lot.

While many of the verse letters seem to have been exchanged with friends as *jeux d'esprit*, some are attempts to influence patrons. A group of poems clearly written with an eye to patronage are the epithalamia. Among the weddings that Donne celebrated was that of Princess Elizabeth to Frederick V, Elector of the Palatinate and later briefly King of Bohemia. Donne also celebrated the wedding of the royal favorite Robert Carr, Earl of Somerset, to Frances Howard, Countess of Essex. Since the Countess was shortly afterward convicted of murdering the essayist Sir Thomas Overbury for having stood in the way of her marriage, this epithalamion must later have been something of an embarrassment to Donne. An occasional poem for which no occasion is ascribed is the "Epithalamion Made at Lincoln's Inn." This is the most interesting of the epithalamia to contemporary taste. Its satiric tone, verbal crudities, and scoffing are a pleasant surprise in a genre usually characterized by reverence, even obsequiousness. The problem of what wedding could have been appropriately celebrated with such a poem has been resolved by David Novarr's suggestion that the "Epithalamion Made at Lincoln's Inn" was written for a mock wedding held as part of the law students' midsummer revels.

Other poems written for patrons are those usually called the epicedes and obsequies. These are eulogies for the dead—elegies in a more modern sense of the term than the one Donne seems to have in mind. Donne was one among the many poets who expressed regret at the death of Prince Henry, the hope of the dynasty.

Also in the general category of memorial verse are the two so-called *Anniversaries* (*An Anatomy of the World: The First Anniversary* and *Of the Progress of the Soule: The Second Anniversary*) but these two poems are so unlike traditional eulogies as to defy inclusion in the genre. In their search for moments of intense feeling, the Metaphysical poets, with their love of paradox, did not often try to write long poems. Most of the attempts they did make are unsatisfactory or at least puzzling in some fundamental way. The *Anniversaries* are, indeed, primary texts in the study of the difficulties of the long poem in the Metaphysical mode.

Ostensibly written as memorial poems to commemorate Elizabeth Drury, who died as a child of fourteen and whom Donne had never seen, these poems range over a broad canvas of history. "Shee," as the subject of the two poems is called, is eulogized in an extravagant fashion beyond anything in the obsequies. While O. B. Hardison has shown that these poems were not regarded as bizarre or fulsome when originally published, they were the first of Donne's works to lose favor with the passing of time. Indeed, of *An Anatomy of the World* Ben Jonson objected to Donne himself that "if it had been writ of the Virgin Marie it had been something." Donne's answer is reported to have been that he was describing not Elizabeth Drury specifically but the idea of woman; but this explanation has not been found wholly satisfactory. Many candidates have been suggested for Shee of the *Anniversaries*—from St. Lucy and Astraea (Goddess of Justice) to the Catholic Church and Christ as Divine *Logos*. Two critics have suggested Queen Elizabeth, but one finds her eulogized and the other sees her as satirized, indicting in a particularly striking way the problematic nature of these difficult, knotty poems.

Hardison, and, more recently Barbara Kiefer Lewalski, have made the case for the poems as part of a tradition of epideictic poetry—poetry of praise. In this tradition, extravagant compliments are the norm rather than the exception, and all of Donne's individual extravagances have precedents. What such a reading leaves out of account is, on the one hand, the extraordinary density of the extravagant praise in Donne's *Anniversaries* and, on the other hand, the presence of satire, not only the possible satire of the heroine but also explicit satire in the exploration of the decay of nature that forms the subject of the poems. Marjorie Hope Nicholson sees the *Anniversaries* as companion poems, the first a lament for the body, the second a meditation on mortality. Louis L. Martz suggests, further, that the *Anniversaries* are structured meditations. Martz sees *An Anatomy of the World* as a mechanical application of Ignatian meditation and *Of the Progress of the Soule* as a more successful organic application. Meditation theory, however, fails to resolve all the interpretive difficulties. Northrop Frye's theory that the poems are Menippian satire, and Frank Manley's that they are wisdom literature, also leave unresolved difficulties.

Perhaps these interpretive difficulties are fundamentally beyond resolution. Rosalie L. Colie has usefully pointed out that, in the *Anniversaries*, Donne seems not to be trying to bring his disparate materials to a conventional resolution. The poems accept contradictions as part of the flux of life and should be seen within the Renaissance tradition of paradox. Donne is demonstrably a student of paradox in many of his other works. More specifically, Daniel B. Rowland has placed *An Anatomy of the World* in the Mannerist tradition because in it Donne succeeded in creating an unresolved tension. His purpose may be just to raise questions about the relative weight of praise and satire and about the identity of the heroine Shee. Mario Praz goes further—perhaps too far—when he sees all the work of Donne as Mannerist, as illustrative not of wit but of the dialectics of passion; Mannerism does, however, provide a useful description for what modern taste finds a strange combination of materials in the *Anniversaries*.

An even more difficult long poem is an unfinished one called "Infinitati Sacrum." This strange parable of original sin adapts Paracelsus' theory of the transmigration of souls to follow through the course of subsequent history the spirit of the apple plucked by Eve. W. A. Murray has seen in this poem the beginnings of a *Paradise Lost* (1667). While few other readers will want to go so far, most will agree with Murray and with George Williamson that "Infinitati Sacrum" is a preliminary use of the materials and themes treated in the *Anniversaries*.

Donne has been called a poet of religious doubt in contrast to Herbert, a poet of religious assurance; but Herbert has real doubts in the context of his assurance, and the bold demand for salvation in audacious, even shocking language characteristic of the holy sonnets suggests, on the contrary, that Donne writes from a deep-seated conviction of election.

Louis Martz, Helen Gardner, and others have shown the influence of Ignatian meditation in the holy sonnets. Dame Helen, in fact, by restoring the manuscript order, has been able to see in these poems a sequential meditative exercise. The sensuous language, however, suggests not so much the meditative technique of St. Ignatius Loyola as the technique of St. Francis de Sales. In addition, Don M. Ricks has argued cogently that the order of the poems in the Westmorland Manuscript may suggest an Elizabethan sonnet sequence and not a meditative exercise at all.

Holy Sonnet XIV (10 in Dame Helen's numbering), "Batter my heart, three-personed God," has been seen by Arthur L. Clements and others as hieroglyphically illustrating the Trinity in its three-part structure. This poem opens with the striking dramatic immediacy typical of Donne's best lyrics. Using both military and sexual imagery, Donne describes the frightening, ambivalent feelings called up by the thought of giving oneself over to God's power and overwhelming grace. The soul is a town ruled by a usurper whom God's viceroy, Reason, is inadequate to overthrow. The soul is also the beloved of God though betrothed to his enemy and longing for divorce. The resolution of this sonnet turns on a paradoxical sexual image as the persona says that his soul will never be chaste unless God ravishes him. A similar complex of imagery is used, though in a less startling fashion, in Holy Sonnet II (1), "As due by many titles I resign."

Holy Sonnet IX (5), "If poisonous minerals," begins audaciously by accusing God of unfairness in the consequences He has decreed for original sin. In the sestet the persona abruptly realizes that he is unworthy to dispute with God in this way and begs that his tears of guilt might form a river of forgetfulness inducing God to overlook his sins rather than actually forgiving them. While this poem does not turn on a sexual image, it does contrast the lot of fallen man unfavorably with that of lecherous goats, who have no decree of damnation hanging over them.

Holy Sonnet XVIII (2 in Dame Helen's separately numbered group from the Westmorland Manuscript), "Show me, dear Christ, Thy spouse so bright and clear," has some of the most shocking sexual imagery in all of religious literature. While the tradition of using erotic imagery to describe the soul's relationship with God has a long history, particularly in exegesis of the Song of Songs, that is helpful in understanding the other holy sonnets, the imagery here is of a different order. Like Satire III, the poem is a discussion of the competing claims of the various Christian churches, but it goes well beyond the courtship imagery of the satire when it praises the Anglican Church because, like a promiscuous woman, it makes itself available to all men.

A distinctly separate series of holy sonnets is "La Corona." Using paradoxes such as the fact that the Virgin is her Maker's maker, and including extensive allusions to the divine office, this sequence of seven poems on the life of Christ has been called by Martz a rosary of sonnets, not so much because of the devotional content as because of the interlaced structure: the last line of each poem is repeated as the first line of the next. While the ingenious patterning renders the sequence less personal than Donne's best religious poetry, within its exquisite compass it does make a beautiful statement of the mysteries of faith.

In "A Hymn to Christ, at the Author's Last Going into Germany," Donne exaggerates the dangers of a Channel crossing to confront his mortality. Then even in the face of death, the persona pictures Christ as a jealous lover to be castigated if He withdraws His love just because it is not reciprocated; yet the persona does call for a bill of divorcement from all his lesser loves. The poem ends with the thought that, just as dark churches (being free of distractions) are best for praying, death is the best refuge from stormy seas.

"Good Friday, 1613: Riding Westward" is a witty paradox built on Ramist dialectic. Forced to make a trip to the West on Good Friday, the persona feels his soul drawn to the East. Although the heavens are ordered for westward motion, he feels a contradiction even as he duplicates their motion because all of Christian iconology urges him to return to the East where life began—both human life in Eden and spiritual life with the Crucifixion. He reasons that through sin he has turned his back on the Cross—but only to receive the correction that his sins merit. He hopes such flagellation will so change his appearance that he will again become recognizable to God as made in His Own image. Then he will at last be able to turn and face God.

Another divine poem of witty paradox is "A Hymn to God the Father." Punning on *Son/sun* and on his own name, Donne demands that God swear to save him. Having done so, God will at last have Donne. Because of its frankness and its very personal use of puns, this poem is not really a hymn despite its title—although it has been included in hymnals.

The chapter headings of *Devotions upon Emergent Occasions* as laid out in the table of contents should also be included among the divine poems. Joan Webber has made the illuminating discovery that this table of contents is a Latin poem in dactylic hexameters. This is a particularly surprising element of artistry in a work composed in such a short time and under such difficult conditions. Thus even more self-conscious than had been supposed, *Devotions upon Emergent Occasions* can finally be seen as an explication of the Latin poem.

## Major publications other than poetry

NONFICTION: *Letters to Several Persons of Honour*, 1651; *A Collection of Letters*, 1660.

RELIGIOUS WRITINGS: *Pseudo-Martyr*, 1610; *Ignatius His Conclave*, 1611; *Devotions upon Emergent Occasions*, 1624; *Death's Duell*, 1632; *Juvenalia: Or, Certain Paradoxes and Problems*, 1633; *Six Sermons on Several Occasions*, 1634; *LXXX Sermons*, 1640; *Biathanatos*, 1646; *Fifty Sermons*, 1649; *Essayes in Divinity*, 1651; *XXVI Sermons*, 1660.

## Bibliography

Bald, R. C. *John Donne: A Life*, 1970.
Gardner, Helen, ed. *John Donne: A Collection of Critical Essays*, 1962.

Lewalski, Barbara Kiefer. *Donne's "Anniversaries" and the Poetry of Praise: The Creation of a Symbolic Mode*, 1973.

Mazzeo, Joseph Anthony. "A Critique of Some Modern Theories of Metaphysical Poetry," in *Modern Philology*. L (1952), pp. 88-96.

Roberts, John R. *John Donne: An Annotated Bibliography of Modern Criticism: 1912-1967*, 1973.

_____ , ed. *John Donne: An Annotated Bibliography of Modern Criticism: 1968-1978*, 1978.

_____ , ed. *Essential Articles for the Study of John Donne's Poetry*, 1975.

Smith, A. J., ed. *John Donne: Essays in Celebration*, 1972.

Webber, Joan. *Contrary Music: The Prose Style of John Donne*, 1963.

Williamson, George. *Six Metaphysical Poets: A Reader's Guide*, 1967.

*Edmund Miller*

# EDWARD DORN

**Born:** Villa Grove, Illinois; April 2, 1929

## Principal poems and collections

*The Newly Fallen*, 1961; *Hands Up!*, 1964; *From Gloucester Out*, 1964; *Idaho Out*, 1965; *Geography*, 1965; *The North Atlantic Turbine*, 1967; *Our Word: Guerrilla Poems from Latin America*, 1968 (translation with Gordon Brotherston); *Gunslinger I*, 1968; *Gunslinger II*, 1969; *Gunslinger I and II*, 1969; *Twenty-Four Love Songs*, 1969; *Trees Between Two Walls*, 1969 (translation with Gordon Brotherston); *The Midwest Is That Space Between the Buffalo Statler and the Lawrence Eldridge*, 1969; *The Cosmology of Finding Your Spot*, 1969; *Songs, Set Two: A Short Count*, 1970; *Spectrum Breakdown: A Microbook*, 1971; *A Poem Called Alexander Hamilton*, 1971; *The Cycle*, 1971; *The Hamadryas Baboon at the Lincoln Park Zoo*, 1972; *Gunslinger Book III*, 1972; *Recollections of Gran Apachería*, 1974; *Semi-Hard*, 1974 (with George Kinball); *Collected Gunslinger*, 1975 (with Book IV); *The Collected Poems: 1956-1974*, 1975; *Manchester Square*, 1975 (with Jennifer Dunbar); *Selected Poems*, 1976 (translation with Gordon Brotherston); *Selected Poems*, 1978 (Donald Allen, editor); *Yellow Lola*, 1981.

## Other literary forms

Edward Dorn has written one novel, *The Rites of Passage: A Brief History* (1965, revised as *By the Sound* in 1971) and one book of short stories, *Some Business Recently Transacted in the White World* (1971). In addition, he has published numerous books of essays and translations.

## Achievements

Dorn's writing has been compared by critics to that of Walt Whitman for its joy in American themes, to that of Ernest Hemingway for its idiomatic speech, to that of Ezra Pound for its humor and erudition, and to that of Thomas Wolfe for its panoramic view. More accurate, however, are the criticisms claiming that his work defies paraphrasing and that his philosophy is likely to be different from that of his reader, who will emerge with a less inhibited and consequently more benevolent and tolerant view of the world. Dorn has been called a "Master of contemporary language," and *Gunslinger* has been called a "masterpiece of contemporary poetry."

Dorn has taught at Idaho State University, at the University of Kansas, at Northeastern Illinois State University, at Kent State University, at the University of Essex (Colchester), at the University of California, Riverside and San Diego, and at Muir College. He is currently an Associate Professor of English at the University of Colorado in Boulder, where he is director of the writing program. He has twice been a Fulbright Lecturer in American Literature at Essex; he received National Endowment for the Arts grants in 1966 and 1968, a fellowship from the University of New Mexico in 1969, and the American Book Award in 1980. He has been Poet-in-Residence at the University of Alaska and at the University of Michigan, Ann Arbor.

He has read at the Folger Library, the Cambridge Poetry Festival, the University of Durham, England, King's College (the University of London), and Westfield College. He gave the Olson lectures at SUNY in 1981.

## Biography

Edward Merton Dorn attended a one-room schoolhouse for most of his first eight grades. The poet he read most frequently was James Whitcomb Riley, whose writing appeared in the local newspapers because he was from the neighboring state of Indiana. Dorn attended the University of Illinois, Urbana, and Black Mountain College, where he was graduated in 1955. At Black Mountain College, in a liberal, creative environment, Dorn was associated with the rector Charles Olson, the poets Robert Creeley, Robert Duncan, Joel Oppenheimer, John Weiners, and Paul Blackburn, as well as the painter Franz Kline, the musician John Cage, and many other stimulating people. Since then he has held such disparate jobs as those of a logger in Washington State and a reference librarian at New Mexico State University in Santa Fe. During the mid-1960's he was the editor of *Wild Dog* magazine.

In 1969 he married Jennifer Dunbar; they have a son, Kidd, and a daughter, Maya.

## Analysis

Usually called a Black Mountain poet, Edward Dorn has commented that there is no Black Mountain "school" with a single style or ideology, but that instead Black Mountain College meant a "school" in the true sense of the word, a climate in which to acquire and satisfy a thirst for the "dazzle of learning" and an appreciation of its value.

Referring to the poetry of the much-revered Charles Olson, Dorn claims that he is not sure what "breath-determined projective verse" is; he simply writes in "clots" of words, and when a line begins to lose its energy, he begins a new one. This intuitional line division leads to free verse, which utilizes some end-rhyme and, more often, internal rhyme. Dorn's long narrative poems ("Idaho Out" and *Gunslinger*) have the structure of an odyssey punctuated by stops and encounters.

Dorn's major themes can be pinpointed by naming certain representative figures in his work. Howard Hughes represents all that is wrong with today's world, from isolation to selfishness to unbounded competitiveness. Daniel Drew, the robber baron, is the prototype of earlier American acquisitiveness. Dick Tracy is a pop figure familiar to all. Parsifal is not only the ideal knight, symbolic of the unrecoverable past in the mistaken view of most Americans, but also a part of the mythology ever-present in Dorn's poetry. John Philip Sousa, associated with a period of history that seems in retrospect more pleasing than the present, elicits both a love for music and an almost sentimental reminiscence about an Illinois childhood. There remains the geranium, the lovely scarlet bloom that flourishes in the West and represents in Dorn's poetry the feminine Indian principle, and the trees—the box elder of his youth and the piñon of his adult years.

Heeding the advice of Olson, his mentor at Black Mountain College, to "dig one thing or place" until he knew more about it than anyone else, Dorn chose the American West. That vast area has become the locus and the vehicle for Dorn's major concerns: displaced persons and minorities, greedy entrepreneurs, ecology, the role of the poet, and, most important, survival. Believing that the United States government created its own first subdivisions with the passage of the Homestead Act, he notes that after a century of "planned greed," what remains are cowboys who live in ranch houses and pull plastic boats behind their highly horsepowered wagons. If a cowboy actually owns a horse, he does not ride it. Although Dorn loves this new world, he sometimes finds it so evil that he thinks it should not even have been discovered. Major villains are the realtors, who have converted SPACE to space by subdividing it, while the victims are the immigrants who came in "long black flea coats," Indians who now "play indian and scoff wieners and Seven Up," and the land itself.

While most ordinary citizens are relatively impotent in the face of money, acquisition, and imperialism, Dorn believes that the poet has the potential to alter perception and thought, to be, in Olson's phrase, "of the company of the gods." Art aids in man's survival. In the poem "Sousa," Dorn suggests that Sousa's music is an antidote to the present crash course on which the world is embarked, and even a means of figuratively irrigating the wasteland. In a Dylan Thomas-like phrase, he recalls "the only May Day of [his] mind," the octagonal bandstand, the girls' billowing summer dresses, and ladybugs— all associated with Sunday afternoon occasions. Pleading with "John" (Philip Sousa) to pick up his "phone," Dorn deplores the fact that the nation, which has lifted the "chalice of explosion," can no longer be amused by Sousa's martial music. Noting that Sousa's marches are benevolent—the kind in which no one is injured—the poet concludes the poem with a brief prayer that the friends he has loved and left will have "cut wood to warm them."

Wood is significant in Dorn's work, not only because it can literally warm bodies, but also because it is one of the natural objects to be lost in the despoliation of the West, and because Dorn himself has worked as a logger. The box elder tree, associated with his youth in Illinois, and the piñon tree of the West and his adult life, appear frequently in the poems. "The Rick of Green Wood," which appears first in both *The Collected Poems* and *Selected*

*Poems*, serves to introduce not only the theme of wood and the comfort it will offer his family, but also the poet himself: "My name is Dorn," he tells the woodcutter as the two converse in the November air. The friendly atmosphere is chilled by the warning that "the world is getting colder"—colder because of a lack of communication between its people and because of a depletion of its resources. Like Robert Frost's invitation to see the new-born calf and clear the pasture spring, and Emily Dickinson's "Letter to the World," Dorn's "The Rick of Green Wood" invites the reader to participate in the poet's world and to read on to learn more about the woodyard and the West beyond it.

As Frost, Pound, and T. S. Eliot did before him, Dorn observed his homeland from England for a time; in all fairness, he admits that America is "no more culpable" than England, and he finally decides that what happens in Minnesota is really more his business than what happens in England. Dorn takes himself back home, but not before advising two jaded English poets who think that everything has already been said that they should make something up, "get laid" and describe that experience, or see what hope they can offer the world.

In the West once more, Dorn parodies the "Home on the Range," where Sacagawea wears a baseball cap and eats a Clark Bar, and cowboys are good ole boys who ride in trucks with gun racks. Concerned as always with the fate of men living in this country and on this continent, Dorn offers suggestions: ignore the rigid patterns of society; the person who is different may be the one worth listening to.

In his Introduction to *The Lost America of Love: Rereading Robert Creeley, Edward Dorn, and Robert Duncan* (1981), Sherman Paul declares that his book concerns, much more than he had expected, the relationship of these poets to their "beloved predecessor," Walt Whitman. Dorn has affinities with the transcendentalists, with Henry David Thoreau (in spite of the fact that he refers to Thoreau as a "god damn sniveler") and his conception of the "different drummer," his attitude toward Civil Disobedience, and his love for land and nature; and with Ralph Waldo Emerson, who claimed to be "an endless seeker—with no past at my back." Dorn is closest, however, to Whitman. His poem, "Wait by the Door Awhile, Death, There Are Others," recalls by its title and subject Whitman's "When Lilacs Last in the Dooryard Bloom'd," and contains several Whitmanesque references to his body, which Dorn says is younger than he is. Inviting himself to enter himself, Dorn confesses that he does so with great pleasure. One can almost smell Whitman's divine armpits. Some of Dorn's many "songs" could have been subtitled "Song of Myself"; in a burst of enthusiasm like that of the transcendentalists, who thought man divine, Dorn announces that many of his gods have been men and women.

Other literary influences are numerous. Dorn's world is frequently like that of Lewis Carroll, where nothing is what it appears to be. "The New Union Dead in Alabama" recalls Allen Tate's "Ode to the Confederate Dead," but with a bitter difference: these men have died as a result of national hypocrisy, a gelding mentality, and a gelding culture. In "Home Again," the "green hand that rocks the cradle" is reminiscent of both Whitman and Dylan Thomas. The quotations and allusions in *North Atlantic Turbine*, published in London, are reminiscent of Eliot. This is not to say that Dorn is not original. The opposite, rather, is true. He weaves old radio characters with Parsifal and Beowulf as adeptly and nimbly as Eliot did in *The Waste Land* (1922).

In spite of, or perhaps because of, all these kinships, Dorn is his own man. As Paul comments, "You don't mess with Dorn; he knows the score, and what is more . . . he has figured it out for himself." The score is, of course lopsided, a fact dramatically expressed in the poem "World Box-Score Cup," whose commentator, Stern Bill, broadcasts, from Yanqui-Go-Home Stadium, a game between the Haves (best fed, mostly English speaking) and the Have-nots of the world. America, who can hardly be expected to be impartial, is the referee, and Al Capp is the captain of the Haves. Because the Havenots have no shirts, numbers are painted on their backs in whitewash, permanent paint considered unnecessary for obvious reasons. Players from the unde-veloped squad have to be carried onto the field, an act distasteful to the developed players because of the smell of their nearly dead opponents. Stern Bill, who constantly uses the jargon of sportscasting, declares that this contest is one of the few places for people from both sides of the aluminum curtain to get together to work off their conflicting ideologies.

Stern Bill explains that the carcasses of undeveloped players will no longer be used in dog food because of the complaints of animal lovers that the meat was neither hygienic nor nutritional. At halftime he interviews Harry Carry (who has a Japanese accent) and John Malcom Fuggeridge, whose strangely dressed companion proves to be Truman Capote (also known as Trustworthy Kaput, a Southern degenerate). The last interviewees are Elizabeth Taylor's four dogs, who are accorded more dignity than are members of the Havenot team. As Dorn has said, democracy has to be "cracked on the head" frequently to keep it in good condition. In this twentieth century "Modest Proposal," he is cracking at his caustic best. In an interview he once stated that one function of the poet is to stay "as removed as possible from permanent asso-ciations with power." Here he strikes out at the tendency of the United States to believe in its own invincibility and to interfere in others' foreign affairs, at the same time condemning selfish greed in all nations—and all of this in sports jargon.

Dorn's satire is pointed, and he is not above using a few gimmicks. As the cover of *Hands Up!* is opened, two hands reach out to the reader, but as the book is closed, the hands suggest a nose-thumbing. In *Hello, La Jolla*, Dorn apologizes for the amount of "calculated" white space and invites the readers to fill it in. As he "roadtests" the language, he uses outrageous puns ("a mews," "pater"-"potter," "tiers of my country," "End-o-China," "Would you Bolivia it?," and "Vee-et," explained as the past tense of "eat"); archaic spelling ("sunne," "starre," "goe"); inversions (An Indian sings in his "daughter" tongue; a vacuum adores Nature; men go to the unemployment agency); and, in an age that has found such exact rhymes unfashionable, places "Trinity" with "infinity," "cuff" with "enough," and "cancer" with "dancer."

His major opus, *Gunslinger*, years in the making, appeared one slim volume at a time but is now available in a one-volume edition. Robert Duncan has called it an American *Canterbury Tales*, and indeed a crew of sophisticated Muppet-pilgrims could say, "To Taos we finally came." George Gugelberger has dubbed the work a space (-d out) epic, but under any name it entertains. The characters, who come out of Western motion pictures, comic books, and science fiction, include the Slinger himself, a "semidios" who drifts along the "selvedge of time," and who is a prototype of the Western strong man. A crack shot, he is headed toward Las Vegas in quest of Howard Hughes, who possesses the power once reserved for the gods. Robart (Rob-art), the foil for Gunslinger, is named for Howard Robard Hughes, and is an evil, lawless, greedy entrepreneur.

"I" is the initiate, the likable dude who dies in Book II but is preserved for "past reference" when he is embalmed with five gallons of acid and finally revived as Parmenides' secretary. Gunslinger explains "I's" function as that of setting up the "bleechers" (*sic*) or booking the hall when the soul plays a date in another town. Lil, who is the Great Goddess, the female principle, and the prostitute with a heart of gold; Cool Everything, an acid freak; the Stoned Horse, Lévi-Strauss; and a "heliocentric" poet complete the list of pilgrims. The horse (horse power) rides *inside* the stage and is, of course, a Pegasus.

The travelers meet a Ph.D. named Doctor Flamboyant, who confesses that he had to "take his degree," because the subject of his dissertation—last winter's icicles—could not be found.

Gunslinger, who observes that all the world is a cinema with Holy Writ as the script, visits a town called Truth or Consequence, whose residents ordered the truth and got the consequences. As the travelers get "inside the outskirts," the Horse is horrified to learn that the green plots of the village contain the kind of grass that has to be *mowed*. When some local horses escape, their owner fires ten rounds so fast that the bullets stick together, his gun falls apart, and he becomes an Old Rugged Statue. The Stoned Horse, who sells the statue for twenty thousand pounds by starting a rumor that it is an Andy Warhol disguise, comments, "There's less to that village than meets the eye."

The townspeople crowd suspiciously around "I" because he looks strange. When they observe, "He has't got a pot. . . ," "I" is saved by the magical appearance of a pot in his right hand. Slinger thanks the assembly for the

"Kiwanis and Lions welcome," and Lil annotates (*sic*), "So this is Universe City," the title suggesting not only "university," but also the fact that people are much alike wherever one goes.

When the travelers "decoach" in Old Town and Cool Everything announces, "We're Here!," Slinger comments, "Sounds like an adverb disguised as a place." Amid puns on "head" and "para-dice," Cool Everything tells Lil his name, and she notes that if he does not stay away from tobacco, he might do just that. After a neat bit of internal rhyme: "'I is dead,' the poet said," Lil complains, "That aint grammatical, poet."

*Gunslinger Book III* introduces J. Edgar Whoever and the date February 31, along with the news that the horse had promised his mother not to join the Sierra Club. Slinger observes that everyone in this state (New Mexico) is fat because the citizens all think that "torque" is a relationship between tongue and fork, Their code is "Sllab," which must be spelled backwards to determine its true seriousness, and the first information it reveals is that Chester A. Arthur was America's first President, no matter what anyone says. The Slinger's quest is unsuccessful because his intended destination, Las Vegas, proves to be a "decoy" controlled by Big Money. The book ends at the Four Corners power plant, with "power" retaining a dual sense.

The speech of *Gunslinger* is that of hipsters, scientists, the media, bureaucracy, computers, comic books, Western slang, metaphysics, and pop culture. Dorn has claimed he handles language like a material, keeping it in "instant repair." In *Gunslinger* he proves to be a virtuoso at juggling words, mining their ambiguous meanings, placing them in surprising positions, and finally using them "to make things cohere."

Why has Dorn chosen the West as his Yoknapatawpha? The most obvious answer is that this is the area in which Americans were the last pioneers; the West is also the locale of America's principal myth—the same myth of the Wild West so effectively debunked by Stephen Crane and now treated more lovingly by Dorn. His poem "Vaquero" describes the last, delicate cowboy, his wrists embossed, his eyes as blue as the top of the sky, a wistful study in color by sometime painter Dorn. A further reason for his choice of the West would be the admiration he holds for the courtesy, humility, and hospitality of the Indians and Spanish-speaking people who live there; he also is attracted to the casual atmosphere of the West, a place which is as figuratively remote as possible from Wall Street, Detroit, and Pittsburgh.

A summary of Dorn's concerns would have to include the tension between man and landscape brought on by greed. While man occasionally appreciates the beauties of landforms, as in *Gunslinger* ("Don't move . . . the sun rests deliberately on the rim of the sierra"), he has imposed a sameness on places by selling fast-food franchises, by constructing look-alike houses, by upsetting nature's balance, by allowing the careless rape of the land, by adopting a universal American dialect as standard, and by recognizing certain pop elements as part of national, not regional, culture. Space and place were at one time important, but thanks to man's avarice, they have lost much of their beauty as well as their identity.

To Dorn, a possible solution to this problem lies in the fact that language is a means of imposing order and discovering the natural order which man has disarrayed. The person who can best utilize language is, of course, the poet, who is equipped to communicate because of his facility with words. He can look objectively at what other men do with language as a means of justifying commerce and even war, at the same time demonstrating through his poetry what a marvelous weapon language can be—directly in the area of criticism, and indirectly by exuberant wordplay.

What, in Dorn's view, is the role of the poet? He wonders aloud about the familiar; he demonstrates the pleasure to be recovered from doubt; he rises above differences; he arbitrates because of his dexterity with words. He is, in short, a shaper.

**Major publications other than poetry**
NOVEL: *The Rites of Passage: A Brief History*, 1965; revised as *By the Sound*, 1971.
SHORT FICTION: *Some Business Recently Transacted in the White World*, 1971.
NONFICTION: *What I See in the Maximus Poems*, 1960; *Prose I*, 1964 (with Michael Rumaker and Warren Tallman); *The Rites of Passage: A History*, 1965; *The Shoshoneans*, 1966 (with photographs by Leroy Lucas); *Book of Daniel Drew*, 1969; *Views and Interviews*, 1978, 1980 (Donald Allen, editor).

**Bibliography**
Davidson, Michael. "Archeologist of Morning: Charles Olson, Edward Dorn and Historical Method," in *ELH*. XLVII (1980), pp. 158-179.
Lockwood, William J. "Ed Dorn's Mystique of the Real: His Poems for North America," in *Contemporary Literature*. XIX, no. 1 (1978), pp. 58-79.
Paul, Sherman. *The Lost America of Love: Rereading Robert Creeley, Edward Dorn, and Robert Duncan*, 1981.

*Sue L. Kimball*

# MICHAEL DRAYTON

**Born:** Hartshill, England; 1563
**Died:** London, England; December 23, 1631

### Principal poems and collections

*The Harmony of the Church*, 1591; *Idea, the Shepherd's Garland*, 1593; *Piers Gaveston*, 1593; *Idea's Mirror*, 1594; *Matilda*, 1594; *Endimion and Phoebe*, 1595; *The Tragical Legend of Robert, Duke of Normandy*, 1596; *Mortimeriados*, 1596; *England's Heroical Epistles*, 1597; *The Barons' Wars*, 1603; *The Owl*, 1604; *Poems Lyric and Pastoral*, 1606; *Legend of the Great Cromwell*, 1607; *Poly-Olbion*, 1612-1622; *Poems*, 1619; *Nimphidia*, 1627; *Shepherd's Sirena*, 1627; *The Battle of Agincourt*, 1627; *The Muses' Elizium*, 1630; *The Works of Michael Drayton*, 1931-1941 (J. W. Hebel, Kathleen Tillotson, and B. H. Newdigate, editors, 5 volumes).

### Other literary forms

Except for brief prefaces to his books and letters, four of which were published in the *Works* of his friend William Drummond of Hawthornden, Michael Drayton wrote exclusively in verse. Between about 1597 and 1602 he is reputed to have written or collaborated on twenty plays, all of which are lost except *The First Part of the True and Honorable History of the Life of Sir John Oldcastle the Good* (1600). The titles indicate that these were chronicle history plays.

### Achievements

According to Francis Meres in 1598, Drayton was "a man of virtuous disposition, honest conversation, and well-governed carriage; which is almost miraculous among good wits in these declining times." His early reputation was as a Spenserian, and as his life went on friends perceived him as a conservative man increasingly out of sorts with the post-Elizabethan world. Though inevitably overshadowed by major contemporaries such as Edmund Spenser, his fellow-Warwickshirite William Shakespeare, John Donne, and Ben Jonson, he wrote well in virtually every popular literary genre of his day, and in his "heroical epistles" and Horatian odes introduced forms which, while not of major importance thereafter in English literature, he practiced with distinction. With reference to his longest work, Charles Lamb called Drayton "that panegyrist of my native earth; who has gone over her soul in his *Poly-Olbion* with the fidelity of a herald, and the painful love of a son." Drayton's odes in praise of English accomplishments, the "Ballad of Agincourt" and "To the Virginian Voyage," remain anthology favorites, as do several poems from *Idea*, one of the finest sonnet sequences in English.

As one of England's first professional poets, Drayton nearly always wrote competently and on occasion superbly, especially in his lyrics. In his best poems he blends an intense love of his native land with a classicism marked by clarity, decorum, careful attention to form, and—with respect to all passions except his patriotic fervor—calm detachment.

## Biography

Most of the available biographical facts derive from Michael Drayton's own poems and dedications. He was born in northern Warwickshire in 1563 and seems to have been reared and well-educated in the household of Sir Henry Goodere at Polesworth, not far from his native village of Hartshill. To fulfill his lifelong desire to be a poet, he moved to London at least by 1591, although more likely in the later 1580's. Beyond reasonable doubt the "Idea" of his sonnets honors Sir Henry's daughter Anne. Drayton may have been in love with Anne; around 1595, however, she married a man of her own class, Sir Henry Rainsford. Of Drayton's ever marrying there is no record. In later years, the poet spent his summers at Clifford Hall, Gloucestershire, the Rainsfords' seat, and he is known to have been treated by Lady Rainsford's physician, Dr. John Hall, who was Shakespeare's son-in-law. Although he apparently lived the last forty years of his life in London, Drayton's fondness for rural England and his admiration for the values of the landed gentry were obviously genuine. He is credited with having been on familiar terms with nearly every important literary Englishman of his time. Dying near the end of 1631, he was buried in Westminster Abbey.

## Analysis

In an age when the writing of poetry was an avocation for actors, courtiers, clergymen, and landed gentlemen, Michael Drayton devoted his life to poetry. In a verse epistle to a friend, Henry Reynolds, Drayton writes of how, at the age of ten, he beseeched his tutor to make him a poet. Being a man of the Renaissance, the teacher started him on eclogues, first those of "honest Mantuan," a currently popular Italian humanist, then the great Vergil himself, after which Drayton studied the English poets, beginning, of course, with Geoffrey Chaucer and working through to contemporaries such as William Shakespeare, Christopher Marlowe, Samuel Daniel, and Ben Jonson (Drayton having of course grown up in the meantime). Both the classics and the native poetical tradition continued to inspire him throughout his long career, and in his most characteristic work he adapts classical models to his own time, place, and language.

To a greater extent, perhaps, than any of his contemporaries, Drayton straddles the sixteenth and seventeenth centuries and raises the question of whether he was more Elizabethan or Jacobean. As he does not fall squarely into the usual categories of "Spenserian," "Jonsonian," or "Metaphysical," his work challenges the usefulness—certainly the inclusiveness—of these categories of English Renaissance poetry. His career may be divided into three stages, the first and last of which are short but enormously energetic and productive, while the long middle stage demonstrates the characteristic development of his art while incidentally furnishing most of the poems for which he is best known today. In the first and, paradoxically, last stages he is most Elizabethan, or, to use a term popularized by C. S. Lewis in his *English Literature in the Sixteenth Century* (1954), most "golden."

His early period begins with the publication in 1591 of a drab religious exercise called *The Harmony of the Church*, but between 1593 and 1595 he brought out three works which typify and enrich that most remarkable period in English letters: *Idea, the Shepherd's Garland*; *Idea's Mirror*; and *Endimion and Phoebe*. The first of these demonstrates a young poet's preliminary pastoral, Vergil having worked from the shepherds' dale to epic heights—a program which the ambitious Spenser had already imitated and which many others, including John Milton, would imitate. The poems are eclogues, shepherds' dialogues on love, death, the decline of the world, and poetry itself; they are meant to exercise a poet's versatility in song. Drayton's are not notable, except perhaps for their unusually frequent references to English topography; they do, however, demonstrate that the poet, at thirty, had long since learned his craft.

*Idea's Mirror* is a sonnet sequence, not a classical form to be sure, but one associated with the great fourteenth century classicist, Petrarch. Since the posthumous publication of Sir Philip Sidney's *Astrophel and Stella* in 1591, poets had flooded England with sonnets featuring graceful tributes to beautiful ladies with stylized and often classical names such as Celia, Delia, and Diana, along with the laments of versifying suitors frustrated by the very aloofness that attracted them so fatally. Shakespeare's "Dark Lady," it might be noted, is in a number of respects the exception to the rule. *Idea's Mirror*, fifty-one sonnets long, is conventionally melancholy, sometimes awkward, and regularly sensuous in the well-bred Elizabethan way.

*Endimion and Phoebe*, in 516 pentameter couplets, is Drayton's contribution to the Ovidian love narrative, a genre that had already generated Shakespeare's *Venus and Adonis* (1593) and Marlowe's *Hero and Leander* (1598). Endimion is a shepherd lad who loves the fair goddess Phoebe at once passionately and chastely; she rewards him by wrapping him in a "fiery mantle" and lofting him to the empyrean, where he is shown a series of splendors both astronomical and divine. The poem is full of rich, smooth-flowing language—not so thoroughly a thing of beauty as John Keats's *Endymion* (1818) but a joy nevertheless.

Myth, pastoral, and love lyrics provided only limited opportunities for another English obsession in the heady years following the defeat of the supposedly invincible Spanish Armada in 1588: the patriotism that rings forth in John of Gaunt's "Methinks I am a prophet new inspired" speech in Shakespeare's *Richard II* (1595-1596) and so many other poems of the 1590's. Thus, 1596 found Drayton issuing *Mortimeriados* on the political struggles of the reign of Edward II. Drayton was again following the lead of other poets, this time Shakespeare and Daniel (who had published the first four books of his *Civil Wars* in 1595) more than Spenser and Marlowe. *Mortimeriados*, which can be considered the last of the poems of Drayton's early phase, is only one of a series, begun three years earlier in his *Piers Gaveston* and continuing throughout most of his life, in which he delves into the history, topography, and presumed national virtues of England.

As the childless Queen Elizabeth grew old and crotchety, ambitious courtiers jockeyed for position, and as the problem of the succession loomed, England's mood changed. Spenser died in 1599, leaving *The Faerie Queene* unfinished and its shadowy heroine Gloriana unwed to Prince Arthur. Shakespeare turned increasingly to the writing of tragedy. Drayton's heart remained, as it always would remain, unabashedly Elizabethan.

As his art matured, however, he welded his classicism and patriotism in poems of much greater originality. *England's Heroical Epistles* marks a turning point. Of this work can be said what surely cannot be said of anything in Drayton's earlier poems: it is something new in English literature. His classical model, Ovid's *Heroides*, had been imitated as far back as Geoffrey Chaucer's *The Legend of Good Women* (1380-1386), but instead of retaining Ovid's subject matter—the plights of a group of legendary and historical women of the ancient world such as Dido, Medea, and Cleopatra—and foregoing Ovid's epistolary form, as had Chaucer, Drayton wrote his poem in the form of letters to and from such women as Eleanor Cobham, Rosamond Clifford, and Alice, Countess of Salisbury—that is, women involved in the political history of England, usually as royal wives or mistresses, although in the case of Lady Jane Grey, as the victim of political intrigue.

Drayton's changes are instructive. All the letters of the *Heroides* are purportedly those of the women, mostly complaints by women abandoned by their consorts, with Ovid avoiding monotony through the exercise of his considerable psychological insight. Drayton, who much preferred to build situations involving the interactions of characters, hit upon the idea of an exchange of letters between the man and the woman, with sometimes hers coming first, sometimes his. Notorious royal mistresses such as Rosamond Clifford and Jane Shore had spoken in verse before, but chiefly in the moralizing vein of that stodgy Elizabethan perennial, *A Mirror for Magistrates* (1599), in which the ghosts of people fallen from high place appear for the purpose of lugubriously advising and admonishing the reader. Thomas Churchyard ends his account of *Shore's Wife* (1563), for example: "A mirror make of my great overthrow;/ Defy this world and all his wanton ways;/ Beware by me that spent so ill her days." Drayton's Jane, on the other hand, concludes her letter to Edward IV: "thou art become my fate,/ And mak'st me love even in the midst of hate." He refuses to subordinate his lovers to an abstract moral, though, to be sure, he has selected them in the first place as manifestations of the national spirit.

Drayton's professionalism drove him to protracted and extensive revisions, and many of the works of his middle period are reworkings of earlier poems. In *The Barons' Wars*, he turns the rhyme royal of *Mortimeriados* into ottava rima, explaining that although the former had "harmony," the latter possesed "majesty, perfection, and solidity." Drayton aspired to an epic, but he was no Vergil, and *The Barons' Wars*, though an improvement on *Mortimeriados*, was no *Aeneid* (c. 29-19 B.C.). In other cases, his critics find his "improvements" made in vain, as in his *Poems Lyric and Pastoral*, which surely made his contemporary readers wonder why, twenty-seven years after Spenser's *Shepheardes Calendar* (1579), Drayton insisted on reworking old eclogues. As for his modern readers, they generally prefer *Endimion and Phoebe* to the new version, *The Man in the Moon*.

The latter volume is nevertheless important for introducing another of Drayton's successful classical adaptations, his odes. A deservedly obscure poet named John Southern had made a few Pindaric odes in the 1580's, but Drayton is the first Englishman to imitate the Horatian type. After acknowledging in his Preface both Pindar's triumphant and Anacreon's amorous odes, Drayton intimates a fondness for the "mixed" odes of Horace. Having written in both the Ovidian and the Vergilian manner, Drayton was now treading in the footsteps of a poet notable for understanding and working within his limitations. In contrast to the high-flying poets, Horace compares himself, in the second ode of his fourth book, to a bee gathering nectar on the banks of the Tiber. Eschewing the heroic and the passionate, he concentrates on such themes as moderation, hospitality, friendship, and the propriety of accepting one's fate. Although Drayton did not easily accept his fate as a leftover Elizabethan in the age of James I, he recognized in the Horatian ode the vehicle for a range of expression that had not found utterance in earlier English poetry. What he suggested in his odes, Ben Jonson and the neoclassicists of the new century would exploit more thoroughly.

For the ode to become a recognizable form in English, Drayton had to find an equivalent of Horace's favorite four-line Alcaic and Sapphic stanzas. He wisely avoided the English imitations of Latin quantitative verse which had so intrigued some of the Elizabethans but had defeated all of them except Thomas Campion in a handful of lyrics. Drayton favored a five- or six-line stanza with short lines and prominent rhymes. Coupled with his usual end-stopped lines, the rhymes not only create an effect entirely different from Horace's but also force Drayton into an unnatural syntax marked by ellipses, inversions, and the omission of transitions. English poets had tended to avoid short lines except in song lyrics, preferring the opposite risk of the hexameter line, which Alexander Pope would later compare to a "wounded snake," and the even longer fourteener. Whether Drayton thought of his odes as singable or not, he knew that short lines and obtrusive rhymes had been used most successfully for satiric and humorous purposes, as in Chaucer's "Tale of Sir Thopas" and John Skelton's *Phillip Sparrow* (c. 1505).

Except in a few instances, such as "The Sacrifice to Apollo," where he fell into a too self-consciously Horatian posture, Drayton avoided servility in the ode as he had in *England's Heroical Epistles*. In the odes on Agincourt and the peak, in "To the New Year" and "To the Virginian Voyage," the reader senses an early seventeenth century Englishman responding directly to his milieu as Horace had responded to Rome in the first century B.C. The similarity between the two poets, less a formal or temperamental likeness than a kind of equivalent spirit grounded in love for land and landscape, kept Drayton from sounding like an "ancient." He did not have to praise Horace's Bandusian fountain and Caecubian wine, for he had "Buxton's delicious baths" and good "strong ale" to celebrate. The whole "Ode Written on the Peak" is built on the proposition that England is as worthy of an ode as anything in ancient Rome. Drayton's classicism, then, takes the form of an Englishman singing his own island in a diction and rhythm assertively Anglo-Saxon. Before Drayton, Englishmen, uncomfortable with Horace's Epicureanism, had valued chiefly the Horace of the moral *Satires* (35, 30 B.C.) and *Epistles* (20-13 B.C.). Having learned from Drayton, the later Cavalier poets achieved (not without some loss of intellectual vigor) the gracefulness and urbanity that Drayton had not caught in their common master's odes.

Drayton expressed the same patriotic convictions in a much more expansive way in his *magnum opus*, *Poly-Olbion*, on which he had been working for many years before its initial publication in 1612. His fondness for myth, the countryside, and antiquarian lore come together in this leisurely survey of England and Wales in which the favorite mode of travel is the river. The poem owes something to the researches of an early Tudor antiquarian, John Leland, and to Drayton's learned contemporary, William Camden. If his preoccupation with rivers needs a model, Spenser, whose *Colin Clout's Come Home Again* (1595), *Prothalamion* (1596), and the now lost *Epithalamion* (1595) all feature rivers, probably is the man.

To assist the reader through his gigantic poem, Drayton employed the services of another learned man, John Selden, who wrote explanatory notes, and an engraver who furnished maps for each section of the poem. Not at all confident that the work would find a ready audience in what he called "this lunatic age," Drayton wrote an introduction excoriating those who would "rather read the fantasies of foreign invention than to see the rarities and history of their own country delivered by a true native muse." Ten years later, having "met with barbarous ignorance and base detraction" in the reception of the first edition, he nevertheless republished the poem with twelve additional sections.

Few readers today negotiate the full *Poly-Olbion*, but it is a pleasant, if sometimes prosaic, journey. Drayton probably did not visit all the localities described in the poem, and it is unlikely that the reader ignorant of his Warwickshire origin could guess it from this poem. It is an interesting section of the poem, however, detailing at length the Forest of Arden, which Shakespeare had used as the setting for much of *As You Like It* (1599-1600). There may be fools in Shakespeare's Arden, but Drayton's is populated by innumerable birds, beasts, hunters, and a happy hermit who has fled "the sottish purblind world." He also traces the several little rivers that flow into the Avon, which he follows past Stratford, though without mentioning Shakespeare. In this poem, Drayton is more interested in the past, and he tells the legend of Guy of Warwick, who is credited with defeating the Danish champion Colbrand and thus turning away the tenth century invasion. Like many historical poems written in late Tudor and early Stuart England, this one shows the transition from the earlier uncritical acceptance of myth and legend to a more skeptical attitude. The legends still have vitality, but the scholars of the seventeenth century—Selden, Francis Bacon, and the Earl of Clarendon—cast increasing doubt on their truthfulness and value.

While at work on *Poly-Olbion*, Drayton was also overhauling his sonnets, now entitled simply *Idea*. In this work his tireless revising paid off handsomely, for by 1619 he had added and rewritten forty-three new sonnets to go with twenty early ones, and the sequence had become a masterpiece. By this time John Donne, the first of the great Metaphysical poets, was writing love poems in other forms and reserving the sonnet for religious purposes, while Ben Jonson and his tribe scorned the sonnet and other nonclassical forms altogether. As a poet born in the decade before Donne and Jonson, Drayton had been enough of a working Elizabethan (and enough of a conservative) to prefer building on the accomplishments of that age. In this endeavor, however, he was alone; all the other Elizabethan poets of consequence—Sidney, Marlowe, Shakespeare, Sir Walter Raleigh, Daniel, all the people he might have wished to please, it must have seemed—were dead. Only Drayton worked on, increasingly testy and ill-humored in his Prefaces but as devoted as ever to the perfection of poems of a kind now out of favor.

As far back as Sidney, English sonneteers had presented the lover as a sometimes comic figure. Despite certain resemblances to his creator, Sidney's Astrophel is a character at whom readers are sometimes encouraged to laugh. In *Idea*, Drayton's speaker even seems to laugh at himself. In the splendid Number 61, "Since there's no help, come let us kiss and part," the speaker, after asserting in a matter-of-fact tone and words chiefly of one syllable—the first thirty-three words, in fact, being monosyllables exclusively—that nothing but a complete break makes any sense, that he is willing to "shake hands" on it, reverts in the third quatrain to a sentimental deathbed scene of love personified, and closes with a couplet the irony of which the speaker surely recognizes: "Now if thou would'st, when all have given him over,/ From death to life, thou might'st him yet recover." The lover in these poems knows that love and passion are silly and that their stylized portrayal in language is sillier yet, but he also knows that to reject them outright is to reject life and the art that attempts to portray it. The perspective here is Horatian: a delicate balance, a golden mean, between involvement and detachment. The poet has mastered his form: he writes English sonnets which frequently retain the capacity of the Italian sonnet for a turning point just past the middle as well as a distinct closing couplet that sometimes brings another, unexpected turn.

Drayton's wit is on display in Number 21, about a "witless gallant" who has asked for and received from the speaker a sonnet to send to his own love. The speaker, however, has written it "as fast as e'er my pen could trot"—just the opposite of the correct, painstaking way. The third quatrain reports that the lady "doted on the dolt beyond all measure," the rueful couplet sadly concluding: "Yet by my troth, this fool his love obtains,/ And I lose you, for all my wit and pains." The reader understands that the "gallant's" success was a hollow one; Idea, whose name is Plato's word for that highest type of beauty and goodness to which all ordinary earthly manifestations are but shadows, is worth the inevitable disappointments.

In Drayton's very Elizabethan sonnets, the reader comes upon many of the witty, argumentative ploys so characteristic of Donne and Jonson. For Drayton, such wit amounted to a perfecting of the now largely abandoned sonnet cycle in which he saw further possibilities for variety within unity, flexibility within firmness. He is not being Metaphysical or neoclassical, only bringing out the latent potential of the earlier poetry, while displaying in the process a wit, irony, and plainness of diction more characteristic of the new poetry that he was supposedly rejecting.

With the publication of the complete *Poly-Olbion*, Drayton's most elaborate tribute to the native land he had been praising so long, the poet, now entering his sixtieth year, might have been expected to taper off. Instead, he brought out two books of largely unpublished poems. The first, named for a long historical poem, *The Battle of Agincourt* (no improvement on his "ballad" and not to be confused with it), included another Horatian genre, the complimentary verse epistle, one of which was the letter to Henry Reynolds revealing his early desire to be a poet. He may not have been the first in the field, for Donne and Jonson were also writing them, but his *Elegies upon Sundrey Occasions*, as he called them, are more carefully adapted to the "occasions," suggesting that his primary aim was communication at once functional, artful, and expressive of genuine feeling. In this aim he came closer to the spirit of his Roman Master than did other poets of the time, whose style and tone tend to vary little with the occasion and the identity of the recipient.

Two poems in *The Battle of Agincourt* illustrate Drayton's final lyrical stage.

*Shepherd's Sirena* sings more purely than any of his earlier pastorals. Sirena dwells in the vicinity of the River Trent, here transmuted into a domestic Arcadia. While vestiges of the competitions and complaints of early English pastoral remain, the best part of the poem is its 170 liquid lines in praise of the lady—praise that never slides into the convolutions of Jacobean wit.

*Nymphidia* is quite different. It can be classified roughly as mock-heroic. Pigwiggen, in love with Queen Mab, entices her away from King Oberon and challenges the latter to a duel for the "dear lady's honor." Having secured seconds and gone through all necessary preliminaries, the champions hack briskly away at each other, though, when the contest threatens to get too bloody, Prosorpina administers the Lethe water that makes them forget their enmity entirely. At the end the King and Queen, as if nothing had happened, are sitting down to a good fairy meal. That the poem has a satirical purpose is indicated by Drayton's name-dropping: Sir Thopas, Pantagruel, and Don Quixote are all mentioned. The poem brims with parodies of heroic clichés. The emphasis, though, is on fun and fantasy in a delicate miniature world made of spider's legs and butterfly's wings. Its eighty-eight tripping stanzas, rhyming aaabcccb (tetrameter except for the b lines, which are a syllable shorter with feminine rhymes), "carry the vein of Sir Thopas into the world of Oberon," as Oliver Elton puts it in *Michael Drayton: A Critical Study* (1966).

Drayton's final volume, issued thirty-nine years after his first and only one year before his death, includes three long "divine poems" on Noah, Moses, and David, but it is best remembered for its title poem, *The Muses' Elizium*. Elizium, a "paradise on earth" whose name honors the queen who had now been dead twenty-seven years, can be seen as a nostalgic retreat from the realities of a nation now entered on the "Eleven Years' Tyranny" of Charles I. Made up of ten eclogues, or "nymphals," the work is, like *Shepherd's Sirena*, almost purely lyrical, full of flowery meadows and crystal springs, with occasional reminders of the prosaic real world.

One of these occurs in the tenth nymphal. Two nymphs discover a "monster" whom the shepherd Corbilus recognizes as an old satyr, a refugee from "Felicia," which is the everyday world, now destroyed by "beastly men." After a suitable opportunity to lament the denuding of the forest by crass builders, the satyr is invited to "live in bliss" in Elizium until such time as the true Felicians reclaim the land. Thus, in his old age, Drayton metamorphosizes his conservativism, love of the land, displeasure with the world of 1630, and perhaps—if readers take the satyr to represent the author—a disposition toward a bit of humor at his own expense, into a calm, dispassionate poem whose very preface is, for a change, sweet-tempered. In this last stage, Drayton has receded from the Stuart milieu to the extent of cultivating a pure, "irrelevant" art. The attitude is that of an old man, but one who has ceased to rage; the lyric freshness is that of a young poet not yet fully aware of the indifferent children of the earth whom Drayton has now forgotten.

With its delight in plain, shaggy, rural life, *The Muses' Elizium* is likely to remind readers of classical pastoral more of Theocritus than of the more polished poet of the Roman Empire, Vergil. The style here is not of the Greek or Roman Golden Ages, but of the Elizabethan. Drayton had outlived his age, but this poem has outlived the seventeenth century strife in the midst of which it seemed so old fashioned.

**Major publication other than poetry**
PLAY: *The First Part of the True and Honorable History of the Life of Sir John Oldcastle the Good*, 1600.

**Bibliography**
Berthelot, Joseph A. *Michael Drayton*, 1967.
Davis, Walter R. "'Fantastickly I Sing': Drayton's *Idea* of 1619," in *Studies in Philology*. LVI (October, 1968), pp. 204-216.
Elton, Oliver. *Michael Drayton: A Critical Study*, 1966.
Hardin, Richard F. *Michael Drayton and the Passing of Elizabethan England*, 1973.
Newdigate, Bernard H. *Michael Drayton and His Circle*, 1941.
Smith, Hallett. *Elizabethan Poetry: A Study in Conventions, Meaning, and Expression*, 1952.
Tuve, Rosemond. *Elizabethan and Metaphysical Imagery*, 1947.

*Robert P. Ellis*

# WILLIAM DRUMMOND OF HAWTHORNDEN

**Born:** Hawthornden, Scotland; December 13, 1585
**Died:** Hawthornden, Scotland; December 4, 1649

## Principal poems and collections

*Teares, on the Death of Moeliades*, 1613; *Poems*, 1616; *Forth Feasting*, 1617; *Flowres of Sion*, 1623; *The Entertainment*, 1633; *To the Exequies*, 1638.

## Other literary forms

William Drummond's only prose work published during his lifetime was *A Midnight's Trance* (1619), a meditation on death. In its revised form it was appended to *Flowres of Sion* as *A Cypresse Grove*. His *History of Scotland from the Year 1423 Until the Year 1542*, his longest piece of prose, appeared posthumously in 1655. This volume also included a selection of Drummond's letters, a reprinting of *A Cypresse Grove*, and "Memorials of State," a sample of the political pamphlets Drummond had written (but never published) in the two decades preceding his death. The 1711 edition of Drummond's works remains the most complete collection of the prose; in this edition *Irene*, *Skiamachia*, and other political pieces first appeared. Here, too, were first published notes on the famous conversations between Drummond and Ben Jonson. In 1831, David Laing published "A Brief Account of the Hawthornden Manuscripts in the Possession of the Society of Antiquaries of Scotland, with Extracts, Containing Several Unpublished Letters with Poems of William Drummond of Hawthornden" (*Transactions of the Society of Antiquaries of Scotland*, Volume IV). In the same volume Laing presented the first complete edition of the *Notes of Ben Jonson's Conversations with William Drummond of Hawthornden* (1832). Subsequent editions of Drummond's poetry have included manuscript material, but the prose remains uncollected.

## Achievements

By 1616 Drummond was known as "the Scottish Petrarch." His first published poem went through three editions within a year, and the 1616 edition of the *Poems* quickly went into a "second impression." John Milton read Drummond with approbation, and Milton's nephew, Edward Phillips, Drummond's first editor, in the Preface to the 1656 edition of the poetry, called Drummond "a genius the most polite and verdant that ever the Scottish nation produced," adding "that neither Tasso, nor Guarini, nor any of the most neat and refined can challenge to themselves any advantage above him." For Charles Lamb, a century and a half later, "The sweetest names, and which carry a perfume in the mention, are, Kit Marlowe, Drayton, Drummond of Hawthornden, and Cowley."

What Alexander Pope observed of the last of these "sweet" poets, however—"Who now reads Cowley?"—is also applicable to Drummond. Though he was the first Scottish poet to produce a substantial body of poetry in English, and though much of that poetry demonstrates technical virtuosity, Drummond does not command many readers today. In large part this neglect has resulted from his theory of composition. Jonson warned him "that oft a man's modesty made a fool of his wit." Drummond's poetic modesty led him to translate and adapt the works of others instead of applying himself to invention. His poetry, therefore, while skillful, is rarely original, and, as Samuel Johnson stated, "No man ever became great by imitation." Drummond's skill with language and the details of prosody guarantee him a secure place among the second rank of Renaissance English poets, but his inability or refusal to go beyond such models as Sir Philip Sidney, Pierre de Ronsard, Petrarch, Giambattista Marino, and Baldassare Castiglione bars him from the first.

His history of the first five Jameses, like his poetry, is stylistically sound but derivative in content. Although much praised by Drummond's contemporaries and reprinted five times, it has not been reissued since 1711. David Laing commented over a century ago in *Archaeoló gia Scotiá* (Volume IV) that the work is "only of subsidiary importance," and so it remains. *A Cypresse Grove* may have influenced Sir Thomas Browne's *Hydriotaphia: Urne-Buriall* (1658), but along with virtually all of Drummond's other prose works it has fallen into neglect after enjoying a contemporary popularity. Yet for most students of early seventeenth century British literature, Drummond owes his reputation to a prose work, though it is one that he merely transcribed and that was never published in his lifetime. *Notes of Ben Jonson's Conversations with William Drummond of Hawthornden*, a record of Jonson's comments on himself and his contemporaries—and hence an invaluable primary source for literary historians—is the best known of Drummond's writings today. It is perhaps fitting that a man who shunned originality should owe his fame almost entirely to his transcription of the pronouncements of another.

### Biography
The eldest son of John Drummond and Susannah Fowler, William Drummond was born on December 13, 1585, at Hawthornden, some seven miles southeast of Edinburgh. In 1590 Drummond's father was appointed Gentleman-usher to King James VI; about this time, too, his uncle, William Fowler, became Private Secretary to Queen Anne. Drummond thus grew up in a court dedicated to literary pursuits. James VI was a poet, and William Fowler translated Petrarch's *The Triumphs* (c. 1352-1374) and composed original verses as well. Such surroundings must have stimulated Drummond's own literary inclinations.

After taking an M.A. degree from the University of Edinburgh in July, 1605, Drummond set out for France to study law at Bourges. During the next four years, Drummond maintained a list of his readings: of the numerous volumes he read, only one concerns jurisprudence—the *Institutes* (533) of Justinian. Other volumes deal in part with religion. Although Drummond was hardly a prejudiced sectarian, his poetry reflects a deep religiosity. Most of Drummond's reading at this time was, however, secular; during his years abroad he familiarized himself with the major works of the Renaissance, both English and Continental, which later served as the models for his own writings. By the time he returned to Scotland in late 1608 he was intimately acquainted with the best of Spanish, French, Italian, and English literatures. These he not only read but also acquired: an inventory of his library in 1611 includes more than five hundred titles. This inventory suggests again that Drummond's interest in the law was less than overwhelming, for only twenty-four of those books deal with that field.

Fortunately for Drummond, he was not obliged to rely on the law for a living. On August 21, 1610, "about Noone," according to Drummond's "Memorials," his father died, leaving him laird of Hawthornden. Here Drummond remained for the rest of his life, reading and writing "farre from the madding Worldlings hoarse Discords" (Sonnet XLIII, Part I, *Poems*).

The death of Prince Henry in November, 1612, inspired Drummond's first published work, *Teares, on the Death of Moeliades*. Shortly afterward, perhaps as early as the next year, another volume appeared, consisting of a sonnet sequence in two parts. In the first section Drummond speaks conventionally of the pains of love, and in the second he mourns his mistress' death. Although both Dante and Petrarch had written of their dead mistresses, no one in English had yet done so. Drummond boasted that he was "The First in the Isle that did celebrate a mistress dead."

Life seems to have imitated art in this case. Drummond apparently had fallen in love with a Miss Cunningham in 1614 and had become engaged to her. Shortly before their marriage—but after the completion of most of the sonnets in *Poems*—Miss Cunningham died. Except for his abandonment of love poetry for religious verse, Drummond's writings do not reflect this personal tragedy, but he remained unmarried until 1632, and the woman he did marry—Elizabeth Logan—attracted him in part because she reminded him of his first love.

When the former James VI of Scotland, then James I of England, returned to his native land after a fourteen-year absence, Drummond welcomed him with the effusive encomium *Forth Feasting*, in which he imagines the river's rejoicing to receive her monarch. In general, the poem pleased the king, though his courtiers, and even James, questioned one line: "No Guard so sure as Love unto a Crowne" (line 246). The sentiment was hardly original with Drummond, going back to Aristotle's *Politics* (between 336 and 322 B.C.). The Stuarts, however, preferred to govern through fear. In his political pamphlets of the 1630's and 1640's Drummond would expand his view, recommending love and mercy to James's successor.

The following year Scotland received another visitor—the prince of poets, Ben Jonson. Jonson probably came to Scotland in search of literary material, but in late December, 1618, and early January of the next year he spent several weeks at Hawthornden conversing with Drummond. It is this visit that has kept Drummond's name alive, for Drummond kept careful notes of Jonson's observations. (The original manuscript apparently has not survived, but a transcription by the antiquary Sir Robert Sibbald [1641-1722] has preserved Jonson's remarks.) These observations contain much material about Jonson himself as well as about his contemporaries and so are invaluable to the student of the period, offering information not available elsewhere. They also suggest why Drummond and Jonson ceased corresponding within six months of the latter's return to England. Drummond's notes justify his comment that Jonson was "a great lover and praiser of himself, a contemner and Scorner of others."

*Flowres of Sion*, a collection of religious poetry, appeared in 1623; in 1630 Drummond published a revised edition of this work. In the interval between these editions, Drummond's thoughts turned for a time to earthly matters: he apparently sired three illegitimate children, and in 1627 he received a letter patent for sixteen military and naval inventions. There is no evidence that he ever went beyond theorizing about these weapons of destruction, but his very proposals suggest a concern with the Thirty Years' War raging on the Continent. The "madding Worldlings hoarse Discords" could penetrate even secluded Hawthornden. More consonant with the tenor of Drummond's temper, in 1626 he donated a large portion of his library—more than five hundred volumes—to his alma mater.

By 1633, when Charles I visited Edinburgh, Drummond was regarded as the unofficial Poet Laureate of Scotland. For the royal visit he wrote *The Entertainment*, a collection of poetry and prose. As in *Forth Feasting*, the praise is lavish. At the same time, just as *Forth Feasting* had advised James I on the proper way to rule, so *The Entertainment* cautions Charles to rule by love rather than by force and to avoid alienating his subjects through the imposition of new taxes or the creation of court favorites.

Unhappily for Charles I and England, Drummond's warnings went unheeded. Instead of attempting to win the love of Scotland, the king alienated the country by attempting to impose Episcopal rites on the Presbyterian Kirk. In 1638, Scottish Presbyterians replied with the National League and Covenant to oppose liturgical alterations, and, after much negotiation, Charles yielded. *Irene*, a work never published during Drummond's lifetime though circulated in manuscript, urged both parties to abandon the quarrel. Drummond criticized the Covenanters for seeking to overthrow the natural order of society by rebelling against the king, but he also warned Charles not to pursue a harsh policy toward his subjects: "The drawing of your sword against them shall be the drawing of it against yourself; instead of triumphs, you shall obtain nothing but sad exequies and mournful funerals."

The struggle did, of course, continue. Though a Royalist, Drummond signed the Covenant in 1639 to escape being "mocked, hissed, plundered, banished hence," as he expressed his plight in one of his late poems. In another unpublished tract he nevertheless prophesied that civil war would lead to "one who will name himself PROTECTOR of the Liberty of the Kingdom. He shall surcharge the people with greater miseries than ever before they did suffer . . . and in the end shall essay to make himself King." Drummond's Royalist sentiments surfaced again when the Parliamentary leader John Pym died; Drummond's poem on the occasion does not suggest regret:

> When Pime last night descended into Hell,
> Ere hee his coupes of Lethe did carouse,
> What place is this (said hee) I pray mee tell?
> To whom a Divell: This is the lower house.

In addition to composing political tracts urging moderation, Drummond was working on a history of Scotland during the reigns of the first five Jameses. He had begun his research at least as early as 1633, perhaps as an outgrowth of genealogical research he had undertaken for his kinsman John Drummond, second Earl of Perth. James I of Scotland, with whom the *History of Scotland from the Year 1423 Until the Year 1542* begins, was the son of Annabella Drummond and so related to the earl. This work, too, shows Drummond's desire for religious toleration and peace. Drummond also wrote "A Speech on Toleration" for one of the privy councillors of James V, urging the monarch to permit religious freedom. Yet Drummond sensed that his calls for moderation would go unheeded; immediately after this speech Drummond notes, "But the King followed not this opinione."

By the time of his death on December 4, 1649, Drummond had witnessed the fulfillment of his direst predictions. He was buried in the church at Lasswade. When he had been near death in 1620, he had written a sonnet to Sir William Alexander, a friend and fellow poet: "I conjure Thee . . ./ To grave this short Remembrance on my Grave./ Heere *Damon* lyes, whose Songes did some-time grace/ The murmuring Eske, may Roses shade the place." In October, 1893, a memorial with this inscription was at last erected over Drummond's grave.

### Analysis

In an undated letter to Dr. Arthur Johnston, court physician to Charles I and himself a poet, William Drummond expressed his theory of poetic composition. Conservative in his literary as in his political philosophy, Drummond objected to the innovations of John Donne and his followers: "What is not like the ancients and conforme to those Rules which hath been agreed unto by all tymes, maye (indeed) be some thing like unto poesie, but it is no more Poesie than a Monster is a Man." Thus, Drummond valued imitation over invention. He would not seek to create new poetic forms or to develop original themes. For Drummond, as for Alexander Pope, the aim of poetry was to give fresh expression to old ideas. The result in Drummond's case is a body of work adapted from classical and Renaissance sources, elegantly phrased and carefully crafted, but lacking the emotion and invention that elevate excellent versifying to the level of first-rate poetry.

Drummond's first published piece, *Teares, on the Death of Moeliades*, exemplifies the poet's habits of composition throughout his life and reveals his skill as a craftsman and his techniques of adaptation. According to L. E. Kastner in his 1913 edition of Drummond's poetry, the model for this elegy is one for Basilius in Sir Philip Sidney's *Arcadia* (1590). Kastner also points out various specific borrowings from Sidney's poem. Thus, Sidney writes, "O Hyacinth let AI be on thee still"; Drummond changes this line only slightly: "O Hyacinthes, for ay your AI keepe still" (line 127). Again, Drummond's lines "Stay Skie thy turning Course, and now become/ A stately Arche, unto the Earth his Tombe" (lines 137-138) echo Sidney's "And well methinks becomes this vaulty sky/ A stately tomb to cover him deceased." Other lines are drawn from *Astrophel and Stella* (1591) and from Sonnet XVI of *Aurora* (1604) by Sir William Alexander. The poem is full of classical allusions, and the consolation, beginning with line 143, suggests Socrates' vision of heaven in Plato's *Phaedo* (probably one of the middle dialogues).

Despite all these borrowings, however, the poem is decidedly Drummond's rather than Sidney's or Alexander's. Drummond has transposed Sidney's lament into iambic pentameter couplets, a verse form which he handles effectively. Aware of the dangers of falling into sing-song monotony, Drummond repeatedly alters the position of the caesura; in the first three lines it occurs after the third, sixth, and fourth syllables respectively. He also alters the iamb. The poem begins with a spondee ("O Heavens!"), as do lines nine and nineteen; line twenty-three begins with a trochee. A potentially monotonous emphasis on the rhyme-words is overcome through frequent enjambment: "That (in a Palsey) quakes to finde so soone/ Her Lover set" (lines 33-34); "A Youth more brave, pale Troy with trembling Walles/ Did never see" (lines 61-62).

Another characteristic evident in this poem is Drummond's musicality. Some of his poetry is clearly intended to be sung, and he was a competent lutanist. Here the refrain—apparently original—repeats the liquid *l* and *r* and combines these with the long *e* and *o* sounds to infuse an appropriately watery sound (since the poet is addressing water spirits) as well as a gentle melancholy tone: "Moeliades sweet courtly Nymphes deplore,/ From Thuly to Hydapses pearlie Shore." (Less happily, this refrain reveals Drummond's fondness for inversion, which occasionally renders a line difficult to decipher.)

Even when he borrows, Drummond frequently improves a verse. He turns Sidney's "I never drank of Aganippe well;/ Nor never did in shade of Tempe sit" into "Chaste Maides which haunt fair Aganippe Well,/ And you in Tempes sacred Shade who dwell" (lines 97-98). The long *u* sounds here, coupled with "haunt," do indeed suggest the "doleful Plaints" that the poet is requesting of the nymphs. Again, Sidney's line about the hyacinths is not much altered, but Drummond does pun on the "AI" that the hyacinth supposedly spells. The sky is to serve as a tomb for both Basilius and Moeliades, but Drummond enriches his couplet by introducing the Copernican world view of a turning rather than a stationary heaven. (Drummond's awareness of the New Science is evident again in *A Cypresse Grove.*)

Drummond's love of natural beauty is evident even as he asks for that beauty to be lessened in mourning: "Delicious *Meades*, whose checkred *Plaine* foorth brings,/ White, golden, azure Flowers, which once were Kings" (lines 121-122); "Queene of the Fields, whose Blush makes blushe the *Morne*,/ Sweet *Rose*" (lines 125-126); "In silver Robe the *Moone*, the *Sunne* in Gold" (line 160). The language is lush, suggesting Edmund Spenser and Sidney. At the same time, the description is general; here is no Romantic nature worship, no minute Wordsworthian observation.

*Teares, on the Death of Moeliades* is as characteristic of Drummond in its themes as in its technique. Drummond's last published poem, like his first, deals with death. He boasted of being the first to write a sonnet sequence in English on the death of a mistress, and the only prose piece he published during his lifetime is an extended meditation on death. The early seventeenth century was obsessed with this subject; yet even those who wrote most eloquently on the theme published on other subjects as well. Not so Drummond. Even his love poems are full of the imagery of graves, grief, and death. Clearly the subject was congenial to him.

Related to Drummond's love of death is a contempt for this world. This theme, too, is conventional, yet even before Drummond was imitating and adapting poetry, he wrote from France to Sir George Keith (February 12, 1607), "And truly considering all our actions, except those which regard the service and adoration of God Almighty, they are either to be lamented or laughed at." In his lament for the death of Prince Henry he presents the moral that he will repeat in numerous poems: "O fading Hopes! O shortwhile-lasting Joy!/ Of Earth-borne Man, which one Houre can destroy!" (lines 9-10). In his elegy on the death of Jane, Countess of Perth, he laments that "fairest Things thus soonest have their End" (line 10). Even in *The Entertainment*, a splendid celebration of temporal power and magnificence, Drummond tells Charles I, "On gorgeous rayments, womanising toyes,/ The workes of wormes, and what a Moth destroyes,/ The Maze of fooles, thou shalt no treasure spend,/ Thy charge to immortality shall tend" (iv, 31-34).

The immortality that Drummond anticipates is decidedly Christian, but it is also Neoplatonic. In *Teares, on the Death of Moeliades* Drummond portrays heaven as the abode of perfection, where "other sumptuous Towres" excel "our poore Bowres" (lines 171-172), where songs are sweetest, where all is immutable; he describes God as the supreme exemplar of love and beauty, which those on earth can never truly experience. This Platonism, too, recurs throughout Drummond's poetry.

*Teares, on the Death of Moeliades* is a tissue of allusions, adaptations, and direct borrowings of phrases and ideas. Still, the poem as a whole is distinctly Drummond's in its techniques and themes. Hence, when Drummond turned from an elegy to a sonnet sequence, the poetry did not assume very different characteristics. One might be hard pressed to find the author of "The Extasie" in "Death Be Not Proud," but one would have no difficulty in recognizing the author of *Tears, on the Death of Moeliades* in *Poems*, despite their disparate subjects.

Like *Teares on the Death of Moeliades*, Drummond's *Poems* are heavily indebted to Sidney. Where Sidney celebrates Stella, Drummond sings of Auristella. Kastner notes that Sonnet XXVII (the first part) is reminiscent of Sidney's Sonnet LXXIV in *Astrophel and Stella*, and Drummond's Sonnet V is reminiscent of Sidney's Sonnet XXX. The sequence also reveals Drummond's intimate knowledge of Italian, French, and Spanish models. The very form is of course traditional, though by 1616 the sonnet sequence was a dying, if not a dead, form. Drummond's use of this poetic model is yet another reflection of his desire to copy the best models instead of striking out on his own.

Drummond invariably ends each sonnet with a two-line summary in the manner of the English rather than the Italian form. Otherwise, however, he is flexible in both rhyme scheme and structure. Sonnet XXIV (the first part) has a rhyme scheme of abab baba cdcd ee. Two sonnets later, one finds abba cddc effe gg, and in the very next sonnet the pattern is different still—abba abba cdcd ee. Sonnet XXXI (the first part) consists of an octet and sestet in the Italian mode (though still with the concluding couplet); Sonnet XVI has three quatrains and a couplet in the English manner.

The lush language and musicality of *Teares, on the Death of Moeliades* are even more fully realized in *Poems*, aided by the use of feminine rhymes not present in the elegy. Song I (the first part) describes a luxuriant landscape. Often rich description appears in conjunction with an unusual word, as in Sonnet XVII (the first part), "The silver Flouds in pearlie Channells flow,/ The late-bare Woods greene Anadeams doe weare" (lines 3-4)—*anadeam* had entered the language only about ten years earlier. A bit later Drummond writes, "With Roses here *Shee* stellified the Ground" (Sonnet XXIII, the first part, line 7), and he writes of "Phoebus in his Chaire/ Ensaffroning Sea and Aire" (Song II, the first part, lines 39-40). This love of exotic diction leads him in at least two instances to new coinings; Drummond's is the only use of *deflourish'd* not rated by the *Oxford English Dictionary* ("Deflourish'd *Mead* where is your heavenly Hue?"—Sonnet XLV, the first part, line 9) and the same authority lists as the first use of *disgarland* his "Thy Lockes disgarland" (Song I, the second part, line 90). The descriptions, though rich, are nevertheless general; the landscape is merely a luxurious background for the human actions occurring there.

As in *Teares, on the Death of Moeliades*, Drummond repeatedly invokes mythology. In Song I (the first part) he invokes Phaeton, Elysian Fields, Venus, Mars, Adonis, and many other mythological figures. His use of mythology is usually conventional. In one instance, though, Drummond does cleverly invert the traditional story. Daphne and Syrinx were both turned into plants to preserve their chastity; Drummond imagines that he sees the process reversed as "three naked Nymphes" emerge from a myrtle (lines 84-86). This reversal of the traditional myths foreshadows a thematic reversal in the poem. Conventionally, the lover praises his mistress' chastity. When Drummond's mistress enters the "Fort of Chastitie," though, he bemoans his fate both asleep and waking.

Such playful invention is all too infrequent in the sonnets, the commonplace lamentations all too frequent. Drummond recognized the artificiality of such writing. In the first of "Galatea's Sonnets," a sequence of five poems that Drummond chose not to publish, a woman rejects Petrarchan conceits:

> I Thinke not love ore thee his wings hath spred,
> Or if that passion hath thy soule opprest,
> Its onlie for some Grecian Mistresse dead,
> Of such old sighs thou dost discharge thy brest.

Occasionally, Drummond can infuse sincerity into those old sighs, as when he regrets his failure to declare his love (Sonnet XXIII, the first part) or when he praises the green color of his mistress' eyes (Sonnet XVIII, the first part); neither of these pieces relies on a specific model. Here the emotions are not exaggerated, the incidents quotidian and hence credible. More often, unfortunately, he is willing to tear a passion to tatters. Sonnet XLVII (the first part) sounds like a parody from the rude mechanical's *Pyramus and Thisbe* in William Shakespeare's *A Midsummer Night's Dream* (1595): "O Night, clear Night, O darke and gloomie Day!/ O wofull Waking! O Soule-pleasing Sleepe" (lines 1-2). Though this is the most egregious example, there are enough borrowings from Petrarch, Giambattista Marino, Pierre de Ronsard, and others to suggest that Drummond's inspiration for his sonnets was his library rather than Miss Cunningham.

The sonnet sequence ends with a vision corresponding to the dream in Song I of the first part. In that earlier song the poet meets his mistress for the first time; in this final song he becomes reconciled to her death. The poem apparently cost Drummond much effort, for among his manuscripts is a fragment of eight lines translated from Passerat, apparently a draft of this piece. Here one can trace the movement from literal translation to adaptation. The eight lines have been expanded to nineteen, the natural setting elaborated, and phrases repeated to heighten the melancholy musicality.

As the poem begins, Drummond's mistress appears to urge him to abandon his grief. Her arguments begin with stoical reflections: "Was shee not mortall borne? (line 45); "Why wouldst thou Here longer wish to bee?" (line 75). With line 93 the argument moves to Platonism, echoing the consolation in *Teares, on the Death of Moeliades*. Whereas *Teares, on the Death of Moeliads* ended with Platonic idealism, however, the song proceeds to a third stage (lines 181-240), explicitly Christian, exhorting the lover to think of heaven's joys rather than earth's sorrows.

*A Cypresse Grove*, which Drummond appended to his next collection of poetry, *Flowres of Sion*, retraces these three stages. Indeed, the prose meditation on death is little more than an expansion of the song, with repetitions of phrases as well as ideas. To cite but one example, in the "Song" Drummond writes, "We bee not made for Earth, though here wee come,/ More than the *Embryon* for the Mothers Wombe" (lines 178-179). In *A Cypresse Grove* these lines become "For though hee bee borne on the Earthe, hee is not borne for the Earth, more than the Embryon for the mothers wombe."

In fact, the entire volume of *Flowres of Sion* stems logically from the "song," elaborating on the Christian message that concludes that piece. In his edition of Drummond's writings, R. H. MacDonald notes that *Flowres of Sion* proceeds through the three stages of the religious meditation: Sonnets I-VI depict the poetry's memory of the evils of this world, Sonnet VII through Hymn III (which treat Christ's birth, life, and death) present an understanding of Christ's solution to those evils, and the rest of the poems adore God's love and meditate on the follies of this world.

The poetic techniques by now familiar to the reader of Drummond remain evident here: the love of exotic words (such as "Jubeling cries" in Hymn II, line 49; the *Oxford English Dictionary* notes only a single fifteenth century use of this word), borrowings from numerous sources, luxurious general description, virtuosity in the handling of the sonnet or couplet form. The themes, too, are familiar—the love of death, contempt for the things of this world, Christianity heavily tinged with Neoplatonism. This sonnet cycle mirrors Drummond's earlier one; both progress from despair to hope, from the pains of this world to the joys of the next. Here, however, the emphasis is on the latter rather than the former, so that, paradoxically, the sequence focusing on death is less depressing than the one supposedly treating love.

In the last twenty-six years of his life Drummond published only two occasional pieces, *The Entertainment* in 1633 for King Charles's visit to Edinburgh, and, five years later, an elegy on the death of the son of his longtime friend and fellow poet, Sir William Alexander. The first of these works combines prose and poetry in an elaborate tribute to the king. For the poetic sections, Drummond uses the heroic couplet almost exclusively, an apt choice to celebrate a grand event, and as usual he handles the verse form competently. Only one poem does not employ the couplet, instead containing three lines of six syllables followed by two lines of ten in each of the four verse paragraphs. This metrical pattern suggests the Italian *canzone*, the madrigal, and the dramatic chorus. The language is ornate, abounding in such epithets as "The Acidalian Queene" (Venus) and "Leucadian Sythe-bearing Sire" (Saturn). As these epithets suggest, Drummond again invokes mythological allusions, as Endymion, Saturn, Jove, Mars, Venus, and Mercury address Charles. In choosing these particular deities, together with the sun and moon, Drummond implies that the entire universe rejoices at Charles's visit. Each of the gods ends his speech with a refrain: "Thus heavens decree, so have ordain'd the Fates," alternating with "Thus heavens ordaine, so doe decree the Fates." Drummond had effectively used this rhetorical device in *Teares, on the Death of Moeliades*; though the refrain here lacks the melody of the earlier one, the slight variation shows a concern for preventing monotony.

Although the excessive flattery is obligatory, it does not lack a hortatory edge. The king is urged to avoid excessive taxation and the raising up of favorites, to aid learning and the arts, and to rule through love rather than through fear. The political message thus anticipates such pamphlets as *Irene*.

*The Entertainment* is largely original, only occasionally hinting at other poets. *A Pastorall Elegie*, on the other hand, is virtually a translation of Baldassare Castiglione's "Alcon"; Drummond even refers to the dead Sir Antony Alexander as Alcon. The highly artificial pastoral form and the lack of originality suggest that Drummond was writing from a sense of obligation to his old friend; there is even less emotion here than in *Teares, on the Death of Moeliades*. The technique is as sound as ever, but only in one place does Drummond surpass his model. Ostensibly unaware of his friend's death, the poet imagines that "the populous City holds him, amongst Harmes/ Of some fierce *Cyclops*, Circe's stronger Charmes" (lines 183-184). These Homeric allusions, absent in Castiglione's poem, suggest that the youth in fact will not return but rather suffer the fate of Odysseus' companions. These references thus foreshadow the poet's discovery of the youth's fate.

During his lifetime Drummond suppressed almost as much poetry as he published. In general, he was a sound editor; few of the pieces published since his death add anything to his reputation. Occasionally, though, one of the posthumous poems demonstrates wit and imagination too often lacking in Drummond's published works. The quatrain on Pym's death quoted earlier is original and clever. The five sonnets of Galatea, supposedly written in response to verses such as those Drummond composed in the first part of *Poems*, wittily undercut the Petrarchan conventions by pointing out their artificiality and logical absurdity. "The Country Maid," though slightly bawdy, is mythopoeic. Drummond's decision not to publish poems such as these may have been less a judgment on their quality than an indication of the kind of literary reputation he wished to cultivate. Less concerned with originality and mythopoesis than with correctness, imitation, and technical virtuosity, Drummond published those works that embodied his poetic ideals. Working with established forms and themes, he was able to make these his own and to find a unique voice. His models rarely led him astray; he produced few bad poems, much competent verse, and a handful of memorable pieces such as the "Song" that closes the second part of the sonnet cycle of *Poems* or his sonnet to Sir William Alexander on his own illness. What Samuel Johnson said of another reclusive poet, Thomas Gray, may also be said of Drummond at his best: "Had [he] written often thus, it had been vain to blame, and useless to praise him."

**Major publications other than poetry**

NONFICTION: *A Midnight's Trance*, 1619; *History of Scotland from the Year 1423 Until the Year 1542*, 1655; *Notes of Ben Jonson's Conversations with William Drummond of Hawthornden*, 1832.

**Bibliography**

Fogle, French Rowe. *A Critical Study of William Drummond of Hawthornden*, 1952.

Masson, David. *Drummond of Hawthornden: The Story of His Life and Writings*, 1873.

Rae, Thomas Ian. "The Political Attitudes of William Drummond of Hawthornden," in *The Scottish Tradition: Essays in Honour of Ronald Gordon Cant*, 1974. Edited by G. W. S. Barrow.

Wallerstein, Ruth C. "The Style of Drummond of Hawthornden in Its Relation to His Translations," in *PMLA*. XLVIII (1933), pp. 1090-1107.

*Joseph Rosenblum*

# JOHN DRYDEN

**Born:** Aldwinckle, England; August 9, 1631
**Died:** London, England; May 1, 1700

### Principal poems and collections

*Heroic Stanzas*, 1659; *Astraea Redux*, 1660; "To My Lord Chancellor," 1662; *Prologues and Epilogues*, 1664-1700; *Annus Mirabilis*, 1667; Ovid's *Epistles*, 1680 (translation); *Absalom and Achitophel*, 1681; *Absalom and Achitophel*, Part II, 1682 (with Nahum Tate); *The Medal*, 1682; *MacFlecknoe*, 1682; *Religio Laici*, 1682; *Threnodia Augustalis*, 1685; *The Hind and the Panther*, 1687; "A Song for St. Cecilia's Day," 1687; *Britannia Rediviva*, 1688; *Eleonora*, 1692; *The Satires of Juvenal and Persius*, 1693 (translation); "To My Dear Friend Mr Congreve," 1693; *Alexander's Feast: Or, The Power of Music*, 1697; *The Works of Vergil*, 1697 (translation); "To My Honour'd Kinsman, John Driden," 1700; *The Secular Masque*, 1700.

### Other literary forms

If one follows the practice of literary historians and assigns John Milton to an earlier age, then John Dryden stands as the greatest literary artist in England between 1660 and 1700, a period sometimes designated the Age of Dryden. In addition to his achievements in poetry, he excelled in drama, translation, and literary criticism. He wrote or coauthored twenty-seven plays over a period of nearly thirty-five years, among them successfully produced tragedies, heroic plays, tragicomedies, comedies of manner, and operas.

For every verse of original poetry that Dryden wrote, he translated two from another poet. Moreover, he translated two long volumes of prose from French originals—Louis Maimbourg's *The History of the League* (1684) and Dominick Bouhours' *The Life of St. Francis Xavier* (1680)—and he had a hand in the translation of Plutarch's *Lives* published by Jacob Tonson in 1683. The translations were usually well received, especially the editions of Juvenal and Persius (1693) and of Vergil (1697).

Dryden's literary criticism consists largely of prefaces and dedications published throughout his career and attached to other works, his only critical work published alone being *An Essay of Dramatic Poesy* (1668). As a critic, Dryden appears at his best when he evaluates an earlier poet or dramatist (Homer, Vergil, Ovid, Geoffrey Chaucer, William Shakespeare, Ben Jonson, John Fletcher), when he seeks to define a genre, or when he breaks new critical ground as in providing, for example, definitions of *wit* or a theory of translation.

### Achievements

The original English poetry of Dryden consists of approximately two hundred titles, or about twenty thousand verses. Slow to develop as a poet, he wrote his first significant poem in his twenty-eighth year, yet his poetic energy continued almost unabated until his death forty-one years later. His poetry reflects the diversity of talent which one finds throughout his literary career, and a wide range of didactic and lyric genre are represented. With *MacFlecknoe* and *Absalom and Achitophel* Dryden raised English satire to a form of high art, surpassing his contemporaries John Oldham, Samuel Butler, and the Earl of Rochester as they had surpassed their Elizabethan predecessors. He left his impression on the ode and the verse epistle, and his religious poem *Religio Laici* may be considered an early example of the verse essay. In the minor genre represented by prologues and epilogues, he stands alone in English literature, unexcelled in both variety and quality.

Of Dryden's poetic achievement Samuel Johnson wrote in his *Life of Dryden*: "What was said of Rome, adorned by Augustus, may be applied by an easy metaphor to English poetry embellished by Dryden . . . he found it brick and he left it marble." Johnson's praise applies primarily to Dryden's significant achievements in style and tone, for Dryden perfected the heroic couplet, the rhymed iambic pentameter form that was to remain the dominant meter of English verse for nearly a century. He demonstrated that a stanza form best suited to lucid and graceful aphoristic wit could be varied and supple enough to produce a range of tones. Building upon the achievements of his predecessors Edmund Waller and John Denham and drawing upon his own wide experience with the couplet in heroic plays, Dryden polished the form that became for him a natural mode of expression. His couplets are usually end-stopped and closed, achieving a complete grammatical unit by the end of the second line. He makes extensive use of colloquial diction to create a rational, almost conversational tone. The lines contain internal pauses that are carefully regulated, and the syntax usually follows that of idiomatic English. To keep tension in the verse, he relies primarily upon balance, antithesis, and other schemes of repetition.

Dryden brought to poetry of his age the energy and directness of expression that critics describe as the most masculine of styles. Accustomed to writing soliloquies and moral arguments in the speeches of heroic drama, he incorporated into his poetry extended passages of reasoning in verse that an age which valued reason found appealing. His inclination to choose for his poetry subjects of interest to contemporaries—science, aesthetics, religion, and politics—enhanced the popularity of his work.

### Biography

John Dryden was the eldest of fourteen children in a landed family of modest means whose sympathies were Puritan on both sides. Little is known of his youth in Northamptonshire, for Dryden, seldom hesitant about his opinions, was reticent about his personal life. At about age fifteen, he was enrolled in Westminster School, then under the headmastership of Dr. Richard Busby, a school notable for its production of poets and bishops. Having attained at Westminster a thorough grounding in Latin, he proceeded to Cambridge, taking the B.A. degree in 1654. After the death of his father brought him a modest inheritance in the form of rents from family land, he left the University and settled in London. Though little is known of his early years there, he served briefly in Cromwell's government in a minor position and may have worked for the publisher Henry Herringman. He produced an elegy on the death of Cromwell, yet when Charles II ascended the throne, Dryden greeted the new ruler with a congratulatory poem, *Astraea Redux*. After the Restoration he turned his main interest to the drama, collaborating with Sir Robert Howard on one heroic play. He married Lady Elizabeth Howard, Sir Robert's sister, in 1663, a marriage which brought him a generous dowry and eventually three sons in whom he took pride.

Throughout his career Dryden was no stranger to controversy, whether literary, political, or religious; in fact, he seemed all too eager to seize an occasion to express his views on these subjects. In literature he challenged Sir Robert Howard's views on the drama, Thomas Rymer's on criticism, and Rochester's and Thomas Shadwell's on questions of literary merit and taste. After receiving encouragement from Charles II, he entered the political controversy over succession to the throne with *Absalom and Achitophel*. Later he explained his religious views by attacking Deists, Catholics, and Dissenters in *Religio Laici*; then he shifted his ground and defended Catholicism in *The Hind and the Panther*.

For a variety of reasons, certainly in some measure because of envy, Dryden was the most often assailed among major poets. In an age when almost everyone prized his own wit, Dryden attained eminence without obviously possessing more of that quality than many others. His willingness to plunge into controversy brought him a host of enemies, and his changes of opinions and beliefs—literary, religious, political—presented an even greater problem. Examining the changes one by one, a biographer or critic can provide a logical explanation for each. This task is perhaps most difficult in literary criticism, however, where Dryden will defend a position with enthusiasm only to abandon it later for another, which he advocates with equal enthusiasm. To his contemporaries, some of his changes coincided with interest, and, rightly or wrongly, he was frequently charged with timeserving.

In 1668, Dryden was appointed poet laureate, a position he held for twenty years, being deprived of it after the Glorious Revolution of 1688. During his term he received a two-hundred-pound annual stipend, which was later increased to three hundred when he became historiographer royal; but this was irregularly paid. His greatest efforts remained with the drama until his satire *MacFlecknoe* and the beginning of the Popish Plot in 1678, when he turned his energies to poetic satire.

When events surrounding the Plot posed a threat to the government of Charles II, Dryden wrote vigorously in behalf of the Tory cause, producing satires, translations, and then his religious poems. Initially he carried the field for the King, but after the fall of James II and the loss of his political cause, he also lost the laureateship and its accompanying pension.

During the final period of his life, 1688-1700, he made a brief return to the theater but devoted most of his considerable energy and talent to translation, achieving success with his patrons and public. Though he had taken unpopular political and religious positions, he experienced no decline in his literary talent; in his final decade he produced some of his best poems. Shortly before his death on May 1, 1700, he could look back upon his century and epitomize the era poetically in *The Secular Masque*. He represented the Stuart Era by Diana (James I), Mars (Charles I and the Civil Wars), and Venus (Charles II):

|  | All, all of a piece throughout; |
| (to Diana) | Thy Chase had a Beast in View; |
| (to Mars) | Thy Wars brought nothing about; |
| (to Venus) | Thy Lovers were all untrue; |
|  | 'Tis well an Old Age is out, |
|  | And time to begin a New. |

**Analysis**

To a greater degree than for most other poets, John Dryden's poems are based upon real and not imaginary occasions or events, often of a public nature. His imaginative power lies not in creating original or dramatic situations but in endowing actual events with poetic and sometimes mythic significance. When one looks beyond the rich variety of his poetry, Dryden's art is likely to impress the reader most strongly for the following: his intricate craftsmanship and style; his sense of genre; and his reliance upon what he termed parallels, analogies used for both structuring and developing his poems. Craft and style are most readily revealed through analysis of selected passages from the poems, but some clarification of genre and the parallels may be useful at the outset.

Though Dryden possessed a keen sense of poetic genre, questions of classification in his poetry are not always easily resolved, for he writes in genres not well defined during his age. A poem may be assigned to one genre on the basis of its theme or purpose (an elegy, for example) and to another on the basis of form (such as an ode). Yet almost any poem by Dryden can be placed with assurance in one of the following genres: lyric forms, especially songs and odes; satires; ratiocinative poems; panegyrics, praising public figures or celebrating public occasions; verse epistles, usually in praise of living persons; epigrams, epitaphs, elegies, commemorating the dead; and prologues and epilogues.

For his parallels, which often reveal his preoccupation with monarchy and hierarchy, Dryden goes to the Bible, classical antiquity, or history. They provide a mythic framework within which he develops rational positions or ideals, aided by a set of conventional metaphors such as the temple, the tree, or the theater. Dryden's use of parallels and conventional metaphors indicates his essentially conservative cast of mind, especially about human nature and political affairs.

The parallels also afford an opportunity for Dryden's favorite mode of thought—that of polarities or opposites. He delights in presenting contrasting viewpoints and then either defending one as an ideal or steering between them in a show of moderation. Normally such polarities or dichotomies contribute to a rational tone, enabling Dryden to ingratiate himself with the reader, as in his "Prologue to *Aureng-Zebe*" (1676). He contemplates retirement from the stage and contrasts his own plays with those of Shakespeare and his younger contemporaries such as William Wycherley:

> As with the greater Dead he dares not strive,
> He wou'd not match his Verse with those who live:
> Let him retire, betwix't two Ages cast,
> The first of this, and hindmost of the last.

The reader accepts the tone of humility, even though he realizes that it is not entirely ingenuous.

Dryden's earliest poems are usually occasional pieces and panegyrics that reveal to some extent a debt to so-called Metaphysical poetry and to Abraham Cowley, an influence he soon rejected for a style more regular and lucid. Yet as late as 1667, in *Annus Mirabilis*, a long poem on the London plague and fire and the Dutch war, Dryden still retains some tendency toward Metaphysical conceits. It is notable too that *Annus Mirabilis* employs the four-line heroic stanza from Sir William Davenant's poem *Gondibert* (1651), which Dryden had used earlier in the elegy on Cromwell. Perhaps a more reliable index to his poetic development during the 1660's is represented by the prologues and epilogues which he began publishing in 1664.

During the Restoration, prologues and epilogues became normal complements to dramatic works. Over nearly four decades, Dryden wrote more than a hundred of them, not only for his own plays but for those of other dramatists as well. They employ straightforward, colloquial diction and syntax, and they are normally written in heroic couplets. In his early examples in this genre, Dryden follows established convention by having the poems appeal for the indulgence of the audience and a favorable reception of the play. Later he adapts the poems to varied subjects and purposes, some having little to do with drama. He writes prologues to introduce special performances at unaccustomed sites, such as Oxford, or to greet an eminent person in the audience (a duke or duchess, perhaps), or to mark some theater occasion, such as the opening of a new playhouse. In some of the poems he reflects upon the poor taste of the audience; in others he explains principles of literary criticism. He may take his audience into his confidence and impart his own personal plans. At times, as in the "Prologue to *The Duke of Guise*" (1684), he outlines his views on political questions, explaining how events chronicled in the play resemble those then current. In more than a few he titillates the audience with sexual humor, allusion, and innuendo. For all their variety, the poems evidence throughout some of Dryden's most characteristic poetic qualities— directness, clarity, colloquial tone, wit, and adaptability.

Neither the occasion nor the time of Dryden's first satire, *MacFlecknoe*, a mock-heroic attack on a rival playwright, Thomas Shadwell, is known with certainty. Dryden selects the demise of the poetaster Richard Flecknoe (d. 1678) as the basis of his poem—a mock coronation, in which Flecknoe, dubbed the reigning prince of dullness, chooses Shadwell as his successor. This situation permits scintillating literary inversion; the kingdom of letters, Augustan Rome, and the seriousness of succession to the throne all provide contrasting analogy and allusion. The poem satirizes not only Shadwell but also bad taste in art. Establishing a polarity between true and false wit, Dryden creates by implication an aesthetic ideal.

In the first section of the poem, Flecknoe arrives at his decision regarding a successor. The poem then describes the festivities preceding Shadwell's coronation and the coronation itself, followed by the long oration and fall of Flecknoe. The opening lines invite the reader to assume that selecting a successor to the throne of dullness is serious business:

> All human things are subject to decay,
> And, when Fate summons, Monarchs must obey.
> This Flecknoe found, who, like Augustus, young
> Was call'd to Empire, and had govern'd long;
> In Prose and Verse, was own'd, without dispute
> Through all the Realms of *Nonsense*, absolute.

The sober aphorism in the opening lines, followed by comparison with Augustus, creates a tone of solemnity, to be overturned by the mockery of "Realms of *Nonsense*." As Flecknoe selects Shadwell, he catalogs a series of personal attributes praiseworthy in a dunce, usually deriving from the plays of Shadwell. Yet Dryden does not refrain from personal satire directed at Shadwell's size, perhaps because Shadwell himself had used his corpulent appearance as a basis for his resemblance to Ben Jonson:

> Besides his goodly Fabrick fills the eyes,
> And seems design'd for thoughtless Majesty:
> Thoughtless as Monarch Oakes that shade the plain,
> And, spread in solemn state, supinely reign.

Another satiric maneuver is to separate poets into two camps, with Shadwell relegated to the company of dullards. An example occurs when Flecknoe describes the site of the coronation:

> Great Fletcher never treads in Buskins here,
> Nor greater Jonson dare in Socks appear.
> But gentle Simkin just reception finds
> Amidst this Monument of vanish't Minds.

The polarity of artists includes such figures as Ben Jonson, John Fletcher, Sir Charles Sedley, and Sir George Etherege at one end; and John Ogleby, Thomas Heywood, John Shirley, Thomas Dekker, and Richard Flecknoe at the other.

As there is a difference between true and false writing, there is also a hierarchy of forms or genres. Flecknoe admonishes Shadwell to abandon the drama and turn to those poems developed through what Dryden's age considered false wit: pattern poems, anagrams, acrostics, and ballads—works appropriate to his dull wit. In *MacFlecknoe* Dryden generally maintains a tone of exuberant good humor and mirth, seldom resorting to lampoon. The poem does, however, illustrate the problem of topicality, since many of its allusions are now obscure and others are altogether lost. Still, as Dryden explores the kingdoms of sense and nonsense, he clearly demonstrates his reliance upon parallels and polarities.

Dryden's three later satiric poems—*Absalom and Achitophel*, *The Medal*, and *Absalom and Achitophel*, Part II (with Nahum Tate)—concern the struggle of the Whigs to alter the succession in England by excluding James, Duke of York, the King's brother, and giving the right of succession to James, Duke of Monmouth, the King's illegitimate son. This enterprise was ably led by the Earl of Shaftesbury (Achitophel), though he could not prevail against the determined opposition of the King. Charles II (David) understood that permitting Parliament to change the established succession would alter the form of monarchy from a royal one, in which the king normally followed law and established tradition but could exercise extraordinary powers in times of crisis, to a constitutional monarchy in which the king's power became subject to parliamentary restrictions. Dryden's objective in the poem is to persuade readers to support the King in the conflict.

Thus in *Absalom and Achitophel*, Dryden (then poet laureate) employed his pen in the King's behalf—according to anecdote, at the King's own suggestion. He makes use of the biblical rebellion against David by his son Absalom, at the instigation of Achitophel (II Samuel 13-18), a parallel familiar to his audience. Dryden freely adds characters and alters the biblical parallel to make it apply to English political leaders and institutions, pointing out that while the biblical account ends with the death of Absalom, he hopes that a peaceful resolution with Monmouth remains possible.

The satire of *Absalom and Achitophel* differs somewhat from that of

*MacFlecknoe*. While Dryden believed satire to be a form of heroic or epic poetry, implying some narrative content, he had in *MacFlecknoe* maintained a tone of ironic mockery and fine raillery throughout. *Absalom and Achitophel* represents a mixed or Varronian kind of satire, perhaps owing something to Juvenal as well as to Varro. The satiric elements are confined chiefly to the first section of the poem, where Dryden discredits the Whig opponents of the King. Instead of implying an ideal, as satire normally does, Dryden explains it directly in a passage that has come to be regarded as an essay on government (vv. 723-810). Finally, Dryden praises the supporters of the King individually and has the King appear in his own person at the poem's end, showing David (Charles II) facing his opponents with firmness and moderation.

In addition to the biblical parallel, Dryden makes effective use of characters, a technique that owes something to classical satirists but more to the character writers of the seventeenth century. A "character" in Dryden is a passage, sometimes satiric, sometimes serious, delineating a person and creating a unified impression. Though Dryden includes both satiric and complimentary characters, the satiric ones—Achitophel (Shaftesbury), Zimri (Buckingham), Shimei (Slingsby Bethel), and Corah (Titus Oates)—are the most memorable. In his character of Zimri (vv. 543-568), Dryden portrays the Duke of Buckingham as foolishly inconsistent: "A man so various, that he seem'd to be/ Not one, but all Mankind's Epitome." In his perversity, Zimri is made to reflect a kind of frenetic energy:

> Stiff in opinions, always in the wrong;
> Was everything by starts, and nothing long;
> But in the course of one revolving Moon,
> Was Chymist, Fidler, States-Man, and Buffoon.

Such an indiscriminate course indicates that Zimri's judgment about human beings and political institutions cannot be trusted, as the character goes on to suggest. The character becomes a major means of discrediting the King's chief opponents, yet it also permits Dryden to praise the King's loyal supporters.

For his religious poem, *Religio Laici* (*A Layman's Faith*), Dryden assigns no genre, giving as the subtitle "A Poem." In a lengthy preface he finds precedent for his work in the epistles of Horace. It is often called a ratiocinative poem, but it closely resembles the genre in English poetry designated "verse essay." It surveys a definite subject, presents a variety of positions, explores their bases, provides reasoned analysis, and gives the poet's personal positions. *Religio Laici* surveys religious movements in England during Dryden's day and rejects all except the established Church, supporting the official view that the Chuch of England represents a *via media*—a middle way— avoiding the extremes of the Deists, Catholics, and Dissenters. Dryden upholds biblical authority against the Deists, citing reasons for belief in scriptural authority and arguing that the religious principles advocated by the Deists were first brought to man by revelation, not innate understanding, as Deists believed, for otherwise the Greeks and Romans would have discovered them. As the Deist relies too heavily on man's reason, the Catholic relies too heavily on tradition and the argument of infallibility, while the Protestant errs in the extreme in another direction, relying excessively on private interpretation of the Scriptures, an extreme which leads to disorder in society.

Dryden's conclusion indicates both his moderation and his intensely conservative outlook. Essential points of faith are few and plain. Since men believe more than is necessary, they should seek guidance from reliable ancient theologians on disputed points. If that does not provide adequate enlightenment, they can either leave the matter unsettled or restrain further speculation and inquiry in the interest of public peace and order.

"To the Memory of Mr. Oldham" (1684), a poem that demonstrates the efficacy of heroic couplets for a serious theme, may be Dryden's finest elegy. John Oldham, a younger poet, had attained success with his satires against the Jesuits and had died young. Dryden pays tribute to a fellow satirist with whom he can identify. The opening lines establish the basic tone: "Farewell, too little, and too lately known,/ Whom I began to think and call my own." The classical simplicity of "farewell," the weight and seriousness of the long vowels and semivowels, and the balance within the lines ("too little and too lately" and "think and call") establish a serious, even tone which Dryden can vary, yet preserve. In a second part of the poem, he stresses the youth of Oldham and his early achievement, acknowledging its imperfection. The tone of unqualified praise has altered, but balance and tonal consistency remain. Dryden next demonstrates his exquisite sense of poetic sound when he turns to the defects of Oldham's poetry, choosing to downplay them: "But Satyr needs not those, and Wit will shine/ Through the harsh cadence of a rugged line." The cadence in the second line sounds harsher because it follows a perfectly balanced line. After further downplaying of the importance of a good ear in the insipid passage, "Maturing time/ But mellow what we write to the dull sweets of Rime," Dryden returns to the balanced and rational tone:

> Once more, hail and farewell; farewell thou young,
> But ah too short, Marcellus of our Tongue;
> Thy Brows with Ivy, and with Laurels bound;
> But Fate and gloomy Night encompass thee around.

Allusion to Marcellus enables Dryden to draw the parallel to Augustan Rome, where the nephew who might have succeeded Augustus dies young. Thus, the kingdom of civilized letters in Dryden's age resembles the finest earlier civilization. The balance within the verse ("Ivy and Laurels," "Fate and gloomy Night") ends the poem in a tone of serious, subdued expression of loss.

As one would expect, in the ode Dryden abandons the heroic couplet for a more complicated stanza and metrical pattern. His odes are occasional poems either upon the death of someone, as in "Threnodia Augustalis," on the death of Charles II, or "To the Pious Memory of the Accomplished Young Lady Mrs. Anne Killigrew," or commemoration of an occasion, as in his two odes for St. Cecilia's Day, written ten years apart (1687 and 1697), both commemorating the patron saint of music. They share a common theme, the power of music to influence man's emotions or passions. In the first "A Song for St. Cecilia's Day," Dryden employs the traditional association of instruments with particular human passions and develops his theme, "What Passion cannot Musick raise and quell," in a kind of linear fashion, the trumpet instilling courage and valor, the flute arousing love, the violin, jealousy, and the organ influencing devotion. Inclusion of the organ enables Dryden to allude to St. Cecilia, who is said to have invented that instrument. According to legend, while playing on her invention she drew an angel to earth, the harmony having caused him to mistake earth for heaven. In a concluding grand chorus, Dryden sees music, an element of the creation, as also befitting the end of creation:

> So, when the last and dreadful hour
> This crumbling Pageant shall devour,
> The Trumpet shall be heard on high,
> The Dead shall live, the Living die,
> And Musick shall untune the sky.

*Alexander's Feast*, the second St. Cecilia ode, is constructed according to a more ambitious plan, for Dryden imagines Alexander celebrating his victory over the Persian King Darius, listening to the music of Timotheus, which has sufficient power to move a hero of Alexander's greatness. The shifts are abrupt, as in the Pindaric ode, yet Dryden preserves the Horatian structure with a regular development of emotional response, as Timotheus causes the monarch to experience a sense of deification, a desire for pleasure, pity for the fallen Darius, and then love. No sooner has Alexander indulged his pleasure than Timotheus, in another strain, incites him to revenge, and the King seizes a torch to set the Persian city aflame. At the poem's end, Dryden compares Cecilia and Timotheus. In this ode Dryden achieves a remarkably complex, forceful, and energetic movement, and he lends dramatic strength to the familiar theme by creating a dramatic parallel that involves historical characters. While the ode attains a kind of Pindaric exuberance, Dryden nevertheless follows a regular, linear organization.

One of Dryden's principal poetic forms is the Horatian verse epistle, a type of poetry he wrote over a period of nearly forty years. The genre permits a poet to address an individual, speaking in his own person, and revealing as much or as little about himself as he wishes. Dryden's epistles are usually poems of praise, though wit may sometimes be the chief purpose. Two of his final epistles, "To My Dear Friend Mr Congreve" and "To My Honor'd Kinsman, John Driden" (a poem addressed to his cousin who then served in Parliament), are among his most memorable. Dryden's reliance on kingdoms and monarchies comes to the fore in each—the state in the epistle to his kinsman and the kingdom of letters in the poem to the dramatist William Congreve.

A favorite device of Dryden's is to set up polarities between differing ages and make comparisons, as he does in his "Epigram on Milton": "Three Poets in three distant ages born/ Greece, Italy, and England did adorn." The contrasts constitute a witty means of expressing praise, an art which Dryden had mastered in both verse and prose—being as skilled in panegyric as he was in satire.

In "To My Dear Friend Mr Congreve," the colloquial tone of the opening line belies a more serious theme and purpose: "Well then; the promis'd hour is come at last;/ The present Age of Wit obscures the past." Speaking of the wits of his time, Dryden acknowledges that, owing to a deficiency of genius, they have not equaled the achievements of Shakespeare and Jonson, and thus, metaphorically, "The second Temple was not like the first." Having introduced his metaphor of the temple, Dryden exploits it by alluding to another age and comparing Congreve to the Roman architect Vitruvius. Dryden goes on to praise Congreve's specific abilities as a dramatist, comparing him with Jonson, Fletcher, George Etherege, Thomas Southerne, and Wycherley, and, in a further allusion to Rome, with Scipio, for achieving greatness in youth.

Becoming more personal, Dryden shifts the parallel to the kingdom of poetry and, specifically, to his own tenure as poet laureate:

> O that your Brows by Lawrel had sustain'd,
> Well had I been Depos'd, if You had reign'd!
> The Father had descended for the Son;
> For only You are lineal to the Throne.

It was a great irony in Dryden's life that the poet he had made successor to the throne of dullness in *MacFlecknoe*, Thomas Shadwell, had succeeded instead to the laureateship. The poem concludes with Dryden speaking of his own departure from the stage and asking the young Congreve to treat his memory kindly, a request which Congreve, to his credit, fulfilled by editing Dryden's plays and writing a personal testimony and memoir favorable to the older poet. The poem is vintage Dryden, displaying the polarities between ages, the temple metaphor, the Roman allusions, and, above all, the monarchical metaphor involving successions, coronations, and reigns.

Dryden is essentially a poet of urbanity, wit, and reason, perhaps seeking more to persuade readers than to move them. It has justly been pointed out that his poetry lacks emotional depth. He would rather arouse indignation and scorn over what he opposes than create admiration and appreciation for what he defends. The topical and occasional nature of his poetry suggest his preoccupation with issues of interest to his own day, which are of course less interesting to subsequent ages. His imagery and figures of speech are derived from classical literature, art, and society, not from nature. Even so, modern readers still find appealing those qualities that Dryden himself prized—grace and subtlety of style, rational tone, and vigorous and direct expression.

## Major publications other than poetry

PLAYS: *The Wild Gallant*, 1663; *The Rival Ladies*, 1664; *The Indian Queen*, 1665 (with Sir Robert Howard); *The Indian Emperor*, 1665; *Secret Love: Or, The Maiden Queen*, 1667; *The Tempest*, 1667 (with Sir William Davenant); *An Evening's Love*, 1668; *Tyrannic Love: Or, The Royal Martyr*, 1669; *The Conquest of Granada, Parts I* and *II*, 1670-1671; *The Assignation: Or, Love in a Nunnery*, 1672; *Amboyna*, 1673; *Aurengzebe*, 1675; *The State of Innocence, and Fall of Man*, 1677; *All for Love*, 1678; *Oedipus*, 1679 (with Nathaniel Lee); *Troilus and Cressida*, 1679; *The Kind Keeper*, 1680; *The Spanish Frair*, 1681; *The Duke of Guise*, 1683 (with Nathaniel Lee); *Albion and Albanius*, 1685; *Don Sebastian*, 1690; *Amphytryon*, 1690; *King Arthur*, 1691; *Cleomenes, the Spartan Hero*, 1692; *Love Triumphant*, 1694.

NONFICTION: *An Essay of Dramatic Poesy*, 1668; "A Defense of *An Essay of Dramatic Poesy*," 1668; "Preface to *An Evening's Love*," 1671; "Of Heroic Plays: An Essay," 1672; "Preface to *All for Love*," 1678; "The Grounds of Criticism in Tragedy," 1679; *The History of the League*, 1684 (translation); "Preface to *Sylvae*," 1685; *The Life of St. Francis Xavier*, 1686; *A Discourse Concerning the Original and Progress of Satire*, 1693; "Dedication of *Examen Poeticum*," 1693; "Dedication of the *Aeneis*," 1697; "Preface to *The Fables*," 1700.

## Bibliography

Hoffman, Arthur. *John Dryden's Imagery*, 1962.

McFadden, George. *Dryden: The Public Poet, 1660-1685*, 1981.

Miner, Earl. *Dryden's Poetry*, 1967.

Ramsey, Paul. *The Art of John Dryden*, 1969.

Roper, Alan. *Dryden's Poetic Kingdoms*, 1965.

Schilling, Bernard. *Dryden and the Conservative Myth*, 1961.

Swedenberg, H. T., Jr., ed. *Essential Articles for the Study of John Dryden*, 1966.

Van Doren, Mark. *The Poetry of John Dryden*, 1931.

Ward, Charles E. *The Life of John Dryden*, 1961.

*Stanley Archer*

# ALAN DUGAN

**Born:** Brooklyn, New York; February 12, 1923

## Principal collections

*Poems*, 1961; *Poems 2*, 1963; *Poems 3*, 1967; *Collected Poems*, 1969; *Poems 4*, 1974.

## Other literary forms

Alan Dugan's literary accomplishments have centered around the medium of poetry.

## Achievements

Dugan had been publishing poems in literary magazines for a number of years—winning an award from *Poetry* as early as 1947—before his first book of poetry was published in 1961. That book, *Poems*, enjoyed one of the greatest critical successes of any first volume of poems in recent decades. Dudley Fitts awarded it the Yale Series of Younger Poets Award; it also won the National Book Award and the Pulitzer Prize. Philip Booth called it "the most original first book that has appeared . . . in a sad long time." Dugan has published three more volumes of poetry, similar in style and range to his first volume, winning the Pulitzer Prize for Poetry again in 1967 for *Poems 3*.

Dugan's language makes it evident that he belongs to the colloquial tradition of American poetry. In a manner somewhat reminiscent of William Carlos Williams, Dugan reverses the expectations of the reader of love or nature poetry, turning sentiment into irony. Like Williams, and like contemporary poets such as James Wright and Philip Levine, Dugan sets his poetry in the city and expresses sympathy for, and identification with, the urban working class. Although Dugan's poems seldom rhyme, they often employ traditional meters and stanza as well as free verse. The emphasis on form—even, on a few occasions, the resort to pattern poems—often creates an interesting tension with his dominant plain style.

Dugan established his insistent ironic tone in his first book, and there has been no significant development in his work since that widely praised collection. This lack of development, the most obvious weakness of his work, can be seen most clearly in his recent volume, *Poems 4*, in which the poems are similar to his earlier work but smaller and thinner.

## Biography

Born in Brooklyn, Alan Dugan has spent most of his life in New York City. His stint in the Army Air Corps during World War II was of importance to him, and a number of his first published poems were portraits of servicemen.

He attended Queens College and Olivet College, and received his B.A. degree from Mexico City College. He married Judith Shahn, the daughter of the painter Ben Shahn. After the war, he held a number of jobs in New York City, working in advertising and publishing and as a maker of models for a medical supply house. These jobs made him dissatisfied with the world of office work that he satirizes in his poetry.

The success of his first book of poems in 1961 led to his winning a series of awards that gave him more time for his poetry. Besides the National Book Award and two Pulitzer prizes, he received a Rome Fellowship from the American Academy of Arts and Letters in 1962-1963, a Guggenheim Fellowship in 1963-1964, and a Rockefeller Foundation Fellowship in 1967-1968. He was a member of the faculty at Sarah Lawrence College from 1967 through 1971, and he has been on the faculty of the Fine Arts Work Center in Provincetown, Massachusetts, since 1971. Dugan has given many poetry readings, and, after adjusting to his high voice and the purposely undramatic, cold presentation, audiences have found that his style of reading fits the poems.

**Analysis**

Alan Dugan brought to his first remarkable volume, *Poems*, a completely developed style. That style was colloquial, spare, and tough, fitting the bleak vision of much of his poetry. Dugan has been characterized as a poet lacking in charm, and truly, there is no attempt to be charming, only intense and truthful. His mocking, ironic style fits the narrowness of his outlook, and both the achievement and the weakness of his poetry rest on it.

Whether Dugan writes of war, love, or work (his key subjects), he confronts them with a similar ironic stance. His poetry is against sentimentality, even against transcendence, a kind of antipoetry. "How We Heard the Name," the poem that Dudley Fitts, the judge of The Yale Series of Younger Poets, selected for its "strangeness" despite "the greyness of diction and versification," is typical of Dugan's work.

In part, the poem depends for its meaning on a classical allusion, a surprisingly common technique in this tough-talking urban poet. At the center of the poem is the battle of Granicus, one of Alexander the Great's most famous victories, but Dugan has singled out a seemingly trivial historical oddity: Alexander wrote that he won the battle "with no help from the Lacedaemonians." In Dugan's poem, the river brings down the debris and dead of the battle until it also brings down a soldier on a log. The speaker of the poem inquires about the source of this grim pollution, and the soldier sardonically tells him of the famous victory won by the Greeks "except/ the Lacedaemonians and/ myself." He explains that this is merely a joke "between me and a man/ named Alexander, whom/ all of you ba-bas/ will hear of as a god." The antiheroic stance, the directness of the language, the casualness of the mention of Alexander, and the comedy of "ba-bas" to characterize those who believe a mere man can be a god, make up a microcosm of Dugan's tone and style. This is a voice that has come to joke about Caesar, not to praise him, yet reserves its greatest contempt for the sheeplike followers of great leaders. No apologies are made for running away from the battle, and the reader is left with the feeling that it was the action of an intelligent man who, like the Lacedaemonians, knew when not to fight.

Dugan often speaks sarcastically of war, whether it is one of Alexander's, the American Civil War, the two World Wars, or the Vietnam War—all of which make appearances in his poetry. In a "Fabrication of Ancestors," Dugan sums up his attitude toward all wars when he praises his ancestor, "shot in the ass," who did not help to win the war for the North but wore on his body a constant "proof/ of the war's obscenity." In the curious "Adultery," Dugan contrasts the insignificance of private immoralities with greater public evils— the world of "McNamara and his band" and "Johnson and his Napalm Boys" who wipe out the lives of entire cities in Vietnam. Dugan does not plan to be among "the ba-bas."

Love is another dominant subject of Dugan's work, and he approaches it in much the same tone of fierceness and irony that informs his poems about war. In these poems he turns to the war between the sexes, its battles and betrayals. "Love Song: I and Thou" is one of Dugan's most skillful poems and is deservedly one of his most frequently anthologized. In a complicated brew, it mixes the techniques of allegory and allusion with Dugan's terse colloquial style. It illustrates the basic paradox of much of his verse: the dominant conversational, flat tone that all the reviewers have emphasized, merging with elaborate poetic devices—devices that only a few commentators have mentioned. The overriding figure is the comparison between a man's life and a house, a badly built house, in this case. The opening line of the poem declares how badly it is built: "Nothing is plumb, level, or square." It is a house with a corresponding life in considerable disarray, a house for which, on one level, the speaker insists on taking responsibility ("I planned it"), yet whose chaos, on some other level, must be blamed on a higher power ("God damned it"). The description of the house becomes a description of the ancient quarrel concerning the roles of free will and determinism in a person's life.

Also running throughout "Love Song: I and Thou" is a comparison-contrast between the speaker and Christ: "By Christ/ I am no carpenter." This reference concludes in the final lines about crucifixion in a passage that suddenly introduces the love song promised by the title. The title's "I and Thou" is a reference to the modern Jewish philosopher Martin Buber; *I-Thou* is the language he used to describe a true and vital love relationship between equals, as opposed to *I-It*. The ending of Dugan's poem, however, creates a highly ambiguous feeling. In what sounds like tender talk, "I need . . . a help, a love, a you, a wife," the speaker is asking for someone to nail his right hand to the cross. He cannot finish his crucifixion by himself; he needs a helpmate, a nailer. One critic finds the language very touching, but there seems to be a bitter joke at the heart of this complex poem.

Although Dugan sometimes praises the world of sexuality ("the red world of love"), his enthusiasms are almost always tempered by irony. In a "Letter to Donald Fall," he makes a list of "my other blessings after friendship/ unencumbered by communion." They include:

> a money making job, time off it, a wife
> I still love sometimes unapproachably
> hammering on picture frames, my own city . . .
> and my new false teeth. . . .

The words "sometimes unapproachably," which manage to go both forward and backward, suggest Dugan's attitude toward love. Even more typical is the comic introduction of his false teeth, which become a parallel to the approaching spring. The teeth seem to him to be "like Grails" and they talk to him, saying, "We are the resurrection/ and the life." Amidst some amusing images of spring coming to the city, Dugan comes as close as he can to satisfaction when he addresses his friend with the symbolic name in the final line of the poem: "Fall, it is not so bad at Dugan's Edge."

The Muse, too, is tough in the poem with the amusing title, "Cooled Heels Lament Against Frivolity, the Mask of Despair"; she is a kind of distant boss, keeping the poet waiting in her office, as she swaps stories with the "star-salesmen of the soul." He seems to speak to her with slim hope of any positive response:

> Dugan's deathward darling; you
> in your unseeable beauty, oh
> fictitious, legal person, need
> be only formally concerned. . . .

If the fanciful Muse seems cold and indifferent, it is because there is not much to look forward to in one's encounters with the real world of bosses and work. That world of work is often portrayed in Dugan's poetry as a necessary but painful evil. "No man should work, but be" is the dream that cannot be fulfilled because "poverty is worse than work." "On a Seven-Day Diary" comically sums up Dugan's attitude with the insistent refrain, "Then I got up and went to work." It is repeated five times for the five weekdays, but "Then it's Saturday, Saturday, Saturday!" The speaker excitedly proclaims that "Love must be the reason for the week!" as he lists the pleasures of the weekend. Yet he drinks so much on Saturday night that most of Sunday is lost, and—as one might expect from Dugan—the poem ends with "Then I got up and went to work."

War, love, and work make a similarly dour pattern in Dugan's poetry—the grayness of Monday always returns. This is a poet whose longest published poem is entitled "On Zero," and whose attitude toward change might be summed up in the closing lines of "General Prothalamion in Populous Times": "the fall/ from summer's marching innocence/ to the last winter of general war." Reading a collection of Dugan's poems can be harrowing. His is a world where freedom is something to be feared, where to meet the morning is to confront "the daily accident," and where "sometimes you can't even lose"; yet Dugan often brings enough skill and humor to his work to overcome the darkness of the vision. What has been said of other writers who have been called cynical or misanthropic can be said of his work as well: The very energy of his language and the vitality of his wit belie his pessimism.

**Bibliography**
Booth, Philip. *Christian Science Monitor*. April 27, 1961, p. 7.
Boyers, Robert. "Alan Dugan: The Poetry of Survival," in *Salmagundi*. Spring-Summer, 1968, pp. 43-52.
Fitts, Dudley. "Foreword" to Alan Dugan's *Poems*, 1961.
Howard, Richard. *Alone with America*, 1980.
Stepanchev, Stephen. *American Poetry Since 1945*, 1965.

*Michael Paul Novak*

# WILLIAM DUNBAR

**Born:** Lothian, Scotland; c. 1460
**Died:** Scotland(?); c. 1525

## Principal poems and collections

"The Thistle and the Rose," 1503; "The Dance of the Seven Deadly Sins," c. 1503-1508; "The Goldyn Targe," c. 1508 ("The Golden Shield"); "Lament for the Poets," c. 1508; "The Two Married Women and the Widow," c. 1508; *The Poems of William Dunbar*, 1883-1913 (John Small, editor); *The Poems of William Dunbar*, 1891-1894 (J. Schipper, editor); *The Poems of William Dunbar*, 1932 (W. MacKay Mackenzie, editor); *Dunbar: Poems*, 1958 (James Kinsley, editor); *The Poems of William Dunbar*, 1979 (James Kinsley, editor).

## Other literary forms

There is currently no evidence that William Dunbar wrote in any genre other than short poetry.

## Achievements

William Dunbar has traditionally been grouped with Robert Henryson, Gavin Douglas, Sir David Lyndsay, and James I of Scotland, author of *The Kingis Quair* (1423-1424, *The King's Choir*), as a "Scottish Chaucerian," because he often used Geoffrey Chaucer's metrical forms and poetic conventions. He may also be considered a Chaucerian in the sense that he and his contemporaries, both in England and Scotland, acknowledged a large debt to Chaucer, the "flower of rhetoricians," who, they believed, raised the English language to a status equal to that of Latin and French, where it could be used for both philosophy and literature. Thus, the Chaucerians felt that one of their important duties was to consolidate this new status by practicing a highly ornate rhetoric, and Dunbar's rhetoric was as self-consciously artful as anyone's. At the same time, however, Dunbar was never a slavish imitator of the great English poet. Indeed, there are more than a few differences between them. Whereas Chaucer was an accomplished storyteller, Dunbar wrote mainly short lyrical poems. Whereas Chaucer was a sensitive creator of literary characters, Dunbar's interests lay elsewhere, and so his characters are never as fully developed. Finally, although Chaucer wrote warm human comedy, the tone of his work is quite different from that of Dunbar's raucous grotesqueries.

One of Dunbar's most noticeable poetic qualities is his professionalism, for he took his job as *makar*, the Scots term for "poet," very seriously. Like his fellow Scots poets, Dunbar had a highly developed sense of the different kinds of poetry that were possible, and thus he cultivated several different poetic forms and levels of language, each of which was chosen expressly to fit differing situations. He was much more a poetic virtuoso than were his contemporaries to the south, and in his small corpus one finds everything from the lowest scatological abuse to the most ornate high-minded panegyric. Furthermore, Dunbar had a gift for picking the correct meter, which he chose from a very extensive repertoire. Finally, Dunbar composed easily on at least three different levels of language: in his eldritch or bawdy poems, he used a very exaggerated Scots voice; in his moral poetry, he used a more normal speaking voice; and in his courtly or panegyric poems, he used a highly literate, aureate voice.

While his lyrical variety looks forward to the Renaissance, Dunbar is more often seen as coming at the end of the long medieval poetic tradition, for his work is usually rooted in traditional forms and themes. Moreover, though his poems may be called lyrical because of their short length and strong musical quality, they are not the products of personal emotion recollected in tranquillity. Dunbar was always a public poet; one never sees him in literary undress. Indeed, Dunbar's interests did not lie with presenting philosophical or moral concepts; still less was he interested in exploring his own emotional depths. He was interested, rather, in presenting traditional materials in highly finished packages. Following medieval thought on poetics, he considered himself primarily a rhetorician, and he wanted his poetry either to explode like colorful and noisy fireworks or to sit "enamelled," "gilded," and "refined," like a delicate piece of china, a precise and static work of art. In short, Dunbar was more concerned with language than with content, and for this reason his poetry has been called a poetry of surface effects. Commenting on Dunbar's unbounded vitality, C. S. Lewis once remarked: "If you like half-tones and nuances you will not enjoy Dunbar; he will deafen you."

## Biography

How much one claims to know about the life of William Dunbar depends on how much one is willing to trust the claims to be found in his poems, for very little external evidence remains. From Dunbar's poetry, for example, John W. Baxter in his book *William Dunbar: A Biographical Study* (1952) surmises that the poet was descended from the noble house of Dunbar, the earls of which were both powerful and controversial figures in the history of Scotland. Descendents of a Northumbrian earl, Cospatrick, they more than once sided with the English in quarrels between the two countries. In 1402, for example, Henry Dunbar, Earl of March, piqued over losses in a personal controversy with the Earl of Douglas, aided King Henry IV of England at the Battle of Homildon Hill, thus earning his family the emnity of James I of Scotland, who stripped the clan of most of its lands. If Dunbar had noble blood, then he belonged to a family whose fortunes had fallen considerably.

However that may be, in many of his poems, Dunbar does speak distastefully of the lower classes and of social climbers. In "To the King" ("Schir, yit remember as befoir"), the poet calls himself a "gentill goishalk." This may be significant since the birds of prey were often associated with the nobility in medieval poetry, as, for example, in Chaucer's *The Parliament of Fowls* (c. 1372-1386). Furthermore, in the same poem Dunbar complains that while still a youth he was thought headed for a bishopric, but upon achieving maturity he stated, "A sempill vicar I can not be." In short, the tone of many of his poems seems to be that of a frustrated aristocrat.

Dunbar appears to have had a good education, and here again there is much speculation as to exactly where he received it. It was customary for Scottish students of the time to study on the Continent, especially at the University of Paris, but there is absolutely no evidence that Dunbar ever studied there. Again, though Dunbar wrote a poem on Oxford, it is doubtful that he ever attended that university. Rather, it is likely that he wrote his poem while visiting Oxford in 1501, when he helped to arrange James IV's marriage to Margaret Tudor, the daughter of Henry VII of England. On the other hand, records of St. Andrew's University in Scotland show that a William Dunbar, probably the poet, received a Bachelor of Arts degree there in 1477 and his Licentiate in 1479.

Evidently not independently wealthy, Dunbar chose a vocation in the Church and was ordained a priest later in life. The Accounts of the Lord High Treasurer of Scotland show that he was given a sum of four pounds eighteen shillings in 1504 as a gift for his first Mass. Moreover, Dunbar spent most of his life waiting for a benefice—a grant of land and a parish from which he could make his living. One of Dunbar's poems, "How Dunbar was Desired to be a Friar," has led some to speculate that the poet spent part of his early life as a traveling Franciscan novice. In the poem, a devil in the guise of St. Francis appears to Dunbar in a dream, exhorting him to take up the Franciscan habit. Dunbar, however, will have none of it, and he retorts that, if he must take a religious habit, he will take that of a bishop, for he has read in "holy legends" that more bishops than friars have become saints. Moreover—and this is the tantalizing part—he claims to have already worn the Franciscan habit all over England and France; to have preached openly; and also to have picked up "many a trick and wile" of the friars, who are "always ready to beguile men." Now, however, those days are long past, says the poet, and he is content to live a more honest life. Whether this poem is a reliable autobiographical document or merely an antifraternal jape cannot be determined.

That Dunbar moved in the aristocratic circles of the court of James IV can be determined. Beginning in 1500, Dunbar was awarded an annual pension of ten pounds per year from the King until he should receive a benefice worth at least forty pounds annually. In 1507, this amount was raised to twenty pounds per year, and in 1510, the poet was awarded a very substantial increase to eighty pounds annually. As a rough measure of what these sums were worth, Baxter reports that, when he was receiving a pension of ten pounds, Dunbar was on the same level as the king's steward and clerk of accounts. When he received a pension of twenty pounds, Dunbar was raised above all other members of the royal household except the keeper of the king's silver vessels. His pension of eighty pounds raised the poet above even the principal of King's College, Hector Boece. Thus, despite Dunbar's frequent complaints to the contrary, he was well appreciated and rewarded by King James.

From these generous pensions, and from his occasional court poetry such as "To Princess Margaret" and "The Ballade of Barnard Stewart Lord of Aubigny," one can infer that Dunbar held the position of unofficial poet laureate. Indeed, when the printing press was finally introduced into Scotland in 1507 by Walter Chepman and Andrew Myllar, Dunbar's poems were among the first writings to be printed.

Entries for Dunbar in the royal records cease in 1513. In June of that year, Henry VIII invaded France, and James IV, responding to calls for help from his old French allies, advanced southward with his armies into England. He met the English at Flodden on September 9, but, although his soldiers fought bravely, he was defeated. Most of the great houses of Scotland lost men in that battle, and the King himself was also killed. In its aftermath, Edinburgh fortified itself against an invasion, but Henry VIII decided not to follow up his victory: the new Scottish king, James V, was the son of Henry's own sister, Margaret, and he thus hoped for better relationships with Scotland. Nevertheless, the defeat was disastrous for the country, and it later led to continuous civil strife.

Dunbar was probably too old to have been among the troops at Flodden, but what became of him after that date is unknown. Did he perhaps finally find his long-awaited benefice, or was his pension simply cut off because of Scotland's financial difficulties? The question is further complicated by the fact that the Treasurer's records are often missing for the years between 1513 and 1529.

One poem, "Quhen the Gouvernour past in Fraunce," is often cited as proof that Dunbar continued to write after 1513, since it refers to the visit to Scotland, from 1515 to 1517, of John Stewart, Duke of Albany, for the purpose of restoring order to the kingdom. Although the poem is ascribed to Dunbar in an important manuscript, however, Dunbar's latest editor, James Kinsley, has deleted it from the poet's corpus, partly because "little else that is attributed to him is as clumsy and undistinguished as this." Since many scholars agree with Kinsley, one can safely say that Dunbar seems to have stopped writing about this time. In any case, in 1530 another Scottish poet, Sir David Lyndsay, noted, in his "Testament of the Papyngo," that Dunbar had died. If Lyndsay listed the poets in the order of their death, then Dunbar died before 1522, for that is when Gavin Douglas, the next poet mentioned, died.

**Analysis**

Because William Dunbar wrote in his native Scots dialect, it is often difficult for modern English speakers to understand his poetry. Middle Scots, the language of the Scotch Lowlanders, was a development from the northern dialects of Middle English. Its rival, the Gaelic tongue spoken by the High-landers, is a Celtic language related to Welsh, Irish, and Breton. Although his own Scots shows the influence of Gaelic, Dunbar often spoke scornfully of the Celtic tongue, as, for example, when he insulted Walter Kennedy, a Highlander, in "The Flyting of Dunbar and Kennedy."

Nevertheless, Scots did borrow many words from Gaelic, some of which, such as "canny," "dour," and "bairn" have been taken over into standard English. The Middle Scots dialect can be easily recognized by its diction, by certain grammatical forms, and also by certain peculiarities in spelling and pronunciation. For example, Scots used "qu" or "quh" in place of "wh" in such words as "quhat" [what], "quhilk" [which], and "quhen" [when]. The dialect also retained the Old English "a" where it had been replaced by a more rounded vowel in the South: "stane" [stone] and "hale" [whole] are good examples. Also, the Northern dialects preferred the plosive consonants "g" and "k" where the Southerners adopted the softer "y" and "ch" sounds; thus one finds "kirk" for "church," "mikel" for "much," and "yaf" for "gave." These are only the most noteworthy of many dialectical peculiarities, but they will be of some help when one first encounters Dunbar's poetry.

Nowhere is Dunbar's ability with language more evident than in his "The Goldyn Targe" ("The Golden Shield"). Although he draws heavily on medieval allegorical traditions, Dunbar here is less interested in the message of the love allegory than in the language with which it is conveyed. Further-more, this display of poetic virtuosity must have been appreciated in his own day, for "The Goldyn Targe" was one of the six poems of Dunbar printed by Chepman and Myllar in 1507, and it was later singled out by Lyndsay in his "Testament of the Papyngo" to prove that Dunbar "language had at large."

"The Goldyn Targe" can be placed in the tradition of *Roman de la Rose* (*The Romance of the Rose*), a long narrative poem written some time in the thirteenth century by the poets Guillaume de Lorris and Jean de Meung. All of the action of the French poem takes place in a dream; the characters are all personifications; and even the settings carry allegorical meanings: the idealized garden represents the life at court, and the rose-plot symbolizes the mind of a young lady. *The Romance of the Rose* was thus a psychological exposition of courtly love.

Although there is some disagreement as to whether courtly love was ever actually practiced or whether it was simply a literary convention, the idea sprang up in the eleventh century in the songs of the French troubadours. Chretien de Troyes' Lancelot and Guinevere are perhaps the best known courtly lovers, though others such as Tristan and Iseult or Chaucer's Troilus and Criseyde could also be cited. The behavior of the lovers was highly codified in this system, with the woman holding the ascendancy. For his part, the man was to be humble, discreet, and courteous, complying with each whim of his mistress. How does one fall in love, and what are its results? Poems such as "The Goldyn Targe" attempted to explain the process through allegory.

Walking through an idealized garden on a fresh May morning, the narrator of "The Goldyn Targe" soon tires, falls asleep, and has a marvelous dream. He spies a beautiful ship laden with a hundred gods and goddesses from antiquity led by Nature and Venus. They are a merry group, dressed entirely in green, a color symbolic of youth, freshness, and vigor. When the Dreamer tries to get a better look at them, however, he is suddenly caught by Venus, who for no apparent reason orders her "troops" to attack him. The attacking platoons are made up of personified feminine qualities such as Beauty, Delight, and Fine Appearance.

The Dreamer is protected from this onslaught for a time by Reason, wielding his golden shield and successfully repelling all the missiles shot by the attackers. Reason is overcome, however, by Presence, who sneaks up and throws a blinding powder into the eyes of the warrior. Thus, Reason is defeated, and the Dreamer is soon enslaved by Venus. The effect of the victory is short-lived, however, for the goddesses and their partners depart as quickly as they came, leaving the Dreamer in a state of despair. A final trumpet blast from the ship wakens the Dreamer, who again finds himself back in the idealized countryside. The poem closes with a panegyric to Chaucer, John Gower, and John Lydgate, and with an envoy in which Dunbar sends his "lytill quair [book]" forth into the world, where it must be obedient to all.

The use of the panegyric and the envoy reinforce the fact that Dunbar was thoroughly grounded in medieval poetic conventions. Chaucer, for example, used much the same sort of envoy in his *Troilus and Criseyde* (c. 1372-1386). Unlike Chaucer, however, Dunbar was not fundamentally interested in the story, his two-dimensional characters, or the obvious moral that the passions must be controlled by the higher faculty of reason, which, unfortunately, is not always invincible. The poem's greatness then, necessarily lies in Dunbar's masterful use of language. His smooth iambic pentameter lines are grouped into nine-line stanzas, rhyming aabaabbab, the very difficult form which Chaucer first employed in *Anelida and Arcite* (1477). Moreover, though Dunbar could use only two different rhymes per stanza, nowhere did that seem to pose any great difficulties for him.

The highly wrought surface of Dunbar's poem is very clearly seen in his descriptions of the garden. What is created here, in the words of Edmund Reiss, *William Dunbar* (1979), is "a world combining heaven and earth, one showing nature in idealized, purified, and rarified splendor." Take, for example, these lines from the second and third stanzas:

> *Anamalit* was the felde wyth all colouris
> The *perly* droppis schake in *silvir* schouris,
> . . . . . . . . . . . . . . . . . . .
> The *purpur* hevyn, ourscailit in *silvir* sloppis,
>     [with silver trailing clouds scattered about]
> *Ourgilt* [gilded over] the treis, branchis, lef
>     and barkis.
>
> (emphasis added)

Here Dunbar uses aureate terms, together with the recurring images of various gems and precious metals, to create a visionary landscape, reminiscent of Paradise in the Middle English *Pearl* (c. 1350-1380). This is obviously not a personally experienced nature like that of the Romantic poets; Dunbar's nature is founded in the tradition of the *locus amoenus*, an idealized pastoral setting, the characteristics of which had already become standardized in late antiquity.

The word "aureate," signifying a highly wrought style and elevated diction, was coined by the English Chaucerian Lydgate, who borrowed many obscure terms from Latin for the sake of sonority and, hence, for dignifying his subject matter. Whereas Lydgate used his aureate terms basically for religious poetry, Dunbar went well beyond his predecessor and used aureate diction in other types of poems. The use of "artificial" words fit well into medieval poetic theory, and it was not until the nineteenth century, when William Wordsworth began to attack "poetic diction," that "aureate" came to have pejorative connotations.

It is a steep descent from the elevated tone and subject matter of "The Goldyn Targe" to the rowdy burlesque of "The Two Married Women and the Widow," though the level of Dunbar's conscious artistry nowhere flags in the latter piece. The poem, written in 530 lines of alliterative verse, begins delicately in the courtly love tradition, but after the first forty lines the reader finds himself thrown into a crude display of female candor, where, in Kinsley's words, "Ideal beauty is exposed as the whited sepulchre of lust and greed."

Walking forth on a midsummer's night, the poet discovers a beautiful little garden, wherein are three courtly ladies, described in the typically idealized way: they all have beautiful blonde hair, white skin, fine features, rich clothing, and jeweled adornment. That they wear green mantles—reminiscent, perhaps, of the gods and goddesses of "The Goldyn Targe"—seems an innocent innovation at this point, but as soon as the poet notes that they "wauchtit" [quaffed] their wine, the reader suspects that something is amiss.

While the narrator discreetly hides, one of the three women, the Widow, sets the dialogue in motion with a *demande d'amour*: "Bewrie [reveal], said the wedo, ye woddit wemen ying,/ Quhat mirth ye fand in maryage sen ye war menis wyffis." She also wishes to know if they have had extramarital affairs; if, given the chance, they would choose another husband; and if they believe the marriage bond to be insoluble. These are hardly the questions one would expect from a "chaste widow," and what follows are hardly the timid responses expected from two modest young wives.

The first is married to an old man who, like Januarius in Chaucer's "The Merchant's Tale" (from *The Canterbury Tales*, c. 1387), guards her jealously. The lusty young wife, however, reveals that her husband lacks the sexual vitality to satisfy fully her womanly desires, and she nonchalantly confesses that, if she were allowed, she would change husbands yearly, like the birds. For the time being her only satisfaction comes from the many gifts which her husband must give her before she consents to lovemaking.

Here, and in many other parts of this poem, Dunbar employs the style used in "The Flyting of Dunbar and Kennedy" to capture suitably the disgust of this young woman toward her spouse. In this style, a Gaelic poetic tradition, the poet piles up lists of epithets, uses various types of wordplay, and polishes the surface with obtrusive alliteration and rhyme. Generally employed when two poets publicly attacked each other, this style creates a tone that is a mixture of aggression, absurdity, and play. Dunbar's ingenuity and wit are shown when he incongruously transplants this harsh technique into the delicate context of courtly conversation.

The second wife is unhappy as well. Her young husband, though outwardly a ladies' man, is totally worn out from his earlier promiscuous behavior. Thus, she too, using suitably graphic metaphors, attacks her husband, reducing him from "rake" to "snivelling faker," and the three ladies laugh loudly, making "game amang the grene leiffis," and quaff more of the "sueit wyne." The two young wives, and the reader as well, are thus prepared for the presentation of the central character of the poem, the Widow, who is a literary cousin of Chaucer's Wife of Bath. Like Dame Alice, the Widow is both lecherous and proud of it. She is also outspoken; and she preaches the gospel of pleasure openly to her audience. Unlike Dame Alice, however, the Widow has no warmth or humanity; she is thoroughly calculating and vicious.

She begins her "sermon" with a mock invocation to God to send her "sentence," the medieval code word for an edifying moral. Religious parody was not uncommon in medieval literature, and, though Dunbar was a priest, he clearly was having fun here at the expense of the sacred rites. This parody, however, is slight compared to the poet's "The Dregy of Dunbar Maid to King James the Fowrth being in Strivilling," where he constructed a mock liturgical Office of the Dead to tease James out of his Lenten retreat.

This unholy preacher, the Widow, had been married twice: first to an old Januarius type, and then to a middle-aged merchant. She recounts all the cruel steps which she took to divest the merchant completely of both his goods and his masculinity. When he finally died, she felt no regrets at all, for then she could begin to play the field in church, at public gatherings, and on pilgrimages. She describes, for example, how her black widow's veil can be used to cover her face while she surveys the crowds of men "To se quhat berne [fellow] is best brand [muscled] or bredest in schulderis." Using the language of courtly love literature, the Widow confesses to being the common property of all her "servants" (lovers), and to being a nymphomaniac who "comforts" them all. As a good preacher, however, she cannot recount a tale without offering her moral as well: the secret of a happy life is guile. Her counsel to the young wives is neatly summed up in the following: "Be dragonis baith and dowis [doves] ay in double forme." Hence her "sentence" is as neatly packaged as proverbial wisdom, and the end of her tale is similarly furnished with religious terminology: "This is the legeand of my lif, thought Latyne it be nane." The reference here is to saints' lives, a very popular form of literature in her day, even among the laity.

Dunbar resumes the high style of courtly literature as the three women retire, having passed the night in drunken camaraderie. The coming of the new day is as pleasantly described as if the narrator had just witnessed the first tryst of Troilus and Criseyde; but he ends the poem with a final ironic question: "Quhilk wald ye waill [choose] to your wif gif ye suld wed one?"

The characters in "The Two Married Women and the Widow" are so outrageous that one wonders whether the poem could ever be considered serious antifeminist satire. Perhaps Dunbar's intention lay no further than to produce belly-laughs from his audience, especially the women. The poem does, however, show Dunbar's skill in blending various medieval traditions: the tradition of the courtly love narrative, the tradition of the eavesdropping narrator, the antifeminist tradition, and the French tradition of *le chanson de la mal mariée* [the song of the unhappy wife].

Not only did Dunbar revive traditional themes, but he also revived, for one of the last times, a very ancient poetic device, the Anglo-Saxon alliterative line used by the poet of *Beowulf* and his contemporaries. This type of poetic line construction was based not on syllable count and not on metrical feet, but on the principle of alliteration. The theory was fairly complex, but basically each verse was constructed from two half-lines, separated by a caesura, each having two, or perhaps three, stressed syllables. Ordinarily the first three stressed syllables per line were alliterated. Thus, Dunbar's "Bewfie, said the wédo/ ye wóddit wémen ying," more than fulfills the requirements, actually adding an unnecessary fourth alliterated syllable. In practice, however, the alliterative line could vary widely in the total number of syllables and in the pattern of stressed alliterations. Moreover, rhyme was normally not used at all as a poetic device.

As Anglo-Saxon evolved into Middle English, chiefly owing to the effects of the Norman Invasion in 1066, alliterative poetry seemed to die out. The

French tradition of decasyllabic rhyming verse came to be favored in England; Chaucer, for example, was highly influenced by just such continental models. His character the Parson, however, does comment on the older verse form in the prologue to his sermon: "But trusteth well, I am a Southren man,/ I kan nat geeste [tell a tale] 'rum, ram, ruf,' by lettre." Nevertheless, there were those in the northwest of England, Chaucer's contemporaries, who could indeed "rum, ram, ruf," and thus English letters experienced an "alliterative revival" in such works as *Sir Gawain and the Green Knight* (c. fourteenth century) and *The Vision of William, Concerning Piers the Plowman* (c. 1360-1399). Dunbar's work, coming as it does roughly one hundred years after these works, attests not only to a sort of poetic conservatism in Scotland, but also to Dunbar's poetic vigor, which enabled him to revive the old form so successfully.

Another traditional form which Dunbar used with imagination was the tail-rhymed stanza, commonly employed by long-winded medieval romancers and parodied by Chaucer in his "The Tale of Sir Thopas" (from *The Canterbury Tales*). The pattern called for four-beat rhyming couplets separated by three-beat lines in the following manner: aabccb, or, if a twelve-line stanza was desired: aabccbddbeeb. Dunbar's "The Dance of the Seven Deadly Sins," Part I of "Fasternes Evening in Hell," is composed of nine twelve-line stanzas with two additional six-line stanzas interspersed. They form another dream poem, like "The Goldyn Targe," but a strange one. The dream takes place on Fasternes Evening, the last day of the carnival before Lent. During this time the public celebrations included colorful pageants, filled with allegorical figures. Baxter notes that one must place the poem in just such a context, imagining the poet reacting to a group of revelers, costumed to represent sins, devils, fairies, and the like, dancing wildly under torchlight in the streets. Dunbar's poem captures them forever in their frenzy.

Indeed, Dunbar's portrait of the Seven Deadly Sins—Pride, Anger, Envy, Cupidity, Sloth, Lechery, and Gluttony—is probably the most lively of all the many such medieval portraits. In the poem, the Dreamer sees "Mahoun" (Satan) give orders for a dance in hell, to which the personified vices immediately respond. The context explains why Dunbar's portraits are fairly realistic, and also why, perhaps, Dunbar took the opportunity to poke fun at his Highland foes. In the last stanza, Mahoun orders a Highland pageant to add some additional music to the festivities. Their Gaelic clatter, however, is too much even for Mahoun, who banishes them to the "depest pit of hell."

An artistic cousin of the "Dance of the Seven Deadly Sins" is perhaps the *danse macabre*, another medieval commonplace. Both in painting and in verse this motif shows the skeletons of men and women of all social classes dancing together as equals—in death. Dunbar takes up this theme in his poem "Lament for the Makaris," which Kinsley calls "one of the great elegiac expressions of a melancholy age." No longer the brazen poet of "The Two

Married Women and the Widow" nor the frenetic poet of "The Dance of the
Seven Deadly Sins," Dunbar here is saddened, pensive, and grave.

The poem is written in twenty-five stanzas of two tetrameter couplets each,
a form which in Old French was called the *kyrielle*. The last line of each
stanza is a Latin quotation from the Office of the Dead, "*Timor mortis conturbat me*" (The fear of death alarms me), a refrain that was often heard in
an age of frequent war, great poverty,and the Black Plague. Lydgate, for
example, used the same refrain in the poem entitled "*Timor Mortis Conturbat
Me*," and it was probably Dunbar's model. Dunbar's poem, however, is much
more compact and understated, and, as Gregory Kratzmann notes in *Anglo-
Scottish Literary Relations, 1430-1550* (1980), these very qualities help give
the poem the rhythm of a sober death dance.

The movement of the poem is from the universal to the particular. It begins
with the sublunary principle that "Our plesance heir is all vane glory,/ This
fals warld is bot transitory"; continues through a catalog of the various classes
and professions, noting especially the deaths of his fellow poets; and concludes
with the realization that his own death must be close at hand. By including
the catalog of his fellow poets, Dunbar particularizes, and thus makes more
poignant, this melancholy poetic form.

Dunbar's creativity, shown very well in "Lament for the Makaris," is manifest throughout his works; he seems always able to reinvest older poetic
forms with new vigor. He is a poet of high energy, but not of inchoate
effusions, for his power is always tightly controlled, each enameled word
fitting carefully into a well-wrought framework. Variety is also a characteristic
of Dunbar's work. His poetry always has a musical quality to it, for he was
a master versifier with an extremely varied repertoire of patterns at his command. Even so, one might be forgiven for clinging to an image of Dunbar
composing only his most energetic pieces, since, like his personified Deadly
Sins, he seems always ready, in a literary sense, to "kast up gamountis [gam-
bols] in the skyis."

**Bibliography**
Baxter, John W. *William Dunbar: A Biographical Study*, 1952.
Brewer, Derek, ed. *Chaucer and Chaucerians*, 1966.
Kratzmann, Gregory. *Anglo-Scottish Literary Relations, 1430-1550*, 1980.
Lewis, C. S. *English Literature in the Sixteenth Century*, 1954.
Reiss, Edmund. *William Dunbar*, 1979.
Ridley, Florence. "William Dunbar," in *A Manual of the Writings in Middle
English, 1050-1500*, 1973.
Scott, Tom. *Dunbar: A Critical Exposition of the Poems*, 1966.
Taylor, Rachel Annand. *Dunbar: The Poet and His Period*, 1931.
Wittig, Kurt. *The Scottish Tradition in Literature*, 1958.

*Gregory M. Sadlek*

# ROBERT DUNCAN

**Born:** Oakland, California; January 7, 1919

### Principal collections

*Heavenly City, Earthly City*, 1947; *Poems 1948-1949*, 1950; *Medieval Scenes*, 1950 (reprinted as *Medieval Scenes 1950 and 1959*, 1978); *Fragments of a Disordered Devotion*, 1952; *Caesar's Gate: Poems 1948-1950*, 1956; *Letters: Poems MCMLIII-MCMLVI*, 1958; *Selected Poems*, 1959; *The Opening of the Field*, 1960; *Writing, Writing: A Composition Book Stein Imitations*, 1964; *Roots and Branches*, 1964; *Passages 22-27 of the War*, 1966; *The Years as Catches: First Poems (1939-1946)*, 1966; *Six Prose Pieces*, 1966; *A Book of Resemblances: Poems 1950-1953*, 1966; *Epilogos*, 1967; *Names of People*, 1968; *Bending the Bow*, 1968; *The First Decade: Selected Poems 1940-1950*, 1969; *Derivations: Selected Poems 1950-1956*, 1969; *Achilles' Song*, 1969; *Play Time: Pseudo Stein*, 1969; *Poetic Disturbances*, 1970; *Tribunals Passages 31-35*, 1970; *Ground Work*, 1971; *Poems from the Margins of Thom Gunn's Moly*, 1972; *A Seventeenth Century Suite in Homage to the Metaphysical Genius in English Poetry 1590/1690*, 1973; *An Ode and Arcadia*, 1974 (with Jack Spicer); *Dante*, 1974; *The Venice Poem*, 1975.

### Other literary forms

Robert Duncan's sensitive readings of his own work and that of others constitute a major contribution to literary history and criticism. Books include *The Sweetness and Greatness of Dante's "Divine Comedy"* (1965) and *The Truth and Life of Myth: An Essay in Essential Autobiography* (1968). "The H. D. Book," a study of H. D. (Hilda Dooiittle) but also a wide-ranging commentary on modernism and poetry, is being published in periodicals. So far, eighteen sections have appeared since 1966; Robert J. Bertholf and Ian W. Reid (*Robert Duncan: Scales of the Marvelous*) provide a bibliographical listing. Other important essays yet to be collected include "Changing Perspectives on Reading Whitman," "Towards an Open Universe," and "Man's Fulfillment in Order and Strife." *Fictive Certainties: Five Essays in Essential Autobiography* was announced by New Directions in 1979 but has not yet appeared. Other titles include *As Testimony: The Poem & the Scene* (1964) and two plays, *Faust Foutu: An Entertainment in Four Parts* (1959) and *Medea at Kolchis: The Maidenhead* (1965). Finally, a Duncan reading is an electric performance, and many tapes are available.

### Achievements

Because of his erudition, his sense of poetic tradition, his mastery of a variety of poetic forms, and, most important, his profoundly metaphysical voice, Duncan is a major contemporary poet. "Each age requires a new confession," Ralph Waldo Emerson declared, and Duncan presents his era with a voice it cannot afford to ignore. While Duncan has called himself a derivative poet, revealing his penetrating readings of Dante, Walt Whitman, Ralph Waldo Emerson, William Shakespeare, William Blake, and others, at the same time he generates comtemporary visions, Emersonian prospects of discovery and renewal. "Turn back the pages as they will," he tells us, "every part of man's story has been re-informed by the creative genius of his own present moment." In his combination (or, as he would put it, "coinherence") of tradition with presence, Duncan attends to the multiple processes of poetic apprehension. His vocabulary itself—"coinherence," "apprehension," "permission," "orders," "first things," "composition by field"—has already begun to shape readers' sense of what poetry is and does. The testimony of his own generation of poets (Charles Olson, Denise Levertov, Thom Gunn, Allen Ginsberg, and others) and of a younger generation as well (Imamu Amiri Baraka, Michael Davidson, Don Byrd, Robert Hass, and many more) attests to his influence and power.

An impressive collection of more than thirty volumes of poetry, drama, and prose constitutes Duncan's literary achievement. His serious notion of the role of the poet is evident in his many statements about his work, including the prefaces to such works as *The Truth and Life of Myth* and "The H. D. Book." Duncan writes in a wide range of voices, including a bardic, visionary persona of high seriousness and metaphysical concerns, but never loses his wit and joy in language-play. Not only a masterful lyricist, capable of penetrating epiphanies such as "Roots and Branches," he also excels in longer closed forms such as the serial poem ("Apprehensions," "The Continent") and the symphonic form of *The Venice Poem*. Finally, Duncan has done some of his finest work in the form which is America's most distinctive contribution to world poetry in the twentieth century: the long, open-ended poem which can accommodate the encyclopedia if need be. Duncan's ongoing open poems, "The Structure of Rime" and "Passages," are in the tradition of Ezra Pound's *Cantos* (beginning in 1925), William Carlos Williams' *Paterson* (1946-1958), Louis Zukofsky's *"A"* (beginning in 1927), and Charles Olson's *The Maximus Poems* (1960).

Duncan's reference to himself as a derivative poet is an odd claim for a high Romantic poet, and it is certain to be taken in a derogatory sense by most readers today. His mannered imitations of other writers have cost him considerable critical admiration, even though a synthesis of one's predecessors and their styles has been a hallmark of such poets as Samuel Taylor Coleridge and Emerson. In that synthesis lies their originality, of course; so while some of Duncan's early poetry may be labored or excessively imitative, his openness to other writers permits him entry into a larger field of poetry, what Percy Bysshe Shelley called "that great poem, which all poets, like the co-operating thoughts of one great mind, have built up since the beginning of the world." For all his formal variety and cultural eclecticism, Duncan may prove to be even more significant for what he has to say. His political and cultural statements give evidence of an uncommon courage, whether opposing war, testifying to his homosexuality, or proclaiming the reality of an essentially religious (but hardly orthodox) experience to a scoffing culture. Duncan admonishes modern critics of poetry because they tend "not to raise a crisis in our consideration of the content or to deepen our apprehension of the content, but to dismiss the content." He unabashedly makes large claims for poetry as a religious, mythological, or metaphysical vehicle. This vehicle, however, is not driven but drives: "In the orders of the poem the poet is commanded by necessities of a form that will not be turned to exemplify moral or aesthetic preconceptions."

Duncan is not an easy poet, but he richly repays repeated readings. His work cannot be neatly categorized, nor can it be turned to particular literary or cultural ends. It does stand as testimony to the integrity of this poet and to the vitality that poetry can have in our time.

## Biography

Robert Duncan was born Edward Howard Duncan in Oakland, California, on January 7, 1919, to Edward Howard and Marguerite Wesley Duncan. His mother died shortly after his birth, and his father was forced to put him up for adoption. His foster parents, "orthodox theosophists," chose him on the basis of his astrological configuration. Duncan grew up as Robert Edward Symmes and published some two dozen poems under that name before resuming his original surname in 1942. The hermetic lore imparted by his family and the fables and nursery rhymes of his childhood constitute a major influence on his work.

He attended the University of California at Berkeley from 1936 to 1938, publishing his first poems in the school's literary magazine, *The Occident*, and joining a circle of friends that included Mary and Lilli Fabilli, Virginia Admiral, and Pauline Kael. For several years he lived in the East, associating with the circle of Anaïs Nin in New York City and with a group of poets in Woodstock which included Sanders Russell and Jack Johnson. Receiving a psychiatric discharge from the Army in 1941, he continued publishing poems, and with Virginia Admiral edited *Ritual* (later *Experimental Review*). In 1944, he published his courageous essay, "The Homosexual in Society," in *Politics*.

Returning to Berkeley in 1946, he studied medieval and Renaissance culture and worked with Kenneth Rexroth, Jack Spicer, and Robin Blaser. In 1951 he began his continuing relationship with Jess Collins, the painter. Duncan directly addresses the significance of his homosexuality to his art: "Perhaps the sexual irregularity underlay and led to the poetic; neither as homosexual nor as poet could one take over the accepted paradigms and conventions of the Protestant ethic."

In 1952, he began publishing in *Origin* and then the *Black Mountain Review*. In the mid-1950's he taught briefly at Black Mountain College, further developing his relationship with Charles Olson, whose important essay, "Projective Verse," had been published in 1950. Duncan remains the strongest link between the Black Mountain poets and the San Francisco Renaissance, although the name of such "schools" must be highly elastic to include such diverse poets as Olson, Robert Creeley, Ed Dorn, Allen Ginsberg, Lawrence Ferlinghetti, and Duncan.

After three active decades which culminated in the three major books of poetry in the 1960's, Duncan announced in 1972 that he would not publish another major collection until 1983; that book would be entitled *Ground Work*. Individual poems and small, often private, printings continue to appear.

**Analysis**

Of the many metaphors that Robert Duncan has applied to his poetry— and very few poets have been so perceptive and articulate about their own practice—those dealing with limits, boundaries, and margins are numerous and permit a coherent if partial survey of his complex work. Such references are frequent in his poetry and are rooted in his life and his way of seeing. Living in San Francisco, at the edge of the continent, Duncan is acutely sensitive to the centrifugal pressures of his culture. Having been an adopted child, his identity and very name were under question during his early years. As a homosexual, he felt distanced from "the accepted paradigms and conventions of the Protestant ethic." As a theosophist, his way of thinking had been influenced by similarly unconventional assumptions. His very vision blurs distinctions and identities: he is cross-eyed, a way of seeing which he eloquently explores in such poems as "A Poem Slow Beginning" and "Crosses of Harmony and Disharmony," and which he relates to Alfred North Whitehead's "presentational immediacy."

Duncan refers to himself as "the artist of the margin," and the term is basic to an understanding of his vision and poetics. While the concept can be traced to a number of eclectic and overlapping influences, William James's *Principles of Psychology* (1890), with its theme of the fluidity of consciousness, provides an instructive point of departure. For James, with his great interest in the "penumbra" of experience, "life is at the transitions." As he says in "A World of Pure Experience," "Our fields of experience have no more definite boundaries than have our fields of view. Both are fringed forever by a *more* that continuously develops and that continuously supersedes them as life proceeds." For Duncan as for James, life is at the edge, at the point of relationship, surprise, novelty—at the transgression of boundaries. Conceiving the universe as a constant rhythm between order and disorder, both writers (with Whitehead and John Dewey) maintain that order develops. Rejecting the extreme poles of a world of mere flux without any stability and a static world without crisis, such a world view embraces the moment of passage as that of most intense life. Appropriately, Duncan's major ongoing poem is entitled the "Passages Poems." Primary here too is Keats's notion of "negative capability," an acceptance of "uncertainties, mysteries, doubts, without any irritable reaching after fact and reason." Indeed, Duncan defines Romanticism as "the intellectual adventure of not knowing."

Duncan is fully cognizant of the implications that such ideas have for his poetics, scoffing in *The Truth and Life of Myth* at the "sensory debunkers" who "would protect our boundaries, the very shape of what we are, by closing our minds to the truth." The poet's charge is to challenge the boundaries of convention, with direct impact on his poetry's form: "Back of each poet's concept of the poem is his concept of the meaning of form itself; and his concept of form in turn where it is serious at all arises from his concept of the nature of the universe." Duncan's poetry challenges the boundaries of conventional ideas and conventional forms. He speaks of his poetry as a collage, an especially appropriate form for a poetry which incessantly inter-rogates boundaries, edges, identities. "The great art of our time," he says in "The H. D. Book," "is the collagist's art, to bring all things into new complexes of meaning."

The theme appears early in his work, developing in the poems of the 1940's and 1950's. From the first decade, in "Heavenly City, Earthly City," the poet as a "man in the solitude of his poetic form/ finds his self-consciousness defined/ by the boundaries of a non-committal sea." He apostrophizes the Pacific Ocean as an "Insistent questioner of our shores!" "A Congregation," similarly, sounds early poetic concerns of field, order, disorder, and frag-mentation. In "The Festival," the fifth poem in *Medieval Scenes*, a strong early series, Duncan uses the motif of the dream to explore the unclear distinctions between wakefulness and sleep and, by extension, between ecstasy and madness, inspiration and inflated foolishness, the unicorn and the ass.

A pervasive concern with boundaries and limits is apparent in "The Venice Poem" (1948), Duncan's first indisputably major poem. In this work, based on Igor Stravinsky's *Symphony in Three Movements*, Duncan relates Berkeley to Venice and links his own lost love and self-questioning to the frustrations of Othello and Desdemona. The awareness of limits and edges crystallizes in a description of an image's coming into being: "She hesitates upon the verge of sound./ She waits upon a sounding impossibility,/ upon the edge of poetry." The final poem collected in *The First Decade*, "The Song of the Borderguard," announces by its very title Duncan's increasing awareness of transgressed boundaries: "The borderlines of sense in the morning light/ are naked as a line of poetry in a war."

The 1950's were productive years; poems written during that period include those published in *Derivations*, *Writing, Writing*, and *Letters*. While many of these poems are all too explicitly derivative, Duncan reprints them as testimony to his roots and his past. In his 1972 Preface to *Caesar's Gate*, Duncan does not use Ezra Pound's term *periplum*, but his description of the writing conveys something of the sense of a poetry "fearfully and with many errors making its way . . . seeking to regain a map in the actual." The first poem collected in *Derivations*, "An Essay at War," opens with a description of the poem "constantly/ under reconstruction," as "a proposition in movement." The poem contrasts the foolish *ad hoc* "design" of war itself with the imperfect pattern or design of a poem true to a changing experience. The Preface to *Letters* argues that a poet's process is one of revision and disorganization which takes place at the threshold. "I attempt the discontinuities of poetry," he announces, opening gaps which "introduce the peril of beauty." While cynics assume that such poetry must be inflated or impossible and while traditionalists abhor his assumption of a godlike role, Duncan answers both in deft lyrics such as "An Owl Is an Only Bird of Poetry," whose sure and witty inclusiveness articulates both design and disorder. Two poems near the end of *Letters*, "Changing Trains" and "The Language of Love," specifically employ the imagery of border-crossing and entering new territory, clear harbingers of Duncan's major phase.

While the early books are significant achievements, Duncan's reputation rests primarily on three major books of poetry published in the 1960's, *The Opening of the Field*, *Roots and Branches*, and *Bending of the Bow*. Each is a unified whole rather than a collection of poems, and each manifests and extends Duncan's use of the theme of boundaries and margins.

The terms of *The Opening of the Field* are proposed in the title, and the book's first and last poems reveal Duncan's awareness of beginnings and endings as they affect this book and much more. "Often I Am Permitted to Return to a Meadow" establishes the basic metaphor of the book, of poetry as an entry into a field of essences, "a scene made-up by the mind,/ that is not mine, but is a made place,/ that is mine." Granted entry into this field of poetic activity, the poet participates in the grand poem through his individual poems. Within this meadow, "the shadows that are forms fall," and in an act of faith ("as if"), the poet accepts it as a "given property of the mind/ that certain bounds hold against chaos." The poems seem to delineate boundaries or fields of order against chaos; but they *only* seem to do so because in the larger view Duncan has of poetry and the universe, chaos or disorder are parts of a larger order. The real boundary of this poem, then, is between a state of awareness and its absence. Delineating that boundary, or more fundamentally recognizing the difference, is the responsibility of the poet. In the "disturbance of words within words," the poet's poems are constructs, architectures, flowers which turn into "flames lit to the lady." The limits and definitions of physical reality must give way before the reality of the visionary imagination.

Duncan returns to these images—indeed he never leaves them—in the final poem of this book, "Food for Fire, Food for Thought," in which he self-consciously comments on the paradox of a last poem in an open poetics: "This is what I wanted for the last poem,/ a loosening of conventions and a return to open form." The attempt to define or limit is frustrating and necessarily progressive rather than definitive. The activity, however, is the poet's preoccupation: "We trace faces in the clouds: they drift apart,/ palaces of air—the sun dying down/ sets them on fire." Fire is the concluding image, again transformed into a flower, as an "unlikely heat/ at the edge of our belief bud[s] forth." In these two poems and those in between, Duncan explores the shifting borderlines between essence and form, childhood and adulthood, flame and flower. Even as Leonardo did, he sees "figures that were stains upon a wall" as he operates "at the edge of our belief."

*The Opening of the Field* includes "A Poem Beginning with a Line by Pindar," perhaps Duncan's best-known poem. Beginning with a misreading of a line from the third Pythian Ode, the poem then proclaims his recognition of a "god-step at the margins of thought." The poem is a mosaic or collage of images playing between light and dark, Cupid-sensuality and Psyche-spirituality, East and West, past and present, and it cannot be summarized here. The fourth section begins, "O yes! Bless the footfall where/ step by step the boundary walker," echoing the footstep of the poem's opening, informs and clarifies the poet's memories and experiences. The poet, as a boundary walker, must be attuned to the elusive image or inspiration, even to a felicitous misreading of Pindar.

Other poems directly addressing the theme of boundaries include "After Reading *Barely and Widely*," a book by Louis Zukofsky, and of course the series "The Structure of Rime," in the second of which the poet interrogates the nature of poetry. "What is the Structure of Rime? I asked," and he is told, "*An absolute scale of resemblance and disresemblance establishes measures that are music in the actual world.*" Such a recognition of pervasive correspondences and rhymes inspires confidence in the face of difficulties and risks inherent in such poetry. In the eighth of the series, the poet is permitted to crawl through "interstices of Earth" in realizing the possible "from a nexus in the Impossible." The entire series, continuing in subsequent books and intersecting at times with other series, addresses major questions of poetry and reality.

Again, *Roots and Branches* enunciates in its title the basic metaphor of the book, "the ramifications below and above the trunk of vegetative life." The title lyric, one of Duncan's best, describes his delight in a Monarch butterfly whose flight traces out an imaginary tree, "unseen roots and branches of sense/ I share in thought." The poet's epiphany, inspired by the correspondence between his spirit and the beauty of the common butterfly, denies yet another boundary respected by common sense, that between physical reality and a transcendent reality. Frank in its Romantic idealism, the poem evokes an Emersonian wonder at the harmony of physical and spiritual facts for a modern audience every bit as skeptical as Emerson's neighbors.

*Roots and Branches* closes with a more extended sequence of poems, the memorable series "The Continent," in which Duncan directly names and accepts his role as "the artist of the margin" who "works abundancies" and who recognizes that the scope of poetry "needs vast terms" because it is "out of earthly proportion to the page." On the literal level, Duncan calls for a long poem which will, like Whitman's, be creative and have "vista." Metaphorically and more significantly, he is calling for a poetry on the edge of consciousness, an expanding awareness of "marginal" realities, an openness to unusual or unconventional apprehensions. Unlike the coastal resident's awareness of the alien or the other, "The mid-Western mind differs in essentials." Without Buddhist temples or variant ways of seeing, midwesterners "stand with feet upon the ground/ against the/ run to the mythic sea, the fabulous." This is not praise for Antaeus.

The poem continues, describing a sparrow smashed upon a sidewalk. More than an allusion to William Carlos Williams' famous poem, the passage illuminates the difference between having a perspective in space and time and being "too close/ for shadow,/ the immediate!" The central image of the poem, the continent, itself examines horizons, especially those between shore and land and night and day. The closing sections link such imagery with Easter (evidently the time of the actual writing of the poem) and its denial of any clear distinction even between life and death.

Far from fragmenting our beliefs and dissociating our sensibilities, such a vision asserts the oneness of things: one time, one god, one promise flaring forth from "the margins of the page." In the apparent chaos of flux and change—"moving in rifts, churning, enjambing"—both continent and poem testify to a dynamic unity. Again, at the border, at the edge of meaning, like Columbus one finds not the abyss but new worlds.

"Apprehensions" is a poem closely related to "The Continent." The central theme is again that which "defines the borderlines of the meaning." The opening chord, "To open Night's eye that sleeps in what we know by day," announces the familiar concern with overcoming common sense and sensory limitations, and with the assertion of paradoxical oneness. Quotidian preoccupations obstruct our perspectives and limit our perceptions. In sharp contrast, the "Sage Architect" awakens "the proportions and scales of the soul's wonder" and lets light and shadow mix. The poem is a song to apprehension—both fearful and perceiving—of excavation of boundaries, resemblances, rhymes. The central apprehension is of concordances which overcome our limited sense of shifting time, place, and boundaries in favor of an overriding order.

Continuing his development, Duncan followed four years later with yet another major book, *Bending the Bow*. In his Introduction, he discusses his poetry with his accustomed insight, beginning by criticizing the Vietnam War which, "as if to hold all China or the ancient sea at bay, breaks out at a boundary we name *ours*. It is a boundary beyond our understanding." Captured by a rigid form, by a fixed image of oneself, one is unable to adapt to new conditions and insights. In contrast, the pulse of the poet in moments of vision "beats before and beyond all proper bounds." The book's title establishes the contrasts of bow and lyre, war and music, Apollo and Hermes, whose tension generates this book's field. Duncan speaks of the poem not as a stream of consciousness but as an area of composition in which "the poet works with a sense of parts fitting in relation to a design that is larger than the poem" and which he knows "will never be completed."

The title lyric develops the bow and lyre analogy, articulating the central Heraclitean themes of design, connection, and unity in diversity: "At this extremity of this/ design/ there is a connexion working in both directions, as in/ the bow and the lyre." As Duncan explains in "Towards an Open Universe," the turn and return of prose and verses of poetry are phases of a dynamic unity, like the alternation of day and night or the systole and diastole of the heart. The focus of his poetry and poetics remains on the intensity of the point of transition.

While "The Structure of Rime" continues in this volume, a new series, the "Passages Poems," is also introduced, beginning with a telling epigraph: "For the even is bounded, but the uneven is without bounds and there is no way through or out of it." The first passage, "Tribal Memories," invokes "Her-Without-Bounds," and the importance of margins, borders, and boundaries continues. Describing "Passages Poems" in his Introduction, Duncan states that "they belong to a series that extends in an area larger than my work in them. I enter the poem as I entered my own life, moving between an initiation and a terminus I cannot name. This is not a field of the irrational; but a field of ratios." Among the poem's many concerns are those ratios or correspondences, and some of the most provocative insights derive from the poetic theme of margins and transitions. "The Architecture, Passages 9" demands recesses so that "there is always something around the corner." In "Wine, Passages 12," the poet celebrates even as he is threatened by "the voice/ . . . the enormous/ sonority at the edge of the void." "In the Place of a Passage 22," the poet prays for passage in "the vast universe/ showing only its boundaries we imagine."

Like "The Structure of Rime," which is continuing at this writing, apparently to terminate only with Duncan's life, "Passages Poems" is an exciting achievement. Like most long poems, it resists the sort of cursory treatment that consideration of space dictates here, and the project may well be victimized by the "magnificent failure" syndrome so characteristic of criticism of American literature. Certainly it is ambitious, as Duncan acknowledges in

"Where It Appears, Passages 4": "Statistically insignificant as a locus of cre-
ation/ I have in this my own/ intense/ area of self creation." Even here, the
telling conditionals of "as if I could cast a shadow ˙/ to surround ˙/ what is
boundless ˙'" indicate Duncan's full, continuing, double-edged apprehension
of his enterprise and its risks.

It is another measure of Duncan's stature and complexity that all his work
is of a piece and should be read entire. A single lyric, for example, can be
read by itself, or as part of a longer series in many cases (several lyrics are
parts of more than one series). It must also be seen as part of the book in
which it appears, since Duncan has carefully ordered his collections, and as
an integral part of Duncan's canon. Finally, as he says in his Introduction to
*The Years as Catches*, "Poems then are immediate presentations of the intention of the whole, the great poem of all poems, a unity." Appropriately, even
the boundaries of his poems are fluid and dynamic.

In his continuing and pervasive border-crossing, Duncan brings his readers
news of an other which is shut out by conventional boundaries. With his artful
disclosures, his imaginative vision transcends false, self-imposed constrictions.
His art ultimately dissolves the very restraints and boundaries he recognizes
in the act of transgressing them, and it thus weds man to nature and to other
men, a familiar but rarely realized ideal of art.

**Major publications other than poetry**

PLAYS: *Faust Foutu: An Entertainment in Four Parts*, 1959; *Medea at Kolchis:
The Maidenhead*, 1965.

NONFICTION: *As Testimony: The Poem & the Scene*, 1964; *The Sweetness
and Greatness of Dante's "Divine Comedy*," 1965; *The Cat and the Blackbird*,
1967; *The Truth and Life of Myth: An Essay in Essential Autobiography*,
1968; "The H. D. Book," published in installments since 1966.

**Bibliography**

Allen, Donald, ed. *The New American Poetry*, 1960.
Allen, Donald, and Warren Tallman, eds. *The Poetics of the New American
Poetry*.
Altieri, Charles. *Enlarging the Temple: New Directions in American Poetry
During the 1960's*, 1979.
Bertholf, Robert J. "Shelley, Stevens, and Robert Duncan: The Poetry of
Approximation," in *Artful Thunder*, 1975. Edited by Robert DeMott and
Sanford Marovitz.
Bertholf, Robert J., and Ian W. Reid, eds. *Robert Duncan: Scales of the
Marvelous*, 1979.
Butterick, George F. "Robert Duncan," in *Dictionary of Literary Biography*,
1980.
Cooley, Dennis. "The Poetics of Robert Duncan," in *Boundary*. VIII, no.

2 (1980), pp. 45-73.

Faas, Ekbert. *Towards a New American Poetics*, 1978.

Mackey, Nathaniel. "The World-Poem in Microcosm: Robert Duncan's 'The Continent,'" in *ELH*. XLVII (1980), pp. 595-618.

Malkoff, Karl. *Crowell's Handbook of Contemporary American Poetry*, 1973.

*Maps*. VI (1974), special issue on Robert Duncan.

Mersmann, James. *Out of the Vietnam Vortex: A Study of Poets and Poetry Against the War*, 1974.

Michelson, Peter. "A Materialist Critique of Robert Duncan's Grand Collage," in *Boundary*. VIII, no. 2 (1980), pp. 21-43.

Nemerov, Howard, ed. "Towards an Open Universe," in *Poets on Poetry*, 1966.

Weatherhead, A. K. "Robert Duncan and the Lyric," in *Contemporary Literature*. XVI (Spring, 1975), pp. 163-174.

*Mark A. Johnson*

# THOMAS D'URFEY

**Born:** Exeter, England; 1653(?)
**Died:** London, England; February 26, 1723

## Principal collections

*Archerie Revived: Or, The Bow-Man's Excellence, an Heroick Poem*, 1676 (with Robert Shotterel); *The Progress of Honesty*, 1681; *Butler's Ghost: Or, Hudibras the Fourth Part*, 1682; *A New Collection of Songs and Poems*, 1683; *Scandalum Magnetum*, 1683; *The Malcontent*, 1683-1684; *Choice New Songs Never Before Printed*, 1684; *Several New Songs*, 1684; *A Third Collection of New Songs, Never Before Printed*, 1685; *A Compleat Collection of Mr. D'Urfey's Songs and Odes Whereof the First Part Never Before Published*, 1687; *A New Collection of Songs and Poems*, 1687 (Part II); *New Poems, Consisting of Satyrs, Elegies, and Odes*, 1690; *A Choice Collection of New Songs and Ballades*, 1699; *Musa et Musica: Or, Honour and Musick*, 1710; *Songs, Compleat, Pleasant and Divertive*, 1719; *Wit and Mirth: Or, Pills to Purge Melancholy*, 1719-1720 (6 volumes).

## Other literary forms

Thomas D'Urfey's popularity as a writer of lyrics and songs may well have been outstripped by the sheer quantity of his writings for the stage, although not all of his thirty-odd dramatic pieces achieved literary merit or public acceptance.

## Achievements

In certain religious and political quarters of late seventeenth and early eighteenth century London Establishment, Thomas D'Urfey's qualities as a poet and entertainer were highly appreciated. The essayist Joseph Addison, writing in 1713, ten years before D'Urfey's death, likened him to Pindar, both being aged lyric poets who endeared themselves to their respective eras and nations with the tuneful strains of their poems. "Our British swan will sing to the last," maintained Addison, although he admitted that D'Urfey's finest efforts were those of his earlier years.

Indeed, time has considerably clipped the wings of D'Urfey's literary achievements, although he may continue to be remembered as one who wrote more odes than Horace and almost four times as many comedies as Terence, as a songster who made ladies merry and sleepy children content. His contemporaries, on the other hand—at least those who shared his political and theological views—appreciated D'Urfey's attacks on the plotting Whigs, claiming that his odes dealt such a blow to the opponents of Charles II that they became, for the remainder of that monarch's reign, little more than impotent noise. D'Urfey received similar notes of gratitude for having attacked and exposed Roman Catholicism with his short, satirical compositions that became extremely popular. He simply latched onto Italian tunes and Italian sonatas and manipulated them for the promotion of English Protestantism; the music of the Papal state was turned against itself. During the height of his popularity as an entertainer, D'Urfey provided the English court with political sonnets, the English nation with dialogue and pastorals, and the cities of London and Westminster with countless descriptions of festivals and festivities.

On a less serious note, D'Urfey gave to English song a host of characters who, although little more than superficial prototypes, nevertheless reflected the breadth of late seventeenth century English life. The likes of Ralph of Redding, Black Bess of the Green, Sir Barnaby Whigg, Colonel Pack, Little Chancellor Tony, Pretty Peg of Windsor, Gillian of Croydon, and hosts of Dollys, Mollys, Tommys, and Johnnys dance upon the lines of his verse, exhibiting (for all of their "flatness") considerable life and gaiety in a time marked by political and theological tension. D'Urfey's contemporaries, from monarch to fellow poets, appreciated his attempts to lighten the burdens of life, no matter how crude those efforts might occasionally be. At the height of his popularity, D'Urfey, like some jocular bard of old, delighted audiences by singing what he had written; the poet was particularly skilled at adapting his verse to existing music.

"Honest Tom D'Urfey," as his contemporaries labeled him, sought to entertain his fellow human beings. Given the general lewdness of the age, an atmosphere partially sponsored by the nation's monarch, it is not surprising that D'Urfey did his best (in the words of Professor James Sutherland) "to keep the dirty old flag flying." The passing of his beloved Charles II did little to bank the fires of his musical-poetic muse. He continued to write: to amuse, to sing, to stutter, and to entertain. In the end, he achieved the status of a popular public figure and maintained, during the reigns of four successive monarchs, the image of a successful court clown.

**Biography**
Tom D'Urfey—his supporters and his enemies rarely, if ever, referred to him as "Thomas"—came from strict Huguenot stock and remained throughout his seventy years the staunchest of Protestants. The family had come from La Rochelle to Exeter in 1628, and the poet's father married a gentlewoman of Huntingdonshire by the name of Frances. Although someone had determined that Thomas must prepare for the law, the young man altered the direction of his life by crowning himself (by way of the prevalent astrological signs) "a knight-errant in the fairy field of poetry." To that end he embarked upon his principal career as a dramatist, eventually publishing ten plays between 1676 and 1682—the high point of his popularity. He seemed to have been able to strike the proper combinations: fast pace, lively dialogue, and

sparkling songs set to music by such friends as Henry Purcell, Thomas Farmer, and John Blow. His reputation reached a point where he was besieged by requests for birthday odes, epithalamia, prologues, and epilogues.

From the opening of *The Siege of Memphis* at the King's Theatre in 1676 until his death forty-seven years later, D'Urfey produced more than thirty plays, the majority of which proved popular—especially those which premiered during the reign of Charles II. The playwright's looseness with the language, however (which did nothing more than to reflect the tastes of those times), got him into trouble with the guardians of the nation's morals, and several pieces were terminated because of their licentiousness and indecency. Interestingly enough, the songs in those plays became even more popular than the plays themselves—particularly those from *A Fool's Preferment*, his adaptation of George Chapman's *Bussy d'Ambois* (1690), from *The Richmond Heiress* (1693), and from *Don Quixote* (1694, 1696) that had been set to music by Purcell. D'Urfey clearly realized the benefits (as well as the profit) of an alliance between music and the stage, and he gained considerable notice in 1706 with his comic opera *Wonders in the Sun*, as set to music by Giovanni Baptiste Draghi.

D'Urfey's contribution to English song cannot be ignored. He achieved much of his recognition in that area by the lively manner in which he performed his own material. He became, *ex officio*, court entertainer to at least three monarchs: Charles II, William III, and Anne. Between 1683 and 1685, for example, D'Urfey published three collections of songs set to music by some of the most noted composers of the Restoration. He became affiliated with the celebrated collection of songs entitled *Wit and Mirth: Or, Pills to Purge Melancholy*, editions of which appeared between 1684 and 1720. Again, as with the plays, complaints arose concerning the gross obscenity in that collection; it remains to this day, however, a most valuable representative of Restoration and Augustan vocal music, especially in its early airs.

Unfortunately, D'Urfey's popularity receded when his political fortunes declined toward the end of the Stuart reign and with the coming of the Hanoverians, the Whigs, and Sir Robert Walpole's ministry. During the last dozen years of his life, he endured poor health under even poorer financial circumstances. He received some assistance in June, 1713, when Sir Richard Steele and Joseph Addison induced the managers of the Drury Lane theater to stage a benefit performance of D'Urfey's *The Fond Husband: Or, The Plotting Sisters*, from which the playwright received the profits. A similar exercise occurred a year later, again at Drury Lane, when D'Urfey appeared and recited his "Oration on the Royal Family and the Prosperous State of the Nation" before the performance of *Court Gallantry: Or, Marriage à-la-Mode*. He continued his struggle to maintain himself as a man of fashion until he was seventy, when he finally died. The Duke of Dorset assumed the poet-playwright's funeral expenses and provided for his burial in St. James's

Church, Piccadilly, then the most fashionable of London churches. Although his stone bears simply his name and the date of his death, D'Urfey would no doubt have been pleased to know that his burial received complete and full attention by the major news-sheets throughout England.

## Analysis

Thomas D'Urfey began his career in poetry as a singer of his own songs and as a semiofficial entertainer at the court of Charles II. In 1681, however, he sought both to escape that role and to relieve, somewhat, the demands created by his prolific dramatic output. Thus, he turned his attention to political satire, writing between 1681 and 1683 four satires on Lord Shaftesbury and the Whigs, whose major objective was to prevent James, Duke of York and Charles II's brother, from succeeding to the throne of England. The results proved not so much that D'Urfey could achieve a high standard of poetic quality, as that he could fall in line behind those who had set the tone and the style for such political and occasional pieces. Thus, his *The Progress of Honesty* (1681), written in the irregular Pindaric stanzas made popular by Abraham Cowley and relying heavily upon eulogies and elegies, warranted reissue in the same year (and again in 1739), even though it seemed to be little more than an imitation of a poem often attributed to Thomas Otway, *The Poet's Complaint of His Muse*. A year later, D'Urfey turned his attention to Samuel Butler's *Hudibras* (1663, 1664, 1678) and produced *Butler's Ghost: Or, Hudibras the Fourth Part* (1682). He continued the burlesque tone of the original by updating the references to fit the political crisis of the moment; Hudibras became a Whig and the poet drew scathing portraits of notorious and notable figures: Titus Oates ("Doctoro"), Slingsby Bethel ("Stalliano"), Anthony Ashley Cooper, third Earl of Shaftesbury ("Pygmy").

The observant student of Restoration poetry will quickly note that 1681 saw the publication of John Dryden's satire on the Popish plots, *Absalom and Achitophel*, while in 1682 the same poet published *The Medall*, his attack on Shaftesbury. D'Urfey obviously drew his *Butler's Ghost* from more than a single source, and his debt to Dryden increased when, also in 1682, he published his third political satire, *Scandalum Magnetum*. Although D'Urfey focused on a phase of Shaftesbury's trial different from that utilized by Dryden, it became obvious that Charles II's jester had borrowed considerably from the laureate of England. D'Urfey's Shaftesbury appears as one Prince Potapski, but the reader still realizes the strong similarity between the Prince's Poland and Dryden's Jerusalem. Finally, the last poem of D'Urfey's political quartet, *The Malcontent* (1683-1684), merely continues the themes of *The Progress of Honesty*, and the piece proved to be both ineffective as political satire and unpopular as poetry intended to entertain.

Perhaps the best assessment of D'Urfey's poetry came from the writer himself, who once declared (in his usual stuttering manner) that "The Town

may da-da-da-mn me as a poet, but they si-si-sing my songs for all that."
Indeed, the degree to which his late seventeenth and early eighteenth century
audiences rallied to those songs reflects their popularity. The theater had
taught him well, had forced him to consider his audience. Without the slightest
pretense or affectation, he gave to the public the very songs they demanded.
Alexander Pope, in a rare moment of praise for a brother poet, remarked in
1710 that D'Urfey's songs were the rage among half-illiterate justices of the
peace and country squires; the bard of Twickenham admitted that he had not
quoted a single Latin author since coming to London, but, instead, had
learned D'Urfey's quick and easy pieces by memory.

The exact number of songs written by D'Urfey may be debated, although
five hundred seems a reasonable approximation. Of greater significance to
scholars and students, however, is the arrangement of those songs into categories (which admittedly may overlap one another): political, country,
dialect, and court. The first group reflects the songster's ability to back a
winner, so to speak. Thus, in "Joy to Great Caesar," a toast to the King's
health, he clearly echoes the sentiments of blind loyalty; the piece preaches
obedience to the sovereign while jeering at "Sneaking Whig" opposition.
Tories must guard Jehovah-like Charles (much like Dryden's David-like
Charles, by the way) from the vipers who would sting him, and, in the end,
faction and folly will dwell together in a utopian land of wit, wine, and beauty.
D'Urfey's loyalty to the sovereign of the present leads him to heights of pure
abuse: Cromwell can now be forgotten and his principal followers allowed
to rot away "Like Sons of Fanatical Whores." D'Urfey's political pieces were
strictly topical, carrying a burden of particular names easily recognized by his
contemporaries. Once those names faded from the memories of British singers, D'Urfey's political songs sank into literary oblivion.

For obvious reasons, D'Urfey's country songs do not create the same problem. Despite the Industrial Revolution of the late eighteenth century and the
growth of the British Empire during the following hundred years, Britons
have always recognized their rural roots. They have always been quick to
express, even in hearty and crude terms, the tradition from which they
emerged. In such pieces as "The Winchester Wedding," "The Gelding of the
Devil," "The Black-Smith," and "The Northumberland Bagpipe," D'Urfey
kept alive both the traditions and the activities: country courtships and rural
weddings, sweet milkmaids and simple farm laborers, love in barnyard and
love in haystack. Indeed, those songs serve as a rotogravure of country life:
totally graphic, outwardly honest, and morally unrestrained. Thus, at the
Winchester union of Ralph of Redding and Black Bess of the Green, a
hundred fiddlers roam about the countryside, gathering members of the wedding party: Ruddy Fac'd Harry, bouncing Nell, melancholy Willy, pert Stephen, and smiling Katy. Everyone eats, drinks, dances, and brawls; then they
go to bed—all within the space of seventy-two lines. The fact that D'Urfey

could sing this song before Charles II—as well as others of similar style—and that Addison could still see fit to discuss it in *The Guardian* some twenty-eight or thirty years later, demonstrates the extent to which the country songs remained popular among a wide social and economic range of the population.

Similarly, the dialect songs were widely accepted, although perhaps not for quite the same reasons. In Scotland, for example, the natives believed that D'Urfey's pieces came not from his pen, but rather from their own ancient bards. They failed to realize, however, that D'Urfey had indeed set foot on Scottish soil on more than one occasion, had visited Edinburgh early in the eighteenth century, and had become closely acquainted with Allan Ramsay and that folk-poet's shop in the Luckenbooths. No matter what the points of origin—Scotland, Ireland, or Wales—D'Urfey was not one to allow dialect to impede the progress of a song on its way to popular acceptance. He could easily gloss over the strong linguistic peculiarities and produce songs of genuine passion, as well as those focusing upon such universal human activities as fishing, hunting, and horse racing. Thus, in a poem such as "The Farmer's Daughter," the few instances of dialect provide proper doses of authenticity and spontaneity: "For I'se take all thy Barley"; "Dagl'd by Winter yearly"; "We'st get a young Kid together." And, of course, when sung to proper melodies (especially *English* melodies), singers were rarely troubled by any rough dialectal or rhythmic edges.

D'Urfey's court songs tend to be highly conventional and thus heavily imitative of certain contemporaries. During the reign of Charles II (1660-1685) especially, such figures as John Wilmot, Earl of Rochester, Sir Charles Sedley, and Charles Sackville, Earl of Dorset constituted a corps of poet-courtiers, rakes, and revelers as much remembered for their escapades and romantic frolics as for the labors of their pens. Nevertheless, they managed to produce easy, free-flowing court verse, graceful in rhythm (although often coarse in language and imagery), focusing on the traditional fictions of loyalty and love. The wits of the Restoration court determined the lyrical tone of the nation. Although D'Urfey was hardly in a position to emulate the nocturnal or romantic experiences of Rochester, Dorset, or Sedley (he had neither the stamina nor the looks), he shared their interests in the general consideration of love—its end as well as its beginning and development. Thus in "A Dirge," from his *Don Quixote*, D'Urfey's narrator gently proclaims a respite, a relief from love, mortal care, and the disease of life. Death emerges in terms of "the Charms of Peace" that isolate the departed from the pains of life's torments. More conventional, however, is the song "Boast no more, fond Love, thy Power," with its clichés of the times and the form: the sun gilds the morning; woman is a fate that can wound a lover; the beautiful Caelia appears sweeter than the blooming rose and whiter than the falling snow, with eyes that the Creator made as lamps to kindle nature.

Unfortunately, D'Urfey's poetic reputation suffered because not all of the court pieces were songs or even longer poems freely and enthusiastically directed toward love. To keep pace with his rivals, notably Tom Brown, Thomas Shadwell, and Dryden, he undertook some occasional verses: odes in honor of St. Cecilia's Day, birthday odes for Queen Mary, and a series of orations, prologues, and epilogues for various productions and festivities. Although his endeavors at that level proved no better or no worse than a hundred other pieces from at least an equal number of versifiers, they did little to advance D'Urfey's stature as a serious poet. Instead, poems such as "Shine Then, My Muse, with Radiance like the Sun," "Success Gave Trophies to Our Monarch's Might," "Our Sovereign's Regal Genius," and "The Loyal Muse [who] . . . sings/ On Themes of Glory and Immortal Things" tended only to obscure him further amid the heap of second-rate versifiers, hacks, and toadies who marched across the poetic stage between the Restoration and the beginning of the Hanoverian dynasty.

At his death, D'Urfey at least had the satisfaction of a certain degree of triumph over his contemporary rivals. His career as a man of letters is a tribute to prolificacy, patronage, and financial success (however temporary or fleeting). If he did not outwrite every Restoration poet and dramatist, he at least out-imitated and out-edited them. Although he really never came close to achieving the artistic excellence of Rochester, William Wycherley, Shadwell, or Dryden, he equaled and on more than one occasion surpassed their abilities to fulfill the literary demands and fashions of the moment. Above everything else, D'Urfey entertained; he made a nation—or at least its principal intellectual agents—laugh. In the end, critics and commentators have little recourse but to agree with the assessment of D'Urfey's twentieth century editor, Professor C. L. Day, that "to have made three generations of one's fellow countrymen laugh is cause enough for a man's memory to be held in some sort of esteem by posterity."

## Major publications other than poetry

PLAYS: *The Siege of Memphis: Or, The Ambitious Queen*, 1676; *The Fond Husband: Or, The Plotting Sisters*, 1676; *Madam Fickle: Or, The Witty False One*, 1677; *The Fool Turn'd Critick*, 1678; *Trick for Trick: Or, The Debauched Hypocrite*, 1678; *Squire Oldsapp: Or, The Night-Adventurers*, 1678; *The Virtuous Wife: Or, Good Luck at Last*, 1680; *Sir Barnaby Whig: Or, No Wit like a Woman's*, 1681; *The Royalist*, 1682; *The Injured Princess: Or, The Fatal Wager*, 1682; *A Commonwealth of Women*, 1685; *The Banditti: Or, A Ladies Distress*, 1686; *A Fool's Preferment*, 1688; *Love for Money: Or, The Boarding School*, 1691; *The Marriage-Hater Matched*, 1692; *The Richmond Heiress: Or, A Woman Once in the Right*, 1693; *The Comical History of Don Quixote, Parts I, II*, and *III*, 1694, 1696; *Cynthia and Endymion: Or, The Loves of the of the Deities*, 1697; *The Intrigues of Versailles: Or, A Jilt in all Humours*, 1697; *The Campaigners: Or, The Pleasant Adventures at Brussels*, 1698; *The*

*Famous History of the Rise and Fall of Massaniello*, 1699; *The Bath: Or, The Western Lass*, 1701; *The Old Mode and the New: Or, The Country Miss and Her Furbelow*, 1703; *Wonders in the Sun: Or, The Kingdom of the Birds*, 1706; *The Modern Prophets: Or, New Wit for a Husband*, 1709.

## Bibliography

Ellis, William D., Jr. "Thomas D'Urfey, the Pope-Philips Quarrel, and *The Shepherd's Week*," in *PMLA*. LXXIV (1959), pp. 203-212.

Hueuston, Edward F. "Gay's Bowzybeus and Thomas D'Urfey," in *Scriblerian*. I (1968), pp. 30-31.

Love, Harold. "Dryden, D'Urfey, and the Standard of Comedy," in *Studies in English Literature*. XIII (1973), pp. 422-436.

Lynch, Kathleen M. "Thomas D'Urfey's Contribution to Sentimental Comedy," in *Philological Quarterly*. IX (1930), pp. 249-259.

Robinson, K. E. "A Glance at Rochester in Thomas D'Urfey's *Madam Fickle*," in *Notes and Queries*. XXII (1975), p. 265.

Simpson, Claude M. *The British Broadside Ballad and Its Music*, 1966.

Solomon, Harry M. "Difficult Beauty: Tom D'Urfey and the Context of Swift's 'The Lady's Dressing Room,'" in *Studies in English Literature*. XIX (1979), pp. 431-444.

Vaughn, Jack A. "Perservering Unexhausted Bard: Tom D'Urfey," in *Quarterly Journal of Speech*. LIII (1967), pp. 342-348.

*Samuel J. Rogal*

# LAWRENCE DURRELL

**Born:** Julundur, India; February 27, 1912

## Principal collections

*Ten Poems*, 1932; *Transition: Poems*, 1934; *A Private Country*, 1943; *Cities, Plains and People*, 1946; *On Seeming to Presume*, 1948; *Private Drafts*, 1955; *The Tree of Idleness*, 1955; *Selected Poems*, 1956; *Collected Poems*, 1960; *The Icons and Other Poems*, 1966.

## Other literary forms

Lawrence Durrell has written novels, plays, travel books, humorous sketches, and poetry. The differences in genre, however, cannot obscure his fundamental and single identity as a poet. He is best known for his novels, especially *The Alexandria Quartet* (1957-1960), one of the major achievements of this century. Any reader of this four-part masterpiece will recognize the same hand at work in Durrell's poems. The beauty of language, the exotic settings, and the subtle treatment of the themes of love, death, and time are elements common to all of Durrell's work. In addition, the novels are rife with interpolated poetry; the characters not only speak poetically, they also quote at length from Greek, Egyptian, French, and English poets. Some have questioned this plethora of verse as unrealistic; others insist that Durrell's use of language and interpolated poetry represents a more intense reality, not a fantasy.

Durrell's poetic drama has inevitably enjoyed less attention than his novels, but it provides an excellent showcase for his skill at characterization and his poetic gifts. Durrell himself considered several passages from *Sappho* (1950) good enough to include in his *Collected Poems*, and most readers would agree. A later play, *Acte* (1966), shows that his drama does not rely entirely on the author's magnificent English: it was first performed in German, three years before its publication.

Ultimately, Durrell is a word artist, a poet. All genres have for him their particular virtues, and he brings to them all a poetic impulse which no change in form can disrupt.

## Achievements

Durrell's accomplishments in prose have overshadowed his work in verse. Most readers will turn to the *Collected Poems* only after having read *The Alexandria Quartet*, or perhaps one of the travel books. Durrell has won no major awards for poetry, despite his consistent excellence from the 1940's on. His name rarely appears on the lists of major English poets of the twentieth century.

All this notwithstanding, Durrell's achievement as a poet is sound and his eventual recognition assured. His success in other genres has left him well-off financially, and under no pressure; he can write poetry as he pleases, with no fear of disappointing expectant readers and no burden of leadership. Precisely because Durrell has made his formidable reputation as a novelist, he can approach his poetry as an alternative. This does not imply that he merely dabbles—on the contrary, every poem shows the mark of craft and diligence—but rather that the wealth of material afforded by his diverse experience and wide-ranging mind can find its expression in pure poetry. Because Durrell need not say everything in verse, he is free to write only those poems that his good judgment tells him to write.

Neither rigidly traditional nor wildly experimental, Durrell's poems represent the subtle innovations of a consummate and independent artist. In this respect, they are reminiscent of the work of Wallace Stevens. Like Stevens, Durrell balances the demands of tradition and the modern psyche, creating poems which the eye and the mind can follow, but which the soul does not reject as obsolete. Some of them compare favorably with the best of this century and will someday be read for their own merits, not merely for their connection with the famous novels by the same author.

**Biography**

Born in India, Lawrence George Durrell has led a wandering life which has profoundly influenced all his work. His formal education was adequate but limited; ironically, he could never gain admission to Cambridge, which may have motivated his half-jesting claim that he became a writer "by sheer ineptitude." In any event, he managed to acquire an astonishing fund of knowledge, becoming competent as a painter, a jazz pianist, a race-car driver, a teacher, and a diplomat. In his turbulent career, he has lived and worked in London, Paris, Cairo, Belgrade, Beirut, Athens, Cyprus, Argentina, and Provence. Naturally enough, he also became an accomplished linguist, particularly in Greek. Many of the places mentioned above are familiar to readers as settings of his novels or travel books; they are also prominent in his poems.

Durrell's personal life has been no less an odyssey than his career. Married three times, he went through two divorces, and became a widower in 1967. His friendships proved more lasting, in particular his evolving relationship with Henry Miller. Beginning as Miller's disciple and admirer, Durrell virtually turned the tables. Even so, the two remained close and mutually stimulating friends, as evidenced by *Lawrence Durrell and Henry Miller: A Private Correspondence* (1964).

After many years of working at odd jobs, teaching, and representing his country in various diplomatic posts, Durrell settled in Provence in 1957 and devoted his full time to writing. Always a rapid worker—he completed the monumental *The Alexandria Quartet* in less than a year of actual writing time—he has published many novels, dramas, and collections of poetry in recent years. His wanderlust appears cured, to such an extent that he stirs only reluctantly, even to go into town. In his reclusion, Durrell imitates Prospero, a favorite character of his, working magic and recalling his life at court. In his poems and his prose, Durrell reveals the fruits of an extraordinary life at many Mediterranean "courts."

## Analysis

Reading Lawrence Durrell's poetry for the first time, a discerning reader might be reminded of T. S. Eliot. He would notice Durrell's sparse but effective rhymes, his facility in finding the *mot juste*, and some of his astonishing single lines, and think of "The Love Song of J. Alfred Prufrock" and *The Waste Land* (1922). Reflecting further, he would perceive that both Durrell and Eliot are philosophical poets, and that their work shows their common preoccupation with the Western tradition and certain of its key philosophical issues. If the reader is truly discerning, however, he will conclude that the resemblance ends there. For all his superficial likeness to Eliot, Durrell has a distinctive voice as a poet. The hypothetical discerning reader might well end up thinking of Durrell as a curious mixture of the qualities of Eliot, D. H. Lawrence, and Gerard Manley Hopkins; but even that remarkable formulation would not cover all the facts. Durrell is unique; he is the Anglo-Indian poet of the Mediterranean, craftsman, and thinker at once.

In an interview printed in the Autumn-Winter issue of the *Paris Review* for 1959-1960, Durrell reveals his guiding principle as a poet: "Poetry is form, and the wooing and seduction of form is the whole game." His poems *seem* rather traditional in their construction; a glance at the printed page reveals few typographical eccentricities. A careful reading, however, will turn up subtle variations in meter, line-length, and rhyme. Durrell has worked hard and successfully at wooing and seducing form. He has altered form almost imperceptibly, so that a sonnet by Durrell does not seem quite a sonnet. One re-counts lines and syllables, and finally admits that the poem *is* a sonnet, but an odd one. Simply put, Durrell has wrested the form away from tradition and made it his own. This victory makes possible—by no means inevitable— the success of the poem.

An example of this phenomenon is the second of the fourteen poems in "A Soliloquy of Hamlet." The poet has already indicated that the fourteen poems are to be regarded as sonnets. The student of the form, however, will demur because of the lack of rhyme and the arrangement into couplets. On intensive reading, he will be compelled to concede that there *is* a six/eight structure, the usual arrangement of a sonnet *à rebours*—in short, that his beloved sonnet form has been seduced.

Durrell offers an intriguing, if somewhat deceptive, insight into his art in a poem entitled "Style." The poet strives for "Something like the sea;/

Unlabored momentum of water;/ But going somewhere. . . ." Subsequently, he wishes to write like "the wind that slits/ Forests from end to end." Finally, he rejects sea and wind for a third alternative:

> But neither is yet
> Fine enough for the line I hunt.
> The dry long blade of the
> Sword-grass might suit me
> Better: an assassin of polish.

The choice is never really made, of course: Durrell can write in all of these manners, and many more. The poem serves more to convey a sense of his unending struggle for perfection, in his verse and in his prose, than to issue any artistic manifesto.

In this struggle for perfection, Durrell differs from other writers only in his relative success. Other differences are easier to define, and more important to the understanding of his poetry. Here it helps to refer to his prose work. Any reader of the novels and travel books knows Durrell's powers of description, his subtlety in handling love relationships between his characters, and his flair for transforming the mundane into the magical. As a poet, he displays the same talents in a different medium.

Durrell, as mentioned above, is the Anglo-Indian poet of the Mediterranean. The phrase is perhaps a trifle awkward, but to omit any element would be to misrepresent the poet. As an Anglo-Indian, he enjoyed at once the benefits of an English education and a childhood in the exotic East. He also suffered, virtually from birth, the plight of the exile, the man without a country. England was alien; English was not. Durrell's work depends on the English literary tradition, even though he could not bear the thought of living in Great Britain. He found a series of homes on the shores of the Mediterranean: Greece, Lebanon, Cyprus, Egypt, France. The Mediterranean is the *sine qua non* of his work; nowhere else could he have found such "cities, plains and people." Thus, every element in the description is vital, because Durrell's birthplace, education, and later environment together help to account for the unique nature of his poetry.

The importance of place in Durrell's poetry is nowhere more evident than in "The Anecdotes," a series of brief lyrics with subtitles such as "In Cairo," "At Rhodes," and "In Patmos." Durrell has an unsurpassed genius for evoking the peculiar atmosphere of locale, and he makes good use of the imagination-stirring names of Mediterranean cities. "The Anecdotes" concern people and emotions, but the geography helps the reader to understand both.

In the third poem, "At Rhodes," Durrell suggests the languorous beauty of Rhodes by way of a few deft images. The memory of the boats in the harbor, the antics of two Greek children, and the town, "thrown as on a screen of watered silk," becomes a compact poem: "twelve sad lines against the dark." The lines express nostalgia for Rhodes through a few well-chosen emblems of the city, suggesting a lovely tranquillity which the poet now lacks. The personal association—Durrell missed Rhodes sorely during his tour of duty in Egypt—becomes a theme.

The sense of place in the poems generally does have an importance beyond mere exotic appeal. The countries, the cities, even the streets and cafés that Durrell mentions have associations with specific moods and memories. Sometimes the connection is obscure; more often, Durrell selects his images so skillfully that the reader shares the mood without quite knowing why. In the best examples, the poet achieves Eliot's ideal, the "objective correlative."

The fourteenth anecdote, "In Beirut," has the reader sighing with the melancholy of "after twenty years another meeting," though Durrell gives few details of the people involved or of their stories. Beirut takes on the withered nature of the old friends, "flesh murky as old horn,/ Hands dry now as sea-biscuit." Even without specific background, the contrast between "breathless harbours north of Tenedos" in April and "in Tunis, winter coming on" is evident. Durrell's beloved Greece comes to represent life and youth; the cities of Asia and North Africa connote aging and death.

One of the best examples of Durrell's artistry in this regard is "Mareotis." The reader need not know beforehand that Mareotis is a salt marsh outside Alexandria; Durrell makes it clear enough, even as he draws the parallel between the atmosphere of the marsh and the climate of his soul. The wind of the place, "Not subtle, not confiding, touches once again,/ The melancholy elbow cheek and paper." The odd blend of discontent and self-knowledge matches the nature of the salt marsh. It misses the changes of spring, remaining the same, just as the poet does. Durrell has performed a sleight of hand, first alluding to a place, then subtly sketching its nature, and ultimately using the finished image to make his poetic point.

It must be noted here that Durrell's reliance on images of place sometimes renders his poetry difficult to understand. Most readers know next to nothing of the world the poet inhabits, beyond a few clichés. In the novels, he overcomes this problem masterfully by means of long descriptions. In the poems, lacking this resource, he depends on a few striking images. This may account in part for the greater popularity of the fiction. To Durrell's credit, relatively few of his poems are seriously marred by his esoteric geography.

In "Cities, Plains and People," one of his major poems, Durrell approaches overwhelming questions in the course of a poetic autobiography. He begins under the shadow of the Himalayas, "in idleness," an innocent tyke to whom "Sex was small,/ Death was small. . . ." Both have become very large for the poet as he has grown, but the early years in British India stand as the time before the Fall. There in the mountains, only "nine marches" from inscrutable Lhasa, the boy grows up. He does not, however, go to Tibet:

> But he for whom steel and running water
> Were roads, went westward only
> To the prudish cliffs and the sad green home
> Of Pudding Island o'er the Victorian foam

The growing artist finds himself repelled and attracted by Europe; though he knows that "London/ Could only be a promise-giving kingdom," there are always "Dante and Homer/ To impress the lame and awkward newcomer." Impressed in both senses of the word, the Anglo-Indian struggles against the insidious examples of Saint Bede, Saint Augustine, and Saint Jerome, those deniers of the flesh, and mourns the dismal reality, "The potential passion hidden, Wordsworth/ In the desiccated bodies of postmistresses." The associations of place here serve to advance the story and to present the thought of the developing poet.

Durrell goes on to discover the escape hatch, the magic of Prospero's island. Here the literal and the fictive landscapes merge. William Shakespeare and the earthly Mediterranean both have a part in the choice, an eclectic mixture of the best of the British literary tradition and the best of the poet's several homes. The conflict is by no means resolved, but the two great forces have at least acknowledged each other. The Englishman born in India has found something worth having from Pudding Island.

The journey continues, of course, because the poet has found only a working arrangement, not an ultimate answer. He still has much to learn of those great matters which the child considered insignificant. He learns much of sex. It becomes "a lesser sort of speech, and the members doors." It is versatile, serving as a means of salvation both spiritual—"man might botch his way/ To God via Valéry, Gide or Rabelais"—and physical: "savage Chatterleys of the new romance/ Get carried off in sex, the ambulance." That Durrell can debunk in one stanza what he affirms so powerfully elsewhere implies not inconsistency, but rather an appreciation of the complexity of the matter. The youth has lost his innocence and has also gone beyond a naïve faith in a simple solution. Sex may be an answer, but not a simple answer.

Durrell goes on to probe beyond knowledge, "in the dark field of sensibility." As in the novels, he comes to no rigid conclusion. At the end of *The Alexandria Quartet*, Darley sits down to write; "Cities, Plains and People" ends with an analogous image:

> For Prospero remains the evergreen
> Cell by the margin of the sea and land,
> Who many cities, plains, and people saw
> Yet by his open door
> In sunlight fell asleep
> One summer with the Apple in his hand.

Between Durrell the poet and Durrell the novelist there lies only the difference in genre: the artist and the resolution are the same. Prospero remains, latent with magic—the magic to bring order and beauty to the chaotic world of cities, plains, and people. Darley on his island off the coast of Egypt and the poet somewhere in the Aegean represent Durrell/Prospero, perhaps the key image of his work.

Durrell's repertoire is by no means limited to extended philosophical ruminations, nor his imagery to geographical references. He has estimable gifts as a lyric poet, which he demonstrates throughout his work. One particularly fine example, "Proffer the loaves of pain," shows Durrell's technical wizardry in the manipulation of rhyme. The four stanzas run the gamut of the seasons, echoing sadly: "they shall not meet." The first three stanzas feature half-rhymes: "quantum/autumn," "saunter/winter," and "roamer/summer." This tantalizing soundplay gives the true rhyme of the conclusion, "ring/spring," a finality not inherent in the words of the stanza. The poem dodges and ducks until the last inexorable rhyme destroys the last hope—in spring, ironically enough.

The poem distinguishes itself in other ways as well. The economy of language requires close attention on the part of the reader, for the clues are subtle. For example, the poet employs the word "this" to modify the seasons in the first two stanzas. Summer and spring, however, serve as objects of the preposition "in." The specific negation of the first half of the poem becomes a chilling "nevermore" in the last two stanzas, by the simple device of a change in grammar.

Durrell's melancholy wit and his fascination with the ever-lurking mystery of death come together in "The Death of General Uncebunke: A Biography in Little," which he labels "Not satire but an exercise in ironic compassion." The biography encompasses not only the general, a Victorian empire builder, but also the dowager Aunt Prudence. Despite the earlier gibes at "Pudding Island," the poet holds true to his word: the poem expresses no contempt for Uncebunke, even if the reader cannot stifle a chuckle or two at the man who "wrote a will in hexameters." Rather, Durrell transmutes the potentially absurd details of the old campaigner's life into symbols of his death. He rides horses, fords rivers, and crosses into Tartary, and the poet invests these adventures with a new and final significance.

Durrell's sentiment is noble and restrained, but his handling of language and form in the poem deserves even more attention. The fourteen "carols" begin in three fashions. Four start with the words "My uncle sleeps in the image of death"; five begin "My uncle has gone beyond astronomy"; the remainder open with references to Aunt Prudence. Thus, the poet achieves at once a compelling repetition and movement; the lines referring to the uncle maintain the elegiac tone, while the stanzas devoted to Prudence reinforce the sense of gradual decay.

A number of phonetic tricks bolster the ironic character of the poem and add to the reader's grasp of the characters. Of the uncle, for example, Durrell says: "he like a faultless liner, finer never took air." The soundplay recalls Gerard Manley Hopkins, although the good Jesuit would probably not have indulged in the irony. Aunt Prudence prays earnestly and ridiculously: "Thy will be done in Baden Baden./ In Ouchy, Lord, and in Vichy." By one of his own favorite ploys, here in a new guise, Durrell uses references of place to provoke a response.

Finally, Durrell tosses off one memorable line after another, each in itself worth an ode. Uncebunke in his dotage lives on a country estate, "devoted to the polo-pony, mesmerized by stamps." Aunt Prudence putters about, "feeding the parrot, pensive over a croquet-hoop." The horses in the stable "champ, stamp, yawn, paw in the straw." One suspects that Hopkins—or any other modern poet, for that matter—would have taken pride in such verses.

To all his other virtues as a poet, Durrell adds a lively and whimsical sense of humor. Though the prevailing literary prejudices of this century keep most readers from appraising humorous verse at its full worth, no one who has suffered the slings and arrows of outrageous Freudians will read the "Ballad of the Oedipus Complex" unmoved. Besides poking fun at overworked psychological truisms, Durrell shows a fine English sense of fair play, plunging his own face into a custard pie:

> I tried to strangle it one day
> While sitting in the Lido
> But it got up and tickled me
> And now I'm all libido.

This ability to snicker at his own literary obsessions betokens a fine sensibility in Durrell, as well as a sense of humor so often lacking in his contemporaries.

Indeed, Durrell has many rare qualities. His multifaceted life has given him a breadth of vision and a balance of mind which, in combination with his natural gifts and hard work, have enabled him to produce a body of poetry remarkable for its beauty, richness, and integrity. His poems afford a glimpse into the changeless world of the Mediterranean, and into the ever-changing lives of the people who live there. Yet the poems never become mere travelogues; part of Durrell's integrity lies in his adherence to the central purpose of poetry: to illuminate the human experience. He remains faithful to that goal throughout "the wooing and seduction of form."

**Major publications other than poetry**

NOVELS: *Pied Piper of Lovers*, 1935; *Panic Spring*, 1937 (under the pseudonym Charles Norden); *The Black Book*, 1938; *Cefalu*, 1947 (republished as *The Dark Labyrinth*, 1958); *The Alexandria Quartet* (*Justine*, 1957; *Balthazar*, 1958; *Mountolive*, 1958; *Clea*, 1960); *Tunc*, 1968; *Nunquam*, 1970.

SHORT FICTION: *Esprit de Corps*, 1957; *Stiff Upper Lip*, 1958.

PLAYS: *Sappho*, 1950; *An Irish Faustus*, 1963; *Acte*, 1966.

NONFICTION: *Prospero's Cell*, 1945; *Reflections on a Marine Venus*, 1953; *Bitter Lemons*, 1957; *Lawrence Durrell and Henry Miller: A Private Correspondence*, 1963.

**Bibliography**

Frazer, George Sutherland. *Lawrence Durrell: A Study*, 1973.

Moore, H. T., ed. *The World of Lawrence Durrell*, 1962.

Unterecker, John. *Lawrence Durrell*, 1964.

Weigel, John A. *Lawrence Durrell*, 1965.

*Philip Krummrich*

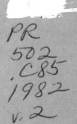